THE
WUERTTEMBERG
EMIGRATION
INDEX

Volume Three

THE
WUERTTEMBERG
EMIGRATION
INDEX

Volume Three

*By Trudy Schenk
and Ruth Froelke*

Ancestry Incorporated
Salt Lake City, Utah
1987

Library of Congress Catalog Card Number 85-052453
ISBN Number 0-916489-25-6 (Hardbound)
ISBN Number 0-916489-26-4   (Paperback)

First Printing 1987
10 9 8 7 6 5 4 3 2 1

Printed in the United States of America

Acknowledgements

I n compiling this book and preparing the manuscript for publication, we wish to express our appreciation to Hans Erwin Froelke for his valuable assistance.

Our appreciation is further directed to the staff of the European Reference section of the Genealogical Library of The Church of Jesus Christ of Latter-day Saints for their encouragement of our endeavor to get this first volume completed and for free use of their equipment.

Finally, we express appreciation to the Wuerttemberg archive officials who made the microfilming of the Ludwigsburg Wuerttemberg emigration records possible.

Foreword

I recall a conversation which took place four or five years ago at the so-called "professional genealogists table" in the cafeteria of the LDS Church Office Building in Salt Lake City. Someone said, "Wouldn't it be nice if there were an index to the Wuerttemberg emigration registers?" We all murmured in agreement, shuddered a bit at the thought of the amount of work involved, and switched the conversation to more congenial topics.

Fortunately, at a nearby table where German was the language of luncheon conversation, three of our professional colleagues decided to do something more than indulge in wishful thinking about the Wuerttemberg registers. The initial results of their labor are in your hands.

Why have professional genealogists and others knowledgeable about German-American genealogy so eagerly awaited the publication of this index? Perhaps the best way to explain this is to cite an example. The name of Otto Walter, born in Ravensburg, Wuerttemberg, in 1832 will appear in Volume II of this work, as will that of his brother Karl, born in 1828. Otto Walter's descendants, like so many Americans of German extraction, wanted to know where he had come from in the Old World. They retained Trudy Schenk to find his exact birthplace.

The case proved to be unusually difficult. According to one family story, Otto came from Wuerttemberg. But another story said his brother Karl emigrated to California from the neighboring German state of Baden. Still another family story said the brothers were from a place called "Oldhouse." This led Mrs. Schenk to search the parish registers of every village in Baden and Wuerttemberg named Altheim, only to come up empty on all counts.

The U.S. Census returns listed only Wuerttemberg or Germany. Since Otto died before 1900, his year of emigration was not known. The naturalization papers of both brothers merely listed Wuerttemberg. All the other available American sources failed to provide the village of origin.

The key to solving the problem proved to be the Wuerttemberg emigration registers. During the preparation of this index, Mrs. Schenk found Otto Walter's name in the emigration registers of Oberamt Ravensburg. But until the publication of this volume, these registers were almost totally inaccessible to the genealogist. One faced the formidable task of reading through hundreds of reels of microfilm containing unindexed records written in difficult (for the novice virtually indecipherable) gothic script.

It should be stressed that this index does not confine itself to emigrants destined for North America. One can find names of individuals headed for the four corners of the earth, e.g. Australia, South America, and even Russia. In fact, many families left Wuerttemberg in the late eighteenth and early nineteenth centuries for a new life on the steppes of southern Russia.

But by the 1870s the threat of serving in the Czar's army caused many of them to look elsewhere for a permanent home. Tens of thousands resettled on the Great Plains of North America. With the passage of time, their descendants have become interested in the saga of the Germans from Russia. But since archives in the Soviet Union do not respond to genealogical inquiries, the quest often seemed quite hopeless. Now, with the publication of this index, many families of German-Russian descent will be able to trace their ancestral lines back to Wuerttemberg.

In summary, the publication of this index rates as a milestone in German emigrant genealogy. By using it, the family historian can avoid years of futile effort. Volume I is at hand and I eagerly await those to follow.

Richard W. Dougherty, Ph.D.

Introduction

The Wuerttemberg emigration records are a unique collection of papers and documents on applicants who filed for permission to emigrate from Wuerttemberg during the nineteenth century. These records are not alphabetized nor are the pages numbered, which makes a search through them complicated and time consuming. In many cases, as many as eight pages were written on one person, including a birth certificate or a family record, military release, and renunciation of citizenship rights. Often the handwriting in these documents is almost indecipherable for even an experienced German researcher. It is almost impossible for a layman to search through these records successfully.

Emigrants leaving without permission are, of course, not listed at the time of emigration. Yet many of these emigrants, later in life, after having arrived in the land of their destination, sent word back to the Wuerttemberg state and town officials renouncing their citizenship rights. Such repudiation is also documented in the Wuerttemberg emigration records.

There were as many as 800,000 people who emigrated to other parts of the world from Wuerttemberg since the late seventeenth century, including the period after World War II. A great number of those who emigrated to the German colonies in the Russian Empire, came to the United States in the nineteenth and early twentieth centuries. Indeed, a significant percentage of all German emigrants to North America have come from Wuerttemberg.

This volume of alphabetized names, containing such vital records as birthdate and place of origin, is a vital work for the genealogist and family historian researching their German heritage.

All information included in this volume of the *Wuerttemberg Emigration Index* has been extracted from the original Wuerttemberg emigration records filmed at Ludwigsburg and available on microfilm at the Genealogical Society of Utah in Salt Lake City. Although all of the records were handwritten by German speaking people, the spelling of names varies from one document to the other. In cases where applicants used their own signature, that spelling was used.

The user of this book should be aware of an anglicized spelling change in the United States and check out several spelling possibilities. All names listed are spelled in the most common German way. For instance a man's name "John" in America can be shown as "Johann" or even "Hans." Place names are all spelled as they will be listed in a German gazetteer or located on a German map.

One important fact should be observed when using a modern map of Germany or a map of Wuerttemberg: Within the last twenty years small villages have merged and often a new name was designated. For example, the village of Kaltenwesten in Oberamt Besigheim does not exist on any map or German gazetteer. It can only be located in conjunction with the village Neckarwestheim. Therefore, it is advisable to consult older maps in trying to locate a given area.

The original Wuerttemberg emigration records were compiled according to the Oberamt to which the applicant belonged. An Oberamt is roughly equivalent to a district town (or county seat in America).

The country of destination for each emigrant is given and regions such as Maehren (Moravia), Siebenbuergen (Transylvania), Rumaenien (Romania), Sudetenland and Czechoslovakia, which were all part of the Austrian empire, are designated as Austria. The actual emigration record gives more details on each single applicant.

Some names may be difficult to locate because of peculiarities in the German language. German surnames that carry an "Umlaut," i.e. a modified vowel (ä, ö, ü), have been changed to their English equivalents; thus ä = ae, ö = oe, ü = ue are indexed as such. Surnames composed of two or more distinct words have been alphabetized under the final word. Thus, von Vogel is found as Vogel von.

When a family or husband and wife applied jointly, the entry would be as follows: Knoedler, Johann & F, with all children listed in alphabetical order if their names were given on the application. The wife would be listed under both her married and maiden name. In a case where children may have left at an earlier time, and if such a notation is made on the application, these children will be listed with the family leaving later. In such an instance, the "Emigration" column will read "bef. 1856" (if this happens to be the date the family is making application). Occasionally the recording official will give the actual date for the early emigrants, but not their names. The reader is advised to follow every lead and check the microfilm originals for possible additional information. In case of a widow with children or a single woman with an illegitimate child, the listing will appear as follows: Widmann, Heinrike & C. A widow also may be listed as Widmann, Heinrike & F.

The date of application for emigration should not be assumed to be the date of emigration. In several cases, emigration was not granted until some time later, or the emigrant had already left secretly before that date.

ABBREVIATIONS

A-dam	=	Amsterdam	Nuernb.	=	Nuernberg
Augsb.	=	Augsburg	Offenb.	=	Offenburg
Austral	=	Australia	Oldenb.	=	Oldenburg
Bessar	=	Bessarabien	Palest	=	Palestine
D-dorf	=	Dusseldorf	Pommer	=	Pommerania
Darmst	=	Darmstadt	Pr.-Pol	=	Prussia Poland
F-burg	=	Freiburg	Regb.	=	Regensburg
Frankf.	=	Frankfurt	Rhld.	=	Rheinland
Hannov.	=	Hannover	Rus-Pol	=	Russia-Poland
Holst	=	Holstein	S. Afri	=	South Africa
Kreuzn.	=	Kreuznach	S.-Amer	=	South America
L-burg	=	Luxemberg	S.-Russ	=	South Russia
Landsb.	=	Landsberg	Slovan	=	Slovania
M-burg	=	Mecklenburg	Switz.	=	Switzerland
M-heim	=	Mannheim	Thur.	=	Thuringia
N.-Amer	=	North America	W.-Prs	=	West Prussia
Neck	=	Neckarsulm	W.-Russ	=	West Russia
Nuer.	=	Nuertingen	Westf.	=	Westphalia

ABBREVIATIONS OF OBERAEMTER = DISTRICT TOWNS

Aal	=	Aalen	Herr	=	Herrenberg*
Bal	=	Balingen*	Hlbr	=	Heilbronn
Bckn	=	Backnang	Hll	=	Hall
Bes	=	Besigheim	Hor	=	Horb
Bib	=	Biberach	Kntl	=	Knittlingen
Bib	=	Blaubeuren	Krch	=	Kirchheim
Boeb	=	Boeblingen	Kzs	=	Kuenzelsau
Brck	=	Brackenheim	Leon	=	Leonberg
Cal	=	Calw*	Lph	=	Laupheim
Can	=	Cannstatt	Ltk	=	Leutkirch
Crls	=	Crailsheim	Lud	=	Ludwigsburg
Eh	=	Ehingen	Marb	=	Marbach
Ellw	=	Ellwangen	Mibr	=	Maulbronn
Essl	=	Esslingen	Mrg	=	Mergentheim
Frd	=	Freudenstadt*	Muens	=	Muensingen
Gld	=	Gaildorf	Nag	=	Nagold*
Gmd	=	Gmuend	Nbg	=	Neuenbuerg
Goep	=	Goeppingen	Nds	=	Neckarsulm
Grb	=	Gerabronn	Ner	=	Neresheim
Gsl	=	Geislingen	Nuert	=	Nuertingen
Hdh	=	Heidenheim	Obd	=	Oberndorf

Oehr	= Oehringen		Tett	= Tettnang
Rav	= Ravensburg		Tueb	= Tuebingen
Rdl	= Riedlingen		Tutt	= Tuttlingen
Rtb	= Rottenburg		Ulm	= Ulm
Rtl	= Reutlingen		Ur	= Urach
Rtw	= Rottweill		Vaih	= Vaihingen
Schd	= Schorndorf		Wbl	= Waiblingen
Slg	= Saulgau		Wlds	= Waldsee
Slz	= Sulz*		Wng	= Wangen
Spch	= Spaichingen		Wnsb	= Weinsberg
Stu	= Stuttgart		Wlz	= Welzheim

*This indicates that the records for this Oberamt are contained in this volume. It *does not* mean that *every* record has been extracted, for new records are being added constantly. The compilers have made every effort to extract an Oberamt as completely as possible, but it cannot be assumed that it is one hundred percent complete. Check every volume of the index for the particular surname you are researching. Listed below are the Oberamts contained in previous volumes.

Volume One = Backnang; Besigheim; Biberach; Blaubeuren; Boeblingen; Brackenheim; Calw; Horb

Volume Two = Nagold; Nuertingen; Rottenburg; Rottweill; Schorndorf

Königreich Württemberg.

Kreis. Oberamt

Bürgerrechts-Verzichts-Urkunde

zur Auswanderung.

Der Unterzeichnete *Adolph Friedrich Kraushar*

geboren den *17 Sept 1856.* evangelischer Confession,

welcher nach *Nord Amerika*

auszuwandern, und sich daselbst häuslich niederzulaſſen geſonnen iſt,

bekennt durch gegenwärtige Urkunde, daß er in dieſem Vorhaben auf sein

bisheriges Gemeindebürger Recht zu *Aich bei Nürtingen* und auf jede Art

von bürgerlichem Verband mit dem Württembergiſchen Staat

wiſſentlich und wohlbedächtig Verzicht leiſtet.

Zugleich verpflichtet

Adolph Friedrich Kraushar

ſich, von dem Wegzug an innerhalb Jahresfriſt gegen Seine Majeſtät den König und das

Königreich Württemberg nicht zu dienen, und eben ſo lange in Hinſicht auf alle nach seinem

Wegzug etwa noch zur Sprache kommenden, vor demſelben an Ihn

erwachſenen Anſprüche vor den obrigkeitlichen Behörden des Königreichs, Recht zu geben, indem er

für die Erfüllung dieſer Verbindlichkeiten

als Bürgen ſtellt, welcher zugleich für alle nachkommenden Schulden mit ſeinem Vermögen haftet.

Gefertigt zu *Aich* den *8 April* 18*78*

Geſehen durch das Königl.

Oberamt

den   18

T. Der Auswanderungsluſtige

Friedrich Kraushar

T. Der Bürge und Selbſtzähler

Wilhelm Kraushar

Example of Wuerttemberg Emigration Application

Schiffs-Accord!

No

Urkundlich, dieses verpflichtet sich der

Verein zur Beförderung deutscher Auswanderer

von

Dr. G. Strecker in Mainz, Anton Joseph Klein in Bingen und Joseph Stöck in Creuznach,

vertreten durch ihren bevollmächtigten und obrigkeitlich concessionirten Hauptagenten für das Königreich Würtemberg, Herrn **Louis Wölffel,** Kaufmann in **Stuttgart** wohnhaft,

Christian Erhard, Taglöhner von Haiterbach, Wittwer,

seine Ehefrau . . . . f. 65.

Alter Bruder Bastian, Christina Barbara, ... " 65.

Magdalena Häußer, Wittwer, ... " 65.

Von den Kinder, von 8, 7, 5 Jahren à f. 43. . . . " 129.

Ein Kind von 3/4 Jahren (Säugling) . . . . f. 324.

Abfahrt auf dem Atlantic am ... September müssen . . . 50.

15 Februar 1852. *in New-York angeregt unter . . . . . . Person an.*

laut Uebereinkunft von *Mannheim* nach *Haiterbach* und von da durch Vermittlung der Herren *Dr. Strecker, Klein und Stöck selbst*

auf dem in der Quittung zu benamenden Schiffe, und an dem dabei zu bestimmenden Abfahrttage unter nachstehenden Bedingungen nach *New-York, à Hauptstamm* zu befördern.

§. 1. Die Passagiere erhalten zur Fahrt von *Mannheim* bis in den Seehafen die nöthigen Billets für die Dampfschiffe und für die Eisenbahn von Cöln bis Antwerpen, wenn letztere benützt wird. Auf dieser Fahrt haben die Passagiere freien Transport von einem Zentner Reisegepäcke pr. Person.

§. 2. Die Kosten der Visitation an den Gränzen und des Durchzugs des wirklichen Reisegepäckes hat der Verein zu tragen. Die Nachtheile unrichtiger Angabe, oder einer Verheimlichung ihrer Effekten und Waaren fallen lediglich den Eigenthümern zur Last.

§. 3. In den Städten, in welchen übernachtet wird, müssen die Passagiere auf ihre eigenen Kosten logiren; dagegen werden ihre Effekten, für sie kostenfrei, von einem Dampfschiffe auf das andere, so wie auf die Eisenbahn und in das Seeschiff gebracht. Die Eigenthümer müssen jedoch ihr Gepäck selbst überwachen, weil der Verein für Verwechselungen, Entwendungen u. s. w. nicht einzustehen hat.

§. 4. In dem Seehafen können die Passagiere spätestens am Tage vor der bestimmten Abfahrt an Bord des für ihre Ueberfahrt bestimmten Schiffes gehen, sich einrichten und wohnen, jedoch nicht kochen und rauchen, so lange dasselbe im Hafen liegt.

§. 5. Der durch gesetzliche Verfügung vorgeschriebene Seeproviant *wird den Reisenden nach dem Maaße geliefert.*

Die nöthigen Säcke, Gefäße *und* Kochgeschirre müssen die Passagiere jedenfalls selbst stellen.

Diejenigen, welchen dieser Seeproviant oder die nöthigen Mittel zu dessen Anschaffung fehlen, können nicht eingeschifft und müssen zurückgewiesen werden.

Example of Wuerttemberg Emigration Application

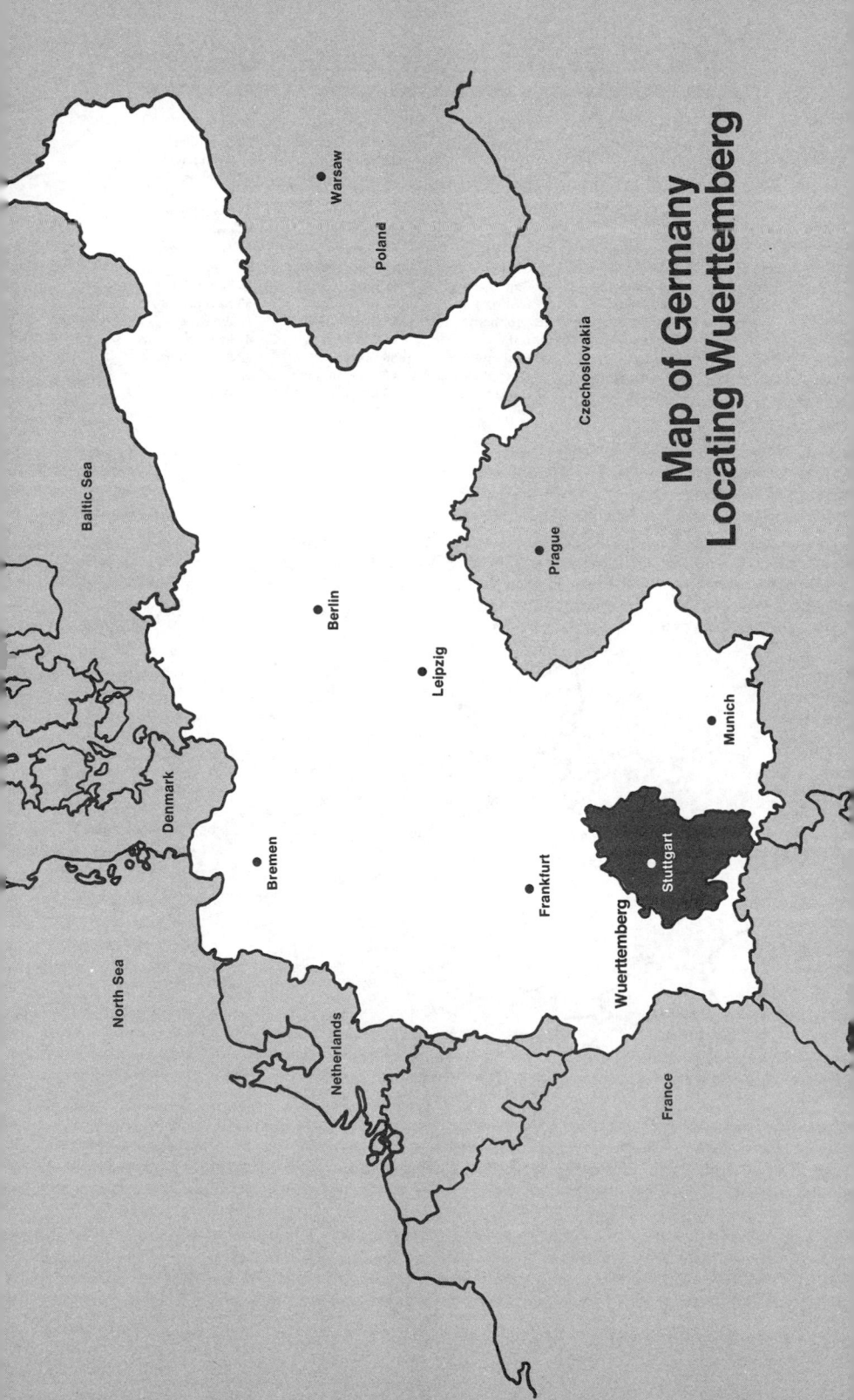

Map of Germany
Locating Wuerttemberg

Map of Wuerttemberg Locating Oberamts

1 Mergentheim
2 Kuenzelsau
3 Gerabronn
4 Oehringen
5 Neckarsulm
6 Weinsberg
7 Hall
8 Crailsheim
9 Heilbronn
10 Brackenheim
11 Knittlingen
12 Besigheim
13 Backnang
14 Gaildorf
15 Ellwangen
16 Maulbronn

17 Vaihingen
18 Marbach
19 Welzheim
20 Ludwigsburg
21 Waiblingen
22 Schorndorf
23 Aalen
24 Neresheim
25 Gmuend
26 Cannstatt
27 Stuttgart
28 Leonberg
29 Calw
30 Esslingen
31 Goeppingen
32 Heidenheim

33 Geislingen
34 Kirchheim
35 Nuertingen
36 Boeblingen
37 Neuenburg
38 Herrenberg
39 Nagold
40 Tuebingen
41 Freudenstadt
42 Horb
43 Rottenburg
44 Reutlingen
45 Urach
46 Ulm
47 Muensingen
48 Blaubeuren

49 Sulz
50 Oberndorf
51 Balingen
52 Ehingen
53 Laupheim
54 Riedlingen
55 Rottweil
56 Spaichingen
57 Biberach
58 Tuttlingen
59 Saulgau
60 Waldsee
61 Leutkirch
62 Ravensburg
63 Tettnang
64 Wangen

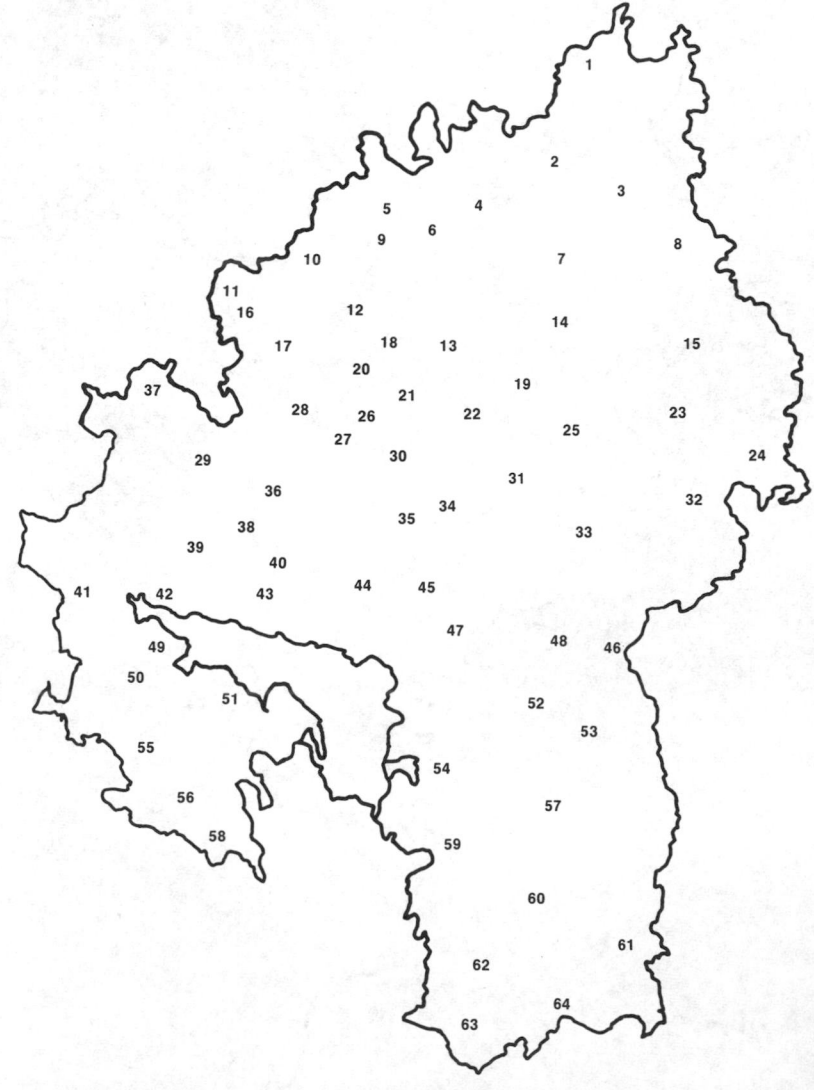

Name	Date	Place	Reg.	Emig.	Dest.	Film
Aberle, Barbara	13 Sep 1809	Wittershausen	Sulz	Jan 1817	Russia	849644
Aberle, Christian	18 May 1816	Wittershausen	Sulz	Mar 1837	N.-Amer	849644
Aberle, Christian	18 May 1816	Wittershausen	Sulz	Jan 1817	Russia	849644
Aberle, Christina	1 Feb 1789	Wittershausen	Sulz	Mar 1837	N.-Amer	849644
Aberle, Christina		Wittershausen	Sulz	Jan 1817	Russia	849644
Aberle, Friedrich	24 Apr 1822	Wittershausen	Sulz	Mar 1837	N.-Amer	849644
Aberle, Georg Jacob	11 Jan 1820	Wittershausen	Sulz	Mar 1837	N.-Amer	849644
Aberle, Jakob Friedrich & F	20 Feb 1782	Wittershausen	Sulz	Jan 1817	Russia	849644
Aberle, Johann Georg		Wittershausen	Sulz	Mar 1817	Russia	849644
Aberle, Johann Georg	18 Aug 1850	Brittheim	Sulz	Mar 1857	N.-Amer	849632
Aberle, Johann Georg & F	48 yrs.	Brittheim	Sulz	Mar 1857	N.-Amer	849632
Aberle, Johannes	9 Nov 1823	Wittershausen	Sulz	Mar 1837	N.-Amer	849644
Aberle, Johannes	30 Apr 1854	Brittheim	Sulz	Mar 1857	N.-Amer	849632
Aberle, Matthias	5 Feb 1834	Wittershausen	Sulz	Mar 1837	N.-Amer	849644
Aberle, Ursula	10 Jul 1812	Wittershausen	Sulz	Jan 1817	Russia	849644
Acker, Andreas	8 Feb 1812	Isingen	Sulz	Mar 1854	N.-Amer	849636
Acker, Anna Maria	1 Nov 1801	Isingen	Sulz	Jun 1817	Russia	849636
Acker, Johann Georg	3 Feb 1852	Isingen	Sulz	Mar 1869	N.-Amer	849636
Acker, Johann Martin	30 Aug 1830	Isingen	Sulz	bef 1870	Switz.	849636
Acker, Maria Barbara & F	10 Sep 1770	Isingen	Sulz	Jun 1817	Russia	849636
Ackerknecht, Christiana Marg.		Nufringen	Herr.	Sep 1836	N.-Amer	834624
Ackerknecht, Christina Heinr.	20 yrs.	Nufringen	Herr.	May 1832	N.-Amer	834624
Ackerknecht, Ferdinand Gottl.	28 Apr 1833	Herrenberg	Herr.	May 1870	N.-Amer	834624
Ackerknecht, Rosine Friedrike	27 Sep 1838	Herrenberg	Herr.	Feb 1870	N.-Amer	834624
Ackermann, Eva Catharina	15 Oct 1822	Unterweissach	Bckn.	bef 1868	N.-Amer	555959
Ade, Christian		Monakam	Calw	1857	N.-Amer	563212
Ade, Christian	20 Jul 1868	Rosenfeld	Sulz	Mar 1884	N.-Amer	849626
Ade, Jakob	18 Jul 1833	Wittendorf	Frd.	Mar 1854	N.-Amer	569273
Ade, Johann Georg		Marschalkenzimmern	Sulz	1833	N.-Amer	849625
Ade, Johann Georg & W	28 yrs.	Bondorf	Herr.	Jun 1832	N.-Amer	834624
Ade, Johann Jacob		Marschalkenzimmern	Sulz	1833	N.-Amer	849625
Ade, Karl	15 Sep 1866	Rosenfeld	Sulz	Mar 1881	N.-Amer	849626
Ade, Karl Ernst Gottlob	1836	Calw	Calw	1856	N.-Amer	563212
Ade, Maria (wid.)	56 yrs.	Obertalheim	Nag.	Feb 1854	N.-Amer	838491
Adler, Theresia		Leinstetten	Sulz	Jun 1854	N.-Amer	849638
Adrion, Andreas		Duerrenmettstetten	Sulz	Feb 1854	N.-Amer	849635
Adrion, Andreas	14 Mar 1832	Dornhan	Sulz	Jun 1854	N.-Amer	849633
Adrion, Anna Maria	11 yrs.	Reinerzau	Frd.	Mar 1817	Russia	569268
Adrion, Dorothea	5 Jan 1830	Dornhan	Sulz	Sep 1854	N.-Amer	849633
Adrion, Dorothee & C	35 yrs.	Reinerzau	Frd.	Mar 1817	Russia	569268
Adrion, Jacob	9 yrs.	Reinerzau	Frd.	Mar 1817	Russia	569268
Adrion, Jacob	20 Sep 1827	Dornhan	Sulz	Jan 1860	Rhld.	849633
Adrion, Johann Georg		Lossburg	Frd.	Apr 1847	N.-Amer	569270
Adrion, Michael		Lossburg	Frd.	bef 1844	Baden	569269
Aener, Johann Georg		Haltscheit	--	Dec 1751	Mas.N-A	550803
Aichele, Barbara		Deckenpfronn	Calw	1868	Bavaria	563212
Aichele, Carl Heinrich		Calw	Calw	1861	N.-Amer	563212
Aichele, Georg Adam & F		Deckenpfronn	Calw	1852	N.-Amer	563212
Aichele, Johann Georg	38 yrs.	Deckenpfronn	Calw	1868	N.-Amer	563212
Aichele, Johann Georg & F		Deckenpfronn	Calw	1852	N.-Amer	563212

Name		Birth		Emigration			Film
Last	First	Date	Place	O'amt	Appl. Date	Dest.	Number
Aicheler, Anna Maria (wife)			Gueltstein	Herr.	Sep 1852	N.-Amer	834627
Aicheler, Barbara (wife)			Nebringen	Herr.	Mar 1831	N.-Amer	834624
Aicheler, Christina		14 Feb 1847	Gueltstein	Herr.	Sep 1852	N.-Amer	834627
Aicheler, Elisabeth		2 Sep 1840	Gueltstein	Herr.	Sep 1852	N.-Amer	834627
Aicheler, Johann Christian		18 Jun 1844	Gueltstein	Herr.	Sep 1852	N.-Amer	834627
Aicheler, Johann Georg		6 May 1841	Gueltstein	Herr.	Sep 1852	N.-Amer	834627
Aicheler, Johannes		17 Sep 1851	Gueltstein	Herr.	Sep 1852	N.-Amer	834627
Aicheler, Johannes & F			Gueltstein	Herr.	Sep 1852	N.-Amer	834627
Aicheler, Martin		13 Jan 1835	Gueltstein	Herr.	Sep 1852	N.-Amer	834627
Aicheler, Peter		20 Sep 1837	Gueltstein	Herr.	Sep 1852	N.-Amer	834627
Aicheler, Peter & F			Gueltstein	Herr.	Sep 1852	N.-Amer	834627
Aicheler, Peter & W			Nebringen	Herr.	Mar 1831	N.-Amer	834624
Aichelmann, Georg & F		19 Apr 1838	Harthausen	Sulz	Jun 1871	N.-Amer	849637
Aimann, Eva Barbara		14 Dec 1792	Steinenberg	Schd.	Apr 1842	N.-Amer	801461
Akerer, Andreas			Holzhausen	Sulz	Jun 1852	N.-Amer	849635
Akerer, Andreas & F			Cresbach	Frd.	Mar 1837	N.-Amer	569269
Akerer, Anna Maria		2 yrs.	Cresbach	Frd.	Mar 1837	N.-Amer	569269
Akerer, Christina		4 yrs.	Cresbach	Frd.	Mar 1837	N.-Amer	569269
Akerer, Jacob & F			Holzhausen	Sulz	May 1817	Russia	849635
Akerer, Johannes		26 Sep 1854	Bergfelden	Sulz	Feb 1872	N.-Amer	849629
Akerer, Johannes		14 yrs.	Holzhausen	Sulz	Jun 1852	N.-Amer	849635
Akerer, Margaretha			Cresbach	Frd.	Mar 1837	N.-Amer	569269
Akerer, Martin & F			Holzhausen	Sulz	Apr 1817	Russia	849635
Alber, Jacob			Onstmettingen	Bal.	Jun 1841	Switz.	555962
Alber, Mathaeus		17 yrs.	Meistern/Bergorte	Calw	1854	N.-Amer	563212
Alber, Michael & F			Meistern/Bergorte	Calw	1854	N.-Amer	563212
Albrecht, Anna Barbara		3 Aug 1840	Brittheim	Sulz	Jul 1884	N.-Amer	849626
Albrecht, Katharina Karolina		4 Aug 1813	Stuttgart	Sulz	Nov 1861	Hesse	849628
Albrecht, Wilhelm			Sulz	Sulz	1836	Austria	849628
Alt, Christiane			Zavelstein	Calw	Jun 1870	Baden	563212
Amann, Anna		3 Apr 1803	Graubuenden/Switz.	Frd.	Mar 1846	N.-Amer	569271
Amann, Anselm			Oberndorf	Herr.	Apr 1830	N.-Amer	834624
Amann, August			Pfeffingen	Bal.	Mar 1844	N.-Amer	555964
Amann, Michael & F			Oberndorf	Herr.	Apr 1831	N.-Amer	834624
Ammann, Catharina			Poltringen	Herr.	Jan 1868	N.-Amer	834624
Ammer, Johann Jakob		26 Jan 1834	Dornstetten	Frd.	Apr 1853	N.-Amer	569272
Ammer, Johann Martin		7 Feb 1835	Dornstetten	Frd.	Mar 1853	N.-Amer	569272
Ammer, Philipp Jakob		11 Sep 1830	Dornstetten	Frd.	Mar 1853	N.-Amer	569272
Andler, Ludwig		35 yrs.	Dornstetten	Frd.	Mar 1866	N.-Amer	577780
Andler, Maria Dorothea		27 Aug 1837	Dornstetten	Frd.	Oct 1866	N.-Amer	577780
Andrae, Ernst Valentin		27 Aug 1844	Liebenzell	Calw	1864	N.-Amer	563212
Andrea, Heinrich Valentin			Liebenzell	Calw	1858	N.-Amer	563212
Andrea, Paul		18 yrs.	Heilbronn	Calw	1869	Turkey	563212
Angerer, Carl Friedr. Julius		7 Nov 1831	Sulz	Sulz	Sep 1858	Austria	849628
Angeshofer, Maria Magdalena			Althengstett	Calw	Feb 1870	N.-Amer	563212
Ansel, Emil			Stuttgart	Calw	Aug 1870	N.-Amer	563212
Appenzeller, Andreas			Tumlingen	Frd.	Aug 1810	Baden	569268
Appenzeller, Jacob			Tumlingen	Frd.	Apr 1752	Pen.N-A	550803
Armbruster, --			Freudenstadt	Frd.	1817	Russia	569269
Armbruster, Barbara (wife)			Duerrenmettstetten	Sulz	Aug 1854	N.-Amer	849635

Armbruster, Bertha Anna	9 Apr 1841	Sulz	Sulz	May 1862	Prussia	849628
Armbruster, Catharina	12 Nov 1836	Hopfau	Sulz	Apr 1860	N.-Amer	849636
Armbruster, Christian & F		Duerrenmettstetten	Sulz	Aug 1854	N.-Amer	849635
Armbruster, Christina	14 yrs.	Duerrenmettstetten	Sulz	Aug 1854	N.-Amer	849635
Armbruster, Eva	17 Sep 1846	Reinerzau	Frd.	Jan 1865	Baden	577779
Armbruster, Gottlieb	9 yrs.	Duerrenmettstetten	Sulz	Aug 1854	N.-Amer	849635
Armbruster, Gottlieb & F		Kniebis	Frd.	Apr 1817	Russia	569267
Armbruster, Jacob & F		Baiersbronn	Frd.	Apr 1817	Rus-Pol	569267
Armbruster, Johann Georg		Kniebis	Frd.	Aug 1817	Baden	569267
Armbruster, Johann Georg	11 yrs.	Duerrenmettstetten	Sulz	Aug 1854	N.-Amer	849635
Armbruster, Johann Jacob	27 yrs.	Sulz	Sulz	1814	Switz.	849625
Armbruster, Joseph	15 Apr 1840	Bettenhausen	Sulz	Mar 1843	Austria	849630
Armbruster, Katharina	19 Jan 1835	Bettenhausen	Sulz	Mar 1843	Austria	849630
Armbruster, Maria (wife)		Bettenhausen	Sulz	Mar 1843	Austria	849630
Armbruster, Martin & F	3 May 1832	Bettenhausen	Sulz	Mar 1843	Austria	849630
Arnold, Adam		Rosenfeld	Sulz	Apr 1854	N.-Amer	849640
Arnold, Christian	5 Mar 1840	Rosenfeld	Sulz	Sep 1860	N.-Amer	849641
Arnold, Christian	6 Mar 1850	Herrenberg	Herr.	Dec 1868	N.-Amer	834624
Arnold, Christina Cath. (wife)	26 Apr 1807	Unterjesingen	Herr.	Aug 1846	Austria	834626
Arnold, Christoph	26 Jul 1826	Rosenfeld	Sulz	bef 1865	N.-Amer	849641
Arnold, Gottlieb Friedrich	30 May 1831	Baiersbronn	Frd.	Feb 1854	N.-Amer	569273
Arnold, Jacob & F	25 Mar 1810	Unterjesingen	Herr.	Aug 1846	Austria	834626
Arnold, Jacob Friedrich	17 Apr 1839	Unterjesingen	Herr.	Aug 1846	Austria	834626
Arnold, Jakob Friedrich	31 Dec 1846	Rosenfeld	Sulz	Sep 1860	N.-Amer	849641
Arnold, Jakob Heinrich	17 Jun 1845	Rosenfeld	Sulz	Sep 1860	N.-Amer	849641
Arnold, Johann Georg	3 Jul 1837	Rosenfeld	Sulz	Jul 1855	N.-Amer	849640
Arnold, Johann Georg		Rosenfeld	Sulz	Apr 1854	N.-Amer	849640
Arnold, Johannes	15 Jun 1839	Rosenfeld	Sulz	Jul 1859	N.-Amer	849640
Arnold, Johannes	20 Jun 1842	Rosenfeld	Sulz	Sep 1860	N.-Amer	849641
Arnold, Johannes	3 Oct 1800	Pfaeffingen	Herr.	Feb 1851	N.-Amer	834627
Arnold, Maria Barbara	23 Apr 1841	Rosenfeld	Sulz	Sep 1860	N.-Amer	849641
Arnold, Mathaeus & F		Dornhan	Frd.	1817	Russia	569269
Arnold, Salome	19 Sep 1840	Unterjesingen	Herr.	Aug 1846	Austria	834626
Arnold, Wilhelmine	22 Jul 1844	Unterjesingen	Herr.	Aug 1846	Austria	834626
Artz, Catharina Christina	44 yrs.	Freudenstadt	Frd.	May 1752	Pen.N-A	550803
Artz, Johann Philipp & F	29 yrs.	Freudenstadt	Frd.	May 1752	Pen.N-A	550803
Artz, Maria Barbara	26 yrs.	Freudenstadt	Frd.	May 1752	Pen.N-A	550803
Artz, Sophia Dorothea	4 yrs.	Freudenstadt	Frd.	May 1752	Pen.N-A	550803
Au von, Josephine Wilh. Henr.	12 Mar 1826	Herrenberg	Herr.	Mar 1862	France	834624
Auer, Anna Maria	28 Mar 1831	Sulz	Sulz	Mar 1888	Switz.	849626
Ayahse, Johann Ludwig	13 Jun 1843	Neuhengstett	Calw	1863	N.-Amer	563212
Ayasse, Johann Jacob	19 yrs.	Neuhengstett	Calw	1869	N.-Amer	563212
Baach, Michel	25 yrs.	Unteriflingen	Frd.	May 1752	Pen.N-A	550803
Baaser, Jacob		Simmozheim	Calw	1861	Afrika	563212
Bacher, Christian	30 Jan 1846	Freudenstadt	Frd.	Jul 1866	N.-Amer	577780
Bacher, Johann Jakob	3 Mar 1839	Gueltlingen	Nag.	Aug 1854	N.-Amer	838491
Bacher, Maria Katharina	25 Jun 1827	Gueltlingen	Nag.	Aug 1854	N.-Amer	838491
Bachmann, Gottfried	10 Jan 1825	Pfalzgrafenweiler	Frd.	Apr 1846	N.-Amer	569271
Bachmann, Johann Adam & F		Hopfau	Sulz	Jan 1817	Russia	849636
Bachteler, Friedrich	10 Jun 1832	Freudenstadt	Frd.	Sep 1854	N.-Amer	569274

Name		Birth		Emigration			Film
Last	First	Date	Place	O'amt	Appl. Date	Dest.	Number
Back, Heinrich			Calw	Calw	1859	N.-Amer	563212
Back, Heinrike Wilhelmine			Calw	Calw	1859	N.-Amer	563212
Backhenni, Christine			Neubulach	Calw	1856	N.-Amer	563212
Bader, Johann Martin			Gueltstein	Herr.	Sep 1835	France	834624
Baechle, Anna Maria & C		17 Apr 1833	Boll	Sulz	Apr 1862	N.-Amer	849632
Baechle, Anna Maria (wid.)		5 Aug 1796	Boll	Sulz	Sep 1865	N.-Amer	849632
Baechle, Johann Georg		20 Jun 1858	Boll	Sulz	Apr 1862	N.-Amer	849632
Baechler, Christina		8 Mar 1831	Langenbach	Frd.	Mar 1854	N.-Amer	569273
Baechtle, Adam & F			Meistern/Bergorte	Calw	1853	N.-Amer	563212
Baechtle, Jacob Friedrich			Aichelberg/Bergorte	Calw	1853	N.-Amer	563212
Baeder, Christoph Friedrich			Haslach	Herr.	Sep 1836	Rus-Pol	834624
Baeder, Friedrich August		3 Aug 1842	Haslach	Herr.	Jun 1866	Switz.	834624
Baer, Johann Philip			Delckheim	– –	Dec 1751	N.-Amer	550803
Baerstecher, Christian		22 Nov 1843	Bondorf	Herr.	Jan 1867	N.-Amer	834624
Baerstecher, Eva Barbara		29 Dec 1819	Oberjettingen	Herr.	Feb 1867	N.-Amer	834624
Baesler, Anna Maria		21 Nov 1838	Muehlheim a.B.	Sulz	Apr 1858	N.-Amer	849639
Baesler, Anna Maria (wife)		24 Dec 1831	Muehlheim a.B.	Sulz	1854	N.-Amer	849639
Baesler, Friedrich Gottlob		7 May 1841	Muehlheim a.B.	Sulz	1858	N.-Amer	849639
Baesler, Jakob & F			Holzhausen	Sulz	Feb 1817	Russia	849635
Baesler, Johann Georg		16 Aug 1831	Brittheim	Sulz	Oct 1860	N.-Amer	849632
Baesler, Johann Jacob		18 Mar 1796	Herrenberg	Herr.	Jul 1846	N.-Amer	834626
Baesler, Johann Peter			Gueltstein	Herr.	Mar 1836	N.-Amer	834624
Baesler, Johannes		19 Sep 1848	Muehlheim a.B.	Sulz	1858	N.-Amer	849639
Baesler, Johannes & F		27 May 1805	Muehlheim a.B.	Sulz	1854	N.-Amer	849639
Baesler, Louisa		2 May 1836	Brittheim	Sulz	Jan 1857	N.-Amer	849632
Baesler, Ludwig		29 Sep 1810	Bergfelden	Sulz	Feb 1836	N.-Amer	849629
Baesler, Mathias			Frutenhof	Frd.	1817	Russia	569269
Baesler, Rosina Katharina		11 May 1828	Brittheim	Sulz	Jan 1857	N.-Amer	849632
Baessler, Anna Maria		21 Nov 1838	Muehlheim a.B.	Sulz	Apr 1858	N.-Amer	849639
Baessler, Barbara			Freudenstadt	Frd.	May 1857	Switz.	577776
Baessler, Christian		7 May 1846	Renfrizhausen	Sulz	Feb 1866	N.-Amer	849639
Baessler, Christian		28 Jan 1864	Renfrizhausen	Sulz	Jan 1866	N.-Amer	849639
Baessler, Dorothea (wife)		17 Jun 1833	Renfrizhausen	Sulz	Jan 1866	N.-Amer	849639
Baessler, Friedrich		26 Sep 1834	Renfrizhausen	Sulz	Jan 1854	N.-Amer	849639
Baessler, Jacob		26 Jun 1832	Renfrizhausen	Sulz	bef 1865	France	849639
Baessler, Jakob Friedrich			Freudenstadt	Frd.	bef 1854	N.-Amer	569275
Baessler, Johannes		15 Jan 1860	Renfrizhausen	Sulz	Jan 1866	N.-Amer	849639
Baessler, Johannes & F		20 Jan 1833	Renfrizhausen	Sulz	Jan 1866	N.-Amer	849639
Baessler, Martin		5 Jul 1842	Renfrizhausen	Sulz	Oct 1859	N.-Amer	849639
Baetzer, Johann Friedrich		19 Mar 1845	Breitenholz	Herr.	Nov 1865	N.-Amer	834624
Baetzmann, Ernestine Cath.		3 May 1843	Reichenbach	Frd.	bef 1863	Baden	577778
Baeuchle, Rosina		7 Jul 1794	Oberurbach	Schd.	Mar 1837	N.-Amer	801461
Baeuerle, Catharina			Wildberg	Frd.	Jun 1856	N.-Amer	569275
Baeuerle, Gottfried & F			Schoenmuenzach	Frd.	Apr 1840	Hungary	569268
Baeuerle, Jacob Friedrich		19 Dec 1839	Oberjesingen	Herr.	Dec 1866	Baden	834624
Baeuerle, Katharina			Boesingen	Nag.	Feb 1854	N.-Amer	838491
Baeuerlein, Eduard			Rosenfeld	Sulz	Nov 1841	E.India	849640
Baeuerlen, Jacob			Herzogsweiler	Frd.	Apr 1752	Pen.N-A	550803
Baezner, Anna Maria			Enztal	Nag.	Jul 1852	N.-Amer	838490
Baezner, Christine			Enztal	Nag.	Jul 1852	N.-Amer	838490

Baezner, Eva Maria & C		Enztal	Nag.	Jul 1852	N.-Amer 838490
Baezner, Friedrich		Enztal	Nag.	Jul 1852	N.-Amer 838490
Baezner, Johann Georg		Enztal	Nag.	Jul 1852	N.-Amer 838490
Baezner, Philipp		Enztal	Nag.	Jul 1852	N.-Amer 838490
Bahlinger, Regina Catharina	29 Jul 1839	Gueltstein	Herr.	Feb 1867	N.-Amer 834624
Baier, Catharina		Oberkollwangen	Calw	1866	Hesse 563212
Baier, Catharina	14 Apr 1844	Marschalkenzimmern	Sulz	Aug 1865	N.-Amer 849638
Baier, Catharina	1830	Altberg	Calw	1855	N.-Amer 563212
Baier, Christian Ludwig	13 Jun 1847	Sulz	Sulz	Nov 1867	N.-Amer 849628
Baier, Christina	21 yrs.	Marschalkenzimmern	Sulz	1861	N.-Amer 849638
Baier, Dorothea		Marschalkenzimmern	Sulz	Aug 1853	N.-Amer 849638
Baier, Karl Leopold	1832	Altberg	Calw	1855	N.-Amer 563212
Baier, Ludwig		Marschalkenzimmern	Sulz	Aug 1855	N.-Amer 849638
Bailharz, Matthaeus	25 Jul 1844	Glatten	Frd.	Apr 1864	N.-Amer 577779
Baisch, Carl	20 Oct 1814	Sulz	Sulz	1841	Russia 849628
Baisch, Georg Christof		Sulz	Sulz	bef 1851	Russia 849628
Baither, Christiane Rosine		Calw	Calw	1857	N.-Amer 563212
Baitinger, Carl Ludwig		Deckenpfronn	Calw	1853	N.-Amer 563212
Baitinger, Johann Jost	22 May 1829	Oberjesingen	Herr.	Jan 1869	N.-Amer 834624
Baittinger, Johann Georg		Deckenpfronn	Calw	Jun 1870	N.-Amer 563212
Baittler, Wilhelm & F		Deckenpfronn	Calw	1853	N.-Amer 563212
Baldenhofer, David & F	11 Feb 1809	Freudenstadt	Frd.	Sep 1846	N.-Amer 569271
Baldenhofer, Franziska	13 Jan 1816	Freudenstadt	Frd.	Sep 1846	N.-Amer 569271
Baldenhofer, Franziska Louise	13 Jul 1836	Pfalzgrafenweiler	Frd.	Sep 1846	N.-Amer 569271
Baldenhofer, Rosine Louise	2 Sep 1841	Pfalzgrafenweiler	Frd.	Sep 1846	N.-Amer 569271
Baldenhofer, Rosine Margaretha	4 Jan 1839	Pfalzgrafenweiler	Frd.	Sep 1846	N.-Amer 569271
Baldenhofer, Wilhelmine Sophie	23 Nov 1843	Pfalzgrafenweiler	Frd.	Sep 1846	N.-Amer 569271
Baltis, Anna Maria	20 yrs.	Sigmarswangen	Sulz	Apr 1817	Rus-Pol 849642
Baltis, Christina (wife)	50 yrs.	Sigmarswangen	Sulz	Apr 1817	Rus-Pol 849642
Baltis, Georg Ferdinand	19 Jan 1860	Sigmarswangen	Sulz	Apr 1877	N.-Amer 849642
Baltis, Georg Ulrich & F	45 yrs.	Sigmarswangen	Sulz	Apr 1817	Rus-Pol 849642
Bantel, Catharina	21 Dec 1831	Oberurbach	Schd.	Mar 1837	N.-Amer 801461
Bantel, Dorothea	21 Dec 1831	Oberurbach	Schd.	Mar 1837	N.-Amer 801461
Bantel, Johann Leonhard	3 May 1834	Oberurbach	Schd.	Mar 1837	N.-Amer 801461
Bantel, Rosina & F	7 Jul 1794	Oberurbach	Schd.	Mar 1837	N.-Amer 801461
Bantle, Christine (wife)		Bickelsberg	Sulz	Feb 1853	N.-Amer 849630
Bantle, Johann Jakob	14 yrs.	Bickelsberg	Sulz	Feb 1853	N.-Amer 849630
Bantle, Johann Martin	20 yrs.	Bickelsberg	Sulz	Feb 1853	N.-Amer 849630
Bantle, Johann Martin & F	4 Jun 1790	Bickelsberg	Sulz	Feb 1853	N.-Amer 849630
Banzinger, Anna Louise	19 Aug 1858	Herrenberg	Herr.	Aug 1867	N.-Amer 834624
Banzinger, Elise	28 Feb 1848	Herrenberg	Herr.	Aug 1867	N.-Amer 834624
Banzinger, Friedrich	11 Jun 1851	Herrenberg	Herr.	Aug 1867	N.-Amer 834624
Baral, Gottlob		Neuhengstett	Calw	Jul 1870	N.-Amer 563212
Barmann, Regine Sophie		Pfalzgrafenweiler	Frd.	Feb 1855	Switz. 569275
Barstecher, Ernestine & F		Calw	Calw	1854	N.-Amer 563212
Bartmaier, Johann Jacob & F		Nufringen	Herr.	Mar 1835	Rus-Pol 834624
Bartok, Johannes	20 Apr 1857	Sigmarswangen	Sulz	Jun 1860	N.-Amer 849642
Bartok, Johannes	25 Dec 1832	Sigmarswangen	Sulz	Jun 1860	N.-Amer 849642
Bartok, Ursula & C	16 Mar 1835	Sigmarswangen	Sulz	Jun 1860	N.-Amer 849642
Bas, Joseph		Montbeilard	– –	Dec 1751	Mas.N-A 550803

| Name | | Birth | | Emigration | | | Film |
Last	First	Date	Place	O'amt	Appl. Date	Dest.	Number
Batsch, Franziska		20 Jul 1810	Schoenmuenzach	Frd.	Jul 1847	Baden	569270
Batsch, Nicodemus		7 Sep 1840	Schoenmuenzach	Frd.	bef 1864	Prussia	577779
Batsch, Simon			Schwarzenberg	Frd.	May 1831	Baden	569268
Bauer, Anna Maria		24 Aug 1851	Ebhausen	Nag.	Sep 1855	N.-Amer	838591
Bauer, Anna Maria		50 yrs.	Spielberg	Nag.	Apr 1853	N.-Amer	838490
Bauer, Anna Maria		31 Dec 1819	Hildrizhausen	Herr.	Jul 1867	N.-Amer	834624
Bauer, Anna Maria & F		14 Feb 1817	Ebhausen	Nag.	Sep 1855	N.-Amer	838591
Bauer, Anna Maria Catharina		30 Jul 1835	Unterjettingen	Herr.	Mar 1848	N.-Amer	834626
Bauer, Barbara & C			Schopfloch	Frd.	Jul 1856	N.-Amer	569275
Bauer, Carl Friedrich			Freudenstadt	Frd.	Mar 1855	N.-Amer	569275
Bauer, Christian		17 Oct 1835	Obermusbach	Frd.	Feb 1854	N.-Amer	569273
Bauer, Christian			Reichenbach	Frd.	bef 1862	Baden	577778
Bauer, Christian		18 Nov 1861	Hallwangen	Frd.	Sep 1865	N.-Amer	577779
Bauer, Christina		7 yrs.	Spielberg	Nag.	Apr 1853	N.-Amer	838490
Bauer, Christine		1852	Ebhausen	Nag.	Sep 1855	N.-Amer	838591
Bauer, Christoph		14 Jul 1833	Gruental	Frd.	Mar 1854	N.-Amer	569273
Bauer, David		23 Oct 1825	Unterjettingen	Herr.	Mar 1848	N.-Amer	834626
Bauer, Elisabeth Catharina		9 Oct 1838	Groembach	Frd.	Aug 1865	N.-Amer	577779
Bauer, Friederike		13 Aor 1811	Hildrizhausen	Herr.	Jul 1867	N.-Amer	834624
Bauer, Friedrich		11 yrs.	Spielberg	Nag.	Apr 1853	N.-Amer	838490
Bauer, Gottfried			Goettelfingen	Frd.	Apr 1860	N.-Amer	577777
Bauer, Gottlieb		31 Dec 1840	Unterjettingen	Herr.	Mar 1848	N.-Amer	834626
Bauer, Gottlieb		26 Aug 1833	Unterjesingen	Herr.	Apr 1851	N.-Amer	834627
Bauer, Gottlieb Friedrich		19 yrs.	Liebenzell	Calw	1868	N.-Amer	563212
Bauer, Heinrich		12 Feb 1838	Moetzingen	Herr.	Mar 1847	N.-Amer	834626
Bauer, Jacob Friedrich			Simmozheim	Calw	1862	N.-Amer	563212
Bauer, Jakob David		22 Oct 1831	Hildrizhausen	Herr.	Feb 1852	N.-Amer	834627
Bauer, Jakob Friedrich & W			Calw	Calw	Oct 1873	N.-Amer	563212
Bauer, Johann Friedrich		25 Jan 1832	Pfaeffingen	Herr.	Apr 1851	N.-Amer	834627
Bauer, Johann Georg		19 yrs.	Spielberg	Nag.	Apr 1853	N.-Amer	838490
Bauer, Johann Georg		4 Mar 1826	Obermusbach	Frd.	Apr 1856	N.-Amer	569275
Bauer, Johann Georg		22 Feb 1829	Unterjesingen	Herr.	Apr 1851	N.-Amer	834627
Bauer, Johann Georg & F			Spielberg	Nag.	Apr 1853	N.-Amer	838490
Bauer, Johann Georg & F		10 Jul 1799	Unterjettingen	Herr.	Mar 1848	N.-Amer	834626
Bauer, Johann Martin		15 Oct 1822	Hildrizhausen	Herr.	Jul 1867	N.-Amer	834624
Bauer, Johannes		11 Nov 1849	Ebhausen	Nag.	Sep 1855	N.-Amer	838591
Bauer, Johannes			Ebhausen	Nag.	1853	N.-Amer	838591
Bauer, Johannes		23 yrs.	Spielberg	Nag.	Apr 1853	N.-Amer	838490
Bauer, Johannes		2 May 1830	Neuneck	Frd.	Feb 1853	N.-Amer	569272
Bauer, Jonathan Ludwig		25 Aug 1799	Sulz	Sulz	Aug 1832	Altona	849627
Bauer, Katharina Agatha		21 yrs.	Unterjesingen	Herr.	Mar 1847	N.-Amer	834626
Bauer, Kunigunde			Groembach	Frd.	1837	N.-Amer	569269
Bauer, Ludwig			Dietersweiler	Frd.	bef 1858	N.-Amer	577776
Bauer, Margaretha Barb. (wife)		26 Jan 1801	Unterjettingen	Herr.	Mar 1848	N.-Amer	834626
Bauer, Maria Catharina			Hallwangen	Frd.	Sep 1865	N.-Amer	577779
Bauer, Maria Charlotte			Hirsau	Calw	1867	Switz.	563212
Bauer, Maria Rosina		8 Jan 1865	Hallwangen	Frd.	Sep 1865	N.-Amer	577779
Bauer, Martin & F			Hallwangen	Frd.	Sep 1865	N.-Amer	577779
Bauer, Mathaeus		25 Nov 1828	Unterjettingen	Herr.	Mar 1848	N.-Amer	834626
Bauer, Michael (wid.) & F		18 May 1783	Groembach	Frd.	Mar 1847	N.-Amer	569271

Bauer, Philipp	14 Dec 1845	Gottelfingen	Frd.	1865	N.-Amer	577779
Bauer, Regina	18 Jan 1822	Groembach	Frd.	Mar 1847	N.-Amer	569771
Bauer, Ulrich		Roetenbach	Calw	1852	N.-Amer	563212
Bauer, Veronika	9 yrs.	Spielberg	Nag.	Apr 1853	N.-Amer	838490
Bauer, Wilhelm Friedrich	21 May 1841	Freudenstadt	Frd.	Jul 1859	N.-Amer	577776
Bauer, Wilhelm Friedrich	5 Nov 1831	Unterjesingen	Herr.	Apr 1851	N.-Amer	834627
Bauerli, Gottlieb & F		Zavelstein	Calw	1867	S.-Amer	563212
Bauernfeind, Emilie Victoria	8 Jul 1840	Sulz	Sulz	May 1869	Baden	849628
Baum, Beda		Leinstetten	Sulz	Jun 1854	N.-Amer	849638
Baumann, Catharina		Schoemberg	Frd.	Jun 1854	N.-Amer	569273
Baumann, Christine		Schoemberg	Frd.	Jun 1854	N.-Amer	569273
Baumann, Dorothea		Schoemberg	Frd.	Jun 1854	N.-Amer	569273
Baumann, Jakob	20 Feb 1862	Marschalkenzimmern	Sulz	Apr 1881	N.-Amer	849626
Baumann, Johann Jacob	4 Mar 1802	Marschalkenzimmern	Sulz	Sep 1832	Baden	849638
Baumann, Johann Jakob & F		Schoemberg	Frd.	Jun 1854	N.-Amer	569273
Baumann, Johann Martin	17 yrs.	Entringen	Herr.	Mar 1852	N.-Amer	834627
Baumann, Johannes		Schoemberg	Frd.	Jun 1854	N.-Amer	569273
Baumann, Johannes	22 Mar 1871	Dornhan	Sulz	May 1886	N.-Amer	849626
Baumann, Michael		Entringen	Herr.	May 1831	Baden	834624
Baumeister, Heinrich Jakob		Balingen	Bal.	bef 1850	Switz.	555963
Baur, (wife)	25 Oct 1807	Altingen	Herr.	Apr 1852	N.-Amer	834627
Baur, Adolph	18 Jun 1837	Reutlingen	Frd.	Sep 1854	N.-Amer	569274
Baur, Anna Maria		Leidringen	Sulz	Jun 1853	N.-Amer	849637
Baur, Charlotte & C		Oberjettingen	Herr.	Jul 1847	N.-Amer	834626
Baur, Christina	3 May 1835	Leidringen	Sulz	Mar 1862	N.-Amer	849637
Baur, Dorothea (wife)	37 yrs.	Oberjettingen	Herr.	Jul 1847	N.-Amer	834626
Baur, Franziska	2 May 1837	Altingen	Herr.	Apr 1852	N.-Amer	834627
Baur, Jakob	13 Oct 1865	Leidringen	Sulz	May 1882	N.-Amer	849626
Baur, Johannes	14 Mar 1844	Altingen	Herr.	Apr 1852	N.-Amer	834627
Baur, Johannes & F	37 yrs.	Oberjettingen	Herr.	Jul 1847	N.-Amer	834626
Baur, Joseph	4 May 1850	Altingen	Herr.	Apr 1852	N.-Amer	834627
Baur, Maria Magdalena	23 Jan 1841	Altingen	Herr.	Apr 1852	N.-Amer	834627
Baur, Matheus & F	15 Sep 1804	Altingen	Herr.	Apr 1852	N.-Amer	834627
Baur, Peter	19 May 1846	Altingen	Herr.	Apr 1852	N.-Amer	834627
Bauser, Carl Louis		Simmozheim	Calw	Feb 1870	N.-Amer	563212
Bauser, Christian Eberhard	24 yrs.	Simmozheim	Calw	Mar 1847	N.-Amer	563212
Bauser, Ernst		Simmozheim	Calw	1852	Hamburg	563212
Bautter, Christian & F		Marschalkenzimmern	Sulz	Feb 1847	N.-Amer	849638
Bayer, Elisabetha	11yrs.	Hofstett	Calw	1866	Baden	563212
Bayer, Elisabetha & C		Hofstett	Calw	1866	Baden	563212
Bayer, Friederike R. & C		Calw	Calw	1868	Baden	563212
Bayer, Johann Georg	23 Oct 1820	Hildrizhausen	Herr.	Mar 1847	N.-Amer	834626
Bayer, Philipp	8 yrs.	Calw	Calw	1868	Baden	563212
Bayerlin, Wilhelmine		Sulz	Sulz	Apr 1838	N.-Amer	849627
Bazer, Anna Maria	6 Sep 1840	Breitenholz	Herr.	Aug 1866	N.-Amer	834624
Bazer, Johann Michael	7 Sep 1847	Breitenholz	Herr.	Aug 1866	N.-Amer	834624
Becherer, Karl August Julius	9 Mar 1866	Stetten	Sulz	bef 1882	N.-Amer	849628
Bechtold, Heinrike Justine	20 yrs.	Nagold	Nag.	Jan 1854	N.-Amer	838491
Bechtold, Johann Georg	16 May 1837	Pfalzgrafenweiler	Frd.	Mar 1854	N.-Amer	569273
Beck, Agnes	10 May 1822	Leidringen	Sulz	Jan 1833	N.-Amer	849637

Name		Birth		Emigration			Film
Last	First	Date	Place	O'amt	Appl. Date	Dest.	Number
Beck, Anna Barbara		25 Sep 1865	Bergfelden	Sulz	Feb 1883	N.-Amer	849626
Beck, Anna Katharina		15 yrs.	Leidringen	Sulz	Feb 1817	Russia	849637
Beck, Anna Maria		19 Oct 1870	Bergfelden	Sulz	Feb 1883	N.-Amer	849626
Beck, Anna Maria (wife)		10 Nov 1841	Bergfelden	Sulz	Feb 1883	N.-Amer	849629
Beck, Christian		13 Nov 1878	Bergfelden	Sulz	Feb 1883	N.-Amer	849626
Beck, Christina		16 Nov 1834	Gundelshausen	Sulz	Aug 1854	N.-Amer	849633
Beck, Christine		27 Sep 1875	Bergfelden	Sulz	Feb 1883	N.-Amer	849626
Beck, Friedrich			Voehringen	Sulz	1836	N.-Amer	849625
Beck, Gustav		19 Jan 1842	Sulz	Sulz	Jan 1869	Berlin	849628
Beck, Jakob		1 Sep 1872	Bergfelden	Sulz	Feb 1883	N.-Amer	849626
Beck, Johann Georg & F			Leidringen	Sulz	Jun 1817	Russia	849637
Beck, Johann Georg & F			Calw	Calw	Mar 1847	N.-Amer	563212
Beck, Johann Jacob		14 May 1842	Leidringen	Sulz	Sep 1859	N.-Amer	849637
Beck, Johann Martin			Leidringen	Sulz	Jan 1855	N.-Amer	849637
Beck, Katharine		21 Dec 1880	Bergfelden	Sulz	Feb 1883	N.-Amer	849626
Beck, Magdalena		17 Feb 1830	Leidringen	Sulz	Jan 1833	N.-Amer	849637
Beck, Margarethe Friederike			Calw	Calw	1868	Switz.	563212
Beck, Martin		13 Oct 1819	Leidringen	Sulz	Jan 1833	N.-Amer	849637
Beck, Martin			Balingen	Bal.	Mar 1863	Switz.	555962
Beck, Martin & F		13 Aug 1838	Bergfelden	Sulz	Feb 1883	N.-Amer	849626
Beck, Mathaeus		17 Apr 1871	Bergfelden	Sulz	Apr 1888	N.-Amer	849626
Beck, Mathias & F		19 Oct 1796	Leidringen	Sulz	Jan 1833	N.-Amer	849637
Beck, Matthaeus			Leidringen	Sulz	Mar 1833	N.-Amer	849637
Beck, Rosine		30 Mar 1821	Leidringen	Sulz	Jan 1833	N.-Amer	849637
Beck, Rosine (wife)			Leidringen	Sulz	Jan 1833	N.-Amer	849637
Beerstecher, Anna Barb. (wife)			Kuppingen	Herr.	Mar 1831	N.-Amer	834624
Beerstecher, Christof		29 yrs.	Moetzingen	Herr.	May 1831	France	834624
Beerstecher, Philipp Jacob & W			Kuppingen	Herr.	Mar 1831	N.-Amer	834624
Behr, Johannes		7 Jun 1848	Trichtingen	Sulz	Nov 1868	N.-Amer	849642
Behr, Michael		7 Oct 1850	Trichtingen	Sulz	May 1869	N.-Amer	849642
Behr, Rosine Friederike			Rosenfeld	Sulz	Jan 1841	Prussia	849640
Beilharz, Anna Maria (wife)			Voehringen	Sulz	Apr 1833	N.-Amer	849643
Beilharz, Christina (wife)			Holzhausen	Sulz	Jun 1832	N.-Amer	849635
Beilharz, Friedrich			Oberbraendi	Frd.	Sep 1860	N.-Amer	577777
Beilharz, Jacob Friedrich		6 Oct 1815	Aach	Frd.	Mar 1837	N.-Amer	569267
Beilharz, Johann Jakob			Wittendorf	Frd.	Jun 1844	France	569269
Beilharz, Johann Jakob		12 Oct 1838	Voehringen	Sulz	bef 1867	Switz.	849643
Beilharz, Johann Martin & W			Voehringen	Sulz	Apr 1833	N.-Amer	849643
Beilharz, Johannes		12 Dec 1829	Aach	Frd.	Mar 1854	N.-Amer	569273
Beilharz, Johannes		11 May 1842	Lossburg	Frd.	Apr 1860	N.-Amer	577777
Beilharz, Johannes & F		27 May 1801	Holzhausen	Sulz	Jun 1832	N.-Amer	849635
Beilharz, Mathaeus		14 Sep 1834	Aach	Frd.	Mar 1854	N.-Amer	569273
Beilharz, Veronika			Holzhausen	Sulz	Apr 1817	Russia	849635
Beisser, Georg Jacob Simon		29 yrs.	Calw	Calw	1866	Bremen	563212
Beisser, Gottlob Heinrich			Calw	Calw	1852	N.-Amer	563212
Beisser, Johannes		1835	Calw	Calw	1854	N.-Amer	563212
Beisser, Maria (wid.) & F			Calw	Calw	1853	N.-Amer	563212
Beisser, Marie Friederike		22 yrs.	Calw	Calw	1867	Switz.	563212
Beisser, Wilhelmine			Calw	Calw	1858	Baden	563212
Bek, Anna Maria		27 Oct 1864	Voehringen	Sulz	Aug 1872	N.-Amer	849643

Bek, Catharina	21 Mar 1834	Voehringen	Sulz	1863	Baden	849643
Bek, Christina & C	19 Jan 1842	Voehringen	Sulz	Aug 1872	N.-Amer	849643
Bek, Friederich	8 Jul 1872	Voehringen	Sulz	Aug 1872	N.-Amer	849643
Bek, Friedrich		Voehringen	Sulz	Apr 1837	N.-Amer	849643
Bek, Jacob (wid.) & F		Breitenholz	Herr.	Aug 1852	N.-Amer	834627
Bek, Jacob Friedrich	19 yrs.	Breitenholz	Herr.	Aug 1852	N.-Amer	834627
Bek, Johann Georg & F		Reusten	Herr.	Apr 1830	N.-Amer	834624
Bek, Maria Agnes	14 yrs.	Breitenholz	Herr.	Aug 1852	N.-Amer	834627
Bekenberger, Barbara		Fuernsal	Sulz	Mar 1837	N.-Amer	849635
Bekenberger, Barbara (wife)		Fuernsal	Sulz	Mar 1837	N.-Amer	849635
Bekenberger, Johannes		Fuernsal	Sulz	Mar 1837	N.-Amer	849635
Bekenberger, Johannes & F		Fuernsal	Sulz	Mar 1837	N.-Amer	849635
Bekenberger, Maria Catharina		Fuernsal	Sulz	Mar 1837	N.-Amer	849635
Beker, Catharina (wife)		Althengstett	Calw	1860	N.-Amer	563212
Beker, Johann Georg & F		Althengstett	Calw	1860	N.-Amer	563212
Benell, Albert		Walddorf	Nag.	Jun 1852	Prussia	838490
Benell, Carl Friedrich	25 yrs.	Walddorf	Nag.	Jun 1852	Prussia	838490
Bengel, Johann Conrad		Gueltstein	Herr.	Mar 1836	N.-Amer	834624
Bengel, Maria Barbara & C		Gueltstein	Herr.	Mar 1836	N.-Amer	834624
Benhard, Johann Christoph & F		Freudenstadt	Frd.	Sep 1854	N.-Amer	569274
Benhard, Sophie Elisabeth		Freudenstadt	Frd.	Sep 1854	N.-Amer	569274
Benhardt, August Friedrich	20 May 1846	Freudenstadt	Frd.	Sep 1854	N.-Amer	569274
Benhardt, Carl August	15 Jun 1848	Freudenstadt	Frd.	Sep 1854	N.-Amer	569274
Benhardt, Caroline	17 Aug 1854	Freudenstadt	Frd.	Sep 1854	N.-Amer	569274
Benhardt, Caroline Wilhelmine	3 Jul 1843	Freudenstadt	Frd.	Sep 1854	N.-Amer	569274
Benhardt, Johann Christian	27 Jul 1837	Freudenstadt	Frd.	Sep 1854	N.-Amer	569274
Benhardt, Johann Friedrich	9 Jan 1840	Freudenstadt	Frd.	Sep 1854	N.-Amer	569274
Benhardt, Maria Dorothea	18 Jun 1841	Freudenstadt	Frd.	Sep 1854	N.-Amer	569274
Benhardt, Sophie Louise	14 Sep 1851	Freudenstadt	Frd.	Sep 1854	N.-Amer	569274
Benro, Adolph Ludwig	1826	Hirsau	Calw	1857	N.-Amer	563212
Benz, Adam & F		Dietersweiler	Frd.	Mar 1854	N.-Amer	569273
Benz, Anna & C	20 Aug 1810	Rodt	Frd.	Apr 1849	N.-Amer	569270
Benz, Barbara		Dietersweiler	Frd.	Mar 1854	N.-Amer	569273
Benz, Catharina (wife)		Dietersweiler	Frd.	Mar 1854	N.-Amer	569273
Benz, Christian		Dietersweiler	Frd.	Mar 1854	N.-Amer	569273
Benz, Dorothea		Dietersweiler	Frd.	Mar 1854	N.-Amer	569273
Benz, Friedrich		Dietersweiler	Frd.	Mar 1854	N.-Amer	569273
Benz, Gottlieb		Dietersweiler	Frd.	Mar 1854	N.-Amer	569273
Benz, Jacob	14 May 1792	Schoemberg	Frd.	Aug 1840	Frankf.	569268
Benz, Johann Adam	18 yrs.	Dietersweiler	Frd.	Feb 1850	N.-Amer	569271
Benz, Johann Georg		Dietersweiler	Frd.	Mar 1854	N.-Amer	569273
Benz, Johannes		Dietersweiler	Frd.	Mar 1854	N.-Amer	569273
Benz, Matthaeus		Dietersweiler	Frd.	Mar 1854	N.-Amer	569273
Benz, Michael	20 Nov 1839	Rodt	Frd.	Apr 1849	N.-Amer	569270
Benz, Michael		Dietersweiler	Frd.	Mar 1854	N.-Amer	569273
Benz, Rudolf	16 Aug 1847	Roseck	Herr.	May 1869	N.-Amer	834624
Benzinger, Adolf	8 May 1842	Hildrizhausen	Herr.	May 1865	N.-Amer	834624
Berg, Christian	18 Feb 1829	Herrenberg	Herr.	Apr 1849	N.-Amer	834627
Berger, Andreas & F		Groembach	Frd.	1837	N.-Amer	569269
Berger, Christina		Groembach	Frd.	1837	N.-Amer	569269

| Name | | Birth | | Emigration | | | Film |
Last	First	Date	Place	O'amt	Appl. Date	Dest.	Number
Berger, Johann Adam		1 Mar 1824	Groembach	Frd.	Jul 1843	N.-Amer	569269
Berger, Johannes & F			Aistaig	Sulz	Mar 1848	N.-Amer	849628
Berger, Philipp		11 Aug 1822	Groembach	Frd.	Jun 1843	N.-Amer	569269
Bernauer, Carolina Friederike			Freudenstadt	Frd.	Sep 1853	N.-Amer	569273
Berneker, Emil		7 Jan 1851	Herrenberg	Herr.	Aug 1866	N.-Amer	834624
Berner, Jacob		24 Sep 184-	Breitenholz	Herr.	Jul 1869	Prussia	834624
Berner, Karl		14 yrs.	Teinach	Calw	1854	N.-Amer	563212
Bernhard, Barbara & C			Muehlheim a.b.	Sulz	Feb 1862	Baden	849639
Bernhard, Eva		5 Jun 1852	Muehlheim a.b.	Sulz	Aug 1854	N.-Amer	849639
Bernhard, Johann Gottlieb & F			Muehlheim a.b.	Sulz	Aug 1854	N.-Amer	849639
Bernhard, Magdalena		31 Aug 1847	Muehlheim a.b.	Sulz	Aug 1854	N.-Amer	849639
Bernhard, Maria Katharina		3 Apr 1860	Muehlheim a.b.	Sulz	Feb 1862	Baden	849639
Bernhard, Maria Magdalena (wife)			Muehlheim a.b.	Sulz	Aug 1854	N.-Amer	849639
Bernhard, Mathaeus		27 Sep 1837	Isingen	Sulz	Feb 1854	N.-Amer	849636
Bernhard, Sophie Frieder.		9 mon.	Freudenstadt	Frd.	Oct 1859	N.-Amer	577776
Bernhard, Sophie Frieder. & C		19 Jan 1831	Freudenstadt	Frd.	Oct 1859	N.-Amer	577776
Bernhardt, Agnes Johanne & F			Freudenstadt	Frd.	Oct 1852	N.-Amer	577778
Bernhardt, Andreas & F			Bickelsberg	Sulz	Mar 1891	Baden	849626
Bernhardt, August		1 yrs.	Freudenstadt	Frd.	Sep 1850	N.-Amer	569271
Bernhardt, Barbara		11 yrs.	Freudenstadt	Frd.	Sep 1850	N.-Amer	569271
Bernhardt, Caroline		3 yrs.	Freudenstadt	Frd.	Oct 1852	N.-Amer	577778
Bernhardt, Caroline		8 yrs.	Freudenstadt	Frd.	Sep 1850	N.-Amer	569271
Bernhardt, Christian David		3 Oct 1841	Freudenstadt	Frd.	Sep 1854	N.-Amer	569274
Bernhardt, Christiana		19 yrs.	Freudenstadt	Frd.	Sep 1850	N.-Amer	569271
Bernhardt, Christiane Frieder.		3 Aug 1844	Freudenstadt	Frd.	Sep 1854	N.-Amer	569274
Bernhardt, David		16 yrs.	Freudenstadt	Frd.	Sep 1850	N.-Amer	569271
Bernhardt, David & F			Freudenstadt	Frd.	Aug 1851	N.-Amer	569271
Bernhardt, Dorothea		20 yrs.	Freudenstadt	Frd.	Aug 1851	N.-Amer	569271
Bernhardt, Elisabetha Marg.			Bergfelden	Sulz	bef 1855	N.-Amer	849629
Bernhardt, Friederike		9 yrs.	Freudenstadt	Frd.	Oct 1852	N.-Amer	577778
Bernhardt, Friederike		23 yrs.	Freudenstadt	Frd.	Sep 1850	N.-Amer	569271
Bernhardt, Friederike Louise		12 Oct 1837	Freudenstadt	Frd.	bef 1863	Baden	577778
Bernhardt, Friedrich		2 yrs.	Freudenstadt	Frd.	Oct 1852	N.-Amer	577778
Bernhardt, Friedrich		6 yrs.	Freudenstadt	Frd.	Aug 1851	N.-Amer	569271
Bernhardt, Friedrich		13 yrs.	Freudenstadt	Frd.	Sep 1850	N.-Amer	569271
Bernhardt, Friedrich & F			Freudenstadt	Frd.	Sep 1854	N.-Amer	569274
Bernhardt, Gustav		5 yrs.	Freudenstadt	Frd.	Oct 1852	N.-Amer	577778
Bernhardt, Heinrich & F			Freudenstadt	Frd.	Mar 1817	Russia	569267
Bernhardt, Jacob			Freudenstadt	Frd.	Mar 1854	N.-Amer	569273
Bernhardt, Jakob Friedrich		11 Apr 1848	Muehlheim a.B.	Sulz	Aug 1871	N.-Amer	849639
Bernhardt, Johann Caspar & F			Freudenstadt	Frd.	Sep 1850	N.-Amer	569271
Bernhardt, Johanne		1831	Freudenstadt	Frd.	1849	N.-Amer	569275
Bernhardt, Karoline Pauline		1842	Freudenstadt	Frd.	Apr 1864	N.-Amer	577779
Bernhardt, Ludwig Friedrich		8 Jul 1835	Freudenstadt	Frd.	Sep 1853	N.-Amer	569274
Bernhardt, Margarethe Barbara			Freudenstadt	Frd.	Sep 1854	N.-Amer	569274
Bernhardt, Maria Sophia		2 Apr 1837	Freudenstadt	Frd.	Jul 1860	N.-Amer	577777
Bernhardt, Rosine Barbara		20 Apr 1852	Freudenstadt	Frd.	Sep 1854	N.-Amer	569274
Bernhardt, Rosine Friederike		1835	Freudenstadt	Frd.	bef 1857	N.-Amer	577776
Bernhardt, Sophie		13 yrs.	Freudenstadt	Frd.	Oct 1852	N.-Amer	577778
Bernhardt, Wilhelm Friedrich		7 yrs.	Freudenstadt	Frd.	Oct 1852	N.-Amer	577778

Dernhardt, Wilhelmine	11 yrs.	Freudenstadt	Frd.	Oct 1852	N.-Amer	577778
Bertermann, Johann Georg		Rheinduerckheim	– –	Dec 1751	N.-Amer	550803
Bertrand, Christiane Frieder.	22 Nov 1839	Sulz	Sulz	Nov 1864	Baden	849628
Bertrand, Gottlob Wilhelm		Sulz	Sulz	May 1853	N.-Amer	849627
Bertrang, Aloisius	20 yrs.	Sigmarswangen	Sulz	Jun 1817	Russia	849642
Bertrang, Anna Maria	12 yrs.	Sigmarswangen	Sulz	Jun 1817	Russia	849642
Bertrang, Anton & F	45 yrs.	Sigmarswangen	Sulz	Jun 1817	Russia	849642
Bertrang, Fidelis	15 yrs.	Sigmarswangen	Sulz	Jun 1817	Russia	849642
Bertrang, Katharina	7 yrs.	Sigmarswangen	Sulz	Jun 1817	Russia	849642
Bertrang, Mathaeus	5 yrs.	Sigmarswangen	Sulz	Jun 1817	Russia	849642
Bertrang, Rosina Elisab. (wife)	45 yrs.	Sigmarswangen	Sulz	Jun 1817	Russia	849642
Bertrang, Sibilla	1 yrs.	Sigmarswangen	Sulz	Jun 1817	Russia	849642
Bertsch, Adalbert	8 Jan 1838	Freudenstadt	Frd.	Aug 1857	N.-Amer	577776
Bertsch, Anna Maria (wife)		Moetzingen	Herr.	Oct 1830	N.-Amer	834624
Bertsch, Carl Friedrich & F		Moetzingen	Herr.	Apr 1834	N.-Amer	834624
Bertsch, Christina (wife)	28 Mar 1809	Moetzingen	Herr.	May 1852	N.-Amer	834627
Bertsch, Christoph	5 Jan 1847	Moetzingen	Herr.	May 1852	N.-Amer	834627
Bertsch, Christoph & F	19 Mar 1793	Moetzingen	Herr.	May 1852	N.-Amer	834627
Bertsch, Eva Maria	9 Dec 1849	Moetzingen	Herr.	May 1852	N.-Amer	834627
Bertsch, Friedrich Otto	7 Jun 1847	Lauffen	Frd.	Jul 1866	N.-Amer	577780
Bertsch, Jakob (wid.) & F		Neuweiler	Calw	1855	N.-Amer	563212
Bertsch, Jakob Friedrich	26 Nov 1837	Moetzingen	Herr.	May 1852	N.-Amer	834627
Bertsch, Jakob Friedrich & F		Ottenbronn	Calw	1854	N.-Amer	563212
Bertsch, Johann Christian	11 Sep 1839	Moetzingen	Herr.	May 1852	N.-Amer	834627
Bertsch, Johannes & F		Moetzingen	Herr.	Oct 1830	N.-Amer	834624
Bertsch, Katharina	23 Jul 1842	Moetzingen	Herr.	May 1852	N.-Amer	834627
Bertsch, Margaretha Barbara		Ottenbronn	Calw	1861	Baden	563212
Bertsch, Rosina		Altburg	Calw	1867	Bavaria	563212
Bertsch, Wilhelm	27 Sep 1840	Moetzingen	Herr.	May 1852	N.-Amer	834627
Besch, Johannes	28 Apr 1851	Hopfau	Sulz	May 1868	N.-Amer	849636
Bessey, Nanette		Gaertringen	Herr.	Oct 1830	N.-Amer	834624
Bessler, Conrad Christoph & W		Nufringen	Herr.	Feb 1848	N.-Amer	834626
Bessler, Elisabetha Catharina		Nufringen	Herr.	Feb 1848	N.-Amer	834626
Bessler, Johann Jacob	31 Aug 1851	Nufringen	Herr.	Apr 1869	N.-Amer	834624
Betzmann, Friedrich	22 Oct 1879	Sachsenhausen	Sulz	bef 1896	N.-Amer	849626
Beutel, Johannes		Muehlheim a.B.	Sulz	May 1817	France	849639
Beuter, Martin		Sulz	Sulz	bef 1812	Rus-Pol	849625
Beutler, Johann Conrad & W		Oberjettingen	Herr.	May 1830	N.-Amer	834624
Beutler, Margaretha (wife)		Oberjettingen	Herr.	May 1830	N.-Amer	834624
Beutter, Eugen	31 Dec 1876	Rosenfeld	Sulz	Dec 1893	N.-Amer	849641
Beutter, Friedrich Wilhelm		Rosenfeld	Sulz	Mar 1853	Baden	849640
Beyerlin, Charlotte H. E. & C	1 Feb 1840	Sulz	Sulz	Sep 1861	Switz.	849628
Beyerlin, Rudolph Oskar Edmund	3 Apr 1859	Stuttgart	Sulz	Sep 1861	Switz.	849628
Beyerlin, Rudolphine Olga The.	17 Aug 1860	Sulz	Sulz	Sep 1861	Switz.	849628
Beyler, Agatha		Altheim	Horb	Apr 1852	N.-Amer	835929
Beyler, Eva & C		Altheim	Horb	Apr 1852	N.-Amer	835929
Bez, Michael		Kayh	Herr.	May 1831	N.-Amer	834624
Biedermann, Andreas	23 Dec 1839	Holzhausen	Sulz	Jul 1860	N.-Amer	849635
Biedermann, Andreas	18 Oct 1812	Holzhausen	Sulz	Jun 1817	Hungary	849635
Biedermann, Anna	15 Sep 1814	Holzhausen	Sulz	Jun 1817	Hungary	849635

Name		Birth		Emigration			Film
Last	First	Date	Place	O'amt	Appl. Date	Dest.	Number
Biedermann, Anna Maria			Holzhausen	Sulz	Jul 1860	N.-Amer	849635
Biedermann, Anna Maria			Renfrizhausen	Sulz	Feb 1817	Russia	849639
Biedermann, Anna Maria (wife)		22 Jan 1788	Isingen	Sulz	Jun 1817	Hungary	849635
Biedermann, Barbara & C			Renfrizhausen	Sulz	Feb 1817	Russia	849639
Biedermann, Christina		30 Jul 1842	Holzhausen	Sulz	Jul 1860	N.-Amer	849635
Biedermann, Georg & F			Aach	Frd.	1817	Russia	569269
Biedermann, Jacob Friedr. & F			Dietersweiler	Frd.	1817	Russia	569269
Biedermann, Jakob		13 Aug 1821	Holzhausen	Sulz	Dec 1865	N.-Amer	849635
Biedermann, Jakob & F			Dietersweiler	Frd.	1817	Russia	569269
Biedermann, Jakob & F			Holzhausen	Sulz	Jul 1817	Russia	849635
Biedermann, Johann Michael & F		6 Aug 1781	Isingen	Sulz	Jun 1817	Hungary	849635
Biedermann, Michael & F			Holzhausen	Sulz	Jun 1817	Hungary	849643
Biedermann, Sabina (wid.) & F		5 Aug 1808	Holzhausen	Sulz	Jul 1860	N.-Amer	849635
Bierle, Sophie Elisabeth & C			Freudenstadt	Frd.	Oct 1853	France	569272
Biesinger, Anton		16 Feb 1844	Oberndorf	Herr.	Jul 1865	N.-Amer	834624
Biesinger, Philipp		3 Dec 1851	Binsdorf	Sulz	Apr 1867	N.-Amer	849631
Bik, Martin & F			Wittershausen	Sulz	Aug 1846	N.-Amer	849644
Bilger, Anna (wife)			Sigmarswangen	Sulz	May 1836	N.-Amer	849642
Bilger, Bernhard		10 yrs.	Sigmarswangen	Sulz	May 1836	N.-Amer	849642
Bilger, Christian & F		26 Nov 1791	Sigmarswangen	Sulz	May 1836	N.-Amer	849642
Bilger, Christian Friedrich		14 yrs.	Sigmarswangen	Sulz	May 1836	N.-Amer	849642
Bilger, Eva		21 yrs.	Sigmarswangen	Sulz	May 1836	N.-Amer	849642
Bilger, Friederike Christine		7 Mar 1837	Freudenstadt	Frd.	Jun 1861	Baden	577778
Bilger, Georg			Boll	Sulz	1852	N.-Amer	849632
Bilger, Georg Jakob		9 Feb 1840	Bickelsberg	Sulz	Oct 1859	N.-Amer	849630
Bilger, Jakob Friedrich		17 yrs.	Sigmarswangen	Sulz	May 1836	N.-Amer	849642
Bilger, Johann Ludwig		14 yrs.	Sigmarswangen	Sulz	May 1836	N.-Amer	849642
Bilger, Johannes & F			Boll	Sulz	Apr 1817	Russia	849632
Bilger, Magdalena			Freudenstadt	Frd.	Nov 1815	Baden	569267
Binder, Agatha		20 Dec 1822	Gueltstein	Herr.	Aug 1866	N.-Amer	834624
Binder, Andreas		26 Sep 1829	Bickelsberg	Sulz	Feb 1873	N.-Amer	849630
Binder, Andreas		6 Oct 1865	Bickelsberg	Sulz	Apr 1880	N.-Amer	849626
Binder, Anna		22 Jul 1847	Bickelsberg	Sulz	Mar 1867	N.-Amer	849630
Binder, Anna & C			Voehringen	Sulz	Jul 1817	Russia	849627
Binder, Anna (wife)		11 May 1821	Bickelsberg	Sulz	Mar 1867	N.-Amer	849630
Binder, Anna Barbara		28 Jan 1843	Voehringen	Sulz	Aug 1854	N.-Amer	849643
Binder, Anna Maria		23 Aug 1849	Voehringen	Sulz	Aug 1854	N.-Amer	849643
Binder, Anna Maria		25 Aug 1844	Bickelsberg	Sulz	Aug 1867	Switz.	849630
Binder, Anna Maria		21 Dec 1818	Gueltstein	Herr.	Aug 1866	N.-Amer	834624
Binder, Anna Maria		11 Mar 1852	Gueltstein	Herr.	Jul 1852	N.-Amer	834627
Binder, Anna Maria		12 Nov 1848	Gueltstein	Herr.	Sep 1852	N.-Amer	834627
Binder, Anna Maria		9 Aug 1860	Gueltstein	Herr.	Apr 1869	N.-Amer	834624
Binder, Anna Maria (wife)		14 Dec 1821	Leidingen	Sulz	Aug 1854	N.-Amer	849643
Binder, Anna Maria (wife)			Gueltstein	Herr.	Sep 1852	N.-Amer	834627
Binder, Barbara			Sigmarswangen	Sulz	Oct 1854	N.-Amer	849642
Binder, Catharina Barbara		5 Apr 1848	Gueltstein	Herr.	Jul 1852	N.-Amer	834627
Binder, Catharina Barbara			Gueltstein	Herr.	Sep 1847	Switz.	834626
Binder, Christian Wilhelm		14 Nov 1867	Gueltstein	Herr.	Apr 1869	N.-Amer	834624
Binder, Christina		7 Jan 1854	Voehringen	Sulz	Aug 1854	N.-Amer	849643
Binder, Christina Barbara (wife)			Gueltstein	Herr.	May 1852	N.-Amer	834627

Binder, Christina Margaretha	25 Nov 1851	Gueltstein	Herr.	Sep 1852	N.-Amer	834627
Binder, Christine	22 Nov 1841	Bickelsberg	Sulz	Mar 1867	N.-Amer	849630
Binder, Dorothea & C		Sigmarswangen	Sulz	Oct 1854	N.-Amer	849642
Binder, Elisabetha Kath. (wife)	7 Jan 1835	Gueltstein	Herr.	Apr 1869	N.-Amer	834624
Binder, Eva Dorothea	20 Mar 1841	Gueltstein	Herr.	Jul 1852	N.-Amer	834627
Binder, Georg Gottlieb	5 Aug 1864	Gueltstein	Herr.	Apr 1869	N.-Amer	834624
Binder, Gottlieb	29 Oct 1838	Gueltstein	Herr.	Jul 1852	N.-Amer	834627
Binder, Jacob Friedrich		Gechingen	Calw	1852	N.-Amer	563212
Binder, Jakob Conrad	3 Oct 1808	Gueltstein	Herr.	Jul 1868	N.-Amer	834624
Binder, Johann Friedrich & F		Gueltstein	Herr.	May 1852	N.-Amer	834627
Binder, Johann Friedrich & F		Gueltstein	Herr.	Mar 1836	N.-Amer	834624
Binder, Johann Georg	21 Jul 1852	Bickelsberg	Sulz	Sep 1871	N.-Amer	849630
Binder, Johann Georg & F	14 Jun 1821	Bickelsberg	Sulz	Mar 1867	N.-Amer	849630
Binder, Johann Jacob	31 Aug 1844	Gueltstein	Herr.	Jul 1852	N.-Amer	834627
Binder, Johann Jacob & F		Gueltstein	Herr.	Jul 1852	N.-Amer	834627
Binder, Johann Jakob	17 Aug 1838	Voehringen	Sulz	Feb 1854	N.-Amer	849643
Binder, Johann Jakob	3 Feb 1847	Gueltstein	Herr.	Sep 1852	N.-Amer	834627
Binder, Johann Martin	2 Dec 1819	Reusten	Herr.	Mar 1867	N.-Amer	834624
Binder, Johann Martin & F		Gueltstein	Herr.	Sep 1852	N.-Amer	834627
Binder, Johann Martin & F	12 Mar 1832	Gueltstein	Herr.	Apr 1869	N.-Amer	834624
Binder, Johannes	4 Nov 1846	Voehringen	Sulz	Aug 1854	N.-Amer	849643
Binder, Johannes	20 Apr 1876	Bickelsberg	Sulz	Apr 1891	N.-Amer	849626
Binder, Johannes & F	10 May 1823	Voehringen	Sulz	Aug 1854	N.-Amer	849643
Binder, Katharina (wid.) & F		Kuppingen	Herr.	Mar 1848	N.-Amer	834626
Binder, Katharina Barbara	21 Mar 1833	Kuppingen	Herr.	Mar 1848	N.-Amer	834626
Binder, Katharina Barbara		Gueltstein	Herr.	Apr 1842	Baden	834625
Binder, Maria Agnes	2 Jun 1845	Gueltstein	Herr.	Sep 1852	N.-Amer	834627
Binder, Maria Katharina	12 Mar 1828	Kuppingen	Herr.	Mar 1848	N.-Amer	834626
Binder, Maria Regina	20 Oct 1843	Gueltstein	Herr.	Sep 1852	N.-Amer	834627
Binder, Martha	12 Dec 1836	Gueltstein	Herr.	Jul 1852	N.-Amer	834627
Binder, Martin	23 Mar 1875	Bickelsberg	Sulz	May 1891	N.-Amer	849626
Binder, Martin	4 Mar 1841	Gueltstein	Herr.	Sep 1852	N.-Amer	834627
Binder, Michael	14 Mar 1860	Bickelsberg	Sulz	May 1876	N.-Amer	849630
Binder, Philipp Jakob	17 Aug 1837	Kuppingen	Herr.	Mar 1848	N.-Amer	834626
Binder, Regina	29 Jun 1829	Kuppingen	Herr.	Mar 1848	N.-Amer	834626
Bindlingmaier, Christof & F		Edlingen	Frd.	1817	Russia	569269
Binger, Xaver & F		Binsdorf	Sulz	Oct 1839	Prussia	849630
Binzin, Anna Maria	6 May 1819	Wittlensweiler	Frd.	Apr 1838	N.-Amer	569268
Bippus, Agatha (wife)	26 Oct 1794	Wittershausen	Sulz	Jul 1817	Russia	849642
Bippus, Agatha (wid.) & F		Sigmarswangen	Sulz	Feb 1854	N.-Amer	849642
Bippus, Andreas	22 Dec 1825	Rotenzimmern	Sulz	May 1866	N.-Amer	849642
Bippus, Andreas	8 Jul 1833	Rotenzimmern	Sulz	bef 1853	N.-Amer	849642
Bippus, Andreas		Boll	Sulz	1841	N.-Amer	849632
Bippus, Anna Catharina		Holzhausen	Sulz	Apr 1832	N.-Amer	849635
Bippus, Anna Maria		Rotenzimmern	Sulz	bef 1857	N.-Amer	849642
Bippus, Barbara		Sigmarswangen	Sulz	Feb 1854	N.-Amer	849642
Bippus, Barbara		Sigmarswangen	Sulz	May 1817	Russia	849642
Bippus, Catharina		Sigmarswangen	Sulz	Apr 1817	Russia	849642
Bippus, Christian		Holzhausen	Sulz	Apr 1832	N.-Amer	849635
Bippus, Christina		Holzhausen	Sulz	Apr 1832	N.-Amer	849635

| Name | | Birth | | Emigration | | | Film |
Last	First	Date	Place	O'amt	Appl. Date	Dest.	Number
Bippus,	Christina (wife)		Holzhausen	Sulz	Apr 1832	N.-Amer	849635
Bippus,	Dorothea		Boll	Sulz	Jan 1837	N.-Amer	849632
Bippus,	Elisabeth		Sigmarswangen	Sulz	May 1817	Russia	849642
Bippus,	Elisabetha		Holzhausen	Sulz	Apr 1832	N.-Amer	849635
Bippus,	Friedrich		Boll	Sulz	Jan 1837	N.-Amer	849632
Bippus,	Georg Jakob		Boll	Sulz	1837	N.-Amer	849632
Bippus,	Gottlieb		Holzhausen	Sulz	Apr 1832	N.-Amer	849635
Bippus,	Jacob		Sigmarswangen	Sulz	May 1817	Russia	849642
Bippus,	Jakob	19 Jul 1848	Rotenzimmern	Sulz	Oct 1868	N.-Amer	849642
Bippus,	Jakob	28 Jan 1850	Hopfau	Sulz	Jul 1870	N.-Amer	849636
Bippus,	Johann & F		Leidringen	Sulz	Jun 1817	Russia	849637
Bippus,	Johann August	5 Jun 1817	Sigmarswangen	Sulz	Jul 1817	Russia	849642
Bippus,	Johann Georg	16 Oct 1861	Bickelsberg	Sulz	May 1871	N.-Amer	849630
Bippus,	Johann Georg	11 Dec 1867	Rotenzimmern	Sulz	Oct 1884	N.-Amer	849642
Bippus,	Johann Georg		Holzhausen	Sulz	Apr 1832	N.-Amer	849635
Bippus,	Johann Georg		Leidringen	Sulz	Jun 1817	Russia	849637
Bippus,	Johann Georg & F	28 May 1785	Holzhausen	Sulz	Apr 1832	N.-Amer	849635
Bippus,	Johann Michael		Wittershausen	Sulz	May 1817	--	849644
Bippus,	Johannes	8 Jul 1845	Rotenzimmern	Sulz	Feb 1859	N.-Amer	849642
Bippus,	Johannes	3 Apr 1832	Hopfau	Sulz	Feb 1854	N.-Amer	849636
Bippus,	Johannes & F	10 Sep 1767	Boll	Sulz	Jan 1837	N.-Amer	849632
Bippus,	Magdalena		Boll	Sulz	Jan 1837	N.-Amer	849632
Bippus,	Mathias & F		Boll	Sulz	Jul 1852	N.-Amer	849632
Bippus,	Matthaeus & F	24 Feb 1792	Sigmarswangen	Sulz	Jul 1817	Russia	849642
Bippus,	Michael		Boll	Sulz	Jan 1837	N.-Amer	849632
Bippus,	Paul Timothan		Holzhausen	Sulz	Apr 1832	N.-Amer	849635
Bippus,	Rosina		Boll	Sulz	Aug 1852	N.-Amer	849632
Bischel,	Christina Rosina		Sulz	Sulz	Feb 1829	Baden	849627
Bischof,	Andreas	20 yrs.	Sigmarswangen	Sulz	May 1856	N.-Amer	849642
Bischoff,	Anna		Leidringen	Sulz	Nov 1855	N.-Amer	849637
Bischoff,	Anna	28 Feb 1845	Leidringen	Sulz	May 1865	N.-Amer	849637
Bischoff,	Anna Barbara & F	19 Oct 1827	Bickelsberg	Sulz	Aug 1853	N.-Amer	849630
Bischoff,	Anna Maria	9 Jul 1851	Fuernsal	Sulz	Apr 1870	N.-Amer	849635
Bischoff,	Anna Maria (wid.)& C		Leidringen	Sulz	Nov 1855	N.-Amer	849637
Bischoff,	Barbara		Wittershausen	Sulz	Apr 1837	N.-Amer	849644
Bischoff,	Christine	21 May 1851	Leidringen	Sulz	Mar 1869	N.-Amer	849637
Bischoff,	Jakob	11 Feb 1847	Leidringen	Sulz	Mar 1866	N.-Amer	849637
Bischoff,	Johann Georg & F		Aistaig	Sulz	1817	N.-Amer	849628
Bischoff,	Johann Gottlieb		Goettelfingen	Frd.	1864	N.-Amer	577779
Bischoff,	Johannes	19 Oct 1827	Bickelsberg	Sulz	Aug 1853	N.-Amer	849630
Bischoff,	Johannes		Bickelsberg	Sulz	Jul 1853	N.-Amer	849637
Bisswurm,	Johannes	27 yrs.	Unteriflingen	Frd.	May 1752	Pen.N-A	550803
Biswurm,	Mathias		Dornhan	Sulz	Apr 1815	Poland	849625
Bitzer,	Anna Maria	31 Dec 1827	Gaertringen	Herr.	Sep 1851	N.-Amer	834627
Bitzer,	Christian	35 yrs.	Simmozheim	Calw	1855	N.-Amer	563212
Bitzer,	Christine		Enztal	Nag.	Aug 1865	N.-Amer	838494
Bizenberger,	Clemens	21 Nov 1838	Poltringen	Herr.	Dec 1865	France	834624
Blaese,	Engelbert	16 Sep 1825	Altheim	Horb	bef 1862	Bavaria	835929
Blaese,	Victoria	23 Oct 1839	Altheim	Horb	bef 1868	Bavaria	835929
Blaich,	Anna Maria	19 yrs.	Zwerenberg	Calw	1859	N.-Amer	563212

Blaich, Anna Maria & C		Oberhaugstett	Calw	1862	N.-Amer	563212
Blaich, Catharina	13 yrs.	Zwerenberg	Calw	1859	N.-Amer	563212
Blaich, Emil Christoph Wilh.		Calw	Calw	1859	N.-Amer	563212
Blaich, Eva Maria & C		Oberhaugstett	Calw	1862	N.-Amer	563212
Blaich, Friedrich	23 yrs.	Zwerenberg	Calw	1859	N.-Amer	563212
Blaich, Jacob		Neuweiler	Calw	Sep 1871	Palest.	563212
Blaich, Johann Georg	20 yrs.	Neuweiler	Calw	1866	N.-Amer	563212
Blaich, Johann Georg		Breitenberg	Calw	1853	N.-Amer	563212
Blaich, Johann Martin & F		Groembach	Frd.	bef 1863	N.-Amer	577778
Blaich, Johann Martin & F		Breitenberg	Calw	1863	N.-Amer	563212
Blaich, Johannes	17 yrs.	Zwerenberg	Calw	1859	N.-Amer	563212
Blaich, Johannes (wid.) & F		Zwerenberg	Calw	1859	N.-Amer	563212
Blaich, Margaretha	21 yrs.	Zwerenberg	Calw	1859	N.-Amer	563212
Bleibel, Anna Maria		Marschalkenzimmern	Sulz	Jul 1817	Russia	849638
Bleich, Eva Katharina	28 yrs.	Oberhaugstett	Calw	1856	N.-Amer	563212
Bleich, Johann David	1834	Aichhalden	Calw	1854	N.-Amer	563212
Bleich, Johann Friedrich	25 yrs.	Stammheim	Calw	May 1848	N.-Amer	563212
Bleich, Johann Georg	1831	Aichhalden	Calw	1854	N.-Amer	563212
Bleich, Johann Georg & F		Aichhalden	Calw	1855	N.-Amer	563212
Bleich, Michael Friedrich		Neuweiler	Calw	Sep 1869	Palest.	563212
Blickle, Andreas		Blitz	Bal.	Feb 1849	N.-Amer	555964
Blocher, Agnes	3 yrs.	Leidringen	Sulz	Mar 1837	N.-Amer	849637
Blocher, Agnes	4 Sep 1862	Leidringen	Sulz	May 1865	N.-Amer	849637
Blocher, Andreas	1 Apr 1873	Dornhan	Sulz	Feb 1889	N.-Amer	849626
Blocher, Anna & F		Baiersbronn	Frd.	Feb 1847	N.-Amer	569271
Blocher, Anna Barbara	19 Sep 1830	Gundelshausen	Sulz	Sep 1854	N.-Amer	849633
Blocher, Anna Maria & C	13 Jun 1840	Leidringen	Sulz	May 1865	N.-Amer	849637
Blocher, Anna Maria (wife)		Leidringen	Sulz	Mar 1837	N.-Amer	849637
Blocher, Christian	23 Apr 1841	Baiersbronn	Frd.	Feb 1847	N.-Amer	569271
Blocher, Elisabetha (wife)		Hopfau	Sulz	May 1847	N.-Amer	849636
Blocher, Friedrich	18 Jun 1880	Dornhan	Sulz	Mar 1896	N.-Amer	849634
Blocher, Georg	10 Mar 1849	Leidringen	Sulz	Aug 1868	N.-Amer	849637
Blocher, Heinrich	28 Apr 1868	Leidringen	Sulz	Mar 1884	N.-Amer	849626
Blocher, Johann Adam & F		Hopfau	Sulz	May 1847	N.-Amer	849636
Blocher, Johann Georg		Wittlensweiler	Frd.	Jul 1865	N.-Amer	577779
Blocher, Johann Georg		Baiersbronn	Frd.	1846	N.-Amer	569271
Blocher, Johann Georg	10 Mar 1873	Voehringen	Sulz	Mar 1891	N.-Amer	849626
Blocher, Johann Georg	10 Mar 1873	Voehringen	Sulz	Mar 1891	N.-Amer	849643
Blocher, Johann Georg		Leidringen	Sulz	bef 1861	Switz.	849637
Blocher, Johannes		Wittlensweiler	Frd.	Jul 1865	N.-Amer	577779
Blocher, Johannes	3 May 1843	Baiersbronn	Frd.	Feb 1847	N.-Amer	569271
Blocher, Johannes	18 yrs.	Dornhan	Sulz	Jan 1853	N.-Amer	849633
Blocher, Martin		Holzhausen	Sulz	bef 1858	N.-Amer	849635
Blocher, Martin & F	23 May 1801	Leidringen	Sulz	Mar 1837	N.-Amer	849637
Blochinger, Anna Catharina	30 Aug 1812	Ostdorf/Balingen	Sulz	Jul 1817	Russia	849629
Bloechle, Johann Georg	12 Nov 1831	Untermusbach	Frd.	Apr 1854	N.-Amer	569273
Blum, Amalie	4 Nov 1827	Schwarzenberg	Frd.	Jun 1847	Bavaria	569271
Blum, Barbara (wife)		Aistaig	Sulz	Apr 1867	N.-Amer	849628
Blum, Erhard		Schoenmuenzach	Frd.	Aug 1857	Prussia	577776
Blum, Jacob Friedrich & F		Baiersbronn	Frd.	bef 1804	Pr.-Pol	550803

| Name | | Birth | | Emigration | | | Film |
Last	First	Date	Place	O'amt	Appl. Date	Dest.	Number
Blum, Johann Georg		26 Feb 1848	Rosenfeld	Sulz	Jun 1866	N.-Amer	849641
Blum, Johannes		26 Jan 1840	Rosenfeld	Sulz	Apr 1860	N.-Amer	849640
Blum, Johannes		25 Dec 1876	Rosenfeld	Sulz	Apr 1893	N.-Amer	849641
Blum, Michael & F			Aistaig	Sulz	Apr 1867	N.-Amer	849628
Bochinger, Christina Louise		28 Dec 1819	Dornstetten	Frd.	Oct 1851	N.-Amer	569271
Bock, Charlotte			Hirsau	Calw	1858	N.-Amer	563212
Bock, Christiane Friederike			Calw	Calw	1869	Prussia	563212
Bodamer, Anna Maria			Agenbach	Calw	1869	N.-Amer	563212
Bodamer, Gottlieb Friedrich			Teinach	Calw	1862	Holst.	563212
Bodner, Caroline Fr.			Hirsau	Calw	Nov 1870	Switz.	563212
Boechle, Andreas		6 Oct 1843	Muehlheim a.B.	Sulz	Feb 1869	N.-Amer	849639
Boechle, August		17 May 1862	Sigmarswangen	Sulz	Sep 1881	N.-Amer	849642
Boechle, Johannes		23 Jul 1846	Aistaig	Sulz	Oct 1866	N.-Amer	849628
Boeckle, Barbara		9 Mar 1809	Gueltstein	Herr.	Mar 1848	N.-Amer	834626
Boeckle, Jacob		11 Mar 1815	Nebringen	Herr.	1836	N.-Amer	834626
Boeckle, Johann Michael		30 yrs.	Herrenberg	Herr.	Sep 1852	N.-Amer	834627
Boeckle, Karl Friedrich		24 Jan 1843	Herrenberg	Herr.	May 1870	Prussia	834624
Boeckle, Maria Catharina & C			Bondorf	Herr.	May 1847	N.-Amer	834626
Boehler, Elisabeth			Altingen	Herr.	Apr 1830	N.-Amer	834624
Boehner, Anna Barbara (wid.)		17 Nov 1759	Duerrenstetten	Sulz	Apr 1833	N.-Amer	849639
Boehner, Auguste (wife)			Muehlheim a.B.	Sulz	Aug 1832	N.-Amer	849639
Boehner, Carl Friedrich		6 yrs.	Muehlheim a.B.	Sulz	Aug 1832	N.-Amer	849639
Boehner, Catharina Doroth.wife			Muehlheim a.B.	Sulz	Apr 1833	N.-Amer	849639
Boehner, Elisabetha		48 yrs.	Holzhausen	Sulz	Sep 1854	N.-Amer	849635
Boehner, Gottfried & F			Holzhausen	Sulz	Sep 1847	N.-Amer	849635
Boehner, Gottlob August		infant	Muehlheim a.B.	Sulz	Aug 1832	N.-Amer	849639
Boehner, Johann Jakob & W		11 Dec 1805	Muehlheim a.B.	Sulz	Apr 1833	N.-Amer	849639
Boehner, Johann Martin		19 yrs.	Muehlheim a.B.	Sulz	Aug 1832	N.-Amer	849639
Boehner, Johann Martin & F			Muehlheim a.B.	Sulz	Mar 1847	N.-Amer	849639
Boehner, Johann Michael		3 yrs.	Muehlheim a.B.	Sulz	Aug 1832	N.-Amer	849639
Boehner, Johann Michael & F		26 Oct 1783	Muehlheim a.B.	Sulz	Aug 1832	N.-Amer	849639
Boehner, Sixt Jakob		17 yrs.	Muehlheim a.B.	Sulz	Aug 1832	N.-Amer	849639
Boehret, Michael			Stammheim	Calw	1853	N.-Amer	563212
Boehringer, Carl August		13 Feb 1835	Buhlbach	Frd.	Sep 1853	N.-Amer	569272
Boehringer, Friederike			Baiersbronn	Frd.	Dec 1813	Baden	569267
Boehringer, Johann Georg		28 Apr 1838	Buhlbach	Frd.	Sep 1853	N.-Amer	569272
Boehringer, Karl Ludwig			Baiersbronn	Frd.	Nov 1809	Baden	569267
Boehringer, Karl Willfried		21 Feb 1832	Baiersbronn	Frd.	Aug 1852	N.-Amer	569271
Boehringer, Wilhelmine		5 Oct 1828	Baiersbronn	Frd.	bef 1853	N.-Amer	569272
Boekle, Anna		16 Jan 1849	Herrenberg	Herr.	Feb 1852	N.-Amer	834627
Boekle, Anna (wife)			Herrenberg	Herr.	Feb 1852	N.-Amer	834627
Boekle, Anna Maria		6 Oct 1851	Herrenberg	Herr.	Feb 1852	N.-Amer	834627
Boekle, Anton		8 Oct 1845	Herrenberg	Herr.	Feb 1852	N.-Amer	834627
Boekle, Gottlieb		15 Jan 1849	Oeschelbronn	Herr.	Mar 1852	N.-Amer	834627
Boekle, Johann Friedrich		18 yrs.	Bondorf	Herr.	May 1831	N.-Amer	834624
Boekle, Johann Michael		4 Dec 1842	Herrenberg	Herr.	Feb 1852	N.-Amer	834627
Boekle, Karl Friedrich & F			Oeschelbronn	Herr.	Mar 1852	N.-Amer	834627
Boekle, Katharina Agatha		12 Dec 1842	Oeschelbronn	Herr.	Mar 1852	N.-Amer	834627
Boekle, Maria Barbara		10 Jul 1838	Herrenberg	Herr.	Feb 1852	N.-Amer	834627
Boekle, Maria Magdalena (wife)			Oeschelbronn	Herr.	Mar 1852	N.-Amer	834627

Boekle, Michael & F		Herrenberg	Herr.	Feb 1852	N.-Amer	834627
Boekle, Regina	19 Mar 1841	Herrenberg	Herr.	Feb 1852	N.-Amer	834627
Boekle, Wilhelm Philipp	9 Nov 1846	Herrenberg	Herr.	Dec 1866	N.-Amer	834624
Boekle, Wilhelmine Heinrika	30 yrs.	Bondorf	Herr.	Dec 1869	N.-Amer	834624
Boesinger, Johann Jacob		Sulz	Sulz	Jun 1825	Prussia	849627
Boess, Christiane Magdalena	12 Jun 1847	Herrenberg	Herr.	Oct 1852	N.-Amer	834627
Boess, Daniel & F	16 May 1811	Herrenberg	Herr.	Oct 1852	N.-Amer	834627
Boess, Daniel Friedrich	27 Jul 1841	Herrenberg	Herr.	Oct 1852	N.-Amer	834627
Boess, Margaretha Magdalena	21 Mar 1845	Herrenberg	Herr.	Oct 1852	N.-Amer	834627
Boess, Rosina Catharina (wife)	7 Oct 1808	Herrenberg	Herr.	Oct 1852	N.-Amer	834627
Boess, Rosine Christine Mag.	30 Aug 1843	Herrenberg	Herr.	Oct 1852	N.-Amer	834627
Boettinger, Carl	16 yrs.	Ostelsheim	Calw	1866	N.-Amer	563212
Boettinger, Gottlob		Ostelsheim	Calw	May 1870	N.-Amer	563212
Boettinger, Jacob	15 yrs.	Ostelsheim	Calw	1866	N.-Amer	563212
Boettinger, Jakob	5 Mar 1837	Hallwangen	Frd.	Jun 1865	N.-Amer	577779
Bohnenberger, Anna Maria		Unterreichenbach	Calw	1852	N.-Amer	563212
Bohnenberger, Anna Maria & C		Unterreichenbach	Calw	1863	Baden	563212
Bohnenberger, Christian	17 Jul 1848	Unterreichenbach	Calw	1868	N.-Amer	563212
Bohnenberger, Elisabeth		Unterhaugstett	Calw	1864	N.-Amer	563212
Bohnenberger, Jacob		Unterreichenbach	Calw	1852	N.-Amer	563212
Bohnenberger, Johann		Unterreichenbach	Calw	Nov 1873	Palest.	563212
Bohnenberger, Johann Martin		Unterreichenbach	Calw	Jul 1870	N.-Amer	563212
Bohnenberger, Johann Michael		Unterreichenbach	Calw	Jul 1870	N.-Amer	563212
Bohnenberger, Louise Juliane	1 yrs.	Unterreichenbach	Calw	1866	Baden	563212
Bohnenberger, Magdalena	1826	Dennjaecht	Calw	1855	Baden	563212
Bohnenberger, Margaretha L.& C		Unterreichenbach	Calw	1866	Baden	563212
Bohnenberger, Michael		Liebenzell	Calw	1853	N.-Amer	563212
Bohnert, Christian Friedrich		Wittlensweiler	Frd.	Nov 1848	N.-Amer	569270
Bohnet, (wife)	29 yrs.	Pfalzgrafenweiler	Frd.	Feb 1854	N.-Amer	569273
Bohnet, Agatha	9 May 1834	Groembach	Frd.	Feb 1860	N.-Amer	577777
Bohnet, Anna Maria		Untermusbach	Frd.	Jul 1854	N.-Amer	569274
Bohnet, Barbara	19 Oct 1868	Waelde	Sulz	Jan 1884	N.-Amer	849626
Bohnet, Carl	26 yrs.	Pfalzgrafenweiler	Frd.	Feb 1854	N.-Amer	569273
Bohnet, Catharina Barbara		Stammheim	Calw	1858	N.-Amer	563212
Bohnet, Christian	14 Jul 1810	Tumlingen	Frd.	Mar 1837	N.-Amer	569268
Bohnet, Christian	16 Dec 1825	Glatten	Frd.	Oct 1846	N.-Amer	569271
Bohnet, Christian Wilhelm	23 Sep 1874	Dornhan	Sulz	Aug 1891	N.-Amer	849626
Bohnet, Christina	22 yrs.	Schernbach	Frd.	Sep 1853	N.-Amer	569272
Bohnet, Christina	6 yrs.	Rodt	Frd.	May 1750	Pen.N-A	550803
Bohnet, Elisabetha Barbara	15 Nov 1816	Herzogsweiler	Frd.	Apr 1846	N.-Amer	569271
Bohnet, Eva Maria	27 Jul 1813	Gruental	Frd.	Mar 1847	N.-Amer	569271
Bohnet, Friedrich	46 yrs.	Pfalzgrafenweiler	Frd.	Feb 1854	N.-Amer	569273
Bohnet, Friedrich	9 Feb 1808	Wittlensweiler	Frd.	Apr 1833	N.-Amer	569268
Bohnet, Friedrich & F	18 Aug 1827	Waelde	Sulz	Jan 1884	N.-Amer	849626
Bohnet, Gottlieb	24 Oct 1838	Schernbach	Frd.	May 1853	France	569272
Bohnet, Jakob & F	35 yrs.	Pfalzgrafenweiler	Frd.	Feb 1854	N.-Amer	569273
Bohnet, Johann	6 yrs.	Pfalzgrafenweiler	Frd.	Feb 1854	N.-Amer	569273
Bohnet, Johann Adam	11 yrs.	Rodt	Frd.	May 1750	Pen.N-A	550803
Bohnet, Johann Georg	28 Jul 1840	Groembach	Frd.	Feb 1860	N.-Amer	577777
Bohnet, Johann Georg	9 Dec 1865	Gundelshausen	Sulz	Mar 1883	N.-Amer	849626

Name		Birth		Emigration			Film
Last	First	Date	Place	O'amt	Appl. Date	Dest.	Number
Bohnet, Johann Martin		22 Jul 1804	Wittlensweiler	Frd.	Apr 1833	N.-Amer	569268
Bohnet, Johann Martin		11 Apr 1842	Dornhan	Sulz	Mar 1861	N.-Amer	849634
Bohnet, Johannes		7 Jul 1834	Schernbach	Frd.	May 1853	France	569272
Bohnet, Johannes			Untermusbach	Frd.	Jul 1854	N.-Amer	569274
Bohnet, Johannes		29 Aug 1871	Waelde	Sulz	Jan 1884	N.-Amer	849626
Bohnet, Karl		24 Sep 1873	Dornhan	Sulz	Aug 1890	N.-Amer	849626
Bohnet, Katharina		21 Jul 1835	Groembach	Frd.	Aug 1860	N.-Amer	577777
Bohnet, Magdalena		26 Sep 1864	Waelde	Sulz	Jan 1884	N.-Amer	849626
Bohnet, Margaretha			Untermusbach	Frd.	Jul 1854	N.-Amer	569274
Bohnet, Maria		14 Aug 1874	Waelde	Sulz	Jan 1884	N.-Amer	849626
Bohnet, Martin		1 yrs.	Pfalzgrafenweiler	Frd.	Feb 1854	N.-Amer	569273
Bohnet, Martin & F			Untermusbach	Frd.	Jul 1854	N.-Amer	569274
Bohnet, Philipp		1 Sep 1840	Schernbach	Frd.	May 1853	France	569272
Bokle, Christiane Friederike		3 Jun 1849	Herrenberg	Herr.	Feb 1867	Baden	834624
Bolhalter, Maria			Reinerzau	Frd.	bef 1844	Switz.	569269
Boller, Ernestine Wilhelm.			Oberjettingen	Herr.	Dec 1833	France	834626
Boller, Julius			Groembach	Frd.	bef 1853	Baden	569272
Boller, Karl Julius Eduard		7 Apr 1825	Groembach	Frd.	Nov 1847	France	569270
Boller, Otto		1 Apr 1834	Groembach	Frd.	Mar 1854	N.-Amer	569273
Bonet, Agatha			Hoerschweiler	Frd.	Sep 1848	N.-Amer	569270
Bonet, Christian & F		37 yrs.	Hoerschweiler	Frd.	Sep 1848	N.-Amer	569270
Bonet, Christiana			Hoerschweiler	Frd.	Sep 1848	N.-Amer	569270
Bonet, Elisabetha			Hoerschweiler	Frd.	Sep 1848	N.-Amer	569270
Bonet, Friederika			Hoerschweiler	Frd.	Sep 1848	N.-Amer	569270
Bonet, Friederika (wife)			Hoerschweiler	Frd.	Sep 1848	N.-Amer	569270
Bonet, Jacob			Hoerschweiler	Frd.	Sep 1848	N.-Amer	569270
Bonnenkant, Andreas			Brittheim	Sulz	Mar 1846	N.-Amer	849632
Bonner, Barbara		5 Feb 1836	Leinstetten	Sulz	Nov 1860	Prussia	849638
Book, Friedrich Daniel		1838	Hirsau	Calw	1854	N.-Amer	563212
Book, Jakob & F			Hirsau	Calw	1854	N.-Amer	563212
Bookser, Anna Maria		4 yrs.	Roetenbach	Calw	1856	N.-Amer	563212
Bookser, Gottlieb		12 yrs.	Roetenbach	Calw	1856	N.-Amer	563212
Bookser, Margaretha Barb. & C		32 yrs.	Roetenbach	Calw	1856	N.-Amer	563212
Borho, Johannes		11 Apr 1848	Glatten	Frd.	Feb 1866	N.-Amer	577780
Borkhardt, Magdalena (wid.)			Sulz	Nag.	Feb 1854	N.-Amer	838491
Borrho, Christina Maria		14 Jun 1853	Wittlensweiler	Frd.	Mar 1861	N.-Amer	577778
Borrho, Salome		26 Nov 1842	Wittlensweiler	Frd.	Mar 1861	N.-Amer	577778
Borrho, Salome		28 Jan 1821	Winzeln	Frd.	Mar 1861	N.-Amer	577778
Bosch, Anna Maria		10 Sep 1828	Wittlensweiler	Frd.	Mar 1847	N.-Amer	569271
Bosch, Anna Maria		6 yrs.	Freudenstadt	Frd.	May 1752	Pen.N-A	550803
Bosch, Anna Maria			Althengstett	Calw	1861	N.-Amer	563212
Bosch, Barbara		37 yrs.	Freudenstadt	Frd.	May 1752	Pen.N-A	550803
Bosch, Christian		18 Apr 1834	Freudenstadt	Frd.	Aug 1854	N.-Amer	569274
Bosch, Conrad			Renfrizhausen	Sulz	Jun 1847	N.-Amer	849639
Bosch, Friedrich		17 Dec 1837	Freudenstadt	Frd.	Aug 1854	N.-Amer	569274
Bosch, Jacob & F		46 yrs.	Freudenstadt	Frd.	May 1752	Pen.N-A	550803
Bosch, Jacob Friedrich			Freudenstadt	Frd.	Oct 1853	N.-Amer	569272
Bosch, Johann Fridrich		2 yrs.	Freudenstadt	Frd.	May 1752	Pen.N-A	550803
Bosch, Johann Jacob		15 yrs.	Freudenstadt	Frd.	May 1752	Pen.N-A	550803
Bosch, Johann Jacob			Althengstett	Calw	1861	N.-Amer	563212

Name	Date/Age	Place	Region	Date	Destination	Code
Bosch, Johann Jakoh & F		Muehlheim a.B.	Sulz	Apr 1847	N.-Amer	849639
Bosch, Johannes	10 yrs.	Freudenstadt	Frd.	May 1752	Pen.N-A	550803
Bosch, Johannes	24 Oct 1833	Muehlheim a.B.	Sulz	1854	N.-Amer	849639
Bosch, Johannes		Muehlheim a.B.	Sulz	Apr 1854	N.-Amer	849639
Bosch, Joseph	4 yrs.	Freudenstadt	Frd.	May 1752	Pen.N-A	550803
Bosch, Joseph Jeremias	28 Feb 1826	Freudenstadt	Frd.	Dec 1860	Hungary	577778
Boss, Baltas	15 Mar 1820	Onstmettingen	Bal.	bef 1845	Switz.	555963
Bossenmeier, Sabina		Leinstetten	Sulz	May 1856	Prussia	849638
Bosser, Georg Christian	11 Nov 1824	Calw	Calw	1854	Hamburg	563212
Bossert, Anna Maria	14 May 1823	Dornhan	Sulz	Oct 1846	N.-Amer	849633
Bossert, Christian & F	2 Aug 1825	Fuernsal	Sulz	Feb 1864	N.-Amer	849635
Bossert, Christina	30 Apr 1860	Fuernsal	Sulz	Feb 1864	N.-Amer	849635
Bossert, Dorothea	7 Dec 1862	Fuernsal	Sulz	Feb 1864	N.-Amer	849635
Bossert, Dorothea (wife)	11 Apr 1836	Fuernsal	Sulz	Feb 1864	N.-Amer	849635
Bossert, Friedrich		Hopfau	Sulz	May 1846	N.-Amer	849636
Bossler, Christiane		Simmozheim	Calw	1854	N.-Amer	563212
Bothner, Adolph	11 May 1838	Freudenstadt	Frd.	Aug 1857	N.-Amer	577776
Bothner, Christian Ludwig		Freudenstadt	Frd.	Jun 1844	Baden	569269
Bothner, Maria Antonie	24 May 1856	Freudenstadt	Frd.	Feb 1864	N.-Amer	577779
Bothner, Rosalie & F		Freudenstadt	Frd.	Feb 1864	N.-Amer	577779
Bothner, Wilhelm	15 Oct 1860	Freudenstadt	Frd.	Feb 1864	N.-Amer	577779
Bothner, Wilhelm		Freudenstadt	Frd.	bef 1864	N.-Amer	577779
Bourell, Antoni		Herzogsweiler	Frd.	Apr 1752	Pen.N-A	550803
Bozenhardt, Catharina Frieder.		Calw	Calw	1868	N.-Amer	563212
Bozenhardt, Christian Friedr.		Calw	Calw	1868	N.-Amer	563212
Bozenhardt, Wilhelm	1835	Calw	Calw	1854	N.-Amer	563212
Bracht, Michael		Boeffingen	Frd.	May 1752	Pen.N-A	550803
Bracht, Peter		Altzen	– –	Dec 1751	Mas.N-A	550803
Braendle, Michael & F		Aach	Frd.	Apr 1817	Russia	569267
Braeuning, Catharina Elis.		Freudenstadt	Frd.	Feb 1853	N.-Amer	569272
Braeuning, Christoph (wid.)		Tailfingen	Herr.	Jun 1837	N.-Amer	834624
Braeuning, Friederike El. & F		Herrenberg	Herr.	Jul 1848	N.-Amer	834626
Braeuning, Georg	1 Mar 1824	Herrenberg	Herr.	Bef 1848	N.-Amer	834626
Braeuning, Johann Georg	29 Sep 1828	Reusten	Herr.	Mar 1862	N.-Amer	834624
Braeuning, Johann Jacob & F		Gueltstein	Herr.	Mar 1836	N.-Amer	834624
Braeuning, Johann Michael	4 Sep 1847	Altingen	Herr.	Oct 1866	N.-Amer	834624
Braeuning, Johannes & F	41 yrs.	Bondorf	Herr.	Jun 1832	N.-Amer	834624
Braeuning, Julius Friedrich	4 Nov 1828	Herrenberg	Herr.	Jul 1848	N.-Amer	834626
Braeuning, Justina (wife)	42 yrs.	Bondorf	Herr.	Jun 1832	N.-Amer	834624
Braeuning, Justine	21 Jan 1830	Kuppingen	Herr.	bef 1862	N.-Amer	834624
Braeuning, Karl Friedrich	9 Jul 1836	Herrenberg	Herr.	Jul 1848	N.-Amer	834626
Braitmaier, Anna Maria (wife)		Gueltstein	Herr.	Apr 1831	N.-Amer	834624
Braitmaier, Catharina Barbara	30 May 1832	Kayh	Herr.	Jun 1865	Baden	834624
Braitmaier, Georg Friedrich	22 Oct 1822	Kayh	Herr.	bef 1852	N.-Amer	834627
Braitmaier, Jacob & W		Gueltstein	Herr.	Apr 1831	N.-Amer	834624
Braitmaier, Jacob (wid.)		Tailfingen	Herr.	Apr 1835	N.-Amer	834624
Braitmaier, Johann Jacob	11 Dec 1827	Nufringen	Herr.	Jul 1867	N.-Amer	834624
Braitmaier, Johann Simon & F		Tailfingen	Herr.	Apr 1835	N.-Amer	834624
Braitmaier, Maria Agnes	2 Jul 1826	Nufringen	Herr.	Jul 1867	N.-Amer	834624
Brand, Anna Maria (wife)	28 Jun 1816	Bondorf	Herr.	Nov 1852	N.-Amer	834627

Name		Birth		Emigration			Film
Last	First	Date	Place	O'amt	Appl. Date	Dest.	Number
Brand, Catharina Elisabeth		22 Jul 1803	Bergzabern/bav.	Sulz	May 1832	N.-Amer	849627
Brand, Christian Engelbert		26 Aug 1844	Bondorf	Herr.	Nov 1852	N.-Amer	834627
Brand, Dorothea		22 Sep 1841	Bondorf	Herr.	Nov 1852	N.-Amer	834627
Brand, Johann Friedrich		17 Oct 1847	Bondorf	Herr.	Nov 1852	N.-Amer	834627
Brand, Johann Jacob		20 Jan 1843	Bondorf	Herr.	Nov 1852	N.-Amer	834627
Brand, Johann Michael		21 Aug 1850	Bondorf	Herr.	Nov 1852	N.-Amer	834627
Brand, Johannes		1 Dec 1838	Bondorf	Herr.	Nov 1852	N.-Amer	834627
Brand, Johannes & F		5 Oct 1810	Bondorf	Herr.	Nov 1852	N.-Amer	834627
Braun Johann Georg		6 Nov 1800	Unterjesingen	Herr.	bef 1863	N.-Amer	834624
Braun, Abraham			Kuppingen	Herr.	Oct 1837	Baden	834624
Braun, Adam & F			Baiersbronn	Frd.	Apr 1856	N.-Amer	569275
Braun, Andreas			Goettelfingen	Frd.	Apr 1860	N.-Amer	577777
Braun, Andreas		23 yrs.	Kuppingen	Herr.	Aug 1832	N.-Amer	834624
Braun, Andreas & F			Kuppingen	Herr.	Mar 1850	N.-Amer	834627
Braun, Anna		1 yrs.	Voehringen	Sulz	Apr 1833	N.-Amer	849643
Braun, Anna (wife)		25 Sep 1818	Tumlingen	Frd.	Jan 1855	N.-Amer	569275
Braun, Anna Maria		2 Nov 1823	Spielberg	Frd.	Jan 1847	N.-Amer	569270
Braun, Anna Maria			Hoerschweiler	Frd.	Apr 1856	N.-Amer	569275
Braun, Anna Maria		6 Jul 1835	Goettelfingen	Frd.	Jan 1864	N.-Amer	577779
Braun, Anna Maria			Huzenbach	Frd.	Sep 1865	N.-Amer	577779
Braun, Anna Maria		18 Mar 1829	Kuppingen	Herr.	Mar 1850	N.-Amer	834627
Braun, Anna Maria (wife)			Baiersbronn	Frd.	Jun 1856	N.-Amer	569275
Braun, Barbara		4 Jan 1794	Enztal	Nag.	Aug 1856	N.-Amer	838492
Braun, Barbara		14 Dec 1814	Tumlingen	Frd.	Jan 1855	N.-Amer	569275
Braun, Barbara			Pfalzgrafenweiler	Frd.	bef 1857	N.-Amer	577776
Braun, Barbara		6 May 1838	Dornhan	Sulz	Feb 1859	N.-Amer	849633
Braun, Barbara & C		16 Sep 1834	Hoerschweiler	Frd.	Apr 1859	N.-Amer	577776
Braun, Bernhard & F		2 Apr 1811	Tumlingen	Frd.	Jan 1855	N.-Amer	569275
Braun, Carl & F			Baiersbronn	Frd.	Jun 1856	N.-Amer	569275
Braun, Carl Friederich		12 May 1834	Wittensweiler	Frd.	Apr 1853	N.-Amer	569272
Braun, Carl Friedrich		14 yrs.	Freudenstadt	Frd.	Sep 1853	N.-Amer	569274
Braun, Carl Gottlob		1 Sep 1840	Sulz	Sulz	Jun 1851	N.-Amer	849627
Braun, Caroline Friederike		10 Aug 1845	Freudenstadt	Frd.	1857	N.-Amer	577778
Braun, Caroline Wilhelmine		13 Sep 1848	Baiersbronn	Frd.	Apr 1856	N.-Amer	569275
Braun, Catharina		7 Mar 1845	Wittlensweiler	Frd.	1857	N.-Amer	577778
Braun, Christian		6 Feb 1839	Wittlensweiler	Frd.	bef 1858	N.-Amer	577776
Braun, Christian			Herzogsweiler	Frd.	Apr 1752	Pen.N-A	550803
Braun, Christian Friederich		17 yrs.	Baiersbronn	Frd.	Jun 1856	N.-Amer	569275
Braun, Christiane Caroline		9 Aug 1845	Freudenstadt	Frd.	Jan 1861	N.-Amer	577778
Braun, Christine		2 Oct 1844	Huzenbach	Frd.	Apr 1865	N.-Amer	577779
Braun, Christine		19 Dec 1835	Hoerschweiler	Frd.	Apr 1859	N.-Amer	577776
Braun, Christine Dorothea & C		17 Mar 1815	Freudenstadt	Frd.	Jul 1856	Baden	569275
Braun, Christine Rosine		19 Sep 1843	Baiersbronn	Frd.	Apr 1856	N.-Amer	569275
Braun, Christoph Friedrich			Besenfeld	Frd.	Apr 1865	N.-Amer	577779
Braun, David & F			Roet	Frd.	Apr 1856	N.-Amer	569275
Braun, Dorothea		29 Apr 1842	Wittlensweiler	Frd.	1857	N.-Amer	577778
Braun, Dorothea (wife)			Unterjesingen	Herr.	Apr 1846	N.-Amer	834626
Braun, Dorothea (wife)			Gueltstein	Herr.	Apr 1831	N.-Amer	834624
Braun, Elisabeth Rosina		5 Mar 1783	Sulz	Sulz	May 1817	N.-Amer	849642
Braun, Esther		31 Oct 1847	Hoerschweiler	Frd.	Apr 1859	N.-Amer	577776

Braun, Eva (wife)		Voehringen	Sulz	Apr 1833	N.-Amer	849643
Braun, Friederike	17 Nov 1851	Hoerschweiler	Frd.	Apr 1859	N.-Amer	577776
Braun, Georg David		Friedrichstal	Frd.	Oct 1848	N.-Amer	569270
Braun, Georg Friedrich		Oberhaugstett	Calw	Feb 1848	N.-Amer	563212
Braun, Georg Jacob		Dornstetten	Frd.	1817	Russia	569269
Braun, Georg Jakob & F		Dornstetten	Frd.	1817	Russia	569269
Braun, Gottfried	10 May 1773	Besenfeld	Frd.	1792	Switz.	569269
Braun, Gottfried	35 yrs.	Oberhaugstett	Calw	1864	France	563212
Braun, Gottfried		Oberhaugstett	Calw	1852	N.-Amer	563212
Braun, Gottfried Franz		Freudenstadt	Frd.	bef 1856	France	569275
Braun, Gottlob	16 yrs.	Baiersbronn	Frd.	Jun 1856	N.-Amer	569275
Braun, Jacob	21 Apr 1833	Durrweiler	Frd.	Mar 1851	N.-Amer	569271
Braun, Jacob	16 yrs.	Voehringen	Sulz	Apr 1833	N.-Amer	849643
Braun, Jacob	26 Jun 1840	Dornhan	Sulz	Sep 1867	N.-Amer	849634
Braun, Jacob Friedrich	6 Jun 1840	Goettelfingen	Frd.	bef 1860	N.-Amer	577777
Braun, Jakob Friedr.		Freudenstadt	Frd.	Apr 1854	N.-Amer	569273
Braun, Jakob Friedrich	3 Jan 1850	Tumlingen	Frd.	Jan 1855	N.-Amer	569275
Braun, Jakob Friedrich	25 Aug 1849	Pfalzgrafenweiler	Frd.	Jan 1866	N.-Amer	577780
Braun, Jakob Friedrich & F		Kuppingen	Herr.	Jun 1833	Rus-Pol	834624
Braun, Johann Friedrich	8 Jul 1841	Baiersbronn	Frd.	Apr 1856	N.-Amer	569275
Braun, Johann Friedrich & W		Gueltstein	Herr.	Apr 1831	N.-Amer	834624
Braun, Johann Georg	27 Jul 1834	Baiersbronn	Frd.	Jun 1856	N.-Amer	569275
Braun, Johann Georg	68 yrs.	Pfalzgrafenweiler	Frd.	Apr 1836	N.-Amer	569268
Braun, Johann Georg		Baiersbronn	Frd.	Mar 1846	N.-Amer	569271
Braun, Johann Georg	13 Jul 1839	Hoerschweiler	Frd.	Apr 1859	N.-Amer	577776
Braun, Johann Georg	22 Feb 1847	Freudenstadt	Frd.	Aug 1866	N.-Amer	577780
Braun, Johann Georg & F	6 Nov 1800	Unterjesingen	Herr.	Apr 1846	N.-Amer	834626
Braun, Johann Gottfried	18 Dec 1820	Woernersberg	Frd.	Oct 1846	N.-Amer	569271
Braun, Johann Jacob	9 Jan 1836	Kuppingen	Herr.	Mar 1850	N.-Amer	834627
Braun, Johann Martin & F		Voehringen	Sulz	Apr 1833	N.-Amer	849643
Braun, Johann Sophie		Freudenstadt	Frd.	Apr 1854	N.-Amer	569273
Braun, Johanna	11 Feb 1843	Durrweiler	Frd.	Apr 1847	N.-Amer	569270
Braun, Johanna	11 Apr 1824	Durrweiler	Frd.	Jun 1854	N.-Amer	569274
Braun, Johanne Friederike		Freudenstadt	Frd.	Sep 1851	France	569271
Braun, Johannes		Schwarzenberg	Frd.	May 1848	N.-Amer	569270
Braun, Johannes	12 May 1833	Schopfloch	Frd.	May 1856	N.-Amer	569275
Braun, Johannes	11 Apr 1816	Durrweiler	Frd.	1836	N.-Amer	577779
Braun, Johannes	13 Sep 1850	Hoerschweiler	Frd.	Apr 1859	N.-Amer	577776
Braun, Johannes	24 yrs.	Freudenstadt	Frd.	May 1752	Pen.N-A	550803
Braun, Johannes		Dornstetten	Frd.	Apr 1752	Pen.N-A	550803
Braun, Johannes		Dietersweiler	Frd.	Jan 1805	Baden	550803
Braun, Johannes		Sulz	Sulz	1854	N.-Amer	849628
Braun, Johannes & F	17 Apr 1789	Schopfloch	Frd.	Apr 1819	N.-Amer	569268
Braun, Johannes & F	20 Aug 1812	Hoerschweiler	Frd.	Apr 1859	N.-Amer	577776
Braun, Johannes & F	28 Jun 1811	Sulz	Sulz	Jun 1851	N.-Amer	849627
Braun, Johannes Leonhardt		Oberhaugstett	Calw	1860	N.-Amer	563212
Braun, Juliana	25 Jun 1805	Pfalzgrafenweiler	Frd.	Apr 1833	N.-Amer	569268
Braun, Katharina	20 Jan 1842	Hoerschweiler	Frd.	Apr 1859	N.-Amer	577776
Braun, Katharina		Neubulach	Calw	1861	Switz.	563212
Braun, Margaretha		Baiersbronn	Frd.	Mar 1847	N.-Amer	569271

| Name | | Birth | | Emigration | | | Film |
Last	First	Date	Place	O'amt	Appl. Date	Dest.	Number
Braun, Margaretha			Aichelberg	Calw	1857	N.-Amer	563212
Braun, Margaretha (wife)			Baiersbronn	Frd.	Apr 1856	N.-Amer	569275
Braun, Maria Dorothea (wife)			Kuppingen	Herr.	Mar 1850	N.-Amer	834627
Braun, Maria Katharina		30 Apr 1845	Baiersbronn	Frd.	Apr 1856	N.-Amer	569275
Braun, Marie Friederike		15 yrs.	Baiersbronn	Frd.	Jun 1856	N.-Amer	569275
Braun, Mathaeus			Schopfloch	Frd.	May 1851	N.-Amer	569271
Braun, Mathaeus Friedrich		21 Nov 1818	Goettelfingen	Frd.	Mar 1847	N.-Amer	569270
Braun, Matthias			Freudenstadt	Frd.	1851	N.-Amer	577778
Braun, Michael		6 Sep 1809	Woernersberg	Frd.	Apr 1833	N.-Amer	569268
Braun, Michael		41 yrs.	Voehringen	Sulz	Aug 1853	N.-Amer	849643
Braun, Paul Wilhelm		25 Jan 1838	Sulz	Sulz	Jun 1851	N.-Amer	849627
Braun, Regina		28 Feb 1843	Tumlingen	Frd.	Jan 1855	N.-Amer	569275
Braun, Regina		22 Jul 1835	Wenden	Frd.	Aug 1853	N.-Amer	569274
Braun, Regina			Oberhaugstett	Calw	1856	N.-Amer	563212
Braun, Rosina Catharina		21 May 1836	Kuppingen	Herr.	Mar 1850	N.-Amer	834627
Braun, Rosine		23 yrs.	Pfalzgrafenweiler	Frd.	Jul 1832	N.-Amer	569268
Braun, Rosine		14 Nov 1843	Hoerschweiler	Frd.	Apr 1859	N.-Amer	577776
Braun, Ulrich & F			Kentheim/Sommenhardt	Calw	1852	N.-Amer	563212
Braun, Wilhelmine		19 yrs.	Baiersbronn	Frd.	Jun 1856	N.-Amer	569275
Brecht, Barbara		10 yrs.	Unteriflingen	Frd.	May 1752	Pen.N-A	550803
Brecht, Elisabetha		32 yrs.	Unteriflingen	Frd.	May 1752	Pen.N-A	550803
Brecht, Louise			Dornstetten	Frd.	Feb 1848	N.-Amer	569270
Brecht, Matthaeus & F		38 yrs.	Unteriflingen	Frd.	May 1752	Pen.N-A	550803
Breining, Conrad Jacob		19 yrs.	Calw	Calw	1867	N.-Amer	563212
Breisinger, Barbara		18 Apr 1848	Sigmarswangen	Sulz	Jun 1880	N.-Amer	849626
Breitenreuter, Johannes		31 Dec 1846	Wittershausen	Sulz	Dec 1866	N.-Amer	849644
Breitenreuter, Johannes		18 yrs.	Wittershausen	Sulz	Mar 1852	N.-Amer	849644
Breithaupt, Gottfried & F			Liebenzell	Calw	1847	N.-Amer	563212
Breithaupt, Jakob		3 Apr 1834	Tumlingen	Frd.	Nov 1844	N.-Amer	569272
Breithaupt, Johann		28 Nov 1823	Boeffingen	Frd.	Aug 1847	N.-Amer	569270
Breithaupt, Johann Georg		13 Jul 1836	Boeffingen	Frd.	Apr 1853	France	569272
Breithaupt, Mathaeus		12 Sep 1843	Duerrenmettstetten	Sulz	Feb 1860	N.-Amer	849635
Breithing, Friedrich			Gechingen	Calw	1859	N.-Amer	563212
Breitling, Anna Maria		30 yrs.	Gechingen	Calw	Mar 1847	N.-Amer	563212
Breitling, Elisabetha & F			Dachtel	Calw	1852	N.-Amer	563212
Breitling, Eva Catharina			Gechingen	Calw	1852	N.-Amer	563212
Breitling, Gottlob & F			Gechingen	Calw	1852	N.-Amer	563212
Breitling, Johann Georg & F			Gechingen	Calw	1854	N.-Amer	563212
Breitling, Johannes			Gechingen	Frd.	1837	France	577779
Breitling, Johannes		16 Jan 1834	Gechingen	Calw	1854	N.-Amer	563212
Breitling, Margaretha & F			Aichhalden	Calw	Jul 1847	N.-Amer	563212
Breitling, Wilhelm			Calw	Calw	1852	N.-Amer	563212
Brener, August		1843	Teinach	Calw	1857	N.-Amer	563212
Brenner, Anna Maria			Egenhausen	Nag.	Jun 1854	N.-Amer	838491
Brenner, Gottfried			Emmingen	Nag.	Feb 1854	N.-Amer	838491
Brenner, Johann Martin			Egenhausen	Nag.	Jun 1854	N.-Amer	838491
Brenner, Johann Michael & F		60 yrs.	Egenhausen	Nag.	Jun 1854	N.-Amer	838491
Brenner, Johannes & F			Egenhausen	Nag.	Jun 1854	N.-Amer	838491
Brenner, Joseph Friedrich			Calw	Calw	Nov 1847	Baden	563212
Brenner, Leo		20 Dec 1866	Altheim	Horb	Apr 1867	N.-Amer	835929

Brenner, Louise Heinrike		Calw	Calw	1864	Holst. 563212
Brenner, Rosina Friederike		Calw	Calw	1869	Bavaria 563212
Breuning, Anna Maria	19 Apr 1811	Bondorf	Herr.	Apr 1847	N.-Amer 834626
Breuning, Catharina		Beutelsbach	Schd.	Feb 1837	N.-Amer 801461
Breuning, Johann Friedrich	18 May 1820	Bondorf	Herr.	Apr 1847	N.-Amer 834626
Brezing, Matthaeus	8 Nov 1829	Baiersbronn	Frd.	Dec 1857	France 577776
Brodbeck, Anna Catharina	23 Dec 1825	Nufringen	Herr.	Apr 1838	N.-Amer 834625
Brodbeck, Anna Maria	11 Dec 1831	Nufringen	Herr.	Apr 1838	N.-Amer 834625
Brodbeck, Auguste (wife)		Sulz	Sulz	Jan 1854	N.-Amer 849627
Brodbeck, Barbara	24 Oct 1827	Nufringen	Herr.	Apr 1838	N.-Amer 834625
Brodbeck, Christina Margar.	30 Jul 1836	Nufringen	Herr.	Apr 1838	N.-Amer 834625
Brodbeck, Elisabetha Ca. (wife)	40 yrs.	Nufringen	Herr.	Apr 1838	N.-Amer 834625
Brodbeck, Friederike	30 Nov 1850	Sulz	Sulz	Jan 1854	N.-Amer 849627
Brodbeck, Friedrich		Herrenberg	Herr.	May 1845	Switz. 834626
Brodbeck, Imanuel Wilhelm		Herrenberg	Herr.	bef 1838	N.-Amer 834625
Brodbeck, Jacob & F		Sulz	Sulz	Jan 1854	N.-Amer 849627
Brodbeck, Jacob & F	39 yrs.	Nufringen	Herr.	Apr 1838	N.-Amer 834625
Brodbeck, Jacob Friedrich	27 Feb 1853	Sulz	Sulz	Jan 1854	N.-Amer 849627
Brodbeck, Johann Georg	19 Jul 1829	Nufringen	Herr.	Apr 1838	N.-Amer 834625
Brodbeck, Johann Jacob	29 Apr 1821	Nufringen	Herr.	Apr 1838	N.-Amer 834625
Brodbeck, Johann Jacob	5 Sep 1849	Nufringen	Herr.	May 1869	N.-Amer 834624
Broesamle, Anna Maria	26 Jul 1831	Herzogsweiler	Frd.	Mar 1847	N.-Amer 569271
Broesamle, Anna Maria	22 Jun 1845	Unterjettingen	Herr.	Oct 1865	N.-Amer 834624
Broesamle, Barbara	6 Jan 1824	Kaelberbronn	Frd.	Mar 1847	N.-Amer 569271
Broesamle, Johann	17 yrs.	Roet	Frd.	Apr 1860	N.-Amer 577777
Broesamle, Johann Jacob	6 Oct 1825	Unterjettingen	Herr.	Sep 1851	N.-Amer 834627
Broesamle, Johannes	12 Jul 1823	Edelweiler	Frd.	bef 1859	N.-Amer 577776
Broesamle, Ludwig	29 Nov 1847	Roet	Frd.	Mar 1864	N.-Amer 577779
Broesamle, Mathaeus	21 yrs.	Unterjettingen	Herr.	Aug 1847	N.-Amer 834626
Brohmer, Anna Maria	18 Mar 1829	Pfalzgrafenweiler	Frd.	1846	N.-Amer 569270
Broner, Catharina Barb. (wife)		Hildrizhausen	Herr.	Mar 1831	N.-Amer 834624
Broner, Johannes & W		Hildrizhausen	Herr.	Mar 1831	N.-Amer 834624
Bronner, Adolf Robert		Boeblingen	Calw	Mar 1870	Saxony 563212
Bronner, Anna Maria	17 yrs.	Pfalzgrafenweiler	Frd.	Apr 1846	N.-Amer 569271
Bronner, Christian	18 Oct 1803	Cresbach	Frd.	Feb 1833	Baden 569269
Bronner, Edmonda		Leinstetten	Sulz	Jun 1854	N.-Amer 849638
Bronner, Franz Anton		Leinstetten	Sulz	Jun 1854	N.-Amer 849638
Bronner, Franziska		Leinstetten	Sulz	Jun 1854	N.-Amer 849638
Bronner, Johannes		Leinstetten	Sulz	Sep 1854	N.-Amer 849638
Bronner, Johannes	9 Dec 1804	Leinstetten	Sulz	Jun 1817	N.-Amer 849638
Bronner, Johannes & F	23 Mar 1775	Leinstetten	Sulz	Jun 1817	N.-Amer 849638
Bronner, Joseph	21 Dec 1815	Leinstetten	Sulz	Jun 1817	N.-Amer 849638
Bronner, Katharina	4 Jul 1806	Leinstetten	Sulz	Jun 1817	N.-Amer 849638
Bronner, Leopold	11 Nov 1821	Leinstetten	Sulz	May 1862	Prussia 849638
Bronner, Lorenz	15 Aug 1840	Leinstetten	Sulz	Aug 1856	N.-Amer 849638
Bronner, Maria	20 May 1842	Leinstetten	Sulz	Jul 1867	Prussia 849638
Bronner, Maria Anna (wife)	17 Oct 1774	Leinstetten	Sulz	Jun 1817	N.-Amer 849638
Bronner, Sophia	4 Jun 1813	Leinstetten	Sulz	Jun 1817	N.-Amer 849638
Bronner, Theresia	21 Oct 1765	Leinstetten	Sulz	Jun 1817	N.-Amer 849638
Bronner, Wilhelmine		Leinstetten	Sulz	Jun 1854	N.-Amer 849638

Name		Birth		Emigration			Film
Last	First	Date	Place	O'amt	Appl. Date	Dest.	Number
Brose, Christina			Groembach	Frd.	1837	N.-Amer	569269
Bross, Anna Maria		1 Nov 1836	Edelweiler	Frd.	Feb 1847	N.-Amer	569271
Bross, Anna Maria		27 Feb 1813	Edelweiler	Frd.	Feb 1847	N.-Amer	569271
Bross, Barbara		18 May 1838	Edelweiler	Frd.	Feb 1847	N.-Amer	569271
Bross, Bernhard		22 Jan 1822	Kaelberbronn	Frd.	Apr 1857	N.-Amer	577776
Bross, David			Baiersbronn	Frd.	Jan 1844	Baden	569269
Bross, Friedrich & F		5 Apr 1811	Edelweiler	Frd.	Feb 1847	N.-Amer	569271
Bross, Heinrike			Ostelsheim	Calw	1868	N.-Amer	563212
Bross, Jacob Friedrich			Baiersbronn	Frd.	Dec 1804	Baden	550803
Bross, Jakob Friedrich		19 Nov 1845	Edelweiler	Frd.	Feb 1847	N.-Amer	569271
Bross, Johannes		7 Feb 1841	Edelweiler	Frd.	Feb 1847	N.-Amer	569271
Bross, Ludwig Friedrich			Ostelsheim	Calw	1859	N.-Amer	563212
Bross, Maria Magdalena		15 Mar 1808	Dornstetten	Frd.	Mar 1846	N.-Amer	569271
Bross, Martin		1839	Ostelsheim	Calw	1857	N.-Amer	563212
Bross, Sophie		31 May 1843	Edelweiler	Frd.	Feb 1847	N.-Amer	569271
Bruder, Anna Maria			Lossburg	Frd.	Mar 1847	N.-Amer	569270
Bruder, David Friedrich		10 Oct 1840	Freudenstadt	Frd.	Jun 1866	N.-Amer	577780
Bruder, Friederike		16 Dec 1835	Freudenstadt	Frd.	Sep 1859	Baden	577776
Bruder, Johann Georg		25 Aug 1842	Freudenstadt	Frd.	Jun 1866	N.-Amer	577780
Brueker, Anna Maria		6 May 1844	Trichtingen	Sulz	Nov 1867	N.-Amer	849642
Bruestle, Friederika			Erzgrube	Frd.	Aug 1865	N.-Amer	577779
Bub, Barbara (wife)		40 yrs.	Freudenstadt	Frd.	May 1752	Pen.N-A	550803
Bub, Georg Fridrich		7 yrs.	Freudenstadt	Frd.	May 1752	Pen.N-A	550803
Bub, Johannes		3 yrs.	Freudenstadt	Frd.	May 1752	Pen.N-A	550803
Bub, Sophia Dorothea		1 yrs.	Freudenstadt	Frd.	May 1752	Pen.N-A	550803
Bub, Tobias		5 yrs.	Freudenstadt	Frd.	May 1752	Pen.N-A	550803
Bub, Tobias & F		42 yrs.	Freudenstadt	Frd.	May 1752	Pen.N-A	550803
Bubenhofer, Katharina			Leinstetten	Sulz	Nov 1854	N.-Amer	849638
Buchfink, Anna Maria		19 Oct 1862	Reusten	Herr.	May 1869	N.-Amer	834624
Buchfink, Anna Maria (wife)		8 Jan 1835	Reusten	Herr.	May 1869	N.-Amer	834624
Buchfink, Catharina Barbara		28 Jun 1861	Reusten	Herr.	May 1869	N.-Amer	834624
Buchfink, Jakob Friedrich			Reusten	Herr.	Apr 1833	France	834624
Buchfink, Johann Martin			Reusten	Herr.	Mar 1849	N.-Amer	834627
Buchfink, Johann Michael & F		24 Apr 1836	Reusten	Herr.	May 1869	N.-Amer	834624
Buchfink, Michael		25 Nov 1863	Reusten	Herr.	May 1869	N.-Amer	834624
Buchmann, Christian Friedrich			Dornstetten	Frd.	Feb 1846	N.-Amer	569271
Buchmann, Gottlieb		5 Dec 1841	Dornstetten	Frd.	Mar 1856	N.-Amer	569275
Buchmann, Jakob		6 Feb 1837	Dornstetten	Frd.	Nov 1853	N.-Amer	569272
Buchmann, Johann David		25 Jul 1839	Dornstetten	Frd.	Mar 1856	N.-Amer	569275
Buchmann, Johann Gottf.		23 Sep 1826	Dornstetten	Frd.	Nov 1853	N.-Amer	569272
Buchmann, Margaretha		26 Oct 1820	Dornstetten	Frd.	Apr 1851	N.-Amer	569271
Buchwald, Ehrenreich			Hildrizhausen	Herr.	Nov 1851	N.-Amer	834627
Bueb, Johannes			Altingen	Herr.	Jun 1826	Hungary	834624
Buechele, Adolph		1 Jan 1860	Binsdorf	Sulz	Sep 1873	N.-Amer	849631
Buechele, Barbara (wid.) & F		31 Oct 1819	Binsdorf	Sulz	Sep 1873	N.-Amer	849631
Buechele, Bibiana		3 Jan 1852	Binsdorf	Sulz	Mar 1868	N.-Amer	849631
Buechele, Carl		28 Feb 1859	Binsdorf	Sulz	Sep 1872	N.-Amer	849631
Buechele, Catharina Elis. (wife)		22 Jul 1803	Bergzabern/Bav.	Sulz	May 1832	N.-Amer	849627
Buechele, Egidius		23 Sep 1849	Binsdorf	Sulz	Sep 1868	N.-Amer	849631
Buechele, Georg Anton		26 May 1858	Binsdorf	Sulz	Sep 1873	N.-Amer	849631

Buechele, Gottlieb		Tischardt	Sulz	Jan 1847	N.-Amer	849633
Buechele, Johann Daniel & F	27 Mar 1794	Sulz	Sulz	May 1832	N.-Amer	849627
Buechele, Johannes	22 Apr 1826	Sulz	Sulz	May 1832	N.-Amer	849627
Buechele, Louise Charlotte	27 Nov 1827	Sulz	Sulz	May 1832	N.-Amer	849627
Buechele, Maria & C		Binsdorf	Sulz	Apr 1855	N.-Amer	849630
Buechele, Mathaeus		Binsdorf	Sulz	Apr 1855	N.-Amer	849630
Buechele, Renate		Binsdorf	Sulz	Apr 1855	N.-Amer	849630
Buecheler, Gottlieb	1 May 1832	Dornhan	Sulz	Nov 1852	N.-Amer	849633
Buechenstein, Johann Michael	29 Apr 1820	Altingen	Herr.	Mar 1844	Bavaria	834626
Buechsenstein, Gottfried	28 Dec 1839	Reichenbach	Frd.	Jan 1866	N.-Amer	577780
Buechsenstein, Johann Adam	4 Aug 1827	Altingen	Herr.	May 1851	N.-Amer	834627
Buechsenstein, Johann Adam & F	3 Apr 1790	Altingen	Herr.	May 1851	N.-Amer	834627
Buechsenstein, Johann Simon	29 Mar 1839	Altingen	Herr.	May 1851	N.-Amer	834627
Buechsenstein, Martha	10 Mar 1835	Altingen	Herr.	May 1851	N.-Amer	834627
Buechsenstein, Martha (wife)	28 Mar 1800	Altingen	Herr.	May 1851	N.-Amer	834627
Bueckle, Johann Jakob	22 yrs.	Liebelsberg	Calw	1855	N.-Amer	563212
Buehle, Ludwig Aug.		Calw	Calw	Feb 1874	Austria	563212
Buehler Johann Georg	20 yrs.	Neuweiler	Calw	1866	N.-Amer	563212
Buehler, Albert & F		Sulz	Sulz	May 1891	N.-Amer	849626
Buehler, Albert Ernst & F	30 May 1845	Sulz	Sulz	Jan 1881	N.-Amer	849628
Buehler, Alfred Christian	15 Feb 1876	Sulz	Sulz	Jan 1881	N.-Amer	849628
Buehler, Andreas	20 Jul 1862	Muehlheim a.B.	Sulz	Jul 1869	N.-Amer	849639
Buehler, Anna Maria	27 Jun 1879	Sulz	Sulz	Jun 1883	N.-Amer	849628
Buehler, Anna Maria	27 Mar 1837	Dornhan	Sulz	Apr 1861	N.-Amer	849634
Buehler, Anna Maria	19 May 1838	Dornhan	Sulz	Mar 1857	N.-Amer	849633
Buehler, Anna Maria	8 Jan 1835	Reusten	Herr.	May 1869	N.-Amer	834624
Buehler, Barbara	16 Feb 1857	Muehlheim a.B.	Sulz	Jul 1869	N.-Amer	849639
Buehler, Carl	6 Mar 1837	Freudenstadt	Frd.	Sep 1853	N.-Amer	569274
Buehler, Christian	1834	Neuweiler	Calw	1854	N.-Amer	563212
Buehler, Christina	23 Dec 1832	Dornhan	Sulz	Mar 1857	N.-Amer	849633
Buehler, Christine	1822	Dornhan	Sulz	Mar 1847	N.-Amer	849633
Buehler, Ernst	14 Feb 1873	Sulz	Sulz	Jun 1883	N.-Amer	849628
Buehler, Eugen	6 Dec 1870	Sulz	Sulz	Jun 1883	N.-Amer	849628
Buehler, Eva	29 May 1817	Reinerzau	Frd.	Jun 1837	Baden	569268
Buehler, Georg Peter	13 Dec 1850	Reusten	Herr.	Jul 1852	N.-Amer	834627
Buehler, Johann Christian	6 Jun 1840	Freudenstadt	Frd.	Oct 1859	N.-Amer	577776
Buehler, Johann Georg		Dornhan	Sulz	Aug 1855	Baden	849633
Buehler, Johann Georg		Gueltstein	Herr.	Jun 1833	Rus-Pol	834624
Buehler, Johann Georg & F		Dornhan	Sulz	Mar 1817	Russia	849633
Buehler, Johann Georg & W		Gueltstein	Herr.	Mar 1831	N.-Amer	834624
Buehler, Johann Jacob		Nagold	Nag.	Jan 1854	N.-Amer	838491
Buehler, Johann Ludwig	12 Oct 1852	Muehlheim a.B.	Sulz	Sep 1866	N.-Amer	849639
Buehler, Johann Martin		Gueltstein	Herr.	Jun 1833	Rus-Pol	834624
Buehler, Johann Michael		Herrenberg	Herr.	Feb 1852	N.-Amer	834627
Buehler, Johannes	15 Oct 1834	Dornhan	Sulz	Sep 1854	N.-Amer	849633
Buehler, Johannes	29 Apr 1845	Muehlheim a.B.	Sulz	Mar 1860	N.-Amer	849639
Buehler, Johannes (wid.)		Herrenberg	Herr.	Mar 1836	Baden	834624
Buehler, Julie	2 Jun 1877	Sulz	Sulz	Jan 1881	N.-Amer	849628
Buehler, Julius	16 Nov 1880	Sulz	Sulz	Jan 1881	N.-Amer	849628
Buehler, Katharina	28 Nov 1849	Muehlheim a.B.	Sulz	Jul 1869	N.-Amer	849639

Name		Birth		Emigration			Film
Last	First	Date	Place	O'amt	Appl. Date	Dest.	Number
Buehler, Lucia (wife)		16 Sep 1820	Reusten	Herr.	Jul 1852	N.-Amer	834627
Buehler, Magdalena Salome (wife)			Gueltstein	Herr.	Mar 1831	N.-Amer	834624
Buehler, Maria (wife)		21 Jul 1849	Sulz	Sulz	Jan 1881	N.-Amer	849628
Buehler, Maria Mag. (wid.)& F		18 Mar 1825	Muehlheim a.B.	Sulz	Jul 1869	N.-Amer	849639
Buehler, Maria Magdalena		10 Nov 1868	Muehlheim a.B.	Sulz	Jul 1869	N.-Amer	849639
Buehler, Mattaeus		15 Apr 1827	Dietersweiler	Frd.	Jun 1854	N.-Amer	569273
Buehler, Matthaeus		19 Dec 1834	Unterwies	Frd.	Aug 1854	N.-Amer	569274
Buehler, Matthias		25 Apr 1842	Dornhan	Sulz	Apr 1859	N.-Amer	849633
Buehler, Michael		28 May 1837	Dornhan	Sulz	Apr 1859	N.-Amer	849633
Buehler, Peter		5 Jul 1814	Reusten	Herr.	Jul 1852	N.-Amer	834627
Buehner, Anna		10 Feb 1812	Muehlheim a.B.	Sulz	Aug 1858	N.-Amer	849639
Buehner, Christine		31 Dec 1816	Oberiflingen	Frd.	Mar 1833	N.-Amer	569268
Buehner, Johann Friedrich & F		15 May 1778	Muehlheim a.B.	Sulz	Aug 1858	N.-Amer	849639
Buehner, Ludwig Friedrich		1 Dec 1843	Muehlheim a.B.	Sulz	Aug 1858	N.-Amer	849639
Buehrer, Johann Georg			Balingen	Bal.	1844	Switz.	555963
Buehrer, Karl Friedrich		2 Oct 1824	Herrenberg	Herr.	May 1870	N.-Amer	834624
Buehrle, Christian & F			Freudenstadt	Frd.	Sep 1854	N.-Amer	569274
Buehrle, Christina			Freudenstadt	Frd.	Sep 1854	N.-Amer	569274
Buerk, Anna Maria		15 Apr 1849	Dornhan	Sulz	Jul 1870	N.-Amer	849634
Buerk, Barbara		22 Apr 1847	Dornhan	Sulz	May 1868	N.-Amer	849634
Buerk, Johannes		15 Jan 1866	Trichtingen	Sulz	Jun 1881	N.-Amer	849642
Buerkle, Anna Catharina		16 Oct 1835	Unterjettingen	Herr.	1840	N.-Amer	834625
Buerkle, Anna Maria		5 Oct 1845	Baiersbronn	Frd.	Dec 1853	N.-Amer	569272
Buerkle, Anna Maria		16 Sep 1831	Unterjettingen	Herr.	1840	N.-Amer	834625
Buerkle, Elisabeth		18 Jan 1849	Baiersbronn	Frd.	Dec 1853	N.-Amer	569272
Buerkle, Elisabeth		12 Feb 1823	Baiersbronn	Frd.	Dec 1853	N.-Amer	569272
Buerkle, Eva		27 Mar 1843	Baiersbronn	Frd.	Dec 1853	N.-Amer	569272
Buerkle, Eva Maria & C		27 Nov 1826	Oberkollwangen	Calw	1854	N.-Amer	563212
Buerkle, Heinrich & F			Unterjettingen	Herr.	1840	N.-Amer	834625
Buerkle, Johann & F			Baiersbronn	Frd.	Apr 1817	Rus-Pol	569267
Buerkle, Johann Adam		18 May 1851	Baiersbronn	Frd.	Dec 1853	N.-Amer	569272
Buerkle, Johann Georg		16 Jun 1828	Unterjettingen	Herr.	1840	N.-Amer	834625
Buerkle, Johann Jacob			Oberkollwangen	Calw	1852	N.-Amer	563212
Buerkle, Johann Martin		26 yrs.	Breitenberg	Calw	1866	N.-Amer	563212
Buerkle, Johann Michael		1853	Oberkollwangen	Calw	1854	N.-Amer	563212
Buerkle, Katharina & C		1828	Oberkollwangen	Calw	1854	N.-Amer	563212
Buerkle, Maria		infant	Oberkollwangen	Calw	1854	N.-Amer	563212
Buerkle, Matthaeus & F		3 Oct 1815	Baiersbronn	Frd.	Dec 1853	N.-Amer	569272
Buerkle, Sidonia Barbara		9 Feb 1839	Unterjettingen	Herr.	1840	N.-Amer	834625
Bugnon, Chaques			Montbeilard	– –	Dec 1751	Mas.N-A	550803
Buhl, Christian & F			Herzogsweiler	Frd.	1817	Russia	569269
Buhl, Franziska			Leinstetten	Sulz	Jun 1817	Prussia	849638
Buhl, Jacob		7 Jul 1839	Enztal	Nag.	Jul 1853	N.-Amer	838490
Buhl, Johannes			Leinstetten	Sulz	Jul 1854	N.-Amer	849638
Buhler, Jacob		26 Oct 1846	Dornhan	Sulz	Sep 1866	N.-Amer	849634
Buhler, Wilhelm		15 Dec 1850	Gueltstein	Herr.	Mar 1869	N.-Amer	834624
Bukenberger, Friedrich & F			Wittendorf	Frd.	Jul 1817	Russia	569268
Bukenberger, Friedrich & F			Boeffingen	Frd.	1817	Russia	569269
Bukenberger, Johann Jakob		26 Sep 1826	Boeffingen	Frd.	Sep 1847	N.-Amer	569270
Bunth, Jacob			Schopfloch	Frd.	Apr 1752	Pen.N-A	550803

Bunth, Matthaeus		Schopfloch	Frd.	Apr 1752	Pen.N-A 550803
Buob, Jacobina Rosina	8 yrs.	Liebenzell	Calw	1866	Baden 563212
Buob, Ludwig	22 yrs.	Calw	Calw	1854	N.-Amer 563212
Buob, Maria Barbara & C		Liebenzell	Calw	1866	Baden 563212
Buob, Maria Catharina		Calw	Calw	Feb 1870	France 563212
Buob, Mathilde		Freudenstadt	Frd.	Feb 1847	Bavaria 569271
Burckardt, Michael		Frutenhof	Frd.	Apr 1752	Pen.N-A 550803
Burckhardt, Johann Jacob		Eichfeldt	– –	Dec 1751	Mas.N-A 550803
Burghardt, Carl Friedrich		Woernersberg	Frd.	bef 1854	N.-Amer 569274
Burghardt, Johannes	2 Aug 1821	Woernersberg	Frd.	bef 1863	Switz. 577778
Burgner, Johann Fried. (wid.)		Unterhaugstett	Calw	1853	N.-Amer 563212
Burk, Adolf		Freudenstadt	Frd.	Oct 1843	Bavaria 569269
Burk, Maria Catharina	44 yrs.	Wintersbach	Schd.	Mar 1833	N.-Amer 801460
Burkhard, Jacob Friedrich & F		Baiersbronn	Frd.	Apr 1817	N.-Amer 569267
Burkhardt, Catharina & F		Unterreichenbach	Calw	1868	N.-Amer 563212
Burkhardt, Catharina Dorothea	28 Aug 1856	Unterreichenbach	Calw	1868	N.-Amer 563212
Burkhardt, Catharina Magdal.		Althengstett	Calw	1863	Switz. 563212
Burkhardt, Christian	26 Sep 1834	Reichenbach	Frd.	Mar 1854	N.-Amer 569273
Burkhardt, Christian Gottlieb		Hirsau	Calw	1853	N.-Amer 563212
Burkhardt, Christiane E.C.wife	16 Jul 1798	Herrenberg	Herr.	Mar 1847	N.-Amer 834626
Burkhardt, Christiane Fried.	4 Jan 1833	Herrenberg	Herr.	Mar 1847	N.-Amer 834626
Burkhardt, Christina		Trichtingen	Sulz	Nov 1853	N.-Amer 849642
Burkhardt, Conrad	18 Nov 1851	Hildrizhausen	Herr.	Jul 1870	N.-Amer 834624
Burkhardt, Eva		Baiersbronn	Frd.	Jul 1832	N.-Amer 569267
Burkhardt, Friedrike	20 Mar 1845	Hildrizhausen	Herr.	Mar 1865	N.-Amer 834624
Burkhardt, Gottlieb Fried. & F	19 Nov 1790	Herrenberg	Herr.	Mar 1847	N.-Amer 834626
Burkhardt, Gottlieb Friedr.	18 May 1864	Hirsau	Calw	Dec 1875	N.-Amer 563212
Burkhardt, Gottlob	22 Jan 1845	Reichenbach	Frd.	Mar 1864	N.-Amer 577779
Burkhardt, Heinrich Gottlieb	4 Nov 1831	Herrenberg	Herr.	Mar 1847	N.-Amer 834626
Burkhardt, Jacob	10 Jun 1839	Liebenzell	Calw	1858	Baden 563212
Burkhardt, Jacob & F		Liebenzell	Calw	1858	Baden 563212
Burkhardt, Jacob Friedrich	6 Feb 1834	Huzenbach	Frd.	Nov 1854	N.-Amer 569274
Burkhardt, Jacob Friedrich	13 yrs.	Unterreichenbach	Calw	1860	N.-Amer 563212
Burkhardt, Jakob Friedrich	14 Jan 1817	Wittlensweiler	Frd.	Apr 1838	N.-Amer 569268
Burkhardt, Johann Adam	9 May 1823	Herrenberg	Herr.	Mar 1847	N.-Amer 834626
Burkhardt, Johann Christian	18 yrs.	Unterreichenbach	Calw	1867	N.-Amer 563212
Burkhardt, Johann Georg		Baiersbronn	Frd.	Apr 1817	Rus-Pol 569267
Burkhardt, Johann Georg		Untermusbach	Frd.	Mar 1837	N.-Amer 569268
Burkhardt, Johann Georg	1851	Roetenbach	Calw	1857	N.-Amer 563212
Burkhardt, Johann Michael	Feb 1850	Unterreichenbach	Calw	1868	N.-Amer 563212
Burkhardt, Johannes	21 yrs.	Breitenberg	Calw	1866	N.-Amer 563212
Burkhardt, Johannes & F		Roetenbach	Calw	1857	N.-Amer 563212
Burkhardt, Katharina	4 Oct 1811	Baiersbronn	Frd.	Jul 1853	N.-Amer 569274
Burkhardt, Ludwig	3 Sep 1834	Baiersbronn	Frd.	May 1854	N.-Amer 569273
Burkhardt, Margaretha		Oberreichenbach	Calw	1861	N.-Amer 563212
Burkhardt, Margaretha Carol.	10 Mar 1836	Herrenberg	Herr.	Mar 1847	N.-Amer 834626
Burkhardt, Margaretha Cathar.	15 Jul 1829	Herrenberg	Herr.	Mar 1847	N.-Amer 834626
Burkhardt, Maria Friederike		Ernstmuehl	Calw	1869	France 563212
Burkhardt, Matthaeus	20 Feb 1837	Hoerschweiler	Frd.	Apr 1854	N.-Amer 569273
Burkhardt, Wilhelm Gottl.	16 May 1857	Unterreichenbach	Calw	1868	N.-Amer 563212

| Name | | Birth | | Emigration | | | Film |
Last	First	Date	Place	O'amt	Appl. Date	Dest.	Number
Burkhardt, Wilhelmine			Unterreichenbach	Calw	1858	Baden	563212
Burkhart, Johann			Unterreichenbach	Calw	Sep 1848	Bavaria	563212
Burkhart, Joseph Sebastian		6 May 1823	Liebenzell	Calw	Mar 1847	N.-Amer	563212
Burster, August		22 Dec 1847	Altheim	Horb	Jul 1866	N.-Amer	835929
Burster, Batholomaeus		44 yrs.	Altheim	Horb	Sep 1853	N.-Amer	835929
Burster, Christian		10 Dec 1838	Altheim	Horb	Sep 1867	Wien	835929
Burster, Josef		9 Apr 1845	Altheim	Horb	Jan 1868	N.-Amer	835929
Buschle, Ernst Caspar		21 Jul 1864	Sulz	Sulz	Mar 1881	N.-Amer	849626
Calmbach, Anna Maria		27 Feb 1813	Edelweiler	Frd.	Feb 1847	N.-Amer	569271
Calmbach, Christian		5 Sep 1846	Woernersberg	Frd.	May 1866	N.-Amer	577780
Calmbach, Christine Cathar.& C			Martinsmoos	Calw	1852	N.-Amer	563212
Calmbach, Georg Friedrich & F			Neuweiler	Calw	1847	N.-Amer	563212
Calmbach, Heinrich		18 yrs.	Liebenzell	Calw	1868	N.-Amer	563212
Calmbach, Maria Margaretha			Martinsmoos	Calw	1852	N.-Amer	563212
Cammerer, Catharina			Sulz	Sulz	bef 1833	S-Russ	849625
Cammerer, Jacob			Sulz	Sulz	bef 1833	S-Russ	849625
Cammerer, Johann Georg			Sigmarswangen	Sulz	Mar 1836	N.-Amer	849625
Carl, Catharina Chr. (wid.)			Oeschelbronn	Herr.	Jun 1832	N.-Amer	834624
Caspar, Anna		8 Oct 1866	Sulz	Sulz	Aug 1876	N.-Amer	849628
Caspar, Christian Gottfried		23 Sep 1831	Sulz	Sulz	Aug 1876	N.-Amer	849628
Caspar, Ferdinand		24 Sep 1817	Freudenstadt	Frd.	Oct 1843	France	569269
Caspar, Friederika Barbara		19 Jul 1828	Freudenstadt	Frd.	bef 1864	France	577779
Caspar, Friederike Dorothea		20 Apr 1835	Sulz	Sulz	Aug 1876	N.-Amer	849628
Caspar, Otto		26 Jul 1846	Freudenstadt	Frd.	Jun 1866	N.-Amer	577780
Caspar, Sophie		20 Feb 1833	Freudenstadt	Frd.	1855	France	577779
Caspar, Sophie Dorothea			Sulz	Sulz	Apr 1835	Hohenz.	849627
Christmann, Paul			Pfalzgrafenweiler	Frd.	bef 1853	N.-Amer	569274
Clauser, Sophie Elisabeth			Freudenstadt	Frd.	Sep 1854	N.-Amer	569274
Clemens, Christina (wife)			Gueltstein	Herr.	Mar 1836	N.-Amer	834624
Clemens, Johann Friedrich & W			Gueltstein	Herr.	Mar 1836	N.-Amer	834624
Conzelmann, Amalie Elisabethe		19 Jan 1824	Heselbach	Frd.	Sep 1847	N.-Amer	569270
Conzelmann, Anna Maria		6 May 1846	Groembach	Frd.	Sep 1847	N.-Amer	569270
Conzelmann, Carl Engelbert		25 Apr 1844	Reichenbach	Frd.	Sep 1847	N.-Amer	569270
Conzelmann, Christian Friedr.		19 Mar 1847	Groembach	Frd.	Sep 1847	N.-Amer	569270
Conzelmann, Israel Gottlob & F		16 Dec 1829	Haiterbach	Frd.	Sep 1847	N.-Amer	569270
Cortes, Karl Wilhelm		16 Apr 1826	Herrenberg	Herr.	Mar 1849	N.-Amer	834627
Craubner, Wilhelm			Freudenstadt	Frd.	Mar 1854	N.-Amer	569273
Currass, Friederike			Calw	Calw	1852	N.-Amer	563212
Daeuble, Agatha		1844	Bergfelden	Sulz	Mar 1857	N.-Amer	849629
Daeuble, Anna Katharina		16 Jun 1838	Muehlheim a.B.	Sulz	May 1858	N.-Amer	849639
Daeuble, Anna Maria		1843	Bergfelden	Sulz	Mar 1857	N.-Amer	849629
Daeuble, Anna Maria & F			Muehlheim a.B.	Sulz	Feb 1854	N.-Amer	849639
Daeuble, Barbara			Dornhan	Sulz	Jan 1827	France	849633
Daeuble, Christine & C		13 Oct 1809	Muehlheim a.B.	Sulz	May 1858	N.-Amer	849639
Daeuble, Elisabetha			Muehlheim a.B.	Sulz	Feb 1854	N.-Amer	849639
Daeuble, Gottfried (wid.) & F		9 Nov 1806	Bergfelden	Sulz	Mar 1857	N.-Amer	849629
Daeuble, Gottlieb		22 Jan 1848	Holzhausen	Sulz	Sep 1865	N.-Amer	849635
Daeuble, Jakob Friedrich			Muehlheim a.B.	Sulz	Apr 1854	N.-Amer	849639
Daeuble, Johann Georg & F			Deckenpfronn	Calw	1852	N.-Amer	563212
Daeuble, Johann Georg & F			Hagelloch/Tuebingen	Herr.	Apr 1833	N.-Amer	834624

Daeuble, Johann Georg & F		Haslach	Herr.	Apr 1835	N.-Amer	834624
Daeuble, Johann Martin		Renfrizhausen	Sulz	bef 1830	Hungary	849625
Daeuble, Johannes	15 yrs.	Muehlheim a.b.	Sulz	Feb 1854	N.-Amer	849639
Daeuble, Ludwig	4 Jun 1841	Muehlheim a.b.	Sulz	May 1858	N.-Amer	849639
Daeuble, Ludwig	26 yrs.	Muehlheim a.b.	Sulz	Feb 1854	N.-Amer	849639
Daiber, Friedrich Oskar	25 Apr 1847	Herrenberg	Herr.	Dec 1867	N.-Amer	834624
Dangelmayer, Anna Barbara	24 Feb 1828	Voehringen	Sulz	Mar 1834	N.-Amer	849643
Dangelmayer, Anna Maria	22 Oct 1826	Voehringen	Sulz	Mar 1834	N.-Amer	849643
Dangelmayer, Anna Maria (wife)		Voehringen	Sulz	Mar 1834	N.-Amer	849643
Dangelmayer, Christina	8 Feb 1824	Voehringen	Sulz	Mar 1834	N.-Amer	849643
Dangelmayer, Conrad	8 Apr 1825	Voehringen	Sulz	Mar 1834	N.-Amer	849643
Dangelmayer, Johann Georg & F		Voehringen	Sulz	Mar 1834	N.-Amer	849643
Dangelmayer, Johann Jacob	13 Nov 1832	Voehringen	Sulz	Mar 1834	N.-Amer	849643
Dannecker, Elisabetha		Bergfelden	Sulz	1817	N.-Amer	849629
Dannecker, Friedrich Jacob & F	20 Oct 1826	Glatten	Frd.	Oct 1854	S.-Amer	569274
Dannecker, Jakob	2 Jan 1864	Bergfelden	Sulz	Jan 1881	N.-Amer	849626
Dannecker, Johann Georg	22 yrs.	Leidringen	Sulz	May 1855	N.-Amer	849637
Dannecker, Johann Georg	29 Nov 1833	Leidringen	Sulz	Nov 1853	N.-Amer	849637
Dannecker, Johann Jacob	17 Dec 1830	Leidringen	Sulz	Oct 1859	N.-Amer	849637
Dannecker, Johann Martin	3 Mar 1836	Bickelsberg	Sulz	Sep 1856	N.-Amer	849630
Dannecker, Magdalena (wife)	27 Jun 1830	Glatten	Frd.	Oct 1854	S.-Amer	569274
Dannecker, Matthaeus	3 Nov 1853	Glatten	Frd.	Oct 1854	S.-Amer	569274
Danneker, Agnes (wife)		Leidringen	Sulz	Jan 1833	N.-Amer	849637
Danneker, Anna	19 Jan 1852	Leidringen	Sulz	Aug 1868	N.-Amer	849637
Danneker, Anna (wife)		Rotenzimmern	Sulz	Apr 1840	N.-Amer	849642
Danneker, Anna Maria	23 Nov 1822	Leidringen	Sulz	Jan 1833	N.-Amer	849637
Danneker, Anna Maria	16 May 1825	Leidringen	Sulz	Jun 1869	N.-Amer	849637
Danneker, Catharina (wife)		Rotenzimmern	Sulz	Apr 1840	N.-Amer	849642
Danneker, Christian	Oct 1826	Rotenzimmern	Sulz	Apr 1840	N.-Amer	849642
Danneker, Jacob	21 Oct 1809	Rotenzimmern	Sulz	Apr 1840	N.-Amer	849642
Danneker, Jakob	7 Jan 1819	Leidringen	Sulz	Jan 1833	N.-Amer	849637
Danneker, Jakob & F	16 Jun 1786	Leidringen	Sulz	Jan 1833	N.-Amer	849637
Danneker, Johann	24 Feb 1852	Leidringen	Sulz	Mar 1870	N.-Amer	849637
Danneker, Johann Christian	23 Jun 1848	Leidringen	Sulz	Mar 1866	N.-Amer	849637
Danneker, Johann Georg	20 Oct 1839	Rotenzimmern	Sulz	Apr 1840	N.-Amer	849642
Danneker, Johann Georg	3 Jan 1831	Leidringen	Sulz	Jan 1833	N.-Amer	849637
Danneker, Johann Georg & F		Rotenzimmern	Sulz	Apr 1840	N.-Amer	849642
Danneker, Johann Georg & F	2 Jan 1791	Leidringen	Sulz	Jun 1869	N.-Amer	849637
Danneker, Johann Georg Sr. & F		Rotenzimmern	Sulz	Apr 1840	N.-Amer	849642
Danneker, Johann Martin	27 Jun 1827	Leidringen	Sulz	Jan 1833	N.-Amer	849637
Danneker, Johann Michael	24 Apr 1814	Leidringen	Sulz	Dec 1816	Poland	849637
Danneker, Johann Michael & F	3 Apr 1783	Leidringen	Sulz	Dec 1816	Poland	849637
Danneker, Maria	25 Dec 1811	Leidringen	Sulz	Dec 1816	Poland	849637
Danneker, Maria Barbara (wife)	32 yrs.	Leidringen	Sulz	Dec 1816	Poland	849637
Danneker, Martin	1 Apr 1838	Rotenzimmern	Sulz	Apr 1840	N.-Amer	849642
Danneker, Martin	2 Apr 1810	Leidringen	Sulz	Dec 1816	Poland	849637
Danneker, Rosina	12 Sep 1816	Leidringen	Sulz	Dec 1816	Poland	849637
Danner, (widow) & F		Sulz	Sulz	Sep 1855	N.-Amer	849627
Danner, Andreas	19 Aug 1826	Wittershausen	Sulz	bef 1861	N.-Amer	849644
Danner, Andreas	28 Aug 1841	Boll	Sulz	Jun 1861	N.-Amer	849632

| Name | | Birth | | Emigration | | | Film |
Last	First	Date	Place	O'amt	Appl. Date	Dest.	Number
Danner, Anna & C			Sigmarswangen	Sulz	Oct 1853	N.-Amer	849642
Danner, Anna Maria		1 Jan 1843	Sigmarswangen	Sulz	Aug 1860	N.-Amer	849642
Danner, Anna Maria			Sigmarswangen	Sulz	Nov 1853	N.-Amer	849642
Danner, Anna Maria		4 Mar 1787	Sigmarswangen	Sulz	May 1817	N.-Amer	849642
Danner, Carl Andreas		1 Feb 1815	Sigmarswangen	Sulz	May 1817	N.-Amer	849642
Danner, Christian		13 Aug 1853	Boll	Sulz	Aug 1871	Switz.	849632
Danner, Christina			Sigmarswangen	Sulz	Oct 1854	N.-Amer	849642
Danner, Dorothea			Weiler	Schd.	Mar 1835	N.-Amer	801460
Danner, Emerenzia			Leinstetten	Sulz	Jun 1854	N.-Amer	849638
Danner, Franziska		5 Jun 1838	Sigmarswangen	Sulz	Sep 1866	Baden	849642
Danner, Gottlob Friedrich		8 Sep 1860	Sigmarswangen	Sulz	Apr 1877	N.-Amer	849642
Danner, Johann Georg		18 Feb 1810	Sigmarswangen	Sulz	May 1817	N.-Amer	849642
Danner, Johann Jacob		29 Aug 1847	Sulz	Sulz	Sep 1855	N.-Amer	849627
Danner, Johann Jakob		17 Oct 1844	Renfrizhausen	Sulz	Jul 1860	N.-Amer	849639
Danner, Johannes			Sigmarswangen	Sulz	Oct 1838	Baden	849642
Danner, Johannes & F		25 Sep 1779	Sigmarswangen	Sulz	May 1817	N.-Amer	849642
Danner, Johannes & F		27 Apr 1784	Boll	Sulz	Feb 1834	Bavaria	849632
Danner, Karl August		14 Aug 1849	Sulz	Sulz	Sep 1855	N.-Amer	849627
Danner, Maria Agatha			Sigmarswangen	Sulz	Oct 1854	N.-Amer	849642
Danner, Maria Agatha		15 Mar 1817	Sigmarswangen	Sulz	May 1817	N.-Amer	849642
Danner, Mathias		10 Sep 1799	Boll	Sulz	May 1832	N.-Amer	849632
Danner, Mathias		11 Apr 1840	Renfrizhausen	Sulz	Feb 1870	France	849639
Danner, Matthaeus		17 May 1805	Sigmarswangen	Sulz	May 1817	N.-Amer	849642
Danner, Matthias		43 yrs.	Sigmarswangen	Sulz	Jun 1817	Hungary	849625
Danner, Matthias		30 Oct 1841	Sigmarswangen	Sulz	Aug 1858	N.-Amer	849642
Danner, Matthias		11 Jul 1838	Sigmarswangen	Sulz	Aug 1858	N.-Amer	849642
Danner, Matthias			Sigmarswangen	Sulz	May 1817	N.-Amer	849642
Danner, Otto Hermann		9 Aug 1853	Dusslingen	Sulz	Jun 1870	N.-Amer	849628
Danner, Philipp & F			Dornhan	Sulz	Mar 1817	Russia	849633
Daucher, Anna Maria			Moettlingen	Calw	1867	Bavaria	563212
Dauerbacher, Johann Michael		1838	Martinsmoos	Calw	1856	N.-Amer	563212
Daunz, Emilie Friederike		25 Jun 1840	Freudenstadt	Frd.	bef 1863	Switz.	577778
Deiss, Christine Sara		29 Dec 1807	Beutelsbach	Schd.	bef 1833	Russia	801460
Deiss, Friederike		8 yrs.	Beutelsbach	Schd.	bef 1833	Russia	801460
Deiss, Israel		25 Aug 1811	Beutelsbach	Schd.	bef 1833	Russia	801460
Deiss, Jakob		22 Aug 1814	Beutelsbach	Schd.	bef 1833	Russia	801460
Deiss, Johann Friedrich		1 Nov 1806	Beutelsbach	Schd.	bef 1833	Russia	801460
Deiss, Johannes		15 Mar 1810	Beutelsbach	Schd.	bef 1833	Russia	801460
Deiss, Michael		8 yrs.	Beutelsbach	Schd.	bef 1833	Russia	801460
Dekler, Jacob			Frutenhof	Frd.	1817	Russia	569269
Demmler, Carl Christian			Calw	Calw	1852	N.-Amer	563212
Demus, Catharina Christiane		26 May 1854	Freudenstadt	Frd.	Aug 1854	N.-Amer	569274
Demus, Catharina Karoline		1 Apr 1844	Freudenstadt	Frd.	Aug 1854	N.-Amer	569274
Demus, Christiane Kathar. (wife)		3 Sep 1812	Freudenstadt	Frd.	Aug 1854	N.-Amer	569274
Demus, Christioph Friedr. & F		15 Feb 1800	Freudenstadt	Frd.	Aug 1854	N.-Amer	569274
Demus, Friederike Wilhelmine		18 Dec 1848	Freudenstadt	Frd.	Aug 1854	N.-Amer	569274
Demuth, Anna			Marschalkenzimmern	Sulz	Nov 1859	Baden	849638
Demuth, Johann Heinrich			Birckenbaeuel	– –	Dec 1751	Mas.N-A	550803
Dendel, Christina Barbara (wife)			Rosenfeld	Sulz	Mar 1837	N.-Amer	849640
Dendel, Heinrich		18 Jan 1817	Rosenfeld	Sulz	Mar 1837	N.-Amer	849640

Dendel, Jacob Friedrich	8 May 1815	Rosenfeld	Sulz	Mar 1837	N.-Amer	849640
Dendel, Johann Jacob		Rosenfeld	Sulz	Mar 1837	N.-Amer	849640
Dendel, Johann Jacob & F	12 Jan 1789	Rosenfeld	Sulz	Mar 1837	N.-Amer	849640
Dendel, Johann Peter	4 May 1819	Rosenfeld	Sulz	Mar 1837	N.-Amer	849640
Dendel, Melchior & F		Rosenfeld	Sulz	Mar 1892	N.-Amer	849626
Dengler, Anna Maria	9 yrs.	Sulz	Nag.	Feb 1854	N.-Amer	838491
Dengler, Anna Maria		Sulz	Nag.	Sep 1853	N.-Amer	838490
Dengler, Carl Ludwig Heinrich	1 yrs.	Sulz	Nag.	Sep 1853	N.-Amer	838490
Dengler, Christian Friedrich	10 Oct 1832	Moetzingen	Herr.	bef 1863	N.-Amer	834624
Dengler, Christina Magdalena	4 yrs.	Sulz	Nag.	Sep 1853	N.-Amer	838490
Dengler, Elisabetha		Erkenbrechtsweiler	Sulz	1854	N.-Amer	849643
Dengler, Eva Katharina	infant	Sulz	Nag.	Feb 1854	N.-Amer	838491
Dengler, Eva Maria	20 yrs.	Sulz	Nag.	Feb 1854	N.-Amer	838491
Dengler, Gottlieb	4 yrs.	Sulz	Nag.	Feb 1854	N.-Amer	838491
Dengler, Gottlieb & F		Sulz	Nag.	Feb 1854	N.-Amer	838491
Dengler, Jakob Friedrich	20 yrs.	Ebhausen	Nag.	Apr 1854	N.-Amer	838591
Dengler, Jakob Friedrich	15 yrs.	Sulz	Nag.	Feb 1854	N.-Amer	838491
Dengler, Jakob Friedrich & F		Sulz	Nag.	Feb 1854	N.-Amer	838491
Dengler, Johann Peter	3 yrs.	Sulz	Nag.	Feb 1854	N.-Amer	838491
Dengler, Johannes	3 yrs.	Sulz	Nag.	Sep 1853	N.-Amer	838490
Dengler, Johannes		Dornstetten	Frd.	Apr 1752	Pen.N-A	550803
Dengler, Margaretha Barbara	11 yrs.	Sulz	Nag.	Feb 1854	N.-Amer	838491
Dengler, Maria Barbara	17 yrs.	Sulz	Nag.	Feb 1854	N.-Amer	838491
Dengler, Maria Magdalena		Sulz	Nag.	Feb 1854	N.-Amer	838491
Dengler, Maria Sara		Sulz	Nag.	Feb 1854	N.-Amer	838491
Deprezin, Carl Friedr. Hugo		Oberhaugstett	Calw	1861	N.-Amer	563212
Deschler, Anna Catharina	19 Dec 1812	Erkenbrechtsweiler	Sulz	Jun 1865	N.-Amer	849643
Dessauer, Louis	28 yrs.	Unterschwandorf	Nag.	Sep 1852	Prussia	838490
Desseker, Jacob Peter	13 Aug 1841	Kayh	Herr.	Apr 1868	N.-Amer	834624
Detscher, Johannes		Aach	Frd.	Mar 1857	Baden	577776
Dettling, Anna Maria	28 Jan 1839	Cresbach	Frd.	Sep 1854	N.-Amer	569274
Dettling, Barbara & C	34 yrs.	Altheim	Horb	Jun 1851	N.-Amer	835929
Dettling, Carolina & C		Freudenstadt	Frd.	Aug 1849	N.-Amer	569270
Dettling, Christina	13 Sep 1849	Cresbach	Frd.	Sep 1854	N.-Amer	569274
Dettling, Christina (wife)	8 Jun 1816	Cresbach	Frd.	Sep 1854	N.-Amer	569274
Dettling, Christina Maria		Freudenstadt	Frd.	bef 1849	Belgium	569270
Dettling, Franziska	11 yrs.	Altheim	Horb	Jun 1851	N.-Amer	835929
Dettling, Johannes	2 yrs.	Altheim	Horb	Jun 1851	N.-Amer	835929
Dettling, Josef	6 yrs.	Altheim	Horb	Jun 1851	N.-Amer	835929
Dettling, Katharina	24 Dec 1853	Cresbach	Frd.	Sep 1854	N.-Amer	569274
Dettling, Michael	20 Apr 1842	Cresbach	Frd.	Sep 1854	N.-Amer	569274
Dettling, Michael & F		Cresbach	Frd.	Sep 1854	N.-Amer	569274
Dettling, Peter	16 Oct 1845	Cresbach	Frd.	Sep 1854	N.-Amer	569274
Dettling, Rosina	46 yrs.	Altheim	Horb	Jun 1851	N.-Amer	835929
Deusch, Heinrich	5 Apr 1849	Rosenfeld	Sulz	Aug 1865	N.-Amer	849641
Deuschle, Christian	1835	Calw	Calw	1854	N.-Amer	563212
Deutschle, Ludwig Heinrich	22 Apr 1848	Calw	Calw	1868	N.-Amer	563212
Deutschle, Wilhelm		Calw	Calw	Aug 1871	N.-Amer	563212
Diebold, Johann Baptist	29 Jan 1848	Altingen	Herr.	Apr 1868	N.-Amer	834624
Diebold, Johannes	36 yrs.	Neuhengstett	Calw	1864	N.-Amer	563212

Name		Birth		Emigration			Film
Last	First	Date	Place	O'amt	Appl. Date	Dest.	Number
Diefenbach, Carl Friedrich & F			Freudenstadt	Frd.	Jun 1817	N.-Amer	569267
Diele, Christiana Louise		22 Nov 1814	Sulz	Sulz	Jul 1817	Russia	849625
Diele, Friederike Elisab. (wife)			Sulz	Sulz	Jul 1817	Russia	849625
Diele, Johann Friedrich		14 Oct 1816	Sulz	Sulz	Jul 1817	Russia	849625
Diele, Johannes & F			Sulz	Sulz	Jul 1817	Russia	849625
Diele, Maria Friederike		25 Feb 1813	Sulz	Sulz	Jul 1817	Russia	849625
Dieterich, Wilhelm Friedrich		19 May 1846	Dietersweiler	Frd.	Aug 1866	N.-Amer	577780
Dieterle, Abraham		5 Nov 1857	Voehringen	Sulz	bef 1883	Bavaria	849643
Dieterle, Albrecht			Voehringen	Sulz	bef.1866	N.-Amer	849643
Dieterle, Andreas		8 Aug 1850	Voehringen	Sulz	Jun 1860	N.-Amer	849643
Dieterle, Andreas & F		50 yrs.	Rosenfeld	Sulz	Jun 1817	Russia	849640
Dieterle, Andreas & F		28 yrs.	Rosenfeld	Sulz	Jun 1817	Russia	849640
Dieterle, Andreas & W			Voehringen	Sulz	Feb 1854	N.-Amer	849643
Dieterle, Anna Maria		31 Jan 1840	Durrweiler	Frd.	Mar 1853	N.-Amer	569272
Dieterle, Anna Maria			Freudenstadt	Frd.	Sep 1854	N.-Amer	569274
Dieterle, Anna Maria (wife)			Durrweiler	Frd.	Mar 1853	N.-Amer	569272
Dieterle, Catharina (wid.)& F			Voehringen	Sulz	Apr 1860	N.-Amer	849643
Dieterle, Christian		9 Sep 1819	Edelweiler	Frd.	Apr 1847	N.-Amer	569270
Dieterle, Christina			Voehringen	Sulz	Feb 1854	N.-Amer	849643
Dieterle, Christina		5 Sep 1814	Voehringen	Sulz	1836	N.-Amer	849643
Dieterle, Elisabeth (wife)		59 yrs.	Rosenfeld	Sulz	Jun 1817	Russia	849640
Dieterle, Eva Maria		10 Jan 1814	Groembach	Frd.	Mar 1846	N.-Amer	569271
Dieterle, Franziska (wife)		21 Aug 1859	Voehringen	Sulz	Aug 1896	Bavaria	849626
Dieterle, Friedrich		30 Apr 1862	Voehringen	Sulz	May 1871	N.-Amer	849643
Dieterle, Helena		4 Jul 1893	Voehringen	Sulz	Aug 1896	Bavaria	849626
Dieterle, Jacob		27 Dec 1797	Pfalzgrafenweiler	Frd.	Sep 1832	N.-Amer	569268
Dieterle, Jakob			Voehringen	Sulz	Aug 1869	Baden	849643
Dieterle, Jakob			Voehringen	Sulz	bef.1866	N.-Amer	849643
Dieterle, Jakob Friedrich		24 Dec 1842	Durrweiler	Frd.	Mar 1853	N.-Amer	569272
Dieterle, Johann Georg		3 Mar 1833	Durrweiler	Frd.	Mar 1853	N.-Amer	569272
Dieterle, Johann Georg		30 Jun 1888	Voehringen	Sulz	Aug 1896	Bavaria	849626
Dieterle, Johann Georg & F		14 Oct 1830	Voehringen	Sulz	May 1871	N.-Amer	849643
Dieterle, Johann Martin		18 Feb 1886	Voehringen	Sulz	Aug 1896	Bavaria	849626
Dieterle, Johannes		14 Feb 1846	Durrweiler	Frd.	Mar 1853	N.-Amer	569272
Dieterle, Johannes		22 Dec 1866	Voehringen	Sulz	May 1871	N.-Amer	849643
Dieterle, Johannes		5 Mar 1842	Erkenbrechtsweiler	Sulz	Jul 1864	France	849643
Dieterle, Johannes		19 Apr 1844	Voehringen	Sulz	Apr 1860	N.-Amer	849643
Dieterle, Johannes			Voehringen	Sulz	May 1855	N.-Amer	849643
Dieterle, Johannes		17 yrs.	Voehringen	Sulz	Feb 1854	N.-Amer	849643
Dieterle, Josepha		20 Apr 1884	Voehringen	Sulz	Aug 1896	Bavaria	849626
Dieterle, Magdalena		5 Sep 1834	Durrweiler	Frd.	Mar 1853	N.-Amer	569272
Dieterle, Maria		25 Jun 1891	Voehringen	Sulz	Aug 1896	Bavaria	849626
Dieterle, Martin		19 yrs.	Voehringen	Sulz	Feb 1854	N.-Amer	849643
Dieterle, Michael		35 yrs.	Voehringen	Sulz	1826	Baden	849643
Dieterle, Michael & F		6 Jun 1807	Durrweiler	Frd.	Mar 1853	N.-Amer	569272
Dieterle, Regina Kathar. (wife)		30 yrs.	Rosenfeld	Sulz	Jun 1817	Russia	849640
Dietterle, Andreas		6 Jan 1863	Leidringen	Sulz	Oct 1879	N.-Amer	849637
Dietterle, Martin		8 Dec 1831	Leidringen	Sulz	bef 1862	N.-Amer	849637
Dimmler, Carl			Calw	Calw	1867	N.-Amer	563212
Dinger, Anna Maria Theresia		32 yrs.	Oberjettingen	Herr.	Apr 1846	N.-Amer	834626

Dinger, Johannes		Calw	Calw	1849	Saxony	563212
Dinger, Salome (wid.) & F	55 yrs.	Oberjettingen	Herr.	Apr 1846	N.-Amer	834626
Dingler, Catharina Barb. (wife)		Hildrizhausen	Herr.	Mar 1832	N.-Amer	834624
Dingler, Christoph & W		Hildrizhausen	Herr.	Mar 1832	N.-Amer	834624
Dipperer, Heinrich		Calw	Calw	1859	Saxony	563212
Disque, Heinrich Jacob		Herrenberg	Herr.	Oct 1850	Saxony	834627
Distelwanger, Georg Jakob & F		Hirsau	Calw	1855	N.-Amer	563212
Dittus, Anna Barbara	29 Apr 1832	Oberjesingen	Herr.	bef 1863	N.-Amer	834624
Dittus, Anna Maria	8 Dec 1835	Oberjesingen	Herr.	bef 1863	N.-Amer	834624
Dittus, Carl		Althengstett	Calw	1858	S.-Amer	563212
Dittus, Gottlieb	8 Apr 1829	Oberjesingen	Herr.	bef 1863	N.-Amer	834624
Dittus, Johann Gottlob		Althengstett	Calw	1862	Austria	563212
Dittus, Michael		Sommenhardt	Calw	Jul 1870	N.-Amer	563212
Dobelmann, Johann Friedrich	2 yrs.	Hebsack	Schd.	Feb 1834	N.-Amer	801460
Dobelmann, Rosina		Hebsack	Schd.	Feb 1834	N.-Amer	801460
Dobelmann, rosina Magdalena	7 yrs.	Hebsack	Schd.	Feb 1834	N.-Amer	801460
Doelker, Andreas	17 Jun 1845	Glatten	Frd.	Mar 1847	N.-Amer	569271
Doelker, Andreas & F		Glatten	Frd.	Mar 1847	N.-Amer	569271
Doelker, Barbara	13 Mar 1809	Glatten	Frd.	Oct 1854	S.-Amer	569274
Doelker, Carolina		Calw	Calw	Apr 1870	Switz.	563212
Doelker, Christian	4 Aug 1807	Wittlensweiler	Frd.	Mar 1837	N.-Amer	569268
Doelker, Christian	24 Dec 1833	Kuppingen	Herr.	Jun 1852	N.-Amer	834627
Doelker, Christina		Glatten	Frd.	Mar 1847	N.-Amer	569271
Doelker, Jacob		Wittlensweiler	Frd.	Jun 1807	France	569268
Doelker, Jacob Friedrich & F	46 yrs.	Kuppingen	Herr.	Jun 1852	N.-Amer	834627
Doelker, Jakob	23 May 1834	Hallwangen	Frd.	Sep 1854	N.-Amer	569274
Doelker, Jakob Friedrich	10 Jan 1850	Wittlensweiler	Frd.	Sep 1866	N.-Amer	577780
Doelker, Jakob Friedrika	3 Mar 1837	Kuppingen	Herr.	Jun 1852	N.-Amer	834627
Doelker, Johann Georg	4 Nov 1844	Kuppingen	Herr.	Jun 1852	N.-Amer	834627
Doelker, Johann Jacob		Wittlensweiler	Frd.	Jun 1807	France	569268
Doelker, Johann Jakob	16 Oct 1840	Kuppingen	Herr.	Jun 1852	N.-Amer	834627
Doelker, Johann Martin	5 Dec 1845	Frutenhof	Frd.	Apr 1864	N.-Amer	577779
Doelker, Johann Michael & W	13 Aug 1832	Hallwangen	Frd.	Feb 1861	N.-Amer	577778
Doelker, Johannes	18 Oct 1843	Glatten	Frd.	Mar 1847	N.-Amer	569271
Doelker, Johannes		Renfrizhausen	Sulz	Jun 1847	N.-Amer	849639
Doelker, Johannes	13 Nov 1848	Kuppingen	Herr.	Jun 1852	N.-Amer	834627
Doelker, Kilian	11 Oct 1842	Hallwangen	Frd.	Feb 1861	N.-Amer	577778
Doelker, Mathaeus	18 Nov 1846	Glatten	Frd.	Mar 1847	N.-Amer	569271
Doelker, Michael	22 yrs.	Cresbach	Frd.	May 1850	N.-Amer	569271
Doelker, Rosine Katharina	25 Feb 1835	Kuppingen	Herr.	Jun 1852	N.-Amer	834627
Doelker, Sophia (wife)		Hallwangen	Frd.	Feb 1861	N.-Amer	577778
Doelker, Wilhelm	25 May 1852	Kuppingen	Herr.	Jun 1852	N.-Amer	834627
Doerr, Christoph & F		Simmozheim	Calw	1867	Baden	563212
Doerr, Johann Georg		Oberjettingen	Herr.	May 1836	N.-Amer	834624
Doettinger, Christian Fr. & F		Gechingen	Calw	1852	N.-Amer	563212
Doettling, Anna Maria	11 Apr 1842	Hallwangen	Frd.	May 1860	N.-Amer	577777
Doettling, Barbara	16 Oct 1820	Betzweiler	Frd.	Apr 1849	N.-Amer	569270
Doettling, Christian		Hallwangen	Frd.	May 1853	N.-Amer	569272
Doettling, Christiane	10 Nov 1845	Wittlensweiler	Frd.	Sep 1853	N.-Amer	569272
Doettling, Friederika	8 Jan 1843	Wittlensweiler	Frd.	Sep 1853	N.-Amer	569272

| Name | | Birth | | Emigration | | | Film |
Last	First	Date	Place	O'amt	Appl. Date	Dest.	Number
Doettling, Georg Friedrich		2 Sep 1829	Wittlensweiler	Frd.	Aug 1854	N.-Amer	569274
Doettling, Georg Gottl.		8 Jul 1849	Wittlensweiler	Frd.	Sep 1853	N.-Amer	569272
Doettling, Jakob		20 May 1851	Wittlensweiler	Frd.	Sep 1853	N.-Amer	569272
Doettling, Johann Martin		24 Mar 1844	Wittlensweiler	Frd.	Sep 1853	N.-Amer	569272
Doettling, Johann Martin & F		23 May 1801	Wittlensweiler	Frd.	Sep 1853	N.-Amer	569272
Doettling, Juliane		18 Mar 1848	Wittlensweiler	Frd.	Sep 1853	N.-Amer	569272
Doettling, Juliane		24 Feb 1812	Pfalzgrafenweiler	Frd.	Sep 1853	N.-Amer	569272
Doettling, Louisa Margaretha		17 Nov 1834	Wittlensweiler	Frd.	Sep 1853	N.-Amer	569272
Doettling, Rosina		31 yrs.	Unterreichenbach	Calw	1864	Bavaria	563212
Dold, Johann			Trichtingen	Sulz	Feb 1846	--	849642
Dold, Maria Katharina (wife)			Entringen	Herr.	May 1852	N.-Amer	834627
Dold, Thomas & W			Entringen	Herr.	May 1852	N.-Amer	834627
Dolmetsch, Alfred Otto			Sulz	Sulz	Feb 1885	N.-Amer	849626
Dolmetsch, Andreas Gottlieb		30 Dec 1813	Sulz	Sulz	bef 1844	N.-Amer	849627
Dolmetsch, Charlotte Regine		15 Sep 1815	Sulz	Sulz	bef 1844	N.-Amer	849627
Dolmetsch, Christiane Sophie		11 Oct 1822	Sulz	Sulz	Apr 1835	Hohenz.	849627
Dolmetsch, Eugen		11 Sep 1855	Sulz	Sulz	bef 1872	N.-Amer	849628
Dolmetsch, Georg Ulrich (wid)		13 Nov 1782	Sulz	Sulz	Apr 1834	N.-Amer	849627
Dolmetsch, Gottlieb Heinr. & F			Sulz	Sulz	Apr 1835	Hohenz.	849627
Dolmetsch, Karl		27 Apr 1849	Sulz	Sulz	Jul 1869	N.-Amer	849628
Dolmetsch, Luise Heinrike		30 Dec 1825	Sulz	Sulz	Apr 1835	Hohenz.	849627
Dolmetsch, Paul Hermann		7 Apr 1856	Sulz	Sulz	Mar 1873	Austria	849628
Dolmetsch, Richard		3 Sep 1865	Sulz	Sulz	Aug 1882	N.-Amer	849626
Dolmetsch, Robert Gottfried		30 Jan 1835	Sulz	Sulz	Apr 1835	Hohenz.	849627
Dolmetsch, Sophie Dorothea			Sulz	Sulz	Apr 1835	Hohenz.	849627
Dolmetsch, Wilhelm Heinrich		22 Jun 1824	Sulz	Sulz	Apr 1835	Hohenz.	849627
Dolmetscher, Alfred Otto		5 May 1868	Sulz	Sulz	1882	N.-Amer	849628
Dongus, Catharina			Deckenpfronn	Calw	1852	N.-Amer	563212
Dongus, Johann Balthas		1828	Deckenpfronn	Calw	1854	N.-Amer	563212
Donner, Christoph Gottlieb			Sulz	Sulz	Mar 1815	Saxony	849625
Dorner, Jakob Friedrich			Rosenfeld	Sulz	Aug 1852	N.-Amer	849640
Dorner, Johann Friedrich		14 Feb 1852	Rosenfeld	Sulz	Feb 1867	N.-Amer	849641
Doser, Johannes			Boll	Sulz	Aug 1850	Baden	849632
Dossinger, Johann Georg			Agenbach	Calw	Jan 1873	N.-Amer	563212
Doster, Jakob		20 yrs.	Untermusbach	Frd.	Jul 1865	N.-Amer	577779
Doster, Johannes		12 Apr 1823	Gruental	Frd.	bef 1859	N.-Amer	577776
Dreher, Andreas & F			Rosenfeld	Sulz	1834	N.-Amer	849625
Dreher, Anna Catharina (wife)			Leidringen	Sulz	Aug 1853	N.-Amer	849637
Dreher, Anna Maria			Pfalzgrafenweiler	Frd.	Apr 1836	N.-Amer	569268
Dreher, Christina		23 Oct 1799	Pfalzgrafenweiler	Frd.	Apr 1836	N.-Amer	569268
Dreher, Christina Barbara			Rosenfeld	Sulz	1834	N.-Amer	849625
Dreher, Christina Margaretha			Pfalzgrafenweiler	Frd.	Apr 1836	N.-Amer	569268
Dreher, Elisabetha			Sulz	Sulz	Apr 1834	N.-Amer	849627
Dreher, Elisabethe Pauline			Pfalzgrafenweiler	Frd.	Apr 1836	N.-Amer	569268
Dreher, Friedrich & F		5 Dec 1797	Pfalzgrafenweiler	Frd.	Apr 1836	N.-Amer	569268
Dreher, Jakob & F		25 Jul 1838	Trichtingen	Sulz	Apr 1882	N.-Amer	849642
Dreher, Johann Georg		2 May 1874	Trichtingen	Sulz	Apr 1882	N.-Amer	849642
Dreher, Johann Jacob			Brittheim	Sulz	Apr 1817	Rus-Pol	849632
Dreher, Johannes		5 Jul 1808	Trichtingen	Sulz	Mar 1833	N.-Amer	849642
Dreher, Johannes		3 Oct 1865	Renfrizhausen	Sulz	Feb 1881	N.-Amer	849626

Name	Date	Place	District	Emigration	Destination	Film
Dreher, Johannes & F		Brittheim	Sulz	Apr 1817	Rus-Pol	849632
Dreher, Louis	31 Oct 1841	Rosenfeld	Sulz	Feb 1868	Frankf.	849641
Dreher, Mathaeus		Leidringen	Sulz	Aug 1853	N.-Amer	849637
Dreher, Mathaeus & F		Leidringen	Sulz	Aug 1853	N.-Amer	849637
Dreher, Matthias	16 May 1802	Trichtingen	Sulz	Mar 1833	N.-Amer	849642
Dreher, Paul Gottlob		Pfalzgrafenweiler	Frd.	Apr 1836	N.-Amer	569268
Dreiss, Emilie Friederike		Calw	Calw	1853	N.-Amer	563212
Dreiss, Eugenie		Calw	Calw	1852	Frankf.	563212
Drescher, Catharina	13 Sep 1863	Gueltstein	Herr.	Mar 1866	N.-Amer	834624
Drescher, Johann Jacob	17 Jan 1861	Gueltstein	Herr.	Mar 1866	N.-Amer	834624
Drescher, Johann Jacob & F	10 Dec 1823	Gueltstein	Herr.	Mar 1866	N.-Amer	834624
Drescher, Johannes	3 Jan 1865	Gueltstein	Herr.	Mar 1866	N.-Amer	834624
Drescher, Maria Salome (wife)	10 Aug 1826	Gueltstein	Herr.	Mar 1866	N.-Amer	834624
Dressle, Anna Maria & C		Goettelfingen	Frd.	Apr 1860	N.-Amer	577777
Dressle, Caroline		Goettelfingen	Frd.	Apr 1860	N.-Amer	577777
Dressle, Eva Maria	9 Aug 1836	Gutwoehr	Frd.	Feb 1854	N.-Amer	569273
Dressle, Jacob Friedrich	17 Aug 1846	Goettelfingen	Frd.	Oct 1866	N.-Amer	577780
Dressle, Johannes		Goettelfingen	Frd.	Apr 1860	N.-Amer	577777
Dressle, Magdalena	19 Feb 1834	Goettelfingen	Frd.	Mar 1857	N.-Amer	577776
Drick, Catharina		Bettenhausen	Sulz	Nov 1869	N.-Amer	849630
Drissler, Adolph Franz	29 May 1845	Freudenstadt	Frd.	Sep 1854	N.-Amer	569274
Drissler, Christiane Sophie	24 Sep 1821	Freudenstadt	Frd.	Sep 1845	Bavaria	569269
Drissler, Friederike & C	23 Jan 1820	Freudenstadt	Frd.	Sep 1854	N.-Amer	569274
Drissler, Friederike Luise	23 Jun 1851	Freudenstadt	Frd.	Sep 1854	N.-Amer	569274
Drissler, Georg David	22 Feb 1838	Freudenstadt	Frd.	Feb 1864	N.-Amer	577779
Druck, Jacob Friedrich & F	34 yrs.	Untermusbach	Frd.	Feb 1833	N.-Amer	569268
Duerlle, Eva Maria	24 May 1804	Erzgrube	Frd.	Jan 1847	Baden	569271
Duerr, (wife) & F		Simmozheim	Calw	1855	N.-Amer	563212
Duerr, Christian Johann		Simmozheim	Calw	1852	N.-Amer	563212
Duerr, Christina Marg.		Sulz	Nag.	Apr 1849	N.-Amer	838490
Duerr, Gottlieb Friedrich & W		Simmozheim	Calw	1854	N.-Amer	563212
Duerr, Jakob Peter		Groembach	Frd.	bef 1866	N.-Amer	577780
Duerr, Johann Georg		Simmozheim	Calw	1852	N.-Amer	563212
Duerr, Johann Jakob	14 Apr 1846	Groembach	Frd.	Aug 1866	N.-Amer	577780
Duerr, Michael		Zwerenberg	Calw	1847	N.-Amer	563212
Dunkel, Barbara	3 Feb 1790	Glatten	Frd.	Mar 1847	N.-Amer	569271
Dupper, Agatha & C	12 May 1829	Groembach	Frd.	Sep 1856	N.-Amer	569275
Dupper, Christian	18 Jun 1854	Groembach	Frd.	Sep 1856	N.-Amer	569275
Dupper, Georg Adam	17 Dec 1832	Groembach	Frd.	Jan 1855	N.-Amer	569275
Dupper, Johann Jacob & W	47 yrs.	Bondorf	Herr.	Jun 1832	N.-Amer	834624
Dupper, Margaretha (wife)	11 Jul 1818	Tailfingen	Herr.	Jan 1868	N.-Amer	834624
Dupper, Rosine Catharina (wife)	46 yrs.	Bondorf	Herr.	Jun 1832	N.-Amer	834624
Dups, Margaretha (wife)	30 yrs.	Nufringen	Herr.	May 1832	N.-Amer	834624
Dups, Michael & W	54 yrs.	Nufringen	Herr.	May 1832	N.-Amer	834624
Dussle, Maria Christina & C	15 Mar 1815	Groembach	Frd.	Apr 1847	France	569270
Dussler, Agatha & C	9 Oct 1786	Salzstetten	Frd.	Oct 1847	N.-Amer	569270
Dussler, Andreas	17 Mar 1842	Durrweiler	Frd.	Oct 1847	N.-Amer	569270
Dussler, Andreas	21 Apr 1851	Groembach	Frd.	Apr 1851	N.-Amer	569271
Dussler, Elisabetha Cath. & C	6 Feb 1820	Durrweiler	Frd.	Apr 1851	N.-Amer	569271
Dussler, Johann Georg	17 Nov 1822	Durrweiler	Frd.	Oct 1847	N.-Amer	569270

| Name | | Birth | | Emigration | | | Film |
Last	First	Date	Place	O'amt	Appl. Date	Dest.	Number
Dussler, Katharina		25 Mar 1833	Durrweiler	Frd.	Oct 1847	N.-Amer	569270
Dutt, Eva Barbara			Simmozheim	Calw	Oct 1847	N.-Amer	563212
Eberhard, Adolf		23 Sep 1851	Rottenburg	Sulz	May 1869	N.-Amer	849631
Eberhard, Anna Dorothea & C			Sulz	Sulz	Jun 1838	Switz.	849627
Eberhard, Anna Katharina		19 Dec 1835	Tumlingen	Frd.	Jan 1855	N.-Amer	569275
Eberhard, Anna Maria		21 May 1842	Moetzingen	Herr.	Mar 1847	N.-Amer	834626
Eberhard, Barbara		11 Sep 1842	Tumlingen	Frd.	Jan 1855	N.-Amer	569275
Eberhard, Barbara (wife)		28 Dec 1805	Tumlingen	Frd.	Jan 1855	N.-Amer	569275
Eberhard, Carl Christian		14 yrs.	Calw	Calw	Sep 1870	N.-Amer	563212
Eberhard, Catharina		17 Jul 1833	Moetzingen	Herr.	Mar 1847	N.-Amer	834626
Eberhard, Christian		25 Jan 1840	Moetzingen	Herr.	Mar 1847	N.-Amer	834626
Eberhard, Christina (wife)		4 Jun 1825	Boll	Sulz	Mar 1873	N.-Amer	849632
Eberhard, Christine			Sulz	Sulz	Aug 1848	N.-Amer	849627
Eberhard, Dorothea Margaretha			Sulz	Sulz	Jun 1838	Switz.	849627
Eberhard, Elisabeth			Boll	Sulz	1815	Switz.	849632
Eberhard, Elisabetha Cathar.		3 Apr 1845	Moetzingen	Herr.	Mar 1847	N.-Amer	834626
Eberhard, Friedrich		15 Jul 1846	Tumlingen	Frd.	Jan 1855	N.-Amer	569275
Eberhard, Friedrich		3 Mar 1809	Baiersbronn	Frd.	bef 1844	N.-Amer	569269
Eberhard, Gottlob		15 Oct 1864	Boll	Sulz	Mar 1873	N.-Amer	849632
Eberhard, Jacob & F		13 May 1802	Moetzingen	Herr.	Mar 1847	N.-Amer	834626
Eberhard, Jakob		2 Mar 1839	Tumlingen	Frd.	Jan 1855	N.-Amer	569275
Eberhard, Jakob		10 Mar 1798	Boll	Sulz	Jul 1838	France	849632
Eberhard, Jakob & F			Unteriflingen	Frd.	Jan 1855	N.-Amer	569275
Eberhard, Johann Georg & F		19 Aug 1828	Boll	Sulz	Mar 1873	N.-Amer	849632
Eberhard, Johannes		5 Nov 1855	Boll	Sulz	Mar 1873	N.-Amer	849632
Eberhard, Joseph		2 Aug 1852	Rottenburg	Sulz	May 1869	N.-Amer	849631
Eberhard, Katharina		17 Dec 1857	Boll	Sulz	Mar 1873	N.-Amer	849632
Eberhard, Margaretha (wife)		25 Oct 1805	Moetzingen	Herr.	Mar 1847	N.-Amer	834626
Eberhard, Mathaeus & F			Boll	Sulz	Jun 1817	N.-Amer	849632
Eberhard, Mathias			Wittendorf	Frd.	1817	Russia	569269
Eberhard, Michael & F			Sterneck	Sulz	Feb 1817	Russia	849635
Eberhardt, Agnes & C			Klosterreichenbach	Frd.	Apr 1848	N.-Amer	569270
Eberhardt, Andreas		20 Nov 1853	Lossburg	Frd.	Sep 1854	N.-Amer	569274
Eberhardt, Andreas		15 yrs.	Fuernsal	Sulz	Sep 1851	N.-Amer	849635
Eberhardt, Anna Maria		2 Nov 1845	Oberiflingen	Frd.	Feb 1850	N.-Amer	569271
Eberhardt, Anna Maria		26 Apr 1851	Lossburg	Frd.	Sep 1854	N.-Amer	569274
Eberhardt, Anna Maria			Fuernsal	Sulz	Sep 1851	N.-Amer	849635
Eberhardt, Barbara		16 Oct 1820	Betzweiler	Frd.	Apr 1849	N.-Amer	569270
Eberhardt, Benhard		29 Apr 1821	Baiersbronn	Frd.	Oct 1846	France	569271
Eberhardt, Bernhard		28 May 1834	Baiersbronn	Frd.	May 1854	N.-Amer	569273
Eberhardt, Catharina			Dietersweiler	Frd.	Mar 1854	N.-Amer	569273
Eberhardt, Catharina		21 yrs.	Tumlingen	Frd.	Sep 1856	N.-Amer	569275
Eberhardt, Christian		12 Jul 1821	Hallwangen	Frd.	Jan 1843	N.-Amer	569269
Eberhardt, Christina			Fuernsal	Sulz	Sep 1851	N.-Amer	849635
Eberhardt, Christine		26 Nov 1822	Neuneck	Frd.	Feb 1850	N.-Amer	569271
Eberhardt, Christine & F		3 Dec 1831	Lossburg	Frd.	Sep 1854	N.-Amer	569274
Eberhardt, Emil Hermann		20 yrs.	Calw	Calw	1867	Austria	563212
Eberhardt, Franz Friedrich		23 Oct 1826	Neuneck	Frd.	bef 1862	N.-Amer	577778
Eberhardt, Friedrich			Baiersbronn	Frd.	May 1837	Baden	569267
Eberhardt, Jakob		13 yrs.	Tumlingen	Frd.	Sep 1856	N.-Amer	569275

Eberhardt, Johann Georg	29 Nov 1845	Betzweiler	Frd.	Apr 1849	N.-Amer	569270
Eberhardt, Johann Georg	29 Oct 1843	Oberiflingen	Frd.	Feb 1850	N.-Amer	569271
Eberhardt, Johannes	29 Jan 1844	Betzweiler	Frd.	Apr 1849	N.-Amer	569270
Eberhardt, Johannes		Rodt	Frd.	Dec 1822	Baden	569268
Eberhardt, Johannes		Fuernsal	Sulz	bef 1846	France	849635
Eberhardt, Johannes	3 Aug 1848	Agenbach	Calw	1868	N.-Amer	563212
Eberhardt, Johannes & F		Hoerschweiler	Frd.	Apr 1854	N.-Amer	569273
Eberhardt, Katharina	13 Nov 1846	Betzweiler	Frd.	Apr 1849	N.-Amer	569270
Eberhardt, Maria Friederika	26 Dec 1842	Baiersbronn	Frd.	Mar 1847	N.-Amer	569271
Eberhardt, Martin & F	14 Jul 1821	Buechenberg	Frd.	Apr 1849	N.-Amer	569270
Eberhardt, Mathaeus	17 Oct 1855	Binsdorf	Sulz	Mar 1872	N.-Amer	849631
Eberhardt, Mathaeus	3 Mar 1825	Hopfau	Sulz	Apr 1852	N.-Amer	849636
Eberhardt, Mathaeus & F		Wittendorf	Frd.	Jun 1817	Russia	569268
Eberhardt, Mathaeus & F	16 Jan 1819	Oberiflingen	Frd.	Feb 1850	N.-Amer	569271
Eberhardt, Tobias		Baiersbronn	Frd.	Aug 1854	N.-Amer	569274
Eberhardt, Wilhelm		Calw	Calw	1859	N.-Amer	563212
Eberhart, Johann Georg	17 May 1853	Boll	Sulz	Mar 1872	N.-Amer	849632
Eberhart, Joseph	20 May 1849	Binsdorf	Sulz	Apr 1869	N.-Amer	849631
Eberhart, Mathias	16 Oct 1806	Boll	Sulz	Oct 1836	France	849632
Eberle, Christian & F		Freudenstadt	Frd.	Sep 1854	N.-Amer	569274
Eberle, Christian Wilhelm	18 Jan 1841	Freudenstadt	Frd.	Sep 1854	N.-Amer	569274
Eberle, Christiane Friederike	3 Nov 1845	Freudenstadt	Frd.	Sep 1854	N.-Amer	569274
Eberle, Fidel		Altingen	Herr.	bef 1863	N.-Amer	834624
Eberle, Franziska	5 Apr 1771	Leinstetten	Sulz	Oct 1836	Prussia	849638
Eberle, Georg Carl	16 Sep 1835	Freudenstadt	Frd.	Sep 1854	N.-Amer	569274
Eberle, Gottlieb	27 Jan 1828	Freudenstadt	Frd.	Jan 1857	France	577776
Eberle, Johann Friedrich	26 Sep 1832	Freudenstadt	Frd.	Sep 1854	N.-Amer	569274
Eberle, Johannes		Altingen	Herr.	bef 1863	N.-Amer	834624
Eberle, Marianne		Leinstetten	Sulz	May 1826	Prussia	849638
Eberle, Rosine	3 Jul 1823	Freudenstadt	Frd.	Sep 1854	N.-Amer	569274
Eberle, Wilhelm	29 Oct 1830	Freudenstadt	Frd.	Sep 1854	N.-Amer	569274
Eberwein, Anna Magdalena		Cresbach	Frd.	Mar 1837	N.-Amer	569269
Eberwein, Maria Anna		Leinstetten	Sulz	bef 1858	Hungary	849638
Ecker, Abraham Wilhelm	1840	Unterreichenbach	Calw	1854	N.-Amer	563212
Ecker, Christian		Unterreichenbach	Calw	1858	N.-Amer	563212
Ecker, Gottlieb	1847	Unterreichenbach	Calw	1867	N.-Amer	563212
Ecker, Philipp	4 Jun 1822	Unterreichenbach	Calw	1856	N.-Amer	563212
Ecker, Wilhelm		Unterreichenbach	Calw	1853	N.-Amer	563212
Eckert or Matt, Andreas	2 Jun 1825	Schoemberg	Frd.	May 1846	N.-Amer	569271
Eckert, Johanna	18 Oct 1823	Breitenholz	Herr.	Mar 1849	N.-Amer	834627
Efus, Michael (wid.) & F		Liebelsberg	Calw	Mar 1847	N.-Amer	563212
Ege, Christina Dorothea & C	16 Jan 1819	Schroeth/Baden	Frd.	Apr 1847	N.-Amer	569270
Ege, Rosina & C	7 May 1787	Durrweiler	Frd.	Apr 1847	N.-Amer	569270
Egeler, Agatha	14 Jul 1864	Oeschelbronn	Herr.	Jun 1868	N.-Amer	834624
Egeler, Anton	15 Dec 1839	Tailfingen	Herr.	May 1847	N.-Amer	834626
Egeler, Carl Friedrich	30 May 1833	Oeschelbronn	Herr.	Apr 1847	N.-Amer	834626
Egeler, Carolina	30 Sep 1862	Oeschelbronn	Herr.	Jun 1868	N.-Amer	834624
Egeler, Catharina	15 Aug 1842	Oeschelbronn	Herr.	Apr 1847	N.-Amer	834626
Egeler, Catharina Barbara (wife)		Rohrau	Herr.	bef 1863	N.-Amer	834624
Egeler, Christian	23 Dec 1867	Oeschelbronn	Herr.	Jun 1868	N.-Amer	834624

Name		Birth		Emigration			Film
Last	First	Date	Place	O'amt	Appl. Date	Dest.	Number
Egeler, Christian Peter		30 Dec 1843	Oberjesingen	Herr.	Apr 1848	N.-Amer	834626
Egeler, Christina Catharina		16 Oct 1836	Oberjesingen	Herr.	Apr 1848	N.-Amer	834626
Egeler, Christoph & F			Tailfingen	Herr.	May 1847	N.-Amer	834626
Egeler, Jakob		28 Mar 1846	Tailfingen	Herr.	May 1847	N.-Amer	834626
Egeler, Jakob Friedrich & F		12 Jan 1810	Oberjesingen	Herr.	Apr 1848	N.-Amer	834626
Egeler, Johann Christoph		1 Jun 1832	Bondorf	Herr.	May 1847	N.-Amer	834626
Egeler, Johann Dorothea		14 Feb 1861	Oeschelbronn	Herr.	Jun 1868	N.-Amer	834624
Egeler, Johann Georg & F		18 Aug 1832	Oeschelbronn	Herr.	Jun 1868	N.-Amer	834624
Egeler, Johann Martin & F			Nebringen	Herr.	May 1836	N.-Amer	834624
Egeler, Johann Melchior		1 Aug 1840	Oberjesingen	Herr.	Apr 1848	N.-Amer	834626
Egeler, Johanna Barbara (wife)		14 Nov 1804	Bondorf	Herr.	May 1847	N.-Amer	834626
Egeler, Johanna Barbara (wife)		23 Nov 1839	Oeschelbronn	Herr.	Jun 1868	N.-Amer	834624
Egeler, Johanna Catharina		7 Dec 1841	Tailfingen	Herr.	May 1847	N.-Amer	834626
Egeler, Johannes		22 May 1838	Bondorf	Herr.	May 1847	N.-Amer	834626
Egeler, Johannes		19 Jun 1866	Oeschelbronn	Herr.	Jun 1868	N.-Amer	834624
Egeler, Johannes & F			Rohrau	Herr.	bef 1863	N.-Amer	834624
Egeler, Johannes & F		10 Oct 1799	Oeschelbronn	Herr.	Apr 1847	N.-Amer	834626
Egeler, Margaretha Barb. (wife)		24 Nov 1807	Oeschelbronn	Herr.	Apr 1847	N.-Amer	834626
Egeler, Maria Christiana		9 Oct 1859	Oeschelbronn	Herr.	Jun 1868	N.-Amer	834624
Egeler, Maria Dorothea		14 Oct 1830	Bondorf	Herr.	May 1847	N.-Amer	834626
Egeler, Maria Margaretha		22 Jan 1841	Oeschelbronn	Herr.	Apr 1847	N.-Amer	834626
Egeler, Sophia (wife)		20 Jun 1817	Oberjesingen	Herr.	Apr 1848	N.-Amer	834626
Eger, Agnes			Binsdorf	Sulz	Jun 1833	Austria	849630
Eger, Andreas			Binsdorf	Sulz	Jun 1833	Austria	849630
Eger, Christian & F			Binsdorf	Sulz	Jun 1833	Austria	849630
Eger, Christina			Binsdorf	Sulz	Jun 1833	Austria	849630
Eger, Jacob & F			Lossburg	Frd.	Sep 1850	N.-Amer	569271
Eger, Johanna (wife)			Binsdorf	Sulz	Jun 1833	Austria	849630
Eger, Leander			Binsdorf	Sulz	Jun 1833	Austria	849630
Eger, Maria			Lossburg	Frd.	Sep 1850	N.-Amer	569271
Eger, Maximillian			Binsdorf	Sulz	Jun 1833	Austria	849630
Eger, Paulina			Binsdorf	Sulz	Jun 1833	Austria	849630
Eger, Romanus			Binsdorf	Sulz	Jun 1833	Austria	849630
Egolf, Jacob		13 Mar 1785	Rosenfeld	Sulz	Sep 1836	France	849640
Egolf, Johannes		17 Sep 1849	Rosenfeld	Sulz	Mar 1864	N.-Amer	849641
Egolf, Michael			Rosenfeld	Sulz	Jan 1829	Hesse	849640
Egolz, Anna Maria			Rosenfeld	Sulz	Aug 1812	France	849625
Ehemann, Friedrich & F			Baiersbronn	Frd.	Apr 1817	N.-Amer	569267
Ehinger, Georg			Balingen	Bal.	Sep 1856	Wien	555962
Ehler, Andreas		28 Nov 1819	Dornhan	Sulz	Mar 1867	Baden	849634
Ehler, Barbara		20 Aug 1829	Dornhan	Sulz	Aug 1853	N.-Amer	849633
Ehler, Christian		1 Jan 1828	Dornhan	Sulz	Mar 1857	Austria	849633
Ehler, Johann		13 Aug 1835	Dornhan	Sulz	Sep 1866	N.-Amer	849634
Ehler, Johannes		15 Aug 1841	Dornhan	Sulz	Sep 1857	N.-Amer	849633
Ehmann, Anna Maria Ros.		18 Sep 1842	Kniebis	Frd.	Dec 1853	N.-Amer	569272
Ehmann, Christine Friederike		10 Nov 1811	Kniebis	Frd.	Dec 1853	N.-Amer	569272
Ehmann, Friederika		3 Jun 1850	Kniebis	Frd.	Dec 1853	N.-Amer	569272
Ehmann, Georg			Renfrizhausen	Sulz	bef 1831	Russia	849625
Ehmann, Jakob Friedrich & F		27 Sep 1813	Kniebis	Frd.	Dec 1853	N.-Amer	569272
Ehmann, Johann Adam		21 Nov 1835	Looch	Frd.	Jul 1853	N.-Amer	569274

Ehmann, Johann Daniel	17 Apr 1824	Freudenstadt	Frd.	bef 1860	N.-Amer	577778
Ehmann, Johanne Friederike	21 Aug 1829	Freudenstadt	Frd.	bef 1862	Switz.	577770
Ehmann, Marie	5 Nov 1808	Freudenstadt	Frd.	May 1832	Switz.	569267
Ehner, Anna Maria & C		Moettlingen	Calw	1869	Baden	563212
Ehner, Christian Friedrich	13 yrs.	Moettlingen	Calw	1869	Baden	563212
Ehninger, Matheus Bernhard & F		Grossaspach	Schd.	Aug 1837	Austria	801461
Ehnis, Jacob	20 yrs.	Oberweiler	Calw	1866	N.-Amer	563212
Ehrsam, Johannes		Emmingen	Nag.	Feb 1854	N.-Amer	838491
Eiber, Agnes		Baiersbronn	Frd.	Mar 1857	N.-Amer	577776
Eicher, Friederike	6 yrs.	Schoenmuenzach	Frd.	Jun 1854	N.-Amer	569273
Eicher, Katharina & C		Schoenmuenzach	Frd.	Jun 1854	N.-Amer	569273
Eilber, Gottfried	27 Aug 1836	Kolsterreichenbach	Frd.	Jun 1853	N.-Amer	569272
Eilber, Gottlob	15 Mar 1839	Reichenbach	Frd.	Jan 1854	N.-Amer	569273
Eilber, Johann Wilhelm	8 Oct 1837	Baiersbronn	Frd.	Sep 1856	N.-Amer	569275
Eilber, Ludwig	13 Jul 1821	Glatten	Frd.	Oct 1854	S.-Amer	569274
Eilber, Ludwig Jacob	16 Aug 1839	Glatten	Frd.	Oct 1854	S.-Amer	569274
Eilbert, Anna Maria (wife)		Aach	Frd.	Apr 1865	N.-Amer	577779
Eilbert, Christian	29 Apr 1824	Frutenhof	Frd.	Jan 1847	N.-Amer	569270
Eilbert, Johannes & W		Aach	Frd.	Apr 1865	N.-Amer	577779
Eipper, Jacob Friedrich		Breitenholz	Herr.	Jun 1830	N.-Amer	834624
Eipper, Johannes	9 Jan 1847	Gueltstein	Herr.	Apr 1867	N.-Amer	834624
Eipper, Johannes		Kayh	Herr.	bef 1851	N.-Amer	834627
Eipperle, Anna Maria	26 Sep 1844	Gaertringen	Herr.	Apr 1867	N.-Amer	834624
Eipperle, Friedrika	5 Apr 1826	Gaertringen	Herr.	Sep 1869	N.-Amer	834624
Eipperle, Johann Georg	7 Nov 1839	Nufringen	Herr.	May 1862	Baden	834624
Eisele, Adam		Aistaig	Sulz	Mar 1849	N.-Amer	849628
Eisele, Anna Barbara	11 Oct 1828	Rosenfeld	Sulz	May 1845	N.-Amer	849640
Eisele, Christiane Friederike	20 Nov 1830	Freudenstadt	Frd.	Feb 1857	Baden	577776
Eisele, Friederika Christiana		Freudenstadt	Frd.	bef 1864	France	577779
Eisele, Friedrich		Balingen	Bal.	Aug 1857	Switz.	555962
Eisele, Jacob Friedrich & F	3 Feb 1785	Rosenfeld	Sulz	May 1845	N.-Amer	849640
Eisele, Johann Friedrich	12 Nov 1814	Dornstetten	Frd.	Jul 1837	Altona	569269
Eisele, Johann Georg		Rosenfeld	Sulz	Aug 1852	N.-Amer	849640
Eisele, Johann Georg & F	15 Apr 1820	Rosenfeld	Sulz	Feb 1849	N.-Amer	849640
Eisele, Johannes	3 Feb 1872	Rosenfeld	Sulz	Jun 1886	N.-Amer	849626
Eisele, Maria Catharina (wife)	25 Sep 1792	Rosenfeld	Sulz	May 1845	N.-Amer	849640
Eisele, Philipp	25 Feb 1830	Rosenfeld	Sulz	Jul 1861	Bremen	849641
Eisele, Salome (wife)		Rosenfeld	Sulz	Feb 1849	N.-Amer	849640
Eisenbeis, Christina	22 yrs.	Gruental	Frd.	Apr 1853	France	569272
Eisenbeis, Jakob	26 Sep 1833	Wittensweiler	Frd.	Apr 1853	N.-Amer	569272
Eisenbeis, Jakob & W	30 yrs.	Gruental	Frd.	Apr 1853	France	569272
Eisenbeiss, Michael		Wittlensweiler	Frd.	May 1857	N.-Amer	577776
Eisenberger, Johann Christian	27 Feb 1808	Schorndorf	Schd.	Jan 1835	Mainz	801460
Eisener, Gottlob	24 yrs.	Calw	Calw	1869	N.-Amer	563212
Eisenhardt, Adolf	19 yrs.	Dachtel	Calw	1867	N.-Amer	563212
Eisenhardt, Christian Friedr.	24 yrs.	Gechingen	Calw	1866	N.-Amer	563212
Eisenhardt, Heinrike Christ.		Dachtel	Calw	Apr 1870	N.-Amer	563212
Eisenhardt, Martin & F		Dachtel	Calw	Apr 1870	N.-Amer	563212
Eisenhardt, Otto	17 yrs.	Dachtel	Calw	1867	N.-Amer	563212
Eisenhardt, Wilhelmine	27 Sep 1863	Dachtel	Calw	Apr 1870	N.-Amer	563212

Name		Birth		Emigration			Film
Last	First	Date	Place	O'amt	Appl. Date	Dest.	Number
Eisenhart, Johann Georg		28 yrs.	Stammheim	Calw	Sep 1847	N.-Amer	563212
Eisenmann, Christine		12 Jun 1838	Dornhan	Sulz	Aug 1857	N.-Amer	849633
Eisenmann, Maria Magdalena		18 Feb 1835	Freudenstadt	Frd.	bef 1862	France	577778
Eitel, Gottlieb Michael & W		3 Jun 1836	Gueltstein	Herr.	Feb 1866	N.-Amer	834624
Eitel, Martha (wife)		12 May 1844	Gueltstein	Herr.	Feb 1866	N.-Amer	834624
Eitelbuss, Carolina Louise		29 Apr 1839	Herrenberg	Herr.	Oct 1866	Tyrol	834624
Eitelbuss, Franz		9 Jan 1807	Gueltstein	Herr.	1833	N.-Amer	834626
Eitelbuss, Gottlieb Friedrich			Gueltstein	Herr.	Jun 1833	Rus-Pol	834624
Eitelbuss, Johann Georg & F			Gueltstein	Herr.	Jun 1832	N.-Amer	834624
Eitelbuss, Johannes			Gueltstein	Herr.	Jun 1833	Rus-Pol	834624
Eith, Catharina (wife)			Binsdorf	Sulz	Mar 1855	N.-Amer	849630
Eith, Christian & W			Binsdorf	Sulz	Mar 1855	N.-Amer	849630
Eith, Emil		20 Nov 1859	Rottenburg	Sulz	Aug 1869	N.-Amer	849631
Eith, Gabriel		25 Oct 1845	Binsdorf	Sulz	Jun 1865	N.-Amer	849631
Eith, Hubert			Geislingen	Bal.	1863	Switz.	555962
Eith, Kaspar		4 Jan 1852	Rottenburg	Sulz	May 1869	N.-Amer	849631
Eith, Maria		20 Mar 1861	Rottenburg	Sulz	Aug 1869	N.-Amer	849631
Eith, Otto		28 Aug 1857	Rottenburg	Sulz	Aug 1869	N.-Amer	849631
Eith, Reinhard		5 Jul 1848	Binsdorf	Sulz	Jun 1865	N.-Amer	849631
Eith, Rudolf		21 yrs.	Binsdorf	Sulz	Sep 1853	Austria	849630
Eith, Rudolf		16 Apr 1848	Binsdorf	Sulz	Sep 1868	N.-Amer	849631
Eith, Sebastian		16 Apr 1848	Binsdorf	Sulz	Oct 1868	N.-Amer	849631
Eith, Ursula & C		21 Oct 1828	Rottenburg	Sulz	Aug 1869	N.-Amer	849631
Eith, Zelestine		17 May 1820	Binsdorf	Sulz	Nov 1860	N.-Amer	849630
Eiting, Johann Georg		14 Jan 1830	Oberjettingen	Herr.	Jul 1866	N.-Amer	834624
Eiting, Johannes		30 Aug 1827	Oberjettingen	Herr.	Jul 1866	N.-Amer	834624
Ekert, Caspar & F			Glatten	Frd.	1817	Russia	569269
Ellinger, Johann Georg		14 Feb 1816	Steinenberg	Schd.	Nov 1842	Bavaria	801461
Emendorfer, Carl		23 Apr 1849	Liebenzell	Calw	1854	N.-Amer	563212
Emendorfer, Johannes		6 Dec 1822	Liebenzell	Calw	1854	N.-Amer	563212
Emendorfer, Sophie & C		17 Oct 1828	Liebenzell	Calw	1854	N.-Amer	563212
Emmendoerfer, Louise		4 yrs.	Liebenzell	Calw	1869	Baden	563212
Emmendoerfer, Maria & C		30 yrs.	Liebenzell	Calw	1869	Baden	563212
Engel, Katharine		17 yrs.	Ostelsheim	Calw	1854	N.-Amer	563212
Engelfein, Katharina		30 yrs.	Calw	Calw	1855	Prussia	563212
Engelfried, Caroline & C			Calw	Calw	1859	France	563212
Engelfried, Johannes		30 Jul 1837	Rosenfeld	Sulz	Mar 1857	N.-Amer	849640
Engelfried, Marie			Calw	Calw	1862	Bavaria	563212
Engelfried, Paul		6 yrs.	Calw	Calw	1859	France	563212
Engelhard, Jacob			Rosenfeld	Sulz	Apr 1854	N.-Amer	849640
Engisch, Jakob		30 Sep 1853	Wittershausen	Sulz	Dec 1871	N.-Amer	849644
Enslin, Christian Julius			Calw	Calw	Oct 1870	N.-Amer	563212
Ensslen, Johann Peter		14 Jun 1836	Ebhausen	Nag.	Aug 1854	N.-Amer	838491
Enzendreiss, Julius		1848	Calw	Calw	1868	England	563212
Epple, Friedrich			Freudenstadt	Frd.	Dec 1845	Baden	569271
Eppler, Johann			Oberdigisheim	Bal.	bef 1849	Switz.	555963
Eppler, Johannes			Wittershausen	Sulz	bef 1855	Switz.	849644
Eppler, Johannes		29 yrs.	Winterbach	Schd.	Apr 1837	N.-Amer	801461
Eppler, Karl Jakob		25 Apr 1872	Muehlheim a.B.	Sulz	May 1889	N.-Amer	849639
Eppler, Martin			Balingen	Bal.	Oct 1862	Switz.	555962

Eppler, Mathias		Balingen	Bal.	Nov 1861	Switz.	555962
Eppler, female		Hossingen	Dal.	Mar 1852	N.-Amer	555961
Epting, Andreas	27 Feb 1836	Wittendorf	Frd.	Feb 1854	N.-Amer	569273
Epting, Maria		Calw	Calw	1849	Prussia	563212
Epting, Sophie Emilie		Calw	Calw	1853	N.-Amer	563212
Erath, Dorothea (wife)		Moetzingen	Herr.	May 1830	N.-Amer	834624
Erath, Simon & F		Moetzingen	Herr.	May 1830	N.-Amer	834624
Ergenzinger, Jakob Friedrich	5 Apr 1846	Freudenstadt	Frd.	May 1866	N.-Amer	577780
Erhard, Johann Carl	28 Jan 1830	Freudenstadt	Frd.	Feb 1860	Bavaria	577777
Erhardt, Christian	1 May 1851	Ueberberg	Nag.	Feb 1852	N.-Amer	838490
Erhardt, Christina		Ueberberg	Nag.	Feb 1852	N.-Amer	838490
Erhardt, Gottlieb	1838	Unterreichenbach	Calw	1854	N.-Amer	563212
Ernde, Johann Gottl.	20 Nov 1767	Sulz	Sulz	1833	N.-Amer	849627
Ernde, Johann Ludwig	15 yrs.	Sulz	Sulz	Apr 1834	N.-Amer	849627
Ernde, Maria	14 yrs.	Sulz	Sulz	Apr 1834	N.-Amer	849627
Ernde, Sophia Agatha & F	6 Dec 1787	Sulz	Sulz	Apr 1834	N.-Amer	849627
Ernst, Regina	42 yrs.	Sulz	Sulz	Mar 1815	Switz.	849625
Eschenhardt, Johann Gottlieb	1828	Gechingen	Calw	1856	N.-Amer	563212
Essig, Anna Barbara	29 Jan 1839	Leidringen	Sulz	Feb 1869	France	849637
Essig, Jakob	27 May 1835	Leidringen	Sulz	Mar 1866	N.-Amer	849637
Essig, Jakob	8 Aug 1829	Leidringen	Sulz	Nov 1862	Switz.	849637
Esslinger, Anna Maria	14 Feb 1839	Hopfau	Sulz	Feb 1860	N.-Amer	849636
Esslinger, Anna Maria		Bergfelden	Sulz	Feb 1883	N.-Amer	849626
Esslinger, August Ehrhardt	8 Nov 1848	Boll	Sulz	bef 1869	N.-Amer	849632
Esslinger, Barbara	17 Mar 1838	Bergfelden	Sulz	Dec 1861	Switz.	849629
Esslinger, Barbara (wife)		Duerrenmettstetten	Sulz	1800	Pol-Rus	849635
Esslinger, Carl Gottlob	9 Apr 1844	Boll	Sulz	Aug 1860	N.-Amer	849632
Esslinger, Catharina		Boll	Sulz	May 1832	N.-Amer	849632
Esslinger, Christian		Duerrenmettstetten	Sulz	bef 1831	Russia	849625
Esslinger, Christian & F		Duerrenmettstetten	Sulz	1800	Pol-Rus	849635
Esslinger, Christina		Boll	Sulz	May 1832	N.-Amer	849632
Esslinger, Elisabetha (wife)		Aistaig	Sulz	Mar 1836	N.-Amer	849628
Esslinger, Friedrich	15 Jun 1840	Boll	Sulz	Aug 1860	N.-Amer	849632
Esslinger, Friedrich Jakob	28 yrs.	Aistaig	Sulz	Mar 1859	France	849628
Esslinger, Johann & F		Dornhan	Sulz	Mar 1817	Russia	849633
Esslinger, Johann Georg		Boll	Sulz	May 1832	N.-Amer	849632
Esslinger, Johann Georg & F	27 Jan 1769	Aistaig	Sulz	Mar 1836	N.-Amer	849628
Esslinger, Johann Martin	29 Dec 1867	Bergfelden	Sulz	Feb 1883	N.-Amer	849626
Esslinger, Johann Martin & F	11 Nov 1795	Sulz	Sulz	Feb 1833	N.-Amer	849627
Esslinger, Johannes		Hopfau-Nennthausen	Sulz	1853	N.-Amer	849642
Esslinger, Johannes	5 Jul 1836	Hopfau	Sulz	Feb 1854	N.-Amer	849636
Esslinger, Maria Gottl. (wife)		Sulz	Sulz	Feb 1833	N.-Amer	849627
Esslinger, Martin & W	14 Oct 1801	Aistaig	Sulz	Mar 1836	N.-Amer	849628
Esslinger, Matheus (wid.) & F	9 May 1778	Boll	Sulz	May 1832	N.-Amer	849632
Esslinger, Rosina	19 Dec 1843	Bergfelden	Sulz	bef 1881	Switz.	849629
Etter, Carl Heinrich	14 Jan 1843	Moetzingen	Herr.	Feb 1847	N.-Amer	834626
Etter, Elisabetha	26 Aug 1846	Moetzingen	Herr.	Feb 1847	N.-Amer	834626
Etter, Johann Jacob	16 Nov 1841	Moetzingen	Herr.	Feb 1847	N.-Amer	834626
Etter, Johann Jacob & F	18 Feb 1815	Moetzingen	Herr.	Feb 1847	N.-Amer	834626
Etter, Johannes & F		Bergfelden	Sulz	Apr 1817	Russia	849629

Name		Birth		Emigration			Film
Last	First	Date	Place	O'amt	Appl. Date	Dest.	Number
Etter, Martin & F			Leidringen	Sulz	Mar 1853	N.-Amer	849637
Etter, Philippine (wife)		1 May 1811	Moetzingen	Herr.	Feb 1847	N.-Amer	834626
Etter, Samuel		8 Sep 1844	Moetzingen	Herr.	Feb 1847	N.-Amer	834626
Etzel, Anna Maria		1 Apr 1847	Oeschelbronn	Herr.	Sep 1852	N.-Amer	834627
Etzel, Catharina		20 Nov 1844	Oeschelbronn	Herr.	Sep 1852	N.-Amer	834627
Etzel, Catharina Doroth. (wife)		16 Sep 1804	Oeschelbronn	Herr.	Sep 1852	N.-Amer	834627
Etzel, Christian		31 Oct 1842	Oeschelbronn	Herr.	Sep 1852	N.-Amer	834627
Etzel, Dorothea		20 Nov 1844	Oeschelbronn	Herr.	Sep 1852	N.-Amer	834627
Etzel, Michael		5 Feb 1840	Oeschelbronn	Herr.	Sep 1852	N.-Amer	834627
Etzel, Michael & F		12 Feb 1804	Emberg	Herr.	Sep 1852	N.-Amer	834627
Eyth, Alois		30 Mar 1856	Binsdorf	Sulz	Sep 1872	N.-Amer	849631
Eyth, Anna			Binsdorf	Sulz	May 1843	Hohenz.	849630
Eyth, August		28 Aug 1856	Binsdorf	Sulz	Sep 1872	N.-Amer	849631
Eyth, August Theodor			Lossburg	Frd.	bef 1855	N.-Amer	569275
Eyth, Genovefa		5 Jan 1822	Binsdorf	Sulz	Apr 1845	Hohenz.	849630
Eyth, Jordan			Binsdorf	Sulz	Mar 1847	N.-Amer	849630
Eyth, Joseph		23 Mar 1858	Binsdorf	Sulz	Aug 1873	N.-Amer	849631
Eyth, Karl		21 Feb 1881	Binsdorf	Sulz	May 1893	N.-Amer	849631
Eyth, Marzelle			Binsdorf	Sulz	Jun 1840	Switz.	849630
Eyth, Mathias			Binsdorf	Sulz	Jun 1840	Hohenz.	849630
Eyth, Oskar		13 Sep 1886	Binsdorf	Sulz	May 1893	N.-Amer	849631
Eyth, Raimund		10 Aug 1808	Binsdorf	Sulz	Mar 1844	Rhld.	849630
Eyth, Rubertus			Binsdorf	Sulz	May 1843	Hohenz.	849630
Eyth, Stefan		24 Dec 1878	Binsdorf	Sulz	May 1893	N.-Amer	849631
Faas, Johann Jakob			Dennjaecht	Calw	1862	Bavaria	563212
Faas, Samuel Friedrich			Calw	Calw	1862	Baden	563212
Faber, Albert		17 yrs.	Hirsau	Calw	1869	Switz.	563212
Faber, Heinrich		22 Apr 1849	Hirsau	Calw	1867	Switz.	563212
Fahrner, Agnes		7 Feb 1835	Baiersbronn	Frd.	Sep 1848	N.-Amer	569270
Fahrner, Ambrosius		28 Nov 1842	Oberndorf	Herr.	Aug 1865	N.-Amer	834624
Fahrner, Andreas		14 May 1858	Roet	Frd.	Jan 1864	N.-Amer	577779
Fahrner, Andreas & F		16 Oct 1826	Roet	Frd.	Jan 1864	N.-Amer	577779
Fahrner, Anna Maria		19 Feb 1856	Goettelfingen	Frd.	Jan 1864	N.-Amer	577779
Fahrner, Anna Maria (wife)		6 Jul 1835	Goettelfingen	Frd.	Jan 1864	N.-Amer	577779
Fahrner, Barbara		24 Sep 1816	Schramberg	Frd.	Aug 1854	N.-Amer	569274
Fahrner, Bernhard		23 Nov 1837	Baiersbronn	Frd.	Sep 1854	N.-Amer	569274
Fahrner, Caroline Catharine		26 Feb 1837	Baiersbronn	Frd.	Jun 1865	N.-Amer	577779
Fahrner, Catharina		6 Dec 1850	Schramberg	Frd.	Aug 1854	N.-Amer	569274
Fahrner, Christian		14 Jun 1844	Roet	Frd.	Jan 1864	N.-Amer	577779
Fahrner, Christian			Freudenstadt	Frd.	May 1828	France	569267
Fahrner, Christian Friedrich		13 Sep 1838	Freudenstadt	Frd.	Sep 1854	N.-Amer	569274
Fahrner, Christine (wife)		24 yrs.	Aach	Frd.	Mar 1837	N.-Amer	569267
Fahrner, Friedrich		22 Nov 1847	Dornhan	Sulz	Oct 1866	N.-Amer	849634
Fahrner, Georg		12 Oct 1842	Baiersbronn	Frd.	Sep 1848	N.-Amer	569270
Fahrner, Gottlieb		30 Jun 1846	Baiersbronn	Frd.	Sep 1848	N.-Amer	569270
Fahrner, Jacob & F		4 Apr 1804	Baiersbronn	Frd.	Sep 1848	N.-Amer	569270
Fahrner, Johann Adam			Aach	Frd.	bef 1851	N.-Amer	569271
Fahrner, Johann Georg		31 Jul 1819	Baiersbronn	Frd.	Nov 1853	N.-Amer	569272
Fahrner, Johann Georg		23 Apr 1848	Baiersbronn	Frd.	Jun 1865	N.-Amer	577779
Fahrner, Johann Georg		30 Sep 1845	Schramberg	Frd.	Aug 1854	N.-Amer	569274

Fahrner, Johann Georg		Oberndorf	Herr.	Apr 1830	N.-Amer	834624
Fahrner, Johanne Auguste	1855	Freudenstadt	Frd.	Nov 1860	France	577777
Fahrner, Johannes	27 yrs.	Aach	Frd.	Mar 1837	N.-Amer	569267
Fahrner, Magdalena	27 Jan 1863	Roet	Frd.	Jan 1864	N.-Amer	577779
Fahrner, Margaretha		Baiersbronn	Frd.	Mar 1847	N.-Amer	569271
Fahrner, Matthaeus	19 Jul 1859	Roet	Frd.	Jan 1864	N.-Amer	577779
Fahrner, Regina	21 Mar 1813	Baiersbronn	Frd.	Sep 1848	N.-Amer	569270
Fahrner, Regina	11 Nov 1848	Schramberg	Frd.	Aug 1854	N.-Amer	569274
Fahrner, Regine		Baiersbronn	Frd.	Dec 1813	Baden	569267
Fahrner, Rosine		Aach	Frd.	Mar 1837	N.-Amer	569267
Fahrner, Rosine Christiane		Freudenstadt	Frd.	Oct 1838	Baden	569267
Fahrner, Rosine Christine	6 mon.	Aach	Frd.	Mar 1837	N.-Amer	569267
Fahrner, Tobias	23 Aug 1839	Baiersbronn	Frd.	Sep 1848	N.-Amer	569270
Fahrner, Tobias & F	16 Nov 1819	Baiersbronn	Frd.	Mar 1847	N.-Amer	569271
Fahrner, Tobias & F	9 Dec 1818	Schramberg	Frd.	Aug 1854	N.-Amer	569274
Faiss, Engelbert	31 Aug 1872	Bettenhausen	Sulz	Jul 1889	N.-Amer	849630
Faisst, Andreas	13 Dec 1835	Looch	Frd.	Mar 1858	N.-Amer	577776
Faisst, Andreas	8 Mar 1860	Sigmarswangen	Sulz	1877	N.-Amer	849642
Faisst, Andreas		Holzhausen	Sulz	Aug 1851	N.-Amer	849635
Faisst, Anna Maria (wife)	12 Jan 1828	Hallwangen	Frd.	Jul 1854	N.-Amer	569274
Faisst, Anna Rosina		Klosterreichenbach	Frd.	Apr 1848	N.-Amer	569270
Faisst, August	9 Jul 1844	Freudenstadt	Frd.	Sep 1859	N.-Amer	577776
Faisst, Barbara (wid.) & F	21 Nov 1825	Sigmarswangen	Sulz	Apr 1880	N.-Amer	849642
Faisst, Barbara Katharina	1 Oct 1865	Sigmarswangen	Sulz	Apr 1880	N.-Amer	849626
Faisst, Bernhard	18 Aug 1835	Roet	Frd.	Apr 1854	N.-Amer	569274
Faisst, Carl	4 Mar 1834	Freudenstadt	Frd.	Sep 1853	N.-Amer	569274
Faisst, Catharina	30 Sep 1832	Neuneck	Frd.	May 1854	N.-Amer	569273
Faisst, Catharina	3 May 1834	Baiersbronn	Frd.	Nov 1854	N.-Amer	569274
Faisst, Catharina Beate	10 Jun 1839	Freudenstadt	Frd.	Sep 1859	N.-Amer	577776
Faisst, Christian	7 Mar 1848	Sigmarswangen	Sulz	Aug 1866	N.-Amer	849642
Faisst, Christian		Holzhausen	Sulz	Aug 1851	N.-Amer	849635
Faisst, Christian Enoch	3 Jan 1863	Sigmarswangen	Sulz	Apr 1880	N.-Amer	849626
Faisst, Christine	19 Aug 1845	Neuneck	Frd.	May 1854	N.-Amer	569273
Faisst, Daniel	24 Sep 1832	Baiersbronn	Frd.	Apr 1856	N.-Amer	569275
Faisst, Dorothea	15 Nov 1806	Unterbraendi	Frd.	May 1854	N.-Amer	569273
Faisst, Eva Christine	10 Dec 1792	Baiersbronn	Frd.	Apr 1847	N.-Amer	569270
Faisst, Eva Maria	5 Aug 1830	Baiersbronn	Frd.	Apr 1847	N.-Amer	569270
Faisst, Friederike Pauline	31 Mar 1849	Freudenstadt	Frd.	Sep 1859	N.-Amer	577776
Faisst, Georg	28 Oct 1853	Sigmarswangen	Sulz	1872	N.-Amer	849642
Faisst, Gottfried	5 Jun 1835	Wittlensweiler	Frd.	Feb 1854	N.-Amer	569273
Faisst, Gottlieb	23 Jul 1833	Baiersbronn	Frd.	Apr 1847	N.-Amer	569270
Faisst, Gottlieb	15 Oct 1868	Sigmarswangen	Sulz	Apr 1880	N.-Amer	849626
Faisst, Jakob & F	24 Mar 1805	Baiersbronn	Frd.	May 1854	N.-Amer	569273
Faisst, Jakob Friedrich	23 Aug 1856	Sigmarswangen	Sulz	1872	N.-Amer	849642
Faisst, Johann Daniel	8 Aug 1832	Baiersbronn	Frd.	Apr 1856	N.-Amer	569275
Faisst, Johann Georg	28 Feb 1827	Baiersbronn	Frd.	Apr 1856	N.-Amer	569275
Faisst, Johann Georg	14 Oct 1825	Baiersbronn	Frd.	Apr 1856	N.-Amer	569275
Faisst, Johann Georg	22 Sep 1853	Aach	Frd.	Jul 1854	N.-Amer	569274
Faisst, Johann Georg & F	15 Jan 1816	Aach	Frd.	Jul 1854	N.-Amer	569274
Faisst, Johann Jakob	6 Mar 1838	Baiersbronn	Frd.	Apr 1856	N.-Amer	569275

Name		Birth		Emigration			Film
Last	First	Date	Place	O'amt	Appl. Date	Dest.	Number
Faisst, Johannes		22 Feb 1843	Neuneck	Frd.	May 1854	N.-Amer	569273
Faisst, Johannes		22 Nov 1850	Sigmarswangen	Sulz	1870	N.-Amer	849642
Faisst, Johannes & F			Sigmarswangen	Sulz	Apr 1880	N.-Amer	849626
Faisst, Magdalena		3 Sep 1837	Neuneck	Frd.	May 1854	N.-Amer	569273
Faisst, Margaretha			Baiersbronn	Frd.	Apr 1856	N.-Amer	569275
Faisst, Maria Christina		11 Mar 1838	Wittlensweiler	Frd.	Jun 1856	N.-Amer	569275
Faisst, Marie Friederike		23 Mar 1837	Edelweiler	Frd.	bef 1857	Switz.	569275
Faisst, Mathias		3 Feb 1871	Sigmarswangen	Sulz	Apr 1880	N.-Amer	849626
Faisst, Mathias		24 Sep 1846	Sigmarswangen	Sulz	Sep 1866	N.-Amer	849642
Faisst, Matthaeus		31 Oct 1828	Baiersbronn	Frd.	Apr 1847	N.-Amer	569270
Faisst, Matthias		30 Nov 1840	Neuneck	Frd.	May 1854	N.-Amer	569273
Faisst, Michael Friedrich		4 Feb 1829	Baiersbronn	Frd.	Apr 1856	N.-Amer	569275
Faisst, Regine		15 Nov 1835	Baiersbronn	Frd.	Apr 1847	N.-Amer	569270
Faisst, Wilhelm Gottfried		23 Dec 1841	Freudenstadt	Frd.	Sep 1859	N.-Amer	577776
Faist, Anna		15 Dec 1816	Bergfelden	Sulz	Jul 1817	Russia	849629
Faist, Anna (wife)		11 Jan 1785	Ostdorf/Balingen	Sulz	Jul 1817	Russia	849629
Faist, Anna Catharina		30 Aug 1812	Ostdorf/Balingen	Sulz	Jul 1817	Russia	849629
Faist, Catharina			Sigmarswangen	Sulz	bef 1821	Pr.-Pol	849625
Faist, Christina & C			Klosterreichenbach	Frd.	Jan 1838	France	569268
Faist, Christine		23 Oct 1827	Baiersbronn	Frd.	Apr 1847	N.-Amer	569270
Faist, Christine Rosine		5 Nov 1826	Klosterreichenbach	Frd.	Jan 1838	France	569268
Faist, Franz Ludwig		7 Aug 1835	Freudenstadt	Frd.	1861	N.-Amer	577778
Faist, Johann Georg & F		11 Apr 1791	Bergfelden	Sulz	Jul 1817	Russia	849629
Faist, Johann Gottlieb & F		13 Sep 1800	Klosterreichenbach	Frd.	Apr 1847	N.-Amer	569270
Faist, Johann Martin		7 Jun 1808	Ostdorf/Balingen	Sulz	Jul 1817	Russia	849629
Faist, Magdalena		24 Jun 1812	Baiersbronn	Frd.	Sep 1846	N.-Amer	569271
Fass, Rosine (wid.)			Dornhan	Sulz	May 1817	Russia	849633
Fassnacht, Anton		14 Feb 1794	Altheim	Horb	1833	N.-Amer	835904
Fassnacht, Johannes			Zwerenberg	Calw	1858	N.-Amer	563212
Fassnacht, Maria			Altheim	Horb	bef 1861	Prussia	835929
Fassnacht, Philipps (wid.)& F			Zwerenberg	Calw	1853	N.-Amer	563212
Fassnacht, Veronika		25 Jan 1850	Altheim	Horb	May 1869	Prussia	835929
Fauser, Anna Maria			Aistaig	Sulz	bef 1846	France	849628
Fauser, Anna Maria		8 Oct 1805	Aistaig	Sulz	1817	N.-Amer	849628
Fauser, Anna Maria (wife)		15 Jun 1780	Aistaig	Sulz	1817	N.-Amer	849628
Fauser, Catharina		5 Jul 1850	Tailfingen	Herr.	May 1851	N.-Amer	834627
Fauser, Catharina (wife)		11 Dec 1831	Tailfingen	Herr.	May 1851	N.-Amer	834627
Fauser, Christina		11 Mar 1851	Sulz	Sulz	Apr 1869	Bavaria	849628
Fauser, Johann Georg & F		8 Oct 1777	Aistaig	Sulz	1817	N.-Amer	849628
Fauser, Johann Georg & F			Tailfingen	Herr.	May 1851	N.-Amer	834627
Fauser, Magdalena			Aistaig	Sulz	Apr 1849	Baden	849628
Fauser, Maria Magdalena		30 Oct 1812	Aistaig	Sulz	1817	N.-Amer	849628
Faust, Jacob			Freudenstadt	Frd.	Mar 1854	N.-Amer	569273
Feber, Ludwig			Hirsau	Calw	1863	Baden	563212
Fecker, Johannes		5 Jan 1829	Altingen	Herr.	Apr 1849	N.-Amer	834627
Federer, Catharina		11 yrs.	Beutelsbach	Schd.	Apr 1833	N.-Amer	801460
Federer, Christina Magdalena		5 yrs.	Beutelsbach	Schd.	Apr 1833	N.-Amer	801460
Federer, Johann Jacob		14 yrs.	Beutelsbach	Schd.	Apr 1833	N.-Amer	801460
Federer, Louise			Beutelsbach	Schd.	Apr 1833	N.-Amer	801460
Federer, Philipp Heinrich		1 yrs.	Beutelsbach	Schd.	Apr 1833	N.-Amer	801460

Feiss, Theresia	30 Aug 1850	Bettenhausen	Sulz	Dec 1884	N.-Amer	849626
Feker, Matheus	23 Jan 1823	Altingen	Herr.	Mar 1847	N.-Amer	834626
Feldenz, Christian Robert		Calw	Calw	1869	N.-Amer	563212
Feldmaier, Adolf	12 Dec 1875	Bergfelden	Sulz	Apr 1883	N.-Amer	849626
Feldmaier, Georg	11 Sep 1869	Bergfelden	Sulz	Apr 1883	N.-Amer	849626
Feldmaier, Gustav	19 Jul 1867	Bergfelden	Sulz	Apr 1883	N.-Amer	849626
Feldmaier, Jakob & F	9 Oct 1830	Bergfelden	Sulz	Apr 1883	N.-Amer	849626
Feldmaier, Jakob Wilhelm	3 Apr 1862	Bergfelden	Sulz	Apr 1883	N.-Amer	849626
Feldmaier, Jakobine Mag. (wife)	20 Jun 1838	Bergfelden	Sulz	Apr 1883	N.-Amer	849626
Feldmaier, Karl Gottlieb	11 Jun 1865	Bergfelden	Sulz	Apr 1883	N.-Amer	849626
Feldmaier, Maria Louise	6 Dec 1863	Bergfelden	Sulz	Apr 1883	N.-Amer	849626
Feldmaier, Martha Margaretha	17 May 1861	Bergfelden	Sulz	Apr 1883	N.-Amer	849626
Fenchel, Johann Jacob		Ostelsheim	Calw	Sep 1869	N.-Amer	563212
Ferber, Carl August		Hirsau	Calw	1866	Bavaria	563212
Ferber, Karl Ludwig	1834	Hirsau	Calw	1854	N.-Amer	563212
Ferber, Wilhelm & F		Hirsau	Calw	1860	Baden	563212
Fessele, Johann Jakob & F		Alzenberg	Frd.	1817	Russia	569269
Fetsch, Andreas	9 Apr 1848	Bergfelden	Sulz	Jul 1860	N.-Amer	849629
Fetsch, Andreas & F	27 Aug 1814	Renfrizhausen	Sulz	Jul 1860	N.-Amer	849639
Fetsch, Andreas & F		Renfrizhausen	Sulz	Mar 1817	Russia	849639
Fetsch, Anna Maria (wife)	18 Jun 1825	Renfrizhausen	Sulz	Jul 1860	N.-Amer	849639
Fetsch, Johann Georg	23 Apr 1843	Bergfelden	Sulz	Jul 1860	N.-Amer	849629
Fetsch, Johannes	4 Mar 1829	Bergfelden	Sulz	Jul 1860	N.-Amer	849629
Fetsch, Johannes & F	4 May 1803	Bergfelden	Sulz	Jul 1860	N.-Amer	849629
Fetsch, Johannes Bernhard	6 Jan 1849	Renfrizhausen	Sulz	Jul 1860	N.-Amer	849639
Fetsch, Margaretha (wife)	20 Apr 1807	Bergfelden	Sulz	Jul 1860	N.-Amer	849629
Feuerbacher, Johannes	18 yrs.	Zwerenberg	Calw	1869	N.-Amer	563212
Fichel, Carl Gottlieb		Liebenzell	Calw	Jun 1870	N.-Amer	563212
Fidel, Johanna		Zwieselberg	Frd.	Nov 1811	Baden	569268
Fiebich, Johannes	19 yrs.	Hildrizhausen	Herr.	Apr 1852	N.-Amer	834627
Fiesel, Eberhardt August & F		Liebenzell	Calw	Mar 1847	N.-Amer	563212
Fiesler, Catharina		Simmozheim	Calw	1852	Prussia	563212
Fingel, Johann Jacob & F		Unterjettingen	Herr.	Aug 1847	N.-Amer	834626
Fink, Christian	20 May 1832	Oberbraendi	Frd.	Oct 1854	N.-Amer	569274
Fink, Christina	22 Sep 1856	Oberbraendi	Frd.	Apr 1858	N.-Amer	577776
Fink, Johannes	29 May 1834	Oberbraendi	Frd.	Oct 1854	N.-Amer	569274
Fink, Johannes	8 Feb 1852	Oberbraendi	Frd.	Apr 1858	N.-Amer	577776
Fink, Johannes & F		Oberbraendi	Frd.	Apr 1858	N.-Amer	577776
Finkbeiner, Adolph August	25 Feb 1844	Freudenstadt	Frd.	Aug 1864	N.-Amer	577779
Finkbeiner, Agnes	5 yrs.	Baiersbronn	Frd.	Aug 1854	N.-Amer	569274
Finkbeiner, Agnes & F	18 Jan 1819	Schoenegruend	Frd.	Feb 1858	N.-Amer	577776
Finkbeiner, Agnes Catharine	30 Mar 1816	Baiersbronn	Frd.	Dec 1853	N.-Amer	569272
Finkbeiner, Anna Maria	8 Jan 1840	Baiersbronn	Frd.	Dec 1853	N.-Amer	569272
Finkbeiner, Anna Maria	7 yrs.	Baiersbronn	Frd.	Aug 1854	N.-Amer	569274
Finkbeiner, Anna Maria	6 Nov 1844	Baiersbronn	Frd.	Aug 1854	N.-Amer	569274
Finkbeiner, Anna Maria & C	17 Nov 1822	Surrbach	Frd.	Sep 1853	N.-Amer	569272
Finkbeiner, Anna Maria (wife)	26 Nov 1816	Baiersbronn	Frd.	Jun 1855	N.-Amer	569275
Finkbeiner, Bernhard		Baiersbronn	Frd.	1851	N.-Amer	577778
Finkbeiner, Bernhard	2 Aug 1819	Baiersbronn	Frd.	May 1845	Baden	569269
Finkbeiner, Bernhard		Baiersbronn	Frd.	May 1851	N.-Amer	569271

Name		Birth		Emigration			Film
Last	First	Date	Place	O'amt	Appl. Date	Dest.	Number
Finkbeiner, Bernhardt		12 Jan 1805	Baiersbronn	Frd.	Mar 1840	France	569267
Finkbeiner, Catharina		29 yrs.	Baiersbronn	Frd.	Sep 1850	N.-Amer	569271
Finkbeiner, Christian			Schoenegruend	Frd.	Jun 1832	N.-Amer	569268
Finkbeiner, Christian & F			Baiersbronn	Frd.	Feb 1846	Austria	569271
Finkbeiner, Christian & F		27 Apr 1812	Baiersbronn	Frd.	Aug 1854	N.-Amer	569274
Finkbeiner, Christian Friedr.		4 Jul 1846	Baiersbronn	Frd.	Dec 1853	N.-Amer	569272
Finkbeiner, Christian Friedr.		17 Apr 1842	Baiersbronn	Frd.	Aug 1854	N.-Amer	569274
Finkbeiner, Christina		24 Nov 1850	Baiersbronn	Frd.	Jun 1855	N.-Amer	569275
Finkbeiner, Christina Barb.			Reichenbach	Frd.	Jul 1848	N.-Amer	569270
Finkbeiner, David		7 Jun 1828	Baiersbronn	Frd.	Mar 1859	Baden	577776
Finkbeiner, Elisabetha		27 Feb 1837	Hoell	Frd.	Mar 1856	Canada	569275
Finkbeiner, Elisabetha		6 mon.	Baiersbronn	Frd.	Sep 1850	N.-Amer	569271
Finkbeiner, Elisabetha Cath.		9 Sep 1829	Tonbach	Frd.	bef 1860	Baden	577778
Finkbeiner, Ernst Gustav		11 Jan 1845	Freudenstadt	Frd.	Aug 1866	N.-Amer	577780
Finkbeiner, Ester		46 yrs.	Freudenstadt	Frd.	May 1752	Pen.N-A	550803
Finkbeiner, Eva Katharina		7 Nov 1822	Baiersbronn	Frd.	Mar 1847	N.-Amer	569271
Finkbeiner, Eva Maria			Baiersbronn	Frd.	bef 1864	Baden	577779
Finkbeiner, Eva Maria		19 Sep 1841	Baiersbronn	Frd.	Sep 1846	N.-Amer	569271
Finkbeiner, Eva Maria		26 Dec 1846	Schoenegruend	Frd.	Feb 1858	N.-Amer	577776
Finkbeiner, Eva Maria (wife)			Schoenegruend	Frd.	Jun 1832	N.-Amer	569268
Finkbeiner, Friderika (wife)		15 Jun 1808	Baiersbronn	Frd.	Aug 1854	N.-Amer	569274
Finkbeiner, Friederika		27 Aug 1827	Baiersbronn	Frd.	Mar 1849	N.-Amer	569270
Finkbeiner, Friederika		26 Nov 1840	Baiersbronn	Frd.	Aug 1854	N.-Amer	569274
Finkbeiner, Friederika & C		14 Dec 1832	Baiersbronn	Frd.	Jul 1864	N.-Amer	577779
Finkbeiner, Friedrich		7 May 1834	Baiersbronn	Frd.	Sep 1854	N.-Amer	569274
Finkbeiner, Gottfried		13 Apr 1842	Schoenegruend	Frd.	Feb 1858	N.-Amer	577776
Finkbeiner, Gottlieb		8 Apr 1849	Schoenegruend	Frd.	Feb 1858	N.-Amer	577776
Finkbeiner, Gottlieb		24 Jun 1847	Huzenbach	Frd.	Jan 1866	N.-Amer	577780
Finkbeiner, Jacob		18 Sep 1806	Baiersbronn	Frd.	Apr 1841	Baden	569267
Finkbeiner, Jacob Friedrich			Freudenstadt	Frd.	Oct 1835	Baden	569267
Finkbeiner, Jakob		21 Jul 1836	Baiersbronn	Frd.	Apr 1856	N.-Amer	569275
Finkbeiner, Jakob & F			Baiersbronn	Frd.	Aug 1854	N.-Amer	569274
Finkbeiner, Johann Adam		8 Jan 1820	Schoenegruend	Frd.	bef 1858	N.-Amer	577776
Finkbeiner, Johann Adam & F		27 Jun 1811	Baiersbronn	Frd.	Dec 1853	N.-Amer	569272
Finkbeiner, Johann Georg		19 Jul 1838	Baiersbronn	Frd.	Dec 1853	N.-Amer	569272
Finkbeiner, Johann Georg		29 Jul 1843	Surrbach	Frd.	Sep 1853	N.-Amer	569272
Finkbeiner, Johann Mathias		1842	Sulz	Sulz	Jul 1854	N.-Amer	849627
Finkbeiner, Johannes		18 Apr 1834	Frutenhof	Frd.	Mar 1854	N.-Amer	569273
Finkbeiner, Johannes			Klosterreichenbach	Frd.	Mar 1837	N.-Amer	569268
Finkbeiner, Johannes		12 May 1807	Klosterreichenbach	Frd.	Jul 1836	N.-Amer	569268
Finkbeiner, Johannes			Baiersbronn	Frd.	Jun 1850	France	569271
Finkbeiner, Johannes		14 May 1847	Baiersbronn	Frd.	Aug 1854	N.-Amer	569274
Finkbeiner, Johannes & F			Baiersbronn	Frd.	Apr 1817	Russia	569267
Finkbeiner, Magdalena		22 yrs.	Kniebis	Frd.	bef 1862	Baden	577778
Finkbeiner, Magdalena & C			Baiersbronn	Frd.	Sep 1850	N.-Amer	569271
Finkbeiner, Maria Magdalena		5 yrs.	Baiersbronn	Frd.	Sep 1850	N.-Amer	569271
Finkbeiner, Matheus		9 Nov 1809	Baiersbronn	Frd.	Sep 1842	Baden	569269
Finkbeiner, Matthaeus		12 Oct 1846	Baiersbronn	Frd.	Jun 1855	N.-Amer	569275
Finkbeiner, Matthaeus & F		17 Dec 1816	Baiersbronn	Frd.	Jun 1855	N.-Amer	569275
Finkbeiner, Michael & F			Klosterreichenbach	Frd.	Apr 1817	Russia	569268

Finkbeiner, Regina	14 Dec 1840	Hoell	Frd.	Mar 1856	Canada	569275
Finkbeiner, Regina	2 yrs.	Baiersbronn	Frd.	Aug 1854	N.-Amer	569274
Finkbeiner, Rosina	3 Jun 1829	Kniebis	Frd.	bef 1863	Baden	577778
Finkbeiner, Rosine	4 Apr 1852	Baiersbronn	Frd.	Dec 1853	N.-Amer	569272
Finkbeiner, Sophie Friederike		Christophstal	Frd.	bef 1858	Baden	577778
Finkbeiner, Tobias & F	30 yrs.	Freudenstadt	– –	Mar 1752	Pen.N-A	550803
Finkbeiner, Wilhelm	3 Mar 1852	Baiersbronn	Frd.	May 1866	N.-Amer	577780
Finkbeiner, Wilhelm Ludwig & F		Reichenbach	Frd.	Jul 1848	N.-Amer	569270
Finkbeiner, Wilhelmine	6 Mar 1843	Kniebis	Frd.	May 1864	N.-Amer	577779
Finkbohner, Catharine Christ.	19 Jun 1839	Sulz	Sulz	Sep 1860	Switz.	849628
Finkbohner, Christian		Schopfloch	Frd.	Feb 1853	N.-Amer	569272
Finkbohner, Christian	18 Jul 1823	Sulz	Sulz	Apr 1833	N.-Amer	849627
Finkbohner, Jacob Bernhard & F	15 Oct 1778	Sulz	Sulz	Apr 1833	N.-Amer	849627
Finkbohner, Johann Georg	2 Apr 1810	Sulz	Sulz	1832	N.-Amer	849627
Finkbohner, Johann Jacob	30 Mar 1808	Sulz	Sulz	1832	N.-Amer	849627
Finkbohner, Johanna Elisabeth		Sulz	Sulz	Apr 1834	N.-Amer	849627
Finkbohner, Karl Friedrich	1 Jan 1814	Sulz	Sulz	Apr 1833	N.-Amer	849627
Finkbohner, Kaspar		Schopfloch	Frd.	Nov 1860	Baden	577777
Finkbohner, Katharina & C		Schopfloch	Frd.	Feb 1853	N.-Amer	569272
Finkbohner, Philipp Ludwig	12 Apr 1821	Sulz	Sulz	Apr 1833	N.-Amer	849627
Finkheimer, Anna Maria		Huzenbach	Frd.	Jun 1865	N.-Amer	577779
Fischer, (widow)		Wittershausen	Sulz	Jul 1847	N.-Amer	849644
Fischer, Andreas & F		Bergfelden	Sulz	Jul 1853	N.-Amer	849629
Fischer, Anna Maria		Baiersbronn	Frd.	Jul 1817	Russia	569268
Fischer, Anna Maria	8 Mar 1835	Moetzingen	Herr.	Mar 1847	N.-Amer	834626
Fischer, Anna Maria	18 Mar 1830	Hildrizhausen	Herr.	Jul 1868	N.-Amer	834624
Fischer, August Ludwig	24 yrs.	Stammheim	Calw	1856	Russia	563212
Fischer, Barbara & C		Lossburg	Frd.	Jun 1848	N.-Amer	569270
Fischer, Beata	28 Feb 1835	Baiersbronn	Frd.	Dec 1853	N.-Amer	569272
Fischer, Bernhard	20 Aug 1779	Ahldorf	Horb	bef 1825	Bavaria	835928
Fischer, Bibiana & C	8 Dec 1791	Binsdorf	Sulz	Apr 1833	N.-Amer	849630
Fischer, Carl Friedrich & F		Herrenberg	Herr.	Jul 1833	N.-Amer	834624
Fischer, Carolina		Herrenberg	Herr.	bef 1840	N.-Amer	834625
Fischer, Catharina		Bickelsberg	Sulz	Feb 1834	N.-Amer	849644
Fischer, Catharina	7 May 1843	Dornhan	Sulz	May 1864	N.-Amer	849634
Fischer, Catharina	8 Aug 1832	Hildrizhausen	Herr.	May 1865	N.-Amer	834624
Fischer, Christian Friedrich		Neubulach	Calw	1863	N.-Amer	563212
Fischer, Christina	16 Nov 1778	Heselbach	Frd.	Apr 1847	N.-Amer	569270
Fischer, Ernst	31 Mar 1877	Rosenfeld	Sulz	Feb 1890	Switz.	849626
Fischer, Eva & F		Oberiflingen	Frd.	May 1854	N.-Amer	569273
Fischer, Friedrich	1 Mar 1838	Wittershausen	Sulz	Jul 1860	N.-Amer	849644
Fischer, Gottlieb & F		Freudenstadt	Frd.	Mar 1817	Russia	569267
Fischer, Gottlob	13 Aug 1874	Rosenfeld	Sulz	Feb 1890	Switz.	849626
Fischer, Gottlob August	1 Nov 1848	Herrenberg	Herr.	Dec 1868	N.-Amer	834624
Fischer, Hanss Michel		Dornstetten	Frd.	Apr 1752	Pen.N-A	550803
Fischer, Heinrich	10 Oct 1872	Rosenfeld	Sulz	Feb 1890	Switz.	849626
Fischer, Imanuel Christian		Geradstetten	Schd.	Oct 1833	England	801460
Fischer, Jacob Friedrich	22 Aug 1822	Hildrizhausen	Herr.	Jul 1868	N.-Amer	834624
Fischer, Jakob	60 yrs.	Rosenfeld	Sulz	Jul 1844	N.-Amer	849640
Fischer, Jakob & F	24 Dec 1836	Rosenfeld	Sulz	Feb 1890	Switz.	849626

Name		Birth		Emigration			Film
Last	First	Date	Place	O'amt	Appl. Date	Dest.	Number
Fischer, Jakob Friedrich		17 yrs.	Gechingen	Calw	1868	N.-Amer	563212
Fischer, Johann Bernhard & F			Moetzingen	Herr.	Apr 1836	N.-Amer	834624
Fischer, Johann Bernhard & F		12 Aug 1807	Moetzingen	Herr.	Mar 1847	N.-Amer	834626
Fischer, Johann Christian			Muehlheim a.B.	Sulz	Aug 1854	N.-Amer	849639
Fischer, Johann Georg & F		16 Jun 1780	Sigmarswangen	Sulz	Mar 1833	N.-Amer	849644
Fischer, Johann Gottlieb		18 Oct 1811	Freudenstadt	Frd.	Feb 1838	France	569267
Fischer, Johann Jakob		17 Sep 1869	Rosenfeld	Sulz	Jun 1886	N.-Amer	849626
Fischer, Johann Michael		18 May 1848	Hildrizhausen	Herr.	Mar 1867	N.-Amer	834624
Fischer, Johannes			Reichenbach	Frd.	Aug 1865	N.-Amer	577779
Fischer, Johannes		20 May 1847	Wittershausen	Sulz	Jan 1867	N.-Amer	849644
Fischer, Johannes			Rosenfeld	Sulz	Jul 1817	Austria	849640
Fischer, Johannes & F			Moetzingen	Herr.	Apr 1836	N.-Amer	834624
Fischer, Josef Heinrich & F		27 yrs.	Pfalzgrafenweiler	Frd.	Apr 1835	N.-Amer	569268
Fischer, Joseph Heinrich		18 mon.	Pfalzgrafenweiler	Frd.	Apr 1835	N.-Amer	569268
Fischer, Karolina Beata			Freudenstadt	Frd.	Feb 1846	Austria	569271
Fischer, Katharina		19 Jan 1880	Rosenfeld	Sulz	Feb 1890	Switz.	849626
Fischer, Katharina Barb. (wife)		6 May 1838	Rosenfeld	Sulz	Feb 1890	Switz.	849626
Fischer, Ludwig Johannes			Calw	Calw	1852	N.-Amer	563212
Fischer, Lukas & W		10 Jul 1799	Ahldorf	Frd.	Apr 1847	N.-Amer	569270
Fischer, Magdalena		26 yrs.	Pfalzgrafenweiler	Frd.	Apr 1835	N.-Amer	569268
Fischer, Maria Catharina (wife)		3 Mar 1805	Moetzingen	Herr.	Mar 1847	N.-Amer	834626
Fischer, Matthias		1 Jun 1844	Wittershausen	Sulz	Aug 1860	N.-Amer	849644
Fischer, Michael		28 yrs.	Hochdorf	Frd.	Mar 1857	N.-Amer	577776
Fischer, Rosina		29 Apr 1827	Brittheim	Sulz	Oct 1860	N.-Amer	849632
Fischer, Sophie			Rosenfeld	Sulz	May 1860	Prussia	849640
Fischer, Stephan			Binsdorf	Sulz	Mar 1862	Austria	849631
Fischer, Susanna			Rosenfeld	Sulz	Jun 1817	Russia	849640
Fischer, Theophil		4 Nov 1881	Rosenfeld	Sulz	Feb 1890	Switz.	849626
Fischer, Wilhelmine Frieder.		13 Dec 1842	Freudenstadt	Frd.	bef 1862	France	577778
Fitting, Johann Jacob		6 Dec 1827	Oberjettingen	Herr.	Apr 1852	N.-Amer	834627
Flad, Caroline Wilhelmine			Calw	Calw	1860	France	563212
Flad, Christian Sigm.		30 yrs.	Calw	Calw	1869	France	563212
Flad, Ludwig Eberhardt		25 yrs.	Calw	Calw	1854	N.-Amer	563212
Flaig, Andreas (wid.) & F			Muehlheim a.B.	Sulz	Nov 1854	N.-Amer	849639
Flaig, Barbara		30 yrs.	Aach	Frd.	Apr 1817	Russia	569267
Flaig, Barbara		9 yrs.	Aach	Frd.	Apr 1817	Russia	569267
Flaig, Elisabetha		17 Nov 1835	Muehlheim a.B.	Sulz	Nov 1854	N.-Amer	849639
Flaig, Georg & F			Aach	Frd.	Apr 1817	Russia	569267
Flaig, Johann Georg			Breitenberg	Calw	1859	N.-Amer	563212
Flaig, Johann Michael		17 Oct 1841	Muehlheim a.B.	Sulz	Nov 1854	N.-Amer	849639
Flaig, Johannes		12 yrs.	Aach	Frd.	Apr 1817	Russia	569267
Flaig, Johannes			Sulz	Sulz	Oct 1852	N.-Amer	849627
Flaig, Margarete		5 yrs.	Aach	Frd.	Apr 1817	Russia	569267
Flaig, Marie Agatha		32 yrs.	Aach	Frd.	Apr 1817	Russia	569267
Flait, Anna		10 yrs.	Neuneck	Frd.	May 1752	Pen.N-A	550803
Flait, Anna Maria		6 mon.	Neuneck	Frd.	May 1752	Pen.N-A	550803
Flait, Johann & F		32 yrs.	Neuneck	– –	Mar 1752	Pen.N-A	550803
Flait, Margaretha		30 yrs.	Neuneck	Frd.	May 1752	Pen.N-A	550803
Flek, Conrad			Entringen	Herr.	Mar 1829	N.-Amer	834624
Flek, Conrad & F		37 yrs.	Entringen	Herr.	May 1829	Hungary	834624

Flek, Friederike (wife)	33 yrs.	Entringen	Herr.	May 1829	Hungary 834624
Flek, Friedrich & F	37 yrs.	Entringen	Herr.	May 1829	Hungary 834624
Flek, Georg Conrad	3 Sep 1826	Entringen	Herr.	Oct 1862	Russia 834624
Flek, Maria Margaretha (wife)	34 yrs.	Entringen	Herr.	May 1829	Hungary 834624
Flek, Wilhelm Friedrich	20 Jan 1838	Entringen	Herr.	Feb 1870	N.-Amer 834624
Foehr, Johannes		Unterjensingen	Herr.	Mar 1833	France 834624
Foell, Christian	17 Oct 1833	Renfrizhausen	Sulz	bef 1856	N.-Amer 849639
Foell, Christian & F		Renfrizhausen	Sulz	Jan 1854	N.-Amer 849639
Foell, Jakob	21 Sep 1831	Renfrizhausen	Sulz	bef 1856	N.-Amer 849639
Foell, Maria Anna (wife)		Renfrizhausen	Sulz	Jan 1854	N.-Amer 849639
Fortenbacher, Christina Barb.		Oberjettingen	Herr.	Apr 1830	N.-Amer 834624
Fortenbacher, Jacob Fried. & W		Oberjettingen	Herr.	Apr 1836	N.-Amer 834624
Fortenbacher, Sophia Margar.		Oberjettingen	Herr.	Apr 1830	N.-Amer 834624
Frank, Anna Maria	7 yrs.	Schietingen	Nag.	Apr 1854	N.-Amer 838491
Frank, Caroline (wife)		Sulz	Sulz	bef 1855	N.-Amer 849627
Frank, Christian	2 yrs.	Schietingen	Nag.	Apr 1854	N.-Amer 838491
Frank, Johann Jakob	11 yrs.	Schietingen	Nag.	Apr 1854	N.-Amer 838491
Frank, Magdalena	9 yrs.	Schietingen	Nag.	Apr 1854	N.-Amer 838491
Frank, Maria Regina	16 Jul 1878	Renfrizhausen	Sulz	Jul 1895	N.-Amer 849639
Frank, Martin Friedrich & F		Schietingen	Nag.	Apr 1854	N.-Amer 838491
Frank, Philipp & W		Sulz	Sulz	bef 1855	N.-Amer 849627
Frank, Rosina	5 yrs.	Schietingen	Nag.	Apr 1854	N.-Amer 838491
Frantz, Andreas		Dornhan	Sulz	Dec 1850	N.-Amer 849633
Franz, Barbara (wife)		Duerrenmettstetten	Sulz	Mar 1833	N.-Amer 849635
Franz, Christine Dorothea	4 May 1869	Sigmarswangen	Sulz	Jul 1885	N.-Amer 849642
Franz, Ernst	19 Jun 1878	Sigmarswangen	Sulz	Jul 1885	N.-Amer 849642
Franz, Friederike	31 May 1872	Sigmarswangen	Sulz	Jul 1885	N.-Amer 849642
Franz, Friedrich	9 Sep 1815	Freudenstadt	Frd.	Nov 1832	Baden 569267
Franz, Johann Georg	19 yrs.	Ursental	Frd.	May 1850	N.-Amer 569271
Franz, Johann Martin	15 Nov 1835	Wittlensweiler	Frd.	Oct 1854	N.-Amer 569274
Franz, Johannes & F		Fuernsal	Sulz	Feb 1817	Russia 849635
Franz, Johannes & F	4 Apr 1787	Duerrenmettstetten	Sulz	Mar 1833	N.-Amer 849635
Franz, Mathias	6 May 1867	Sigmarswangen	Sulz	Jul 1885	N.-Amer 849642
Franz, Pauline	8 Oct 1873	Sigmarswangen	Sulz	Jul 1885	N.-Amer 849642
Frauz, Alexander Heinrich	11 Jan 1834	Freudenstadt	Frd.	Dec 1848	N.-Amer 569274
Frech, Johannes	12 yrs.	Ostelsheim	Calw	1858	N.-Amer 563212
Frei, Adam	29 Oct 1841	Allmandle	Frd.	Oct 1861	N.-Amer 577778
Frei, Agathe	23 Oct 1842	Goettelfingen	Frd.	May 1855	N.-Amer 569275
Frei, Anna Maria (wife)	5 Aug 1815	Goettelfingen	Frd.	May 1855	N.-Amer 569275
Frei, Catharina	13 Feb 1825	Huzenbach	Frd.	Feb 1847	N.-Amer 569271
Frei, Christian		Goettelfingen	Frd.	Apr 1860	N.-Amer 577777
Frei, Christian & F	7 Apr 1801	Goettelfingen	Frd.	May 1855	N.-Amer 569275
Frei, Christiana	14 Mar 1817	Woernersberg	Frd.	Feb 1847	N.-Amer 569271
Frei, Christina	3 Dec 1793	Hallwangen	Frd.	1846	N.-Amer 569271
Frei, Christina	13 Nov 1823	Woernersberg	Frd.	Feb 1847	N.-Amer 569271
Frei, Friedrich	25 Jun 1828	Hallwangen	Frd.	1846	N.-Amer 569271
Frei, Georg Adam	27 Nov 1852	Goettelfingen	Frd.	May 1855	N.-Amer 569275
Frei, Johann Adam	15 Nov 1831	Hallwangen	Frd.	1846	N.-Amer 569271
Frei, Johann Adam & F	24 Jan 1783	Untermusbach	Frd.	Jan 1847	N.-Amer 569271
Frei, Johann Georg	17 Jul 1846	Goettelfingen	Frd.	May 1855	N.-Amer 569275

Name		Birth		Emigration			Film
Last	First	Date	Place	O'amt	Appl. Date	Dest.	Number
Frei, Karolina			Isingen	Sulz	Sep 1883	Switz.	849626
Frei, Louise		24 Nov 1837	Allmandle	Frd.	Oct 1861	N.-Amer	577778
Frei, Matthaeus		23 Feb 1840	Frutenhof	Frd.	Apr 1856	N.-Amer	569275
Frei, Rosina		5 Nov 1848	Goettelfingen	Frd.	May 1855	N.-Amer	569275
Frei, Rosina		20 Jun 1833	Allmandle	Frd.	Oct 1861	N.-Amer	577778
Freiberger, Luise (wife)			Rohr/Stuttgart	Sulz	Apr 1852	N.-Amer	849633
Freiberger, Wilhelm Friedr.& F			Rohr/Stuttgart	Sulz	Apr 1852	N.-Amer	849633
Freude, Anna Maria			Unterreichenbach	Calw	1862	Baden	563212
Frey, Adam		20 yrs.	Roet	Frd.	Aug 1865	N.-Amer	577779
Frey, Adam & F			Aichhalden	Calw	1853	N.-Amer	563212
Frey, Agatha		18 Oct 1812	Groembach	Frd.	Jun 1854	N.-Amer	569273
Frey, Andreas		4 Jul 1845	Huzenbach	Frd.	Nov 1865	N.-Amer	577779
Frey, Anna		6 Aug 1864	Schwarzenberg	Frd.	Sep 1865	N.-Amer	577779
Frey, Anna (wife)		24 Dec 1832	Schwarzenberg	Frd.	Sep 1865	N.-Amer	577779
Frey, Anna (wife)			Hopfau	Sulz	Jun 1834	N.-Amer	849636
Frey, Anna Barbara		27 Jul 1822	Beuren	Frd.	May 1853	N.-Amer	569272
Frey, Anna Maria			Huzenbach	Frd.	Jan 1847	N.-Amer	569270
Frey, Anna Maria		16 Nov 1843	Durrweiler	Frd.	Apr 1844	N.-Amer	569269
Frey, Anna Maria		22 Jan 1814	Cresbach	Frd.	Apr 1844	N.-Amer	569269
Frey, Anna Maria & F		1 Jan 1823	Dornstetten	Frd.	Aug 1848	N.-Amer	569270
Frey, Anna Maria (wife)			Aistaig	Sulz	Mar 1836	N.-Amer	849628
Frey, Auguste Catharina			Sulz	Sulz	Feb 1854	N.-Amer	849627
Frey, Barbara Magdalena		30 Mar 1815	Hallwangen	Frd.	Sep 1853	N.-Amer	569274
Frey, Benedikt & F		11 Jan 1815	Goettelfingen	Frd.	May 1851	N.-Amer	569271
Frey, Carl		2 yrs.	Freudenstadt	Frd.	Jun 1853	N.-Amer	569272
Frey, Carl & F			Freudenstadt	Frd.	Sep 1848	N.-Amer	569270
Frey, Christian		26 Jul 1835	Heselbach	Frd.	Mar 1853	N.-Amer	569272
Frey, Christian		14 May 1834	Freudenstadt	Frd.	Sep 1853	N.-Amer	569274
Frey, Christian		13 Feb 1849	Gruental	Frd.	Jan 1866	N.-Amer	577780
Frey, Christian & F		29 Jun 1816	Huzenbach	Frd.	Apr 1844	N.-Amer	569269
Frey, Christina		5 Mar 1819	Goettelfingen	Frd.	May 1851	N.-Amer	569271
Frey, Elisabeth			Baiersbronn	Frd.	Jun 1815	Baden	569267
Frey, Elisabetha			Schwarzenberg	Frd.	Mar 1825	Baden	569268
Frey, Franz Carl August		7 Jun 1815	Freudenstadt	Frd.	May 1840	N.-Amer	569267
Frey, Friederika		17 Jan 1838	Groembach	Frd.	Apr 1864	N.-Amer	577779
Frey, Friederike		5 yrs.	Altenstaig	Nag.	Aug 1854	N.-Amer	838491
Frey, Friederike			Pfalzgrafenweiler	Frd.	bef 1830	Russia	569268
Frey, Friedrich		20 Jan 1834	Schoenegruend	Frd.	Mar 1854	N.-Amer	569273
Frey, Friedrich		30 Jan 1840	Heselbach	Frd.	May 1864	N.-Amer	577779
Frey, Friedrich			Freudenstadt	Frd.	Aug 1853	N.-Amer	569274
Frey, Friedrich		13 Apr 1849	Goettelfingen	Frd.	Oct 1866	N.-Amer	577780
Frey, Friedrich & F		6 Nov 1801	Groenbach	Sulz	Jun 1834	N.-Amer	849636
Frey, Georg & F		20 Nov 1805	Schwarzenberg	Frd.	Jan 1866	N.-Amer	577780
Frey, Gottfried & F			Obermusbach	Frd.	Sep 1853	N.-Amer	569272
Frey, Gottlieb		8 Sep 1846	Huzenbach	Frd.	Jan 1866	N.-Amer	577780
Frey, Gottlob		4 Jul 1845	Schwarzenberg	Frd.	Jun 1865	N.-Amer	577779
Frey, Jacob		22 Feb 1807	Wittlensweiler	Frd.	Apr 1833	N.-Amer	569268
Frey, Jacob Bernhadt			Roet	Frd.	Jul 1859	Baden	577776
Frey, Jacob Friedrich		17 yrs.	Altenstaig	Nag.	Aug 1854	N.-Amer	838491
Frey, Jacob Friedrich & F			Altenstaig	Nag.	Aug 1854	N.-Amer	838491

Frey, Jacob Ludwig		Freudenstadt	Frd.	1851	N.-Amer	577778
Frey, Jacob Ludwig	30 yrs.	Baiersbronn	Frd.	Jul 1851	N.-Amer	569271
Frey, Johann Christian		Hallwangen	Frd.	1817	Russia	569269
Frey, Johann Georg		Pfalzgrafenweiler	Frd.	bef 1830	Russia	569268
Frey, Johann Georg & F	1 Dec 1825	Huzenbach	Frd.	Sep 1865	N.-Amer	577779
Frey, Johann Georg & F	8 Sep 1789	Aistaig	Sulz	Mar 1836	N.-Amer	849628
Frey, Johann Martin	19 Jan 1834	Groembach	Frd.	Jun 1854	N.-Amer	569274
Frey, Johann Martin	3 Sep 1847	Renfrizhausen	Sulz	Apr 1865	N.-Amer	849639
Frey, Johann Michael		Schwarzenberg	Frd.	1851	N.-Amer	577778
Frey, Johann Michael		Unterreichenbach	Calw	1852	N.-Amer	563212
Frey, Johanna Rosina	16 Jun 1837	Dornstetten	Frd.	May 1857	N.-Amer	577776
Frey, Johannes	8 yrs.	Altenstaig	Nag.	Aug 1854	N.-Amer	838491
Frey, Johannes	13 Nov 1848	Huzenbach	Frd.	Jan 1866	N.-Amer	577780
Frey, Johannes	9 Aug 1847	Huzenbach	Frd.	Jan 1866	N.-Amer	577780
Frey, Karoline & C		Freudenstadt	Frd.	Jun 1853	N.-Amer	569272
Frey, Katharina (wife)	14 Feb 1829	Gruental	Frd.	Jan 1866	N.-Amer	577780
Frey, Luise Mathilde		Schwarzenberg	Frd.	Apr 1859	France	577776
Frey, Margaretha	15 yrs.	Altenstaig	Nag.	Aug 1854	N.-Amer	838491
Frey, Maria	1 yrs.	Altenstaig	Nag.	Aug 1854	N.-Amer	838491
Frey, Maria		Freudenstadt	Frd.	Mar 1854	N.-Amer	569273
Frey, Maria Friederike		Calw	Calw	Apr 1870	Baden	563212
Frey, Maria Magdalena	10 Apr 1806	Huzenbach	Frd.	Mar 1854	N.-Amer	569273
Frey, Marie Christiane		Freudenstadt	Frd.	Sep 1854	N.-Amer	569274
Frey, Martin	28 Jul 1811	Freudenstadt	Frd.	May 1840	N.-Amer	569267
Frey, Martin & F		Freudenstadt	Frd.	Sep 1848	N.-Amer	569270
Frey, Martin & F		Freudenstadt	Frd.	Apr 1817	Russia	569267
Frey, Michael & F		Schoenegrund	Frd.	Jun 1832	N.-Amer	569268
Frey, Michael Friedrich	3 Dec 1849	Huzenbach	Frd.	Jan 1866	N.-Amer	577780
Frey, Sophia Rosine	16 Jan 1847	Freudenstadt	Frd.	Aug 1848	N.-Amer	569270
Frey, Veronika	23 Feb 1832	Goettelfingen	Frd.	Mar 1854	N.-Amer	569273
Frick, Anna Dorothea	28 Feb 1792	Alpiersbach	Frd.	Apr 1846	N.-Amer	569271
Frick, Anna Maria		Lombach	Frd.	Apr 1865	N.-Amer	577779
Frick, Elisabeta	26 yrs.	Unteriflingen	Frd.	May 1752	Pen.N-A	550803
Frick, Friederike	4 Apr 1847	Lombach	Frd.	Apr 1866	N.-Amer	577780
Frick, Friedrich		Rodt	Frd.	Dec 1866	Switz.	577780
Frick, Jakob	25 Jul 1837	Lombach	Frd.	Aug 1854	N.-Amer	569274
Frick, Jakobine Magdalena	20 Jun 1838	Bergfelden	Sulz	Apr 1883	N.-Amer	849626
Frick, Johann Adam	27 Mar 1847	Aach	Frd.	Apr 1865	N.-Amer	577779
Frick, Johann Georg	28 Oct 1837	Dornhan	Sulz	Feb 1860	N.-Amer	849633
Frick, Johannes	9 Aug 1846	Wittlensweiler	Frd.	Oct 1866	N.-Amer	577780
Frick, Johannes		Dornhan	Sulz	Apr 1839	France	849633
Frick, Magdalena		Rodt	Frd.	Jul 1853	N.-Amer	569272
Friedrich, Carl & son		Calw	Calw	Dec 1873	Saxony	563212
Friedrich, Ludwig	2 Dec 1815	Freudenstadt	Frd.	bef 1856	France	569275
Frik, Adam & F		Pfalzgrafenweiler	Frd.	Feb 1817	Russia	569268
Frik, Catharina		Durrweiler	Frd.	Feb 1847	N.-Amer	569271
Frik, Friedrich & F		Reinerzau	Frd.	bef 1844	Switz.	569269
Frik, Gottlieb & F		Durrweiler	Frd.	Feb 1847	N.-Amer	569271
Frik, Jakob		Dornhan	Sulz	bef 1856	N.-Amer	849633
Frik, Johann & F		Lombach	Frd.	Jul 1817	Russia	569268

Name		Birth		Emigration			Film
Last	First	Date	Place	O'amt	Appl. Date	Dest.	Number
Frik, Johannes		22 Jul 1845	Durrweiler	Frd.	Feb 1847	N.-Amer	569271
Frik, Maria			Reinerzau	Frd.	bef 1844	Switz.	569269
Frisch, Bernhard		8 Feb 1824	Tailfingen	Herr.	Jun 1867	N.-Amer	834624
Fritz, Baptist			Balingen	Bal.	Mar 1860	Switz.	555962
Fritz, Johann Georg Fritz		9 Jan 1860	Baiersbronn	Frd.	Jul 1864	N.-Amer	577779
Fritz, Regina Christina		23 Dec 1808	Schorndorf	Schd.	Aug 1843	Baden	801461
Friz, Johann Baptist			Messstetten	Bal.	bef 1847	Switz.	555963
Froederer, Sophie		25 Jun 1841	Schoenmuenzach	Frd.	bef 1864	Switz.	577779
Frohemueller, Friederike		19 yrs.	Calw	Calw	1869	N.-Amer	563212
Frohmueller, Wilhelm			Calw	Calw	Apr 1873	N.-Amer	563212
Frohnmaier, Anna Barbara & F			Freudenstadt	Frd.	Jun 1817	N.-Amer	569267
Frommer, Adam		15 yrs.	Isingen	Sulz	Sep 1854	N.-Amer	849636
Frommer, Anna		28 Feb 1850	Isingen	Sulz	1866	N.-Amer	849636
Frommer, Anna			Isingen	Sulz	Mar 1854	N.-Amer	849636
Frommer, Anna			Isingen	Sulz	Apr 1850	N.-Amer	849636
Frommer, Anna Katharina (wife)			Isingen	Sulz	Apr 1880	N.-Amer	849626
Frommer, Anna Maria		17 Jun 1848	Isingen	Sulz	1866	N.-Amer	849636
Frommer, Anna Maria (wife)			Isingen	Sulz	Mar 1854	N.-Amer	849636
Frommer, Catharina			Oberjettingen	Herr.	Oct 1846	Baden	834626
Frommer, Catharina (wid.) & F			Isingen	Sulz	Apr 1850	N.-Amer	849636
Frommer, Christoph		27 Oct 1795	Bickelsberg	Sulz	Jun 1846	N.-Amer	849630
Frommer, Daniel			Isingen	Sulz	1853	N.-Amer	849636
Frommer, Gottlieb			Isingen	Sulz	Mar 1854	N.-Amer	849636
Frommer, Jacob			Isingen	Sulz	Jun 1816	Austria	849638
Frommer, Johann Georg		5 Dec 1847	Isingen	Sulz	Mar 1866	N.-Amer	849636
Frommer, Johann Georg		28 Jan 1823	Isingen	Sulz	Mar 1845	N.-Amer	849636
Frommer, Johann Jakob		25 Nov 1842	Isingen	Sulz	1866	N.-Amer	849636
Frommer, Johann Martin		7 Nov 1841	Isingen	Sulz	Mar 1870	Saxony	849636
Frommer, Johann Martin		26 yrs.	Isingen	Sulz	Jan 1857	N.-Amer	849636
Frommer, Johann Martin			Isingen	Sulz	Mar 1854	N.-Amer	849636
Frommer, Johannes		28 May 1860	Isingen	Sulz	Apr 1880	N.-Amer	849626
Frommer, Johannes		17 yrs.	Isingen	Sulz	Sep 1854	N.-Amer	849636
Frommer, Johannes & F			Isingen	Sulz	Apr 1880	N.-Amer	849626
Frommer, Katharina		14 Feb 1859	Isingen	Sulz	Apr 1880	N.-Amer	849626
Frommer, Konrad		4 Feb 1844	Isingen	Sulz	1866	N.-Amer	849636
Frommer, Konrad & F			Isingen	Sulz	Mar 1854	N.-Amer	849636
Frommer, Luise		6 Aug 1857	Isingen	Sulz	1866	N.-Amer	849636
Frommer, Martin		26 Jan 1786	Isingen	Sulz	1801	Austria	849636
Frommer, Rosina			Isingen	Sulz	Apr 1850	N.-Amer	849636
Frommer, Rosine		11 Mar 1862	Isingen	Sulz	Apr 1880	N.-Amer	849626
Frommer, Rosine		16 Jan 1839	Isingen	Sulz	bef 1869	N.-Amer	849636
Frueck, Adam			Freudenstadt	Frd.	1817	Russia	569269
Frueth, Susanna			Dietersweiler	Frd.	Apr 1752	Pen.N-A	550803
Fuchs, Barbara		43 yrs.	Pfalzgrafeneiler	Frd.	1862	N.-Amer	577778
Fuchs, Catharina			Liebenzell	Calw	1866	N.-Amer	563212
Fuchs, Gottlob Friedrich		33 yrs.	Liebenzell	Calw	1866	N.-Amer	563212
Fuchs, Johann Andreas		40 yrs.	Liebenzell	Calw	1866	N.-Amer	563212
Fuerst, Catharina Barbara			Boeffingen	Frd.	Jul 1852	Switz.	569271
Fuerthmueller, Georg Jacob & F			Stammheim	Calw	1852	N.-Amer	563212
Fues, Carl		13 Jul 1849	Freudenstadt	Frd.	Sep 1854	N.-Amer	569274

Fues, Christine & C	29 Jul 1816	Freudenstadt	Frd.	Sep 1854	N.-Amer	569274
Fues, Regina	29 Sep 1820	Freudenstadt	Frd.	Sep 1854	N.-Amer	569274
Fues, Wilhelm Friedrich	7 May 1844	Freudenstadt	Frd.	Sep 1854	N.-Amer	569274
Funk, Barbara & C		Breitenberg	Calw	1860	N.-Amer	563212
Funk, Heinrich	6 Jul 1838	Entringen	Herr.	Jan 1866	N.-Amer	834624
Funk, Johann Friedrich	1 yrs.	Breitenberg	Calw	1860	N.-Amer	563212
Funk, Johann Martin	22 yrs.	Reusten	Herr.	May 1831	N.-Amer	834624
Funk, Maria Magdalena		Reusten	Herr.	May 1830	N.-Amer	834624
Funk, Regina		Reusten	Herr.	Mar 1830	N.-Amer	834624
Funkler, Franz		Friedrichstal	Frd.	Nov 1819	Bavaria	569267
Funkler, Georg		Friedrichstal	Frd.	Nov 1819	Bavaria	569267
Fuoss, Agnesia Catharina		Leidringen	Sulz	Mar 1854	N.-Amer	849637
Fuoss, Anna	7 yrs.	Trichtingen	Sulz	Mar 1833	N.-Amer	849642
Fuoss, Anna (wid.) & F	28 May 1808	Muehlheim a.B.	Sulz	May 1869	N.-Amer	849639
Fuoss, Christina		Trichtingen	Sulz	bef 1863	N.-Amer	849642
Fuoss, Dorothea (wife)		Trichtingen	Sulz	Mar 1833	N.-Amer	849642
Fuoss, Jakob & F	31 Aug 1783	Trichtingen	Sulz	Mar 1833	N.-Amer	849642
Fuoss, Johann Jakob	12 yrs.	Trichtingen	Sulz	Mar 1833	N.-Amer	849642
Fuoss, Johannes		Leidringen	Sulz	bef 1859	N.-Amer	849642
Fuoss, Johannes	4 Nov 1853	Muehlheim a.B.	Sulz	May 1869	N.-Amer	849639
Fuoss, Leonhard	6 Nov 1847	Leidringen	Sulz	Mar 1866	N.-Amer	849637
Fuoss, Ursula		Leidringen	Sulz	Mar 1854	N.-Amer	849637
Furer, Anna		Freudenstadt	Frd.	Mar 1854	N.-Amer	569273
Fuss, Christine		Schoemberg	Frd.	Jun 1854	N.-Amer	569273
Fuss, Gottlieb & F		Schoemberg	Frd.	Jun 1854	N.-Amer	569273
Fuss, Johann Friedrich		Schoemberg	Frd.	Jun 1854	N.-Amer	569273
Fuss, Louise		Schoemberg	Frd.	Jun 1854	N.-Amer	569273
Fuss, Magdalena		Schoemberg	Frd.	Jun 1854	N.-Amer	569273
Gack, Ernst Benedict	18 Jun 1848	Unterjesingen	Herr.	Apr 1868	N.-Amer	834624
Gackenheimer, Agnes Barbara		Gueltlingen	Nag.	Feb 1854	N.-Amer	838491
Gackenheimer, Anton	24 Mar 1850	Gueltlingen	Nag.	Apr 1854	N.-Amer	838491
Gackenheimer, Carl Wilhelm		Calw	Calw	Jun 1876	Holland	563212
Gackenheimer, Christian		Althengstett	Calw	Feb 1870	N.-Amer	563212
Gackenheimer, Christiane & C		Zavelstein	Calw	1853	N.-Amer	563212
Gackenheimer, Christiane Er.	20 yrs.	Liebenzell	Calw	1854	N.-Amer	563212
Gackenheimer, Elisabetha	30 Dec 1842	Gueltlingen	Nag.	Apr 1854	N.-Amer	838491
Gackenheimer, Elisabetha		Gueltlingen	Nag.	Apr 1854	N.-Amer	838491
Gackenheimer, Jakob Gottlieb	1837	Zavelstein	Calw	1854	N.-Amer	563212
Gackenheimer, Johann Georg	5 Mar 1845	Gueltlingen	Nag.	Apr 1854	N.-Amer	838491
Gackenheimer, Johann Georg & F	14 Nov 1813	Gueltlingen	Nag.	Apr 1854	N.-Amer	838491
Gackenheimer, Johann Jakob	13 Feb 1840	Gueltlingen	Nag.	Apr 1854	N.-Amer	838491
Gaehring, Anna Maria (wife)		Aistaig	Sulz	Mar 1833	N.-Amer	849628
Gaehring, Johann Friedrich	1 yrs.	Aistaig	Sulz	Mar 1833	N.-Amer	849628
Gaehring, Johann Jacob & F	17 Sep 1802	Aistaig	Sulz	Mar 1833	N.-Amer	849628
Gaekle, Xaver		Leinstetten	Sulz	1828	Switz.	849638
Gaensle, Dorothea		Walddorf	Nag.	bef 1861	N.-Amer	838493
Gaerter, Martin		Oberdigisheim	Bal.	bef 1847	Switz.	555963
Gaertner, Christian	15 Mar 1838	Pfalzgrafenweiler	Frd.	Mar 1854	N.-Amer	569273
Gaertner, Crescentia & C		Loechgau	Sulz	Nov 1853	N.-Amer	849633
Gaertner, Georg		Dornhan	Sulz	May 1817	N.-Amer	849633

| Name | | Birth | | Emigration | | | Film |
Last	First	Date	Place	O'amt	Appl. Date	Dest.	Number
Gaertner, George & F			Dornhan	Sulz	Jul 1835	France	849633
Gaertner, Johannes		4 Feb 1835	Herzogsweiler	Frd.	Apr 1855	N.-Amer	569275
Gaertner, Kordula		19 yrs.	Dornhan	Sulz	May 1817	N.-Amer	849633
Gaertner, Martin		15 Mar 1838	Pfalzgrafenweiler	Frd.	Mar 1854	N.-Amer	569273
Gaessler, Christiane		2 Aug 1854	Pfalzgrafenweiler	Frd.	Sep 1864	N.-Amer	577779
Gaessler, Gottlob		11 Feb 1862	Pfalzgrafenweiler	Frd.	Sep 1864	N.-Amer	577779
Gaessler, Jakob		3 Dec 1855	Pfalzgrafenweiler	Frd.	Mar 1861	N.-Amer	577778
Gaessler, Johannes & F		17 Jul 1823	Pfalzgrafenweiler	Frd.	Sep 1864	N.-Amer	577779
Gaessler, Magdalena		31 Oct 1853	Pfalzgrafenweiler	Frd.	Mar 1861	N.-Amer	577778
Gaessler, Maria Emerenzia		7 Sep 1858	Pfalzgrafenweiler	Frd.	Sep 1864	N.-Amer	577779
Gaessler, Matthias		25 Mar 1851	Pfalzgrafenweiler	Frd.	Mar 1861	N.-Amer	577778
Gaessler, Paul		28 Jun 1857	Pfalzgrafenweiler	Frd.	Sep 1864	N.-Amer	577779
Gaessler, Sybilla & F		7 Jun 1820	Dietersweiler	Frd.	Mar 1861	N.-Amer	577778
Gaier, Ernst		19 Sep 1847	Dornhan	Sulz	Apr 1867	England	849634
Gaiger, Karl Christian		9 Apr 1838	Freudenstadt	Frd.	Aug 1863	N.-Amer	577778
Gaiser, Agatha		25 Aug 1840	Baiersbronn	Frd.	Jul 1853	N.-Amer	569274
Gaiser, Agnes		26 Dec 1808	Baiersbronn	Frd.	Dec 1853	N.-Amer	569272
Gaiser, Agnes			Baiersbronn	Frd.	Apr 1860	France	577777
Gaiser, Anna Maria		1 Feb 1795	Baiersbronn	Frd.	Mar 1849	N.-Amer	569270
Gaiser, Anna Maria			Hopfau-Nennthausen	Sulz	bef 1812	Pr.-Pol	849625
Gaiser, Bernhard & F			Kniebis	Frd.	Jul 1854	N.-Amer	569274
Gaiser, Bernhard Heinrich		7 Jan 1833	Baiersbronn	Frd.	Aug 1853	N.-Amer	569272
Gaiser, Carl August		5 Aug 1844	Freudenstadt	Frd.	Feb 1863	N.-Amer	577778
Gaiser, Carl Friedrich		23 Jun 1836	Baiersbronn	Frd.	Jul 1853	N.-Amer	569274
Gaiser, Carl Philipp		23 Oct 1847	Baiersbronn	Frd.	May 1856	N.-Amer	569275
Gaiser, Caroline Christine		12 Jul 1848	Baiersbronn	Frd.	Jul 1853	N.-Amer	569274
Gaiser, Caroline Friederike		17 Jan 1850	Baiersbronn	Frd.	May 1856	N.-Amer	569275
Gaiser, Caroline Margarethe		4 Sep 1851	Freudenstadt	Frd.	Sep 1854	N.-Amer	569274
Gaiser, Catharina		27 yrs.	Aach	Frd.	May 1857	N.-Amer	577776
Gaiser, Christian		20 Dec 1834	Baiersbronn	Frd.	Jul 1853	N.-Amer	569274
Gaiser, Christine (wife)		23 yrs.	Kniebis	Frd.	Jul 1854	N.-Amer	569274
Gaiser, Elisabeth		9 May 1837	Baiersbronn	Frd.	Jul 1853	N.-Amer	569274
Gaiser, Elisabetha		20 Jun 1815	Gaertenbuehl	Frd.	Jun 1849	N.-Amer	569270
Gaiser, Elisabetha & C		28 yrs.	Igelsberg	Frd.	Apr 1857	N.-Amer	577776
Gaiser, Eva Magdalena		25 Feb 1840	Baiersbronn	Frd.	Jul 1853	N.-Amer	569274
Gaiser, Eva Maria		26 Jul 1839	Baiersbronn	Frd.	Dec 1853	N.-Amer	569272
Gaiser, Friederika		8 Dec 1836	Baiersbronn	Frd.	bef 1866	France	577780
Gaiser, Friederike		7 Dec 1834	Baiersbronn	Frd.	Dec 1853	N.-Amer	569272
Gaiser, Friedrich		29 yrs.	Aach	Frd.	May 1857	N.-Amer	577776
Gaiser, Gottlob Friedrich		26 Oct 1843	Baiersbronn	Frd.	Jul 1853	N.-Amer	569274
Gaiser, Gustav Adolf		10 Dec 1853	Baiersbronn	Frd.	Jul 1853	N.-Amer	569274
Gaiser, Heinrich Julius		26 Sep 1841	Baiersbronn	Frd.	Jul 1853	N.-Amer	569274
Gaiser, Jacob		18 yrs.	Aach	Frd.	May 1857	N.-Amer	577776
Gaiser, Jacob Friedrich		11 Mar 1844	Mitteltal	Frd.	Apr 1864	N.-Amer	577779
Gaiser, Jakob		9 Sep 1837	Baiersbronn	Frd.	Dec 1853	N.-Amer	569272
Gaiser, Jakob		30 Mar 1845	Baiersbronn	Frd.	Jul 1853	N.-Amer	569274
Gaiser, Johann Adam		24 Mar 1835	Baiersbronn	Frd.	Aug 1852	N.-Amer	569271
Gaiser, Johann Georg		7 Jul 1838	Baiersbronn	Frd.	Jul 1853	N.-Amer	569274
Gaiser, Johann Georg		28 yrs.	Baiersbronn	Frd.	May 1805	Baden	550803
Gaiser, Johann Georg & F		19 Aug 1803	Baiersbronn	Frd.	Dec 1853	N.-Amer	569272

Gaiser, Johann Martin	31 Dec 1834	Freudenstadt	Frd.	Sep 1853	N.-Amer	569274
Gaiser, Johann Matthias	15 Jul 1831	Baiersbronn	Frd.	Apr 1856	N.-Amer	569275
Gaiser, Johannes	8 Mar 1833	Baiersbronn	Frd.	Jul 1853	N.-Amer	569274
Gaiser, Johannes	21 yrs.	Aach	Frd.	May 1857	N.-Amer	577776
Gaiser, Johannes & F	8 Nov 1803	Baiersbronn	Frd.	Jul 1853	N.-Amer	569274
Gaiser, Karl	7 Dec 1842	Baiersbronn	Frd.	Dec 1853	N.-Amer	569272
Gaiser, Katharina	18 Jul 1833	Edelweiler	Frd.	Apr 1853	N.-Amer	569272
Gaiser, Katharina	4 Oct 1811	Baiersbronn	Frd.	Jul 1853	N.-Amer	569274
Gaiser, Katharine Regine	9 Mar 1852	Baiersbronn	Frd.	Jul 1853	N.-Amer	569274
Gaiser, Louise	28 Nov 1844	Baiersbronn	Frd.	Dec 1853	N.-Amer	569272
Gaiser, Magdalena		Schoemberg	Frd.	Jun 1854	N.-Amer	569273
Gaiser, Maria		Salzstetten	Nag.	Jun 1856	N.-Amer	838492
Gaiser, Marie Louise	10 Aug 1845	Baiersbronn	Frd.	Jul 1853	N.-Amer	569274
Gaiser, Martin & F		Aach	Frd.	Sep 1817	Poland	569267
Gaiser, Mathaeus	16 yrs.	Aach	Frd.	May 1857	N.-Amer	577776
Gaiser, Matthaeus	6 Mar 1841	Baiersbronn	Frd.	Dec 1853	N.-Amer	569272
Gaiser, Regina		Baiersbronn	Frd.	Sep 1854	N.-Amer	569274
Gaiser, Regina Magdalena	30 Sep 1847	Baiersbronn	Frd.	Dec 1853	N.-Amer	569272
Gaiser, Rosina	infant	Kniebis	Frd.	Jul 1854	N.-Amer	569274
Gaiser, Rosina Regina & C	1 Nov 1824	Baiersbronn	Frd.	May 1856	N.-Amer	569275
Gaiser, Sophia Paulina	30 May 1849	Baiersbronn	Frd.	Dec 1853	N.-Amer	569272
Gaiser, Sophie & C	30 Mar 1830	Freudenstadt	Frd.	Sep 1854	N.-Amer	569274
Gaiser, Wilhelm David	22 Jan 1838	Baiersbronn	Frd.	Jul 1853	N.-Amer	569274
Gaiser, Wilhelmine Regine	25 Apr 1842	Baiersbronn	Frd.	Jul 1853	N.-Amer	569274
Gaisser, Anna Maria	18 yrs.	Neuneck	Frd.	May 1752	Pen.N-A	550803
Gaisser, Barbara	50 yrs.	Neuneck	Frd.	May 1752	Pen.N-A	550803
Gaisser, Christian		Freudenstadt	Frd.	Aug 1850	N.-Amer	569271
Gaisser, Elisabeth		Freudenstadt	Frd.	Mar 1851	N.-Amer	569271
Gaisser, Friederike		Freudenstadt	Frd.	Aug 1850	N.-Amer	569271
Gaisser, Friedrich		Freudenstadt	Frd.	May 1854	N.-Amer	569273
Gaisser, Friedrich		Freudenstadt	Frd.	Aug 1850	N.-Amer	569271
Gaisser, Gottlieb	20 yrs.	Roet	Frd.	Aug 1865	N.-Amer	577779
Gaisser, Hans Georg & F	51 yrs.	Neuneck	Frd.	May 1752	Pen.N-A	550803
Gaisser, Heinrich		Freudenstadt	Frd.	Aug 1850	N.-Amer	569271
Gaisser, Heinrich & F		Freudenstadt	Frd.	Aug 1850	N.-Amer	569271
Gaisser, Johann		Freudenstadt	Frd.	Aug 1850	N.-Amer	569271
Gaisser, Johann & F		Freudenstadt	Frd.	Mar 1851	N.-Amer	569271
Gaisser, Johanna	18 yrs.	Neuneck	Frd.	May 1752	Pen.N-A	550803
Gaisser, Katharina	20 Apr 1820	Freudenstadt	Frd.	bef 1847	Switz.	569270
Gaisser, Louise		Freudenstadt	Frd.	Aug 1850	N.-Amer	569271
Gaisser, Martin		Glatten	Frd.	1817	Russia	569269
Gaisser, Rosine	11 yrs.	Freudenstadt	Frd.	Mar 1851	N.-Amer	569271
Gaisser, Sophie		Freudenstadt	Frd.	Aug 1850	N.-Amer	569271
Gaisser, Sophie (wife)		Freudenstadt	Frd.	Aug 1850	N.-Amer	569271
Gak, Catharina Valeria		Sulz	Sulz	Apr 1834	N.-Amer	849627
Gak, Georg	7 Aug 1829	Unterjesingen	Herr.	Feb 1865	N.-Amer	834624
Gall, Anna Maria	26 Oct 1824	Edelweiler	Frd.	Jun 1854	N.-Amer	569273
Gall, Johann Georg	2 Nov 1812	Edelweiler	Frd.	Jun 1854	N.-Amer	569273
Galster, Anna Maria		Trichtingen	Sulz	Nov 1853	N.-Amer	849642
Galster, Jakob		Trichtingen	Sulz	Nov 1853	N.-Amer	849642

| Name | | Birth | | Emigration | | | Film |
Last	First	Date	Place	O'amt	Appl. Date	Dest.	Number
Galster, Johann			Trichtingen	Sulz	Nov 1853	N.-Amer	849642
Galster, Johann Jakob		31 Mar 1841	Bickelsberg	Sulz	Mar 1867	N.-Amer	849630
Galster, Martin		28 May 1821	Trichtingen	Sulz	1847	N.-Amer	849642
Galster, Matthias & F			Trichtingen	Sulz	May 1847	N.-Amer	849642
Galster, Michael			Bickelsberg	Sulz	bef 1834	Russia	849625
Gammerdinger, Gottfried		6 Feb 1833	Entringen	Herr.	Sep 1862	France	834624
Gandenbein, Jacob			Freudenstadt	Frd.	1817	Russia	569269
Ganser, Christina		23 yrs.	Voehringen	Sulz	Jul 1854	N.-Amer	849643
Ganser, Elisabeth		19 yrs.	Voehringen	Sulz	Jul 1854	N.-Amer	849643
Ganser, Johannes		28 yrs.	Voehringen	Sulz	Jul 1854	N.-Amer	849643
Gantenbein, Jacob & F			Pfalzgrafenweiler	Frd.	Feb 1817	Russia	569268
Ganter, Wilhelmine Chr. Soph.			Rohrau	Herr.	Feb 1845	Frankf.	834626
Garn, Johann Georg			Unterhaugstett	Calw	1852	N.-Amer	563212
Gastpar, Gustav Adolph			Calw	Calw	1849	N.-Amer	563212
Gauser, Catharina			Simmozheim	Calw	Apr 1870	Erbach	563212
Gauss, (wid.) & F			Freudenstadt	Frd.	Sep 1854	N.-Amer	569274
Gauss, Christian Friedrich		12 Nov 1848	Reusten	Herr.	Dec 1868	N.-Amer	834624
Gauss, Christian Wilhelm		17 Mar 1842	Freudenstadt	Frd.	Sep 1854	N.-Amer	569274
Gauss, Christoph Friedrich & W			Hirsau	Calw	Mar 1847	N.-Amer	563212
Gauss, Elisabetha			Gueltlingen	Nag.	Apr 1854	N.-Amer	838491
Gauss, Ernst Wilhelm		20 Jan 1839	Haiterbach	Nag.	Feb 1854	N.-Amer	838491
Gauss, Eva Maria			Oberkollbach	Calw	1852	N.-Amer	563212
Gauss, Friedrich		20 1847	Oberweiler	Calw	1867	N.-Amer	563212
Gauss, Imanuel Friedrich			Hildrizhausen	Herr.	1835	N.-Amer	834625
Gauss, Jakob		10 Jan 1838	Gaertringen	Herr.	Sep 1863	N.-Amer	834624
Gauss, Johann Gustav		19 Sep 1840	Freudenstadt	Frd.	Sep 1854	N.-Amer	569274
Gauss, Johann Michael		6 Feb 1844	Hildrizhausen	Herr.	Mar 1869	N.-Amer	834624
Gauss, Maria Barbara		27 Mar 1820	Reusten	Herr.	Oct 1865	N.-Amer	834624
Gauss, Stephan			Tailfingen	Herr.	Feb 1846	Austria	834626
Gausser, Christoph Ludwig		17 Apr 1830	Rosenfeld	Sulz	Oct 1850	N.-Amer	849640
Gaussler, Franz Wilhelm			Calw	Calw	May 1870	N.-Amer	563212
Gayer, Anna Margaretha		14 yrs.	Sulz	Nag.	Feb 1854	N.-Amer	838491
Gayer, Eva Catharina			Sulz	Nag.	Feb 1854	N.-Amer	838491
Gayer, Eva Maria		8 yrs.	Sulz	Nag.	Feb 1854	N.-Amer	838491
Gayer, Jakob Friedrich		18 yrs.	Sulz	Nag.	Feb 1854	N.-Amer	838491
Gayer, Johann Georg		10 yrs.	Sulz	Nag.	Feb 1854	N.-Amer	838491
Gayer, Johann Jakob		7 yrs.	Sulz	Nag.	Feb 1854	N.-Amer	838491
Gayer, Johann Michael		16 yrs.	Sulz	Nag.	Feb 1854	N.-Amer	838491
Gayer, Johannes		19 yrs.	Sulz	Nag.	Feb 1854	N.-Amer	838491
Gayer, Johannes & F			Sulz	Nag.	Feb 1854	N.-Amer	838491
Gayer, Maria Agnes		12 yrs.	Sulz	Nag.	Feb 1854	N.-Amer	838491
Gayer, Maria Katharina		22 yrs.	Sulz	Nag.	Feb 1854	N.-Amer	838491
Gayer, Pauline		inf.	Sulz	Nag.	Feb 1854	N.-Amer	838491
Gegenbach, Heinrich			Unterreichenbach	Calw	1876	N.-Amer	563212
Gegenbach, Jacob (wid.) & C			Unterreichenbach	Calw	1858	N.-Amer	563212
Gegenbach, Johann Heinrich		23 May 1847	Unterreichenbach	Calw	1867	N.-Amer	563212
Gegenbach, Johannes			Dennjaecht	Calw	1854	Baden	563212
Gegenbach, Rosine			Liebenzell	Calw	1853	N.-Amer	563212
Gehring, Christian			Ostelsheim	Calw	1868	N.-Amer	563212
Gehring, Jacob			Gechingen	Calw	1852	N.-Amer	563212

Gehring, Jacob Friedrich	1839	Ostelsheim	Calw	1857	N.-Amer	563212
Gehring, Johann Georg	May 1838	Ostelsheim	Calw	1854	N.-Amer	563212
Gehring, Johann Georg		Gechingen	Calw	1853	N.-Amer	563212
Gehring, Johann Michael	6 Feb 1836	Ostelsheim	Calw	1854	N.-Amer	563212
Gehring, Johannes & F		Ostelsheim	Calw	1860	Switz.	563212
Gehring, Michael & F		Gechingen	Calw	1853	N.-Amer	563212
Gehring, Rosine	26 Oct 1834	Ostelsheim	Calw	1854	N.-Amer	563212
Geier, Friedrich	26 yrs.	Liebenzell	Calw	1854	N.-Amer	563212
Geier, Louise & C		Liebenzell	Calw	1854	N.-Amer	563212
Geiger, Andreas	13 Apr 1846	Hochdorf	Frd.	Jan 1866	N.-Amer	577780
Geiger, Anna Christina		Edelweiler	Frd.	Mar 1847	N.-Amer	569271
Geiger, Anna Maria		Bergfelden	Sulz	1858	N.-Amer	849629
Geiger, Anna Maria		Voehringen	Sulz	Apr 1833	N.-Amer	849643
Geiger, Anton		Bergfelden	Sulz	1858	N.-Amer	849629
Geiger, Margaretha		Bergfelden	Sulz	1858	N.-Amer	849629
Geigle, Michael	13 Feb 1817	Moetzingen	Herr.	May 1852	N.-Amer	834627
Geiser, Andreas		Voehringen	Sulz	May 1859	N.-Amer	849643
Geiser, Anna Maria	26 Nov 1873	Waelde	Sulz	Aug 1885	N.-Amer	849644
Geiser, Barbara Friederike	22 May 1840	Bergfelden	Sulz	Sep 1856	N.-Amer	849629
Geiser, Friedrich	25 Sep 1881	Waelde	Sulz	Aug 1885	N.-Amer	849626
Geiser, Johann Georg	1 Jun 1872	Waelde	Sulz	Aug 1885	N.-Amer	849644
Geiser, Johann Georg (wid.)& F	21 Sep 1837	Waelde	Sulz	Aug 1885	N.-Amer	849644
Geisser, Christoph		Freudenstadt	Frd.	Mar 1854	N.-Amer	569273
Geisser, Magdalena		Marschalkenzimmern	Sulz	Oct 1853	N.-Amer	849638
Geisser, Michael		Protenhof	Frd.	1817	Russia	569269
Gengenbach, Catharina	13 Apr 1842	Moetzingen	Herr.	Mar 1847	N.-Amer	834626
Gengenbach, Christine		Dennjaecht	Calw	1861	Baden	563212
Gengenbach, Friederike		Unterreichenbach	Calw	1858	Prussia	563212
Gengenbach, Friedrich		Unterreichenbach	Calw	1852	N.-Amer	563212
Gengenbach, Jacob Friedr. & F	2 Mar 1803	Moetzingen	Herr.	Mar 1847	N.-Amer	834626
Gengenbach, Jacob Friedrich	19 Sep 1833	Moetzingen	Herr.	Mar 1847	N.-Amer	834626
Gengenbach, Johann Friedrich	11 Mar 1821	Oeschelbronn	Herr.	Nov 1867	N.-Amer	834624
Gengenbach, Johann Martin	49 yrs.	Oeschelbronn	Herr.	May 1832	N.-Amer	834624
Gengenbach, Johannes	13 Jul 1807	Bondorf	Herr.	Aug 1866	N.-Amer	834624
Gengenbach, Johannes	26 Jan 1838	Moetzingen	Herr.	Mar 1847	N.-Amer	834626
Gengenbach, Sara (wife)	28 Jun 1802	Moetzingen	Herr.	Mar 1847	N.-Amer	834626
Genkinger, Friederika		Dornstetten	Frd.	Apr 1853	N.-Amer	569272
Genkinger, Jakob		Dornstetten	Frd.	bef 1853	N.-Amer	569272
Genther, Jacob		Zwerenberg	Calw	1860	N.-Amer	563212
Genthner, Friederike & F		Zwerenberg	Calw	1859	N.-Amer	563212
Genthner, Jacob		Sommenhardt	Calw	1858	Baden	563212
Georgi, Hermann		Calw	Calw	Feb 1871	Switz.	563212
Gerber, Agatha		Sulz	Sulz	Jul 1813	Baden	849625
Gerber, Karl Ludwig	14 Apr 1849	Sulz	Sulz	bef 1885	Switz.	849626
Gerber, Ludwig	12 Jan 1786	Sulz	Sulz	May 1846	N.-Amer	849627
Gerlach, Catharina Dorothea	10 Oct 1803	Gueltstein	Herr.	Apr 1839	N.-Amer	834625
Gerlach, Charlotte	27 May 1815	Herrenberg	Herr.	Jan 1851	N.-Amer	834627
Gerlach, Christian Franz	14 Apr 1822	Gueltstein	Herr.	Mar 1847	N.-Amer	834626
Gerlach, Christian Jacob	22 Jun 1836	Hildrizhausen	Herr.	May 1865	N.-Amer	834624
Gerlach, Johann Christian & F		Gueltstein	Herr.	Apr 1835	N.-Amer	834624

Name		Birth		Emigration			Film
Last	First	Date	Place	O'amt	Appl. Date	Dest.	Number
Gerlach, Johann Wilhelm			Herrenberg	Herr.	May 1840	Prussia	834625
Gern, Johann Jacob		31 Mar 1811	Ebingen	Bal.	bef 1847	Switz.	555963
Gerst, Caroline		23 Feb 1837	Grumbach	Schd.	Mar 1844	Austria	801461
Gerst, Christian David		18 May 1831	Grunbach	Schd.	Mar 1844	Austria	801461
Gerst, Christiane Helene		31 Mar 1835	Grunbach	Schd.	Mar 1844	Austria	801461
Gerst, Christina Dorothea			Grunbach	Schd.	Mar 1844	Austria	801461
Gerst, Friedrich		15 Oct 1839	Grumbach	Schd.	Mar 1844	Austria	801461
Gerst, Gottlieb		18 Oct 1842	Grumbach	Schd.	Mar 1844	Austria	801461
Gerst, Helene Sophia		15 May 1806	Grumbach	Schd.	Jul 1844	Austria	801461
Gerst, Johann Wilhelm & F			Grunbach	Schd.	Mar 1844	Austria	801461
Gerst, Wilhelm Thomas		20 Dec 1825	Grunbach	Schd.	Mar 1844	Austria	801461
Gerster, Anna & C		22 Feb 1826	Bergfelden	Sulz	May 1857	N.-Amer	849629
Gerster, Christine		14 Jan 1857	Bergfelden	Sulz	May 1857	N.-Amer	849629
Gerster, Johann Georg		14 Nov 1855	Bergfelden	Sulz	May 1857	N.-Amer	849629
Gerster, Joseph		30 Jul 1851	Bergfelden	Sulz	May 1857	N.-Amer	849629
Gerster, Maria Barbara		1823	Bergfelden	Sulz	Mar 1857	N.-Amer	849629
Gess, Georg Ludwig			Dennjaecht	Calw	Jul 1875	N.-Amer	563212
Gessler, Jakob & W		26 Sep 1841	Dietersweiler	Frd.	Sep 1866	N.-Amer	577780
Gessler, Luise (wife)		28 Apr 1839	Goettelfingen	Frd.	Sep 1866	N.-Amer	577780
Geuser, Andreas		3 Feb 1847	Bergfelden	Sulz	Aug 1854	N.-Amer	849629
Geuser, Anna Maria		25 May 1850	Bergfelden	Sulz	Aug 1854	N.-Amer	849629
Geuser, Johannes		23 Jan 1840	Bergfelden	Sulz	Aug 1854	N.-Amer	849629
Geuser, Johannes & F			Bergfelden	Sulz	Aug 1854	N.-Amer	849629
Geuser, Mattheus		15 Feb 1843	Bergfelden	Sulz	Aug 1858	N.-Amer	849629
Geuss, Marie Luise		24 Apr 1842	Sulz	Sulz	Feb 1865	Nassau	849628
Gfoerer, Anna Maria Juliana			Berneck	Nag.	Apr 1854	N.-Amer	838591
Giebenrath, Caroline Frieder.			Calw	Calw	1869	L-burg	563212
Gierbach, Georg Franz		4 yrs.	Altbulach	Calw	1869	Bavaria	563212
Gierbach, Johann Michael			Zwerenberg	Calw	1862	N.-Amer	563212
Gierbach, Margaretha & C			Altbulach	Calw	1869	Bavaria	563212
Giering, Christian Ludwig & W		19 Dec 1847	Dornstetten	Frd.	Oct 1866	N.-Amer	577780
Giering, Gottlieb		30 yrs.	Dornstetten	Frd.	bef 1864	N.-Amer	577779
Giering, Johann Friedrich		18 Jul 1827	Groembach	Frd.	Dec 1848	N.-Amer	569270
Giering, Johann Jacob			Dornstetten	Frd.	bef 1832	Rhld.	569269
Giering, Johann Jacob		19 Jul 1846	Dornstetten	Frd.	Oct 1866	N.-Amer	577780
Giering, Maria Dorothea (wife)		27 Aug 1837	Dornstetten	Frd.	Oct 1866	N.-Amer	577780
Giering, Matthias		24 Feb 1836	Groembach	Frd.	Mar 1854	N.-Amer	569273
Giering, Rosine Catharine		31 Dec 1848	Dornstetten	Frd.	Oct 1866	N.-Amer	577780
Giesinger, Louise Philipp.			Freudenstadt	Frd.	Sep 1854	N.-Amer	569274
Ginader, Johann Daniel			Gechingen	Calw	1862	N.-Amer	563212
Ginader, Johann Georg			Gechingen	Calw	1862	N.-Amer	563212
Ginader, Johann Georg		1830	Gechingen	Calw	1856	N.-Amer	563212
Ginader, Katharina Magdalena			Gechingen	Calw	1862	N.-Amer	563212
Ginader, Rosine Elisabethe			Gechingen	Calw	1862	N.-Amer	563212
Ginkinger, Michael Gottlob			Tailfingen	Herr.	Apr 1842	Baden	834625
Girrbach, Catharina Barbara			Altbulach	Calw	1869	Bavaria	563212
Glammer, Johann Ludwig		11 Mar 1801	Freudenstadt	Frd.	Jul 1835	France	569267
Glaser, Carl		4 Mar 1838	Ellbach	Frd.	Sep 1854	N.-Amer	569274
Glaser, Caroline Friederike			Altburg	Calw	1864	N.-Amer	563212
Glaser, Friederike		20 Sep 1827	Baiersbronn	Frd.	Mar 1856	N.-Amer	569275

Glaser, Johann Georg		Baiersbronn	Frd.	bef 1833	Berlin	569267
Glaser, Johann Michael	3 Jun 1846	Baiersbronn	Frd.	Nov 1866	N.-Amer	577780
Glaser, Maria Agnes (wife)	20 Jul 1813	Nufringen	Herr.	Mar 1866	N.-Amer	834624
Glaser, Mathaeus & F	26 yrs.	Baiersbronn	Frd.	Jul 1832	N.-Amer	569267
Glaser, Rosina Dorothea	28 Jan 1815	Weissenbach	Frd.	Oct 1848	N.-Amer	569270
Glauner, Barbara		Freudenstadt	Frd.	Oct 1854	N.-Amer	569274
Glauner, Barbara	16 Jun 1819	Freudenstadt	Frd.	Sep 1854	N.-Amer	569274
Glauner, David & F		Freudenstadt	Frd.	Apr 1817	Russia	569267
Glauner, Jakob Ferdinand	20 Oct 1839	Freudenstadt	Frd.	Sep 1853	N.-Amer	569274
Glauner, Margarethe Barbara		Freudenstadt	Frd.	Sep 1854	N.-Amer	569274
Glausser, Johann August	2 Jul 1839	Freudenstadt	Frd.	Aug 1859	N.-Amer	577776
Glueck, Gustav Ludwig	4 Jan 1850	Sulz	Sulz	May 1869	N.-Amer	849628
Glueck, Peter Paul	7 Jun 1871	Bettenhausen	Sulz	May 1891	N.-Amer	849630
Goehring, Anna	10 Jul 1817	Bickelsberg	Sulz	Feb 1845	Paris	849630
Goehring, Anna (wid.) & F	28 Sep 1757	Bergfelden	Sulz	May 1817	Russia	849629
Goehring, Anna Barbara	21 Jun 1862	Leidringen	Sulz	Jun 1869	N.-Amer	849637
Goehring, Anna Barbara	17 Nov 1847	Muehlheim a.B.	Sulz	Mar 1869	N.-Amer	849639
Goehring, Anna Barbara		Muehlheim a.B.	Sulz	bef 1869	N.-Amer	849639
Goehring, Anna Barbara & C	19 Dec 1836	Leidringen	Sulz	Jun 1871	N.-Amer	849637
Goehring, Anna Maria	24 Aug 1868	Bickelsberg	Sulz	May 1871	N.-Amer	849630
Goehring, Anna Maria	30 Jul 1867	Leidringen	Sulz	Jun 1869	N.-Amer	849637
Goehring, Anna Maria	7 Jul 1873	Leidringen	Sulz	Oct 1879	N.-Amer	849641
Goehring, Anna Maria & C	21 Jan 1828	Muehlheim a.B.	Sulz	Mar 1869	N.-Amer	849639
Goehring, Anna Maria (wife)		Bickelsberg	Sulz	Oct 1852	N.-Amer	849630
Goehring, Anna Maria (wife)	4 Jun 1834	Leidringen	Sulz	Jun 1869	N.-Amer	849637
Goehring, Barbara	14 Sep 1817	Bickelsberg	Sulz	Jul 1853	N.-Amer	849630
Goehring, Barbara	21 yrs.	Bickelsberg	Sulz	Oct 1852	N.-Amer	849630
Goehring, Christian	4 Mar 1799	Bergfelden	Sulz	May 1817	Russia	849629
Goehring, Dorothea & C	20 Dec 1833	Leidringen	Sulz	Jun 1869	N.-Amer	849637
Goehring, Jacob	1 Sep 1812	Bickelsberg	Sulz	bef 1847	N.-Amer	849630
Goehring, Jakob	10 May 1851	Bickelsberg	Sulz	Sep 1871	N.-Amer	849630
Goehring, Jakob Hugo	23 Apr 1857	Muehlheim a.B.	Sulz	Mar 1869	N.-Amer	849639
Goehring, Johann & F		Holzhausen	Sulz	Mar 1817	Russia	849635
Goehring, Johann Georg	23 May 1876	Leidringen	Sulz	Nov 1892	N.-Amer	849626
Goehring, Johann Georg	20 Feb 1849	Bickelsberg	Sulz	Apr 1868	N.-Amer	849630
Goehring, Johann Georg	29 Nov 1848	Bickelsberg	Sulz	Dec 1867	N.-Amer	849630
Goehring, Johann Georg	1 Jun 1827	Bickelsberg	Sulz	Jan 1854	N.-Amer	849630
Goehring, Johann Georg	8 May 1839	Leidringen	Sulz	Feb 1859	N.-Amer	849637
Goehring, Johann Georg	18 Apr 1863	Leidringen	Sulz	Jun 1871	N.-Amer	849637
Goehring, Johann Georg	27 Dec 1868	Leidringen	Sulz	Jun 1869	N.-Amer	849637
Goehring, Johann Georg & F		Wittershausen	Sulz	1817	Russia	849625
Goehring, Johann Jacob & F		Bergfelden	Sulz	Apr 1817	Russia	849629
Goehring, Johann Jakob	14 Jul 1867	Leidringen	Sulz	Mar 1884	N.-Amer	849626
Goehring, Johann Jakob & F	25 Apr 1810	Bickelsberg	Sulz	Oct 1852	N.-Amer	849630
Goehring, Johannes		Bergfelden	Sulz	May 1817	Russia	849629
Goehring, Johannes	8 Jan 1832	Dornhan	Sulz	Feb 1857	N.-Amer	849633
Goehring, Josias	16 Sep 1855	Bickelsberg	Sulz	Apr 1872	N.-Amer	849630
Goehring, Josias	24 May 1851	Bickelsberg	Sulz	May 1869	N.-Amer	849630
Goehring, Martin	16 Dec 1865	Leidringen	Sulz	Jun 1869	N.-Amer	849637
Goehring, Martin & F	9 Aug 1837	Leidringen	Sulz	Jun 1869	N.-Amer	849637

Name		Birth		Emigration			Film
Last	First	Date	Place	O'amt	Appl. Date	Dest.	Number
Goehring, Martin Evangelist		20 Jan 1861	Leidringen	Sulz	Jun 1871	N.-Amer	849637
Goehring, Mathaeus		21 Jul 1877	Bickelsberg	Sulz	Mar 1894	N.-Amer	849626
Goehring, Matheus		10 Mar 1812	Bickelsberg	Sulz	Mar 1837	N.-Amer	849630
Goehring, Michael		23 Feb 1808	Nufringen	Herr.	Sep 1840	Austria	834625
Goehringer, Anna Maria			Bickelsberg	Sulz	Jan 1811	Baden	849625
Goekeler, Anna Maria & C			Schnait	Schd.	Apr 1834	N.-Amer	801460
Goekeler, Christiane		12 May 1830	Schnait	Schd.	Apr 1834	N.-Amer	801460
Goering, Jacob & F			Dornhan	Sulz	Mar 1817	Russia	849633
Goessler, August		13 yrs.	Ostelsheim	Calw	1866	N.-Amer	563212
Goessler, Jacob Friedrich		32 yrs.	Ostelsheim	Calw	May 1847	N.-Amer	563212
Goessler, Joseph		24 yrs.	Ostelsheim	Calw	1866	N.-Amer	563212
Goessmann, Wilhelm			Ostelsheim	Calw	Sep 1847	N.-Amer	563212
Goetsche, Jacob Friedrich			Zwerenberg	Calw	1852	N.-Amer	563212
Goettler, Franziska		5 Mar 1808	Altheim	Horb	Oct 1853	N.-Amer	835929
Goettler, Georg Gustav			Calw	Calw	1853	N.-Amer	563212
Goettler, Jakobina & C		20 Jul 1840	Altheim	Horb	Feb 1867	N.-Amer	835929
Goettler, Justin		20 Aug 1866	Altheim	Horb	Feb 1867	N.-Amer	835929
Goettler, Maria		7 May 1846	Altheim	Horb	Feb 1867	N.-Amer	835929
Goettler, Maria		15 Aug 1836	Altheim	Horb	Aug 1866	Hungary	835929
Goetz, Agatha		8 Dec 1846	Goettelfingen	Frd.	Oct 1866	N.-Amer	577780
Goetz, Christian		21 Jan 1850	Goettelfingen	Frd.	Oct 1866	N.-Amer	577780
Goetz, Christian			Ostdorf	Bal.	Apr 1857	Switz.	555962
Goetz, Jacob			Rosenfeld	Sulz	Mar 1840	France	849640
Goetz, Jacob			Laufen	Bal.	Feb 1857	Switz.	555962
Goetz, Jakob Friedrich		19 Apr 1853	Goettelfingen	Frd.	Mar 1854	N.-Amer	569273
Goetz, Regina Friederike & C		25 Dec 1831	Goettelfingen	Frd.	Mar 1854	N.-Amer	569273
Goez, Andreas		19 Mar 1784	Dornhan	Sulz	Nov 1835	France	849633
Goez, Anna Maria			Dornhan	Sulz	Mar 1817	Russia	849633
Goez, Christina		3 Dec 1793	Hallwangen	Frd.	1846	N.-Amer	569271
Goez, Johann Georg		14 Nov 1786	Dornhan	Sulz	Nov 1835	France	849633
Goez, Johann Michael		14 Oct 1775	Dornhan	Sulz	Nov 1835	France	849633
Goezinger, Gottfried			Duerrenmettstetten	Sulz	Sep 1853	N.-Amer	849635
Gommel, Christian			Stammheim	Calw	1863	France	563212
Gossler, Joseph		1841	Ostelsheim	Calw	1857	N.-Amer	563212
Gossweiler, Catharina			Schwarzenberg	Frd.	May 1817	Poland	569268
Gossweiler, Johann			Schwarzenberg	Frd.	May 1817	Poland	569268
Gossweiler, Johannes		55 yrs.	Unterwies	Frd.	Aug 1854	N.-Amer	569274
Gottschalk, Anna Maria			Unterhaugstett	Calw	1852	N.-Amer	563212
Gottschalk, Friedrich & F			Unterhaugstett	Calw	1853	N.-Amer	563212
Gottschalk, Leonhardt & F			Althengstett	Calw	1854	N.-Amer	563212
Gottwein, Johannes		1 Apr 1834	Ellbach	Frd.	Sep 1854	N.-Amer	569274
Goud, Daniel			Montbeilard	– –	Dec 1751	Mas.N-A	550803
Goud, Jean Geo.			Montbeilard	– –	Dec 1751	Mas.N-A	550803
Gouser, Conrad			Voehringen	Sulz	Dec 1855	Baden	849643
Gouser, Margaretha		23 yrs.	Voehringen	Sulz	Jul 1848	N.-Amer	849643
Graeber, Christian Heinrich		20 yrs.	Hechingen	Calw	1867	N.-Amer	563212
Graeber, Georg Jacob		38 yrs.	Ostelsheim	Calw	1867	N.-Amer	563212
Graeber, Georg Simon			Gechingen	Calw	Feb 1872	N.-Amer	563212
Graeber, Gottlieb & F			Althengstett	Calw	1854	N.-Amer	563212
Graeber, Johann Georg		1839	Ostelsheim	Calw	1859	N.-Amer	563212

Graeber, Johann Jakob & F		Gechingen	Calw	1854	N.-Amer	563212
Graf, Adam		Freudenstadt	Frd.	Oct 1853	N.-Amer	569272
Graf, Andreas	18 yrs.	Schoemberg	Frd.	Sep 1854	N.-Amer	569274
Graf, Andreas		Dietersweiler	Frd.	Apr 1804	Pr.-Pol	550803
Graf, Andreas	17 Sep 1841	Fuernsal	Sulz	Aug 1866	N.-Amer	849635
Graf, Anna Maria	7 yrs.	Schoemberg	Frd.	Sep 1854	N.-Amer	569274
Graf, Barbara	13 yrs.	Schoemberg	Frd.	Sep 1854	N.-Amer	569274
Graf, Barbara		Boll	Sulz	bef 1864	Baden	849632
Graf, Carl Ludwig	16 Dec 1831	Freudenstadt	Frd.	Feb 1857	France	577776
Graf, Christiane	27 Jul 1834	Simmonzheim	Calw	1854	N.-Amer	563212
Graf, Christine	14 yrs.	Schoemberg	Frd.	Sep 1854	N.-Amer	569274
Graf, Christine (wife)		Schoemberg	Frd.	Sep 1854	N.-Amer	569274
Graf, Elisabeth	18 Feb 1754	Dietersweiler	Frd.	Apr 1804	Pr.-Pol	550803
Graf, Friederike Barbara	6 Aug 1834	Christophstal	Frd.	bef 1864	Baden	577779
Graf, Georg		Liebenzell	Calw	1853	N.-Amer	563212
Graf, Jacob	20 yrs.	Schoemberg	Frd.	Sep 1854	N.-Amer	569274
Graf, Jakob	12 Sep 1836	Freudenstadt	Frd.	Feb 1854	N.-Amer	569273
Graf, Jakob	28 Oct 1841	Schopfloch	Frd.	Jun 1860	N.-Amer	577777
Graf, Johann	10 Sep 1835	Wittershausen	Sulz	bef 1869	N.-Amer	849644
Graf, Johann Georg	9 Dec 1832	Durrweiler	Frd.	Apr 1853	Baden	569272
Graf, Johann Georg	4 Feb 1873	Salzenweiler	Sulz	May 1890	N.-Amer	849626
Graf, Johannes	3 Dec 1840	Lossburg	Frd.	Mar 1864	Baden	577779
Graf, Johannes	19 yrs.	Boll	Sulz	Apr 1853	N.-Amer	849632
Graf, Johannes	25 Aug 1815	Fuernsal	Sulz	Mar 1837	N.-Amer	849635
Graf, Johannes	25 Apr 1845	Renfrizhausen	Sulz	Sep 1865	N.-Amer	849639
Graf, Katharina		Fuernsal	Sulz	1853	N.-Amer	849635
Graf, Martin & F		Schoemberg	Frd.	Sep 1854	N.-Amer	569274
Graf, Mathias	2 Sep 1862	Waelde	Sulz	Apr 1880	N.-Amer	849626
Graff, Andreas		Dietersweiler	Frd.	Apr 1804	Pr.-Pol	550803
Graff, Elisabeth		Dietersweiler	Frd.	Apr 1804	Pr.-Pol	550803
Grall, Anna Maria & C		Althengstett	Calw	1869	Bavaria	563212
Grall, Johann Gottlieb		Althengstett	Calw	1860	N.-Amer	563212
Grall, Maria Catharina	2 yrs.	Althengstett	Calw	1869	Bavaria	563212
Grammel, Christian Friedr. & F	13 Jul 1833	Freudenstadt	Frd.	May 1865	N.-Amer	577779
Grammel, David Christoph	15 Dec 1834	Freudenstadt	Frd.	Sep 1853	N.-Amer	569274
Grammel, Friederike Lou. (wife)	16 Oct 1840	Freudenstadt	Frd.	May 1865	N.-Amer	577779
Grammel, Georg	19 yrs.	Huzenbach	Frd.	Apr 1860	N.-Amer	577777
Grammel, Georg		Klosterreichenbach	Frd.	Oct 1860	N.-Amer	577777
Grammel, Jakob Friedrich	10 May 1840	Huzenbach	Frd.	Jan 1866	N.-Amer	577780
Grammel, Karl	17 yrs.	Huzenbach	Frd.	Apr 1860	N.-Amer	577777
Grammel, Maria Friederike	7 Dec 1858	Freudenstadt	Frd.	May 1865	N.-Amer	577779
Grammel, Sophie Friederike	28 Oct 1863	Freudenstadt	Frd.	May 1865	N.-Amer	577779
Grammel, Sophie Rosine	19 Feb 1828	Freudenstadt	Frd.	May 1858	Baden	577776
Grammel, Wilhelm Ludwig	19 May 1821	Freudenstadt	Frd.	bef 1847	N.-Amer	569270
Grandt, Johann Michael	34 yrs.	Stammheim	Calw	1867	N.-Amer	563212
Grass, Johannes & F	58 yrs.	Oberurbach	Schd.	Mar 1836	N.-Amer	801460
Grasset, Ernestine Adelheid	30 May 1826	Pfalzgrafenweiler	Frd.	Aug 1860	N.-Amer	577777
Grathwohl, August	28 Aug 1874	Bergfelden	Sulz	Jul 1891	N.-Amer	849626
Grathwohl, Catharina	10 Jun 1836	Bergfelden	Sulz	Dec 1860	N.-Amer	849629
Grathwohl, Johannes	27 Sep 1826	Bergfelden	Sulz	Oct 1860	Denmark	849629

Name		Birth		Emigration			Film
Last	First	Date	Place	O'amt	Appl. Date	Dest.	Number
Grathwohl, Johannes		17 Mar 1850	Sigmarswangen	Sulz	Jan 1869	N.-Amer	849642
Grathwol, Johann Georg		14 Aug 1804	Isingen	Sulz	Dec 1834	Bavaria	849636
Gratz, Johann		20 Apr 1820	Voehringen	Sulz	bef 1869	France	849643
Grau, Christina			Sulz	Sulz	Aug 1812	France	849625
Grau, Christina & C		2 Mar 1778	Sulz	Sulz	May 1817	N.-Amer	849627
Grau, Josef		20 Aug 1811	Strassburg/France	Sulz	May 1817	N.-Amer	849627
Grau, Maria Christina		26 Jan 1814	Strassburg/France	Sulz	May 1817	N.-Amer	849627
Graz, Louise Wilhelmine			Hirsau	Calw	1864	Hesse	563212
Graze, Anna Maria			Simmozheim	Calw	1853	N.-Amer	563212
Graze, Christiane Katharina			Hirsau	Calw	1866	Bavaria	563212
Graze, Marie Magdalena			Simmozheim	Calw	1869	Prussia	563212
Greb, Johannes & F			Liebenzell	Calw	Feb 1848	N.-Amer	563212
Greiner, Christian & F			Sulz	Sulz	Apr 1881	Switz.	849626
Greiner, Christian Ludwig		14 Dec 1830	Sulz	Sulz	bef 1882	Switz.	849628
Greiner, Emilie (wife)			Sulz	Sulz	Apr 1882	N.-Amer	849626
Greiner, Johann Friedrich		15 Sep 1827	Sulz	Sulz	Oct 1864	Baden	849628
Greiner, Julius Friedrich		13 Feb 1866	Sulz	Sulz	Apr 1881	Switz.	849626
Greiner, Marie		1809	Liebenzell	Calw	1854	N.-Amer	563212
Greiss, Charlotte Cathari. & C			Calw	Calw	1858	N.-Amer	563212
Grell, Johann Adolf Ferdinand			Nagold	Nag.	Dec 1853	Wien	838491
Greth, Elisabeth Katharina		1839	Oberkollwangen	Calw	1857	N.-Amer	563212
Greule, Johann Michael		22 yrs.	Breitenberg	Calw	1866	N.-Amer	563212
Greule, Johannes			Breitenberg	Calw	Apr 1873	N.-Amer	563212
Greuss, Jacob Friedrich Jr.			Calw	Calw	May 1847	N.-Amer	563212
Greuss, Jacob Friedrich Sr.			Calw	Calw	May 1847	N.-Amer	563212
Grieb, Catharina		17 Nov 1817	Oberndorf	Herr.	Aug 1867	N.-Amer	834624
Grieshaber, Friedrich			Ursental	Frd.	Feb 1847	N.-Amer	569271
Grieshaber, Friedrich			Muehlheim a.B.	Sulz	bef 1854	N.-Amer	849627
Grieshuber, Maria Magdalena			Muehlheim a.B.	Sulz	Feb 1856	N.-Amer	849639
Grobenheimer, Katharina		1835	Zavelstein	Calw	1854	N.-Amer	563212
Groeber, Caroline			Gechingen	Calw	1853	N.-Amer	563212
Groezinger, Adam			Dornhan	Sulz	Sep 1852	France	849634
Groezinger, Adelheid Esther			Dornhan	Sulz	Sep 1851	Switz.	849634
Groezinger, Andreas		13 May 1842	Fuernsal	Sulz	Sep 1860	N.-Amer	849635
Groezinger, Anna			Baiersbronn	Frd.	Feb 1847	N.-Amer	569271
Groezinger, Anna		28 Jan 1838	Duerrenmettstetten	Sulz	Mar 1860	N.-Amer	849635
Groezinger, Anna Maria		15 May 1843	Dornhan	Sulz	Sep 1864	N.-Amer	849634
Groezinger, Anna Maria		15 Jan 1842	Dornhan	Sulz	Mar 1860	N.-Amer	849633
Groezinger, Barbara		5 yrs.	Sigmarswangen	Sulz	Mar 1836	N.-Amer	849642
Groezinger, Barbara		10 Feb 1845	Dornhan	Sulz	Apr 1861	N.-Amer	849634
Groezinger, Barbara (wife)			Sigmarswangen	Sulz	Mar 1836	N.-Amer	849642
Groezinger, Christian			Boll	Sulz	Jun 1837	N.-Amer	849632
Groezinger, Christian		5 Apr 1852	Dornhan	Sulz	May 1868	N.-Amer	849634
Groezinger, Christina			Boll	Sulz	Jun 1837	N.-Amer	849632
Groezinger, Christina Fried.		13 yrs.	Sigmarswangen	Sulz	Mar 1836	N.-Amer	849642
Groezinger, Emilie		4 May 1857	Dornhan	Sulz	Jun 1860	N.-Amer	849633
Groezinger, Georg		20 yrs.	Fuernsal	Sulz	Oct 1854	N.-Amer	849635
Groezinger, Jakob & F		9 Oct 1808	Sigmarswangen	Sulz	Mar 1836	N.-Amer	849642
Groezinger, Johann Georg		5 Dec 1822	Durrweiler	Frd.	Apr 1847	N.-Amer	569270
Groezinger, Johanna Jac. (wife)		20 Oct 1833	Dornhan	Sulz	Jun 1860	N.-Amer	849633

Groezinger, Johannes	18 mon.	Sigmarswangen	Sulz	Mar 1836	N.-Amer	849642
Groezinger, Johannes		Boll	Sulz	Jun 1837	N.-Amer	849632
Groezinger, Johannes	10 Sep 1815	Dornhan	Sulz	Apr 1862	N.-Amer	849634
Groezinger, Johannes	30 Oct 1840	Dornhan	Sulz	Mar 1860	N.-Amer	849633
Groezinger, Johannes	6 Dec 1832	Loechgau	Sulz	Feb 1854	N.-Amer	849633
Groezinger, Johannes & F	2 Mar 1827	Dornhan	Sulz	Jun 1860	N.-Amer	849633
Groezinger, Rosina	24 May 1838	Dornhan	Sulz	Jun 1860	N.-Amer	849633
Grosshans, Adam Friedrich	19 yrs.	Oberweiler	Calw	1866	N.-Amer	563212
Grosshans, Christian & F		Teinach	Calw	1854	N.-Amer	563212
Grosshans, Christine Dor. Fr.	9 Apr 1812	Klosterreichenbach	Frd.	Dec 1835	Baden	569268
Grosshans, Friederike	18 yrs.	Oberweiler	Calw	1867	N.-Amer	563212
Grosshans, Friedrich	24 yrs.	Oberweiler	Calw	1867	N.-Amer	563212
Grosshans, Johann Georg	1847	Oberweiler	Calw	1867	N.-Amer	563212
Grosshans, Johannes & F		Meistern/Bergorte	Calw	1852	N.-Amer	563212
Grossmann, Johann Georg & F		Aichhalden	Calw	1854	N.-Amer	563212
Grossmann, Johanna Cathar. & C		Hirsau	Calw	1854	Hesse	563212
Grossmann, Johannes & F		Hornberg	Calw	1855	Canada	563212
Grossmann, Margaretha Heinr.		Unterreichenbach	Calw	1863	N.-Amer	563212
Grotz, Johannes		Tieringen	Bal.	bef 1852	Baden	555962
Gruber, Christine & C		Dornhan	Sulz	May 1817	Russia	849633
Gruber, Jacob Friedrich & F		Dornhan	Sulz	May 1817	Russia	849633
Gruber, Magdalena		Dornhan	Sulz	May 1817	Russia	849633
Grubler, Anna	10 May 1840	Bickelsberg	Sulz	Apr 1860	N.-Amer	849644
Gruehler, Johannes & F		Sigmarswangen	Sulz	Oct 1853	N.-Amer	849642
Gruendler, Caroline		Ostelsheim	Calw	1858	Baden	563212
Grueninger, Christian Friedr.	infant	Nagold	Nag.	Jan 1854	N.-Amer	838491
Grueninger, Jacob Friedr. & F		Nagold	Nag.	Jan 1854	N.-Amer	838491
Grueninger, Johanne Margaretha		Nagold	Nag.	Jan 1854	N.-Amer	838491
Gruenwald, Juliane	22 Oct 1844	Schorndorf	Schd.	Nov 1844	Austria	801461
Gruhler, Barbara	11 Dec 1824	Boll	Sulz	bef 1859	N.-Amer	849632
Gruhler, Johann Georg	27 Aug 1853	Boll	Sulz	May 1871	N.-Amer	849632
Grundler, Christiane Gottl.	Mar 1835	Sulz	Sulz	1854	N.-Amer	849628
Grundler, Friedrich Wilhelm		Tuttlingen	Sulz	Sep 1840	Austria	849627
Grundler, Pauline Amalie	5 Jul 1837	Sulz	Sulz	Dec 1863	Baden	849628
Gschwind, Anton		Leinstetten	Sulz	Oct 1816	--	849638
Guckelberger, Jakob	7 Oct 1845	Gruental	Frd.	Nov 1865	N.-Amer	577779
Guckenheimer, Dorothea		Moettlingen	Calw	1869	Saxony	563212
Guehring, Jacob	5 Oct 1833	Muehlheim a.B.	Sulz	Oct 1859	N.-Amer	849639
Guehring, Jakob	1811	Erzingen	Bal.	1845	Switz.	555963
Guehring, Jakob & F	61 yrs.	Bickelsberg	Sulz	Jan 1846	N.-Amer	849640
Guehring, Johannes	17 Apr 1840	Leidringen	Sulz	Jul 1858	N.-Amer	849637
Guehring, Martin	20 Oct 1796	Brittheim	Sulz	bef 1836	Switz.	849632
Guenter, Franziska	18 May 1829	Baiersbronn	Frd.	Apr 1855	N.-Amer	569275
Guenter, Johann Georg & F		Freudenstadt	Frd.	bef 1839	Russia	569267
Guenter, Johannes	18 Dec 1834	Tannenfels	Frd.	Dec 1855	N.-Amer	569275
Guenter, Tobias	12 Aug 1835	Oedenhof	Frd.	Nov 1855	N.-Amer	569275
Guenther, Agathe	26 May 1831	Baiersbronn	Frd.	Apr 1857	N.-Amer	577776
Guenther, Agathe Magdalena	21 Apr 1846	Baiersbronn	Frd.	Mar 1847	N.-Amer	569271
Guenther, Andreas	3 Jun 1857	Boll	Sulz	Feb 1873	N.-Amer	849632
Guenther, Andreas		Fuernsal	Sulz	Feb 1860	N.-Amer	849635

Name		Birth		Emigration			Film
Last	First	Date	Place	O'amt	Appl. Date	Dest.	Number
Guenther, Anna Maria		25 May 1847	Baiersbronn	Frd.	Nov 1853	N.-Amer	569272
Guenther, Anna Maria (wife)			Gruental	Frd.	Mar 1833	N.-Amer	569268
Guenther, Anton			Leinstetten	Sulz	Jul 1854	N.-Amer	849638
Guenther, Barbara		28 Feb 1812	Fuernsal	Sulz	May 1866	N.-Amer	849644
Guenther, Caroline		27 Feb 1847	Baiersbronn	Frd.	May 1864	N.-Amer	577779
Guenther, Christian		1 Oct 1876	Waelde	Sulz	Oct 1892	N.-Amer	849644
Guenther, Christine		15 May 1847	Baiersbronn	Frd.	Nov 1853	N.-Amer	569272
Guenther, Christoph Friedrich			Freudenstadt	Frd.	bef 1826	France	569267
Guenther, David		30 May 1842	Baiersbronn	Frd.	Nov 1853	N.-Amer	569272
Guenther, David		19 Mar 1837	Baiersbronn	Frd.	Mar 1857	N.-Amer	577776
Guenther, David & F		12 Nov 1804	Baiersbronn	Frd.	Nov 1853	N.-Amer	569272
Guenther, Dorothea		20 Apr 1835	Baiersbronn	Frd.	Nov 1853	N.-Amer	569272
Guenther, Elisabeth		13 Apr 1844	Baiersbronn	Frd.	Nov 1853	N.-Amer	569272
Guenther, Elisabeth		12 Feb 1823	Baiersbronn	Frd.	Dec 1853	N.-Amer	569272
Guenther, Elisabetha		23 Feb 1835	Kniebis	Frd.	Apr 1860	France	577777
Guenther, Engelbert		30 Jan 1837	Leinstetten	Sulz	Dec 1859	Hungary	849638
Guenther, Eva Maria			Altburg	Calw	1868	M-burg	563212
Guenther, Eva Maria & C		7 Apr 1841	Baiersbronn	Frd.	May 1864	N.-Amer	577779
Guenther, Franz Jacob		10 Jul 1806	Baiersbronn	Frd.	bef 1843	N.-Amer	569269
Guenther, Franz Joseph			Leinstetten	Sulz	Jun 1854	N.-Amer	849638
Guenther, Franziska		31 Dec 1844	Baiersbronn	Frd.	May 1864	N.-Amer	577779
Guenther, Franziska (wid.)& F			Leinstetten	Sulz	Dec 1859	Hungary	849638
Guenther, Friederike & C			Teinach	Calw	May 1848	Bavaria	563212
Guenther, Genovefa		3 Jan 1842	Leinstetten	Sulz	Dec 1859	Hungary	849638
Guenther, Gottlieb		12 May 1847	Baiersbronn	Frd.	Feb 1865	N.-Amer	577779
Guenther, Jakob		9 Mar 1848	Boll	Sulz	Feb 1864	N.-Amer	849632
Guenther, Johann Georg		14 Apr 1840	Baiersbronn	Frd.	Mar 1865	N.-Amer	577779
Guenther, Johann Georg		13 May 1849	Boll	Sulz	Sep 1867	N.-Amer	849632
Guenther, Johann Georg & F		19 Dec 1793	Oberiflingen	Frd.	Mar 1833	N.-Amer	569268
Guenther, Johanna		27 Aug 1838	Hohreute	Frd.	Apr 1856	N.-Amer	569275
Guenther, Johannes		10 Nov 1839	Baiersbronn	Frd.	Nov 1853	N.-Amer	569272
Guenther, Johannes		1 Dec 1834	Wittershausen	Sulz	bef 1864	N.-Amer	849644
Guenther, Johannes		27 Nov 1865	Boll	Sulz	Aug 1865	N.-Amer	849632
Guenther, Johannes		25 Oct 1840	Leinstetten	Sulz	Jun 1871	Baden	849638
Guenther, Johannes			Leinstetten	Sulz	Jul 1854	N.-Amer	849638
Guenther, Johannes & F		26 yrs.	Schoenmuenzach	Frd.	Jul 1832	N.-Amer	569267
Guenther, Johannes & F		14 Aug 1817	Baiersbronn	Frd.	Jan 1846	N.-Amer	569271
Guenther, Johannes & F			Bettenhausen	Sulz	May 1866	N.-Amer	849630
Guenther, Johannes & F			Leinstetten	Sulz	Jul 1854	N.-Amer	849638
Guenther, Josef Gotthard		9 Jul 1870	Bettenhausen	Sulz	Feb 1887	N.-Amer	849626
Guenther, Joseph			Leinstetten	Sulz	Jul 1854	N.-Amer	849638
Guenther, Katharina & C		27 Aug 1805	Oberiflingen	Frd.	Mar 1833	N.-Amer	569268
Guenther, Ludwig		3 Aug 1820	Baiersbronn	Frd.	Nov 1853	N.-Amer	569272
Guenther, Magdalena			Leinstetten	Sulz	Jul 1854	N.-Amer	849638
Guenther, Maria			Lossburg	Frd.	Mar 1859	Switz.	577776
Guenther, Maria Magdalena		22 Dec 1836	Baiersbronn	Frd.	May 1864	N.-Amer	577779
Guenther, Marina		12 Dec 1863	Bettenhausen	Sulz	May 1866	N.-Amer	849630
Guenther, Martin		23 Aug 1814	Oberiflingen	Frd.	Aug 1860	N.-Amer	577777
Guenther, Mathaeus		20 Nov 1809	Baiersbronn	Frd.	bef 1843	N.-Amer	569269
Guenther, Mathias		6 Jan 1861	Boll	Sulz	Feb 1873	N.-Amer	849632

Guenther, Matthias	?? Sep 1850	Baiersbronn	Frd.	Mar 1865	N.-Amer	577779
Guenther, Michael	15 Jan 1834	Oedenhof	Frd.	Sep 1854	N.-Amer	569274
Guenther, Pauline (wife)		Bettenhausen	Sulz	May 1866	N.-Amer	849630
Guenther, Regina	12 May 1849	Baiersbronn	Frd.	May 1864	N.-Amer	577779
Guenther, Regina	16 Jan 1864	Baiersbronn	Frd.	May 1864	N.-Amer	577779
Guenther, Regine Katharine	6 Jan 1837	Baiersbronn	Frd.	Jul 1855	N.-Amer	569275
Guenther, Rosina		Baiersbronn	Frd.	Jun 1865	N.-Amer	577779
Guenther, Rosina & C	3 Sep 1814	Baiersbronn	Frd.	Mar 1847	N.-Amer	569271
Guenther, Rosine	10 Mar 1809	Oberiflingen	Frd.	Mar 1833	N.-Amer	569268
Guenther, Rudolf		Leinstetten	Sulz	bef 1858	Austria	849638
Guenther, Theresia	9 Oct 1838	Leinstetten	Sulz	Dec 1859	Hungary	849638
Guenther, Theresia (wife)		Leinstetten	Sulz	Jul 1854	N.-Amer	849638
Guenther, Tobias	1 Feb 1837	Baiersbronn	Frd.	Mar 1857	N.-Amer	577776
Guenther, Xaver	11 Oct 1840	Bettenhausen	Sulz	May 1857	N.-Amer	849630
Guenther, Xaver		Leinstetten	Sulz	Jul 1854	N.-Amer	849638
Guenther, Xaver & F		Leinstetten	Sulz	Oct 1839	Hungary	849638
Guenthner, Immanuel Friedrich	30 Jan 1827	Herrenberg	Herr.	Oct 1865	Berlin	834624
Guerthner, Johann Georg	16 Jun 1829	Gaertringen	Herr.	Aug 1865	N.-Amer	834624
Gugel, Johann Georg & F		Stammheim	Calw	1854	N.-Amer	563212
Guhl, Andreas	6 Jan 1869	Dornhan	Sulz	Sep 1884	N.-Amer	849634
Guhl, Andreas	17 Jan 1865	Dornhan	Sulz	Jun 1881	N.-Amer	849626
Guhl, Anna Barbara		Voehringen	Sulz	Sep 1852	N.-Amer	849643
Guhl, Anna Maria	21 May 1875	Muehlheim a.B.	Sulz	May 1883	N.-Amer	849639
Guhl, Barbara	1 Nov 1830	Glatten	Frd.	Oct 1854	S.-Amer	569274
Guhl, Christine Barbara	14 Aug 1876	Muehlheim a.B.	Sulz	May 1883	N.-Amer	849639
Guhl, Eva Margaretha	26 May 1833	Glatten	Frd.	Oct 1854	S.-Amer	569274
Guhl, Friederike		Glatten	Frd.	Jan 1855	N.-Amer	569275
Guhl, Georg & F	4 Oct 1851	Muehlheim a.B.	Sulz	May 1883	N.-Amer	849639
Guhl, Jakob		Aistaig	Sulz	Jan 1867	N.-Amer	849628
Guhl, Johann Jakob	3 Oct 1878	Muehlheim a.B.	Sulz	May 1883	N.-Amer	849639
Guhl, Johannes	24 Aug 1847	Hopfau	Sulz	Apr 1864	N.-Amer	849636
Guhl, Johannes	19 Mar 1872	Dornhan	Sulz	Aug 1886	N.-Amer	849626
Guhl, Johannes & F		Muehlheim a.B.	Sulz	Jul 1847	N.-Amer	849639
Guhl, Katharina	10 Jun 1881	Muehlheim a.B.	Sulz	May 1883	N.-Amer	849639
Guhl, Margaretha (wife)	23 Dec 1853	Muehlheim a.B.	Sulz	May 1883	N.-Amer	849639
Guhl, Mathias	14 Nov 1869	Dornhan	Sulz	Apr 1886	N.-Amer	849626
Gukelberger, Anna Maria	27 Jul 1839	Gruental	Frd.	Jan 1865	N.-Amer	577779
Gukelberger, Georg Friedrich	7 Apr 1841	Freudenstadt	Frd.	Mar 1862	N.-Amer	577778
Gukelberger, Wilhelmine Fr.		Freudenstadt	Frd.	bef 1848	Baden	569270
Gukenrath, Christian	15 yrs.	Calw	Calw	1854	N.-Amer	563212
Gulde, Conrad	23 yrs.	Altingen	Herr.	Jul 1852	N.-Amer	834627
Gulde, Johann Georg	18 Mar 1831	Altingen	Herr.	Sep 1869	N.-Amer	834624
Gulde, Maria Martha & C	50 yrs.	Altingen	Herr.	Jul 1852	N.-Amer	834627
Gulde, Philipp Jacob	22 Sep 1850	Altingen	Herr.	Apr 1869	N.-Amer	834624
Gundel, Anna Maria & F		Liebenzell	Calw	1855	N.-Amer	563212
Gundel, Catharina		Liebenzell	Calw	1869	N.-Amer	563212
Gundel, Elisabetha		Liebenzell	Calw	1861	Switz.	563212
Gundel, Maria Catharina		Liebenzell	Calw	1855	N.-Amer	563212
Gunser, Johannes & W		Tischardt	Sulz	bef 1847	N.-Amer	849633
Gunzenhauser, Anna Maria	16 Jan 1849	Hopfau	Sulz	Feb 1869	N.-Amer	849636

| Name | | Birth | | Emigration | | | Film |
Last	First	Date	Place	O'amt	Appl. Date	Dest.	Number
Gunzenhauser, Christian		23 Jul 1857	Hopfau	Sulz	Aug 1871	N.-Amer	849636
Gunzenhauser, Johannes			Ottenbronn	Calw	1863	N.-Amer	563212
Gunzenhauser, Johannes		27 Oct 1850	Hopfau	Sulz	Feb 1868	N.-Amer	849636
Gutekunst, Anna Maria & C		5 Nov 1848	Goettelfingen	Frd.	Sep 1866	N.-Amer	577780
Gutekunst, Christian		27 Apr 1848	Cresbach	Frd.	Aug 1865	N.-Amer	577779
Gutekunst, Christian			Herzogsweiler	Frd.	Oct 1860	N.-Amer	577777
Gutekunst, Christiane Magd.		25 Jun 1838	Moetzingen	Herr.	Feb 1847	N.-Amer	834626
Gutekunst, Gottfried		8 Feb 1834	Haiterbach	Nag.	Dec 1851	N.-Amer	838491
Gutekunst, Gottlieb		20 yrs.	Holzhausen	Sulz	Jan 1833	N.-Amer	849635
Gutekunst, Jacob		3 Jan 1820	Moetzingen	Herr.	Apr 1847	N.-Amer	834626
Gutekunst, Johann Georg & F		3 Mar 1784	Holzhausen	Sulz	Jan 1833	N.-Amer	849635
Gutekunst, Johann Georg & F			Gueltstein	Herr.	Apr 1835	N.-Amer	834624
Gutekunst, Johann Jakob		15 yrs.	Holzhausen	Sulz	Jan 1833	N.-Amer	849635
Gutekunst, Johanna Gottl. (wife)			Holzhausen	Sulz	Jan 1833	N.-Amer	849635
Gutekunst, Luise		28 Apr 1839	Goettelfingen	Frd.	Sep 1866	N.-Amer	577780
Gutekunst, Michael		18 Aug 1844	Goettelfingen	Frd.	Apr 1860	N.-Amer	577777
Gutekunst, Rebekka		3 Apr 1814	Moetzingen	Herr.	Feb 1847	N.-Amer	834626
Gutman, Maria Gottliebin		14 Jul 1823	Herrenberg	Herr.	Feb 1849	N.-Amer	834627
Gutmann, Johann Andreas		15 May 1848	Affstaett	Herr.	Apr 1867	N.-Amer	834624
Gutmann, Johann Georg		7 Jun 1809	Herrenberg	Herr.	bef 1847	Austria	834626
Gutmann, Johannes		29 Oct 1837	Ostelsheim	Calw	1854	N.-Amer	563212
Gutruh, Johann Friedrich		1822	Calw	Calw	1855	Hamburg	563212
Gutwein, Elisabetha Margar.		18 Feb 1801	Groembach	Frd.	Jun 1854	N.-Amer	569274
Gwinner, Maria			Altenstaig	Nag.	Jul 1862	France	838493
Gwinner, Maria Auguste		5 Jul 1840	Kuppingen	Herr.	May 1865	Bavaria	834624
Haab, (male) & F			Freudenstadt	Frd.	Sep 1854	N.-Amer	569274
Haab, Anna Maria (wife)			Freudenstadt	Frd.	Sep 1854	N.-Amer	569274
Haab, August		28 Aug 1832	Freudenstadt	Frd.	Sep 1854	N.-Amer	569274
Haab, Catharina Sophie		12 Sep 1842	Freudenstadt	Frd.	bef 1866	Switz.	577780
Haab, Friederike Barbara		14 Sep 1838	Freudenstadt	Frd.	Sep 1854	N.-Amer	569274
Haab, Friedrich & F			Freudenstadt	Frd.	Sep 1854	N.-Amer	569274
Haab, Georg Friedrich		23 Sep 1842	Freudenstadt	Frd.	Sep 1854	N.-Amer	569274
Haab, Johann Friedrich		26 Nov 1830	Freudenstadt	Frd.	bef 1854	N.-Amer	569274
Haab, Justine Elisabethe		23 Jun 1838	Freudenstadt	Frd.	Sep 1854	N.-Amer	569274
Haab, Karoline Juliane		9 Feb 1836	Freudenstadt	Frd.	Sep 1854	N.-Amer	569274
Haab, Marie Louise		23 Jul 1842	Freudenstadt	Frd.	Sep 1854	N.-Amer	569274
Haab, Marie Sophie		20 Feb 1849	Freudenstadt	Frd.	Sep 1854	N.-Amer	569274
Haab, Mathilde Luise		14 Oct 1851	Freudenstadt	Frd.	Sep 1854	N.-Amer	569274
Haag, Friedrich			Bickelsberg	Sulz	Jun 1817	Hungary	849625
Haag, Katharina (wid) & F			Sulz	Sulz	May 1817	N.-Amer	849627
Haage, Christina Cathar. (wife)		48 yrs.	Unterjesingen	Herr.	Jan 1829	N.-Amer	834624
Haage, Gottlieb & F		45 yrs.	Unterjesingen	Herr.	Jan 1829	N.-Amer	834624
Haage, Jakob		28 Feb 1846	Bickelsberg	Sulz	Sep 1866	N.-Amer	849630
Haags, Daniel		1 May 1810	Wittershausen	Sulz	May 1817	N.-Amer	849644
Haags, Friedrich		8 Dec 1807	Wittershausen	Sulz	May 1817	N.-Amer	849644
Haags, Jakob		5 Jun 1792	Wittershausen	Sulz	May 1817	N.-Amer	849644
Haags, Johann Georg		23 Mar 1798	Wittershausen	Sulz	May 1817	N.-Amer	849644
Haags, Johannes		14 Apr 1805	Wittershausen	Sulz	May 1817	N.-Amer	849644
Haags, Katharina (wid.) & F		29 May 1764	Wittershausen	Sulz	May 1817	N.-Amer	849644
Haags, Maria Katharina & C		25 Jun 1787	Wittershausen	Sulz	May 1817	N.-Amer	849644

Name	Date	Place		Emigr.	Dest.	ID
Haan, Adam		Glatten	Frd.	1817	Russia	569269
Haan, Jacob		Glatten	Frd.	1817	Russia	569269
Haar, Anna Maria	28 Mar 1848	Moetzingen	Herr.	May 1852	N.-Amer	834627
Haar, Auguste Barbara & C	9 Aug 1840	Pfaeffingen	Herr.	Oct 1866	Hesse	834624
Haar, Barbara	10 Nov 1842	Moetzingen	Herr.	May 1852	N.-Amer	834627
Haar, Barbara (wife)		Pfaeffingen	Herr.	Apr 1831	N.-Amer	834624
Haar, Christian & W		Pfaeffingen	Herr.	Apr 1831	N.-Amer	834624
Haar, Constantin & W	15 Aug 1835	Poltringen	Herr.	May 1866	N.-Amer	834624
Haar, Dorothea Mathilde (wife)	14 Feb 1836	Poltringen	Herr.	May 1866	N.-Amer	834624
Haar, Johann Georg & W		Pfaeffingen	Herr.	Apr 1831	N.-Amer	834624
Haar, Juliane	8 Nov 1865	Pfaeffingen	Herr.	Oct 1866	Hesse	834624
Haar, Katharina & C	21 Apr 1816	Moetzingen	Herr.	May 1852	N.-Amer	834627
Haarer, Anna Maria (wife)	26 Jun 1840	Kuppingen	Herr.	May 1867	N.-Amer	834624
Haarer, Johann Georg & F	29 Apr 1840	Kuppingen	Herr.	May 1867	N.-Amer	834624
Haarer, Josef Friedrich	9 Jun 1865	Kuppingen	Herr.	May 1867	N.-Amer	834624
Haarer, Justina Catharina	27 May 1866	Kuppingen	Herr.	May 1867	N.-Amer	834624
Haarer, Simon Friedrich	17 Jan 1851	Kuppingen	Herr.	May 1867	N.-Amer	834624
Haas, Adam & F		Aach	Frd.	May 1817	Poland	569267
Haas, Andreas	7 Apr 1840	Glatten	Frd.	Oct 1858	N.-Amer	577776
Haas, Andreas	17 Mar 1882	Dornhan	Sulz	Sep 1896	N.-Amer	849634
Haas, Anna	28 May 1841	Erkenbrechtsweiler	Sulz	May 1864	France	849643
Haas, Anna Barbara	29 May 1851	Leidringen	Sulz	Mar 1869	N.-Amer	849637
Haas, Anna Maria		Neuneck	Frd.	bef 1843	N.-Amer	569269
Haas, Anna Maria	26 Sep 1847	Leidringen	Sulz	Mar 1870	N.-Amer	849637
Haas, Anna Maria & C	16 Sep 1809	Glatten	Frd.	Oct 1854	S.-Amer	569274
Haas, Barbara & F	2 Aug 1827	Boll	Sulz	Oct 1867	N.-Amer	849632
Haas, Carl Jakob	30 Dec 1833	Freudenstadt	Frd.	Sep 1854	N.-Amer	569274
Haas, Christian		Freudenstadt	Frd.	Mar 1854	N.-Amer	569273
Haas, Christian	8 Feb 1839	Oberiflingen	Frd.	Feb 1854	N.-Amer	569273
Haas, Christian Gustav Albert	22 Jan 1831	Sulz	Sulz	bef 1876	N.-Amer	849628
Haas, Christina	2 Aug 1860	Boll	Sulz	Oct 1867	N.-Amer	849632
Haas, Christina	2 Feb 1861	Dornhan	Sulz	Mar 1870	N.-Amer	849634
Haas, Christoph & F		Freudenstadt	Frd.	Sep 1854	N.-Amer	569274
Haas, Elisabetha	24 Jan 1790	Oberiflingen	Frd.	Mar 1833	N.-Amer	569268
Haas, Elisabetha Rosina	26 Sep 1820	Sulz	Sulz	May 1832	N.-Amer	849627
Haas, Friedrich	17 Apr 1827	Oberiflingen	Frd.	Mar 1847	N.-Amer	569270
Haas, Friedrich	5 Jan 1834	Freudenstadt	Frd.	Feb 1854	N.-Amer	569273
Haas, Friedrich	13 May 1846	Glatten	Frd.	Oct 1854	S.-Amer	569274
Haas, Friedrich		Boll	Sulz	1826	France	849632
Haas, Friedrich	30 Apr 1846	Dornhan	Sulz	Mar 1866	N.-Amer	849634
Haas, Friedrich		Dornhan	Sulz	Aug 1853	N.-Amer	849633
Haas, Gottlieb & F		Hopfau/Nennthausen	Sulz	Jan 1817	Russia	849636
Haas, Jacob		Dornhan	Sulz	Sep 1853	N.-Amer	849633
Haas, Jacob & F		Aach	Frd.	Sep 1817	Poland	569267
Haas, Jacob Friedrich	14 Jul 1835	Aach	Frd.	Apr 1846	N.-Amer	569271
Haas, Jakob Friedrich	6 Jun 1829	Sulz	Sulz	May 1832	N.-Amer	849627
Haas, Johann Christoph	4 Jul 1827	Sulz	Sulz	May 1832	N.-Amer	849627
Haas, Johann Friedrich	28 Jan 1838	Freudenstadt	Frd.	Feb 1859	France	577776
Haas, Johann Georg	11 Nov 1851	Freudenstadt	Frd.	Sep 1854	N.-Amer	569274
Haas, Johann Georg	13 Mar 1825	Sulz	Sulz	May 1832	N.-Amer	849627

Name		Birth		Emigration			Film
Last	First	Date	Place	O'amt	Appl. Date	Dest.	Number
Haas, Johann Georg			Boll	Sulz	bef 1857	N.-Amer	849632
Haas, Johann Georg		5 Mar 1825	Holzhausen	Sulz	May 1832	N.-Amer	849635
Haas, Johann Georg (wid.) & F		14 Mar 1784	Holzhausen	Sulz	May 1832	N.-Amer	849635
Haas, Johann Jacob			Sulz	Sulz	1833	N.-Amer	849627
Haas, Johann Jakob		3 Sep 1823	Sulz	Sulz	May 1832	N.-Amer	849627
Haas, Johann Jakob		16 Mar 1829	Holzhausen	Sulz	May 1832	N.-Amer	849635
Haas, Johann Jakob & F		29 Nov 1793	Sulz	Sulz	May 1832	N.-Amer	849627
Haas, Johann Wilhelm		Dec 1810	Freudenstadt	Frd.	Aug 1835	Baden	569267
Haas, Johanna Christiana		24 Dec 1834	Freudenstadt	Frd.	Sep 1854	N.-Amer	569274
Haas, Johanna Ernestine			Schoemberg	Frd.	Jun 1821	Baden	569268
Haas, Johannes			Oberiflingen	Sulz	bef 1844	N.-Amer	849625
Haas, Johannes		17 Dec 1835	Glatten	Frd.	Oct 1854	S.-Amer	569274
Haas, Johannes		1 Sep 1820	Holzhausen	Sulz	May 1832	N.-Amer	849635
Haas, Johannes		17 Jun 1863	Leidringen	Sulz	Oct 1879	N.-Amer	849637
Haas, Jokob Friedrich		18 Nov 1836	Freudenstadt	Frd.	Sep 1854	N.-Amer	569274
Haas, Katharina		13 May 1846	Glatten	Frd.	Oct 1854	S.-Amer	569274
Haas, Magdalena		27 Jun 1830	Glatten	Frd.	Oct 1854	S.-Amer	569274
Haas, Maria Barbara		26 Oct 1841	Freudenstadt	Frd.	Sep 1854	N.-Amer	569274
Haas, Maria Magdalena (wife)			Freudenstadt	Frd.	Sep 1854	N.-Amer	569274
Haas, Martin		25 Nov 1835	Oberiflingen	Frd.	Feb 1854	N.-Amer	569273
Haas, Martin		19 Nov 1815	Oberiflingen	Frd.	Oct 1845	Baden	569269
Haas, Mathias & F			Hopfau	Sulz	Feb 1817	Russia	849636
Haas, Matthaeus		4 Aug 1839	Glatten	Frd.	Oct 1854	S.-Amer	569274
Haas, Michael			Boll	Sulz	Dec 1828	France	849632
Haas, Rosina & C		19 Mar 1839	Dornhan	Sulz	Mar 1870	N.-Amer	849634
Haas, Rosina Catharina (wife)		12 Aug 1785	Sulz	Sulz	May 1832	N.-Amer	849627
Haas, Rosina Maria		20 May 1865	Dornhan	Sulz	Mar 1870	N.-Amer	849634
Haas, Wilhelmine		9 Feb 1816	Freudenstadt	Frd.	bef 1860	N.-Amer	577777
Haas, Wilhelmine Friederike		11 Dec 1844	Freudenstadt	Frd.	Sep 1854	N.-Amer	569274
Haasis, Ludwig		11 Feb 1813	Duerrwangen	Bal.	bef 1846	Switz.	555963
Haberer, Jakob Friedrich		4 Jun 1848	Bergfelden	Sulz	Jul 1868	N.-Amer	849629
Haberer, Johannes		26 Apr 1847	Bergfelden	Sulz	Apr 1860	N.-Amer	849629
Habisreitinger, Johann David		30 Mar 1844	Freudenstadt	Frd.	Jun 1864	N.-Amer	577779
Habisreitinger, Johannes			Freudenstadt	Frd.	bef 1845	N.-Amer	569269
Habisreitter, Jacob Friedr.		29 Jul 1836	Freudenstadt	Frd.	bef 1856	N.-Amer	569275
Habisrittinger, Christian		15 Nov 1839	Freudenstadt	Frd.	bef 1860	N.-Amer	577777
Habisrittinger, Friederika C.		17 Nov 1845	Freudenstadt	Frd.	Jan 1861	N.-Amer	577778
Habisrittinger, Jakob Friedr.		16 Mar 1842	Freudenstadt	Frd.	Jan 1861	N.-Amer	577778
Habisrittinger, Johann Michael			Freudenstadt	Frd.	Oct 1820	France	569267
Habisrittinger, Karl David			Freudenstadt	Frd.	Feb 1855	N.-Amer	569275
Habisrittninger, August		14 yrs.	Freudenstadt	Frd.	Jul 1853	N.-Amer	569272
Habisrittninger, Caroline		18 yrs.	Freudenstadt	Frd.	Jul 1853	N.-Amer	569272
Habisrittninger, Emilia		4 yrs.	Freudenstadt	Frd.	Jul 1853	N.-Amer	569272
Habisrittninger, Friederike		22 yrs.	Freudenstadt	Frd.	Jul 1853	N.-Amer	569272
Habisrittninger, Johann Georg			Freudenstadt	Frd.	Jul 1853	N.-Amer	569272
Habisrittninger, Louise		11 yrs.	Freudenstadt	Frd.	Jul 1853	N.-Amer	569272
Habisrittninger, Maria		19 yrs.	Freudenstadt	Frd.	Jul 1853	N.-Amer	569272
Habisrittninger, Wilhelm		21 yrs.	Freudenstadt	Frd.	Jul 1853	N.-Amer	569272
Habmann, Jacob Friedrich		1834	Gechingen	Calw	1854	N.-Amer	563212
Habmann, Johann Georg			Gechingen	Calw	1856	Baden	563212

Hack, Johann Conrad		Gaertringen	Herr.	bef 1851	Switz.	834627
Hack, Johann Jacob		Gaertringen	Herr.	Jun 1846	Switz.	834626
Hack, Johann Jakob	2 Feb 1864	Sigmarswangen	Sulz	Mar 1885	N.-Amer	849642
Hack, Johannes	1812	Herrenberg	Herr.	bef 1847	Switz.	834626
Hack, Maria Barbara		Gaertringen	Herr.	Mar 1844	Switz.	834626
Hackenjos, (widow) & F		Freudenstadt	Frd.	Sep 1854	N.-Amer	569274
Hackenjos, Christian Michael	20 Apr 1837	Freudenstadt	Frd.	Sep 1854	N.-Amer	569274
Hackenjos, Georg Friedrich	23 Nov 1845	Freudenstadt	Frd.	Sep 1854	N.-Amer	569274
Hackenjos, Louise	6 Dec 1846	Freudenstadt	Frd.	Sep 1854	N.-Amer	569274
Hackenjos, Mathias Friedrich	5 Jun 1848	Freudenstadt	Frd.	Sep 1854	N.-Amer	569274
Hackenjos, Sophie Marie	3 Feb 1840	Freudenstadt	Frd.	Sep 1854	N.-Amer	569274
Haeberle, Adam	1823	Simmozheim	Calw	1854	Wien	563212
Haehnle, Michael	30 Nov 1834	Oeschelbronn	Herr.	Jul 1869	N.-Amer	834624
Haemmerle, Anna	5 Nov 1786	Trichtingen	Sulz	Apr 1817	Russia	849642
Haemmerle, Christian	9 Jul 1842	Leidringen	Sulz	Apr 1860	N.-Amer	849637
Haemmerle, Christiane Dor.		Gueltstein	Herr.	Apr 1831	N.-Amer	834624
Haemmerle, Jacob Friedrich	15 Jun 1834	Leidringen	Sulz	Aug 1852	N.-Amer	849637
Haemmerle, Johann Jacob	3 Mar 1834	Gaertringen	Herr.	May 1862	N.-Amer	834624
Haemmerle, Maria (wid.) & F		Leidringen	Sulz	Jun 1854	N.-Amer	849637
Haemmerle, Michael	30 Apr 1840	Leidringen	Sulz	Jul 1858	N.-Amer	849637
Haendler, Johann Baptist	15 Aug 1821	Zwieselberg	Frd.	bef 1863	France	577778
Haendler, Johanna		Zwieselberg	Frd.	Dec 1812	Baden	569268
Haendler, Kunigunde		Zwieselberg	Frd.	May 1866	France	577780
Haenssler, Jakob	7 Jul 1836	Stutztal	Frd.	Mar 1854	N.-Amer	569273
Haerter, Anna (wife)	26 Aug 1819	Rotenzimmern	Sulz	May 1846	N.-Amer	849642
Haerter, Christian	18 Aug 1850	Rotenzimmern	Sulz	May 1866	N.-Amer	849642
Haerter, Christina	3 May 1843	Rotenzimmern	Sulz	May 1866	N.-Amer	849642
Haerter, Gottlieb	10 Oct 1852	Rotenzimmern	Sulz	May 1866	N.-Amer	849642
Haerter, Jacob	13 Jan 1854	Rotenzimmern	Sulz	May 1866	N.-Amer	849642
Haerter, Johann & F		Leidringen	Sulz	Jun 1817	Russia	849640
Haerter, Johann Georg	19 Aug 1841	Rotenzimmern	Sulz	Feb 1859	N.-Amer	849642
Haerter, Johann Jakob & F	11 Oct 1811	Rotenzimmern	Sulz	May 1866	N.-Amer	849642
Haerter, Leonhard	5 Jan 1860	Rotenzimmern	Sulz	May 1866	N.-Amer	849642
Haerter, Martin	4 Nov 1837	Rotenzimmern	Sulz	Sep 1857	N.-Amer	849642
Haertner, (widow) & F		Freudenstadt	Frd.	Sep 1854	N.-Amer	569274
Haertner, Anna Maria (wife)		Freudenstadt	Frd.	Sep 1854	N.-Amer	569274
Haertner, August	10 Jun 1850	Freudenstadt	Frd.	Sep 1854	N.-Amer	569274
Haertner, Carl		Freudenstadt	Frd.	May 1854	N.-Amer	569273
Haertner, Carl Friedrich	12 Sep 1837	Freudenstadt	Frd.	Sep 1854	N.-Amer	569274
Haertner, Christian Friedrich	6 Jan 1834	Freudenstadt	Frd.	Sep 1854	N.-Amer	569274
Haertner, Christian Wilhelm	3 Mar 1842	Freudenstadt	Frd.	Sep 1854	N.-Amer	569274
Haertner, Christoph & F		Freudenstadt	Frd.	Sep 1854	N.-Amer	569274
Haertner, Christoph Friedrich	31 May 1845	Freudenstadt	Frd.	Sep 1854	N.-Amer	569274
Haertner, Johann Georg	25 Aug 1831	Freudenstadt	Frd.	Sep 1854	N.-Amer	569274
Haertner, Marie Sophie	5 May 1844	Freudenstadt	Frd.	Sep 1854	N.-Amer	569274
Haertner, Sophie Friederike	22 Apr 1843	Freudenstadt	Frd.	Sep 1854	N.-Amer	569274
Haertner, Wilhelm	24 Apr 1838	Freudenstadt	Frd.	Sep 1854	N.-Amer	569274
Haertner, Wilhelmine & C		Freudenstadt	Frd.	May 1854	N.-Amer	569273
Haertter, Catharina		Sulz	Nag.	Feb 1854	N.-Amer	838491
Haetinger, Barbara		Kayh	Herr.	bef 1846	Switz.	834626

Name		Birth		Emigration			Film
Last	First	Date	Place	O'amt	Appl. Date	Dest.	Number
Haetinger, Simon		21 Jan 1847	Unterjettingen	Herr.	May 1867	N.-Amer	834624
Haeusermann, Jacob			Dennjaecht	Calw	1853	N.-Amer	563212
Haeusler, Gottlob		17 Nov 1835	Nagold	Nag.	Mar 1854	N.-Amer	838491
Haeusler, Rosina		31 Jan 1816	Pfalzgrafenweiler	Frd.	bef 1844	N.-Amer	569269
Haeussler, Christian Friedr.		19 Mar 1824	Kayh	Herr.	Mar 1868	N.-Amer	834624
Haffner, Magdalena		25 Sep 1826	Kuppingen	Herr.	Jul 1866	N.-Amer	834624
Hafner, Anna Maria			Sulz	Sulz	May 1856	N.-Amer	849627
Hafner, Daniel & F			Holzhausen	Sulz	Feb 1855	N.-Amer	849635
Hafner, Johann Daniel		18 Aug 1872	Holzhausen	Sulz	Mar 1881	N.-Amer	849626
Hafner, Johann Jakob		27 Dec 1867	Holzhausen	Sulz	Mar 1881	N.-Amer	849635
Hafner, Johann Jakob		27 Dec 1869	Holzhausen	Sulz	Mar 1881	N.-Amer	849626
Hafner, Joseph Daniel		18 Aug 1872	Holzhausen	Sulz	Mar 1881	N.-Amer	849635
Hafner, Ludwig		18 yrs.	Holzhausen	Sulz	Aug 1854	N.-Amer	849635
Hag, Anna Maria		3 Jan 1837	Unterjettingen	Herr.	Apr 1847	N.-Amer	834626
Hag, Johann Conrad & F		9 May 1808	Unterjettingen	Herr.	Apr 1847	N.-Amer	834626
Hag, Johann Georg		18 Aug 1840	Unterjettingen	Herr.	Apr 1847	N.-Amer	834626
Hag, Johann Heinrich			Pfalzgrafenweiler	Frd.	Apr 1752	Pen.N-A	550803
Hag, Margaretha (wife)		30 Aug 1811	Unterjettingen	Herr.	Apr 1847	N.-Amer	834626
Hagenloch, Catharina			Klosterreichenbach	Frd.	Sep 1830	Russia	569268
Hagenlocher, Ulrich Carl		23 Jul 1838	Pfaeffingen	Herr.	Mar 1865	N.-Amer	834624
Hahn, Anna Catharina		30 May 1841	Gueltstein	Herr.	Apr 1869	N.-Amer	834624
Hahn, Carolina Magdalena			Hildrizhausen	Herr.	bef 1863	N.-Amer	834624
Hahn, Johann David			Gueltstein	Herr.	Jun 1834	Austria	834624
Hahn, Johann Georg & F			Gueltstein	Herr.	Jun 1833	Rus-Pol	834624
Hahn, Johann Gottlieb		4 Aug 1846	Gueltstein	Herr.	Nov 1867	N.-Amer	834624
Hahn, Johann Jacob		11 Jun 1843	Gueltstein	Herr.	Apr 1869	N.-Amer	834624
Hahn, Johannes		9 Jun 1838	Gueltstein	Herr.	Apr 1869	N.-Amer	834624
Hahrer, Eva Catharina (wife)			Oeschelbronn	Herr.	May 1832	N.-Amer	834624
Hahrer, Johann Jacob & F			Oeschelbronn	Herr.	May 1832	N.-Amer	834624
Haiber, Anna		16 Sep 1846	Brittheim	Sulz	Apr 1867	N.-Amer	849632
Haiber, Anna Maria		4 Nov 1835	Brittheim	Sulz	Oct 1859	N.-Amer	849632
Haiber, Friedrich		3 Jul 1864	Brittheim	Sulz	Apr 1866	N.-Amer	849632
Haiber, Rudolph		12 Dec 1862	Brittheim	Sulz	Apr 1866	N.-Amer	849632
Haiber, Ursula & C		13 Oct 1842	Brittheim	Sulz	Apr 1866	N.-Amer	849632
Haibt, Afra		14 Apr 1846	Leinstetten	Sulz	Jul 1867	Prussia	849638
Haibt, Amalia			Leinstetten	Sulz	Jun 1854	N.-Amer	849638
Haibt, Anton			Bettenhausen	Sulz	Aug 1849	Hohenz.	849630
Haibt, Apolonia			Leinstetten	Sulz	Jun 1854	N.-Amer	849638
Haibt, Christina		26 Dec 1802	Bettenhausen	Sulz	Sep 1835	Hohenz.	849630
Haibt, Elisabeth			Leinstetten	Sulz	Jun 1854	N.-Amer	849638
Haibt, Franz Xaver		15 Nov 1846	Leinstetten	Sulz	Sep 1866	N.-Amer	849638
Haibt, Franziska			Leinstetten	Sulz	Jun 1854	N.-Amer	849638
Haibt, Josef		24 Aug 1872	Leinstetten	Sulz	Mar 1891	N.-Amer	849626
Haibt, Joseph & F			Leinstetten	Sulz	Jun 1854	N.-Amer	849638
Haibt, Katharina (wife)		29 Oct 1844	Leinstetten	Sulz	Aug 1869	N.-Amer	849638
Haibt, Mathias & F			Leinstetten	Sulz	Aug 1869	N.-Amer	849638
Haibt, Stephan		16 Feb 1869	Leinstetten	Sulz	Aug 1869	N.-Amer	849638
Haich, Johann Georg		13 Aug 1865	Dornhan	Sulz	Sep 1881	N.-Amer	849626
Haid, Andreas		7 Apr 1823	Dornhan	Sulz	bef 1861	Austria	849634
Haid, Georg Gottlob		13 Jul 1815	Sigmarswangen	Sulz	Jan 1845	N.-Amer	849642

Haid, Johannes	14 Apr 1845	Hopfau	Sulz	Feb 1860	N.-Amer	849636
Haidt, Anna Maria	27 Oct 1846	Hopfau	Sulz	Apr 1866	N.-Amer	849636
Haier, Catharina		Pfalzgrafenweiler	Frd.	1817	Russia	569269
Haier, Christian Friedr. & F		Freudenstadt	Frd.	1851	N.-Amer	577778
Haier, Christoph Friedrich & F		Groembach	Frd.	Aug 1851	N.-Amer	569271
Haier, Jakob		Pfalzgrafenweiler	Frd.	Jan 1866	N.-Amer	577780
Haier, Johann Adam		Freudenstadt	Frd.	1851	N.-Amer	577778
Haier, Johann Adam	9 Jun 1811	Groembach	Frd.	Aug 1851	N.-Amer	569271
Haier, Karoline Jul. Ernest.	1850	Groembach	Frd.	Aug 1851	N.-Amer	569271
Haier, Louise Mathilde	1849	Groembach	Frd.	Aug 1851	N.-Amer	569271
Haier, Regina		Groembach	Frd.	Aug 1851	N.-Amer	569271
Haier, Wilhelmine		Pfalzgrafenweiler	Frd.	Jul 1851	Switz.	569271
Haier, Wilhelmine Regina	1846	Groembach	Frd.	Aug 1851	N.-Amer	569271
Haigis, Anna Maria (wife)		Aistaig	Sulz	Jun 1837	N.-Amer	849628
Haigis, Christian & F		Renfrizhausen	Sulz	Apr 1817	Rus-Pol	849639
Haigis, Friedrich	8 Jan 1870	Rosenfeld	Sulz	Aug 1886	N.-Amer	849626
Haigis, Georg Heinrich & F	30 Sep 1801	Holzhausen	Sulz	Apr 1832	N.-Amer	849635
Haigis, Gottlieb Friedrich	1 yrs.	Holzhausen	Sulz	Jul 1831	N.-Amer	849635
Haigis, Heinrich & F		Holzhausen	Sulz	Jul 1831	N.-Amer	849635
Haigis, Johann Heinrich	5 yrs.	Holzhausen	Sulz	Jul 1831	N.-Amer	849635
Haigis, Johann Heinrich		Holzhausen	Sulz	Apr 1832	N.-Amer	849635
Haigis, Ludwig & F	31 May 1790	Aistaig	Sulz	Jun 1837	N.-Amer	849628
Haigis, Maria Catharina		Holzhausen	Sulz	Apr 1832	N.-Amer	849635
Haigis, Sibilla (wife)		Holzhausen	Sulz	Jul 1831	N.-Amer	849635
Haigis, Sibilla (wife)		Holzhausen	Sulz	Apr 1832	N.-Amer	849635
Hais, Jacob & F		Pfalzgrafenweiler	Frd.	Feb 1817	Russia	569268
Hais, Martin & F		Pfalzgrafenweiler	Frd.	Feb 1817	Russia	569268
Haisch, Elias		Breitenberg	Calw	1864	Baden	563212
Haisch, Georg	10 Jan 1840	Reichenbach	Frd.	Jun 1866	Switz.	577780
Haisch, Johannes		Breitenberg	Calw	1860	N.-Amer	563212
Haisler, Johann Georg & F		Wuerzbach	Calw	1853	N.-Amer	563212
Haist, Anna Maria	1 Feb 1795	Baiersbronn	Frd.	Mar 1849	N.-Amer	569270
Haist, August	7 Nov 1839	Baiersbronn	Frd.	Mar 1849	N.-Amer	569270
Haist, Carl	26 Nov 1846	Baiersbronn	Frd.	Mar 1865	N.-Amer	577779
Haist, Carl	23 yrs.	Freudenstadt	Frd.	Sep 1850	Baden	569271
Haist, Carl August	20 Oct 1838	Baiersbronn	Frd.	Aug 1854	N.-Amer	569274
Haist, Christian	14 Aug 1828	Baiersbronn	Frd.	Mar 1849	N.-Amer	569270
Haist, Christian	11 yrs.	Baiersbronn	Frd.	May 1817	N.-Amer	569267
Haist, Christian & F	3 Sep 1800	Baiersbronn	Frd.	Aug 1854	N.-Amer	569274
Haist, Christian David	30 Jun 1828	Baiersbronn	Frd.	Aug 1854	N.-Amer	569274
Haist, Christina	22 yrs.	Gruental	Frd.	Apr 1853	France	569272
Haist, Christina	28 Nov 1838	Reichenbach	Frd.	Jun 1864	N.-Amer	577779
Haist, Christof Simon	17 Jul 1841	Baiersbronn	Frd.	Mar 1857	N.-Amer	577776
Haist, David	25 yrs.	Baiersbronn	Frd.	May 1817	N.-Amer	569267
Haist, Dorothea	28 Jul 1839	Baiersbronn	Frd.	bef 1865	Baden	577779
Haist, Elisabetha	14 Sep 1811	Baiersbronn	Frd.	Jul 1832	N.-Amer	569267
Haist, Elisabetha	5 yrs.	Baiersbronn	Frd.	May 1817	N.-Amer	569267
Haist, Eva Catharina	9 yrs.	Baiersbronn	Frd.	May 1817	N.-Amer	569267
Haist, Friederich	16 Aug 1834	Baiersbronn	Frd.	Mar 1849	N.-Amer	569270
Haist, Friederika	36 yrs.	Freudenstadt	Frd.	bef 1865	Switz.	577779

Name		Birth			Emigration		Film
Last	First	Date	Place	O'amt	Appl. Date	Dest.	Number
Haist, Friederika		31 Oct 1846	Baiersbronn	Frd.	Mar 1847	N.-Amer	569271
Haist, Heinrich		12 Jun 1842	Baiersbronn	Frd.	Aug 1854	N.-Amer	569274
Haist, Jacob		21 Sep 1835	Freudenstadt	Frd.	Jun 1864	N.-Amer	577779
Haist, Jacob & F		7 Jan 1791	Baiersbronn	Frd.	Mar 1849	N.-Amer	569270
Haist, Johann		11 Mar 1834	Tonbach	Frd.	Feb 1854	N.-Amer	569273
Haist, Johann Daniel		21 yrs.	Baiersbronn	Frd.	May 1817	N.-Amer	569267
Haist, Johann Daniel & F			Baiersbronn	Frd.	May 1817	N.-Amer	569267
Haist, Johann Georg		16 Nov 1837	Baiersbronn	Frd.	Aug 1854	N.-Amer	569274
Haist, Johann Georg & F			Baiersbronn	Frd.	Jul 1832	N.-Amer	569267
Haist, Johann Georg (wid) & F		21 Jan 1795	Baiersbronn	Frd.	Mar 1857	N.-Amer	577776
Haist, Johann Georg Christ.		23 Nov 1827	Baiersbronn	Frd.	Aug 1854	N.-Amer	569274
Haist, Johannes		23 Dec 1837	Baiersbronn	Frd.	Mar 1854	N.-Amer	569273
Haist, Johannes		23 yrs.	Baiersbronn	Frd.	May 1817	N.-Amer	569267
Haist, Johannes & F			Baiersbronn	Frd.	May 1817	N.-Amer	569267
Haist, Joseph & F			Baiersbronn	Frd.	Jul 1832	N.-Amer	569267
Haist, Justine		7 Apr 1832	Baiersbronn	Frd.	Mar 1849	N.-Amer	569270
Haist, Katharina & C		20 Jan 1806	Baiersbronn	Frd.	Mar 1847	N.-Amer	569271
Haist, Ludwig		21 yrs.	Baiersbronn	Frd.	Aug 1854	N.-Amer	569274
Haist, Margaretha		24 Aug 1804	Baiersbronn	Frd.	Aug 1854	N.-Amer	569274
Haist, Michael & F			Baiersbronn	Frd.	Jul 1832	N.-Amer	569267
Haist, Peter		15 yrs.	Baiersbronn	Frd.	May 1817	N.-Amer	569267
Haist, Regine		17 yrs.	Baiersbronn	Frd.	May 1817	N.-Amer	569267
Haist, Rosina		19 Nov 1830	Baiersbronn	Frd.	Mar 1849	N.-Amer	569270
Haist, Rosina		3 Mar 1825	Baiersbronn	Frd.	Aug 1854	N.-Amer	569274
Haist, Rosine			Baiersbronn	Frd.	Aug 1815	Hess-D.	569267
Haist, Sofie Dorothea		17 yrs.	Freudenstadt	Frd.	Apr 1844	France	561269
Haist, Wilhelm Friedrich		19 Feb 1835	Baiersbronn	Frd.	Aug 1854	N.-Amer	569274
Haitzmann, Anna Maria		17 Aug 1839	Duerrenmettstetten	Sulz	Feb 1860	N.-Amer	849635
Halblizel, Catharina Barbara			Sulz	Sulz	May 1817	N.-Amer	849627
Halblizel, Christina Gottlieb.		21 Sep 1810	Sulz	Sulz	Jun 1835	Bavaria	849627
Halblizel, Johann Ludwig			Sulz	Sulz	1815	--	849627
Halblizel, Philipp Jacob			Sulz	Sulz	Dec 1826	Saxony	849627
Haldenwang, Carl			Simmozheim	Calw	1853	N.-Amer	563212
Haldenwang, Carl Georg			Simmozheim	Calw	1853	N.-Amer	563212
Hallauer, Anna Maria		7 Mar 1821	Bondorf	Herr.	Jul 1869	Switz.	834624
Haller, -- & F			Freudenstadt	Frd.	Sep 1854	N.-Amer	569274
Haller, Agnes Katharina (wife)			Sulz	Sulz	Jan 1833	N.-Amer	849627
Haller, Anna Maria			Freudenstadt	Frd.	Sep 1854	N.-Amer	569274
Haller, Anna Maria (wife)			Gueltstein	Herr.	Sep 1852	N.-Amer	834627
Haller, Carl Adolph		6 yrs.	Sulz	Sulz	Jan 1833	N.-Amer	849627
Haller, Caroline Sophie		3 Apr 1854	Freudenstadt	Frd.	Sep 1854	N.-Amer	569274
Haller, Christian		16 Dec 1839	Bondorf	Herr.	Oct 1866	N.-Amer	834624
Haller, Christian Friedrich		10 yrs.	Sulz	Sulz	Jan 1833	N.-Amer	849627
Haller, Christiane Margar.wife			Freudenstadt	Frd.	Sep 1854	N.-Amer	569274
Haller, Friedrich & F		28 Jul 1793	Sulz	Sulz	Jan 1833	N.-Amer	849627
Haller, Johann Carl		16 Jan 1847	Freudenstadt	Frd.	Sep 1854	N.-Amer	569274
Haller, Johann Georg		6 Mar 1843	Gueltstein	Herr.	Sep 1852	N.-Amer	834627
Haller, Johann Georg & W		24 Mar 1824	Bondorf	Herr.	Apr 1869	N.-Amer	834624
Haller, Johann Martin		3 Jan 1824	Gueltstein	Herr.	Sep 1852	N.-Amer	834627
Haller, Johanne Margarethe		30 Jan 1849	Freudenstadt	Frd.	Sep 1854	N.-Amer	569274

Haller, Johannes	9 Jul 1836	Gueltstein	Herr.	Sep 1852	N.-Amer	834627
Haller, Johannes & F		Gueltstein	Herr.	Sep 1852	N.-Amer	834627
Haller, Katharina Barbara	13 Feb 1833	Gueltstein	Herr.	Sep 1852	N.-Amer	834627
Haller, Katharina Magdalena	19 Jun 1825	Gueltstein	Herr.	Sep 1852	N.-Amer	834627
Haller, Maria Catharina (wife)	24 Mar 1811	Bondorf	Herr.	Apr 1869	N.-Amer	834624
Haller, Marie Pauline	19 Sep 1850	Freudenstadt	Frd.	Sep 1854	N.-Amer	569274
Halm, Friedrich		Gaertringen	Herr.	Apr 1830	N.-Amer	834624
Halter, Anna	26 Jun 1829	Rosenfeld	Sulz	Jul 1865	Baden	849641
Halter, Christian	16 Jul 1875	Rosenfeld	Sulz	Mar 1892	N.-Amer	849626
Halter, Gottlieb	29 Aug 1870	Rosenfeld	Sulz	Apr 1887	N.-Amer	849626
Halter, Johann Jakob	21 Feb 1881	Rosenfeld	Sulz	Apr 1895	N.-Amer	849641
Halter, Johann Jakob	24 Jun 1847	Rosenfeld	Sulz	Jun 1866	N.-Amer	849641
Halter, Johann Jakob	17 Jun 1872	Rosenfeld	Sulz	Apr 1887	N.-Amer	849626
Halter, Michael	12 Oct 1865	Rosenfeld	Sulz	Jun 1881	N.-Amer	849626
Hamann, Agnes	26 Mar 1814	Trichtingen	Sulz	May 1867	N.-Amer	849642
Hamann, Anna Maria	5 May 1775	Trichtingen	Sulz	May 1817	Polen	849642
Hamann, Johann Georg	7 Oct 1848	Trichtingen	Sulz	Oct 1866	N.-Amer	849642
Hamann, Johannes	22 May 1833	Hallwangen	Frd.	Aug 1851	N.-Amer	569271
Hamann, Martin	8 Feb 1836	Glatten	Frd.	Jun 1855	N.-Amer	569275
Hamberger, Magdalena	1837	Oberreichenbach	Calw	1857	N.-Amer	563212
Hammann, Anna Maria		Breitenberg	Calw	1858	N.-Amer	563212
Hammann, Johann Georg	25 yrs.	Aichelberg	Calw	1864	N.-Amer	563212
Hammann, Johann Martin		Hofstett	Calw	1860	N.-Amer	563212
Hammann, Lorenz	1838	Breitenberg	Calw	1858	N.-Amer	563212
Hammer, Carl Wolf	17 yrs.	Calw	Calw	Sep 1870	N.-Amer	563212
Hammer, Catharina & C	30 Apr 1813	Altingen	Herr.	Aug 1846	N.-Amer	834626
Hammer, Christian Jacob		Calw	Calw	1860	N.-Amer	563212
Hammer, Georg Christian		Calw	Calw	Jun 1873	N.-Amer	563212
Hammer, Helena	1 Mar 1838	Altingen	Herr.	Jan 1867	N.-Amer	834624
Hammer, Johannes	26 Dec 1847	Altingen	Herr.	Jan 1866	N.-Amer	834624
Hammer, Kresentia (wife)		Altingen	Herr.	Mar 1838	Austria	834625
Hammer, Louise		Calw	Calw	May 1870	Baden	563212
Hammer, Magnus		Altingen	Herr.	Apr 1836	N.-Amer	834624
Hammer, Philipp Friedrich & W		Altingen	Herr.	Mar 1838	Austria	834625
Hammer, Rosina	4 Jan 1839	Altingen	Herr.	Feb 1867	N.-Amer	834624
Hammer, Thekla	11 Sep 1847	Altingen	Herr.	Nov 1868	Prussia	834624
Hamp, Susanna	4 Jul 1853	Hopfau	Sulz	Nov 1889	Switz.	849626
Hampp, Johann Georg		Grunbach	Schd.	Mar 1844	Austria	801461
Hanger, Jordan & F		Monakam	Calw	1852	N.-Amer	563212
Hanselmann, Johannes	1836	Zwerenberg	Calw	1856	N.-Amer	563212
Hardtle, Johann Adam	6 Oct 1823	Entringen	Herr.	Jul 1866	Switz.	834624
Harr, Andreas	4 APr 1827	Tumlingen	Frd.	Jul 1856	N.-Amer	569275
Harr, Anna Maria	14 Aug 1831	Dornstetten	Frd.	Apr 1849	N.-Amer	569270
Harr, Anna Maria & C		Unterjettingen	Herr.	Apr 1836	N.-Amer	834624
Harr, Barbara	17 Jun 1839	Dornstetten	Frd.	Oct 1864	N.-Amer	577779
Harr, Catharina	9 Feb 1822	Moetzingen	Herr.	Apr 1847	N.-Amer	834626
Harr, Christian	8 Jul 1829	Tumlingen	Frd.	Feb 1857	Frankf.	577776
Harr, Christine (wife)	12 Jun 1793	Moetzingen	Herr.	May 1852	N.-Amer	834627
Harr, Christine Barbara	16 May 1849	Moetzingen	Herr.	May 1852	N.-Amer	834627
Harr, David		Groembach	Frd.	1817	Russia	569269

Name		Birth		Emigration			Film
Last	First	Date	Place	O'amt	Appl. Date	Dest.	Number
Harr, Dorothea		27 Oct 1826	Moetzingen	Herr.	May 1852	N.-Amer	834627
Harr, Friederike		14 May 1849	Moetzingen	Herr.	May 1852	N.-Amer	834627
Harr, Friedrich			Glatten	Frd.	1817	Russia	569269
Harr, Gottlieb		27 Aug 1823	Moetzingen	Herr.	May 1852	N.-Amer	834627
Harr, Jacob		27 yrs.	Altingen	Herr.	Jun 1839	Baden	834625
Harr, Jacob Friedrich		18 Jul 1826	Gaertringen	Herr.	bef 1863	N.-Amer	834624
Harr, Jakob		9 Jun 1830	Moetzingen	Herr.	May 1852	N.-Amer	834627
Harr, Johann Jacob (wid.) & F			Unterjettingen	Herr.	Apr 1836	N.-Amer	834624
Harr, Johann Jakob		27 Apr 1826	Dornstetten	Frd.	Apr 1849	N.-Amer	569270
Harr, Johannes		19 Feb 1847	Moetzingen	Herr.	May 1852	N.-Amer	834627
Harr, Johannes & F		10 Nov 1819	Moetzingen	Herr.	May 1852	N.-Amer	834627
Harr, Johannes Sr. & F		22 May 1795	Moetzingen	Herr.	May 1852	N.-Amer	834627
Harr, Jokob		13 Feb 1845	Gruental	Frd.	Oct 1865	N.-Amer	577779
Harr, Katharina		31 May 1833	Glatten	Frd.	Oct 1854	S.-Amer	569274
Harr, Katharina Justina		27 Nov 1850	Moetzingen	Herr.	May 1852	N.-Amer	834627
Harr, Katharina Martha (wife)		30 Dec 1820	Moetzingen	Herr.	May 1852	N.-Amer	834627
Harr, Ludwig		13 Jul 1821	Glatten	Frd.	Oct 1854	S.-Amer	569274
Harr, Martin		3 Mar 1820	Moetzingen	Herr.	Mar 1847	N.-Amer	834626
Harre, Agatha		30 yrs.	Rotenzimmern	Sulz	Sep 1854	N.-Amer	849642
Harre, Anna		10 yrs.	Rotenzimmern	Sulz	Sep 1854	N.-Amer	849642
Harre, Anna (wife)			Rotenzimmern	Sulz	Sep 1854	N.-Amer	849642
Harre, Anna Barbara		15 Jan 1844	Rotenzimmern	Sulz	Jan 1861	N.-Amer	849642
Harre, Anna Barbara		17 yrs.	Rotenzimmern	Sulz	Sep 1854	N.-Amer	849642
Harre, Anna Katharina		26 Apr 1834	Rotenzimmern	Sulz	Oct 1868	N.-Amer	849642
Harre, Anna Maria		16 Nov 1866	Rotenzimmern	Sulz	May 1869	N.-Amer	849642
Harre, Anna Maria		6 yrs.	Rotenzimmern	Sulz	Sep 1854	N.-Amer	849642
Harre, Anna Maria			Isingen	Sulz	Mar 1854	N.-Amer	849636
Harre, Barbara			Schoemberg	Frd.	Jun 1854	N.-Amer	569273
Harre, Catharina		13 yrs.	Rotenzimmern	Sulz	Sep 1854	N.-Amer	849642
Harre, Christian		3 yrs.	Rotenzimmern	Sulz	Sep 1854	N.-Amer	849642
Harre, Christina		4 Apr 1838	Rotenzimmern	Sulz	Mar 1859	N.-Amer	849642
Harre, Christina (wife)			Rotenzimmern	Sulz	Sep 1854	N.-Amer	849642
Harre, Friedrich & F			Schoemberg	Frd.	Jun 1854	N.-Amer	569273
Harre, Heinrich		14 yrs.	Rotenzimmern	Sulz	Sep 1854	N.-Amer	849642
Harre, Heinrich & F		44 yrs.	Rotenzimmern	Sulz	Sep 1854	N.-Amer	849642
Harre, Johann Jakob & F		42 yrs.	Rotenzimmern	Sulz	Sep 1854	N.-Amer	849642
Harre, Katharina			Isingen	Sulz	Mar 1854	N.-Amer	849636
Harre, Magdalena			Schoemberg	Frd.	Jun 1854	N.-Amer	569273
Harre, Matthias			Schoemberg	Frd.	Jun 1854	N.-Amer	569273
Harre, Rosina		25 Sep 1839	Rotenzimmern	Sulz	Jun 1866	N.-Amer	849642
Harre, Ursula & C		23 Feb 1841	Rotenzimmern	Sulz	May 1869	N.-Amer	849642
Harrer, Gottlieb		14 Feb 1849	Pfaeffingen	Herr.	Aug 1869	N.-Amer	834624
Harsch, Karl		10 May 1865	Binsdorf	Sulz	Apr 1881	N.-Amer	849631
Harsch, Maximillian		6 Aug 1866	Binsdorf	Sulz	Mar 1882	N.-Amer	849631
Harsch, Otto		5 Oct 1872	Binsdorf	Sulz	Jun 1888	N.-Amer	849631
Hartdorn, Albrecht		14 Aug 1839	Freudenstadt	Frd.	Mar 1854	N.-Amer	569273
Hartdorn, Anna		14 Feb 1843	Freudenstadt	Frd.	Mar 1854	N.-Amer	569273
Hartdorn, Anna (wife)			Freudenstadt	Frd.	Mar 1854	N.-Amer	569273
Hartdorn, Carl Friedrich		20 Jan 1836	Freudenstadt	Frd.	Mar 1854	N.-Amer	569273
Hartdorn, Carl Friedrich & F			Freudenstadt	Frd.	Mar 1854	N.-Amer	569273

Hartdorn, Franz	1 May 1838	Freudenstadt	Frd.	Mar 1854	N.-Amer	569273
Hartdorn, Gottfried	2 Jan 1853	Freudenstadt	Frd.	Mar 1854	N.-Amer	569273
Hartdorn, Gottlieb	6 Apr 1847	Freudenstadt	Frd.	Mar 1854	N.-Amer	569273
Hartdorn, Heinrice		Freudenstadt	Frd.	bef 1848	Basel	569270
Hartdorn, Jakob	27 Feb 1851	Freudenstadt	Frd.	Mar 1854	N.-Amer	569273
Hartdorn, Johann Friedr.	11 May 1845	Freudenstadt	Frd.	Mar 1854	N.-Amer	569273
Hartdorn, Johann Jacob		Freudenstadt	Frd.	Aug 1816	France	569267
Hartdorn, Maria Anna	17 Dec 1840	Freudenstadt	Frd.	Mar 1854	N.-Amer	569273
Hartdorn, Rosina	5 Dec 1836	Freudenstadt	Frd.	Mar 1854	N.-Amer	569273
Hartdorn, Wilhelm	12 Aug 1849	Freudenstadt	Frd.	Mar 1854	N.-Amer	569273
Hartenstein, Christioph Gottf.	21 yrs.	Sulz	Sulz	Jan 1815	Holland	849625
Harter, Johann Georg	19 Apr 1835	Goettelfingen	Frd.	Aug 1853	N.-Amer	569274
Harter, Vinzens	4 Apr 1834	Goettelfingen	Frd.	Aug 1853	N.-Amer	569274
Hartmaier, Catharina Magdal.	24 Oct 1820	Herrenberg	Herr.	May 1852	N.-Amer	834627
Hartmaier, Johannes	17 Apr 1823	Herrenberg	Herr.	bef 1851	N.-Amer	834627
Hartmaier, Sophie	5 Apr 1834	Herrenberg	Herr.	May 1852	N.-Amer	834627
Hartmann, Andreas	26 Feb 1845	Oberndorf	Herr.	Apr 1865	N.-Amer	834624
Hartmann, Anna Maria(wid.)& F		Meistern/Bergorte	Calw	1852	N.-Amer	563212
Hartmann, Carl		Gechingen	Calw	1853	N.-Amer	563212
Hartmann, Carl Ludwig		Oberhaugstett	Calw	1859	N.-Amer	563212
Hartmann, Christian	25 Jun 1828	Allmandle	Frd.	Feb 1856	N.-Amer	569275
Hartmann, Christoph Friedrich	29 yrs.	Aichelberg	Calw	1864	N.-Amer	563212
Hartmann, Dorothea		Liebenzell	Calw	1859	Austria	563212
Hartmann, Felix	21 May 1848	Oberndorf	Herr.	Apr 1867	N.-Amer	834624
Hartmann, Gottlieb Ehrenreich		Liebenzell	Calw	1853	Baden	563212
Hartmann, Jacob Imanuel		Oberhaugstett	Calw	1859	N.-Amer	563212
Hartmann, Johann Georg	12 Sep 1843	Gruental	Frd.	Apr 1865	N.-Amer	577779
Hartmann, Johann Jakob	1827	Althengstett	Calw	1855	Baden	563212
Hartmann, Johann Martin	2 Jun 1838	Gruental	Frd.	Aug 1857	N.-Amer	577776
Hartmann, Johannes	1834	Breitenberg	Calw	1854	N.-Amer	563212
Hartmann, Karl Ludwig	27 yrs.	Oberhaugstett	Calw	1856	N.-Amer	563212
Hartmann, Margaretha	1836	Breitenberg	Calw	1854	N.-Amer	563212
Hartmann, Vincenz	30 May 1839	Oberndorf	Herr.	Aug 1867	N.-Amer	834624
Haselschwerdt, Jacob		Meistern/Bergorte	Calw	1853	N.-Amer	563212
Haselschwerdt, Johann Georg	1828	Ostelsheim	Calw	1856	N.-Amer	563212
Hass, Anna Maria		Schnait	Schd.	Apr 1834	N.-Amer	801460
Hauber, August Friedrich Her.	30 Nov 1809	Herrenberg	Herr.	Sep 1848	N.-Amer	834626
Hauck, Johann Daniel	23 Nov 1818	Schorndorf	Schd.	Jul 1844	Baden	801461
Haudelette, Charles Etienne		Isenburg	– –	Dec 1751	Mas.N-A	550803
Haudte, Georg Martin	17 Dec 1852	Rosenfeld	Sulz	Jul 1870	N.-Amer	849641
Hauer, Barbara	14 May 1801	Tumlingen	Frd.	Mar 1837	N.-Amer	569268
Hauer, Catharina	25 Feb 1849	Tumlingen	Frd.	Jan 1854	N.-Amer	569273
Hauer, Christina	12 Oct 1828	Tumlingen	Frd.	Jan 1854	N.-Amer	569273
Hauer, Elisabetha	21 Aug 1833	Tumlingen	Frd.	Jan 1855	N.-Amer	569275
Hauer, Gottfried	2 Jul 1826	Tumlingen	Frd.	bef 1860	N.-Amer	577777
Hauer, Johannes & F	12 Sep 1811	Tumlingen	Frd.	Jan 1854	N.-Amer	569273
Hauer, Maria Auguste	13 Mar 1847	Tumlingen	Frd.	Jan 1854	N.-Amer	569273
Hauer, Theodor Friedrich	25 yrs.	Neubulach	Calw	1868	N.-Amer	563212
Hauff, Jacob Friedrich	14 yrs.	Beutelsbach	Schd.	Apr 1833	N.-Amer	801460
Hauff, Joseph & F		Beutelsbach	Schd.	Apr 1833	N.-Amer	801460

Name		Birth		Emigration			Film
Last	First	Date	Place	O'amt	Appl. Date	Dest.	Number
Hauff, Katharina Barbara			Beutelsbach	Schd.	Apr 1833	N.-Amer	801460
Haug, Adam			Dornstetten	Frd.	Mar 1833	N.-Amer	569269
Haug, Adam		12 Jul 1835	Edelweiler	Frd.	Mar 1847	N.-Amer	569271
Haug, Anna Maria		13 Sep 1797	Klosterreichenbach	Frd.	Mar 1847	N.-Amer	569271
Haug, Carl August		1 Jul 1834	Freudenstadt	Frd.	Feb 1854	N.-Amer	569273
Haug, Christian		21 Mar 1845	Gruental	Frd.	Apr 1865	N.-Amer	577779
Haug, Christiane		20 Jul 1847	Sigmarswangen	Sulz	Feb 1869	Switz.	849642
Haug, Christine		3 Feb 1830	Edelweiler	Frd.	Mar 1847	N.-Amer	569271
Haug, Conrad & F		12 Jan 1800	Edelweiler	Frd.	Mar 1847	N.-Amer	569271
Haug, Franz Ferdinand		27 Mar 1853	Freudenstadt	Frd.	Mar 1858	Austria	577776
Haug, Georg Jakob		21 Mar 1874	Rosenfeld	Sulz	Feb 1891	N.-Amer	849626
Haug, Georg Jakob		20 Sep 1834	Marschalkenzimmern	Sulz	Jul 1860	N.-Amer	849638
Haug, Gottlieb		23 Apr 1807	Freudenstadt	Frd.	Mar 1865	N.-Amer	577779
Haug, Gottlieb		8 Jul 1841	Edelweiler	Frd.	Mar 1847	N.-Amer	569271
Haug, Hans Martin			Herzogsweiler	Frd.	Apr 1752	Pen.N-A	550803
Haug, Heinrich		17 Feb 1877	Rosenfeld	Sulz	Dec 1893	N.-Amer	849641
Haug, Jacob			Dornstetten	Frd.	1817	Russia	569269
Haug, Jacob & F			Dornstetten	Frd.	1817	Russia	569269
Haug, Jacob Friedrich		32 yrs.	Calw	Calw	1866	N.-Amer	563212
Haug, Johann Georg		22 Jul 1829	Hallwangen	Frd.	Sep 1854	N.-Amer	569274
Haug, Johann Georg		Jul 1849	Freudenstadt	Frd.	Jul 1866	N.-Amer	577780
Haug, Johann Georg		25 Jun 1838	Sigmarswangen	Sulz	bef 1870	Switz.	849642
Haug, Johannes		26 Apr 1838	Edelweiler	Frd.	Mar 1847	N.-Amer	569271
Haug, Johannes			Dornhan	Sulz	Dec 1815	France	849633
Haug, Karl Heinrich		19 Aug 1880	Rosenfeld	Sulz	Feb 1891	N.-Amer	849626
Haug, Margaretha Barbara			Freudenstadt	Frd.	bef 1864	Darmst.	577779
Haug, Matthaeus		12 Jul 1832	Edelweiler	Frd.	Mar 1847	N.-Amer	569271
Haug, Michael & F			Dornstetten	Frd.	Jul 1854	N.-Amer	569274
Haug, Rosina		25 Aug 1827	Edelweiler	Frd.	Mar 1847	N.-Amer	569271
Haug, Sophie & C			Freudenstadt	Frd.	Mar 1858	Austria	577776
Hauk, Michael			Schietingen	Nag.	bef 1856	N.-Amer	838492
Haupt, Magdalena			Entringen	Herr.	Sep 1852	N.-Amer	834627
Hausch, Nathanuel			Sulz	Sulz	bef 1834	N.-Amer	849625
Hauser, Agatha (wife)		8 Apr 1792	Voehringen	Herr.	Jan 1848	N.-Amer	834626
Hauser, Andreas			Wittendorf	Frd.	Mar 1856	N.-Amer	569275
Hauser, Andreas		24 Jul 1856	Sigmarswangen	Sulz	Feb 1872	N.-Amer	849642
Hauser, Andreas		25 yrs.	Oberkollwangen	Calw	1866	N.-Amer	563212
Hauser, Anna		6 Sep 1848	Ueberberg	Nag.	Feb 1852	N.-Amer	838490
Hauser, Anna (wid.)		1 Jan 1817	Bergfelden	Sulz	Apr 1867	N.-Amer	849629
Hauser, Anna Barbara		12 yrs.	Bergfelden	Sulz	Feb 1872	N.-Amer	849629
Hauser, Anna Barbara		8 Jul 1849	Bergfelden	Sulz	Mar 1857	N.-Amer	849629
Hauser, Anna Maria		25 Nov 1850	Bergfelden	Sulz	Sep 1866	N.-Amer	849629
Hauser, Anna Maria		1849	Bergfelden	Sulz	Mar 1857	N.-Amer	849629
Hauser, Anna Maria		20 Sep 1833	Wittershausen	Sulz	bef 1868	N.-Amer	849644
Hauser, Anna Maria (wid) & F			Bergfelden	Sulz	Nov 1853	N.-Amer	849629
Hauser, Barbara		1 Apr 1822	Hildrizhausen	Herr.	Aug 1862	N.-Amer	834624
Hauser, Barbara (wife)			Bergfelden	Sulz	Apr 1833	N.-Amer	849629
Hauser, Christian		11 Feb 1846	Bergfelden	Sulz	Sep 1866	N.-Amer	849629
Hauser, Christian			Sigmarswangen	Sulz	1867	N.-Amer	849642
Hauser, Christian		10 Feb 1848	Sigmarswangen	Sulz	Jun 1867	N.-Amer	849642

Hauser, Christian & F		Moetzingen	Herr.	Feb 1834	N.-Amer	834624
Hauser, Christina	8 May 1836	Bergfelden	Sulz	Mar 1857	N.-Amer	849629
Hauser, Christina Barbara	26 May 1845	Ueberberg	Nag.	Feb 1852	N.-Amer	838490
Hauser, Christina Barbara	31 Oct 1837	Moetzingen	Herr.	May 1852	N.-Amer	834627
Hauser, Christine	12 Apr 1842	Bergfelden	Sulz	Sep 1854	N.-Amer	849629
Hauser, Elisabetha (wid.) & F	17 Jul 1814	Bergfelden	Sulz	Sep 1866	N.-Amer	849629
Hauser, Elisabetha Barbara	23 Feb 1843	Bergfelden	Sulz	Sep 1866	N.-Amer	849629
Hauser, Elisabetha Barbara	2 yrs.	Bergfelden	Sulz	Apr 1833	N.-Amer	849629
Hauser, Elisabetha Barbara & C	1823	Bergfelden	Sulz	Mar 1857	N.-Amer	849629
Hauser, Fridrich & F	17 Sep 1765	Moetzingen	Herr.	Jan 1848	N.-Amer	834626
Hauser, Friederike	25 May 1849	Sigmarswangen	Sulz	Jun 1867	N.-Amer	849642
Hauser, Friederike & C	30 Jan 1820	Moetzingen	Herr.	Jan 1848	N.-Amer	834626
Hauser, Friedrich	4 Mar 1866	Sigmarswangen	Sulz	Mar 1881	N.-Amer	849626
Hauser, Georg Jacob		Bergfelden	Sulz	Aug 1847	N.-Amer	849629
Hauser, Georg Jakob	15 Feb 1844	Ueberberg	Nag.	Feb 1852	N.-Amer	838490
Hauser, Gottliebin	7 Oct 1838	Altingen	Herr.	May 1869	N.-Amer	834624
Hauser, Gottlob	53 yrs.	Erzingen	Bal.	1868	N.-Amer	555964
Hauser, Hedwig Friederike		Rosenfeld	Sulz	Sep 1854	N.-Amer	849640
Hauser, Jacob	19 May 1816	Moetzingen	Herr.	Jan 1848	N.-Amer	834626
Hauser, Jacob Friedrich	17 Dec 1841	Sulz	Sulz	Mar 1868	Augsb.	849628
Hauser, Jacob Friedrich	29 Oct 1840	Moetzingen	Herr.	May 1852	N.-Amer	834627
Hauser, Jakob	1 May 1856	Leidringen	Sulz	Mar 1870	N.-Amer	849637
Hauser, Jeremias		Ostelsheim	Calw	1853	N.-Amer	563212
Hauser, Johann & F		Erzingen	Bal.	Aug 1847	N.-Amer	555964
Hauser, Johann Georg		Durrweiler	Frd.	Aug 1860	N.-Amer	577777
Hauser, Johann Georg	21 May 1836	Bergfelden	Sulz	Mar 1857	N.-Amer	849629
Hauser, Johann Georg	1 Aug 1842	Sigmarswangen	Sulz	bef 1872	Baden	849642
Hauser, Johann Georg		Leidringen	Sulz	Aug 1853	N.-Amer	849637
Hauser, Johann Georg	17 Oct 1859	Leidringen	Sulz	Aug 1865	N.-Amer	849637
Hauser, Johann Georg & F		Ostelsheim	Calw	1852	N.-Amer	563212
Hauser, Johann Jacob	25 Mar 1846	Bergfelden	Sulz	Sep 1854	N.-Amer	849629
Hauser, Johann Jacob	30 Apr 1834	Sigmarswangen	Sulz	Nov 1853	N.-Amer	849642
Hauser, Johann Jacob		Oberkollwangen	Calw	1859	N.-Amer	563212
Hauser, Johann Jacob & F		Bergfelden	Sulz	May 1817	Russia	849629
Hauser, Johanna (wid.) & F		Moetzingen	Herr.	May 1852	N.-Amer	834627
Hauser, Johannes	24 yrs.	Klosterreichenbach	Frd.	Oct 1850	Baden	569271
Hauser, Johannes	19 Jul 1851	Bergfelden	Sulz	Apr 1867	N.-Amer	849629
Hauser, Johannes	16 Aug 1843	Bergfelden	Sulz	Sep 1859	N.-Amer	849629
Hauser, Johannes	2 Jan 1837	Bergfelden	Sulz	May 1855	N.-Amer	849629
Hauser, Johannes	31 May 1845	Wittershausen	Sulz	Feb 1865	N.-Amer	849644
Hauser, Johannes	20 Jul 1820	Voehringen	Sulz	Jan 1858	N.-Amer	849643
Hauser, Johannes	29 Jan 1867	Bergfelden	Sulz	May 1883	N.-Amer	849626
Hauser, Johannes	20 Jan 1873	Bergfelden	Sulz	Oct 1889	N.-Amer	849626
Hauser, Johannes	4 Jul 1863	Sigmarswangen	Sulz	Jun 1880	N.-Amer	849626
Hauser, Johannes	5 Feb 1840	Sigmarswangen	Sulz	Sep 1857	N.-Amer	849642
Hauser, Johannes	12 yrs.	Ostelsheim	Calw	1858	N.-Amer	563212
Hauser, Johannes	28 Aug 1833	Moetzingen	Herr.	May 1852	N.-Amer	834627
Hauser, Johannes & F		Bergfelden	Sulz	Feb 1872	N.-Amer	849629
Hauser, Joseph	9 Jun 1842	Sigmarswangen	Sulz	Aug 1866	N.-Amer	849642
Hauser, Karl Friedrich	4 Mar 1866	Sigmarswangen	Sulz	Mar 1882	N.-Amer	849642

Name		Birth		Emigration			Film
Last	First	Date	Place	O'amt	Appl. Date	Dest.	Number
Hauser, Katharina & C		30 Apr 1839	Leidringen	Sulz	Aug 1865	N.-Amer	849637
Hauser, Louise		5 Jul 1839	Moetzingen	Herr.	May 1852	N.-Amer	834627
Hauser, Magdalena & C		1829	Bergfelden	Sulz	Mar 1857	N.-Amer	849629
Hauser, Magdalena & F			Ueberberg	Nag.	Feb 1852	N.-Amer	838490
Hauser, Maria Agnes (wid.) & F			Bergfelden	Sulz	Sep 1854	N.-Amer	849629
Hauser, Martin			Oberwaldach	Frd.	1817	Russia	569269
Hauser, Martin & F			Bergfelden	Sulz	Jul 1853	N.-Amer	849629
Hauser, Mathaeus & F		8 Oct 1797	Bergfelden	Sulz	Apr 1833	N.-Amer	849629
Hauser, Matheus		4 yrs.	Bergfelden	Sulz	Apr 1833	N.-Amer	849629
Hauser, Philipp Adoph		15 Mar 1837	Rosenfeld	Sulz	Oct 1864	N.-Amer	849641
Hauser, Rosine Catharina		23 Jun 1826	Moetzingen	Herr.	Apr 1847	N.-Amer	834626
Hauss, Anna Maria			Oberreichenbach	Calw	1853	N.-Amer	563212
Hauss, Barbara			Oberreichenbach	Calw	1853	N.-Amer	563212
Hauss, Gottlieb		27 May 1827	Entringen	Herr.	Jun 1869	N.-Amer	834624
Hauss, Michael		1840	Oberkollbach	Calw	1857	N.-Amer	563212
Hausser, Anna Maria		7 Feb 1833	Moetzingen	Herr.	Mar 1869	N.-Amer	834624
Hausser, Barbara		8 Nov 1831	Glatten	Frd.	Oct 1854	S.-Amer	569274
Hausser, Jakob & F			Boll	Sulz	Jun 1817	Russia	849632
Hausser, Joseph Friedrich		3 Aug 1786	Schorndorf	Schd.	Aug 1833	N.-Amer	801460
Hausser, Karl Friedrich		12 Jun 1841	Herrenberg	Herr.	Jul 1870	Bavaria	834624
Hausser, Margaretha		23 Apr 1835	Glatten	Frd.	Oct 1854	S.-Amer	569274
Haussmann, Johann Gottlob			Calw	Calw	1852	N.-Amer	563212
Hauter, Stephan			Balingen	Bal.	Jul 1854	Switz.	555962
Hayd, Christian		20 Dec 1878	Hopfau	Sulz	Nov 1889	Switz.	849626
Hayd, Ernst		28 Feb 1880	Hopfau	Sulz	Nov 1889	Switz.	849626
Hayd, Susanna (wife)		4 Jul 1853	Hopfau	Sulz	Nov 1889	Switz.	849626
Hayer, Anna Barbara		15 yrs.	Cresbach	Frd.	Mar 1837	N.-Amer	569269
Hayer, Anna Catharina		18 yrs.	Dornstetten	Frd.	Mar 1837	N.-Amer	569269
Hayer, Anna Maria			Pfalzgrafenweiler	Frd.	Aug 1853	N.-Amer	569274
Hayer, Anna Maria & C		1 Sep 1822	Pfalzgrafenweiler	Frd.	Aug 1854	N.-Amer	569274
Hayer, Catharina		20 yrs.	Pfalzgrafenweiler	Frd.	Feb 1817	Russia	569268
Hayer, Catharina			Dornstetten	Frd.	Mar 1837	N.-Amer	569269
Hayer, Christiana		22 yrs.	Cresbach	Frd.	Mar 1837	N.-Amer	569269
Hayer, Christine		11 Apr 1830	Cresbach	Frd.	Jul 1842	N.-Amer	569269
Hayer, David		7 May 1836	Cresbach	Frd.	Jul 1842	N.-Amer	569269
Hayer, Dorothea & F		50 yrs.	Cresbach	Frd.	Jul 1842	N.-Amer	569269
Hayer, Elisabetha		20 yrs.	Cresbach	Frd.	Mar 1837	N.-Amer	569269
Hayer, Eva Rosina		10 yrs.	Dornstetten	Frd.	Mar 1837	N.-Amer	569269
Hayer, Gottfried		12 Mar 1828	Cresbach	Frd.	Jul 1842	N.-Amer	569269
Hayer, Gottlieb		15 yrs.	Dornstetten	Frd.	Mar 1837	N.-Amer	569269
Hayer, Jakob Friedrich		2 yrs.	Dornstetten	Frd.	Mar 1837	N.-Amer	569269
Hayer, Johann Wilhelm		12 yrs.	Dornstetten	Frd.	Mar 1837	N.-Amer	569269
Hayer, Matheus		6 yrs.	Dornstetten	Frd.	Mar 1837	N.-Amer	569269
Hayer, Wilhelm & F			Dornstetten	Frd.	Mar 1837	N.-Amer	569269
Hechler, Imanuel Christlieb		15 yrs.	Unterjesingen	Herr.	May 1852	N.-Amer	834627
Heck, Johann David		33 yrs.	Geradstetten	Schd.	Sep 1833	Bavaria	801460
Heckel, Johann Georg		4 Nov 1846	Trichtingen	Sulz	bef 1874	Switz.	849642
Heckele, Martin			Leidringen	Sulz	Jan 1855	N.-Amer	849637
Heckele, Martin (wid.) & F			Trichtingen	Sulz	Jun 1817	Kaukas.	849642
Heckele, Michael			Trichtingen	Sulz	Jun 1817	Kaukas.	849642

Heckele, Michael	6 Nov 1847	Leidringen	Sulz	Mar 1867	N.-Amer	849637
Hegel, Martin	8 Sep 1847	Voehringen	Sulz	Sep 1865	N.-Amer	849643
Hehr, Christian	14 Dec 1839	Freudenstadt	Frd.	Jun 1864	N.-Amer	577779
Hehr, Christiana	21 Sep 1822	Groembach	Frd.	bef 1853	N.-Amer	569272
Hehr, Jeramias Carl	4 Mar 1844	Freudenstadt	Frd.	Jul 1864	N.-Amer	577779
Hehr, Kunigunda	21 Jan 1827	Groembach	Frd.	Aug 1848	N.-Amer	569270
Hehr, Sophie		Freudenstadt	Frd.	Aug 1850	N.-Amer	569271
Heid, Anna Maria (wife)		Dornhan	Sulz	Mar 1817	Russia	849633
Heid, Jacob Friedrich & F		Dornhan	Sulz	Mar 1817	Russia	849633
Heidlauf, Christian Andreas	25 May 1828	Pfaeffingen	Herr.	Dec 1848	N.-Amer	834627
Heidlauf, Christina Franz & F		Gueltstein	Herr.	Apr 1834	N.-Amer	834624
Heidlauf, Elisabetha Cathar.	24 Apr 1852	Gueltstein	Herr.	Jul 1852	N.-Amer	834627
Heidlauf, Johannes & F		Gueltstein	Herr.	May 1831	N.-Amer	834624
Heidlauf, Margaretha Barb. & C		Gueltstein	Herr.	Apr 1835	N.-Amer	834624
Heidlauf, Maria Katharina (wife)		Gueltstein	Herr.	Jul 1852	N.-Amer	834627
Heidlauf, Martin & F		Gueltstein	Herr.	Apr 1834	N.-Amer	834624
Heidlauf, Michael & F		Gueltstein	Herr.	Jul 1852	N.-Amer	834627
Heidlauf, Regina Maria	22 Sep 1850	Gueltstein	Herr.	Jul 1852	N.-Amer	834627
Heilemann, Georg		Liebenzell	Calw	1861	Baden	563212
Heiler, Carl Otten		Calw	Calw	Jun 1877	Belgium	563212
Heim, Anna Maria & C		Gechingen	Calw	1852	N.-Amer	563212
Heim, Barbara		Sulz	Sulz	Jan 1833	N.-Amer	849627
Heim, Catharina Magdalena	28 yrs.	Beutelsbach	Schd.	Apr 1833	N.-Amer	801460
Heim, Christina Barbara	26 yrs.	Beutelsbach	Schd.	Apr 1833	N.-Amer	801460
Heim, Georg Ludwig		Gechingen	Calw	1860	N.-Amer	563212
Heim, Gottlieb	30 yrs.	Beutelsbach	Schd.	Apr 1833	N.-Amer	801460
Heim, Gottlieb		Gechingen	Calw	1860	N.-Amer	563212
Heim, Jacob		Gechingen	Calw	1860	N.-Amer	563212
Heim, Jacob Friedrich & F	15 Jun 1786	Sulz	Sulz	Jan 1833	N.-Amer	849627
Heim, Johann Daniel	24 yrs.	Beutelsbach	Schd.	Apr 1833	N.-Amer	801460
Heim, Maria Barbara		Beutelsbach	Schd.	Apr 1833	N.-Amer	801460
Heim, Marie Elisabetha		Sulz	Sulz	Sep 1855	Baden	849627
Hein, Carl August	17 yrs.	Gechingen	Calw	1868	N.-Amer	563212
Heininger, Maria Antionette	23 Dec 1846	Altingen	Herr.	Feb 1868	N.-Amer	834624
Heinrich, (Female) & C	Apr 1823	Deckenpfronn	Calw	1854	N.-Amer	563212
Heinrich, Balthas		Deckenpfronn	Calw	1852	N.-Amer	563212
Heinrich, Catharina	17 Feb 1822	Oberurbach	Schd.	Mar 1844	N.-Amer	801461
Heinrich, Jakob	1845	Deckenpfronn	Calw	1854	N.-Amer	563212
Heinrich, Johann Georg & F		Deckenpfronn	Calw	1852	N.-Amer	563212
Heins, Elisabeth Catha. (wife)		Gechingen	Calw	1869	N.-Amer	563212
Heins, Jacob Friedrich & F		Gechingen	Calw	1869	N.-Amer	563212
Heins, Ludwig Samuel	18 mon.	Gechingen	Calw	1869	N.-Amer	563212
Heins, Theresia Louise	5 yrs.	Gechingen	Calw	1869	N.-Amer	563212
Heins, Wilhelmine Caroline	16 yrs.	Gechingen	Calw	1869	N.-Amer	563212
Heintzmann, Mathias		Aistaig	Sulz	bef 1846	N.-Amer	849628
Heinzelmann, Agatha	27 Apr 1844	Gruental	Frd.	Mar 1847	N.-Amer	569271
Heinzelmann, Agatha		Voehringen	Sulz	Jul 1837	N.-Amer	849643
Heinzelmann, Agathe	29 Dec 1802	Gruental	Frd.	Mar 1847	N.-Amer	569271
Heinzelmann, Andreas	11 Dec 1833	Rodt	Frd.	Mar 1853	N.-Amer	569272
Heinzelmann, Andreas	41 yrs.	Sulz	Sulz	Sep 1860	N.-Amer	849628

Name		Birth		Emigration			Film
Last	First	Date	Place	O'amt	Appl. Date	Dest.	Number
Heinzelmann, Anna Barbara		24 yrs.	Freudenstadt	Frd.	May 1752	Pen.N-A	550803
Heinzelmann, Anna Maria			Dietersweiler	Frd.	Jan 1823	Russia	569269
Heinzelmann, Anna Maria		28 Mar 1829	Gruental	Frd.	Mar 1847	N.-Amer	569271
Heinzelmann, Anna Maria		13 Sep 1797	Klosterreichenbach	Frd.	Mar 1847	N.-Amer	569271
Heinzelmann, Barbara		26 Mar 1832	Gruental	Frd.	Mar 1847	N.-Amer	569271
Heinzelmann, Barbara		16 Dec 1846	Glatten	Frd.	Oct 1854	S.-Amer	569274
Heinzelmann, Barbara (wife)		20 Jun 1818	Glatten	Frd.	Oct 1854	S.-Amer	569274
Heinzelmann, Catharina & C		3 Jun 1836	Reinerzau	Frd.	Sep 1862	N.-Amer	577778
Heinzelmann, Christian		24 Mar 1839	Reinerzau	Frd.	Nov 1855	N.-Amer	569275
Heinzelmann, Christian		7 Apr 1836	Gruental	Frd.	Apr 1864	N.-Amer	577779
Heinzelmann, Christian		25 Nov 1800	Bergfelden	Sulz	bef 1830	Hungary	849625
Heinzelmann, Christian		19 Oct 1846	Hopfau	Sulz	bef 1872	N.-Amer	849636
Heinzelmann, Christina		24 Aug 1809	Bergfelden	Sulz	bef 1830	Hungary	849625
Heinzelmann, Christina			Dietersweiler	Frd.	Jan 1823	Russia	569269
Heinzelmann, Christina		11 Oct 1835	Gruental	Frd.	Mar 1847	N.-Amer	569271
Heinzelmann, Christine		3 Dec 1831	Lossburg	Frd.	Sep 1854	N.-Amer	569274
Heinzelmann, Elisabetha		6 Apr 1794	Bergfelden	Sulz	bef 1830	Hungary	849625
Heinzelmann, Eva			Dietersweiler	Frd.	Jan 1823	Russia	569269
Heinzelmann, Eva		7 Feb 1824	Schoemberg	Frd.	Sep 1852	N.-Amer	569271
Heinzelmann, Jacob		6 Mar 1845	Lossburg	Frd.	Apr 1860	N.-Amer	577777
Heinzelmann, Johann Adam		1 Mar 1811	Klosterreichenbach	Frd.	Apr 1837	N.-Amer	569268
Heinzelmann, Johann Georg		14 May 1807	Edelweiler	Frd.	bef 1839	N.-Amer	569268
Heinzelmann, Johann Georg		20 yrs.	Reinerzau	Frd.	Sep 1854	N.-Amer	569274
Heinzelmann, Johann Jakob		18 yrs.	Voehringen	Sulz	Jul 1854	N.-Amer	849643
Heinzelmann, Johann Martin			Bergfelden	Sulz	bef 1834	Hungary	849625
Heinzelmann, Johann Martin		6 May 1816	Bergfelden	Sulz	bef 1830	Hungary	849625
Heinzelmann, Johann Martin & F			Bergfelden	Sulz	bef 1830	Hungary	849625
Heinzelmann, Johannes & F		4 Sep 1801	Gruental	Frd.	Mar 1847	N.-Amer	569271
Heinzelmann, Johannes & F		20 Jan 1819	Glatten	Frd.	Oct 1854	S.-Amer	569274
Heinzelmann, Louise Chr.			Voehringen	Sulz	Jul 1837	N.-Amer	849643
Heinzelmann, Maria Elis. (wife)		32 yrs.	Freudenstadt	Frd.	May 1752	Pen.N-A	550803
Heinzelmann, Maria Margaretha		18 Aug 1841	Glatten	Frd.	Oct 1854	S.-Amer	569274
Heinzelmann, Mathaeus		14 Nov 1869	Waelde	Sulz	Apr 1884	N.-Amer	849644
Heinzelmann, Mathaeus		14 Nov 1869	Breitenau/Waelde	Sulz	Mar 1884	N.-Amer	849626
Heinzelmann, Mathias		30 Dec 1795	Lombach	Frd.	May 1847	France	569271
Heinzelmann, Matthias		16 Oct 1841	Dornhan	Sulz	Feb 1860	N.-Amer	849633
Heinzelmann, Michael		30 Jul 1849	Hopfau	Sulz	Feb 1868	N.-Amer	849636
Heinzelmann, Sibilla Cathar.			Freudenstadt	Frd.	Sep 1854	N.-Amer	569274
Heinzmann, Agatha		5 Feb 1830	Baiersbronn	Frd.	Oct 1852	N.-Amer	569271
Heinzmann, Anna Maria & C		21 May 1845	Nufringen	Herr.	Oct 1868	N.-Amer	834624
Heinzmann, Johann Martin		15 Nov 1866	Nufringen	Herr.	Oct 1868	N.-Amer	834624
Heinzmann, Matthaeus		9 Jan 1851	Nufringen	Herr.	Oct 1868	N.-Amer	834624
Heitzmann, Jakob			Tumlingen	Frd.	Dec 1840	Wien	569268
Heitzmann, Johann Georg		20 May 1823	Herzogsweiler	Frd.	Aug 1853	N.-Amer	569274
Heitzmann, Matthaeus		14 Oct 1844	Tumlingen	Frd.	Apr 1859	N.-Amer	577776
Heizmann, Agatha (wife)			Holzhausen	Sulz	Apr 1836	N.-Amer	849635
Heizmann, Anna		21 Feb 1870	Brittheim	Sulz	May 1882	N.-Amer	849632
Heizmann, Anna Maria		25 Jan 1845	Wittershausen	Sulz	Oct 1860	N.-Amer	849644
Heizmann, Anna Maria		14 Aug 1864	Brittheim	Sulz	May 1882	N.-Amer	849632
Heizmann, Anna Maria			Hopfau	Sulz	May 1841	Baden	849636

Heizmann, Barbara	10 Mar 1834	Wittershausen	Sulz	1853	N.-Amer	849644
Heizmann, Christian	18 Feb 1835	Duerrenmettstetten	Sulz	Feb 1854	N. Amer	849635
Heizmann, Christian & C	18 Oct 1814	Baiersbronn	Frd.	Jun 1855	N.-Amer	569275
Heizmann, Christina	2 Aug 1839	Wittershausen	Sulz	1853	N.-Amer	849644
Heizmann, Friedrich	7 Aug 1835	Wittershausen	Sulz	1853	N.-Amer	849644
Heizmann, Georg Friedrich	20 May 1840	Baiersbronn	Frd.	Jun 1855	N.-Amer	569275
Heizmann, Georg Michael & W	31 Jul 1809	Holzhausen	Sulz	Apr 1836	N.-Amer	849635
Heizmann, Jakob	30 Oct 1842	Wittershausen	Sulz	Oct 1860	N.-Amer	849644
Heizmann, Jakob & F	21 Nov 1808	Wittershausen	Sulz	1853	N.-Amer	849644
Heizmann, Johann Georg		Duerrenmettstetten	Sulz	Feb 1854	N.-Amer	849635
Heizmann, Johannes	13 Nov 1853	Wittershausen	Sulz	Oct 1860	N.-Amer	849644
Heizmann, Mathaeus		Duerrenmettstetten	Sulz	1857	N.-Amer	849635
Heizmann, Mathias		Duerrenmettstetten	Sulz	bef 1854	N.-Amer	849635
Heizmann, Rosina		Duerrenmettstetten	Sulz	Feb 1854	N.-Amer	849635
Heizmann, Ursula	12 May 1849	Wittershausen	Sulz	Oct 1860	N.-Amer	849644
Heizmann, Ursula & F	18 Jun 1809	Wittershausen	Sulz	Oct 1860	N.-Amer	849644
Hek, Christian		Nufringen	Herr.	Mar 1837	N.-Amer	834624
Hek, Christian	28 Sep 1828	Moenchberg	Herr.	Jan 1867	N.-Amer	834624
Hekele, Anna	21 yrs.	Trichtingen	Sulz	Jul 1817	Hungary	849625
Hekele, Barbara	17 Nov 1843	Trichtingen	Sulz	Mar 1869	N.-Amer	849642
Hekele, Christina	24 Feb 1842	Trichtingen	Sulz	Mar 1867	N.-Amer	849642
Hekele, Martin & F	47 yrs.	Trichtingen	Sulz	Jul 1817	Hungary	849625
Hekele, Michael	14 yrs.	Trichtingen	Sulz	Jul 1817	Hungary	849625
Helber, Anna Maria	4 Jun 1822	Iselshausen	Nag.	Feb 1854	N.-Amer	838491
Helber, Christian Immanuel	7 Jan 1849	Iselshausen	Nag.	Feb 1854	N.-Amer	838491
Helber, Eugen Socrates J.	12 Nov 1846	Pfalzgrafenweiler	Frd.	Mar 1854	N.-Amer	569273
Helber, Faiter Christian & F	44 yrs.	Pfalzgrafenweiler	Frd.	Mar 1854	N.-Amer	569273
Helber, Friederike	10 Jul 1826	Wildberg	Nag.	Feb 1856	Bavaria	838492
Helber, Gustav Adolph	9 Jul 1845	Pfalzgrafenweiler	Frd.	Mar 1854	N.-Amer	569273
Helber, Hanna Lyd. Chr.	8 Sep 1850	Pfalzgrafenweiler	Frd.	Mar 1854	N.-Amer	569273
Helber, Jakob	23 Oct 1853	Iselshausen	Nag.	Feb 1854	N.-Amer	838491
Helber, Johannes	10 Sep 1846	Iselshausen	Nag.	Feb 1854	N.-Amer	838491
Helber, Konrad Gottlob & F	25 May 1818	Iselshausen	Nag.	Feb 1854	N.-Amer	838491
Helber, Louise Agatha (wife)		Pfalzgrafenweiler	Frd.	Mar 1854	N.-Amer	569273
Helber, Maria Tabitha	26 Jun 1848	Pfalzgrafenweiler	Frd.	Mar 1854	N.-Amer	569273
Held, Anna Maria	25 Nov 1847	Nufringen	Herr.	Mar 1868	N.-Amer	834624
Held, Johannes		Rosenfeld	Sulz	bef 1867	N.-Amer	849641
Held, Wilhelm	26 Jan 1845	Rosenfeld	Sulz	Jun 1865	N.-Amer	849641
Heldmaier, Jacob		Moettlingen	Calw	1868	Baden	563212
Heldmaier, Jacob & F		Ostelsheim	Calw	1852	N.-Amer	563212
Heldmaier, Justine Dorothea		Moettlingen	Calw	1863	N.-Amer	563212
Heller, Anna	1850	Bergfelden	Sulz	Mar 1857	N.-Amer	849629
Heller, Anna Maria (wife)	19 Jan 1803	Bergfelden	Sulz	Mar 1857	N.-Amer	849629
Heller, Eva Katharina	1843	Bergfelden	Sulz	Mar 1857	N.-Amer	849629
Heller, Friedrich & F	2 Jun 1803	Bergfelden	Sulz	Mar 1857	N.-Amer	849629
Heller, Johann Georg	29 Aug 1831	Bergfelden	Sulz	Aug 1861	N.-Amer	849629
Heller, Johann Martin	29 Oct 1840	Bergfelden	Sulz	Mar 1857	N.-Amer	849629
Heller, Johannes		Bergfelden	Sulz	Aug 1854	N.-Amer	849629
Heller, Maria Katharina		Bergfelden	Sulz	Mar 1857	N.-Amer	849629
Heller, Paul Friedrich		Weiden	Sulz	1848	N.-Amer	849644

Name		Birth		Emigration			Film
Last	First	Date	Place	O'amt	Appl. Date	Dest.	Number
Hellerich, Louise Caroline			Schorndorf	Frd.	Nov 1853	N.-Amer	569272
Hellstern, Hermann		1 Jan 1845	Sulz	Sulz	Dec 1865	Switz.	849628
Hemminger, August		5 Sep 1835	Klosterreichenbach	Frd.	Sep 1853	N.-Amer	569272
Henger, Andreas & F			Bergfelden	Sulz	Dec 1854	N.-Amer	849629
Henger, Anna		4 yrs.	Bergfelden	Sulz	Dec 1854	N.-Amer	849629
Henger, Anna (wife)			Bergfelden	Sulz	Dec 1854	N.-Amer	849629
Henger, Anna Maria		infant	Bergfelden	Sulz	Dec 1854	N.-Amer	849629
Henger, Anna Maria		20 yrs.	Bergfelden	Sulz	Nov 1853	N.-Amer	849629
Henger, Anna Maria		9 yrs.	Bergfelden	Sulz	Apr 1833	N.-Amer	849629
Henger, Barbara		12 yrs.	Bergfelden	Sulz	Apr 1833	N.-Amer	849629
Henger, Christian		9 Oct 1852	Bergfelden	Sulz	Apr 1860	N.-Amer	849629
Henger, Christian		2 yrs.	Bergfelden	Sulz	Dec 1854	N.-Amer	849629
Henger, Christian		25 yrs.	Bergfelden	Sulz	Nov 1853	N.-Amer	849629
Henger, Christian		14 Mar 1866	Bergfelden	Sulz	Feb 1883	N.-Amer	849626
Henger, Jakob			Bergfelden	Sulz	Nov 1852	Austria	849629
Henger, Johann Georg		7 yrs.	Bergfelden	Sulz	Dec 1854	N.-Amer	849629
Henger, Johann Georg		2 yrs.	Bergfelden	Sulz	Apr 1833	N.-Amer	849629
Henger, Johann Jacob		31 yrs.	Bergfelden	Sulz	Nov 1853	N.-Amer	849629
Henger, Johann Jacob		6 yrs.	Bergfelden	Sulz	Apr 1833	N.-Amer	849629
Henger, Johann Jacob & F		25 Apr 1793	Bergfelden	Sulz	Apr 1833	N.-Amer	849629
Henger, Johann Jacob & F			Bergfelden	Sulz	Jun 1817	Russia	849629
Henger, Johanna		15 yrs.	Bergfelden	Sulz	Nov 1853	N.-Amer	849629
Henger, Johannes			Sulz	Sulz	Jul 1854	N.-Amer	849627
Henger, Johannes		30 yrs.	Bergfelden	Sulz	Nov 1853	N.-Amer	849629
Henger, Maria Catharina		22 yrs.	Bergfelden	Sulz	Nov 1853	N.-Amer	849629
Henger, Matheus & F			Bergfelden	Sulz	Nov 1853	N.-Amer	849629
Henger, Rosine Catharine		8 yrs.	Bergfelden	Sulz	Nov 1853	N.-Amer	849629
Henger, Sabina		7 yrs.	Bergfelden	Sulz	Apr 1833	N.-Amer	849629
Henger, Sabina (wife)			Bergfelden	Sulz	Apr 1833	N.-Amer	849629
Hengsteler, Agatha		5 Mar 1824	Leidringen	Sulz	Jan 1833	N.-Amer	849637
Hengsteler, Andreas			Leidringen	Sulz	Mar 1837	N.-Amer	849637
Hengsteler, Anna		2 Apr 1829	Leidringen	Sulz	Jan 1833	N.-Amer	849637
Hengsteler, Anna Barbara			Leidringen	Sulz	Mar 1837	N.-Amer	849637
Hengsteler, Anna Maria			Leidringen	Sulz	bef 1850	W.-Prs.	849625
Hengsteler, Anna Maria		17 Mar 1835	Trichtingen	Sulz	bef 1857	N.-Amer	849642
Hengsteler, Anna Maria		22 yrs.	Leidringen	Sulz	Mar 1837	N.-Amer	849637
Hengsteler, Anna Maria		11 Jan 1819	Leidringen	Sulz	Jan 1833	N.-Amer	849637
Hengsteler, Anna Regina			Rosenfeld	Sulz	Jun 1812	Leipzig	849625
Hengsteler, Barbara		24 Aug 1821	Leidringen	Sulz	Jan 1833	N.-Amer	849637
Hengsteler, Georg			Leidringen	Sulz	Mar 1837	N.-Amer	849637
Hengsteler, Georg (wid.) & F		23 Apr 1784	Leidringen	Sulz	Mar 1837	N.-Amer	849637
Hengsteler, Johann Georg			Leidringen	Sulz	Mar 1837	N.-Amer	849637
Hengsteler, Johann Jacob & F		22 Jul 1790	Leidringen	Sulz	Jan 1833	N.-Amer	849637
Hengsteler, Johann Jakob			Trichtingen	Sulz	Nov 1811	Austria	849625
Hengsteler, Johann Martin		31 May 1868	Boll	Sulz	Jul 1884	N.-Amer	849632
Hengsteler, Karl		11 Jun 1836	Leidringen	Sulz	Feb 1854	N.-Amer	849637
Hengsteler, Ludwig			Leidringen	Sulz	Mar 1837	N.-Amer	849637
Hengsteler, Martin		28 Jun 1831	Leidringen	Sulz	Jan 1833	N.-Amer	849637
Hengsteler, Sophie (wife)			Leidringen	Sulz	Jan 1833	N.-Amer	849637
Hengsteler, Ursula		7 yrs.	Leidringen	Sulz	Mar 1837	N.-Amer	849637

Hengstler, Martin	14 Jul 1811	Leidringen	Sulz	bef 1843	N.-Amer	849637
Henne, Anna		Minderobach	Nag.	Sep 1854	N.-Amer	838491
Henne, Catharina		Zwerenberg	Calw	1852	N.-Amer	563212
Henne, Christina		Zwerenberg	Calw	1852	N.-Amer	563212
Henne, Christine	24 yrs.	Zwerenberg	Calw	1855	N.-Amer	563212
Henne, Dorothea		Zwerenberg	Calw	1852	N.-Amer	563212
Henne, Dorothea		Unterjesingen	Herr.	Apr 1830	N.-Amer	834624
Henne, Hedwig	1 Nov 1838	Unterjettingen	Herr.	1847	N.-Amer	834626
Henne, Jakob Martin	1824	Hirsau	Calw	1856	Bavaria	563212
Henne, Johann Christof	3 Sep 1847	Nufringen	Herr.	Apr 1867	N.-Amer	834624
Hennefahrt, Johann Georg & F		Breitenberg	Calw	1852	N.-Amer	563212
Hennefarth, Michael	17 yrs.	Breitenberg	Calw	1869	N.-Amer	563212
Henninger, Johannes		Herzogsweiler	Frd.	Apr 1752	Pen.N-A	550803
Hensler, Johann Wilhelm		Pfalzgrafenweiler	Frd.	bef 1839	N.-Amer	569268
Henssler, Anna Maria		Altenstaig	Nag.	Jun 1856	N.-Amer	838492
Henssler, Christian	6 Jan 1839	Pfalzgrafenweiler	Frd.	Apr 1854	N.-Amer	569273
Henssler, Elisabetha		Igelsberg	Frd.	bef 1854	N.-Amer	569274
Henssler, Elisabetha & C	22 Nov 1815	Altenstaig	Nag.	Jun 1856	N.-Amer	838492
Henssler, Friederika	27 Jan 1826	Dornstetten	Frd.	Jan 1849	N.-Amer	569270
Henssler, Johannes	5 Aug 1850	Altenstaig	Nag.	Jun 1856	N.-Amer	838492
Henzel, Anna Maria		Deckenpfronn	Calw	1854	N.-Amer	563212
Henzler, Carl Theodor	Jun 1835	Pfaeffingen	Herr.	Oct 1869	Boppard	834624
Heppting, Agnes (wife)		Freudenstadt	Frd.	Sep 1854	N.-Amer	569274
Heppting, August Wilhelm	18 Feb 1842	Freudenstadt	Frd.	Sep 1854	N.-Amer	569274
Heppting, Christine Margar.& C	14 Oct 1832	Freudenstadt	Frd.	Sep 1854	N.-Amer	569274
Heppting, Georg Friedrich		Freudenstadt	Frd.	Oct 1852	N.-Amer	577778
Heppting, Jakob & F		Freudenstadt	Frd.	Sep 1854	N.-Amer	569274
Heppting, Johann Carl	3 Jun 1854	Freudenstadt	Frd.	Sep 1854	N.-Amer	569274
Heppting, Johann Friedrich	6 Jun 1849	Freudenstadt	Frd.	Sep 1854	N.-Amer	569274
Heppting, Johann Jakob	17 Nov 1839	Freudenstadt	Frd.	Sep 1854	N.-Amer	569274
Heppting, Maria	25 Sep 1830	Freudenstadt	Frd.	bef 1863	Hesse	577778
Heppting, Pauline Sophie	23 Nov 1853	Freudenstadt	Frd.	Sep 1854	N.-Amer	569274
Heppting, Rosine Louise	26 Feb 1834	Freudenstadt	Frd.	Sep 1854	N.-Amer	569274
Heppting, Sophie Caroline	28 May 1845	Freudenstadt	Frd.	Sep 1854	N.-Amer	569274
Hepting, Adam & F		Wittershausen	Sulz	Jul 1846	N.-Amer	849644
Hepting, Carl		Freudenstadt	Frd.	bef 1854	N.-Amer	569274
Herb, Johannes	15 Oct 1796	Schorndorf	Schd.	Dec 1842	Austria	801461
Herbstreit, Andreas	14 Jul 1851	Schoemberg	Frd.	Mar 1861	N.-Amer	577778
Herbstreit, Anna Maria	17 Dec 1844	Wittlensweiler	Frd.	Mar 1863	N.-Amer	577778
Herbstreit, Anna Maria & C	3 Aug 1807	Aach	Frd.	Apr 1833	N.-Amer	569267
Herbstreit, Christoph	28 May 1832	Aach	Frd.	Apr 1833	N.-Amer	569267
Herbstreit, Karl Friedrich	10 Nov 1846	Schoemberg	Frd.	Mar 1861	N.-Amer	577778
Herbstreit, Salome (wid) & F	28 Jan 1821	Winzeln	Frd.	Mar 1861	N.-Amer	577778
Herbstreuth, Michael	7 May 1834	Glatten	Frd.	Nov 1853	N.-Amer	569272
Hermann, Anna	6 Nov 1847	Muehlheim a.B.	Sulz	Jun 1865	N.-Amer	849639
Hermann, Anna (wid.) & F	6 Oct 1803	Muehlheim a.B.	Sulz	Jun 1865	N.-Amer	849639
Hermann, August Heinrich		Calw	Calw	1852	N.-Amer	563212
Hermann, Gottlieb	36 yrs.	Hirsau	Calw	1864	N.-Amer	563212
Hermann, Johann Jakob	15 Oct 1835	Muehlheim a.B.	Sulz	Oct 1865	N.-Amer	849639
Hermann, Maria Friederike	52 yrs.	Oeschelbronn	Herr.	May 1832	N.-Amer	834624

| Name | | Birth | | Emigration | | | Film |
Last	First	Date	Place	O'amt	Appl. Date	Dest.	Number
Hermann, Maria Susanna		18 Aug 1842	Sulz	Sulz	Mar 1868	Switz.	849628
Herre, Carl & F			Renfrizhausen	Sulz	Mar 1817	Russia	849639
Herre, Johannes		24 Feb 1810	Sigmarswangen	Sulz	Mar 1817	Russia	849642
Herrman, Catharina Barb. (wife)		37 yrs.	Oberjettingen	Herr.	Jul 1847	N.-Amer	834626
Herrman, Johann Georg & F		36 yrs.	Oberjettingen	Herr.	Jul 1847	N.-Amer	834626
Herrmann, Jacob		43 yrs.	Sulz	Sulz	Feb 1812	Switz.	849625
Herter, Andreas			Balingen	Bal.	Feb 1859	Switz.	555962
Herter, Anna Maria			Sulz	Nag.	Sep 1853	N.-Amer	838490
Herter, Ludwig		26 Dec 1833	Burgfelden	Bal.	bef 1861	Switz.	555962
Herter, Ludwig			Balingen	Bal.	Apr 1861	Switz.	555962
Hertmaier, Johann Lukas		14 Dec 1827	Gueltstein	Herr.	Aug 1868	N.-Amer	834624
Hertmaier, Ludwig Friedrich		18 Jun 1830	Herrenberg	Herr.	Aug 1868	N.-Amer	834624
Hertner, Regine			Freudenstadt	Frd.	bef 1813	Baden	569267
Hertner, Regine Catharine			Friedrichstal	Frd.	Jun 1813	Baden	569267
Herzer, Philipp		29 Jun 1844	Tumlingen	Frd.	Sep 1860	N.-Amer	577777
Herzog, Emilie			Sulz	Sulz	Apr 1882	N.-Amer	849626
Heselschwerdt, Anna			Zwerenberg	Calw	1866	Palest.	563212
Heselschwerdt, Eva Maria & C			Meistern/Bergorte	Calw	1852	N.-Amer	563212
Heselschwerdt, Jacob		20 yrs.	Zwerenberg	Calw	1867	Palest.	563212
Heselschwerdt, Jacob			Zwerenberg	Calw	1866	N.-Amer	563212
Heselschwerdt, Johann Geo. & F			Huernerberg/BergorteCalw		1854	N.-Amer	563212
Heselschwerdt, Johannes		22 yrs.	Zwerenberg	Calw	1866	N.-Amer	563212
Hess, Elisabetha Kathar. (wife)		28 Aug 1804	Glatten	Frd.	Oct 1854	S.-Amer	569274
Hess, Elisabetha Margaretha		9 Oct 1844	Glatten	Frd.	Oct 1854	S.-Amer	569274
Hess, Gottfried			Nagold	Nag.	Jan 1854	N.-Amer	838491
Hess, Johann & F			Dornhan	Sulz	Mar 1817	Russia	849633
Hess, Johann Ludwig & F			Nagold	Nag.	Jan 1854	N.-Amer	838491
Hess, Johannes & F		20 Feb 1816	Glatten	Frd.	Oct 1854	S.-Amer	569274
Hess, Katharina		21 Nov 1840	Glatten	Frd.	Oct 1854	S.-Amer	569274
Hess, Maria		1 yrs.	Nagold	Nag.	Jan 1854	N.-Amer	838491
Hess, Maria			Nagold	Nag.	Jan 1854	N.-Amer	838491
Hess, Robert Christian Heinr.		13 Mar 1842	Cresbach	Frd.	Feb 1857	N.-Amer	577776
Hess, Robert Christian Heinr.		1 Feb 1848	Woernersberg	Frd.	Feb 1857	N.-Amer	577776
Hetzel, Andreas		25 Apr 1822	Schoemberg	Frd.	Apr 1846	N.-Amer	569271
Hetzel, Anna Barbara		6 Apr 1820	Schoemberg	Frd.	Apr 1846	N.-Amer	569271
Hetzel, Anna Dorothea		28 Feb 1792	Alpiersbach	Frd.	Apr 1846	N.-Amer	569271
Hetzel, Anna Maria & C		17 Apr 1814	Schoemberg	Frd.	Apr 1846	N.-Amer	569271
Hetzel, Barbara			Schoemberg	Frd.	Jun 1854	N.-Amer	569273
Hetzel, Barbara		6 Jan 1842	Peterzell	Frd.	Apr 1846	N.-Amer	569271
Hetzel, Caroline			Schoemberg	Frd.	Jun 1854	N.-Amer	569273
Hetzel, Christian			Schoemberg	Frd.	Jun 1854	N.-Amer	569273
Hetzel, Christiane		26 Nov 1825	Schoemberg	Frd.	Apr 1846	N.-Amer	569271
Hetzel, Christine			Schoemberg	Frd.	Jun 1854	N.-Amer	569273
Hetzel, Friedrich & F			Schoemberg	Frd.	Jun 1854	N.-Amer	569273
Hetzel, Friedrich & F		18 Nov 1784	Voehringen	Frd.	Apr 1846	N.-Amer	569271
Hetzel, Jakob Friedrich		28 Apr 1830	Schoemberg	Frd.	Apr 1846	N.-Amer	569271
Hetzel, Johann Conrad			Voehringen	Sulz	1848		849643
Hetzel, Johann Friedrich			Sulz	Sulz	Jan 1817	Augsb.	849627
Hetzel, Johann Georg		18 Mar 1834	Sigmarswangen	Sulz	Aug 1854		849642
Hetzel, Johann Gottlieb			Sulz	Sulz	Jan 1817	Augsb.	849627

Hetzer, Anna Maria	4 Jun 1822	Iselshausen	Nag.	Feb 1854	N.-Amer	838491
Heumesser, Vincenz	26 Jan 1837	Oberndorf	Herr.	Mai 1869	N.-Amer	834024
Heyd, Christian & F	15 Apr 1854	Hopfau	Sulz	1889	Switz.	849636
Heyd, Jakob	11 Oct 1856	Hopfau	Sulz	Mar 1871	N.-Amer	849636
Heyd, Wilhelm Andreas	5 Jun 1848	Gueltstein	Herr.	Apr 1866	N.-Amer	834624
Heydlauf, Christiane Hedwig	15 Oct 1845	Gueltstein	Herr.	Mar 1869	N.-Amer	834624
Heydlauf, Elisabeth Katharina	7 Jan 1835	Gueltstein	Herr.	Apr 1869	N.-Amer	834624
Heyer, Friedrich Wilhelm		Hagelloch/Tuebingen Herr.		Aug 1836	N.-Amer	834624
Hezel, Agnes Catharina		Sulz	Sulz	May 1834	N.-Amer	849627
Hezel, Andreas		Voehringen	Sulz	May 1852	N.-Amer	849643
Hezel, Andreas	19 Jun 1880	Holzhausen	Sulz	Mar 1881	N.-Amer	849635
Hezel, Anna Maria	16 Aug 1839	Voehringen	Sulz	May 1852	N.-Amer	849643
Hezel, Anna Maria	4 Mar 1787	Sigmarswangen	Sulz	May 1817	N.-Amer	849642
Hezel, Barbara (wife)		Voehringen	Sulz	May 1852	N.-Amer	849643
Hezel, Christine Barb.		Sigmarswangen	Sulz	May 1834	N.-Amer	849627
Hezel, Elisabetha (mother)		Muehlheim a.B.	Sulz	May 1817	Russia	849639
Hezel, Eva (wife)	22 Nov 1845	Holzhausen	Sulz	Mar 1881	N.-Amer	849635
Hezel, Georg Adam & F		Bergfelden	Sulz	Oct 1853	N.-Amer	849629
Hezel, Gottlieb Friedrich	14 Oct 1812	Sigmarswangen	Sulz	May 1834	N.-Amer	849627
Hezel, Jacob		Voehringen	Sulz	Jun 1817	Russia	849643
Hezel, Jacob	14 Jan 1850	Marschalkenzimmern Sulz		Dec 1870	N.-Amer	849638
Hezel, Jacob & W		Sigmarswangen	Sulz	May 1817	--	849642
Hezel, Jakob & F		Muehlheim a.B.	Sulz	Aug 1847	N.-Amer	849639
Hezel, Jakob & F		Muehlheim a.B.	Sulz	May 1817	Russia	849639
Hezel, Johann Georg	12 yrs.	Aistaig	Sulz	Mar 1833	N.-Amer	849628
Hezel, Johann Martin	9 May 1843	Voehringen	Sulz	May 1852	N.-Amer	849643
Hezel, Johannes	27 May 1877	Holzhausen	Sulz	Mar 1881	N.-Amer	849635
Hezel, Johannes	12 Oct 1846	Muehlheim a.B.	Sulz	Sep 1866	N.-Amer	849639
Hezel, Johannes & F		Bergfelden	Sulz	Jun 1817	Russia	849629
Hezel, Johannes & F	8 Sep 1845	Holzhausen	Sulz	Mar 1881	N.-Amer	849635
Hezel, Joseph		Sigmarswangen	Sulz	Oct 1854	N.-Amer	849642
Hezel, Katharina	5 Feb 1876	Holzhausen	Sulz	Mar 1881	N.-Amer	849635
Hezel, Ludwig		Wittershausen	Sulz	bef 1810	Switz.	849625
Hezel, Ludwig	30 Aug 1855	Muehlheim a.B.	Sulz	Jan 1870	N.-Amer	849639
Hezel, Maria Catharina	11 Mar 1826	Wildberg	Nag.	Feb 1861	H-Nass.	838493
Hezel, Matthias	25 Mar 1851	Wittershausen	Sulz	Feb 1869	N.-Amer	849644
Hezel, Salome & F		Boll	Sulz	Jul 1852	N.-Amer	849632
Hezel, Sibilla Regina & F	20 Dec 1777	Aistaig	Sulz	Mar 1833	N.-Amer	849628
Hezle, Katharina	2 May 1845	Muehlheim a.B.	Sulz	Mar 1868	N.-Amer	849639
Hildt, Maria Barbara		Calw	Calw	Mar 1848	France	563212
Hilfinger, Friederike (wife)		Oberiflingen	Frd.	Mar 1833	N.-Amer	569268
Hilfinger, Mathias & F	18 Dec 1806	Oberiflingen	Frd.	Mar 1833	N.-Amer	569268
Hiller, Adam Friedrich	6 Mar 1836	Moetzingen	Herr.	Aug 1847	N.-Amer	834626
Hiller, Adam Friedrich & F	22 Mar 1807	Moetzingen	Herr.	May 1852	N.-Amer	834627
Hiller, Andreas	18 Mar 1834	Oeschelbronn	Herr.	May 1852	N.-Amer	834627
Hiller, Anna Catharina	27 yrs.	Oeschelbronn	Herr.	May 1852	N.-Amer	834627
Hiller, Anna Maria	14 Nov 1843	Schietingen	Nag.	Feb 1852	N.-Amer	838490
Hiller, Anna Maria	15 Jan 1847	Moetzingen	Herr.	May 1852	N.-Amer	834624
Hiller, Anna Maria		Moetzingen	Herr.	Apr 1831	N.-Amer	834624
Hiller, Anna Maria (wife)		Oeschelbronn	Herr.	May 1852	N.-Amer	834627

Name		Birth		Emigration			Film
Last	First	Date	Place	O'amt	Appl. Date	Dest.	Number
Hiller, August		23 Sep 1848	Holzhausen	Sulz	Jun 1868	N.-Amer	849635
Hiller, Christian		30 Apr 1835	Moetzingen	Herr.	Aug 1847	N.-Amer	834626
Hiller, Christian		5 Feb 1838	Oeschelbronn	Herr.	May 1852	N.-Amer	834627
Hiller, Christian Friedrich		24 Aug 1806	Herrenberg	Herr.	Jul 1844	N.-Amer	834626
Hiller, Christina		7 Jul 1839	Oeschelbronn	Herr.	May 1852	N.-Amer	834627
Hiller, Christina Barb. (wife)		11 Jun 1819	Moetzingen	Herr.	May 1852	N.-Amer	834627
Hiller, Christina Barbara (wife)		15 Oct 1808	Moetzingen	Herr.	Aug 1847	N.-Amer	834626
Hiller, Dorothea		14 Feb 1844	Moetzingen	Herr.	May 1852	N.-Amer	834627
Hiller, Gottfried		7 Mar 1861	Tuebingen	Sulz	Aug 1881	N.-Amer	849642
Hiller, Gottlieb & F			Oeschelbronn	Herr.	May 1852	N.-Amer	834627
Hiller, Gottlieb & F			Moetzingen	Herr.	Apr 1834	N.-Amer	834624
Hiller, Gottlieb (wid.) & F			Moetzingen	Herr.	Jun 1832	N.-Amer	834624
Hiller, Heinrich & W			Moetzingen	Herr.	Jun 1832	N.-Amer	834624
Hiller, Johann Friedrich		4 Sep 1839	Schietingen	Nag.	Feb 1852	N.-Amer	838490
Hiller, Johann Georg		11 May 1834	Frutenhof	Frd.	Sep 1856	N.-Amer	569275
Hiller, Johannes		14 Aug 1841	Schietingen	Nag.	Feb 1852	N.-Amer	838490
Hiller, Johannes		11 Jun 1834	Moetzingen	Herr.	Aug 1847	N.-Amer	834626
Hiller, Johannes		8 Aug 1845	Moetzingen	Herr.	May 1852	N.-Amer	834627
Hiller, Johannes & F			Schietingen	Nag.	Feb 1852	N.-Amer	838490
Hiller, Johannes & F		15 Aug 1809	Moetzingen	Herr.	Aug 1847	N.-Amer	834626
Hiller, Johannes & W		28 yrs.	Moetzingen	Herr.	Jun 1832	N.-Amer	834624
Hiller, Karl		16 Aug 1845	Moetzingen	Herr.	Aug 1847	N.-Amer	834626
Hiller, Katharina Barbara		13 Feb 1842	Moetzingen	Herr.	May 1852	N.-Amer	834627
Hiller, Lucas		30 Apr 1841	Moetzingen	Herr.	Aug 1847	N.-Amer	834626
Hiller, Maria (wife)			Moetzingen	Herr.	Jun 1832	N.-Amer	834624
Hiller, Maria Magdalena (wife)			Moetzingen	Herr.	Jun 1832	N.-Amer	834624
Hiller, Matthias Friedrich			Dornhan	Sulz	Jan 1860	France	849633
Hiller, Michael Friedrich		22 Jan 1849	Moetzingen	Herr.	May 1852	N.-Amer	834627
Hiller, Rebecca		29 Oct 1846	Moetzingen	Herr.	Aug 1847	N.-Amer	834626
Hiller, Rosina		20 Jan 1837	Schietingen	Nag.	Feb 1852	N.-Amer	838490
Hiller, Wilhelm Gottlieb		10 Oct 1812	Herrenberg	Herr.	Apr 1851	N.-Amer	834627
Hils, Andreas		18 Feb 1834	Boll	Sulz	Jul 1853	N.-Amer	849632
Hils, Christian Ludwig		7 Jul 1837	Sulz	Sulz	May 1857	N.-Amer	849628
Hilzinger, Johann Georg			Freudenstadt	Frd.	Sep 1822	Bavaria	569267
Hindelang, Christian			Klosterreichenbach	Frd.	1805	Hungary	569268
Hindennach, Gottlieb Fr.		11 Nov 1835	Herzogsweiler	Frd.	Feb 1854	N.-Amer	569273
Hindennach, Johann Georg		17 Feb 1838	Herzogsweiler	Frd.	Jun 1854	N.-Amer	569273
Hindennach, Johannes		16 Mar 1837	Pfalzgrafenweiler	Frd.	Apr 1853	N.-Amer	569272
Hindennach, Johannes		20 Apr 1838	Herzogsweiler	Frd.	Mar 1853	N.-Amer	569272
Hinderer, Johann Michael		8 Aug 1792	Gaertringen	Herr.	Oct 1851	N.-Amer	834627
Hineisen, Gottlieb & F			Gechingen	Calw	1852	N.-Amer	563212
Hipp, Ernst Gottlieb		5 Apr 1846	Binsdorf	Sulz	Jan 1866	N.-Amer	849631
Hipp, Johannes		4 Mar 1848	Boll	Sulz	Dec 1868	N.-Amer	849632
Hirlinger, Christian			Leidringen	Sulz	May 1853	N.-Amer	849637
Hirlinger, Christina (wife)			Leidringen	Sulz	Mar 1837	N.-Amer	849637
Hirlinger, Maria Salome		23 Feb 1836	Leidringen	Sulz	Sep 1866	N.-Amer	849637
Hirlinger, Matheis		2 yrs.	Leidringen	Sulz	Mar 1837	N.-Amer	849637
Hirlinger, Wilhelm		3 yrs.	Leidringen	Sulz	Mar 1837	N.-Amer	849637
Hirlinger, Wilhelm & F		5 Nov 1799	Leidringen	Sulz	Mar 1837	N.-Amer	849637
Hirlinger, Wilhelm Ludwig		28 Dec 1850	Leidringen	Sulz	Aug 1867	N.-Amer	849637

Hirsch, Karoline Friederike	1 Jul 1883	Dornhan	Sulz	Jun 1885	N.-Amer	849626
Hirth, Jacob	2 Feb 1842	Tailfingen	Herr.	Nov 1865	N.-Amer	834624
Hirth, Johann Georg & F		Haslach	Herr.	Apr 1835	N.-Amer	834624
Hirth, Johannes	1 Nov 1828	Dornstetten	Frd.	bef 1856	France	569275
Hirth, Johannes	22 Feb 1846	Reusten	Herr.	Apr 1866	N.-Amer	834624
Hitzinger, Johann Friedrich		Freudenstadt	Frd.	Dec 1817	Bavaria	569267
Hochstetter, Carl Chr. Heinr.	8 Dec 1814	Sulz	Sulz	bef 1846	Bavaria	849627
Hodderlin, Carl Albert	1840	Deckenpfronn	Calw	1860	N.-Amer	563212
Hoeckh, Jacob		Reusten	Herr.	Apr 1830	N.-Amer	834624
Hoeckh, Johann Christian	4 Feb 1839	Unterjesingen	Herr.	May 1852	N.-Amer	834627
Hoeckh, Johann Christian & F		Unterjesingen	Herr.	May 1852	N.-Amer	834627
Hoeckh, Maria Katharina (wife)		Unterjesingen	Herr.	May 1852	N.-Amer	834627
Hoefel, Anna Magdalena	5 Mar 1834	Gaertringen	Herr.	Oct 1867	N.-Amer	834624
Hoehing, Jacob		Nagold	Nag.	Mar 1854	N.-Amer	838491
Hoehn, Agnes (wife)		Rosenfeld	Sulz	Jun 1817	Russia	849640
Hoehn, Andreas	9 yrs.	Rosenfeld	Sulz	Jun 1817	Russia	849640
Hoehn, Anna	6 yrs.	Rosenfeld	Sulz	Jun 1817	Russia	849640
Hoehn, Anna Maria	7 May 1842	Bickelsberg	Sulz	Apr 1854	N.-Amer	849630
Hoehn, Anna Maria	10 Nov 1784	Muehlheim a.B.	Sulz	May 1833	N.-Amer	849639
Hoehn, Anna Maria	15 yrs.	Rosenfeld	Sulz	Jun 1817	Russia	849640
Hoehn, Anna Maria (wife)		Isingen	Sulz	Mar 1817	Russia	849636
Hoehn, Barbara	12 yrs.	Rosenfeld	Sulz	Jun 1817	Russia	849640
Hoehn, Christian		Rosenfeld	Sulz	Dec 1842	Austria	849640
Hoehn, Christian	9 yrs.	Rosenfeld	Sulz	Jun 1817	Russia	849640
Hoehn, Christiane	11 Jul 1830	Freudenstadt	Frd.	Sep 1854	N.-Amer	569274
Hoehn, Christina	22 Feb 1850	Bickelsberg	Sulz	Apr 1854	N.-Amer	849630
Hoehn, Christina (wife)	3 Jun 1809	Bickelsberg	Sulz	Apr 1854	N.-Amer	849630
Hoehn, Elisabetha (wife)	39 yrs.	Rosenfeld	Sulz	Jun 1817	Russia	849640
Hoehn, Friederike	17 Apr 1827	Freudenstadt	Frd.	Sep 1854	N.-Amer	569274
Hoehn, Georg	23 Jun 1837	Bickelsberg	Sulz	Apr 1854	N.-Amer	849630
Hoehn, Gottlieb	28 Sep 1871	Isingen	Sulz	Jul 1888	N.-Amer	849636
Hoehn, Jakob	1 Jun 1833	Wittendorf	Frd.	Jan 1861	N.-Amer	577778
Hoehn, Johann Friedrich	25 Apr 1839	Baiersbronn	Frd.	Sep 1856	N.-Amer	569275
Hoehn, Johann Georg	8 Apr 1841	Baiersbronn	Frd.	Nov 1859	N.-Amer	577776
Hoehn, Johann Georg	7 yrs.	Isingen	Sulz	Mar 1817	Russia	849636
Hoehn, Johann Georg	7 yrs.	Rosenfeld	Sulz	Jun 1817	Russia	849640
Hoehn, Johann Georg & F		Rosenfeld	Sulz	bef 1831	Odessa	849640
Hoehn, Johann Georg & F	40 yrs.	Rosenfeld	Sulz	Jun 1817	Russia	849640
Hoehn, Johann Jakob & F		Bickelsberg	Sulz	Apr 1854	N.-Amer	849630
Hoehn, Johann Martin		Isingen	Sulz	Mar 1853	N.-Amer	849636
Hoehn, Johann Martin	18 yrs.	Isingen	Sulz	Mar 1817	Russia	849636
Hoehn, Johann Martin & F	47 yrs.	Rosenfeld	Sulz	Jun 1817	Russia	849640
Hoehn, Johannes	5 yrs.	Rosenfeld	Sulz	Jun 1817	Russia	849640
Hoehn, Johannes	17 yrs.	Rosenfeld	Sulz	Jun 1817	Russia	849640
Hoehn, Johannes & F		Isingen	Sulz	Mar 1817	Russia	849636
Hoehn, Johannes & W	12 Feb 1819	Voehringen	Sulz	bef 1834	N.-Amer	849643
Hoehn, Maria Rosina	2 yrs.	Rosenfeld	Sulz	Jun 1817	Russia	849640
Hoehn, Rudolph	9 Jul 1837	Baiersbronn	Frd.	Sep 1856	N.-Amer	569275
Hoehne, Jacob	26 Feb 1858	Reinerzau	Frd.	Sep 1862	N.-Amer	577778
Hoek, Johann Georg	Mar 1850	Pfaeffingen	Herr.	Feb 1869	N.-Amer	834624

Name		Birth		Emigration			Film
Last	First	Date	Place	O'amt	Appl. Date	Dest.	Number
Hoek, Johann Heinrich		10 Sep 1812	Pfaeffingen	Herr.	bef 1847	Austria	834626
Hoekh, Christian Friedrich		30 Dec 1849	Pfaeffingen	Herr.	Feb 1869	N.-Amer	834624
Hoelder, Theodor Traugott		1848	Deckenpfronn	Calw	1868	N.-Amer	563212
Hoelle, Agnes & C		24 yrs.	Binsdorf	Sulz	Sep 1863	Hohenz.	849631
Hoelle, Andreas			Bickelsberg	Sulz	Jul 1853	N.-Amer	849630
Hoelle, Andreas			Leidringen	Sulz	Aug 1853	N.-Amer	849637
Hoelle, Andreas		11 Feb 1840	Leidringen	Sulz	Jul 1865	N.-Amer	849637
Hoelle, Andreas		18 Aug 1817	Leidringen	Sulz	May 1864	N.-Amer	849637
Hoelle, Anna			Bickelsberg	Sulz	Jul 1853	N.-Amer	849630
Hoelle, Anna Barbara			Bickelsberg	Sulz	Jul 1853	N.-Amer	849630
Hoelle, Anna Catharina			Bickelsberg	Sulz	Jul 1853	N.-Amer	849630
Hoelle, Anna Maria			Bickelsberg	Sulz	Jul 1853	N.-Amer	849630
Hoelle, Anna Maria (wife)		18 Feb 1813	Bickelsberg	Sulz	Jul 1853	N.-Amer	849630
Hoelle, Anna Maria (wife)			Leidringen	Sulz	Aug 1853	N.-Amer	849637
Hoelle, Barbara			Leidringen	Sulz	Jun 1854	N.-Amer	849637
Hoelle, Catharina			Leidringen	Sulz	Jun 1854	N.-Amer	849637
Hoelle, Catharina			Leidringen	Sulz	Aug 1853	N.-Amer	849637
Hoelle, Franz Joseph			Binsdorf	Sulz	Jul 1828	Austria	849630
Hoelle, Franz Xaver			Rottenburg	Sulz	bef 1869	N.-Amer	849631
Hoelle, Friedrich		25 Mar 1852	Leidringen	Sulz	Mar 1871	N.-Amer	849637
Hoelle, Friedrich & F			Bickelsberg	Sulz	Jul 1853	N.-Amer	849630
Hoelle, Gottlieb		23 Mar 1859	Binsdorf	Sulz	Aug 1873	N.-Amer	849631
Hoelle, Jacob		2 Feb 1834	Leidringen	Sulz	Jan 1854	N.-Amer	849637
Hoelle, Jakob		31 Oct 1848	Leidringen	Sulz	Sep 1866	N.-Amer	849637
Hoelle, Johann		2 Apr 1846	Leidringen	Sulz	May 1864	N.-Amer	849637
Hoelle, Johann Georg			Leidringen	Sulz	Jun 1854	N.-Amer	849637
Hoelle, Johann Jacob			Leidringen	Sulz	Jun 1854	N.-Amer	849637
Hoelle, Johannes			Leidringen	Sulz	Jul 1845	Prussia	849637
Hoelle, Johannes			Leidringen	Sulz	Jun 1854	N.-Amer	849637
Hoelle, Johannes		19 Feb 1816	Leidringen	Sulz	Jan 1845	Prussia	849637
Hoelle, Leonhard			Binsdorf	Sulz	Aug 1839	Austria	849630
Hoelle, Leonhart & F			Leidringen	Sulz	Aug 1853	N.-Amer	849637
Hoelle, Magdalena		10 Feb 1840	Binsdorf	Sulz	Jan 1857	N.-Amer	849630
Hoelle, Martin			Leidringen	Sulz	Jun 1854	N.-Amer	849637
Hoelle, Martin		1 Dec 1841	Leidringen	Sulz	May 1864	N.-Amer	849637
Hoelle, Martin		16 Oct 1853	Leidringen	Sulz	Mar 1881	N.-Amer	849626
Hoelle, Nanette			Binsdorf	Sulz	Aug 1841	Switz.	849630
Hoelle, Peter			Binsdorf	Sulz	Jul 1852	Austria	849630
Hoelle, Remigius		18 Nov 1871	Binsdorf	Sulz	Jul 1886	N.-Amer	849631
Hoelle, Rosina			Bickelsberg	Sulz	Jul 1853	N.-Amer	849630
Hoelle, Rosina			Leidringen	Sulz	Jun 1854	N.-Amer	849637
Hoelle, Rosina			Leidringen	Sulz	Aug 1853	N.-Amer	849637
Hoelle, Rosina		4 Nov 1844	Leidringen	Sulz	Apr 1867	N.-Amer	849637
Hoelle, Ursula			Leidringen	Sulz	Aug 1853	N.-Amer	849637
Hoelle, Veronika		3 Jul 1863	Binsdorf	Sulz	Sep 1863	Hohenz.	849631
Hoelzle, Leonhart			Althengstett	Calw	Jan 1848	Austria	563212
Hoenecker, Mathias			Schopfloch	Frd.	1817	Russia	569269
Hoepfer, Anna Maria		10 Aug 1839	Kuppingen	Herr.	Feb 1847	N.-Amer	834626
Hoepfer, Anna Maria (wife)			Kuppingen	Herr.	Feb 1847	N.-Amer	834626
Hoepfer, Georg Jakob & F			Kuppingen	Herr.	Feb 1847	N.-Amer	834626

Hoepfer, Jacob & F		Deckenpfronn	Calw	1852	N.-Amer	563212
Hoepfer, Jakob Friedrich	13 Sep 1835	Kuppingen	Herr.	Feb 1847	N.-Amer	834626
Hoepfer, Johann Georg	29 Dec 1845	Kuppingen	Herr.	Feb 1847	N.-Amer	834626
Hoepfer, Johann Konrad	26 Feb 1837	Kuppingen	Herr.	Feb 1847	N.-Amer	834626
Hoepfer, Margaretha		Deckenpfronn	Calw	1852	N.-Amer	563212
Hoepfer, Maria Katharina	24 Jul 1842	Kuppingen	Herr.	Feb 1847	N.-Amer	834626
Hoermann, Agatha	26 Oct 1794	Wittershausen	Sulz	Jul 1817	Russia	849642
Hoerrmann, Johann Georg	30 Jan 1832	Oeschelbronn	Herr.	bef 1869	N.-Amer	834624
Hoerrmann, Johann Georg	49 yrs.	Reusten	Herr.	Apr 1852	N.-Amer	834627
Hoeschle, Johann Abraham	18 Jul 1823	Herrenberg	Herr.	Jun 1849	N.-Amer	834627
Hof, Carl Friedrich		Cresbach	Frd.	Mar 1866	N.-Amer	577780
Hof, Ulrich	16 Jan 1836	Cresbach	Frd.	Mar 1854	N.-Amer	569273
Hofer, Anna Maria	5 Oct 1828	Kaelberbronn	Frd.	Apr 1853	N.-Amer	569272
Hofer, Anna Maria	9 May 1798	Kaelberbronn	Frd.	Apr 1853	N.-Amer	569272
Hofer, Anna Maria	12 Jan 1829	Obermusbach	Frd.	Jun 1854	N.-Amer	569274
Hofer, Anna Maria Magdalena	6 May 1841	Gruental	Frd.	May 1866	N.-Amer	577780
Hofer, Carl	19 Mar 1841	Aach	Frd.	Apr 1846	N.-Amer	569271
Hofer, Catharina (wid.) & F	24 Apr 1802	Baiersbronn	Frd.	Apr 1846	N.-Amer	569271
Hofer, Christian	8 Jan 1835	Aach	Frd.	Apr 1846	N.-Amer	569271
Hofer, Christiane	22 May 1810	Aach	Frd.	Mar 1837	N.-Amer	569267
Hofer, Christina	31 Dec 1831	Kaelberbronn	Frd.	Apr 1853	N.-Amer	569272
Hofer, Christina	13 Apr 1837	Aach	Frd.	Apr 1846	N.-Amer	569271
Hofer, Elise	12 Sep 1824	Dornhan	Sulz	Mar 1859	N.-Amer	849633
Hofer, Georg	22 Apr 1814	Aach	Frd.	Mar 1837	N.-Amer	569267
Hofer, Gottfried	17 Jul 1836	Kaelberbronn	Frd.	Apr 1853	N.-Amer	569272
Hofer, Jakob Friedrich	23 Nov 1832	Obermusbach	Frd.	Sep 1853	N.-Amer	569272
Hofer, Jakob Friedrich	2 Oct 1839	Kaelberbronn	Frd.	Apr 1853	N.-Amer	569272
Hofer, Jakob Friedrich & F	17 Nov 1794	Obermusbach	Frd.	Jun 1854	N.-Amer	569274
Hofer, Johann Adam	7 Mar 1827	Obermusbach	Frd.	Feb 1854	N.-Amer	569273
Hofer, Johann Georg	18 Oct 1846	Kaelberbronn	Frd.	Apr 1853	N.-Amer	569272
Hofer, Johann Martin	36 yrs.	Aach	Frd.	Mar 1833	N.-Amer	569267
Hofer, Johann Martin	20 Jan 1831	Aach	Frd.	bef 1859	N.-Amer	577776
Hofer, Johann Michael	17 Jul 1824	Kaelberbronn	Frd.	Apr 1853	N.-Amer	569272
Hofer, Johannes	30 Apr 1827	Kaelberbronn	Frd.	Apr 1853	N.-Amer	569272
Hofer, Johannes	27 Oct 1831	Obermusbach	Frd.	Jun 1854	N.-Amer	569274
Hofer, Johannes & F	21 Oct 1793	Untermusbach	Frd.	Apr 1853	N.-Amer	569272
Hofer, Johannes Matthaeus	24 May 1831	Klosterreichenbach	Frd.	Jul 1860	Frankf.	577777
Hofer, Margaretha	2 Nov 1822	Kaelberbronn	Frd.	Apr 1853	N.-Amer	569272
Hoffacker, Mathias	28 Dec 1804	Schorndorf	Schd.	Jul 1837	Austria	801461
Hoffer, Mathias	27 Nov 1848	Renfrizhausen	Sulz	Feb 1877	N.-Amer	849639
Hoffmann, Christian Fr. Fried.	28 May 1840	Calw	Calw	1858	N.-Amer	563212
Hofstaetter, Martin	20 Oct 1828	Marschalkenzimmern	Sulz	bef 1858	France	849638
Hohl, Jakob		Ostelsheim	Calw	1862	N.-Amer	563212
Hohlmayer, Rosina		Grunbach	Schd.	May 1834	N.-Amer	801460
Hohnecker, Matheus		Schopfloch	Frd.	Apr 1817	Russia	569268
Hol, Johann Heinrich		Elsstadt	--	Dec 1751	N.-Amer	550803
Holder, Alfred Theophil	4 Apr 1840	Hildrizhausen	Herr.	bef 1862	Baden	834624
Holdweg, Carl Ernst Leopold		Calw	Calw	1853	N.-Amer	563212
Holl, Anna Barbara (wife)		Sulz	Sulz	Aug 1855	N.-Amer	849627
Holl, Johann Melchior & W	38 yrs.	Sulz	Sulz	Aug 1855	N.-Amer	849627

Name		Birth		Emigration			Film
Last	First	Date	Place	O'amt	Appl. Date	Dest.	Number
Holle, Ludwig			Balingen	Bal.	Sep 1856	Switz.	555962
Holler, Anna Maria		21 Jan 1821	Schornbach	Schd.	Apr 1834	N.-Amer	801460
Holler, Catharina		9 Jun 1819	Schornbach	Schd.	Apr 1834	N.-Amer	801460
Holler, Dorothea (wife)		28 Feb 1789	Schornbach	Schd.	Apr 1834	N.-Amer	801460
Holler, Eva Dorothea		10 Jun 1824	Schornbach	Schd.	Apr 1834	N.-Amer	801460
Holler, Jacob Friedrich		30 Jan 1826	Schornbach	Schd.	Apr 1834	N.-Amer	801460
Holler, Jacob Friedrich & F		10 Jul 1792	Schornbach	Schd.	Apr 1834	N.-Amer	801460
Holler, Johann Georg		19 Aug 1827	Schornbach	Schd.	Apr 1834	N.-Amer	801460
Holler, Johanna		18 Jul 1831	Schornbach	Schd.	Apr 1834	N.-Amer	801460
Holler, Johannes		21 Mar 1822	Schornbach	Schd.	Apr 1834	N.-Amer	801460
Holweger, Agnes			Leidringen	Sulz	Feb 1830	Switz.	849637
Holweger, Andreas			Leidringen	Sulz	Feb 1817	Rus-Pol	849637
Holweger, Anna Maria		5 Jan 1848	Leidringen	Sulz	Oct 1860	N.-Amer	849637
Holweger, Anna Maria		9 Apr 1841	Leidringen	Sulz	Feb 1859	N.-Amer	849637
Holweger, Anna Maria & C		23 Oct 1831	Leidringen	Sulz	Oct 1860	N.-Amer	849637
Holweger, Christian		14 Aug 1846	Leidringen	Sulz	Mar 1864	N.-Amer	849637
Holweger, Christina (wid.)& F		21 Jun 1805	Leidringen	Sulz	Oct 1860	N.-Amer	849637
Holweger, Jacob		1833	Leidringen	Sulz	Nov 1853	N.-Amer	849637
Holweger, Johann & F			Leidringen	Sulz	Jun 1817	Russia	849640
Holweger, Johann Georg		8 Nov 1835	Leidringen	Sulz	Oct 1855	N.-Amer	849637
Holweger, Johann Georg		3 Jul 1872	Leidringen	Sulz	Mar 1889	N.-Amer	849626
Holweger, Johann Jakob		22 Dec 1850	Leidringen	Sulz	Apr 1869	N.-Amer	849637
Holweger, Johannes			Leidringen	Sulz	Mar 1853	N.-Amer	849637
Holweger, Johannes & F			Leidringen	Sulz	Feb 1817	Russia	849637
Holweger, Ludwig		30 May 1849	Leidringen	Sulz	Mar 1868	N.-Amer	849637
Holweger, Thomas		19 Dec 1844	Leidringen	Sulz	Sep 1861	N.-Amer	849637
Holz, Johann Martin			Unterjesingen	Herr.	Apr 1830	N.-Amer	834624
Holzaepfel, Anna & F			Schoenbronn	Nag.	Jul 1852	N.-Amer	838490
Holzaepfel, Anna Margaretha		12 yrs.	Schoenbronn	Nag.	Jul 1852	N.-Amer	838490
Holzaepfel, Anna Maria		10 yrs.	Schoenbronn	Nag.	Jul 1852	N.-Amer	838490
Holzaepfel, Dorothea		44 yrs.	Liebenzell	Calw	1855	N.-Amer	563212
Holzaepfel, Eberhard		1828	Liebenzell	Calw	1857	N.-Amer	563212
Holzaepfel, Hermann		3 yrs.	Schoenbronn	Nag.	Jul 1852	N.-Amer	838490
Holzaepfel, Jakob		1830	Liebenzell	Calw	1857	N.-Amer	563212
Holzaepfel, Johann Jacob			Oberhaugstett	Calw	1852	Algier	563212
Holzaepfel, Johanna		35 yrs.	Liebenzell	Calw	1855	N.-Amer	563212
Holzaepfel, Sophie		6 yrs.	Schoenbronn	Nag.	Jul 1852	N.-Amer	838490
Holzapfel, Johann Friedrich		23 Jul 1837	Herrenberg	Herr.	Aug 1866	Baden	834624
Holzapfel, Johann Friedrich		9 Jun 1865	Herrenberg	Herr.	Aug 1866	Baden	834624
Holzwart, Gottlieb			Unterjesingen	Herr.	May 1831	Baden	834624
Hopf, Julius Ferdinand		19 Jul 1839	Sulz	Sulz	Jan 1859	N.-Amer	849628
Hopf, Paul Arthur		10 Apr 1843	Sulz	Sulz	Jun 1866	N.-Amer	849628
Horn, Charlotte Gottliebin		23 Apr 1777	Sulz	Sulz	Jun 1833	N.-Amer	849627
Horn, Gustav Hermann Eugen		29 Apr 1869	Karlsruhe/Baden	Sulz	Feb 1886	N.-Amer	849626
Horn, Luise Friedrike			Sulz	Sulz	Jun 1833	N.-Amer	849627
Horn, Theodor		10 May 1835	Sulz	Sulz	Oct 1854	N.-Amer	849627
Hornbacher, Anna Maria		4 Sep 1822	Cresbach	Frd.	May 1835	N.-Amer	569269
Hornbacher, Christina		26 Mar 1825	Cresbach	Frd.	May 1835	N.-Amer	569269
Hornbacher, Friedrich & F			Herzogsweiler	Frd.	1817	Russia	569269
Hornbacher, Gottfried		12 Dec 1840	Herzogsweiler	Frd.	Apr 1853	N.-Amer	569272

Hornbacher, Johann Georg		Cresbach	Frd.	bef 1840	Russia	569269
Hornbacher, Johann Georg & F		Cresbach	Frd.	May 1835	N.-Amer	569269
Hornbacher, Magdalena	25 yrs.	Cresbach	Frd.	May 1835	N.-Amer	569269
Hornbacher, Michael	1848	Oberkollwangen	Calw	1868	Palest.	563212
Hornbacher, Regina		Tonbach	Frd.	Aug 1854	N.-Amer	569274
Hornberger, Amalie Elisabethe	19 Jan 1824	Heselbach	Frd.	Sep 1847	N.-Amer	569270
Hornberger, Andreas & F		Aach	Frd.	Sep 1817	Rus-Pol	569267
Hornberger, Barbara	6 Mar 1843	Gruental	Frd.	Mar 1847	N.-Amer	569271
Hornberger, Carl Matheus Da.		Freudenstadt	Frd.	Sep 1860	N.-Amer	577777
Hornberger, Catharina	9 Oct 1839	Gruental	Frd.	Mar 1847	N.-Amer	569271
Hornberger, Christian	6 Oct 1822	Gruental	Frd.	Feb 1848	France	569270
Hornberger, Christian	21 Dec 1840	Gruental	Frd.	Mar 1847	N.-Amer	569271
Hornberger, Christian	25 Jan 1846	Aach	Frd.	Sep 1866	N.-Amer	577780
Hornberger, Christina	28 Dec 1823	Gruental	Frd.	Mar 1847	N.-Amer	569271
Hornberger, Christine		Schoemberg	Frd.	Sep 1854	N.-Amer	569274
Hornberger, Emanuel	18 May 1827	Freudenstadt	Frd.	bef 1861	France	577778
Hornberger, Eva Catharina	29 Nov 1841	Reichenbach	Frd.	1866	Switz.	577780
Hornberger, Eva Maria	27 Jul 1813	Gruental	Frd.	Mar 1847	N.-Amer	569271
Hornberger, Georg	8 Aug 1835	Freudenstadt	Frd.	Sep 1854	N.-Amer	569274
Hornberger, Johann Andreas	11 Oct 1835	Gruental	Frd.	Mar 1847	N.-Amer	569271
Hornberger, Johann Georg	29 Jan 1845	Gruental	Frd.	Mar 1847	N.-Amer	569271
Hornberger, Johann Georg	19 Nov 1848	Aach	Frd.	Sep 1866	N.-Amer	577780
Hornberger, Johannes	8 Sep 1848	Wittlensweiler	Frd.	Jun 1862	N.-Amer	577778
Hornberger, Johannes	6 Nov 1850	Hallwangen	Frd.	Sep 1866	N.-Amer	577780
Hornberger, Johannes & F		Schoenegruend	Frd.	May 1832	N.-Amer	569268
Hornberger, Johannes & F	22 Aug 1813	Gruental	Frd.	Mar 1847	N.-Amer	569271
Hornberger, Matthaeus	21 Sep 1833	Tumlingen	Frd.	Jun 1857	N.-Amer	577776
Hornberger, S. Friederike		Freudenstadt	Frd.	Mar 1854	N.-Amer	569273
Hornberger, Wilhelm		Freudenstadt	Frd.	Oct 1854	N.-Amer	569274
Hornberger, Wilhelmine		Freudenstadt	Frd.	Sep 1860	N.-Amer	577777
Hornung, Christina Magdalena	8 Aug 1821	Kuppingen	Herr.	bef 1862	N.-Amer	834624
Horsch, Wilhelmine Louise M.	18 Apr 1849	Herrenberg	Herr.	Jul 1865	N.-Amer	834624
Hosch, Caroline Friederike	5 Oct 1853	Freudenstadt	Frd.	Sep 1854	N.-Amer	569274
Hosch, David & F		Freudenstadt	Frd.	Sep 1854	N.-Amer	569274
Hosch, Dorothea Magdal. (wife)		Freudenstadt	Frd.	Sep 1854	N.-Amer	569274
Hosch, Friedrich	11 Apr 1850	Freudenstadt	Frd.	Sep 1854	N.-Amer	569274
Hottmann, Heinrike	31 May 1825	Grunbach	Schd.	Mar 1835	N.-Amer	801460
Hottmann, Johanna	18 Jan 1820	Grunbach	Schd.	Jan 1834	N.-Amer	801460
Hotzmann, Johannes Ludwig	23 Nov 1859	Muehlheim a.B.	Sulz	May 1866	N.-Amer	849639
Hotzmann, Katharina (wid.)& F	8 Nov 1833	Muehlheim a.B.	Sulz	May 1866	N.-Amer	849639
Hotzmann, Philipp	5 Sep 1857	Muehlheim a.B.	Sulz	May 1866	N.-Amer	849639
Hounker, Anna	26 Aug 1819	Rotenzimmern	Sulz	May 1866	N.-Amer	849642
Huanker, Carl Ludwig	11 May 1843	Freudenstadt	Frd.	Feb 1853	N.-Amer	569272
Huanker, Catharina Elis.	11 Nov 1852	Freudenstadt	Frd.	Feb 1853	N.-Amer	569272
Huanker, Catharina Elis.		Freudenstadt	Frd.	Feb 1853	N.-Amer	569272
Huanker, Franz	4 Oct 1848	Freudenstadt	Frd.	Feb 1853	N.-Amer	569272
Huanker, Georg Ludwig & F		Freudenstadt	Frd.	Feb 1853	N.-Amer	569272
Huanker, Johann Carl	23 Feb 1845	Freudenstadt	Frd.	Feb 1853	N.-Amer	569272
Huber, Franz Joseph	1793	Bettenhausen	Sulz	Jun 1817	N.-Amer	849630
Huber, Friederike		Calw	Calw	1852	N.-Amer	563212

Name		Birth		Emigration			Film
Last	First	Date	Place	O'amt	Appl. Date	Dest.	Number
Huber, Gottlob		11 Mar 1844	Teinach	Calw	1863	N.-Amer	563212
Huck, Heinrich Joseph Anton		29 Sep 1846	Ulm	Frd.	Nov 1866	England	577780
Huels, Johann Georg & F		8 Feb 1829	Wittershausen	Sulz	bef 1857	Switz.	849644
Huerrbach, Johann Georg			Wuerzbach	Calw	1853	N.-Amer	563212
Hummel, Anna			Cresbach	Frd.	Jun 1833	N.-Amer	569269
Hummel, Christian			Bondorf	Herr.	bef 1837	N.-Amer	834625
Hummel, Christina Agatha			Cresbach	Frd.	Jun 1833	N.-Amer	569269
Hummel, Johannes		5 Sep 1859	Leidringen	Sulz	Feb 1874	N.-Amer	849637
Hummel, Wilhelmine Franziska			Freudenstadt	Frd.	bef 1849	Bern	569270
Hummer, Catharina		6 Oct 1850	Altingen	Herr.	Feb 1868	N.-Amer	834624
Hunker, Anna Maria		24 Oct 1845	Voehringen	Sulz	Jun 1853	N.-Amer	849643
Hunker, Friedrich		10 Oct 1848	Voehringen	Sulz	Jun 1853	N.-Amer	849643
Hunker, Jakob		16 Dec 1842	Voehringen	Sulz	Jun 1853	N.-Amer	849643
Hunker, Jakob & F			Voehringen	Sulz	Jun 1853	N.-Amer	849643
Hunker, Martin		22 Aug 1836	Voehringen	Sulz	Jun 1853	N.-Amer	849643
Hunker, Mathias		31 Aug 1840	Voehringen	Sulz	Jun 1853	N.-Amer	849643
Hunoker, Jacob		23 Mar 1854	Leidringen	Sulz	Dec 1871	N.-Amer	849637
Huonker, Andreas		20 Jan 1851	Leidringen	Sulz	Mar 1869	N.-Amer	849637
Huonker, Anna			Voehringen	Sulz	Mar 1837	N.-Amer	849643
Huonker, Anna		26 May 1847	Leidringen	Sulz	Jun 1865	N.-Amer	849637
Huonker, Anna (wife)			Leidringen	Sulz	Mar 1837	N.-Amer	849643
Huonker, Anna Barbara		24 Jan 1832	Leidringen	Sulz	bef 1869	N.-Amer	849637
Huonker, Anna Barbara (wife)		4 May 1828	Leidringen	Sulz	Oct 1852	N.-Amer	849637
Huonker, Anna Maria		12 Sep 1827	Leidringen	Sulz	bef 1869	N.-Amer	849637
Huonker, Anna Maria (wife)			Leidringen	Sulz	Apr 1833	N.-Amer	849637
Huonker, Anna Maria (wid.)& F		4 Apr 1805	Leidringen	Sulz	Sep 1869	N.-Amer	849637
Huonker, Christian		17 May 1859	Leidringen	Sulz	Jun 1869	N.-Amer	849637
Huonker, Christina			Voehringen	Sulz	Mar 1837	N.-Amer	849643
Huonker, Christoph & F		5 Oct 1803	Leidringen	Sulz	Apr 1833	N.-Amer	849637
Huonker, Friedrich			Leidringen	Sulz	Mar 1837	N.-Amer	849643
Huonker, Friedrich & F		21 Jun 1824	Leidringen	Sulz	Oct 1852	N.-Amer	849637
Huonker, Georg Friedrich & F			Leidringen	Sulz	May 1839	N.-Amer	849637
Huonker, Jakob		23 Mar 1856	Leidringen	Sulz	Dec 1871	N.-Amer	849637
Huonker, Jakob		5 Sep 1870	Leidringen	Sulz	Mar 1887	N.-Amer	849626
Huonker, Johann		19 Nov 1849	Leidringen	Sulz	Mar 1866	N.-Amer	849637
Huonker, Johann Georg			Leidringen	Sulz	May 1853	N.-Amer	849637
Huonker, Johann Georg		4 Jul 1852	Leidringen	Sulz	Oct 1852	N.-Amer	849637
Huonker, Johann Georg		18 Sep 1837	Leidringen	Sulz	bef 1869	N.-Amer	849637
Huonker, Johann Martin		5 May 1850	Leidringen	Sulz	Oct 1852	N.-Amer	849637
Huonker, Johann georg		9 May 1872	Leidringen	Sulz	Mar 1889	N.-Amer	849626
Huonker, Johannes			Voehringen	Sulz	Mar 1837	N.-Amer	849643
Huonker, Johannes		28 Jul 1836	Leidringen	Sulz	Dec 1856	N.-Amer	849637
Huonker, Johannes & F		8 Oct 1795	Leidringen	Sulz	Mar 1837	N.-Amer	849643
Huonker, Karl		11 Mar 1875	Leidringen	Sulz	Feb 1892	N.-Amer	849626
Huonker, Katharina			Voehringen	Sulz	Mar 1837	N.-Amer	849643
Huonker, Katharine		8 Dec 1834	Leidringen	Sulz	Sep 1869	N.-Amer	849637
Huonker, Leonhard		30 Jun 1874	Leidringen	Sulz	May 1891	N.-Amer	849626
Huonker, Leonhard			Leidringen	Sulz	Feb 1869	N.-Amer	849637
Huonker, Leonhardt			Voehringen	Sulz	Mar 1837	N.-Amer	849643
Huonker, Ludwig			Voehringen	Sulz	Mar 1837	N.-Amer	849643

Huonker, Ludwig		Leidringen	Sulz	May 1852	N.-Amer 849637
Huonker, Ludwig	19 Dec 1852	Leidringen	Sulz	Sep 1869	N.-Amer 849637
Huonker, Maria Salome & C	29 Jan 1841	Leidringen	Sulz	Sep 1869	N.-Amer 849637
Huonker, Martin		Voehringen	Sulz	Mar 1837	N.-Amer 849643
Huonker, Martin		Leidringen	Sulz	Jul 1853	N.-Amer 849637
Huonker, Martin	26 Jun 1806	Leidringen	Sulz	Feb 1833	N.-Amer 849637
Huonkern, Leonhard	27 Jan 1844	Rotenzimmern	Sulz	bef 1878	Switz. 849642
Huss, Anna	20 Jan 1834	Lombach	Frd.	Oct 1854	N.-Amer 569274
Huss, Anna Maria	12 Nov 1835	Glatten	Frd.	Mar 1847	N.-Amer 569270
Huss, Catharina		Wittendorf	Frd.	Jun 1855	N.-Amer 569275
Huss, Christina	28 Mar 1841	Glatten	Frd.	Mar 1847	N.-Amer 569270
Huss, Christina	25 Nov 1830	Lombach	Frd.	Oct 1854	N.-Amer 569274
Huss, Christina	30 Jun 1865	Duerrenmettstetten	Sulz	Sep 1867	N.-Amer 849635
Huss, Jacob	12 Aug 1838	Glatten	Frd.	Mar 1847	N.-Amer 569270
Huss, Jacob Friedrich	20 May 1807	Freudenstadt	Frd.	bef 1848	Switz. 569270
Huss, Johann Georg		Duerrenmettstetten	Sulz	bef 1858	N.-Amer 849635
Huss, Johann Georg	24 Dec 1806	Duerrenmettstetten	Sulz	Apr 1832	Prussia 849635
Huss, Johann Georg Christoph	7 May 1783	Freudenstadt	Frd.	May 1827	France 569267
Huss, Margaretha & C	23 Oct 1844	Duerrenmettstetten	Sulz	Sep 1867	N.-Amer 849635
Huss, Matthaes & F		Glatten	Frd.	Mar 1847	N.-Amer 569270
Huss, Matthias	24 Feb 1833	Glatten	Frd.	Mar 1847	N.-Amer 569270
Huss, Michael	26 Oct 1794	Duerrenmettstetten	Sulz	Mar 1830	Prussia 849635
Huss, Wilhelm	9 Aug 1845	Glatten	Frd.	Mar 1847	N.-Amer 569270
Hutt, Andreas	8 Jul 1848	Binsdorf	Sulz	Oct 1868	N.-Amer 849631
Hutt, Friedrich	6 May 1868	Binsdorf	Sulz	Jul 1881	N.-Amer 849631
Hutt, Jacob & F		Binsdorf	Sulz	May 1817	Rus-Pol 849630
Hutt, Joseph	15 Nov 1873	Binsdorf	Sulz	Mar 1889	N.-Amer 849631
Hutt, Viktoria		Binsdorf	Sulz	May 1817	Rus-Pol 849630
Huttenlocher, Jacob Friedrich		Aach	Frd.	Sep 1852	N.-Amer 569271
Igel, Maria Gottliebin	3 Aug 1825	Herrenberg	Herr.	Jun 1850	Hesse 834627
Irion, Andreas		Brittheim	Sulz	Mar 1846	N.-Amer 849632
Irion, Anna Barbara (wife)	3 Aug 1840	Brittheim	Sulz	Jul 1884	N.-Amer 849626
Irion, Barbara & C	9 Dec 1835	Brittheim	Sulz	Jul 1860	N.-Amer 849632
Irion, Catharina	10 Dec 1826	Altburg	Calw	1847	N.-Amer 563212
Irion, Christian	5 Nov 1820	Wittershausen	Sulz	Mar 1847	N.-Amer 849644
Irion, Gottfried	7 May 1814	Wittershausen	Sulz	1835¢170 47	N.-Amer 849644
Irion, Gustav	6 Aug 1870	Brittheim	Sulz	Jul 1884	N.-Amer 849626
Irion, Jacob	16 Jan 1860	Brittheim	Sulz	Jul 1860	N.-Amer 849632
Irion, Jacob & F		Holzhausen	Sulz	Apr 1817	Russia 849635
Irion, Jakob (wid.)		Wittershausen	Sulz	Mar 1847	N.-Amer 849644
Irion, Johannes	23 Sep 1822	Wittershausen	Sulz	Mar 1847	N.-Amer 849644
Irion, Martin & F		Wittershausen	Sulz	Mar 1840	N.-Amer 849644
Irion, Mathias & F	3 Mar 1839	Brittheim	Sulz	Jul 1884	N.-Amer 849626
Irion, Ursula	28 May 1811	Wittershausen	Sulz	Mar 1847	N.-Amer 849644
Iserloh, Isaac		Elsstadt	– –	Dec 1751	N.-Amer 550803
Jacob, Johann Caspar	14 Jul 1834	Rosenfeld	Sulz	Jun 1854	N.-Amer 849640
Jacob, Johann David		Rosenfeld	Sulz	1847	N.-Amer 849640
Jacob, Johann David	18 Feb 1836	Rosenfeld	Sulz	Jun 1869	N.-Amer 849641
Jacob, Johann Georg	16 Dec 1845	Rosenfeld	Sulz	May 1859	N.-Amer 849640
Jacob, Johann Jacob	4 Jun 1839	Rosenfeld	Sulz	Jun 1854	N.-Amer 849640

| Name | | Birth | | Emigration | | | Film |
Last	First	Date	Place	O'amt	Appl. Date	Dest.	Number
Jacob, Tobias		2 Oct 1840	Rosenfeld	Sulz	Jan 1865	Bavaria	849641
Jaeck, Friederike			Groembach	Frd.	Aug 1844	Hesse	569269
Jaecklin, Barbara (wid.) & F		15 Feb 1827	Marschalkenzimmern	Sulz	Sep 1882	N.-Amer	849626
Jaecklin, Mathaeus		27 Dec 1862	Marschalkenzimmern	Sulz	Sep 1882	N.-Amer	849626
Jaeger, Agnes Katharina		19 Sep 1861	Rosenfeld	Sulz	Jul 1863	N.-Amer	849641
Jaeger, Albert Friedrich			Calw	Calw	Jan 1870	Bavaria	563212
Jaeger, Anna Maria			Gaertringen	Herr.	May 1837	Baden	834624
Jaeger, Anna Maria & C		3 Apr 1839	Rosenfeld	Sulz	Jul 1863	N.-Amer	849641
Jaeger, Jakob			Rosenfeld	Sulz	bef 1863	N.-Amer	849641
Jaeger, Jakob Gottlob		21 Nov 1873	Rosenfeld	Sulz	Sep 1887	N.-Amer	849626
Jaeger, Johann Georg			Rosenfeld	Sulz	Dec 1845	Bavaria	849640
Jaeger, Maria Christine			Calw	Calw	1868	Bavaria	563212
Jaeger, Martin		4 Feb 1839	Rosenfeld	Sulz	Dec 1861	Bavaria	849641
Jaeger, Rudolf Gottlob		20 Jan 1835	Calw	Calw	1854	N.-Amer	563212
Jaekle, Anna			Duerrenmettstetten	Sulz	Mar 1854	N.-Amer	849635
Jaekle, Georg		29 Jun 1874	Duerrenmettstetten	Sulz	Feb 1891	N.-Amer	849626
Jaekle, Jakob		Apr 1841	Duerrenmettstetten	Sulz	Feb 1860	N.-Amer	849635
Jaekle, Johann Christian		20 Mar 1839	Duerrenmettstetten	Sulz	Feb 1859	N.-Amer	849635
Jaekle, Johann Georg			Duerrenmettstetten	Sulz	Mar 1852	N.-Amer	849635
Jahr, Tobias		19 yrs.	Neuweiler	Calw	1869	N.-Amer	563212
Jakob, Gottlob		8 Jun 1845	Renfrizhausen	Sulz	Jan 1860	N.-Amer	849639
Jakob, Wilhelm		7 Aug 1842	Renfrizhausen	Sulz	Jan 1860	N.-Amer	849639
Jauch, Anna		30 Apr 1846	Leidringen	Sulz	Aug 1867	N.-Amer	849637
Jauch, Bernhard		4 Mar 1873	Binsdorf	Sulz	bef 1896	Switz.	849631
Jauch, Jacob		20 yrs.	Wittershausen	Sulz	Jan 1854	N.-Amer	849644
Jauch, Jacob		22 Mar 1842	Leidringen	Sulz	Jan 1857	N.-Amer	849637
Jauch, Jacob (Wid)			Wittershausen	Sulz	Apr 1858	N.-Amer	849644
Jauch, Jakob		11 Dec 1833	Leidringen	Sulz	Aug 1852	N.-Amer	849637
Jauch, Johann Georg		1 Dec 1855	Leidringen	Sulz	Sep 1868	N.-Amer	849637
Jauss, Johannes		21 yrs.	Haslach	Herr.	Dec 1852	N.-Amer	834627
Jeitter, Maria Magdalena			Winterbach	Schd.	Apr 1844	Austria	801461
Jenter, Carolina		3 Jul 1859	Dornhan	Sulz	Jun 1860	N.-Amer	849633
Jenter, Elisabetha Kathar. & C		22 Oct 1838	Dornhan	Sulz	Jun 1860	N.-Amer	849633
Jenter, Johann Georg			Balingen	Bal.	bef 1848	Switz.	555962
Jenter, Karolina		11 Oct 1841	Dornhan	Sulz	Jul 1867	N.-Amer	849634
Jenther, Catharina (wife)		2 Dec 1766	Dornhan	Sulz	Jun 1817	N.-Amer	849633
Jenther, Johannes & F		25 Jul 1760	Dornhan	Sulz	Jun 1817	N.-Amer	849633
Jerg, (widow)			Bergfelden	Sulz	Aug 1854	N.-Amer	849629
Jerg, Anna Maria			Voehringen	Sulz	Apr 1832	N.-Amer	849643
Jerg, Christina		8 yrs.	Voehringen	Sulz	Apr 1832	N.-Amer	849643
Jerg, Christine (wife)			Voehringen	Sulz	Apr 1832	N.-Amer	849643
Jerg, Johann Georg		3 mon.	Voehringen	Sulz	Apr 1832	N.-Amer	849643
Jerg, Johann Jakob & F		24 Oct 1799	Voehringen	Sulz	Apr 1832	N.-Amer	849643
Jerger, Johann Georg		24 Sep 1800	Trichtingen	Sulz	bef 1835	France	849642
Jetter, Gottliebin Sybilla		19 Mar 1794	Sulz	Sulz	May 1832	France	849627
Jetter, Jacob			Onstmettingen	Bal.	Jan 1856	Switz.	555962
Jetter, Johann Ferdinand			Engstlatt	Bal.	bef 1847	Switz.	555963
Jetter, Johann Georg			Balingen	Bal.	Sep 1863	France	555962
Jetter, Johann Martin		23 Feb 1817	Balingen	Bal.	Oct 1846	France	555963
Jetter, Johannes		11 Oct 1846	Goettelfingen	Frd.	Sep 1866	N.-Amer	577780

Jetter, Johannes		Balingen	Bal.	bef 1846	Switz.	555963
Jettich, Maria Magdalena		Voehringen	Sulz	May 1855	N.-Amer	849643
Joerger, Elisabetha Barbara	10 May 1837	Renfrizhausen	Sulz	Apr 1860	N.-Amer	849639
Joerger, Johann Hilebrand	12 Apr 1839	Renfrizhausen	Sulz	Oct 1859	N.-Amer	849639
John, Gottlob Fried. Wil. Ed.	24 Feb 1845	Herrenberg	Herr.	Nov 1865	Baden	834624
Johr, Caroline Friederike		Calw	Calw	1869	Prussia	563212
Joos, (widow)	59 yrs.	Voehringen	Sulz	Feb 1854	N.-Amer	849643
Joos, Christian		Oberiflingen	Frd.	Mar 1851	N.-Amer	569271
Joos, Christina		Voehringen	Sulz	Feb 1854	N.-Amer	849643
Jordan, Sara		Neuhengstett	Calw	1866	Prussia	563212
Jost, Anna Maria	3 Jan 1848	Trichtingen	Sulz	May 1867	N.-Amer	849642
Jost, Anna Maria	9 mon.	Trichtingen	Sulz	Jul 1854	N.-Amer	849642
Jost, Anna Maria	15 Nov 1799	Trichtingen	Sulz	May 1817	Polen	849642
Jost, Anna Maria (wife)	5 May 1775	Trichtingen	Sulz	May 1817	Polen	849642
Jost, Christina	22 Nov 1802	Trichtingen	Sulz	May 1817	Polen	849642
Jost, Christina & C		Trichtingen	Sulz	Jul 1854	N.-Amer	849642
Jost, Johann Georg	29 Jul 1810	Trichtingen	Sulz	May 1817	Polen	849642
Jost, Johannes	20 Dec 1852	Bergfelden	Sulz	Mar 1872	N.-Amer	849629
Jost, Johannes	3 Feb 1805	Trichtingen	Sulz	bef 1837	Baden	849642
Jost, Johannes	10 Feb 1805	Trichtingen	Sulz	May 1817	Polen	849642
Jost, Johannes & F	12 Aug 1769	Trichtingen	Sulz	May 1817	Polen	849642
Jost, Katharina	20 Nov 1812	Trichtingen	Sulz	May 1817	Polen	849642
Jost, Lorenz		Trichtingen	Sulz	Mar 1836	N.-Amer	849642
Jost, Maria Katharina	26 Sep 1815	Trichtingen	Sulz	May 1817	Polen	849642
Jost, Matthias	22 Feb 1797	Trichtingen	Sulz	May 1817	Polen	849642
Jourdan, Peter		Neuhengstett	Calw	1852	N.-Amer	563212
Jung, Christian	11 Dec 1845	Goettelfingen	Frd.	Mar 1846	N.-Amer	569271
Jung, Eva Maria	10 Jan 1814	Groembach	Frd.	Mar 1846	N.-Amer	569271
Jung, Friedrich	13 Dec 1840	Goettelfingen	Frd.	Mar 1846	N.-Amer	569271
Jung, Johann Georg	1 Oct 1837	Goettelfingen	Frd.	Mar 1846	N.-Amer	569271
Jung, Johann Georg & F	6 Nov 1812	Goettelfingen	Frd.	Mar 1846	N.-Amer	569271
Jung, Philipp	29 Oct 1842	Goettelfingen	Frd.	Mar 1846	N.-Amer	569271
Junghorn, Eva Catharina		Alzenberg	Calw	Dec 1868	Baden	563212
Junk, Johannes		Schoemberg	Frd.	Jun 1854	N.-Amer	569273
Junker, Pauline		Freudenstadt	Frd.	Jan 1855	N.-Amer	569275
Junt, Agatha (wife)		Voehringen	Sulz	Apr 1833	N.-Amer	849643
Junt, Anna Maria		Voehringen	Sulz	Apr 1833	N.-Amer	849643
Junt, Eva		Voehringen	Sulz	Apr 1833	N.-Amer	849643
Junt, Gottlieb	5 May 1840	Lombach	Frd.	Jul 1866	Baden	577780
Junt, Johannes & F		Voehringen	Sulz	Apr 1833	N.-Amer	849643
Junth, Anna Maria	28 Jun 1819	Glatten	Frd.	Oct 1854	S.-Amer	569274
Junth, Barbara	29 Mar 1832	Glatten	Frd.	Oct 1854	S.-Amer	569274
Kade, Carl Adolph	4 Aug 1830	Freudenstadt	Frd.	Jan 1857	Baden	577776
Kade, Friederich	5 Jul 1847	Pfalzgrafenweiler	Frd.	Jun 1866	N.-Amer	577780
Kade, Heinrich	28 Jul 1849	Pfalzgrafenweiler	Frd.	Jan 1866	N.-Amer	577780
Kaempf, Carl		Calw	Calw	1853	N.-Amer	563212
Kaiser, Adelheid	22 yrs.	Calw	Calw	1867	Baden	563212
Kaiser, Adolph Friedrich	26 yrs.	Calw	Calw	1866	Russia	563212
Kaiser, Andreas	9 Oct 1878	Bickelsberg	Sulz	Jul 1893	N.-Amer	849626
Kaiser, Anna Maria	12 Feb 1824	Herzogsweiler	Frd.	May 1847	N.-Amer	569270

| Name | | Birth | | Emigration | | | Film |
Last	First	Date	Place	O'amt	Appl. Date	Dest.	Number
Kaiser,	Christian Friedrich	28 Jan 1855	Unterjesingen	Herr.	May 1869	N.-Amer	834624
Kaiser,	Christof G.(wid.) & F	30 Dec 1820	Unterjesingen	Herr.	May 1869	N.-Amer	834624
Kaiser,	Ernst Jacob	25 Jul 1850	Unterjesingen	Herr.	Apr 1869	N.-Amer	834624
Kaiser,	Gottlieb	6 Mar 1834	Herzogsweiler	Frd.	Dec 1854	N.-Amer	569274
Kaiser,	Imanuel Gottlobe	6 Sep 1853	Unterjesingen	Herr.	Apr 1869	N.-Amer	834624
Kaiser,	Johann August	12 Aug 1847	Unterjesingen	Herr.	Feb 1867	N.-Amer	834624
Kaiser,	Johann Georg		Herzogsweiler	Frd.	bef 1854	N.-Amer	569274
Kaiser,	Johann Georg	20 Nov 1847	Herzogsweiler	Frd.	Dec 1865	N.-Amer	577780
Kaiser,	Johannes	13 Nov 1874	Bickelsberg	Sulz	Jun 1891	N.-Amer	849626
Kaiser,	Maria Barbara	25 Jan 1852	Unterjesingen	Herr.	May 1869	N.-Amer	834624
Kaiser,	Rosina		Hebsack	Schd.	Feb 1834	N.-Amer	801460
Kaiser,	Salome	4 Aug 1857	Unterjesingen	Herr.	May 1869	N.-Amer	834624
Kaiser,	Wilhelm Gottlieb	23 Mar 1846	Unterjesingen	Herr.	Apr 1869	N.-Amer	834624
Kalenbach,	Johann Georg	19 Aug 1835	Glatten	Frd.	bef 1853	N.-Amer	569273
Kall,	Anna Catharina	24 yrs.	Unterjesingen	Herr.	Mar 1846	N.-Amer	834626
Kalmbach,	Andreas	14 May 1833	Edelweiler	Frd.	Apr 1853	N.-Amer	569272
Kalmbach,	Anna Maria	27 Dec 1831	Edelweiler	Frd.	Mar 1854	N.-Amer	569273
Kalmbach,	Anna Maria		Schoenegruend	Frd.	bef 1856	N.-Amer	569275
Kalmbach,	Christine	14 yrs.	Roet	Frd.	Mar 1854	N.-Amer	569273
Kalmbach,	Gottfried	11 Apr 1840	Pfalzgrafenweiler	Frd.	Mar 1854	N.-Amer	569273
Kalmbach,	Johann Georg	5 Feb 1855	Isingen	Sulz	Jan 1856	N.-Amer	849636
Kalmbach,	Johann Georg	26 Aug 1864	Sterneck	Sulz	Jun 1881	N.-Amer	849626
Kalmbach,	Johann Michael		Berneck	Nag.	1857	N.-Amer	838492
Kalmbach,	Johannes		Berneck	Nag.	1857	N.-Amer	838492
Kalmbach,	Johannes & F		Breitenberg	Calw	1854	N.-Amer	563212
Kalmbach,	Michael	16 yrs.	Roet	Frd.	Mar 1854	N.-Amer	569273
Kalmbach,	Ulrich		Emberg	Calw	1852	N.-Amer	563212
Kalmbacher,	Johannes	30 yrs.	Oberkollbach	Calw	1869	Baden	563212
Kaltenbach,	Anna Maria	11 Sep 1810	Dornstetten	Frd.	Apr 1854	N.-Amer	569273
Kaltenbach,	Christian Friedr.		Calw	Calw	1868	Baden	563212
Kaltenbach,	Christiane Kathar.	3 Sep 1812	Freudenstadt	Frd.	Aug 1854	N.-Amer	569274
Kammerer,	Anna Katharina	10 Feb 1850	Pfalzgrafenweiler	Frd.	Feb 1861	N.-Amer	577778
Kammerer,	Anna Maria		Wittershausen	Sulz	Dec 1854	N.-Amer	849644
Kammerer,	Barbara	13 Sep 1853	Pfalzgrafenweiler	Frd.	Feb 1861	N.-Amer	577778
Kammerer,	Carolina	29 Aug 1857	Pfalzgrafenweiler	Frd.	Feb 1861	N.-Amer	577778
Kammerer,	Christina		Wittershausen	Sulz	Dec 1854	N.-Amer	849644
Kammerer,	Eva		Wittershausen	Sulz	Dec 1854	N.-Amer	849644
Kammerer,	Eva Maria	28 Jan 1852	Pfalzgrafenweiler	Frd.	Feb 1861	N.-Amer	577778
Kammerer,	Georg Friedrich	31 Dec 1838	Bebenhausen	Frd.	Aug 1853	N.-Amer	569272
Kammerer,	Johann Georg	41 yrs.	Durrweiler	Frd.	Apr 1864	N.-Amer	577779
Kammerer,	Johann Georg	12 Jul 1808	Sigmarswangen	Sulz	1829	N.-Amer	849625
Kammerer,	Johann Georg		Sigmarswangen	Sulz	bef 1840	N.-Amer	849642
Kammerer,	Johannes	20 Jul 1859	Pfalzgrafenweiler	Frd.	Feb 1861	N.-Amer	577778
Kammerer,	Johannes & F	14 Aug 1821	Pfalzgrafenweiler	Frd.	Feb 1861	N.-Amer	577778
Kammerer,	Juliana	15 Oct 1855	Pfalzgrafenweiler	Frd.	Feb 1861	N.-Amer	577778
Kammerer,	Juliane & C		Cresbach	Frd.	Mar 1866	N.-Amer	577780
Kammerer,	Justina (wife)	6 Nov 1819	Altensteig	Frd.	Feb 1861	N.-Amer	577778
Kammerer,	Luise	26 Nov 1858	Cresbach	Frd.	Mar 1866	N.-Amer	577780
Kammerer,	Mathias	13 Dec 1814	Sigmarswangen	Sulz	1835	N.-Amer	849625
Kammerer,	Ursula		Wittershausen	Sulz	Dec 1854	N.-Amer	849644

Kantlehner, Friedrich C.	22 Sep 1842	Freudenstadt	Frd.	Jun 1865	N.-Amer	577779
Kapp, Anna (wife)		Gueltstein	Herr.	Sep 1852	N.-Amer	834627
Kapp, Anna Katharina	24 Jul 1849	Leidringen	Sulz	Jun 1871	N.-Amer	849637
Kapp, Anna Katharina	15 Feb 1836	Gueltstein	Herr.	Sep 1852	N.-Amer	834627
Kapp, Anna Maria	16 Sep 1858	Leidringen	Sulz	Jun 1871	N.-Amer	849637
Kapp, Anna Maria	14 Dec 1833	Gueltstein	Herr.	Sep 1852	N.-Amer	834627
Kapp, Christian Franz	28 Jun 1830	Gueltstein	Herr.	Sep 1852	N.-Amer	834627
Kapp, Dorothea	3 Aug 1831	Gueltstein	Herr.	Sep 1852	N.-Amer	834627
Kapp, Franz	25 Nov 1810	Gueltstein	Herr.	Apr 1862	N.-Amer	834624
Kapp, Jakob	1 Oct 1853	Leidringen	Sulz	Jun 1871	N.-Amer	849637
Kapp, Johann Friedrich	9 Dec 1832	Gueltstein	Herr.	Sep 1852	N.-Amer	834627
Kapp, Johann Georg	14 Oct 1850	Leidringen	Sulz	1869	N.-Amer	849637
Kapp, Johann Georg	20 Mar 1841	Gueltstein	Herr.	Sep 1852	N.-Amer	834627
Kapp, Johann Jacob	29 Sep 1844	Gueltstein	Herr.	Sep 1852	N.-Amer	834627
Kapp, Johann Martin	7 Jun 1843	Gueltstein	Herr.	Sep 1852	N.-Amer	834627
Kapp, Johannes	10 Apr 1829	Gueltstein	Herr.	Sep 1852	N.-Amer	834627
Kapp, Johannes & F	23 Jan 1833	Leidringen	Sulz	Jun 1871	N.-Amer	849637
Kapp, Johannes & F		Gueltstein	Herr.	Sep 1852	N.-Amer	834627
Kapp, Johannes & F		Gueltstein	Herr.	Sep 1852	N.-Amer	834627
Kapp, Katharina Frieder. (wife)	22 May 1825	Leidringen	Sulz	Jun 1871	N.-Amer	849637
Kapp, Leonhard	31 Dec 1864	Leidringen	Sulz	Jun 1871	N.-Amer	849637
Kapp, Matthaeus	17 Apr 1834	Glatten	Frd.	Jul 1854	N.-Amer	569274
Kappeler, Agnes	30 Sep 1885	Binsdorf	Sulz	Feb 1894	Austria	849631
Kappeler, Andreas	28 Nov 1843	Binsdorf	Sulz	bef 1867	N.-Amer	849631
Kappeler, Anton		Binsdorf	Sulz	bef 1859	N.-Amer	849630
Kappeler, Bernhartine (wife)		Binsdorf	Sulz	Jun 1852	N.-Amer	849630
Kappeler, Caecilie	20 Nov 1820	Binsdorf	Sulz	Oct 1851	Austria	849630
Kappeler, Emerenzia	8 Jan 1812	Binsdorf	Sulz	bef 1867	N.-Amer	849631
Kappeler, Fina	17 yrs.	Binsdorf	Sulz	Jun 1852	N.-Amer	849630
Kappeler, Franz Xaver	6 Dec 1891	Binsdorf	Sulz	Feb 1894	Austria	849631
Kappeler, Ignatz	10 Feb 1808	Binsdorf	Sulz	bef 1867	N.-Amer	849631
Kappeler, Johann	26 Jan 1883	Binsdorf	Sulz	Feb 1894	Austria	849631
Kappeler, Johann & F		Binsdorf	Sulz	Jan 1817	Russia	849630
Kappeler, Joseph	7 yrs.	Binsdorf	Sulz	Jun 1852	N.-Amer	849630
Kappeler, Karl	1 Jul 1889	Binsdorf	Sulz	Feb 1894	Austria	849631
Kappeler, Karoline	22 May 1848	Binsdorf	Sulz	bef 1867	N.-Amer	849631
Kappeler, Leopoldine	2 Oct 1879	Binsdorf	Sulz	Feb 1894	Austria	849631
Kappeler, Luzia	19 Oct 1807	Binsdorf	Sulz	Jun 1834	Wien	849630
Kappeler, Maria	14 Jun 1881	Binsdorf	Sulz	Feb 1894	Austria	849631
Kappeler, Maria (wife)	26 Nov 1851	Binsdorf	Sulz	Feb 1894	Austria	849631
Kappeler, Othmar	11 yrs.	Binsdorf	Sulz	Jun 1852	N.-Amer	849630
Kappeler, Peter	10 Jan 1849	Binsdorf	Sulz	Aug 1868	N.-Amer	849631
Kappeler, Raphael & F	25 Oct 1844	Binsdorf	Sulz	Feb 1894	Austria	849631
Kappeler, Richard	8 yrs.	Binsdorf	Sulz	Jun 1852	N.-Amer	849630
Kappeler, Rosalia	12 yrs.	Binsdorf	Sulz	Jun 1852	N.-Amer	849630
Kappeler, Rudolf	7 Sep 1875	Binsdorf	Sulz	Feb 1894	Austria	849631
Kappeler, Theresia		Binsdorf	Sulz	Feb 1838	Hohenz.	849630
Kappeler, Theresia	22 Apr 1841	Binsdorf	Sulz	bef 1867	N.-Amer	849631
Kappeler, Vinzenz & F		Binsdorf	Sulz	Jun 1852	N.-Amer	849630
Kappeler, Wilhelmine	29 Oct 1842	Binsdorf	Sulz	bef 1867	N.-Amer	849631

Name		Birth		Emigration			Film
Last	First	Date	Place	O'amt	Appl. Date	Dest.	Number
Kappeler, Xaver			Binsdorf	Sulz	Apr 1836	Vienna	849630
Kappeler, Zacharias		5 yrs.	Binsdorf	Sulz	Jun 1852	N.-Amer	849630
Kappler, Adolph		9 yrs.	Meistern/Bergorte	Calw	1854	N.-Amer	563212
Kappler, Anna		16 yrs.	Meistern/Bergorte	Calw	1854	N.-Amer	563212
Kappler, Anna Maria			Huzenbach	Frd.	Aug 1851	Baden	569271
Kappler, Gottliebin			Pfalzgrafenweiler	Frd.	Jul 1832	N.-Amer	569268
Kappler, Johann Georg		15 Nov 1831	Kuppingen	Herr.	Mar 1869	N.-Amer	834624
Kappler, Johann Jacob		27 yrs.	Roetenbach	Calw	1857	N.-Amer	563212
Kappler, Ludwig		16 Feb 1827	Freudenstadt	Frd.	Jul 1859	Baden	577776
Kappler, Magdalena			Huzenbach	Frd.	Sep 1866	Baden	577780
Kappler, Martin		14 yrs.	Meistern/Bergorte	Calw	1854	N.-Amer	563212
Kappler, Wilhelm		11 yrs.	Meistern/Bergorte	Calw	1854	N.-Amer	563212
Kast, Maria			Oberhengstett	Calw	1868	Switz.	563212
Katz, Anna Barbara		5 Nov 1836	Leidringen	Sulz	May 1867	N.-Amer	849637
Katz, Anna Catharina (wife)		12 Jun 1841	Leidringen	Sulz	Dec 1884	N.-Amer	849626
Katz, Anna Maria			Leidringen	Sulz	Mar 1854	N.-Amer	849637
Katz, Christian		17 Feb 1871	Leidringen	Sulz	Dec 1884	N.-Amer	849626
Katz, Christian & F		2 Jun 1840	Leidringen	Sulz	Dec 1884	N.-Amer	849626
Katz, Christina		29 Oct 1838	Bergfelden	Sulz	bef 1859	N.-Amer	849629
Katz, Christina		23 Sep 1839	Leidringen	Sulz	Mar 1864	N.-Amer	849637
Katz, Johann Georg		11 Sep 1828	Leidringen	Sulz	bef 1859	N.-Amer	849637
Katz, Johann Georg		12 Dec 1869	Leidringen	Sulz	Dec 1884	N.-Amer	849626
Katz, Johannes		30 Jun 1856	Bergfelden	Sulz	Jan 1857	N.-Amer	849629
Katz, Johannes & F			Oberbraendi	Frd.	Jul 1817	Russia	569268
Katz, Katharina		5 Aug 1883	Leidringen	Sulz	Dec 1884	N.-Amer	849626
Katz, Maria Catharina & C		11 May 1830	Bergfelden	Sulz	Jan 1857	N.-Amer	849629
Katz, Martin			Leidringen	Sulz	Aug 1853	N.-Amer	849637
Kauffman, Agatha		32 yrs.	Neuneck	Frd.	May 1752	Pen.N-A	550803
Kauffman, Bernhard		8 yrs.	Neuneck	Frd.	May 1752	Pen.N-A	550803
Kauffman, Johanna		3 yrs.	Neuneck	Frd.	May 1752	Pen.N-A	550803
Kauffman, Johannes		13 yrs.	Neuneck	Frd.	May 1752	Pen.N-A	550803
Kauffmann, Anna		28 yrs.	Unteriflingen	Frd.	May 1752	Pen.N-A	550803
Kauffmann, Barbara & C			Hopfau/Nennthausen	Sulz	Jan 1817	Russia	849636
Kaufman, Johannes		6 Mar 1841	Bickelsberg	Sulz	Aug 1858	N.-Amer	849644
Kaufmann, Agatha		28 May 1842	Sigmarswangen	Sulz	Aug 1860	N.-Amer	849642
Kaufmann, Andreas		8 May 1867	Dornhan	Sulz	Jan 1882	N.-Amer	849634
Kaufmann, Andreas		9 Oct 1800	Marschalkenzimmern	Sulz	Mar 1836	N.-Amer	849638
Kaufmann, Anna			Aistaig	Sulz	1817	N.-Amer	849628
Kaufmann, Anna Maria			Aistaig	Sulz	Jun 1837	N.-Amer	849628
Kaufmann, Christina		20 Sep 1839	Hopfau	Sulz	Jul 1864	N.-Amer	849636
Kaufmann, Dorothea			Unterbraendi	Frd.	May 1854	N.-Amer	569273
Kaufmann, Elisabeth		20 Sep 1839	Hopfau	Sulz	Sep 1868	N.-Amer	849636
Kaufmann, Hans Bernhart & F		40 yrs.	Neuneck	Frd.	May 1752	Pen.N-A	550803
Kaufmann, Johann Andreas		27 Jan 1852	Sulz	Sulz	Sep 1869	N.-Amer	849628
Kaufmann, Johann Friedrich		33 yrs.	Gechingen	Calw	1855	N.-Amer	563212
Kaufmann, Johann Georg		8 Oct 1846	Dornhan	Sulz	Oct 1866	N.-Amer	849634
Kaufmann, Johann Georg		7 Dec 1871	Dorhan	Sulz	Oct 1889	N.-Amer	849626
Kaufmann, Johannes		5 Jul 1829	Dornhan	Sulz	Sep 1854	N.-Amer	849633
Kaufmann, Johannes		15 Apr 1833	Dorhan	Sulz	Jan 1890	N.-Amer	849626
Kaufmann, Regina & F			Oberkollbach	Calw	Feb 1848	N.-Amer	563212

Kaup, Johann Georg		Rosenfeld	Sulz	Aug 1852	N.-Amer	849640
Kaupp, Barbara & C	19 Dec 1832	Stuttgart	Sulz	Oct 1872	N.-Amer	849635
Kaupp, Barbara & C		Leinstetten	Sulz	Feb 1854	N.-Amer	849638
Kaupp, Christian	18 Sep 1851	Freudenstadt	Frd.	Sep 1854	N.-Amer	569274
Kaupp, Christian & F		Freudenstadt	Frd.	Sep 1854	N.-Amer	569274
Kaupp, Christian Friedrich	10 Jul 1867	Holzhausen	Sulz	Oct 1872	N.-Amer	849635
Kaupp, Dorothea	30 May 1837	Lossburg	Frd.	bef 1865	France	577779
Kaupp, Elisabethe Sophie	13 Jul 1846	Freudenstadt	Frd.	Sep 1854	N.-Amer	569274
Kaupp, Georg Friedrich	15 Jun 1844	Freudenstadt	Frd.	Sep 1854	N.-Amer	569274
Kaupp, Gottlieb	7 Apr 1807	Holzhausen	Sulz	Apr 1833	Prussia	849635
Kaupp, Johann Martin	25 Jan 1856	Stuttgart	Sulz	Oct 1872	N.-Amer	849635
Kaupp, Johann Mathaeus		Holzhausen	Sulz	Feb 1846	Altona	849635
Kaupp, Johannes		Schopfloch	Frd.	Mar 1837	N.-Amer	569268
Kaupp, Josef	19 yrs.	Altheim	Horb	Mar 1853	N.-Amer	835929
Kaupp, Joseph	21 Apr 1832	Leinstetten	Sulz	May 1862	Baden	849638
Kaupp, Karl	42 yrs.	Calw	Calw	1857	N.-Amer	563212
Kaupp, Maria Catharina	10 Oct 1827	Hildrizhausen	Herr.	Mar 1844	N.-Amer	834626
Kaupp, Mathaeus	12 Apr 1834	Schopfloch	Frd.	Apr 1851	N.-Amer	569271
Kaupp, Rosine Dorothea (wife)		Freudenstadt	Frd.	Sep 1854	N.-Amer	569274
Kaupp, Sophia		Freudenstadt	Frd.	Aug 1842	Switz.	569269
Kaupp, Theresia		Leinstetten	Sulz	Jun 1854	N.-Amer	849638
Kaz, Anna	11 Oct 1845	Bergfelden	Sulz	Jul 1854	N.-Amer	849629
Kaz, Christiana Friederika		Bondorf	Herr.	Apr 1836	N.-Amer	834624
Kaz, Johann		Wittendorf	Frd.	1817	Russia	569269
Kaz, Johanna Friederike		Calw	Calw	Aug 1847	Hesse	563212
Keck, Adam	9 yrs.	Wittershausen	Sulz	Sep 1854	N.-Amer	849644
Keck, Agatha	5 Feb 1841	Besenfeld	Frd.	bef 1863	Switz.	577778
Keck, Agathe	21 yrs.	Roet	Frd.	Jul 1852	N.-Amer	569271
Keck, Andreas		Hallwangen	Frd.	Apr 1752	Pen.N-A	550803
Keck, Anna	8 Apr 1839	Leidringen	Sulz	May 1867	N.-Amer	849637
Keck, Anna	21 Aug 1878	Leidringen	Sulz	Aug 1885	Switz.	849626
Keck, Anna Barbara		Leidringen	Sulz	Mar 1837	N.-Amer	849637
Keck, Anna Catharina		Leidringen	Sulz	Mar 1837	N.-Amer	849637
Keck, Anna Maria	10 May 1773	Freudenstadt	Frd.	bef 1839	Russia	569267
Keck, Anna Maria		Leidringen	Sulz	Mar 1837	N.-Amer	849637
Keck, Anna Maria (wife)		Leidringen	Sulz	Mar 1837	N.-Amer	849637
Keck, Catharina	13 yrs.	Wittershausen	Sulz	Sep 1854	N.-Amer	849644
Keck, Christian	3 Aug 1866	Dornhan	Sulz	Jul 1884	N.-Amer	849634
Keck, Christian	13 Sep 1837	Leidringen	Sulz	Sep 1865	N.-Amer	849637
Keck, Christian	18 Aug 1871	Leidringen	Sulz	Aug 1885	Switz.	849626
Keck, Christian Friedrich	26 yrs.	Liebenzell	Calw	1866	N.-Amer	563212
Keck, Christiana	18 Dec 1832	Schoenengrund	Frd.	Jul 1860	N.-Amer	577777
Keck, Christiane	13 yrs.	Roet	Frd.	Jul 1852	N.-Amer	569271
Keck, Christina (wife)	30 Nov 1851	Leidringen	Sulz	Aug 1885	Switz.	849626
Keck, Christoph Friedrich		Leidringen	Sulz	Feb 1818	Rus-Pol	849637
Keck, Christoph Friedrich		Leidringen	Sulz	1817	Rus-Pol	849637
Keck, David & F		Roet	Frd.	Jul 1852	N.-Amer	569271
Keck, Frieda	6 Jul 1884	Leidringen	Sulz	Aug 1885	Switz.	849626
Keck, Georg	17 Dec 1850	Leidringen	Sulz	Aug 1867	N.-Amer	849637
Keck, Georg Friedrich	25 Oct 1831	Edelweiler	Frd.	Jul 1852	N.-Amer	569271

Name		Birth		Emigration			Film
Last	First	Date	Place	O'amt	Appl. Date	Dest.	Number
Keck,	Gottlieb	13 May 1863	Dornhan	Sulz	Sep 1883	N.-Amer	849634
Keck,	Gottliebin		Deckenpfronn	Calw	1853	N.-Amer	563212
Keck,	Jakob	3 Dec 1841	Leidringen	Sulz	Sep 1865	N.-Amer	849637
Keck,	Jakob Friedrich	15 Jan 1848	Leidringen	Sulz	Apr 1866	N.-Amer	849637
Keck,	Jakob Friedrich	27 May 1877	Leidringen	Sulz	Aug 1885	Switz.	849626
Keck,	Jakob Friedrich & F	1 Dec 1841	Leidringen	Sulz	Aug 1885	Switz.	849626
Keck,	Johann Adam		Leidringen	Sulz	May 1853	N.-Amer	849637
Keck,	Johann Adam		Leidringen	Sulz	Mar 1837	N.-Amer	849637
Keck,	Johann Christian	7 yrs.	Roet	Frd.	Jul 1852	N.-Amer	569271
Keck,	Johann David	15 yrs.	Roet	Frd.	Jul 1852	N.-Amer	569271
Keck,	Johann Georg	28 Mar 1831	Aistaig	Sulz	Feb 1851	N.-Amer	849628
Keck,	Johann Georg		Wittershausen	Sulz	Sep 1854	N.-Amer	849644
Keck,	Johann Georg	12 yrs.	Wittershausen	Sulz	Sep 1854	N.-Amer	849644
Keck,	Johann Georg		Leidringen	Sulz	Mar 1837	N.-Amer	849637
Keck,	Johann Georg	5 Feb 1828	Leidringen	Sulz	Mar 1866	N.-Amer	849637
Keck,	Johann Georg	5 Sep 1868	Leidringen	Sulz	Aug 1885	Switz.	849626
Keck,	Johann Jacob		Leidringen	Sulz	bef 1812	Poland	849637
Keck,	Johann Jakob	15 Oct 1838	Leidringen	Sulz	Jul 1865	N.-Amer	849637
Keck,	Johann Karl	11 yrs.	Roet	Frd.	Jul 1852	N.-Amer	569271
Keck,	Johann Wilhelm	5 yrs.	Roet	Frd.	Jul 1852	N.-Amer	569271
Keck,	Johanna Friederike	18 yrs.	Roet	Frd.	Jul 1852	N.-Amer	569271
Keck,	Johanna Maria	9 yrs.	Roet	Frd.	Jul 1852	N.-Amer	569271
Keck,	Johannes	28 Jan 1833	Aistaig	Sulz	Feb 1851	N.-Amer	849628
Keck,	Johannes	19 May 1838	Wittershausen	Sulz	May 1857	N.-Amer	849644
Keck,	Johannes	23 Feb 1877	Hopfau	Sulz	May 1891	N.-Amer	849636
Keck,	Johannes		Leidringen	Sulz	Aug 1853	N.-Amer	849637
Keck,	Johannes	17 Sep 1843	Leidringen	Sulz	Jul 1863	N.-Amer	849637
Keck,	Johannes Michael	14 Aug 1874	Leidringen	Sulz	Aug 1885	Switz.	849626
Keck,	Karl	13 Sep 1867	Dornhan	Sulz	Sep 1883	N.-Amer	849634
Keck,	Leonhard	12 Apr 1849	Leidringen	Sulz	Apr 1866	N.-Amer	849637
Keck,	Luise	19 Mar 1841	Schoenegruend	Frd.	Jul 1860	N.-Amer	577777
Keck,	Magdalena	5 Mar 1880	Leidringen	Sulz	Aug 1885	Switz.	849626
Keck,	Martin & F		Aichhalden	Calw	1854	N.-Amer	563212
Keck,	Mathaeus	16 Nov 1866	Hopfau	Sulz	May 1883	N.-Amer	849636
Keck,	Matheis		Leidringen	Sulz	Mar 1837	N.-Amer	849637
Keck,	Matheis & F	1770	Leidringen	Sulz	Mar 1837	N.-Amer	849637
Keck,	Michael		Leidringen	Sulz	Mar 1837	N.-Amer	849637
Keck,	Michael & F	25 Nov 1800	Leidringen	Sulz	Mar 1837	N.-Amer	849637
Keck,	Paulus	12 Jun 1837	Schoenegruend	Frd.	Jul 1860	N.-Amer	577777
Keck,	Rosina		Leidringen	Sulz	Mar 1837	N.-Amer	849637
Keck,	Rosina	3 Jun 1873	Leidringen	Sulz	Aug 1885	Switz.	849626
Keck,	Rosine Catharina	17 yrs.	Roet	Frd.	Jul 1852	N.-Amer	569271
Keck,	Theodor	21 Oct 1848	Liebenzell	Calw	1867	N.-Amer	563212
Keck,	Ursula	6 Mar 1870	Leidringen	Sulz	Aug 1885	Switz.	849626
Keck,	Wilhelm	6 Jan 1846	Freudenstadt	Frd.	Nov 1865	N.-Amer	577779
Kehle,	Anna Marie		Neubulach	Calw	1862	Switz.	563212
Keiper,	Constantia (wife)		Binsdorf	Sulz	Apr 1847	N.-Amer	849630
Keiper,	Jakob & W	24 Jan 1814	Binsdorf	Sulz	Apr 1847	N.-Amer	849630
Keiser,	Mathias & F		Dornhan	Sulz	Mar 1817	Russia	849633
Kek,	Andreas		Oberiflingen	Frd.	Mar 1833	N.-Amer	569268

Kek, Catharina		Oberiflingen	Frd.	Mar 1833	N.-Amer	569268
Kek, Christian		Oberiflingen	Frd.	Mar 1833	N. Amer	569268
Kek, Christiane Rosine	24 Feb 1819	Freudenstadt	Frd.	Mar 1851	Switz.	569271
Kek, Christina	3 Dec 1799	Wittershausen	Sulz	Apr 1868	N.-Amer	849644
Kek, Christine		Oberiflingen	Frd.	Mar 1833	N.-Amer	569268
Kek, Jacob		Oberiflingen	Frd.	Mar 1833	N.-Amer	569268
Kek, Jacob & F	1 Oct 1796	Oberiflingen	Frd.	Mar 1833	N.-Amer	569268
Kek, Johannes		Kaelberbronn	Frd.	1817	Russia	569269
Kek, Marie		Oberiflingen	Frd.	Mar 1833	N.-Amer	569268
Kek, Martin	22 Apr 1802	Oberiflingen	Frd.	Mar 1833	N.-Amer	569268
Keller, Anna & F		Rosenfeld	Sulz	Jun 1854	N.-Amer	849640
Keller, Anna Maria		Liebelsberg	Calw	1859	Baden	563212
Keller, Anna Maria	2 yrs.	Liebelsberg	Calw	1859	Baden	563212
Keller, Anna Maria		Rosenfeld	Sulz	Jun 1854	N.-Amer	849640
Keller, Anna Maria (wid.)		Rehmuehle	Calw	1868	N.-Amer	563212
Keller, Anton		Rosenfeld	Sulz	Jul 1854	N.-Amer	849640
Keller, Augustin & F		Poltringen	Herr.	Apr 1848	N.-Amer	834626
Keller, Christian	15 Dec 1841	Nufringen	Herr.	Jul 1868	N.-Amer	834624
Keller, Christoph		Rosenfeld	Sulz	Jul 1853	N.-Amer	849640
Keller, Elisabetha (wife)	22 Jun 1822	Rosenfeld	Sulz	Sep 1869	N.-Amer	849641
Keller, Emilie Therese		Calw	Calw	Jan 1870	Coblenz	563212
Keller, Eugen	25 Sep 1872	Ulm	Sulz	Sep 1888	N.-Amer	849626
Keller, Friederike Elisabeth		Calw	Calw	1859	Baden	563212
Keller, Friedrich & F		Liebenzell	Calw	1852	N.-Amer	563212
Keller, Johann Christian	25 Jun 1849	Bondorf	Herr.	Oct 1866	N.-Amer	834624
Keller, Johann Georg		Liebelsberg	Calw	1861	N.-Amer	563212
Keller, Johann Georg	23 Aug 1812	Rosenfeld	Sulz	Mar 1857	N.-Amer	849640
Keller, Johann Georg & F	11 Mar 1824	Rosenfeld	Sulz	Sep 1869	N.-Amer	849641
Keller, Johann Jakob	16 Nov 1872	Rosenfeld	Sulz	Apr 1889	N.-Amer	849626
Keller, Johannes		Rosenfeld	Sulz	Mar 1842	N.-Amer	849640
Keller, Johannes	Apr 1858	Rosenfeld	Sulz	Sep 1869	N.-Amer	849641
Keller, Judita Emilie		Calw	Calw	1849	Switz.	563212
Keller, Ludwig Friedrich	1831	Calw	Calw	1855	Austria	563212
Keller, Wilhelm	20 Dec 1812	Engstlatt	Bal.	bef 1847	Switz.	555963
Kemmler, Wilhelm	30 Dec 1856	Marschalkenzimmern	Sulz	bef 1873	Switz.	849638
Kempf, Christian	1840	Calw	Calw	1860	N.-Amer	563212
Kempf, Christiane Friederike		Calw	Calw	Feb 1870	Bavaria	563212
Kempf, Johann Friedrich		Unterjettingen	Herr.	Apr 1836	N.-Amer	834624
Kempf, Maria Luise	5 Oct 1826	Calw	Calw	1849	N.-Amer	563212
Kennerknecht, Georg Josef	12 yrs.	Bettenhausen	Sulz	May 1866	N.-Amer	849630
Keppler, Johannes	28 Sep 1834	Goettelfingen	Frd.	Mar 1854	N.-Amer	569273
Keppler, Wilhelm	5 May 1823	Freudenstadt	Frd.	Jul 1845	Baden	569269
Kern, Adam & F		Aichhalden	Calw	1854	N.-Amer	563212
Kern, Anna Barbara	1837	Aichhalden	Calw	1854	N.-Amer	563212
Kern, Anton & F	10 Nov 1792	Pfalzgrafenweiler	Frd.	Apr 1836	N.-Amer	569268
Kern, Christine		Oberweiler/Aichh.	Calw	1853	N.-Amer	563212
Kern, Elisabeth	16 Mar 1802	Pfalzgrafenweiler	Frd.	Apr 1836	N.-Amer	569268
Kern, Elisabeth		Oberweiler	Calw	1866	N.-Amer	563212
Kern, Elisabetha	4 Apr 1817	Pfalzgrafenweiler	Frd.	Apr 1836	N.-Amer	569268
Kern, Jacobine		Gruental	Frd.	1852	N.-Amer	577776

Name		Birth		Emigration			Film
Last	First	Date	Place	O'amt	Appl. Date	Dest.	Number
Kern, Jakob Friedrich		1841	Aichhalden	Calw	1857	N.-Amer	563212
Kern, Johannes		1840	Aichhalden	Calw	1857	N.-Amer	563212
Kern, Michael		1833	Aichhalden	Calw	1854	N.-Amer	563212
Kerner, Andreas		4 Nov 1856	Holzhausen	Sulz	Feb 1872	N.-Amer	849635
Kerner, Anna Maria		5 Jan 1835	Moetzingen	Herr.	Apr 1847	N.-Amer	834626
Kerner, Anna Maria (wife)		11 Apr 1812	Moetzingen	Herr.	Apr 1847	N.-Amer	834626
Kerner, Dorothea		18 Feb 1833	Moetzingen	Herr.	Apr 1847	N.-Amer	834626
Kerner, Elisabeth Rosina (wife)		5 Mar 1783	Sulz	Sulz	May 1817	N.-Amer	849642
Kerner, Gottfried Michael		1 Oct 1814	Sigmarswangen	Sulz	May 1817	N.-Amer	849642
Kerner, Johann Christian		29 Nov 1840	Moetzingen	Herr.	Apr 1847	N.-Amer	834626
Kerner, Johannes		25 Nov 1837	Moetzingen	Herr.	Apr 1847	N.-Amer	834626
Kerner, Johannes & F		17 Aug 1803	Moetzingen	Herr.	Apr 1847	N.-Amer	834626
Kerner, Joseph & F			Sigmarswangen	Sulz	1817	Hungary	849643
Kerner, Joseph & F		11 Nov 1778	Sigmarswangen	Sulz	May 1817	N.-Amer	849642
Kerner, Karl		4 Dec 1865	Sigmarswangen	Sulz	Dec 1882	N.-Amer	849626
Kerner, Maria Agatha		22 Nov 1804	Sigmarswangen	Sulz	May 1817	N.-Amer	849642
Kerner, Rebecca		16 Oct 1846	Moetzingen	Herr.	Apr 1847	N.-Amer	834626
Kerner, Wilhelm Heinrich		3 Dec 1843	Moetzingen	Herr.	Apr 1847	N.-Amer	834626
Kessler, Heinrich			Frutenhof	Frd.	Apr 1752	Pen.N-A	550803
Ketteraff, Wilhelm		28 Mar 1810	Winterbach	Schd.	Jan 1837	Bavaria	801461
Ketterer, Anton			Alpirsbach	Frd.	May 1752	Pen.N-A	550803
Keuler, Johann Bernhardt		18 Mar 1839	Oberjettingen	Herr.	Oct 1865	Prussia	834624
Keuss, Robert Gottfried Val.			Neubulach	Calw	1859	Switz.	563212
Khoenle, Julius		7 Jan 1847	Herrenberg	Herr.	Dec 1867	N.-Amer	834624
Kibler, Conrad			Klosterreichenbach	Frd.	1817	Russia	569269
Kibler, Jacob			Dietersweiler	Frd.	1817	Russia	569269
Kibler, Michael			Wittlensweiler	Frd.	1817	Russia	569269
Kiefer, Heinrich		28 yrs.	Zwerenberg	Calw	1854	N.-Amer	563212
Kiefer, Johann Georg		21 Mar 1851	Isingen	Sulz	1854	Switz.	849636
Kieffer, Johann Martin			Isingen	Sulz	Apr 1853	N.-Amer	849636
Kienzle, Andreas		26 Oct 1822	Nufringen	Herr.	May 1838	N.-Amer	834625
Kienzle, Anna Margaretha		24 Mar 1813	Nufringen	Herr.	bef 1838	N.-Amer	834625
Kienzle, Anna Maria		13 Jul 1815	Nufringen	Herr.	May 1838	N.-Amer	834625
Kienzle, Anna Maria (wife)		39 yrs.	Affstaett	Herr.	May 1832	N.-Amer	834624
Kienzle, Anton		29 Dec 1841	Tailfingen	Herr.	Apr 1847	N.-Amer	834626
Kienzle, Barbara		15 Sep 1850	Nufringen	Herr.	Mar 1868	N.-Amer	834624
Kienzle, Bartholomaeus		37 yrs.	Affstaett	Herr.	Apr 1847	France	834626
Kienzle, Christian Phil.Fried.		16 Jan 1874	Sulz	Sulz	1879	N.-Amer	849628
Kienzle, Christina (wife)		19 May 1810	Besenfeld	Herr.	Apr 1847	N.-Amer	834626
Kienzle, Elisabetha Dorothea		9 Jul 1819	Nufringen	Herr.	May 1838	N.-Amer	834625
Kienzle, Georg Heinrich & F		21 May 1783	Nufringen	Herr.	May 1838	N.-Amer	834625
Kienzle, Gottlob Friedrich & F			Sulz	Sulz	Apr 1891	N.-Amer	849626
Kienzle, Gottlob Friedrich & F		12 Dec 1844	Sulz	Sulz	1879	N.-Amer	849628
Kienzle, Jacob		16 May 1846	Tailfingen	Herr.	Apr 1847	N.-Amer	834626
Kienzle, Johann Georg		3 Aug 1852	Nufringen	Herr.	Mar 1868	N.-Amer	834624
Kienzle, Johann Jacob		2 Sep 1810	Nufringen	Herr.	bef 1838	N.-Amer	834625
Kienzle, Johann Jacob & W		45 yrs.	Affstaett	Herr.	May 1832	N.-Amer	834624
Kienzle, Johann Michael		19 Dec 1847	Oberjesingen	Herr.	Aug 1867	N.-Amer	834624
Kienzle, Johann Michael		24 Feb 1833	Nufringen	Herr.	May 1838	N.-Amer	834625
Kienzle, Johann Michael		11 Nov 1848	Nufringen	Herr.	Mar 1868	N.-Amer	834624

Kienzle, Johannes	27 Apr 1843	Tailfingen	Herr.	Apr 1847	N.-Amer	834626
Kienzle, Johannes & F	12 Sep 1806	Tailfingen	Herr.	Apr 1847	N.-Amer	834626
Kienzle, Louise Marie (wife)		Sulz	Sulz	Apr 1891	N.-Amer	849626
Kienzle, Ludwig & W	37 yrs.	Nufringen	Herr.	May 1832	N.-Amer	834624
Kienzle, Luise (wife)		Stuttgart	Sulz	1878	N.-Amer	849628
Kienzle, Margaretha (wife)	34 yrs.	Nufringen	Herr.	May 1832	N.-Amer	834624
Kienzle, Maria Salome	15 Sep 1836	Tailfingen	Herr.	Apr 1847	N.-Amer	834626
Kieple, Catharina		Beutelsbach	Schd.	Feb 1837	N.-Amer	801461
Kiercker, Carl Franz Emil	21 Aug 1840	Freudenstadt	Frd.	Jun 1856	N.-Amer	569275
Kiferle, Maximillian	Jan 1851	Rottenburg	Sulz	Dec 1870	N.-Amer	849631
Kilgus, Barbara	12 Mar 1856	Pfalzgrafenweiler	Frd.	May 1860	N.-Amer	577777
Kilgus, Christian	8 Nov 1842	Schopfloch	Frd.	Dec 1860	N.-Amer	577777
Kilgus, Elisabetha & C	2 Jul 1824	Pfalzgrafenweiler	Frd.	May 1860	N.-Amer	577777
Kilgus, Johann Georg		Rodt	Frd.	Jul 1817	France	569268
Kilgus, Johann Georg	12 Nov 1828	Gruental	Frd.	Mar 1865	N.-Amer	577779
Killgus, Anna & C	12 Sep 1808	Hallwangen	Frd.	Apr 1860	N.-Amer	577777
Killgus, Christina	30 Mar 1803	Hallwangen	Frd.	Apr 1860	N.-Amer	577777
Killgus, Christina	24 yrs.	Hallwangen	Frd.	Apr 1860	N.-Amer	577777
Killguss, Friedrich		Schopfloch	Frd.	Apr 1752	Pen.N-A	550803
Killinger, Anna Maria	12 Mar 1838	Bergfelden	Sulz	Sep 1856	N.-Amer	849629
Killinger, Anna Maria(wid.)& F	53 yrs.	Bergfelden	Sulz	Sep 1865	N.-Amer	849629
Killinger, Johann Georg	10 Sep 1840	Bergfelden	Sulz	Aug 1858	N.-Amer	849629
Killinger, Johann Martin	19 yrs.	Bergfelden	Sulz	Sep 1865	N.-Amer	849629
Killinger, Johannes	31 Oct 1843	Bergfelden	Sulz	Oct 1860	N.-Amer	849629
Kimig, – –		Sindelfingen	– –	1752	Pen.N-A	550803
Kimmich, Andreas & F		Muehlheim a.B.	Sulz	May 1817	Russia	849639
Kimmich, Anna (wife)		Renfrizhausen	Sulz	May 1832	N.-Amer	849639
Kimmich, Anna Rosina (wife)	7 Jan 1814	Voehringen	Sulz	Mar 1860	N.-Amer	849639
Kimmich, Christina & F		Renfrizhausen	Sulz	Jul 1885	N.-Amer	849639
Kimmich, Christine	20 Mar 1849	Renfrizhausen	Sulz	Mar 1860	N.-Amer	849639
Kimmich, Conrad		Bergfelden	Sulz	Oct 1853	N.-Amer	849629
Kimmich, Conrad	6 Oct 1851	Renfrizhausen	Sulz	Mar 1860	N.-Amer	849639
Kimmich, Jacob		Renfrizhausen	Sulz	bef 1885	N.-Amer	849639
Kimmich, Jakob		Renfrizhausen	Sulz	1832	N.-Amer	849639
Kimmich, Johann Georg	9 Dec 1844	Renfrizhausen	Sulz	Mar 1860	N.-Amer	849639
Kimmich, Johann Georg & F	29 Jan 1812	Renfrizhausen	Sulz	Mar 1860	N.-Amer	849639
Kimmich, Johann Jakob	29 Jul 1842	Renfrizhausen	Sulz	Mar 1860	N.-Amer	849639
Kimmich, Johann Martin	1 Jun 1858	Renfrizhausen	Sulz	Mar 1860	N.-Amer	849639
Kimmich, Johannes	27 Aug 1840	Renfrizhausen	Sulz	Mar 1860	N.-Amer	849639
Kimmich, Johannes	9 Aug 1869	Muehlheim a.B.	Sulz	Jan 1884	N.-Amer	849639
Kimmich, Johannes & F	9 Feb 1807	Renfrizhausen	Sulz	May 1832	N.-Amer	849639
Kimmich, Maria Jacobine	25 Jun 1873	Renfrizhausen	Sulz	Jul 1885	N.-Amer	849639
Kimmich, Paul Ludwig	25 Jan 1872	Renfrizhausen	Sulz	Jul 1885	N.-Amer	849639
Kindler, Johannes	31 yrs.	Ehningen, Boebl.	Herr.	Mar 1844	N.-Amer	834626
Kipp, Andreas	3 Jun 1849	Voehringen	Sulz	Nov 1865	N.-Amer	849643
Kipp, Andreas	9 Oct 1850	Leidringen	Sulz	Aug 1867	N.-Amer	849637
Kipp, Anna	12 Mar 1840	Voehringen	Sulz	Aug 1852	N.-Amer	849643
Kipp, Anna	3 yrs.	Bickelsberg	Sulz	Jun 1853	N.-Amer	849630
Kipp, Anna (wife)		Voehringen	Sulz	Aug 1852	N.-Amer	849643
Kipp, Anna Maria	8 Apr 1843	Voehringen	Sulz	Aug 1852	N.-Amer	849643

Name		Birth		Emigration			Film
Last	First	Date	Place	O'amt	Appl. Date	Dest.	Number
Kipp, Anna Maria			Bickelsberg	Sulz	Jun 1853	N.-Amer	849630
Kipp, Anna Maria (wife) & F			Voehringen	Sulz	1866	N.-Amer	849643
Kipp, Barbara		13 Sep 1845	Bergfelden	Sulz	Nov 1865	N.-Amer	849629
Kipp, Barbara		5 Sep 1845	Voehringen	Sulz	Aug 1852	N.-Amer	849643
Kipp, Carl		23 Sep 1849	Bergfelden	Sulz	Sep 1866	N.-Amer	849629
Kipp, Christian		infant	Holzhausen	Sulz	Oct 1854	N.-Amer	849635
Kipp, Christina			Bickelsberg	Sulz	Jun 1853	N.-Amer	849630
Kipp, Elisabetha		20 Oct 1850	Voehringen	Sulz	May 1868	N.-Amer	849643
Kipp, Elisabetha Barbara		22 Jun 1839	Bergfelden	Sulz	Nov 1867	N.-Amer	849629
Kipp, Eva		31 Oct 1853	Voehringen	Sulz	1866	N.-Amer	849643
Kipp, Eva Katharina		9 Mar 1842	Bergfelden	Sulz	Sep 1865	N.-Amer	849629
Kipp, Hermann		22 Oct 1870	Rosenfeld	Sulz	Jan 1889	N.-Amer	849626
Kipp, Jacob		11 Jul 1843	Leidringen	Sulz	Jul 1863	N.-Amer	849637
Kipp, Jacob & F			Bergfelden	Sulz	1817	Russia	849625
Kipp, Jakob			Voehringen	Sulz	May 1855	N.-Amer	849643
Kipp, Jakob		15 May 1855	Bergfelden	Sulz	Aug 1882	N.-Amer	849626
Kipp, Jakob		22 Jul 1877	Bickelsberg	Sulz	Sep 1894	N.-Amer	849626
Kipp, Jakob			Bickelsberg	Sulz	Jun 1853	N.-Amer	849630
Kipp, Jakob			Holzhausen	Sulz	Sep 1846	N.-Amer	849635
Kipp, Jakob & F			Voehringen	Sulz	Aug 1852	N.-Amer	849643
Kipp, Johann Bernhardt		19 Sep 1850	Bergfelden	Sulz	Sep 1865	N.-Amer	849629
Kipp, Johann Georg			Voehringen	Sulz	bef 1844	N.-Amer	849643
Kipp, Johann Georg		22 Apr 1846	Bickelsberg	Sulz	Oct 1866	N.-Amer	849630
Kipp, Johann Jacob		21 Oct 1844	Bickelsberg	Sulz	bef 1868	N.-Amer	849630
Kipp, Johann Jakob		23 Apr 1842	Bergfelden	Sulz	Nov 1867	N.-Amer	849629
Kipp, Johann Jakob		3 yrs.	Holzhausen	Sulz	Oct 1854	N.-Amer	849635
Kipp, Johann Martin			Bickelsberg	Sulz	Jun 1853	N.-Amer	849630
Kipp, Johannes		15 Oct 1832	Bergfelden	Sulz	Oct 1855	N.-Amer	849629
Kipp, Johannes		19 Nov 1872	Isingen	Sulz	May 1888	N.-Amer	849636
Kipp, Johannes & F			Holzhausen	Sulz	Oct 1854	N.-Amer	849635
Kipp, Josias			Bickelsberg	Sulz	Jun 1853	N.-Amer	849630
Kipp, Kaspar		18 Sep 1847	Bickelsberg	Sulz	Dec 1867	N.-Amer	849630
Kipp, Leonhard		12 Apr 1868	Rotenzimmern	Sulz	May 1885	N.-Amer	849642
Kipp, Maria		27 Apr 1861	Voehringen	Sulz	1866	N.-Amer	849643
Kipp, Maria		5 yrs.	Holzhausen	Sulz	Oct 1854	N.-Amer	849635
Kipp, Michael		26 Feb 1849	Bickelsberg	Sulz	Nov 1869	N.-Amer	849630
Kipp, Michael			Bickelsberg	Sulz	Jun 1853	N.-Amer	849630
Kipp, Michael & F		5 Sep 1806	Bickelsberg	Sulz	Jun 1853	N.-Amer	849630
Kipp, Wilhelm		15 May 1875	Bickelsberg	Sulz	Oct 1890	N.-Amer	849626
Kipp, Wilhelm		14 Apr 1832	Rosenfeld	Sulz	Aug 1852	N.-Amer	849640
Kirchherr, Anna Maria		21 yrs.	Oberkollbach	Calw	Apr 1848	N.-Amer	563212
Kirchherr, Eva Barbara		22 yrs.	Altburg	Calw	Mar 1847	N.-Amer	563212
Kirchherr, Johann Martin & F			Oberkollbach	Calw	1847	N.-Amer	563212
Kirchherr, Johannes		19 yrs.	Simmozheim	Calw	1861	N.-Amer	563212
Kirchherr, Johannes			Stammheim	Calw	1854	N.-Amer	563212
Kirchherr, Michael		38 yrs.	Oberkollbach	Calw	1868	Baden	563212
Kirgis, Caspar & F			Balingen	Bal.	May 1854	N.-Amer	555964
Kirgus, Eleonore			Sulz	Sulz	Apr 1833	N.-Amer	849627
Kirgus, Jacob			Sulz	Sulz	Apr 1833	N.-Amer	849627
Kirgus, Jakob & F		25 Jul 1772	Sulz	Sulz	Apr 1833	N.-Amer	849627

Kirgus, Johann		Sulz	Sulz	Apr 1833	N.-Amer	849627
Kirgus, Johann Daniel	1 Aug 1810	Sulz	Sulz	Apr 1833	N. Amer	849627
Kirgus, Johann Jonathan	30 Dec 1813	Sulz	Sulz	Apr 1833	N.-Amer	849627
Kirgus, Rosina Catharina (wife)		Sulz	Sulz	Apr 1833	N.-Amer	849627
Kirn, (wife)	27 Dec 1793	Unterjettingen	Herr.	Jul 1852	N.-Amer	834627
Kirn, Agatha	23 Sep 1843	Groembach	Frd.	Jun 1854	N.-Amer	569273
Kirn, Agatha	18 Oct 1812	Groembach	Frd.	Jun 1854	N.-Amer	569273
Kirn, Agatha		Besenfeld	Frd.	Aug 1865	N.-Amer	577779
Kirn, Caroline		Groembach	Frd.	Aug 1844	Hesse	569269
Kirn, Catharina		Roet	Frd.	bef 1855	N.-Amer	569275
Kirn, Christian	28 Dec 1827	Unterjettingen	Herr.	Apr 1847	N.-Amer	834626
Kirn, Christian Heinrich	3 Nov 1825	Unterjettingen	Herr.	Apr 1847	N.-Amer	834626
Kirn, Conrad & F	8 Jul 1799	Unterjettingen	Herr.	Jul 1852	N.-Amer	834627
Kirn, David	1 Feb 1822	Unterjettingen	Herr.	Apr 1847	N.-Amer	834626
Kirn, Eva Maria	25 Nov 1849	Groembach	Frd.	Jun 1854	N.-Amer	569273
Kirn, Eva Maria	22 Jul 1827	Besenfeld	Frd.	Mar 1855	N.-Amer	569275
Kirn, Friederike & C		Groembach	Frd.	Aug 1844	Hesse	569269
Kirn, Friederike Dorothea	6 Feb 1825	Unterjettingen	Herr.	Jul 1852	N.-Amer	834627
Kirn, Georg Michael	10 Mar 1827	Unterjettingen	Herr.	Apr 1847	N.-Amer	834626
Kirn, Jakob Friedrich	19 Apr 1853	Goettelfingen	Frd.	Mar 1854	N.-Amer	569273
Kirn, Jakob Friedrich	17 Jul 1817	Besenfeld	Frd.	Feb 1854	N.-Amer	569273
Kirn, Johann Conrad	2 Dec 1832	Unterjettingen	Herr.	Jul 1852	N.-Amer	834627
Kirn, Johann Jacob (wid.) & F	15 Feb 1795	Unterjettingen	Herr.	Apr 1847	N.-Amer	834626
Kirn, Johann Matthaeus & F	22 Nov 1815	Groembach	Frd.	Jun 1854	N.-Amer	569273
Kirn, Johann Ulrich & F		Oberhaugstett	Calw	Mar 1847	N.-Amer	563212
Kirn, Johannes	19 Jul 1839	Unterjettingen	Herr.	Jul 1852	N.-Amer	834627
Kirn, Johannes & F		Groembach	Frd.	Mar 1851	N.-Amer	569271
Kirn, Konrad		Besenfeld	Frd.	Mar 1850	N.-Amer	569271
Kirn, Maria Katharina	28 Nov 1834	Unterjettingen	Herr.	Jul 1852	N.-Amer	834627
Kirn, Wilhelm August		Altenstaig	Nag.	Apr 1856	N.-Amer	838492
Kirschenmann, Barbara	22 Nov 1820	Durrweiler	Frd.	Sep 1853	N.-Amer	569274
Kirschenmann, Christian	11 Mar 1837	Durrweiler	Frd.	Mar 1853	N.-Amer	569272
Kirschenmann, Elisabetha	16 Mar 1802	Pfalzgrafenweiler	Frd.	Apr 1836	N.-Amer	569268
Kirschenmann, Johann Adam	8 Apr 1833	Durrweiler	Frd.	Mar 1851	N.-Amer	569271
Kirschenmann, Johann Georg	20 Nov 1839	Durrweiler	Frd.	Mar 1853	N.-Amer	569272
Kirschenmann, Johann Georg	31 Dec 1827	Durrweiler	Frd.	Mar 1851	N.-Amer	569271
Kirschenmann, Matthias	23 Oct 1835	Tumlingen	Frd.	Apr 1866	N.-Amer	577780
Kissling, Lisete	21 Jul 1833	Pfalzgrafenweiler	Frd.	Nov 1844	N.-Amer	569272
Kistler, Jakob		Ebingen	Bal.	1857	Switz.	555962
Kittel, Christiana		Unterjesingen	Herr.	Aug 1838	France	834625
Kittel, Louise Charlotte		Unterjesingen	Herr.	bef 1851	France	834627
Kittel, Ludwig	23 yrs.	Poltringen	Herr.	Apr 1847	N.-Amer	834626
Kittel, Margaretha (wife)	47 yrs.	Poltringen	Herr.	Apr 1847	N.-Amer	834626
Kittel, Simon & F	58 yrs.	Poltringen	Herr.	Apr 1847	N.-Amer	834626
Kittel, Thaddaeus & W		Tailfingen	Herr.	Apr 1831	N.-Amer	834624
Kitzlinger, Marie Agnes		Sulz	Sulz	Aug 1838	Switz.	849627
Klaeger, Anna Katharina	10 Nov 1835	Tumlingen	Frd.	Jan 1855	N.-Amer	569275
Klaeger, Anna Katharina & C		Tumlingen	Frd.	Aug 1860	N.-Amer	577777
Klaeger, Anna Maria	10 Jan 1844	Tumlingen	Frd.	Jan 1855	N.-Amer	569275
Klaeger, Anna Maria	17 Jan 1804	Tumlingen	Frd.	Mar 1837	N.-Amer	569268

Name		Birth		Emigration			Film
Last	First	Date	Place	O'amt	Appl. Date	Dest.	Number
Klaeger, Anton		20 Sep 1850	Altheim	Horb	Feb 1852	N.-Amer	835929
Klaeger, Christian			Dornstetten	Frd.	bef 1860	N.-Amer	577777
Klaeger, Christian & F		26 Oct 1798	Tumlingen	Frd.	Jan 1855	N.-Amer	569275
Klaeger, Christine		10 Jun 1838	Tumlingen	Frd.	Jan 1855	N.-Amer	569275
Klaeger, Christine (wife)		3 Nov 1808	Neunuifra	Frd.	Jan 1855	N.-Amer	569275
Klaeger, Christoph Adam		14 Feb 1836	Baiersbronn	Frd.	Mar 1854	N.-Amer	569273
Klaeger, Elisabethe		6 May 1825	Tumlingen	Frd.	Feb 1851	N.-Amer	569271
Klaeger, Friederike		28 yrs.	Altheim	Horb	bef 1869	Baden	835929
Klaeger, Gottlob		1 Feb 1846	Tumlingen	Frd.	Jan 1855	N.-Amer	569275
Klaeger, Johann Georg		1 Mar 1848	Tumlingen	Frd.	Jan 1855	N.-Amer	569275
Klaeger, Johann Georg			Neunuifra	Frd.	bef 1866	Baden	577780
Klaeger, Johann Georg (wid)		50 yrs.	Tumlingen	Frd.	Jul 1856	N.-Amer	569275
Klaeger, Johannes		13 Jan 1851	Tumlingen	Frd.	Jan 1855	N.-Amer	569275
Klaeger, Mathias		13 yrs.	Tumlingen	Frd.	Aug 1860	N.-Amer	577777
Klaeger, Michael		5 Sep 1829	Tumlingen	Frd.	Jul 1856	N.-Amer	569275
Klaeger, Rosina Catharina		13 Sep 1823	Dornstetten	Frd.	Jan 1849	N.-Amer	569270
Klaeger, Victoria			Altheim	Horb	Aug 1868	N.-Amer	835929
Klaeger, Wilhelm			Altheim	Horb	Mar 1853	N.-Amer	835929
Klaiber, Dominikus & F			Poltringen	Herr.	May 1834	Hungary	834624
Klaiber, Johannes		10 May 1865	Wittershausen	Sulz	Sep 1881	N.-Amer	849626
Klaiber, Silvester & F			Poltringen	Herr.	May 1834	Hungary	834624
Klaile, Gottlieb		7 Apr 1850	Unterreichenbach	Calw	1868	N.-Amer	563212
Klais, Elisabetha Catharina		19 Apr 1837	Herzogsweiler	Frd.	Apr 1857	N.-Amer	577776
Klais, Jakob		8 Oct 1834	Herzogsweiler	Frd.	Apr 1857	N.-Amer	577776
Klais, Johannes		27 Jul 1839	Herzogsweiler	Frd.	Apr 1857	N.-Amer	577776
Klaiss, Anna Maria		31 May 1823	Cresbach	Frd.	Sep 1846	N.-Amer	569271
Klaiss, Christina		8 Jun 1816	Cresbach	Frd.	Sep 1854	N.-Amer	569274
Klaiss, Elisabetha Catharina		4 Jan 1827	Cresbach	Frd.	Sep 1846	N.-Amer	569271
Klaiss, Friedrich & F		11 Feb 1814	Cresbach	Frd.	Sep 1846	N.-Amer	569271
Klaiss, Jacob Friedrich			Sommenhardt	Calw	1862	N.-Amer	563212
Klaiss, Johann Georg		28 Nov 1843	Cresbach	Frd.	Sep 1846	N.-Amer	569271
Klaiss, Magdalena		24 Jun 1812	Baiersbronn	Frd.	Sep 1846	N.-Amer	569271
Klauber, Christine		7 Mar 1865	Enztal	Nag.	Aug 1865	N.-Amer	838494
Klauber, Dorothea		30 Oct 1845	Enztal	Nag.	Aug 1865	N.-Amer	838494
Klauber, Georg Friedrich & F			Enztal	Nag.	Aug 1865	N.-Amer	838494
Klauber, Johann F. Carl		20 Mar 1859	Enztal	Nag.	Aug 1865	N.-Amer	838494
Klauber, Mathias		11 Oct 1851	Enztal	Nag.	Aug 1865	N.-Amer	838494
Klaus, Marie Dorothee		27 Apr 1810	Freudenstadt	Frd.	Dec 1841	Switz.	569267
Kleib, Wilhelm			Nagold	Nag.	May 1855	Hungary	838591
Klein, Christine Cath. El.			Stammheim	Calw	May 1870	N.-Amer	563212
Klein, Friedrich			Wittlensweiler	Frd.	Jul 1865	N.-Amer	577779
Klein, Georg Friedrich		11 yrs.	Stammheim	Calw	May 1870	N.-Amer	563212
Klein, Heinrich & F			Muehlheim a.B.	Sulz	May 1817	Russia	849639
Klein, Jacob			Sulz	Sulz	bef 1821	Russia	849625
Klein, Johann Christian		8 yrs.	Stammheim	Calw	May 1870	N.-Amer	563212
Klein, Johann Martin		19 May 1821	Wittlensweiler	Frd.	Dec 1846	N.-Amer	569270
Klein, Johannes		22 Jan 1846	Wittlensweiler	Frd.	Oct 1866	N.-Amer	577780
Klein, Johannes & F			Wittendorf	Frd.	Apr 1847	N.-Amer	569271
Klein, Martin		2 Nov 1835	Wittlensweiler	Frd.	Jun 1854	N.-Amer	569274
Klein, Matthaeus			Hopfau/Nennthausen	Sulz	Oct 1835	France	849636

Kleinconrad, Anna Maria & C	26 Mar 1825	Renfrizhausen	Sulz	Jul 1861	N.-Amer	849639
Kleindienst, August	10 Dec 1842	Bettenhausen	Sulz	Jan 1870	N.-Amer	849630
Kleindienst, Reinhard	28 Aug 1849	Binsdorf	Sulz	Feb 1866	N.-Amer	849631
Kleinkonrad, Anna Barbara	1 Apr 1811	Renfrizhausen	Sulz	Mar 1817	Hungary	849639
Kleinkonrad, Christian wid.& F	7 Jan 1780	Renfrizhausen	Sulz	Mar 1817	Hungary	849639
Kleinkonrad, Katharina	25 Jul 1804	Renfrizhausen	Sulz	Mar 1837	N.-Amer	849639
Kleinkonrad, Katharina	25 Jul 1804	Renfrizhausen	Sulz	Mar 1817	Hungary	849639
Kleinkonrad, Mathias		Renfrizhausen	Sulz	Feb 1853	N.-Amer	849639
Kleiss, Christian Friedrich	25 Feb 1798	Pfalzgrafenweiler	Frd.	bef 1838	A-dam	569268
Klick, Jacob	27 yrs.	Neuweiler	Calw	1864	N.-Amer	563212
Klinck, Georg Adam	19 yrs.	Neuweiler	Calw	1869	N.-Amer	563212
Kling, Louise		Calw	Calw	1861	Berlin	563212
Klingele, Johann Martin		Voehringen	Sulz	1856	Switz.	849643
Klingele, Josias	2 Apr 1807	Voehringen	Sulz	bef 1854	Frankf.	849643
Klingele, Josias		Voehringen	Sulz	Mar 1839	M-heim	849643
Klink, Anna Maria		Hornberg	Calw	1866	N.-Amer	563212
Klink, Bernhardt	25 Aug 1808	Untertalheim	Nag.	Dec 1849	Baden	838490
Klink, Crezentia & C	6 Feb 1829	Leinstetten	Sulz	Jun 1860	Prussia	849638
Klink, Franz Xaver	2 Dec 1858	Leinstetten	Sulz	Jun 1860	Prussia	849638
Klink, Johann Georg	1832	Hornberg	Calw	1855	N.-Amer	563212
Klink, Johannes & F		Hornberg	Calw	1854	N.-Amer	563212
Klink, Michael & F		Altbulach	Calw	1847	N.-Amer	563212
Klink, Rosina		Untertalheim	Horb	Feb 1849	N.-Amer	835929
Kloepfer, Auguste (wife)		Muehlheim a.B.	Sulz	Mar 1858	N.-Amer	849639
Kloepfer, Auguste Beate Julie		Muehlheim a.B.	Sulz	Mar 1858	N.-Amer	849639
Kloepfer, Carl Ludwig	13 Jun 1813	Schorndorf	Schd.	Aug 1833	N.-Amer	801460
Kloepfer, Carl Wilhelm	25 Aug 1819	Schorndorf	Schd.	Aug 1833	N.-Amer	801460
Kloepfer, Friederike Dorothea		Schorndorf	Schd.	Aug 1833	N.-Amer	801460
Kloepfer, Johann Friedrich	14 Feb 1823	Schorndorf	Schd.	Aug 1833	N.-Amer	801460
Kloepfer, Johann Gottfried & F		Schorndorf	Schd.	Aug 1833	N.-Amer	801460
Kloepfer, Louise Magdalena	16 Jul 1821	Schorndorf	Schd.	Aug 1833	N.-Amer	801460
Kloepfer, Otto Albert		Muehlheim a.B.	Sulz	Mar 1858	N.-Amer	849639
Kloepfer, Rudolf & F		Muehlheim a.B.	Sulz	Mar 1858	N.-Amer	849639
Kloepfer, Rudolf Carl Robert		Muehlheim a.B.	Sulz	Mar 1858	N.-Amer	849639
Kloepfer, Wilhelm Heinrich	9 Jun 1826	Schorndorf	Schd.	Aug 1833	N.-Amer	801460
Kloess, Anna Christina		Edelweiler	Frd.	Mar 1847	N.-Amer	569271
Kloess, Christian		Edelweiler	Frd.	Mar 1847	N.-Amer	569271
Kloess, Jakob Friedrich & F		Edelweiler	Frd.	Mar 1847	N.-Amer	569271
Klotz, Christina	19 yrs.	Breitenholz	Herr.	May 1831	N.-Amer	834624
Klotz, Christina Cathar. & F		Breitenholz	Herr.	May 1831	N.-Amer	834624
Klotz, Dorothea		Altingen	Herr.	Oct 1852	France	834627
Klotz, Elisabetha	21 yrs.	Zwerenberg	Calw	1854	N.-Amer	563212
Klotz, Georg Friedrich & F		Breitenholz	Herr.	May 1830	N.-Amer	834624
Klotz, Jocob Friedrich		Breitenholz	Herr.	May 1830	N.-Amer	834624
Klotz, Johann & F		Stammheim	Calw	1853	N.-Amer	563212
Klotz, Johannes		Breitenholz	Herr.	May 1830	N.-Amer	834624
Klotz, Katharina	25 yrs.	Zwerenberg	Calw	1854	N.-Amer	563212
Klotz, Maria Catharina	17 Jun 1843	Altingen	Herr.	Mar 1869	N.-Amer	834624
Kloz, Johann Georg	7 Dec 1824	Altingen	Herr.	Apr 1852	N.-Amer	834627
Kloz, Johannes	18 Mar 1814	Altingen	Herr.	Jan 1848	N.-Amer	834626

Name		Birth		Emigration			Film
Last	First	Date	Place	O'amt	Appl. Date	Dest.	Number
Kloz, Maria Catharina		30 Nov 1827	Altingen	Herr.	Apr 1852	N.-Amer	834627
Klump, Eva & C			Protenhof	Frd.	1817	Russia	569269
Klumpp, Agatha		29 Dec 1841	Baiersbronn	Frd.	bef 1866	France	577780
Klumpp, Anna Barbara		30 Apr 1825	Besenfeld	Frd.	Jun 1854	N.-Amer	569274
Klumpp, Anna Maria			Baiersbronn	Frd.	Jun 1856	N.-Amer	569275
Klumpp, Anna Maria		7 Nov 1831	Hegenbach	Frd.	Aug 1854	N.-Amer	569274
Klumpp, Barbara		1823	Klosterreichenbach	Frd.	Mar 1847	N.-Amer	569271
Klumpp, Carl Ferdinand		31 Jul 1832	Besenfeld	Frd.	Apr 1853	N.-Amer	569272
Klumpp, Caroline Louise			Schwarzenberg	Frd.	Jan 1845	Switz.	569269
Klumpp, Catharina			Kniebis	Frd.	Jun 1853	N.-Amer	569272
Klumpp, Christina			Schwarzenberg	Frd.	Mar 1842	Baden	569269
Klumpp, Daniel		2 Oct 1836	Baiersbronn	Frd.	Apr 1856	N.-Amer	569275
Klumpp, Ernst Ludwig		27 yrs.	Calw	Calw	1849	N.-Amer	563212
Klumpp, Franz Jacob & F			Tannenfels	Frd.	Jul 1832	N.-Amer	569267
Klumpp, Friederike Christiane		13 Sep 1831	Freudenstadt	Frd.	Sep 1854	N.-Amer	569274
Klumpp, Friedrich			Glatten	Frd.	1851	N.-Amer	569275
Klumpp, Friedrich			Schoenegruend	Frd.	Apr 1832	N.-Amer	569268
Klumpp, Friedrich & F			Rodt	Frd.	Mar 1847	N.-Amer	569271
Klumpp, Georg Friedrich		10 Feb 1846	Rodt	Frd.	Mar 1847	N.-Amer	569271
Klumpp, Jacob Bernhardt			Kniebis	Frd.	Jun 1853	N.-Amer	569272
Klumpp, Johann Adam			Klosterreichenbach	Frd.	bef 1839	N.-Amer	569268
Klumpp, Johann Gottlieb		30 yrs.	Schwarzenberg	Frd.	Dec 1858	Baden	577776
Klumpp, Johannes		22 Apr 1830	Schoenmuenzach	Frd.	Jun 1862	Baden	577778
Klumpp, Johannes			Roet	Frd.	bef 1858	N.-Amer	577776
Klumpp, Karl		19 Mar 1837	Klosterreichenbach	Frd.	Mar 1853	N.-Amer	569272
Klumpp, Maria Catharina			Tonbach	Frd.	Mar 1847	N.-Amer	569271
Klumpp, Mathaeus			Baiersbronn	Frd.	bef 1836	N.-Amer	569267
Klumpp, Matthaeus		11 Jan 1835	Loch	Frd.	bef 1855	N.-Amer	569275
Klumpp, Michael		24 yrs.	Roet	Frd.	Apr 1856	N.-Amer	569275
Klumpp, Michael Friedrich			Besenfeld	Frd.	Sep 1865	N.-Amer	577779
Klumpp, Philipp Andreas		20 Nov 1825	Gruental	Frd.	Mar 1855	N.-Amer	569275
Klumpp, Philippina		28 Nov 1820	Schwarzenberg	Frd.	Aug 1838	Baden	569268
Klumpp, Regina Catharina		8 Jul 1834	Baiersbronn	Frd.	Apr 1856	N.-Amer	569275
Klumpp, Sophia			Kniebis	Frd.	Jun 1853	N.-Amer	569272
Klumpp, Wilhelm Ernst		9 Feb 1835	Baiersbronn	Frd.	Mar 1854	N.-Amer	569273
Klumpp, Wilhelm Ernst		6 Aug 1836	Baiersbronn	Frd.	Mar 1854	N.-Amer	569273
Klumpp, Wilhelm Friedrich		4 Mar 1840	Freudenstadt	Frd.	Sep 1854	N.-Amer	569274
Klumpp, Wilhelm Ludwig		12 Jan 1846	Roet	Frd.	Oct 1866	N.-Amer	577780
Knaeussler, Anna Maria		12 Sep 1775	Sulz	Sulz	Jul 1817	Russia	849627
Knap, Jacob			Untermusbach	Frd.	1817	Russia	569269
Knapp, Christiane & C			Simmozheim	Calw	1854	N.-Amer	563212
Knapp, Jacob & F			Untermusbach	Frd.	Apr 1817	Russia	569268
Knauer, Johann Daniel		16 May 1802	Grunbach	Schd.	1833	Russia	801460
Knaus, Anna			Marschalkenzimmern	Sulz	Aug 1854	N.-Amer	849638
Knaus, Johannes		14 Nov 1785	Oberiflingen	Frd.	Mar 1833	N.-Amer	569268
Knaus, Johannes			Oberiflingen	Frd.	Jun 1817	Russia	569268
Knauss, Agatha (wife)		20 Feb 1825	Dornhan	Sulz	Feb 1860	N.-Amer	849633
Knauss, Anna Maria		30 Sep 1858	Dornhan	Sulz	Feb 1860	N.-Amer	849633
Knauss, Christina		12 Jun 1835	Loechgau	Sulz	Feb 1854	N.-Amer	849633
Knauss, Georg Friedrich			Sulz	Sulz	Jun 1817	Switz.	849625

Knauss, Jacob		Gruental	Frd.	Apr 1752	Pen.N-A 550803
Knauss, Johannes & F		Dornhan	Sulz	Feb 1860	N. Amer 849633
Knauss, Josefa	3 Apr 1850	Dornhan	Sulz	Feb 1860	N.-Amer 849633
Knauss, Walburga	6 Jun 1856	Dornhan	Sulz	Feb 1860	N.-Amer 849633
Kniess, Friedrich August	5 Nov 1838	Baiersbronn	Frd.	Feb 1854	N.-Amer 569273
Knoedler, Helene		Grunbach	Schd.	Mar 1834	N.-Amer 801460
Knoeller, Maria Magdalena		Sulz	Nag.	Feb 1854	N.-Amer 838491
Knoepfe, Matthias	16 Sep 1873	Marschalkenzimmern	Sulz	Mar 1892	N.-Amer 849638
Knoepfle, Anna Maria		Dornhan	Sulz	Jun 1817	Russia 849633
Knoepfle, Anna Maria (wife)		Dornhan	Sulz	Jun 1817	Russia 849633
Knoepfle, Barbara (wife)		Marschalkenzimmern	Sulz	Apr 1846	N.-Amer 849638
Knoepfle, Catharina		Dornhan	Sulz	Jun 1817	Russia 849633
Knoepfle, Christina		Dornhan	Sulz	Jun 1817	Russia 849633
Knoepfle, Georg Friedrich		Dornhan	Sulz	Jun 1817	Russia 849633
Knoepfle, Jacob & F	23 Jan 1799	Marschalkenzimmern	Sulz	Apr 1846	N.-Amer 849638
Knoepfle, Johann Georg & F		Dornhan	Sulz	Jun 1817	Russia 849633
Knoeri, Michael & W		Althengstett	Calw	1852	N.-Amer 563212
Knoll, Adolf	14 Apr 1850	Binsdorf	Sulz	Apr 1868	N.-Amer 849631
Knoll, Alois	19 Jan 1851	Binsdorf	Sulz	bef 1890	Switz. 849631
Knupfer, Oscar Alois	20 Jun 1849	Binsdorf	Sulz	Sep 1868	Switz. 849631
Knyfle, Christina	18 Aug 1845	Dornhan	Sulz	Sep 1864	N.-Amer 849634
Kober, Georg	14 yrs.	Liebelsberg	Calw	1860	N.-Amer 563212
Kober, Johann Jacob		Hirsau	Calw	Mar 1847	N.-Amer 563212
Kober, Johannes	20 Jul 1833	Dornstetten	Frd.	Aug 1864	N.-Amer 577779
Kober, Maria Agnes	17 yrs.	Liebelsberg	Calw	1856	N.-Amer 563212
Kober, Valentin		Stammheim	Calw	1853	N.-Amer 563212
Koch, Anna Catharina		Tumlingen	Frd.	Jan 1826	Prussia 569268
Koch, Anna Maria		Pfalzgrafenweiler	Frd.	Mar 1817	Russia 569268
Koch, Anna Maria	23 Oct 1838	Brittheim	Sulz	Mar 1857	N.-Amer 849632
Koch, Barbara	20 Jun 1818	Glatten	Frd.	Oct 1854	S.-Amer 569274
Koch, Catharina		Durrweiler	Frd.	Feb 1847	N.-Amer 569271
Koch, Christiane		Pfalzgrafenweiler	Frd.	Mar 1817	Russia 569268
Koch, Christina	18 yrs.	Pfalzgrafenweiler	Frd.	May 1833	N.-Amer 569268
Koch, Elisabetha Catharina	8 Jun 1825	Kuppingen	Herr.	Jul 1868	N.-Amer 834624
Koch, Friedrich	14 Sep 1842	Gaertringen	Herr.	Oct 1851	N.-Amer 834627
Koch, Friedrich & F		Boeffingen	Frd.	1817	Russia 569269
Koch, Georg	26 May 1839	Gaertringen	Herr.	Oct 1851	N.-Amer 834627
Koch, Gottlieb	1824	Dornstetten	Frd.	bef 1854	N.-Amer 569275
Koch, Gottlieb Ludwig	1827	Hirsau	Calw	1857	N.-Amer 563212
Koch, Hermann Mathaeus	20 Jun 1850	Sulz	Sulz	Jul 1867	N.-Amer 849628
Koch, Jacob	20 Oct 1849	Isingen	Sulz	Apr 1868	N.-Amer 849636
Koch, Jacob Friedrich		Kuppingen	Herr.	May 1829	Baden 834624
Koch, Jakob Friedrich		Sulz	Sulz	Mar 1809	-- 849625
Koch, Johann Georg		Herzogsweiler	Frd.	1817	Russia 569269
Koch, Johann Georg & F	30 Apr 1806	Gaertringen	Herr.	Oct 1851	N.-Amer 834627
Koch, Johann Philipp & F		Marbach	Frd.	1817	Russia 569269
Koch, Josefine	24 Jan 1867	Binsdorf	Sulz	Apr 1889	Switz. 849626
Koch, Karl Heinrich Amandus		Duerrwangen	Bal.	1844	Baden 555963
Koch, Karoline Wilhelmine	19 Mar 1836	Groembach	Frd.	Jul 1853	N.-Amer 569274
Koch, Margaretha	7 Feb 1831	Gaertringen	Herr.	Oct 1851	N.-Amer 834627

Name		Birth		Emigration			Film
Last	First	Date	Place	O'amt	Appl. Date	Dest.	Number
Koch, Maria Katharina			Ernstmuehl	Calw	1861	Switz.	563212
Koch, Maria Louise		27 Nov 1832	Gaertringen	Herr.	Oct 1851	N.-Amer	834627
Koch, Matthaeus		5 Aug 1815	Balingen	Bal.	Nov 1844	Prussia	555963
Koch, Pauline		6 Mar 1835	Groembach	Frd.	Jul 1853	N.-Amer	569274
Koch, Sophia Heinrike (wife)		16 Dec 1800	Gaertringen	Herr.	Oct 1851	N.-Amer	834627
Kodweiss, Sophie Friederika		25 Jan 1833	Freudenstadt	Frd.	bef 1864	France	577779
Koegele, Johann Martin		7 Jun 1808	Ostdorf/Balingen	Sulz	Jul 1817	Russia	849629
Koehler, Anna Barbara		11 Mar 1866	Marschalkenzimmern	Sulz	Feb 1880	N.-Amer	849626
Koehler, Anna Maria		34 yrs.	Breitenholz	Herr.	Aug 1852	N.-Amer	834627
Koehler, Anna Maria		7 Nov 1851	Kuppingen	Herr.	Feb 1852	N.-Amer	834627
Koehler, Anna Maria (wid.)& F			Breitenholz	Herr.	Aug 1852	N.-Amer	834627
Koehler, Caroline		17 yrs.	Breitenholz	Herr.	Aug 1852	N.-Amer	834627
Koehler, Catharina		12 Aug 1823	Breitenholz	Herr.	Aug 1851	N.-Amer	834627
Koehler, Christian Wilhelm		15 Aug 1872	Marschalkenzimmern	Sulz	Feb 1880	N.-Amer	849626
Koehler, Christian Wilhelm & F			Marschalkenzimmern	Sulz	Feb 1880	N.-Amer	849626
Koehler, Christine		15 Jul 1864	Marschalkenzimmern	Sulz	Feb 1880	N.-Amer	849626
Koehler, Christoph Friedrich		6 Nov 1867	Marschalkenzimmern	Sulz	Feb 1880	N.-Amer	849626
Koehler, Dorothea (wife)			Marschalkenzimmern	Sulz	Feb 1880	N.-Amer	849626
Koehler, Dorothea (wife)		37 yrs.	Kuppingen	Herr.	Feb 1852	N.-Amer	834627
Koehler, Friedrich August		17 Nov 1862	Marschalkenzimmern	Sulz	Feb 1880	N.-Amer	849626
Koehler, Georg Friedrich		22 yrs.	Breitenholz	Herr.	Aug 1852	N.-Amer	834627
Koehler, Gottliebin		20 yrs.	Breitenholz	Herr.	Aug 1852	N.-Amer	834627
Koehler, Hermann		20 Sep 1877	Marschalkenzimmern	Sulz	Feb 1880	N.-Amer	849626
Koehler, Johann Georg		17 Oct 1866	Marschalkenzimmern	Sulz	Feb 1880	N.-Amer	849626
Koehler, Johannes		23 Dec 1845	Kuppingen	Herr.	Feb 1852	N.-Amer	834627
Koehler, Philipp Friedrich		26 Jul 1870	Marschalkenzimmern	Sulz	Feb 1880	N.-Amer	849626
Koehler, Regina Dorothea		12 Jan 1841	Kuppingen	Herr.	Feb 1852	N.-Amer	834627
Koehler, Regina Elisabeth		11 May 1848	Kuppingen	Herr.	Feb 1852	N.-Amer	834627
Koehler, Rudolph		2 Oct 1879	Marschalkenzimmern	Sulz	Feb 1880	N.-Amer	849626
Koehler, Simon & F			Kuppingen	Herr.	Feb 1852	N.-Amer	834627
Koehler, Susanna Barbara (wid)		3 Feb 1790	Glatten	Frd.	Mar 1847	N.-Amer	569271
Koehlreuter, Carolina Johanna			Sulz	Sulz	Aug 1831	Bavaria	849627
Koehne, Christian		23 Dec 1805	Oberjettingen	Herr.	Apr 1869	N.-Amer	834624
Koehrer, Abraham & F			Dornstetten	Frd.	Oct 1854	N.-Amer	569274
Koehrer, Anna Maria		19 Jun 1837	Dornstetten	Frd.	Oct 1854	N.-Amer	569274
Koehrer, Barbara		26 yrs.	Dornstetten	Frd.	Oct 1860	N.-Amer	577777
Koehrer, Christian			Dornstetten	Frd.	Apr 1857	N.-Amer	577776
Koehrer, Christian		2 yrs.	Dornstetten	Frd.	Apr 1857	N.-Amer	577776
Koehrer, Erhard & F			Dornstetten	Frd.	1817	Russia	569269
Koehrer, Friedrich		2 Aug 1840	Dornstetten	Frd.	Oct 1854	N.-Amer	569274
Koehrer, Gottlieb		15 Aug 1817	Dornstetten	Frd.	Jun 1854	N.-Amer	569274
Koehrer, Jakob Friedrich			Dornstetten	Frd.	Sep 1854	N.-Amer	569274
Koehrer, Jakob Friedrich			Dornstetten	Frd.	Apr 1857	N.-Amer	577776
Koehrer, Johann Friedrich		25 Jun 1804	Dornstetten	Frd.	Apr 1846	Switz.	569271
Koehrer, Johannes			Dornstetten	Frd.	May 1857	N.-Amer	577776
Koehrer, Katharina		10 Sep 1825	Dornstetten	Frd.	Sep 1850	N.-Amer	569271
Kohler, Adolf		3 Feb 1864	Binsdorf	Sulz	1878	N.-Amer	849631
Kohler, Anna		10 yrs.	Sigmarswangen	Sulz	Jul 1855	N.-Amer	849642
Kohler, Anna			Duerrenmettstetten	Sulz	Mar 1854	N.-Amer	849635
Kohler, Anna Barbara		21 Aug 1824	Sulz	Sulz	Jul 1856	Augsb.	849628

Kohler, Anna Maria	6 Jun 1830	Pfalzgrafenweiler	Frd.	Mar 1854	N.-Amer	569273
Kohler, Auguste		Sulz	Sulz	Jan 1854	N. Amer	849627
Kohler, Barbara		Dornstetten	Frd.	Apr 1838	N.-Amer	569269
Kohler, Barbara	1 Nov 1830	Glatten	Frd.	Oct 1854	S.-Amer	569274
Kohler, Carl	11 Nov 1851	Herrenberg	Herr.	Feb 1867	N.-Amer	834624
Kohler, Carl Christian		Freudenstadt	Frd.	Jan 1851	Baden	569271
Kohler, Catharina Margaretha	14 Feb 1822	Glatten	Frd.	Mar 1847	N.-Amer	569270
Kohler, Christian	28 Jul 1869	Binsdorf	Sulz	Jul 1886	N.-Amer	849631
Kohler, Christian	1837	Calw	Calw	1857	N.-Amer	563212
Kohler, Christian Friedrich	11 Jan 1846	Kuppingen	Herr.	Feb 1865	N.-Amer	834624
Kohler, Clemenz	9 mon.	Binsdorf	Sulz	Jun 1854	N.-Amer	849630
Kohler, Dorothea	14 Feb 1820	Binsdorf	Sulz	Sep 1854	N.-Amer	849630
Kohler, Elisabetha Kathar.	28 Aug 1804	Glatten	Frd.	Oct 1854	S.-Amer	569274
Kohler, Franz Xaver	5 Aug 1867	Binsdorf	Sulz	May 1884	N.-Amer	849631
Kohler, Gabriel & F	24 May 1823	Binsdorf	Sulz	Jun 1854	N.-Amer	849630
Kohler, Gertrud		Binsdorf	Sulz	Apr 1836	Hohenz.	849630
Kohler, Gottlieb		Calw	Calw	1854	N.-Amer	563212
Kohler, Jacob Christof		Calw	Calw	1852	N.-Amer	563212
Kohler, Jakob Friedrich	27 Jun 1827	Gaertringen	Herr.	Apr 1852	N.-Amer	834627
Kohler, Johann Georg	16 yrs.	Sigmarswangen	Sulz	Jul 1855	N.-Amer	849642
Kohler, Johann Jacob		Calw	Calw	1853	N.-Amer	563212
Kohler, Johann Jacob & F		Sulz	Sulz	Jun 1854	N.-Amer	849627
Kohler, Johanna Auguste	12 Nov 1829	Sulz	Sulz	Feb 1854	N.-Amer	849627
Kohler, Johanna Dorothea	18 Sep 1824	Freudenstadt	Frd.	bef 1857	Baden	577778
Kohler, Johannes	20 yrs.	Sigmarswangen	Sulz	Jul 1855	N.-Amer	849642
Kohler, Johannes	15 Sep 1865	Binsdorf	Sulz	Jan 1881	N.-Amer	849626
Kohler, Johannes & F		Oberkollbach	Calw	1847	N.-Amer	563212
Kohler, Joseph Friedrich		Haslach	Herr.	Aug 1842	N.-Amer	834625
Kohler, Katharina		Sulz	Sulz	bef 1850	Hungary	849627
Kohler, Katherine Rosine (wife)		Sulz	Sulz	Jun 1854	N.-Amer	849627
Kohler, Louise Friederike	28 Feb 1819	Freudenstadt	Frd.	Nov 1838	Baden	569267
Kohler, Ludwig Ernst	6 Apr 1853	Herrenberg	Herr.	Aug 1868	N.-Amer	834624
Kohler, Magdalena	18 Feb 1845	Rottenburg	Sulz	Apr 1869	Prussia	849631
Kohler, Mathaeus	8 Dec 1831	Boeffingen	Frd.	Jan 1847	N.-Amer	569271
Kohler, Peter	28 Oct 1867	Binsdorf	Sulz	Jul 1881	N.-Amer	849631
Kohler, Regina (wife)		Binsdorf	Sulz	Jun 1854	N.-Amer	849630
Kohler, Sara	33 yrs.	Binsdorf	Sulz	Aug 1863	Switz.	849631
Kohler, Veronica	3 yrs.	Binsdorf	Sulz	Jun 1854	N.-Amer	849630
Kohler, Wilhelm	26 Jun 1837	Binsdorf	Sulz	Sep 1864	N.-Amer	849631
Kohler, Wilhelm Friedrich	24 Dec 1848	Herrenberg	Herr.	Dec 1868	N.-Amer	834624
Kohler, Wilhelm Ludwig		Sulz	Sulz	bef 1834	N.-Amer	849625
Kohlreuter, Christian Ludwig		Dornhan	Sulz	Jun 1817	Russia	849633
Kolb, Gottlieb Friedrich	24 Nov 1850	Sulz	Sulz	Oct 1870	N.-Amer	849628
Kommer, Christian		Endingen	Bal.	Dec 1844	N.-Amer	555964
Konzelmann, Christian Gottl.		Onstmettingen	Bal.	bef 1852	Switz.	555962
Konzelmann, Jacob		Streichen	Bal.	Jan 1845	Switz.	555963
Konzelmann, Johann Georg		Balingen	Bal.	Apr 1855	Switz.	555962
Kopf, Anna & C		Leidringen	Sulz	Mar 1857	N.-Amer	849637
Kopf, Anna Barbara	25 Nov 1864	Leidringen	Sulz	Feb 1869	N.-Amer	849637
Kopf, Anna Barbara	2 Oct 1847	Leidringen	Sulz	May 1865	N.-Amer	849637

Name		Birth		Emigration			Film
Last	First	Date	Place	O'amt	Appl. Date	Dest.	Number
Kopf, Anna Katharina (wife)		2 Aug 1840	Leidringen	Sulz	Feb 1869	N.-Amer	849637
Kopf, Anna Maria		18 mon.	Leidringen	Sulz	May 1856	N.-Amer	849637
Kopf, Anna Maria			Leidringen	Sulz	bef 1866	N.-Amer	849637
Kopf, Catharina & C		1826	Leidringen	Sulz	May 1856	N.-Amer	849637
Kopf, Christina		Oct 1851	Leidringen	Sulz	Jul 1863	N.-Amer	849637
Kopf, Christine			Leidringen	Sulz	bef 1859	N.-Amer	849637
Kopf, Jacob		18 Oct 1837	Leidringen	Sulz	Jun 1863	N.-Amer	849637
Kopf, Jakob		28 Apr 1836	Leidringen	Sulz	Feb 1859	N.-Amer	849637
Kopf, Johann Adam		20 Dec 1865	Leidringen	Sulz	Feb 1869	N.-Amer	849637
Kopf, Johann Georg		23 Jun 1795	Isingen	Sulz	Jan 1817	Russia	849635
Kopf, Johann Georg		30 Nov 1839	Leidringen	Sulz	Feb 1859	N.-Amer	849637
Kopf, Johann Georg			Leidringen	Sulz	Aug 1853	N.-Amer	849637
Kopf, Johann Georg		28 Jan 1855	Leidringen	Sulz	Aug 1871	N.-Amer	849637
Kopf, Johann Georg		19 Dec 1866	Leidringen	Sulz	Feb 1869	N.-Amer	849637
Kopf, Johann Georg		29 Jan 1868	Leidringen	Sulz	Oct 1884	N.-Amer	849626
Kopf, Johann Michael			Leidringen	Sulz	bef 1859	N.-Amer	849637
Kopf, Johannes & F		16 Aug 1837	Leidringen	Sulz	Feb 1869	N.-Amer	849637
Kopf, Karl Friedrich		5 Jan 1863	Leidringen	Sulz	Dec 1879	N.-Amer	849637
Kopf, Katharina		24 Dec 1861	Bickelsberg	Sulz	Mar 1881	N.-Amer	849626
Kopf, Louise Friederika			Sulz	Sulz	Jun 1862	Hohenz.	849628
Kopf, Ludwig		26 Jan 1857	Leidringen	Sulz	Mar 1857	N.-Amer	849637
Kopf, Ludwig		11 May 1845	Leidringen	Sulz	Apr 1867	N.-Amer	849637
Kopf, Rosina & C			Leidringen	Sulz	Mar 1857	N.-Amer	849637
Kopf, Rosine		26 Mar 1849	Leidringen	Sulz	Mar 1857	N.-Amer	849637
Kopp, Amand (wife)		1 Jun 1849	Sulz	Sulz	Dec 1888	Baden	849626
Kopp, Andreas		31 Mar 1876	Dornhan	Sulz	May 1892	N.-Amer	849626
Kopp, Andreas		17 Oct 1857	Hopfau	Sulz	May 1868	N.-Amer	849636
Kopp, Andreas		16 Apr 1863	Dornhan	Sulz	Apr 1881	N.-Amer	849626
Kopp, Andreas & F		3 Oct 1843	Dornhan	Sulz	Apr 1881	N.-Amer	849626
Kopp, Anna Maria		27 Feb 1846	Aach	Frd.	Apr 1846	N.-Amer	569271
Kopp, Anna Maria		1 Aug 18496	Gueltstein	Herr.	May 1869	N.-Amer	834624
Kopp, Barbara (wife)			Dornhan	Sulz	Apr 1881	N.-Amer	849626
Kopp, Barbara (wid.) & F		14 Oct 1823	Hopfau	Sulz	May 1867	N.-Amer	849636
Kopp, Carl Wilhelm Robert		7 May 1824	Nufringen	Herr.	Apr 1838	N.-Amer	834625
Kopp, Christian		6 Feb 1845	Aach	Frd.	Apr 1846	N.-Amer	569271
Kopp, Christian		3 Sep 1863	Hopfau	Sulz	May 1867	N.-Amer	849636
Kopp, Christina		17 May 1841	Aach	Frd.	Apr 1846	N.-Amer	569271
Kopp, Christina		8 May 1849	Fuernsal	Sulz	Sep 1865	N.-Amer	849635
Kopp, Eberhardine Elisabetha		8 Jan 1834	Nufringen	Herr.	Apr 1838	N.-Amer	834625
Kopp, Eva Maria		16 Apr 1851	Gueltstein	Herr.	May 1869	N.-Amer	834624
Kopp, Friedrich		25 Jul 1828	Nufringen	Herr.	Apr 1838	N.-Amer	834625
Kopp, Isaak		21 Feb 1834	Aach	Frd.	Apr 1846	N.-Amer	569271
Kopp, Jacob			Busenweiler	Sulz	Apr 1816	Baden	849632
Kopp, Johann Friedrich & F		6 Sep 1801	Lossburg	Frd.	Apr 1846	N.-Amer	569271
Kopp, Johann Georg		1 Feb 1851	Hopfau	Sulz	Oct 1867	N.-Amer	849636
Kopp, Johann Georg		13 Feb 1826	Nufringen	Herr.	Feb 1865	N.-Amer	834624
Kopp, Johann Georg		5 Nov 1852	Gueltstein	Herr.	May 1869	N.-Amer	834624
Kopp, Johann Jacob			Nufringen	Herr.	Apr 1845	Hesse	834626
Kopp, Johann Martin		27 Jan 1832	Aach	Frd.	Apr 1846	N.-Amer	569271
Kopp, Johann Mathias & F		9 May 1851	Sulz	Sulz	Dec 1888	Baden	849626

Kopp, Johann Michael & F		Nufringen	Herr.	Jun 1833	Rus-Pol 834624
Kopp, Johann Simon	22 Sep 1856	Gueltstein	Herr.	May 1869	N.-Amer 834624
Kopp, Johanna Elisabetha & F	44 yrs.	Nufringen	Herr.	Apr 1838	N.-Amer 834625
Kopp, Johannes	24 Jun 1849	Hopfau	Sulz	Oct 1867	N.-Amer 849636
Kopp, Johannes	6 Dec 1833	Renfrizhausen	Sulz	Jan 1854	N.-Amer 849639
Kopp, Justine	29 yrs.	Nagold	Nag.	Jan 1854	N.-Amer 838491
Kopp, Louisa Johanna	16 Feb 1813	Nufringen	Herr.	Apr 1838	N.-Amer 834625
Kopp, Maria	4 Apr 1812	Lombach	Frd.	Apr 1846	N.-Amer 569271
Kopp, Maria Catharina	10 Aug 1846	Gueltstein	Herr.	May 1869	N.-Amer 834624
Kopp, Mathias	11 Jul 1844	Hopfau	Sulz	Apr 1864	N.-Amer 849636
Kopp, Michael	16 yrs.	Nufringen	Herr.	May 1832	N.-Amer 834624
Kopp, Otto		Rosenfeld	Sulz	Jul 1883	N.-Amer 849626
Kopp, Philipp Jacob	1 May 1848	Gueltstein	Herr.	Aug 1868	N.-Amer 834624
Kopp, Sabina	27 Oct 1861	Gueltstein	Herr.	May 1869	N.-Amer 834624
Korn, Friedrich	29 Mar 1844	Calw	Calw	1863	N.-Amer 563212
Korn, Katharina Magdalena		Gechingen	Calw	1862	N.-Amer 563212
Kornwell, Johann Martin	9 Apr 1846	Reusten	Herr.	Apr 1869	N.-Amer 834624
Kraemer, Christiane Sib. (wife)		Sulz	Sulz	Feb 1833	N.-Amer 849627
Kraemer, Dorothea		Sulz	Sulz	Nov 1856	Africa 849628
Kraemer, Friedrich		Sulz	Sulz	Jan 1793	Russia 849625
Kraemer, Gottlieb Friedrich	27 Sep 1797	Sulz	Sulz	Feb 1833	N.-Amer 849627
Kraemer, Jakob	32 yrs.	Sulz	Sulz	Mar 1815	France 849625
Kraemer, Karl August		Wittershausen	Sulz	bef 1810	France 849625
Kraeusler, Jacob		Freudenstadt	Frd.	Mar 1817	Russia 569267
Kraeusler, Johannes		Untermusbach	Frd.	Jul 1854	N.-Amer 569274
Krafft, Johann Gottfried	28 yrs.	Baiersbronn	Frd.	Jun 1804	Pr.-Pol 550803
Kraft, Andreas	30 Nov 1839	Duerrenmettstetten	Sulz	Feb 1859	N.-Amer 849635
Kraft, Anna Maria	40 yrs.	Baiersbronn	Frd.	May 1817	N.-Amer 569267
Kraft, Anna Maria	25 yrs.	Altburg	Calw	Mar 1847	N.-Amer 563212
Kraft, Anna Maria (wife)	23 Dec 1816	Pfalzgrafenweiler	Frd.	Jul 1854	N.-Amer 569274
Kraft, Catharina Barbara (wife)	13 Apr 1805	Breitenholz	Herr.	May 1829	Hungary 834624
Kraft, Christian	8 Mar 1849	Pfalzgrafenweiler	Frd.	Jul 1854	N.-Amer 569274
Kraft, Dorothea (wife)		Oberkollwangen	Calw	Apr 1875	Palest. 563212
Kraft, Elisabetha & C	8 Sep 1822	Pfalzgrafenweiler	Frd.	Apr 1847	N.-Amer 569270
Kraft, Jacob		Dornstetten	Frd.	Feb 1805	France 550803
Kraft, Johann Adam	13 Nov 1846	Pfalzgrafenweiler	Frd.	Jul 1854	N.-Amer 569274
Kraft, Johann Adam & F	29 Jun 1816	Pfalzgrafenweiler	Frd.	Jul 1854	N.-Amer 569274
Kraft, Johann Franz & F		Baiersbronn	Frd.	Jun 1817	N.-Amer 569267
Kraft, Johann Georg	22 Jan 1834	Breitenholz	Herr.	Jul 1870	N.-Amer 834624
Kraft, Johann Gottlob		Ernstmuehl	Calw	1849	N.-Amer 563212
Kraft, Johann Jacob	9 Mar 1845	Breitenholz	Herr.	May 1862	N.-Amer 834624
Kraft, Johannes	7 Apr 1826	Pfalzgrafenweiler	Frd.	Apr 1847	N.-Amer 569270
Kraft, Johannes	19 yrs.	Oberkollwangen	Calw	1866	N.-Amer 563212
Kraft, Johannes & F		Roetenbach	Calw	1852	N.-Amer 563212
Kraft, Johannes & F	25 Sep 1795	Breitenholz	Herr.	May 1829	Hungary 834624
Kraft, Mathias		Duerrenmettstetten	Sulz	Mar 1854	N.-Amer 849635
Kraft, Philipp & F		Oberkollwangen	Calw	Apr 1875	Palest. 563212
Kraft, Ulrich	25 Feb 1860	Oberkollwangen	Calw	Apr 1875	Palest. 563212
Kraibuhler, Anna Maria	2 Jul 1852	Fuernsal	Sulz	May 1883	N.-Amer 849626
Kraubner, Friedrich & F		Freudenstadt	Frd.	Apr 1817	Russia 569267

Name		Birth		Emigration			Film
Last	First	Date	Place	O'amt	Appl. Date	Dest.	Number
Kraubner, Gottfried		1802	Freudenstadt	Frd.	bef 1864	N.-Amer	577779
Kraus, Michael			Hebsack	Schd.	Jun 1833	Russia	801460
Krauss, Anna Catharina & F			Althengstett	Calw	1869	N.-Amer	563212
Krauss, Anna Magdalena & F			Gechingen	Calw	1869	N.-Amer	563212
Krauss, August Wilhelm		30 yrs.	Dornstetten	Frd.	Jul 1861	N.-Amer	577778
Krauss, Carl Christian		5 Apr 1832	Herrenberg	Herr.	Jul 1849	N.-Amer	834627
Krauss, Catharina & C		34 yrs.	Liebenzell	Calw	Mar 1847	N.-Amer	563212
Krauss, Christian Henrich		20 yrs.	Gechingen	Calw	1869	N.-Amer	563212
Krauss, Friedrike Cath. (wife)		11 Sep 1798	Herrenberg	Herr.	Jul 1849	N.-Amer	834627
Krauss, Georg Heinrich & F		5 Sep 1798	Herrenberg	Herr.	Jul 1849	N.-Amer	834627
Krauss, Gustav Friedrich		27 Oct 1838	Herrenberg	Herr.	Jul 1849	N.-Amer	834627
Krauss, Johann Georg		6 Apr 1849	Gueltstein	Herr.	Apr 1869	N.-Amer	834624
Krauss, Johann Gottl. Fr. & W			Herrenberg	Herr.	Mar 1831	N.-Amer	834624
Krauss, Johannes & W			Tailfingen	Herr.	Apr 1832	N.-Amer	834624
Krauss, Justine		14 yrs.	Liebenzell	Calw	Mar 1847	N.-Amer	563212
Krauss, Magdalena		16 yrs.	Gechingen	Calw	1869	N.-Amer	563212
Krauss, Margaretha			Altburg	Calw	Sep 1870	Baden	563212
Krauss, Paul Immanuel		17 Jul 1841	Herrenberg	Herr.	Jul 1849	N.-Amer	834627
Krauss, Rosine Catharina (wife)			Herrenberg	Herr.	Mar 1831	N.-Amer	834624
Krauss, Wilhelm Heinrich		1 Sep 1830	Herrenberg	Herr.	Jul 1849	N.-Amer	834627
Kraut, Christian		28 Jan 1843	Hopfau	Sulz	May 1866	N.-Amer	849636
Krauth, Anna Maria		3 Sep 1840	Hopfau	Sulz	Mar 1869	N.-Amer	849636
Krauth, Christian		2 Oct 1850	Hopfau	Sulz	Mar 1869	N.-Amer	849636
Krauth, Gottlieb		29 Jul 1845	Hopfau	Sulz	Sep 1866	N.-Amer	849636
Krauth, Luise		7 Sep 1865	Goettelfingen	Frd.	Sep 1866	N.-Amer	577780
Krautmann, Jacob Friedrich		2 Aug 1847	Sulz	Sulz	Sep 1853	N.-Amer	849627
Krautmann, Johann Andreas		21 Nov 1841	Sulz	Sulz	Sep 1853	N.-Amer	849627
Krautmann, Johann Friedrich		11 Jun 1843	Sulz	Sulz	Sep 1853	N.-Amer	849627
Krautmann, Johann Georg & F			Sigmarswangen	Sulz	Jul 1817	Russia	849627
Krautmann, Johannes		24 Feb 1810	Sigmarswangen	Sulz	Mar 1817	Russia	849642
Krautmann, Kath. Frieder. & C			Sulz	Sulz	Sep 1853	N.-Amer	849627
Krautmann, Maria Elisabetha			Sulz	Sulz	Mar 1833	N.-Amer	849627
Krehl, Maximilian Friedrich			Sulz	Sulz	bef 1834	N.-Amer	849627
Kreidler, Jakob		2 Nov 1836	Altheim	Horb	Jul 1854	N.-Amer	835929
Kreissler, Johann Georg			Boeffingen	Frd.	Jan 1810	Poland	569269
Kreitmann, Anna Maria & C		17 Feb 1779	Sigmarswangen	Sulz	Mar 1817	Russia	849642
Kreitmann, Christina		18 Apr 1804	Sigmarswangen	Sulz	Mar 1817	Russia	849642
Kreitmann, Maria Katharina		21 Aug 1792	Sigmarswangen	Sulz	Mar 1817	Russia	849642
Kretz, Andreas		6 yrs.	Reinerzau	Frd.	Aug 1856	Baden	569275
Kretz, Christian		1 mon.	Reinerzau	Frd.	Aug 1856	Baden	569275
Kretz, Christine & C			Reinerzau	Frd.	Aug 1856	Baden	569275
Kreut, Gottlieb & F			Dornhan	Sulz	Jul 1846	N.-Amer	849633
Krieg, Adam & W		32 yrs.	Bondorf	Herr.	Jun 1832	N.-Amer	834624
Krieg, Maria Barbara (wife)		44 yrs.	Bondorf	Herr.	Jun 1832	N.-Amer	834624
Krimmel, Barbara (wife) & F			Voehringen	Sulz	Feb 1854	N.-Amer	849643
Krimmel, Catharina Barbara		8 Jan 1850	Voehringen	Sulz	Feb 1854	N.-Amer	849643
Krimmel, Jakob		22 Feb 1839	Voehringen	Sulz	Feb 1854	N.-Amer	849643
Krimmel, Johann Martin			Voehringen	Sulz	1853	N.-Amer	849643
Krimmel, Johannes			Voehringen	Sulz	1853	N.-Amer	849643
Krimmel, Paulina		20 Jul 1852	Voehringen	Sulz	Feb 1854	N.-Amer	849643

Krin, Regine Helene		Sulz	Sulz	Mar 1836	N.-Amer	849627
Krock, Pauline		Liebenzell	Calw	1869	Baden	563212
Kroeck, Johann Philipp	26 yrs.	Liebenzell	Calw	1866	N.-Amer	563212
Kromer, Wilhelm	5 Aug 1873	Marschalkenzimmern	Sulz	Jan 1892	N.-Amer	849626
Kronenbitter, Andreas	29 Jul 1873	Dornhan	Sulz	Aug 1890	N.-Amer	849626
Kronenbitter, Christina	3 Jun 1842	Dornhan	Sulz	Aug 1866	N.-Amer	849634
Kronenbitter, Johann Georg		Dornhan	Sulz	Mar 1817	Russia	849633
Kronenbitter, Johannes	26 Mar 1867	Dornhan	Sulz	Dec 1883	N.-Amer	849634
Kruck, Johanne Rosine		Liebenzell	Calw	1858	Hesse	563212
Kruppinger, Hartmann (wid.)		Liebenzell	Calw	1854	N.-Amer	563212
Kuebler, Anna	22 Jan 1835	Cresbach	Frd.	Feb 1853	N.-Amer	569272
Kuebler, Anna		Wittlensweiler	Frd.	1817	Hungary	569268
Kuebler, Anna	22 Jan 1835	Vesperweiler	Frd.	bef 1859	N.-Amer	577776
Kuebler, Anna Maria		Durrweiler	Frd.	Mar 1853	N.-Amer	569272
Kuebler, Anna Maria	23 Aug 1842	Glatten	Frd.	Oct 1854	S.-Amer	569274
Kuebler, Anna Maria	24 yrs.	Dornstetten	Frd.	May 1805	Pr.-Pol	550803
Kuebler, Anna Maria	26 Mar 1829	Sulz	Sulz	1855	N.-Amer	849628
Kuebler, Anna Maria	22 Nov 1812	Dornhan	Sulz	Jul 1817	Russia	849633
Kuebler, Anna Maria (wife)	25 Mar 1806	Tumlingen	Frd.	Jan 1855	N.-Amer	569275
Kuebler, Anna Maria (wife)	29 Apr 1784	Tuebingen	Sulz	Jul 1817	Russia	849633
Kuebler, Barbara & C		Pfalzgrafenweiler	Frd.	May 1833	N.-Amer	569268
Kuebler, Barbara (wife)		Sulz	Sulz	Jan 1833	N.-Amer	849627
Kuebler, Catharina	7 Jun 1810	Dornhan	Sulz	Jul 1817	Russia	849633
Kuebler, Christian	28 Jun 1847	Wittlensweiler	Frd.	Mar 1864	N.-Amer	577779
Kuebler, Christian	24 Sep 1874	Dornhan	Sulz	May 1892	N.-Amer	849626
Kuebler, Christian	4 May 1850	Pfalzgrafenweiler	Frd.	Jul 1854	N.-Amer	569274
Kuebler, Christian & F		Pfalzgrafenweiler	Frd.	Jul 1854	N.-Amer	569274
Kuebler, Christina	20 Oct 1839	Tumlingen	Frd.	Jan 1855	N.-Amer	569275
Kuebler, Christina	7 Jun 1840	Glatten	Frd.	Oct 1854	S.-Amer	569274
Kuebler, Christine		Hornberg	Calw	1861	N.-Amer	563212
Kuebler, Christine Rosine		Sulz	Sulz	Sep 1838	Prussia	849627
Kuebler, Elisabeth	16 Feb 1838	Sulz	Sulz	Apr 1866	Switz.	849628
Kuebler, Elisabeth Kathar.	2 Apr 1845	Tumlingen	Frd.	Jan 1855	N.-Amer	569275
Kuebler, Elisabetha		Pfalzgrafenweiler	Frd.	Jul 1854	N.-Amer	569274
Kuebler, Eva		Dietersweiler	Frd.	1817	Russia	569269
Kuebler, Friederike		Muehlheim a.B.	Sulz	bef 1869	N.-Amer	849639
Kuebler, Georg		Vesperweiler	Frd.	Apr 1854	N.-Amer	569274
Kuebler, Georg Friedrich		Hochdorf	Frd.	Dec 1848	Baden	569270
Kuebler, Gottfried & F		Vesperweiler	Frd.	Mar 1817	Russia	569269
Kuebler, Jacob	25 yrs.	Rodt	Frd.	May 1752	Pen.N-A	550803
Kuebler, Jacob & F		Dietersweiler	Frd.	1817	Russia	569269
Kuebler, Jakob	29 Jan 1847	Tumlingen	Frd.	Jan 1855	N.-Amer	569275
Kuebler, Jakob Friedrich	19 Feb 1853	Dornhan	Sulz	Apr 1881	N.-Amer	849626
Kuebler, Johann Adam	12 Aug 1853	Pfalzgrafenweiler	Frd.	Jul 1854	N.-Amer	569274
Kuebler, Johann Friedrich		Berneck	Nag.	Mar 1853	N.-Amer	838491
Kuebler, Johann Friedrich & F	3 Apr01785	Sulz	Sulz	Jan 1833	N.-Amer	849627
Kuebler, Johann Georg		Hoerschweiler	Frd.	Apr 1853	N.-Amer	569272
Kuebler, Johann Georg	11 Apr 1833	Schopfloch	Frd.	Apr 1851	N.-Amer	569271
Kuebler, Johann Georg		Vesperweiler	Frd.	bef 1859	N.-Amer	577776
Kuebler, Johann Jacob	28 Aug 1779	Marschalkenzimmern	Sulz	Jun 1817	N.-Amer	849638

| Name | | Birth | | Emigration | | | Film |
Last	First	Date	Place	O'amt	Appl. Date	Dest.	Number
Kuebler, Johann Martin		1 Oct 1823	Untermusbach	Frd.	Apr 1854	N.-Amer	569273
Kuebler, Johann Martin		29 Jun 1843	Wittlensweiler	Frd.	Oct 1866	N.-Amer	577780
Kuebler, Johann Michael & F			Wittlensweiler	Frd.	Apr 1817	Russia	569268
Kuebler, Johann Georg		8 Oct 1808	Dornhan	Sulz	Jul 1817	Russia	849633
Kuebler, Johannes		30 Jun 1811	Hoerschweiler	Frd.	Apr 1842	N.-Amer	569269
Kuebler, Johannes		28 Dec 1851	Pfalzgrafenweiler	Frd.	Jul 1854	N.-Amer	569274
Kuebler, Johannes		26 Oct 1816	Dornhan	Sulz	Jul 1817	Russia	849633
Kuebler, Johannes		15 Sep 1847	Hornberg	Calw	1864	N.-Amer	563212
Kuebler, Johannes & F		13 Jul 1791	Pfalzgrafenweiler	Frd.	Jul 1854	N.-Amer	569274
Kuebler, Karolina Rosina		2 Jun 1833	Sulz	Sulz	1855	N.-Amer	849628
Kuebler, Katharina & C		11 May 1809	Glatten	Frd.	Oct 1854	S.-Amer	569274
Kuebler, Katharina (wid.)			Berneck	Nag.	Mar 1853	N.-Amer	838491
Kuebler, Konrad & F			Klosterreichenbach	Frd.	Jun 1817	N.-Amer	569268
Kuebler, Ludwig		19 Mar 1813	Sulz	Sulz	Feb 1869	Switz.	849628
Kuebler, Magdalena			Muehlheim a.B.	Sulz	bef 1869	N.-Amer	849639
Kuebler, Martin			Pfalzgrafenweiler	Frd.	May 1833	N.-Amer	569268
Kuebler, Martin			Dietersweiler	Frd.	1817	Russia	569269
Kuebler, Mathaeus		1828	Hornberg	Calw	1854	N.-Amer	563212
Kuebler, Mathias		18 Apr 1841	Tumlingen	Frd.	Jan 1855	N.-Amer	569275
Kuebler, Mathias & F			Sulz	Sulz	Jul 1817	Russia	849627
Kuebler, Matthaeus			Schopfloch	Frd.	Apr 1752	Pen.N-A	550803
Kuebler, Matthias		12 May 1847	Tumlingen	Frd.	Oct 1866	N.-Amer	577780
Kuebler, Michael			Dertingen		Dec 1751	Mas.N-A	550803
Kuebler, Michael			Martinsmoss	Calw	1863	N.-Amer	563212
Kuebler, Rosina (wife)			Pfalzgrafenweiler	Frd.	May 1833	N.-Amer	569268
Kuebler, Stephan			Dornhan	Sulz	1817	Rus-Pol	849637
Kuebler, Stephan & F			Dornhan	Sulz	Jul 1817	Russia	849633
Kuebler, Ulrich		21 Oct 1831	Tumlingen	Frd.	Jan 1855	N.-Amer	569275
Kuebler, Ulrich			Neubulach	Calw	1864	Baden	563212
Kuebler, Ulrich & F		6 Jun 1808	Pfalzgrafenweiler	Frd.	Jan 1855	N.-Amer	569275
Kueblinger, Johann Jacob			Rheinduerckheim		Dec 1751	N.-Amer	550803
Kueblinger, Johannes			Rheinduerckheim		Dec 1751	N.-Amer	550803
Kuegler, Anna Maria		13 Oct 1813	Gruental	Frd.	Apr 1819	N.-Amer	569268
Kuehn, Andreas & F			Leidringen	Sulz	Apr 1854	N.-Amer	849637
Kuehn, Catharina		3 yrs.	Leidringen	Sulz	Apr 1854	N.-Amer	849637
Kuehn, Catharina (wife)			Leidringen	Sulz	Apr 1854	N.-Amer	849637
Kuehn, Johann Jakob		1838	Gechingen	Calw	1854	N.-Amer	563212
Kuehn, Simon		1834	Gechingen	Calw	1854	N.-Amer	563212
Kuehne, Franziska			Binsdorf	Sulz	Feb 1835	Hungary	849630
Kuehne, Maria Barbara		28 Apr 1845	Bergfelden	Sulz	Mar 1863	N.-Amer	849629
Kuehnle, Barbara & C		6 Apr 1822	Herzogsweiler	Frd.	Mar 1847	N.-Amer	569271
Kuehnle, Eva Maria		5 Dec 1844	Herzogsweiler	Frd.	Mar 1847	N.-Amer	569271
Kuehnle, Gottlieb			Pfalzgrafenweiler	Frd.	Mar 1817	Russia	569268
Kuehnle, Gottlieb		15 Jan 1841	Herzogsweiler	Frd.	Feb 1857	N.-Amer	577776
Kuemmerle, Elisabetha (wife)			Rosenfeld	Sulz	bef 1826	Odessa	849640
Kuemmerle, Friedrich & F			Rosenfeld	Sulz	bef 1826	Odessa	849640
Kuemmerle, Georg Heinrich			Calw	Calw	1860	Switz.	563212
Kuemmerle, Johannes		19 Nov 1784	Gaertringen	Herr.	Nov 1825	Baden	834624
Kuemmerle, Luise Wilhelm. K.		2 Feb 1846	Wittershausen	Sulz	Jan 1881	Switz.	849626
Kuenlin, Christiane Katharine			Freudenstadt	Frd.	Oct 1809	Baden	569267

Kuenzler, Johann Jacob	34 yrs.	Winterbach	Schd.	Jan 1833	Bremen	801460
Kuesterer, Catharine		Sommenhardt	Calw	1869	N.-Amer	563212
Kugel, Johannes & F		Calw	Frd.	1817	Russia	569269
Kugler, Anna Maria		Frutenhof	Frd.	Jun 1856	N.-Amer	569275
Kugler, Anna Maria		Boeffingen	Frd.	bef 1856	N.-Amer	569275
Kugler, Elisabetha		Gruental	Frd.	Apr 1819	N.-Amer	569268
Kugler, Jakob	12 Sep 1835	Freudenstadt	Frd.	Sep 1853	N.-Amer	569274
Kugler, Johann Michael		Freudenstadt	Frd.	bef 1855	Prussia	569275
Kugler, Leonhard		Schopfloch	Frd.	Mar 1805	Augsb.	550803
Kugler, Mathaeus		Schopfloch	Frd.	Mar 1817	Russia	569268
Kugler, Mathias		Schopfloch	Frd.	1817	Russia	569269
Kuhn, Friedrich	16 Feb 1831	Erzgrube	Frd.	bef 1864	Baden	577779
Kuhnle, Johann Martin	24 Apr 1838	Herzogsweiler	Frd.	Oct 1854	N.-Amer	569274
Kull, Gottfried Theodor	14 Apr 1840	Entringen	Herr.	Jun 1867	N.-Amer	834624
Kummer, Christian		Glatten	Frd.	Jan 1855	N.-Amer	569275
Kummer, Christian	27 Mar 1848	Hallwangen	Frd.	Jan 1866	N.-Amer	577780
Kummer, Johann Georg	23 Apr 1846	Hallwangen	Frd.	Jan 1866	N.-Amer	577780
Kummler, Johann Michael	5 May 1838	Reusten	Herr.	Mar 1868	Koeln	834624
Kunz, Barbara (wid.)		Rosenfeld	Sulz	Mar 1853	N.-Amer	849640
Kunz, Conrad & F		Rosenfeld	Sulz	Jan 1846	N.-Amer	849640
Kunz, Margaretha	10 May 1800	Dornstetten	Frd.	Feb 1847	N.-Amer	569271
Kuonath, Ernestine		Nagold	Nag.	Oct 1854	N.-Amer	838491
Kuonath, Gottlob Fried.		Nagold	Nag.	Oct 1854	N.-Amer	838491
Kuonath, Karoline		Nagold	Nag.	Oct 1854	N.-Amer	838491
Kuonath, Nicolaus & F		Nagold	Nag.	Oct 1854	N.-Amer	838491
Kupp, Anna Maria	26 Apr 1831	Gueltstein	Herr.	Mar 1866	N.-Amer	834624
Kupp, Christina Barbara	6 Jun 1838	Gueltstein	Herr.	Mar 1866	N.-Amer	834624
Kupp, Franz	19 Feb 1842	Gueltstein	Herr.	Mar 1866	N.-Amer	834624
Kupp, Johann Jacob	10 Oct 1826	Gueltstein	Herr.	Mar 1866	N.-Amer	834624
Kupp, Maria Catharina	24 Mar 1861	Gueltstein	Herr.	Mar 1866	N.-Amer	834624
Kupp, Maria Catharina & C	17 Jul 1839	Gueltstein	Herr.	Mar 1866	N.-Amer	834624
Kurz, Barbara	25 Feb 1792	Leinstetten	Sulz	Jun 1817	N.-Amer	849638
Kurz, Felicia		Leinstetten	Sulz	Jun 1817	N.-Amer	849638
Kurz, Theresia	4 May 1789	Leinstetten	Sulz	Jun 1817	N.-Amer	849638
Kussmaul, Andreas	14 Nov 1832	Moetzingen	Herr.	Apr 1847	N.-Amer	834626
Kussmaul, Anna Maria	26 Nov 1811	Moetzingen	Herr.	Apr 1847	N.-Amer	834626
Kussmaul, Christian Andr. & F	22 Jul 1785	Moetzingen	Herr.	Apr 1847	N.-Amer	834626
Kussmaul, Jacob		Nebringen	Herr.	Apr 1836	N.-Amer	834624
Kussmaul, Johann Friedrich	24 Dec 1819	Moenchberg	Herr.	Aug 1847	N.-Amer	834626
Kussmaul, Johann Georg	29 Sep 1811	Moenchberg	Herr.	Aug 1847	N.-Amer	834626
Kussmaul, Johann Georg	9 May 1841	Nebringen	Herr.	May 1847	N.-Amer	834626
Kussmaul, Johannes		Moenchberg	Herr.	bef 1838	N.-Amer	834625
Kussmaul, Maria Barbara & C	30 Jul 1786	Nebringen	Herr.	May 1847	N.-Amer	834626
Kuster, Jakob & F		Hofstett/Neuweiler	Calw	1854	N.-Amer	563212
Kusterer, Adam & F		Oberkollwangen	Calw	1854	N.-Amer	563212
Kusterer, Friederike		Unterreichenbach	Calw	Nov 1847	Baden	563212
Kusterer, Georg Adam & F		Roetenbach	Calw	1853	N.-Amer	563212
Kusterer, Martin & F		Altburg	Calw	1853	N.-Amer	563212
L'armic, Heinrich		Neuhengstett	Calw	Feb 1873	N.-Amer	563212
Labadie, Caroline Rosine		Hirsau	Calw	1862	Hesse	563212

Name		Birth		Emigration			Film
Last	First	Date	Place	O'amt	Appl. Date	Dest.	Number
Labadie, Rosine Katharine			Hirsau	Calw	1862	Hesse	563212
Lachenmaier, Johann Georg			Agenbach	Calw	1869	N.-Amer	563212
Lachenmaier, Johannes			Agenbach	Calw	1869	N.-Amer	563212
Lachenmayer, Johann Jacob		19 Feb 1810	Steinenberg	Schd.	Dec 1842	Bavaria	801461
Ladenburger, Christina			Freudenstadt	Frd.	Jan 1816	Baden	569267
Ladenburger, Johann Christian			Sulz	Sulz	May 1815	Baden	849627
Ladenburger, Johann Christian			Sulz	Sulz	May 1807	Switz.	849625
Ladenburger, Otto & F			Dornhan	Sulz	1838	Baden	849633
Laegerle, Johannes & F			Oberbraendi	Frd.	Jul 1817	Russia	569268
Laemmle, Christina Dorothea			Grunbach	Schd.	Mar 1844	Austria	801461
Laemmle, Friederika			Grunbach	Schd.	Feb 1834	N.-Amer	801460
Laemmle, Helene & F			Grunbach	Schd.	Feb 1834	N.-Amer	801460
Laemmle, Helene Christinah			Grunbach	Schd.	Feb 1834	N.-Amer	801460
Laemmle, Imanuel Friedrich			Grunbach	Schd.	Feb 1834	N.-Amer	801460
Laemmle, Johann			Grunbach	Schd.	Mar 1834	N.-Amer	801460
Laemmle, Johann Georg			Grunbach	Schd.	Feb 1834	N.-Amer	801460
Laemmle, Johann Georg & F		14 Feb 1792	Grunbach	Schd.	Mar 1834	N.-Amer	801460
Laemmle, Marie Friederike			Grunbach	Schd.	1833	N.-Amer	801460
Lais, Anna Maria		23 yrs.	Hebsack	Schd.	Jun 1833	Russia	801460
Lambart, Jakob		12 Nov 1848	Edelweiler	Frd.	Mar 1861	N.-Amer	577778
Lambart, Matthaeus & F		3 May 1810	Edelweiler	Frd.	Mar 1861	N.-Amer	577778
Lambarter, Johann Martin		29 yrs.	Pfalzgrafenweiler	Frd.	Apr 1804	Pr.-Pol	550803
Lambarth, Abraham		22 Sep 1850	Baiersbronn	Frd.	Aug 1854	N.-Amer	569274
Lambarth, Christian		20 Nov 1847	Baiersbronn	Frd.	Aug 1854	N.-Amer	569274
Lambarth, Elisabeth (wife)		19 Jan 1817	Unterwies	Frd.	Aug 1854	N.-Amer	569274
Lambarth, Jacob			Edelweiler	Frd.	Aug 1842	Dresden	569269
Lambarth, Jacob Friedrich		4 Nov 1843	Baiersbronn	Frd.	Aug 1854	N.-Amer	569274
Lambarth, Jakob & F		19 Oct 1819	Unterwies	Frd.	Aug 1854	N.-Amer	569274
Lambarth, Johannes		19 Sep 1841	Baiersbronn	Frd.	Aug 1854	N.-Amer	569274
Lambarth, Michael Friedrich		28 Feb 1806	Cresbach	Frd.	Feb 1833	N.-Amer	569269
Lamberger, Caroline		10 Feb 1829	Freudenstadt	Frd.	Aug 1850	France	569271
Lamberger, Christiane Margar.		2 Mar 1811	Freudenstadt	Frd.	May 1836	France	569267
Lampart, Johannes		14 Aug 1834	Kniebis	Frd.	Aug 1854	N.-Amer	569274
Lamparter, Friedrich & F			Dornhan	Sulz	Mar 1817	Russia	849633
Lampprecht, Barbara		24 Oct 1837	Busenweiler	Sulz	May 1866	N.-Amer	849632
Lampprecht, Johann Georg		7 Jan 1833	Busenweiler	Sulz	bef 1867	N.-Amer	849632
Lampprecht, Johannes			Busenweiler	Sulz	Sep 1853	N.-Amer	849632
Lamprecht, (widow)			Wittershausen	Sulz	Jul 1847	N.-Amer	849644
Lamprect, Anna Maria		11 Apr 1853	Dornhan	Sulz	Sep 1853	N.-Amer	849633
Landenberger, Johannes			Balingen	Bal.	Oct 1861	Austria	555962
Landenberger, Katharina (wife)		43 yrs.	Oberndorf	Herr.	Feb 1833	N.-Amer	834624
Landenberger, Urban & W		45 yrs.	Oberndorf	Herr.	Feb 1833	N.-Amer	834624
Landenberger, Vincenz		20 Jun 1848	Oberndorf	Herr.	Aug 1866	N.-Amer	834624
Landerer, Auguste Wilhelmine			Schoemberg	Frd.	bef 1850	Switz.	569271
Landherr, Christine (wife)			Monakam	Calw	1866	N.-Amer	563212
Landherr, Jacob Friedrich		3 yrs.	Monakam	Calw	1866	N.-Amer	563212
Landherr, Johann Georg		15 Oct 1840	Freudenstadt	Frd.	Sep 1854	N.-Amer	569274
Landherr, Johann Georg & F			Monakam	Calw	1866	N.-Amer	563212
Landherr, Johann Jacob		1 yrs.	Monakam	Calw	1866	N.-Amer	563212
Landherr, Rosine & C		5 Apr 1818	Freudenstadt	Frd.	Sep 1854	N.-Amer	569274

Landskorn, Robert	1834	Althengstetten	Çalw	1854	N.-Amer	563212
Lang, Anna Maria		Hornberg	Calw	1847	N.-Amer	563212
Lang, Christian	28 Mar 1840	Glatten	Frd.	Feb 1859	N.-Amer	577776
Lang, Christian		Martinsmoss	Calw	1864	N.-Amer	563212
Lang, Christina Barbara		Martinsmoss	Calw	1864	N.-Amer	563212
Lang, Christine Catharine		Martinsmoos	Calw	1855	N.-Amer	563212
Lang, Johann Friedrich		Schmieh	Calw	1868	N.-Amer	563212
Lang, Johannes		Hornberg	Calw	1863	N.-Amer	563212
Lang, Martin		Zwerenberg	Calw	1853	N.-Amer	563212
Lang, Martin & F		Hornberg	Calw	1852	N.-Amer	563212
Lang, Matthaeus	22 yrs.	Zwerenberg	Calw	1867	N.-Amer	563212
Langenbacher, (male)	22 May 1858	Sigmarswangen	Sulz	Aug 1858	N.-Amer	849642
Langenbacher, Anna		Voehringen	Sulz	Mar 1836	N.-Amer	849643
Langenbacher, Anna (wife)		Voehringen	Sulz	Mar 1836	N.-Amer	849643
Langenbacher, Anna Katharina		Voehringen	Sulz	Mar 1836	N.-Amer	849643
Langenbacher, Charlotte & C	13 Sep 1829	Sigmarswangen	Sulz	Aug 1858	N.-Amer	849642
Langenbacher, Christina		Voehringen	Sulz	Mar 1836	N.-Amer	849643
Langenbacher, Johann Georg	11 Oct 1823	Sigmarswangen	Sulz	Aug 1858	N.-Amer	849642
Langenbacher, Johann Georg & F	24 Jan 1792	Voehringen	Sulz	Mar 1836	N.-Amer	849643
Langenbacher, Johann Georg & F		Sigmarswangen	Sulz	Oct 1853	N.-Amer	849642
Langenbacher, Johann Martin		Voehringen	Sulz	Mar 1836	N.-Amer	849643
Langenbacher, Maria Agnes		Voehringen	Sulz	Mar 1836	N.-Amer	849643
Langenstrass, Anna Maria	30 Apr 1802	Nufringen	Herr.	Apr 1838	N.-Amer	834625
Langenstrass, Johann Jacob	25 Feb 1811	Nufringen	Herr.	Apr 1838	N.-Amer	834625
Langenstrass, Maria Cath. & F		Nufringen	Herr.	Apr 1838	N.-Amer	834625
Langjahr, Friedrich		Freudenstadt	Frd.	Apr 1817	Russia	569267
Langjahr, Johann Christian		Freudenstadt	Frd.	Apr 1817	Russia	569267
Langjahr, Mathias	22 yrs.	Freudenstadt	Frd.	Mar 1817	Russia	569267
Lanken v. d., Franz Carl		Spesshardt	Calw	1853	N.-Amer	563212
Lanz, Anton	23 Feb 1839	Altingen	Herr.	Jan 1867	N.-Amer	834624
Lanz, Anton	infant	Altingen	Herr.	Jan 1867	N.-Amer	834624
Lanz, Carl Friedrich	1 Jul 1847	Altingen	Herr.	Mar 1867	N.-Amer	834624
Lanz, Christina	17 Dec 1842	Voehringen	Sulz	Sep 1867	N.-Amer	849643
Lanz, Christina Barbara (wife)	4 Jun 1806	Altingen	Herr.	Jan 1867	N.-Amer	834624
Lanz, Heinrich		Stammheim	Calw	1860	Bavaria	563212
Lanz, Johannes	14 Dec 1786	Muehlheim a.B.	Sulz	May 1817	Russia	849639
Lanz, Matheus	23 Aug 1832	Altingen	Herr.	Jul 1852	N.-Amer	834627
Lanz, Matthaeus & F	21 Sep 1798	Altingen	Herr.	Jan 1867	N.-Amer	834624
Lanz, Theresia & C	15 May 1842	Altingen	Herr.	Jan 1867	N.-Amer	834624
Lau, Franz	5 Aug 1856	Leidringen	Sulz	Mar 1880	N.-Amer	849626
Laufer, Johann Bernhard	12 May 1835	Freudenstadt	Frd.	Sep 1853	N.-Amer	569274
Laufer, Johann Christian	26 Apr 1839	Freudenstadt	Frd.	Aug 1853	N.-Amer	569274
Laufer, Sophia Agatha	6 Dec 1787	Sulz	Sulz	Apr 1834	N.-Amer	849627
Lauffer, Johann Georg		Freudenstadt	Frd.	bef 1855	N.-Amer	569275
Lauser, Louise		Calw	Calw	1869	N.-Amer	563212
Laux, Anna Barbara	29 Aug 1850	Reusten	Herr.	Jul 1870	N.-Amer	834624
Laux, Anna Maria	27 Sep 1848	Oeschelbronn	Herr.	Jul 1852	N.-Amer	834627
Laux, Anna Maria (wife)	9 Sep 1823	Reusten	Herr.	Jul 1852	N.-Amer	834627
Laux, Anna Maria (wife)	22 Oct 1824	Oeschelbronn	Herr.	Jul 1852	N.-Amer	834627
Laux, Johannes	5 Jul 1850	Oeschelbronn	Herr.	Jul 1852	N.-Amer	834627

| Name | | Birth | | Emigration | | | Film |
Last	First	Date	Place	O'amt	Appl. Date	Dest.	Number
Laux, Johannes & F		27 Apr 1819	Oeschelbronn	Herr.	Jul 1852	N.-Amer	834627
Laux, Rosina Catharina		30 Jan 1853	Reusten	Herr.	Jul 1870	N.-Amer	834624
Laux, Stephan		27 Nov 1816	Reusten	Herr.	1846	Switz.	834626
Laux, Stephan		2 Apr 1852	Oeschelbronn	Herr.	Jul 1852	N.-Amer	834627
Laux, Stephan & W		28 Oct 1824	Reusten	Herr.	Jul 1852	N.-Amer	834627
Layer, Eberhardine		8 Jan 1822	Unterjesingen	Herr.	Aug 1849	Bavaria	834627
Layer, Friedrich		3 Sep 1803	Schnait	Schd.	Mar 1834	N.-Amer	801460
Layer, Johann Heinrich		1 Sep 1849	Pfaeffingen	Herr.	Feb 1869	N.-Amer	834624
Layer, Johannes		11 Feb 1831	Pfaeffingen	Herr.	Apr 1851	N.-Amer	834627
Lechler, Johannes		8 May 1834	Altheim	Horb	Mar 1854	N.-Amer	835929
Lederer, Johann Gottlieb			Sulz	Sulz	Jan 1817	Paris	849627
Lehman, Johann Jakob		27 Apr 1809	Sulz	Sulz	Aug 1833	Bavaria	849627
Lehmann, Andreas		28 Oct 1875	Dornhan	Sulz	Mar 1893	N.-Amer	849626
Lehmann, Andreas			Voehringen	Sulz	Jul 1817	Russia	849627
Lehmann, Andreas		34 yrs.	Voehringen	Sulz	Jun 1817	Hungary	849625
Lehmann, Andreas		24 Feb 1871	Hopfau	Sulz	May 1887	N.-Amer	849636
Lehmann, Anna Pauline		28 May 1866	Holzhausen	Sulz	Apr 1882	N.-Amer	849635
Lehmann, Christian		29 Apr 1880	Dornhan	Sulz	Feb 1896	N.-Amer	849634
Lehmann, Elisa			Voehringen	Sulz	Mar 1837	N.-Amer	849643
Lehmann, Eva		22 Nov 1845	Holzhausen	Sulz	Mar 1881	N.-Amer	849626
Lehmann, Friedrich		23 Jan 1812	Tumlingen	Frd.	Jan 1839	N.-Amer	569268
Lehmann, Jacob			Voehringen	Sulz	bef 1814	France	849625
Lehmann, Jacob & F		10 Aug 1809	Voehringen	Sulz	Mar 1837	N.-Amer	849643
Lehmann, Johann Georg		14 Dec 1866	Bergfelden	Sulz	Jul 1883	N.-Amer	849626
Lehmann, Johann Georg		3 Apr 1876	Dornhan	Sulz	Mar 1894	N.-Amer	849626
Lehmann, Johann Jakob		27 Sep 1850	Dornhan	Sulz	Mar 1870	N.-Amer	849634
Lehmann, Johann Ludwig		16 Mar 1868	Holzhausen	Sulz	Mar 1881	N.-Amer	849635
Lehmann, Johannes			Voehringen	Sulz	Mar 1837	N.-Amer	849643
Lehmann, Johannes		21 Apr 1868	Bergfelden	Sulz	Jul 1883	N.-Amer	849626
Lehmann, Johannes		24 Feb 1871	Hopfau	Sulz	May 1887	N.-Amer	849636
Lehmann, Johannes		22 Dec 1878	Dornhan	Sulz	Mar 1894	N.-Amer	849626
Lehmann, Johannes		13 Jan 1876	Bickelsberg	Sulz	Sep 1893	N.-Amer	849626
Lehmann, Ludwig		1 Mar 1881	Dornhan	Sulz	Feb 1897	N.-Amer	849626
Lehmann, Magdalena (wife)			Voehringen	Sulz	Mar 1837	N.-Amer	849643
Lehmann, Mathias			Leinstetten	Sulz	May 1835	Prussia	849638
Lehmann, Matthias		18 Jan 1843	Trichtingen	Sulz	Mar 1869	N.-Amer	849642
Lehmann, Melchior			Voehringen	Sulz	bef 1814	France	849625
Lehmann, Michael			Aistaig	Sulz	Jul 1837	N.-Amer	849628
Lehrer, Anna Barbara		12 Jul 1791	Rotenberg	Sulz	1817	Russia	849627
Lehrer, Johann Georg & F			Deckenpfronn	Calw	1854	N.-Amer	563212
Leibrand, Johannes & F			Weissach	Frd.	1817	Russia	569269
Leicht, Anna Maria		18 Sep 1840	Wittershausen	Sulz	Apr 1868	N.-Amer	849644
Leicht, Anna Maria		23 Jul 1833	Wittershausen	Sulz	Jul 1860	N.-Amer	849644
Leicht, Catharina			Sigmarswangen	Sulz	Aug 1852	N.-Amer	849642
Leicht, Christina & F		3 Dec 1799	Wittershausen	Sulz	Apr 1868	N.-Amer	849644
Leicht, Jacob		20 yrs.	Wittershausen	Sulz	Sep 1854	N.-Amer	849644
Leicht, Ludwig		13 Dec 1851	Wittershausen	Sulz	Jul 1869	N.-Amer	849644
Leicht, Matthias		17 yrs.	Wittershausen	Sulz	Sep 1854	N.-Amer	849644
Leins, Anna		20 Feb 1846	Brittheim	Sulz	Apr 1853	N.-Amer	849632
Leins, Anna Maria (wid.)			Leidringen	Sulz	Jul 1853	N.-Amer	849637

Leins, Jacob	9 Sep 1859	Bickelsberg	Sulz	Apr 1876	N.-Amer	849630
Leins, Johann Georg		Brittheim	Sulz	1855	Austria	049632
Leins, Johann Jacob & F	16 Jul 1796	Brittheim	Sulz	Apr 1853	N.-Amer	849632
Leins, Johannes		Brittheim	Sulz	Aug 1810	Pfalz	849625
Leins, Johannes & F		Beutelsbach	Schd.	Apr 1833	N.-Amer	801460
Leins, Louise Sibille	14 yrs.	Beutelsbach	Schd.	Apr 1833	N.-Amer	801460
Leins, Maria Katharina	8 yrs.	Beutelsbach	Schd.	Apr 1833	N.-Amer	801460
Leins, Maria Katharina (wife)		Beutelsbach	Schd.	Apr 1833	N.-Amer	801460
Leins, Martin		Brittheim	Sulz	Apr 1853	N.-Amer	849632
Leins, Michael		Brittheim	Sulz	Mar 1843	N.-Amer	849632
Leinz, Johannes		Muehlheim	Sulz	May 1817	Russia	849625
Leipold, Caspar	10 Jan 1817	Lautlingen	Bal.	bef 1847	Switz.	555963
Leipold, Georg		Weilheim	Bal.	1844	Switz.	555963
Leitenberger, Johann Felix	22 Dec 1827	Herrenberg	Herr.	Aug 1852	N.-Amer	834627
Leitle, Barbara		Oberiflingen	Frd.	Jun 1817	Russia	569268
Leitle, Jacob & F		Oberiflingen	Frd.	Jun 1817	Russia	569268
Leix, Adam		Untermusbach	Frd.	Sep 1853	N.-Amer	569272
Leix, Eva Maria & C		Untermusbach	Frd.	Sep 1853	N.-Amer	569272
Leix, Friedrich & F		Untermusbach	Frd.	Sep 1853	N.-Amer	569272
Leix, Johann Adam	23 Feb 1826	Untermusbach	Frd.	Feb 1854	N.-Amer	569273
Leix, Michael		Untermusbach	Frd.	Apr 1752	Pen.N-A	550803
Leng, Bertha	30 Jul 1884	Sulz	Sulz	Jan 1889	Baden	849628
Leng, Bertha (wife)		Sulz	Sulz	Jan 1889	Baden	849628
Leng, Catharina Charlotte		Sulz	Sulz	Apr 1832	France	849627
Leng, Christine (wife)		Sulz	Sulz	Aug 1848	N.-Amer	849627
Leng, Emma Bertha	2 Nov 1879	Sulz	Sulz	Jan 1889	Baden	849628
Leng, Ferdinand Gustav & F	24 Jul 1850	Sulz	Sulz	Jan 1889	Baden	849626
Leng, Johann & F		Sulz	Sulz	Aug 1848	N.-Amer	849627
Leng, Karl Gustav	18 Nov 1886	Sulz	Sulz	Jan 1889	Baden	849628
Lenk, Rosine Dorothee		Freudenstadt	Frd.	May 1835	Switz.	569267
Lensing, Maria Catharina	17 Sep 1826	Sulz	Sulz	Feb 1854	N.-Amer	849627
Lentz, Eberhardt	28 Feb 1819	Schnait	Schd.	1842	N.-Amer	801461
Lenz, Johann Jacob	6 Jun 1807	Schorndorf	Schd.	Oct 1833	H-Nass.	801460
Leo, Ludwig Friedrich	19 Feb 1837	Schoenmuenzach	Frd.	bef 1855	N.-Amer	569275
Leo, Philipp Ernst	16 May 1828	Schoenmuenzach	Frd.	bef 1856	France	569275
Leopold, Agatha	1 Feb 1835	Bickelsberg	Sulz	Mar 1864	Switz.	849630
Leopold, Agatha (wife)		Bickelsberg	Sulz	Apr 1838	N.-Amer	849630
Leopold, Anna Maria & C	26 Oct 1820	Bickelsberg	Sulz	Feb 1854	N.-Amer	849630
Leopold, Christian		Bickelsberg	Sulz	Apr 1838	N.-Amer	849630
Leopold, Christian	10 Jul 1870	Trichtingen	Sulz	Jun 1890	N.-Amer	849642
Leopold, Christine		Bergfelden	Sulz	Mar 1840	N.-Amer	849629
Leopold, Elisabeth	8 yrs.	Bickelsberg	Sulz	Apr 1838	N.-Amer	849630
Leopold, Georg & F	3 Mar 1800	Bickelsberg	Sulz	Apr 1838	N.-Amer	849630
Leopold, Georg & F		Voehringen	Sulz	May 1817	Polen	849643
Leopold, Jacob		Bergfelden	Sulz	Mar 1840	N.-Amer	849629
Leopold, Johann Georg		Bergfelden	Sulz	Mar 1840	N.-Amer	849629
Leopold, Johann Georg	5 May 1866	Bickelsberg	Sulz	Feb 1882	N.-Amer	849626
Leopold, Johann Georg & F		Bergfelden	Sulz	Mar 1840	N.-Amer	849629
Leopold, Johannes		Bergfelden	Sulz	Mar 1840	N.-Amer	849629
Leopold, Johannes	10 May 1839	Bickelsberg	Sulz	Oct 1869	Hamburg	849630

Name		Birth		Emigration			Film
Last	First	Date	Place	O'amt	Appl. Date	Dest.	Number
Leopold, Maria (wife)			Bergfelden	Sulz	Mar 1840	N.-Amer	849629
Leopold, Martin			Bergfelden	Sulz	Mar 1840	N.-Amer	849629
Leopold, Martin		2 yrs.	Bickelsberg	Sulz	Apr 1838	N.-Amer	849630
Leppler, Anna Maria			Agenbach	Calw	1849	N.-Amer	563212
Leser, Agnes Catharina		24 Aug 1829	Oberjesingen	Herr.	Mar 1847	N.-Amer	834626
Leser, Elisabetha Dorothea		15 Aug 1831	Oberjesingen	Herr.	Mar 1847	N.-Amer	834626
Leser, Johann Georg		20 Mar 1844	Oberjesingen	Herr.	Mar 1847	N.-Amer	834626
Leser, Johann Georg & F		8 Mar 1801	Oberjesingen	Herr.	Mar 1847	N.-Amer	834626
Leser, Regina Magdalena		10 Aug 1837	Oberjesingen	Herr.	Mar 1847	N.-Amer	834626
Leser, Sibylla (wife)		9 Jul 1805	Oberjesingen	Herr.	Mar 1847	N.-Amer	834626
Leser, Sibylle		29 May 1841	Oberjesingen	Herr.	Mar 1847	N.-Amer	834626
Lety, Christiane Cath, (wid.)			Oeschelbronn	Herr.	Apr 1831	N.-Amer	834624
Leucht, Johann Ludwig		4 Jan 1846	Muehlheim a.B.	Sulz	Sep 1866	N.-Amer	849639
Leucht, Johann Martin			Muehlheim a.B.	Sulz	Apr 1855	N.-Amer	849639
Leyer, Christina			Untermusbach	Frd.	1817	Russia	569269
Lieb, Adolf & F			Freudenstadt	Frd.	Oct 1852	N.-Amer	577778
Lieb, Adolph & F			Freudenstadt	Frd.	Oct 1852	N.-Amer	569271
Lieb, Georg		23 Apr 1815	Freudenstadt	Frd.	Sep 1854	N.-Amer	569274
Lieb, Johannes		21 yrs.	Hildrizhausen	Herr.	Mar 1831	N.-Amer	834624
Lieb, Johannes & F		57 yrs.	Rodt	Frd.	May 1752	Pen.N-A	550803
Lieb, Margaretha Barbara		57 yrs.	Rodt	Frd.	May 1752	Pen.N-A	550803
Lieb, Rosina Catharina			Freudenstadt	Frd.	Aug 1827	Switz.	569267
Lieb, Wilhelm David			Freudenstadt	Frd.	bef 1846	France	569270
Liekenheil, Christian Ludwig			Calw	Calw	1868	N.-Amer	563212
Lienhardt, Christine			Freudenstadt	Frd.	Mar 1816	Baden	569267
Linck, Matthias		16 Oct 1839	Geroldsweiler	Frd.	Sep 1866	N.-Amer	577780
Lindheim, Gottlieb Friedrich			Calw	Calw	1859	N.-Amer	563212
Ling, Regine		1 Mar 1834	Baiersbronn	Frd.	Feb 1866	France	577780
Link, Albert August		20 Oct 1851	Plieningen	Sulz	Jun 1865	N.-Amer	849643
Link, Andreas			Hopfau	Sulz	Aug 1843	Switz.	849636
Link, Anna Cath. (wid.) & F		19 Dec 1812	Erkenbrechtsweiler	Sulz	Jun 1865	N.-Amer	849643
Link, Anna Maria		29 Nov 1838	Voehringen	Sulz	bef 1869	N.-Amer	849643
Link, Christian		26 Jul 1827	Duerrenmettstetten	Sulz	Mar 1857	N.-Amer	849635
Link, Christina		19 Feb 1857	Dornhan	Sulz	May 1882	N.-Amer	849634
Link, Christina		12 Mar 1858	Hopfau	Sulz	Oct 1865	N.-Amer	849636
Link, Christina & C		5 Jun 1837	Hopfau	Sulz	Oct 1865	N.-Amer	849636
Link, Dorothea			Lombach	Frd.	Oct 1859	France	577776
Link, Dorothea		6 Mar 1846	Dornhan	Sulz	Jun 1865	N.-Amer	849634
Link, Jakob		21 Dec 1868	Leidringen	Sulz	Feb 1869	N.-Amer	849637
Link, Jakob & F		2 Feb 1841	Leidringen	Sulz	Feb 1869	N.-Amer	849637
Link, Johann Georg			Duerrenmettstetten	Sulz	Apr 1817	Russia	849635
Link, Johannes			Dornhan	Sulz	Feb 1853	N.-Amer	849633
Link, Sophie Pauline			Voehringen	Sulz	Jun 1865	N.-Amer	849643
Link, Ursula (wife)		1839	Leidringen	Sulz	Feb 1869	N.-Amer	849637
Linkenheil, Heinrich			Calw	Calw	1861	Bavaria	563212
Lippsin, Christina		18 Apr 1804	Sigmarswangen	Sulz	Mar 1817	Russia	849642
Locher, Carl Christoph			Liebenzell	Calw	1869	Baden	563212
Locher, Louise Friederike			Neubulach	Calw	Nov 1870	Baden	563212
Locher, Ludwig		18 yrs.	Neubulach	Calw	1869	N.-Amer	563212
Locher, Michael & F			Oberkollwangen	Calw	1868	N.-Amer	563212

Lochlaiter, Anna Maria		Sulz	Sulz	1771	Hungary	849625
Lochlaiter, Franziska		Bettenhausen	Sulz	Jan 1811	Baden	849625
Lochlaiter, Johannes		Sulz	Sulz	1771	Hungary	849625
Lochlaiter, Karl & F		Sulz	Sulz	1771	Hungary	849625
Lockmayer, Christina	25 yrs.	Neuneck	Frd.	May 1752	Pen.N-A	550803
Lockmayer, Hans Georg & F	52 yrs.	Neuneck	Frd.	May 1752	Pen.N-A	550803
Lockmayer, Hans Michael	22 yrs.	Neuneck	Frd.	May 1752	Pen.N-A	550803
Lockmayer, Johannes	16 yrs.	Neuneck	Frd.	May 1752	Pen.N-A	550803
Lockmayer, Magdalena	50 yrs.	Neuneck	Frd.	May 1752	Pen.N-A	550803
Lodholz, Anna Maria	31 May 1833	Ebhausen	Nag.	Oct 1854	N.-Amer	838491
Loeffler, Andreas		Schoemberg	Frd.	Jun 1854	N.-Amer	569273
Loeffler, Andreas		Schoemberg	Frd.	Jun 1854	N.-Amer	569273
Loeffler, Barbara		Schoemberg	Frd.	Jun 1854	N.-Amer	569273
Loeffler, Carl Gottlieb	13 Apr 1848	Breitenholz	Herr.	Aug 1869	N.-Amer	834624
Loeffler, Caroline		Schoemberg	Frd.	Jun 1854	N.-Amer	569273
Loeffler, Christina		Schoemberg	Frd.	Jun 1854	N.-Amer	569273
Loeffler, Christoph Friedrich	3 May 1832	Nufringen	Herr.	Mar 1848	N.-Amer	834626
Loeffler, Dorothea & C		Schoemberg	Frd.	Jun 1854	N.-Amer	569273
Loeffler, Elisabetha & C		Schoemberg	Frd.	Jun 1854	N.-Amer	569273
Loeffler, Heinrike Dorothea	18 Dec 1847	Nufringen	Herr.	Sep 1866	N.-Amer	834624
Loeffler, Jacob Andreas	4 Jul 1844	Breitenholz	Herr.	Oct 1867	N.-Amer	834624
Loeffler, Johann Georg		Schoemberg	Frd.	Jun 1854	N.-Amer	569273
Loeffler, Johann M.(wid.) & F	51 yrs.	Nufringen	Herr.	Mar 1848	N.-Amer	834626
Loeffler, Kordula & C		Schoemberg	Frd.	Jun 1854	N.-Amer	569273
Loeffler, Maria		Schoemberg	Frd.	Jun 1854	N.-Amer	569273
Loeffler, Maria		Breitenberg	Calw	1856	Baden	563212
Loeffler, Matthias		Schoemberg	Frd.	Jun 1854	N.-Amer	569273
Loefler, Johann Jakob	25 Jul 1797	Voehringen	Sulz	Apr 1817	Polen	849642
Loehmann, Mathias		Oberjesingen	Herr.	Apr 1852	N.-Amer	834627
Loehrer, Barbara	22 yrs.	Duerrenmettstetten	Sulz	Aug 1854	N.-Amer	849635
Loehrer, Johann Georg	25 yrs.	Duerrenmettstetten	Sulz	Aug 1854	N.-Amer	849635
Loehrer, Rosina	8 Jan 1839	Duerrenmettstetten	Sulz	Mar 1860	N.-Amer	849635
Loehrer, Rosina (wid.) & F	1 Feb 1808	Duerrenmettstetten	Sulz	Mar 1860	N.-Amer	849635
Loehrer, Wilhelm	23 Mar 1841	Duerrenmettstetten	Sulz	Mar 1860	N.-Amer	849635
Loercher, Christiana	8 Nov 1845	Herrenberg	Herr.	Jan 1868	N.-Amer	834624
Loercher, Christiane Gottlieb.		Spesshardt	Calw	1858	Hesse	563212
Loercher, Friedrich	26 yrs.	Oberkollwangen	Calw	1869	N.-Amer	563212
Loercher, Gottlieb Friedrich		Liebenzell	Calw	1853	N.-Amer	563212
Loercher, Johann Georg		Oberkollwangen	Calw	1867	N.-Amer	563212
Loercher, Michael	42 yrs.	Altburg	Calw	1847	N.-Amer	563212
Loercher, Michael & F		Breitenberg	Calw	Aug 1874	N.-Amer	563212
Loersch, Casimir		Hofheim	– –	Dec 1751	N.-Amer	550803
Loetterle, Gottfried Michael	2 Jan 1841	Teinach	Calw	1857	N.-Amer	563212
Loetterle, Johannes	1837	Althengstett	Calw	1854	N.-Amer	563212
Lohre, Jacob	53 yrs.	Althengstett	Calw	1854	N.-Amer	563212
Lohrer, (wid.) & F		Altingen	Herr.	Jul 1852	N.-Amer	834627
Lorenz, Catharina		Winterbach	Schd.	Jan 1844	France	801461
Lorz, Friedrich Daniel	24 Apr 1841	Glatten	Frd.	May 1858	N.-Amer	577776
Lotsch, Anna Maria		Pfalzgrafenweiler	Frd.	Aug 1853	N.-Amer	569274
Lotter, Eduard	21 Nov 1862	Rosenfeld	Sulz	Aug 1879	N.-Amer	849641

| Name | | Birth | | Emigration | | | Film |
Last	First	Date	Place	O'amt	Appl. Date	Dest.	Number
Lubadie, Carl Gottlieb		10 yrs.	Hirsau	Calw	1860	N.-Amer	563212
Lubadie, Catharina Regina & C			Hirsau	Calw	1860	N.-Amer	563212
Luedle, Christiana		6 Jan 1835	Streich	Schd.	Apr 1842	N.-Amer	801461
Luedle, Eva Kathrina		29 Apr 1828	Streich	Schd.	Apr 1842	N.-Amer	801461
Luedle, Gottlob		22 Jan 1837	Streich	Schd.	Apr 1842	N.-Amer	801461
Luedle, Jacob Friedrich		16 Sep 1840	Streich	Schd.	Apr 1842	N.-Amer	801461
Luedle, Johann Jacob & F		28 Feb 1801	Streich	Schd.	Apr 1842	N.-Amer	801461
Luedle, Sabina		8 Jun 1807	Streich	Schd.	Apr 1842	N.-Amer	801461
Luethi, Elisabetha		4 Apr 1817	Pfalzgrafenweiler	Frd.	Apr 1836	N.-Amer	569268
Luff, Andreas		28 Dec 1839	Bondorf	Herr.	Mar 1846	N.-Amer	834626
Luff, Fidelis		28 Jan 1842	Bondorf	Herr.	Mar 1846	N.-Amer	834626
Luff, Fidelius		28 yrs.	Bondorf	Herr.	May 1843	N.-Amer	834625
Luff, Johann Baptist & F		48 yrs.	Bondorf	Herr.	Mar 1846	N.-Amer	834626
Luff, Johann Georg		30 Apr 1833	Bondorf	Herr.	Mar 1846	N.-Amer	834626
Luff, Sophia		5 Mar 1846	Bondorf	Herr.	Mar 1846	N.-Amer	834626
Luff, Sophie (wife)		45 yrs.	Bondorf	Herr.	Mar 1846	N.-Amer	834626
Luff, Waldburga		25 May 1837	Bondorf	Herr.	Mar 1846	N.-Amer	834626
Luger, Maria			Herzogsweiler	Frd.	Oct 1846	N.-Amer	569271
Luipold, Barbara (wife)		4 Jun 1842	Bergfelden	Sulz	Jul 1867	N.-Amer	849629
Luipold, Mathaeus & F		12 Sep 1842	Bergfelden	Sulz	Jul 1867	N.-Amer	849629
Luithardt, Friederike Doroth.			Schorndorf	Schd.	Aug 1833	N.-Amer	801460
Lukenberger, Anna Maria		1 Dec 1856	Oberiflingen	Frd.	Apr 1860	N.-Amer	577777
Lukenberger, Christian		15 Aug 1858	Oberiflingen	Frd.	Apr 1860	N.-Amer	577777
Lukenberger, Christine & C		22 Mar 1836	Oberiflingen	Frd.	Apr 1860	N.-Amer	577777
Lukenberger, Elisabetha & C		11 Jul 1838	Oberiflingen	Frd.	Apr 1860	N.-Amer	577777
Lutz, Andreas		19 Nov 1838	Oberjettingen	Herr.	Jun 1867	N.-Amer	834624
Lutz, Anna Magdalena			Gaertringen	Herr.	Dec 1845	Bavaria	834626
Lutz, Anna Maria		16 Sep 1828	Wittlensweiler	Frd.	Jul 1847	N.-Amer	569270
Lutz, Anna Maria		12 Jan 1828	Hallwangen	Frd.	Jul 1854	N.-Amer	569274
Lutz, Anna Maria		19 Jan 1849	Pfalzgrafenweiler	Frd.	Jan 1866	N.-Amer	577780
Lutz, Carl August		23 Feb 1820	Vesperweiler	Frd.	Oct 1853	Switz.	569272
Lutz, Carl August			Vesperweiler	Frd.	bef 1851	Switz.	569271
Lutz, Caroline Louise			Nagold	Nag.	Jan 1854	N.-Amer	838491
Lutz, Christian			Huzenbach	Frd.	bef 1853	France	569272
Lutz, Christian		6 Jan 1848	Pfalzgrafenweiler	Frd.	Jun 1864	N.-Amer	577779
Lutz, Christian		1 Sep 1848	Deckenpfronn	Calw	1868	N.-Amer	563212
Lutz, Christian		8 Jan 1849	Kuppingen	Herr.	Mar 1865	N.-Amer	834624
Lutz, Christina		16 Sep 1828	Wittlensweiler	Frd.	Jul 1847	N.-Amer	569270
Lutz, Christoph Friedrich			Dornstetten	Frd.	bef 1817	Frankf.	569269
Lutz, Conrad			Pfalzgrafenweiler	Frd.	Mar 1811	Baden	569268
Lutz, Elisabetha			Oberreichenbach	Calw	1860	N.-Amer	563212
Lutz, Elisabetha Barbara & C		21 Mar 1840	Gaertringen	Herr.	May 1868	N.-Amer	834624
Lutz, Eva		26 Mar 1824	Wittlensweiler	Frd.	1846	N.-Amer	569270
Lutz, Eva			Schopfloch	Frd.	Sep 1815	Switz.	569268
Lutz, Filipp		11 Jun 1849	Pfalzgrafenweiler	Frd.	Sep 1866	N.-Amer	577780
Lutz, Friederike		1 Dec 1833	Freudenstadt	Frd.	Aug 1853	N.-Amer	569274
Lutz, Jakob Friedrich		29 Feb 1828	Pfalzgrafenweiler	Frd.	Oct 1852	N.-Amer	569271
Lutz, Jakob Friedrich			Roetenbach	Calw	1854	N.-Amer	563212
Lutz, Jakob Friedrich & F		3 Dec 1795	Wittlensweiler	Frd.	Jul 1847	N.-Amer	569270
Lutz, Johann Balthas		2 Aug 1842	Gaertringen	Herr.	May 1868	N.-Amer	034024

Lutz, Johann Friedrich & W		Deckenpfronn	Calw	1852	N.-Amer	563212
Lutz, Johann Georg	7 Jul 1837	Pfalzgrafenweiler	Frd.	Mar 1854	N.-Amer	569273
Lutz, Johann Georg	31 Mar 1831	Schopfloch	Frd.	Mar 1850	N.-Amer	569271
Lutz, Johann Georg	1849	Deckenpfronn	Calw	1869	N.-Amer	563212
Lutz, Johann Georg		Deckenpfronn	Calw	1852	N.-Amer	563212
Lutz, Johann Gottlieb		Nagold	Nag.	Jan 1854	N.-Amer	838491
Lutz, Johann Gottlieb		Hirsau	Calw	1854	N.-Amer	563212
Lutz, Johannes	17 Apr 1820	Nagold	Nag.	Jun 1849	France	838490
Lutz, Johannes	7 Sep 1849	Gaertringen	Herr.	Jun 1867	N.-Amer	834624
Lutz, Johannes	11 Dec 1863	Gaertringen	Herr.	May 1868	N.-Amer	834624
Lutz, Katharina	12 Jul 1797	Wittlensweiler	Frd.	Jul 1847	N.-Amer	569270
Lutz, Ludwig		Deckenpfronn	Calw	Oct 1848	France	563212
Lutz, Margaretha & F		Deckenpfronn	Calw	1853	N.-Amer	563212
Lutz, Maria Catharina	24 Dec 1865	Gaertringen	Herr.	May 1868	N.-Amer	834624
Lutz, Martin	27 Sep 1823	Herzogsweiler	Frd.	bef 1851	N.-Amer	569271
Lutz, Mathaeus & F		Herzogsweiler	Frd.	1817	Russia	569269
Lutz, Matthias	7 Dec 1847	Oberwaldach	Frd.	Jan 1866	N.-Amer	577780
Lutz, Nikolaus	18 Mar 1830	Gaertringen	Herr.	Sep 1852	N.-Amer	834627
Lutz, Regina		Deckenpfronn	Calw	1867	France	563212
Lutz, Regina Sophia	6 Aug 1837	Goettelfingen	Frd.	Feb 1855	N.-Amer	569275
Lutz, Wilhelm Gottlieb	9 Sep 1829	Moettlingen	Calw	1853	N.-Amer	563212
Luz, Anna Maria		Herzogsweiler	Frd.	bef 1843	N.-Amer	569269
Luz, Carl August		Vesperweiler	Frd.	1851	Switz.	577778
Luz, Carl Friedrich	14 yrs.	Freudenstadt	Frd.	Mar 1851	N.-Amer	569271
Luz, Carl Wilhelm		Freudenstadt	Frd.	Oct 1856	N.-Amer	569275
Luz, Catharina Friederike	10 yrs.	Freudenstadt	Frd.	Mar 1851	N.-Amer	569271
Luz, Christian	34 yrs.	Aach	Frd.	Apr 1865	N.-Amer	577779
Luz, Christian & F		Freudenstadt	Frd.	Mar 1851	N.-Amer	569271
Luz, Daniel Friedrich	12 Jan 1808	Pfalzgrafenweiler	Frd.	Mar 1848	N.-Amer	569270
Luz, Friedrich Ludwig	27 Feb 1806	Dornstetten	Frd.	bef 1849	Baden	569270
Luz, Gustav	6 yrs.	Freudenstadt	Frd.	Mar 1851	N.-Amer	569271
Luz, Johann Georg		Cresbach	Frd.	bef 1847	N.-Amer	569270
Luz, Johann Georg	39 yrs.	Pfalzgrafenweiler	Frd.	May 1817	N.-Amer	569268
Luz, Johannes	19 Jan 1832	Glatten	Frd.	1854	N.-Amer	577778
Luz, Johannes	17 Jul 1779	Dornstetten	Frd.	Oct 1806	Frankf.	569269
Luz, Louise	1 yrs.	Freudenstadt	Frd.	Mar 1851	N.-Amer	569271
Luz, Martin		Herzogsweiler	Frd.	1851	N.-Amer	577778
Luz, Michael & F		Dornstetten	Frd.	Feb 1817	Russia	569269
Luz, Paulina	3 yrs.	Freudenstadt	Frd.	Mar 1851	N.-Amer	569271
Luz, Sophie	9 yrs.	Freudenstadt	Frd.	Mar 1851	N.-Amer	569271
Mabold, Carl Friedrich		Balingen	Bal.	bef 1866	Switz.	555962
Mack, (child)	28 Sep 1871	Sulz	Sulz	Mar 1888	Switz.	849626
Mack, Anna Maria (wife)	28 Mar 1831	Sulz	Sulz	Mar 1888	Switz.	849626
Mack, Margaretha		Geradstetten	Schd.	Mar 1837	N.-Amer	801461
Mack, Mathias & F	20 Dec 1829	Sulz	Sulz	Mar 1888	Switz.	849626
Mader, Christian	21 Oct 1809	Pfalzgrafenweiler	Frd.	Jun 1836	Baden	569268
Maeder, Andreas		Trichtingen	Sulz	bef 1830	Baden	849642
Maeder, Jakob	27 yrs.	Edelweiler	Frd.	bef 1864	Baden	577779
Maeder, Johann Adam		Cresbach	Frd.	1817	Russia	569269
Maentele, Jakob	3 Apr 1844	Weiden	Sulz	Oct 1874	N.-Amer	849644

| Name | | Birth | | Emigration | | | Film |
Last	First	Date	Place	O'amt	Appl. Date	Dest.	Number
Maestle, Anna Maria		8 Apr 1830	Wittendorf	Frd.	Sep 1854	N.-Amer	569274
Maestle, Elisabetha		11 Jun 1833	Wittendorf	Frd.	Sep 1854	N.-Amer	569274
Maestling, Johann Martin		17 yrs.	Isingen	Sulz	Aug 1853	N.-Amer	849636
Maestling, Johannes		2 Dec 1874	Rosenfeld	Sulz	Apr 1891	N.-Amer	849626
Maeuel, Barbara		26 yrs.	Freudenstadt	Frd.	Feb 1851	N.-Amer	569271
Maeuel, Jakob Friedrich		27 yrs.	Freudenstadt	Frd.	Feb 1851	N.-Amer	569271
Maeusel, Caroline		4 yrs.	Freudenstadt	Frd.	Feb 1851	N.-Amer	569271
Maeusel, Catharina		20 yrs.	Freudenstadt	Frd.	Feb 1851	N.-Amer	569271
Maeusel, Christian Gottlieb		17 yrs.	Freudenstadt	Frd.	Feb 1851	N.-Amer	569271
Maeusel, Jakob Friedrich & F			Freudenstadt	Frd.	Feb 1851	N.-Amer	569271
Maeusel, Rosina & C		24 yrs.	Freudenstadt	Frd.	Feb 1851	N.-Amer	569271
Maeusel, Sophie		13 yrs.	Freudenstadt	Frd.	Feb 1851	N.-Amer	569271
Mager, Peter			Erlaheim	Bal.	bef 1848	Switz.	555963
Maichel, Catharina		18 Dec 1806	Kniebis	Frd.	Aug 1854	N.-Amer	569274
Maichel, Christian		17 Dec 1831	Kniebis	Frd.	Aug 1854	N.-Amer	569274
Maichel, Christof		13 May 1832	Kniebis	Frd.	Aug 1854	N.-Amer	569274
Maichel, David		13 Jan 1845	Kniebis	Frd.	Aug 1854	N.-Amer	569274
Maichel, Johann Georg		11 Oct 1849	Kniebis	Frd.	Aug 1854	N.-Amer	569274
Maichel, Johann Jacob		15 Dec 1835	Kniebis	Frd.	Aug 1854	N.-Amer	569274
Maichel, Joseph		18 Mar 1828	Erisdorf	Rdl.	Jul 1868	N.-Amer	841072
Maichel, Michael & F		16 Mar 1806	Kniebis	Frd.	Aug 1854	N.-Amer	569274
Maier, Agatha			Hoerschweiler	Frd.	Jul 1853	N.-Amer	569272
Maier, Andreas		9 Jan 1832	Durrweiler	Frd.	Mar 1853	N.-Amer	569272
Maier, Andreas			Hopfau	Sulz	Mar 1816	France	849636
Maier, Anna			Hoerschweiler	Frd.	Jul 1853	N.-Amer	569272
Maier, Anna & C			Muehlheim a.B.	Sulz	Mar 1854	N.-Amer	849639
Maier, Anna Maria			Hoerschweiler	Frd.	Jul 1853	N.-Amer	569272
Maier, Anna Maria		4 Aug 1848	Sulz	Sulz	Jul 1869	Switz.	849628
Maier, Anna Maria		21 yrs.	Bickelsberg	Sulz	Jun 1849	N.-Amer	849630
Maier, Anna Maria		22 Aug 1846	Dornhan	Sulz	Aug 1866	N.-Amer	849634
Maier, Anna Maria		12 May 1842	Renfrizhausen	Sulz	Dec 1865	N.-Amer	849639
Maier, Anna Maria		infant	Oberreichenbach	Calw	Mar 1847	N.-Amer	563212
Maier, Anna Maria		18 Jul 1836	Bondorf	Herr.	Nov 1865	N.-Amer	834624
Maier, Anna Maria & F		8 Sep 1839	Brittheim	Sulz	May 1882	N.-Amer	849632
Maier, Anna Maria (wife)			Pfalzgrafenweiler	Frd.	Jul 1832	N.-Amer	569268
Maier, Anna Maria (wife)			Oberjettingen	Herr.	Jun 1830	N.-Amer	834624
Maier, Anna Marie		19 yrs.	Pfalzgrafenweiler	Frd.	Jul 1832	N.-Amer	569268
Maier, Caroline (widow)			Hirsau	Calw	1862	N.-Amer	563212
Maier, Catharina		12 Mar 1817	Pfalzgrafenweiler	Frd.	May 1833	N.-Amer	569268
Maier, Catharina (wife)			Kuppingen	Herr.	Feb 1847	N.-Amer	834626
Maier, Christian		28 Jun 1838	Unteriflingen	Frd.	Oct 1853	N.-Amer	569272
Maier, Christian			Brittheim	Sulz	May 1882	N.-Amer	849632
Maier, Christian		17 Sep 1851	Duerrenmettstetten	Sulz	Jan 1870	N.-Amer	849635
Maier, Christiana		14 Nov 1845	Renfrizhausen	Sulz	1865	N.-Amer	849639
Maier, Christiane			Dornstetten	Frd.	Apr 1817	France	569269
Maier, Christiane		9 Oct 1848	Muehlheim a.B.	Sulz	Oct 1865	N.-Amer	849639
Maier, Christiane			Muehlheim a.B.	Sulz	Apr 1844	N.-Amer	849639
Maier, Christina		17 Jan 1771	Pfalzgrafenweiler	Frd.	Apr 1836	N.-Amer	569268
Maier, Christina & C			Oberreichenbach	Calw	Mar 1847	N.-Amer	563212
Maier, Christine			Unteriflingen	Frd.	bef 1858	N.-Amer	577776

Maier, Christine	19 Dec 1843	Muehlheim a.B.	Sulz	bef 1865	N.-Amer	849639
Maier, Christine & C	24 Nov 1842	Holzhausen	Sulz	May 1872	N.-Amer	849635
Maier, Christine (wid.) & F		Muehlheim a.B.	Sulz	Apr 1844	N.-Amer	849639
Maier, Christoph Ludwig	13 Jan 1839	Dornstetten	Frd.	Mar 1856	N.-Amer	569275
Maier, Elisabetha (wife)	12 Jan 1820	Renfrizhausen	Sulz	Dec 1865	N.-Amer	849639
Maier, Elisabetha Barbara	3 May 1851	Renfrizhausen	Sulz	Dec 1865	N.-Amer	849639
Maier, Esther	21 yrs.	Hoerschweiler	Frd.	Feb 1855	N.-Amer	569275
Maier, Friederike Barbara	20 Oct 1835	Sulz	Sulz	Oct 1868	Baden	849628
Maier, Friederike Elisabetha		Calw	Calw	1852	N.-Amer	563212
Maier, Friederike Philippine	20 Mar 1827	Herrenberg	Herr.	Jul 1846	N.-Amer	834626
Maier, Friedrich Christian	24 Sep 1837	Bondorf	Herr.	Jun 1866	N.-Amer	834624
Maier, Friedrich Roman	5 May 1843	Sulz	Sulz	Oct 1865	N.-Amer	849628
Maier, Georg Michael & F		Gueltstein	Herr.	Jun 1833	Rus-Pol	834624
Maier, Gottlieb		Muehlheim a.B.	Sulz	Apr 1844	N.-Amer	849639
Maier, Gottliebin		Pfalzgrafenweiler	Frd.	Jul 1832	N.-Amer	569268
Maier, Gottlob		Oberjettingen	Herr.	Jun 1843	Baden	834625
Maier, Gottlob Friedrich		Deckenpfronn	Calw	1852	N.-Amer	563212
Maier, Jacob		Marschalkenzimmern	Sulz	Jul 1845	Baden	849638
Maier, Jacob		Oberjettingen	Herr.	Nov 1852	N.-Amer	834627
Maier, Jacob Friedrich		Unterjesingen	Herr.	Jan 1843	Austria	834625
Maier, Jacob Friedrich & F		Neuhengstett	Calw	Oct 1847	N.-Amer	563212
Maier, Jacob Martin	16 Feb 1822	Kuppingen	Herr.	bef 1863	N.-Amer	834624
Maier, Jakob	22 Jan 1815	Unteriflingen	Frd.	Oct 1853	N.-Amer	569272
Maier, Jakob	14 yrs.	Pfalzgrafenweiler	Frd.	Jul 1832	N.-Amer	569268
Maier, Jakob	28 Mar 1847	Duerrenmettstetten	Sulz	Apr 1867	N.-Amer	849635
Maier, Jakob	28 Mar 1851	Muehlheim a.B.	Sulz	Oct 1865	N.-Amer	849639
Maier, Jakob (wid.) & F	27 Mar 1815	Muehlheim a.B.	Sulz	Oct 1865	N.-Amer	849639
Maier, Johann Bernhardt		Althengstett	Calw	Feb 1873	N.-Amer	563212
Maier, Johann Christian	29 Sep 1819	Gueltstein	Herr.	Mar 1847	N.-Amer	834626
Maier, Johann Daniel	18 Oct 1801	Balingen	Bal.	1843	Switz.	555963
Maier, Johann Friedrich	7 Feb 1807	Pfalzgrafenweiler	Frd.	May 1833	N.-Amer	569268
Maier, Johann Friedrich	3 Sep 1832	Kuppingen	Herr.	Aug 1852	N.-Amer	834627
Maier, Johann Friedrich & W		Kuppingen	Herr.	Feb 1847	N.-Amer	834626
Maier, Johann Georg	11 Jul 1834	Sulz	Sulz	Sep 1854	N.-Amer	849627
Maier, Johann Georg		Muehlheim a.B.	Sulz	bef 1846	N.-Amer	849639
Maier, Johann Georg		Pfeffingen	Bal.	Jan 1845	Switz.	555963
Maier, Johann Gottlob	1836	Calw	Calw	1854	N.-Amer	563212
Maier, Johann Jacob	23 Feb 1856	Gueltstein	Herr.	Sep 1867	N.-Amer	834624
Maier, Johann Jakob Fr. & F		Oeschelbronn	Herr.	Jul 1852	N.-Amer	834627
Maier, Johann Konrad	1836	Oberhaugstett	Calw	1856	N.-Amer	563212
Maier, Johanna Heinrike		Hirsau	Calw	1858	N.-Amer	563212
Maier, Johannes		Walddorf	Frd.	1817	Russia	569269
Maier, Johannes	4 Mar 1844	Marschalkenzimmern	Sulz	May 1865	N.-Amer	849638
Maier, Johannes	14 Nov 1857	Renfrizhausen	Sulz	Dec 1865	N.-Amer	849639
Maier, Johannes	30 Sep 1840	Muehlheim a.B.	Sulz	Mar 1857	N.-Amer	849639
Maier, Johannes	1839	Moettlingen	Calw	1854	N.-Amer	563212
Maier, Johannes	2 Oct 1854	Gueltstein	Herr.	Sep 1867	N.-Amer	834624
Maier, Johannes		Gueltstein	Herr.	1836	N.-Amer	834625
Maier, Johannes & C		Hoerschweiler	Frd.	Jul 1853	N.-Amer	569272
Maier, Johannes & F		Pfalzgrafenweiler	Frd.	Jul 1832	N.-Amer	569268

Name		Birth		Emigration			Film
Last	First	Date	Place	O'amt	Appl. Date	Dest.	Number
Maier, Johannes & F		21 Feb 1814	Renfrizhausen	Sulz	Dec 1865	N.-Amer	849639
Maier, Johannes & F		20 Jan 1822	Gueltstein	Herr.	Sep 1867	N.-Amer	834624
Maier, Johannes & F			Oberjettingen	Herr.	Jun 1830	N.-Amer	834624
Maier, Jost		22 Apr 1844	Kuppingen	Herr.	Mar 1848	N.-Amer	834626
Maier, Jost & F			Kuppingen	Herr.	Mar 1848	N.-Amer	834626
Maier, Justine		13 Feb 1859	Gueltstein	Herr.	Sep 1867	N.-Amer	834624
Maier, Karoline		7 Sep 1873	Brittheim	Sulz	May 1882	N.-Amer	849632
Maier, Katharina Barbara		4 Jun 1860	Gueltstein	Herr.	Sep 1867	N.-Amer	834624
Maier, Magdalena		12 yrs.	Muehlheim a.b.	Sulz	Mar 1854	N.-Amer	849639
Maier, Maria			Obertalheim	Nag.	Feb 1854	N.-Amer	838491
Maier, Maria		1846	Pfaeffingen	Herr.	Jan 1865	Baden	834624
Maier, Maria Agnes (wife)		12 Apr 1823	Gueltstein	Herr.	Sep 1867	N.-Amer	834624
Maier, Maria Barbara		24 Oct 1841	Muehlheim a.B.	Sulz	bef 1865	N.-Amer	849639
Maier, Maria Barbara		4 Mar 1851	Oeschelbronn	Herr.	Jul 1852	N.-Amer	834627
Maier, Maria Magdalena		18 May 1865	Holzhausen	Sulz	May 1872	N.-Amer	849635
Maier, Maria Theresia		20 Mar 1827	Herrenberg	Herr.	Jul 1846	N.-Amer	834626
Maier, Marie Agnes			Deckenpfronn	Calw	1858	Hesse	563212
Maier, Martin			Onstmettingen	Bal.	1843	Switz.	555963
Maier, Matthias			Hoerschweiler	Frd.	Jul 1853	N.-Amer	569272
Maier, Paul Josef		24 Jun 1837	Buhlbach	Frd.	Jul 1856	N.-Amer	569275
Maier, Philipp & F			Renfrizhausen	Sulz	Mar 1817	Russia	849639
Maier, Philipp Adam & F			Deckenpfronn	Calw	1852	N.-Amer	563212
Maier, Rosine		22 yrs.	Pfalzgrafenweiler	Frd.	Jul 1832	N.-Amer	569268
Maier, Rosine (wid.) & F			Moenchberg	Herr.	May 1831	N.-Amer	834624
Maier, Rudolf			Calw	Calw	1853	N.-Amer	563212
Maier, Sophie Emilie		18 Jul 1840	Sulz	Sulz	Aug 1867	Baden	849628
Maier, Tobias			Moenchberg	Herr.	May 1830	N.-Amer	834624
Maierle, Catharina Magdalena		19 yrs.	Hebsack	Schd.	Jun 1833	Russia	801460
Maierle, Catharina Margaretha			Hebsack	Schd.	Jun 1833	Russia	801460
Maierle, Johann Daniel		21 yrs.	Hebsack	Schd.	Jun 1833	Russia	801460
Maierle, Johann Georg		12 yrs.	Hebsack	Schd.	Jun 1833	Russia	801460
Maierle, Johann Georg & F			Hebsack	Schd.	Jun 1833	Russia	801460
Maihofer, Andreas		14 yrs.	Sigmarswangen	Sulz	May 1836	N.-Amer	849642
Maihofer, Christina (wife)			Sigmarswangen	Sulz	May 1836	N.-Amer	849642
Maihofer, Jakob & W		22 Mar 1796	Sigmarswangen	Sulz	May 1836	N.-Amer	849642
Maihofer, Johann Heinrich		9 Jan 1835	Sigmarswangen	Sulz	Jan 1864	N.-Amer	849642
Maihofer, Johannes		20 Apr 1857	Sigmarswangen	Sulz	Jun 1860	N.-Amer	849642
Maihofer, Johannes			Sigmarswangen	Sulz	Apr 1817	Polen	849642
Maisch, Agnes Catharina (wife)			Sulz	Sulz	May 1834	N.-Amer	849627
Maisch, Carl		24 Dec 1852	Entringen	Herr.	Sep 1868	N.-Amer	834624
Maisch, Catharine Dorothea		4 May 1833	Sulz	Sulz	May 1834	N.-Amer	849627
Maisch, Elisabetha		15 Nov 1819	Sulz	Sulz	May 1834	N.-Amer	849627
Maisch, Friedrich		25 Oct 1851	Entringen	Herr.	Sep 1868	N.-Amer	834624
Maisch, Jacob Friedrich		4 Apr01829	Sulz	Sulz	May 1834	N.-Amer	849627
Maisch, Johann Georg & F		26 Jul 1796	Kayh/Herrenberg	Sulz	May 1834	N.-Amer	849627
Maisch, Johann Michael			Nagold	Nag.	Jan 1854	N.-Amer	838491
Maisch, Johann Michael		26 Mar 1844	Kuppingen	Herr.	May 1867	N.-Amer	834624
Maisch, Johann Michael		21 Mar 1843	Kayh	Herr.	May 1869	N.-Amer	834624
Maisch, Louise Catharine		14 Jul 1831	Sulz	Sulz	May 1834	N.-Amer	849627
Maisch, Simon		28 Feb 1839	Kuppingen	Herr.	Feb 1847	N.-Amer	834626

Malbon, Daniel		Montbeilard	– –	Dec 1751	Mas.N-A 550803
Maltz, Christian		Wittlensweiler	Frd.	1817	Russia 569269
Mammel, Anna Barbara (wife)		Kuppingen	Herr.	Feb 1847	N.-Amer 834626
Mammel, Anna Maria		Moettlingen	Calw	1857	Bavaria 563212
Mammel, Carolina	23 May 1831	Kuppingen	Herr.	Feb 1847	N.-Amer 834626
Mammel, Christoph Friedrich	13 May 1828	Kuppingen	Herr.	bef 1863	N.-Amer 834624
Mammel, Elisabeth	23 Aug 1825	Kuppingen	Herr.	bef 1863	N.-Amer 834624
Mammel, Ernst Gottlieb		Kuppingen	Herr.	Apr 1835	N.-Amer 834624
Mammel, Gottlieb Friedrich & F		Kuppingen	Herr.	Feb 1847	N.-Amer 834626
Mammel, Johannes	20 Jun 1837	Kuppingen	Herr.	Feb 1847	N.-Amer 834626
Mammel, Maria Margaretha	5 Mar 1846	Kuppingen	Herr.	Feb 1847	N.-Amer 834626
Mammel, Philipp Jakob	29 Aug 1832	Kuppingen	Herr.	Feb 1847	N.-Amer 834626
Mammel, Regina Dorothea	12 Jan 1841	Kuppingen	Herr.	Feb 1852	N.-Amer 834627
Mandel, Jacob & F		Dornstetten	Frd.	Apr 1817	Odessa 569269
Mann, Anna Maria (wid.) & F		Althengstett	Calw	1861	N.-Amer 563212
Mann, Caroline Wilhelmine		Calw	Calw	1869	Bavaria 563212
Mann, Christoph David	8 Aug 1828	Kuppingen	Herr.	bef 1863	N.-Amer 834624
Manz, Jacob		Voehringen	Sulz	bef 1844	France 849643
Marbold, Gustav Adolph	2 Nov 1850	Sulz	Sulz	Mar 1869	N.-Amer 849628
Marlok, Christian	6 May 1847	Baiersbronn	Frd.	Oct 1866	N.-Amer 577780
Marlok, Jacob Friederich	13 Jun 1839	Baiersbronn	Frd.	bef 1866	N.-Amer 577780
Marquardt, Conrad		Dornstetten	Frd.	Apr 1752	Pen.N-A 550803
Marquardt, Gottfried	23 Apr 1824	Unterjesingen	Herr.	Nov 1865	N.-Amer 834624
Marquardt, Johann	28 Dec 1831	Nufringen	Herr.	Feb 1866	N.-Amer 834624
Marquardt, Johann Georg		Althengstett	Calw	1868	N.-Amer 563212
Marquardt, Johannes	19 yrs.	Gueltstein	Herr.	May 1852	N.-Amer 834627
Marquardt, Johannes	8 Jun 1823	Nufringen	Herr.	Sep 1869	N.-Amer 834624
Marquardt, Ludwig	27 Feb 1824	Nufringen	Herr.	bef 1862	N.-Amer 834624
Marquardt, Michael		Dornstetten	Frd.	Apr 1752	Pen.N-A 550803
Marquardt, Sophie (wife)		Gueltstein	Herr.	Apr 1831	N.-Amer 834624
Marquardt, Stephan & W		Gueltstein	Herr.	Apr 1831	N.-Amer 834624
Marquart, Johann Friedrich		Calw	Calw	1852	N.-Amer 563212
Marquart, Justina Salomea	1 Dec 1826	Kuppingen	Herr.	Apr 1847	N.-Amer 834626
Marquart, Michael	40 yrs.	Dornstetten	Frd.	May 1752	Pen.N-A 550803
Marquart, Philipp Jacob & W	9 Mar 1819	Kuppingen	Herr.	Apr 1847	N.-Amer 834626
Martin, Barbara & C		Wittlensweiler	Frd.	Apr 1847	N.-Amer 569270
Martin, Carl Friedrich	4 Dec 1846	Wittlensweiler	Frd.	Apr 1847	N.-Amer 569270
Martin, Jacob & F		Dietersweiler	Frd.	1817	Russia 569269
Martin, Johann Jacob		Dietersweiler	Frd.	1817	Russia 569269
Martinet, Heinrich		Neuhengstett	Calw	1862	Luebeck 563212
Martz, Ernst Gustav	9 Mar 1846	Sulz	Sulz	Apr 1883	Switz. 849626
Marx, Anna Maria		Brittheim	Sulz	Apr 1852	N.-Amer 849632
Marx, Johann Martin & F	29 May 1812	Brittheim	Sulz	Apr 1852	N.-Amer 849632
Marx, Johannes		Brittheim	Sulz	Apr 1852	N.-Amer 849632
Maser, Friedrich	12 Jan 1850	Dornstetten	Frd.	Oct 1866	N.-Amer 577780
Maser, Gottfried	30 Jul 1839	Sulz	Sulz	Jul 1858	N.-Amer 849628
Maser, Johannes & F		Wittendorf	Frd.	Apr 1817	Russia 569268
Maser, Karl August	27 Dec 1836	Sulz	Sulz	Dec 1856	N.-Amer 849628
Mast, Agatha	26 yrs.	Klosterreichenbach	Frd.	Aug 1853	N.-Amer 569272
Mast, Agnes Barbara		Sulz	Sulz	bef 1857	N.-Amer 849628

Name		Birth		Emigration			Film
Last	First	Date	Place	O'amt	Appl. Date	Dest.	Number
Mast, Anna Maria			Tumlingen	Frd.	Apr 1854	N.-Amer	569273
Mast, Barbara		1823	Klosterreichenbach	Frd.	Mar 1847	N.-Amer	569271
Mast, Bernhard & F		5 May 1820	Klosterreichenbach	Frd.	Mar 1847	N.-Amer	569271
Mast, Bernhardt		9 Dec 1822	Klosterreichenbach	Frd.	Jul 1846	France	569271
Mast, Carl		28 Apr 1839	Baiersbronn	Frd.	bef 1865	Bavaria	577779
Mast, Caroline			Freudenstadt	Frd.	Oct 1854	N.-Amer	569274
Mast, Catharina			Freudenstadt	Frd.	Feb 1838	Baden	569267
Mast, Catharina		25 Sep 1814	Woernersberg	Frd.	Aug 1845	N.-Amer	569269
Mast, Christian		14 Dec 1835	Pfalzgrafenweiler	Frd.	Apr 1853	N.-Amer	569272
Mast, Christian Friedrich		6 Nov 1839	Sulz	Sulz	Aug 1857	N.-Amer	849628
Mast, Christina & F			Tumlingen	Frd.	Sep 1854	N.-Amer	569274
Mast, Christina Catharina		2 Aug 1821	Reichenbach	Frd.	Jun 1849	France	569270
Mast, Christine		18 Jan 1850	Tumlingen	Frd.	Sep 1854	N.-Amer	569274
Mast, Christine (wife)			Dornhan	Sulz	Sep 1846	Austria	849633
Mast, David			Urnagold	Frd.	bef 1847	N.-Amer	569270
Mast, Dorothea		19 Sep 1804	Klosterreichenbach	Frd.	Mar 1837	France	569268
Mast, Esther		15 Jun 1826	Tumlingen	Frd.	Mar 1850	N.-Amer	569271
Mast, Eva			Untermusbach	Frd.	Mar 1833	N.-Amer	569268
Mast, Eva Maria			Hochdorf	Frd.	bef 1849	Basel	569270
Mast, Friederike			Freudenstadt	Frd.	Oct 1854	N.-Amer	569274
Mast, Friedrich			Freudenstadt	Frd.	Dec 1853	N.-Amer	569272
Mast, Georg Friedrich			Hofstett/Neuweiler	Calw	1854	N.-Amer	563212
Mast, Gottlob		14 Oct 1839	Dornhan	Sulz	Feb 1854	N.-Amer	849633
Mast, Jacob		17 Dec 1801	Bondorf	Herr.	Feb 1838	Austria	834625
Mast, Jacob Friedrich		25 Dec 1830	Dornhan	Sulz	Mar 1854	N.-Amer	849633
Mast, Johann		18 Dec 1848	Dornhan	Sulz	Jun 1865	N.-Amer	849634
Mast, Johann & F		21 Feb 1804	Dornhan	Sulz	Sep 1846	Austria	849633
Mast, Johann Georg		19 Dec 1830	Boesingen	Nag.	bef 1861	N.-Amer	838493
Mast, Johann Georg		20 Sep 1843	Tumlingen	Frd.	Sep 1854	N.-Amer	569274
Mast, Johann Georg		8 Aug 1844	Huzenbach	Frd.	bef 1866	Baden	577780
Mast, Johann Michael		12 Aug 1832	Neuweiler	Calw	1854	N.-Amer	563212
Mast, Johanna		13 May 1838	Hochdorf	Frd.	bef 1861	Switz.	577778
Mast, Johannes		27 Sep 1845	Tumlingen	Frd.	Sep 1854	N.-Amer	569274
Mast, Johannes		31 Oct 1840	Dornhan	Sulz	Feb 1854	N.-Amer	849633
Mast, Johannes & F		50 yrs.	Baiersbronn	Frd.	Jul 1832	N.-Amer	569267
Mast, Karl		23 Sep 1867	Bergfelden	Sulz	May 1883	N.-Amer	849626
Mast, Karl Wilhelm		14 Nov 1848	Freudenstadt	Frd.	Jun 1866	N.-Amer	577780
Mast, Katharina		5 Jan 1852	Tumlingen	Frd.	Sep 1854	N.-Amer	569274
Mast, Katharina		14 Feb 1829	Gruental	Frd.	Jan 1866	N.-Amer	577780
Mast, Maria Louise		14 Feb 1841	Freudenstadt	Frd.	Aug 1864	N.-Amer	577779
Mast, Mathias			Tumlingen	Frd.	bef 1854	N.-Amer	569274
Mast, Mathias		2 Oct 1845	Dornhan	Sulz	Jun 1865	N.-Amer	849634
Mast, Matthias		29 Dec 1850	Tumlingen	Frd.	Sep 1854	N.-Amer	569274
Mast, Michael		3 Mar 1817	Hallwangen	Frd.	Mar 1847	N.-Amer	569271
Mast, Regina		13 Aug 1846	Klosterreichenbach	Frd.	Mar 1847	N.-Amer	569271
Mast, Rosina			Klosterreichenbach	Frd.	Mar 1815	Baden	569268
Mast, Rosina		1845	Klosterreichenbach	Frd.	Mar 1847	N.-Amer	569271
Mast, Wilhelmine Friederike		18 Feb 1835	Freudenstadt	Frd.	1852	N.-Amer	577779
Master, Johannes			Wittendorf	Frd.	1817	Russia	569269
Mathes, Andreas			Holzhausen	Sulz	bef 1854	N.-Amer	849635

Mathes, Johann Martin		Donnhan	Sulz	bef 1819	Switz.	849625
Mathis, Johannes & F		Zavelstein	Calw	1853	N.-Amer	563212
Matt, Christian & F		Glatten	Frd.	1817	Russia	569269
Matt, Christine (wife)		Bickelsberg	Sulz	Jun 1852	N.-Amer	849630
Matt, Dorothea		Schoemberg	Frd.	Jul 1851	N.-Amer	569271
Matt, Gottfried		Glatten	Frd.	1817	Russia	569269
Matt, Johann Georg		Bickelsberg	Sulz	Jun 1852	N.-Amer	849630
Matt, Johann Georg & F	18 Mar 1822	Bickelsberg	Sulz	Jun 1852	N.-Amer	849630
Matt, Johanna Magdalena & C	9 Aug 1805	Wittlensweiler	Frd.	Apr 1838	N.-Amer	569268
Matt, Johannes	8 Jun 1839	Schoemberg	Frd.	Jun 1860	N.-Amer	577777
Matt, Michael		Bickelsberg	Sulz	Jun 1852	N.-Amer	849630
Matz, Johann Georg		Freudenstadt	Frd.	Dec 1850	Baden	569271
Mau, Johann Jakob		Stammheim	Calw	Jun 1868	N.-Amer	563212
Mauer, Wilhelm	12 Apr 1875	Wittershausen	Sulz	Sep 1892	N.-Amer	849626
Maulbetsch, Eva Christina	14 Feb 1839	Goettelfingen	Frd.	Mar 1854	N.-Amer	569273
Maulbetsch, Georg Adam	9 May 1851	Goettelfingen	Frd.	Sep 1866	N.-Amer	577780
Maulbetsch, Georg Adam & F	6 Apr 1806	Goettelfingen	Frd.	Mar 1854	N.-Amer	569273
Maulbetsch, Johann Georg	30 Nov 1837	Goettelfingen	Frd.	Feb 1855	N.-Amer	569275
Maulbetsch, Veronika	13 Nov 1846	Goettelfingen	Frd.	Oct 1866	N.-Amer	577780
Maurer, Anna Maria	27 Sep 1850	Breitenholz	Herr.	Sep 1868	N.-Amer	834624
Maurer, Christian	5 Apr 1846	Reusten	Herr.	Apr 1869	N.-Amer	834624
Maurer, Friedrich	21 Oct 1868	Rosenfeld	Sulz	Aug 1884	N.-Amer	849626
Maurer, Heinrich	31 Aug 1876	Dornhan	Sulz	Aug 1891	N.-Amer	849626
Maurer, Johann Friedrich		Ebingen	Bal.	bef 1853	Switz.	555962
Maurer, Johann Georg	27 Dec 1875	Rosenfeld	Sulz	Mar 1891	N.-Amer	849626
Maurer, Johann Heinrich	29 Nov 1835	Rosenfeld	Sulz	Apr 1854	N.-Amer	849640
Maurer, Johann Michael	26 Jun 1850	Reusten	Herr.	Apr 1869	N.-Amer	834624
Maurer, Karl Eugen	2 May 1874	Trossingen/Tuttl.	Sulz	Jan 1889	N.-Amer	849626
Maut, Maria		Leidringen	Sulz	Jun 1817	Russia	849637
Mauth, Andreas	3 Dec 1834	Leidringen	Sulz	Mar 1854	N.-Amer	849637
Mauth, Johann Martin	9 Mar 1842	Boll	Sulz	Apr 1860	N.-Amer	849632
Mauth, Johannes	3 Aug 1844	Boll	Sulz	Feb 1864	N.-Amer	849632
Mauthe, Maria & C		Leidringen	Sulz	Apr 1817	Russia	849637
Mautz, Theresia	22 Sep 1846	Renfrizhausen	Sulz	Feb 1887	N.-Amer	849626
Mayer, Andreas	3 Dec 1849	Bergfelden	Sulz	Oct 1860	N.-Amer	849629
Mayer, Andreas	20 Apr 1856	Hopfau	Sulz	Feb 1872	N.-Amer	849636
Mayer, Anna Maria	13 Dec 1841	Bergfelden	Sulz	Oct 1860	N.-Amer	849629
Mayer, Anna Maria	23 Sep 1857	Kuppingen	Herr.	May 1867	N.-Amer	834624
Mayer, Anna Maria		Entringen	Herr.	Aug 1847	Hesse	834626
Mayer, Anna Maria & C	17 Sep 1821	Kuppingen	Herr.	May 1867	N.-Amer	834624
Mayer, Carl & F		Freudenstadt	Frd.	Mar 1849	N.-Amer	569270
Mayer, Christiane Elisabeth		Calw	Calw	1859	N.-Amer	563212
Mayer, Christina (wife)	19 Jun 1813	Bergfelden	Sulz	Oct 1860	N.-Amer	849629
Mayer, Conrad Christoph		Nufringen	Herr.	1848	N.-Amer	834627
Mayer, Friederike	7 yrs.	Gaertringen	Herr.	Oct 1846	N.-Amer	834626
Mayer, Gottlieb	23 yrs.	Wittlensweiler	Frd.	Mar 1837	N.-Amer	569268
Mayer, Jacob Friedrich	5 Apr 1806	Herrenberg	Herr.	Sep 1862	N.-Amer	834624
Mayer, Jacob Friedrich	30 Dec 1830	Kuppingen	Herr.	May 1867	N.-Amer	834624
Mayer, Johann Georg		Marschalkenzimmern	Sulz	Mar 1847	N.-Amer	849638
Mayer, Johann Georg	29 Jan 1846	Nufringen	Herr.	bef 1863	N.-Amer	834624

| Name | | Birth | | Emigration | | | Film |
Last	First	Date	Place	O'amt	Appl. Date	Dest.	Number
Mayer, Johann Martin		27 yrs.	Gueltstein	Herr.	May 1831	N.-Amer	834624
Mayer, Johann Michael		23 Jan 1831	Breitenholz	Herr.	Mar 1849	N.-Amer	834627
Mayer, Johannes		18 Jul 1845	Bergfelden	Sulz	Oct 1860	N.-Amer	849629
Mayer, Johannes		infant	Gaertringen	Herr.	Oct 1846	N.-Amer	834626
Mayer, Johannes & F		3 Jan 1813	Bergfelden	Sulz	Oct 1860	N.-Amer	849629
Mayer, Joseph Friedrich		1825	Muehlheim a.B.	Sulz	1848	N.-Amer	849639
Mayer, Leonhardt			Simmozheim	Calw	1861	France	563212
Mayer, Maria		3 yrs.	Gaertringen	Herr.	Oct 1846	N.-Amer	834626
Mayer, Paul Wilhelm Moriz		18 May 1860	Sulz	Sulz	Jun 1877	N.-Amer	849628
Mayer, Pauline			Deckenpfronn	Calw	1861	Frankf.	563212
Mayer, Rosina Clara		5 yrs.	Gaertringen	Herr.	Oct 1846	N.-Amer	834626
Mayer, Rosine & C		31 yrs.	Gaertringen	Herr.	Oct 1846	N.-Amer	834626
Mayerhofer, Johannes		18 Apr 1816	Renfrizhausen	Sulz	Jun 1866	Baden	849639
Mayhoefer, Agatha		2 yrs.	Sigmarswangen	Sulz	Apr 1817	Russia	849642
Mayhoefer, Anna Barbara (wife)		45 yrs.	Sigmarswangen	Sulz	Apr 1817	Russia	849642
Mayhoefer, Anna Maria		8 yrs.	Sigmarswangen	Sulz	Apr 1817	Russia	849642
Mayhoefer, Barbara		5 yrs.	Sigmarswangen	Sulz	Apr 1817	Russia	849642
Mayhoefer, Christina		19 yrs.	Sigmarswangen	Sulz	Apr 1817	Russia	849642
Mayhoefer, Johann Martin & F		46 yrs.	Sigmarswangen	Sulz	Apr 1817	Russia	849642
Mayhoefer, Johannes		15 yrs.	Sigmarswangen	Sulz	Apr 1817	Russia	849642
Mayhoefer, Mathaeus		12 yrs.	Sigmarswangen	Sulz	Apr 1817	Russia	849642
Mayhofer, Bernhard		13 yrs.	Sigmarswangen	Sulz	Jun 1817	N.-Amer	849642
Mayhofer, Christina		15 yrs.	Sigmarswangen	Sulz	Jun 1817	N.-Amer	849642
Mayhofer, Christina (wife)		51 yrs.	Sigmarswangen	Sulz	Jun 1817	N.-Amer	849642
Mayhofer, Friedrich		4 yrs.	Sigmarswangen	Sulz	Jun 1817	N.-Amer	849642
Mayhofer, Georg Jakob		17 yrs.	Sigmarswangen	Sulz	Jun 1817	N.-Amer	849642
Mayhofer, Johann Georg		7 yrs.	Sigmarswangen	Sulz	Jun 1817	N.-Amer	849642
Mayhofer, Maria Anna		2 yrs.	Sigmarswangen	Sulz	Jun 1817	N.-Amer	849642
Mayhofer, Mathaeus		9 yrs.	Sigmarswangen	Sulz	Jun 1817	N.-Amer	849642
Mayhofer, Matthias & F		49 yrs.	Sigmarswangen	Sulz	Jun 1817	N.-Amer	849642
Meebold, Johann Gottlieb		20 yrs.	Sulz	Sulz	Oct 1816	Frankf.	849625
Meier, Christina			Bondorf	Herr.	Feb 1830	Leipzig	834624
Meier, Jacob Friedrich			Dornstetten	Frd.	bef 1844	Prussia	569269
Meier, Johann Friedrich		3 yrs.	Dornstetten	Frd.	Oct 1860	N.-Amer	577777
Meier, Johann Georg		17 Oct 1835	Baiersbronn	Frd.	Feb 1847	N.-Amer	569271
Meier, Johann Georg		17 Jul 1811	Duerrenmettstetten	Sulz	Aug 1839	N.-Amer	849635
Meier, Johannes		17 Dec 1828	Lossburg	Frd.	May 1857	Baden	577776
Meier, Johannes (wid.) & F		53 yrs.	Pfalzgrafenweiler	Frd.	Feb 1847	N.-Amer	569271
Meier, Maria & C		30 yrs.	Dornstetten	Frd.	Oct 1860	N.-Amer	577777
Meier, Wilhelm Gottfried		13 yrs.	Pfalzgrafenweiler	Frd.	Feb 1847	N.-Amer	569271
Meinhardt, Johann Fr.			Hirsau	Calw	Jan 1877	N.-Amer	563212
Meisenbach, Christine & C			Unterreichenbach	Calw	1854	N.-Amer	563212
Meisenbach, Heinrich		1 yrs.	Unterreichenbach	Calw	1854	N.-Amer	563212
Meisenbacher, Johann Michael			Liebenzell	Calw	1849	Frankf.	563212
Menger, August		22 Sep 1865	Boll	Sulz	Jun 1866	Baden	849632
Mennikheim, Johann Georg		12 Feb 1880	Bettenhausen	Sulz	Oct 1896	N.-Amer	849630
Merbold, Agnes Katharina			Sulz	Sulz	Jan 1833	N.-Amer	849627
Merkle, Anna Katharina			Isingen	Sulz	Apr 1880	N.-Amer	849626
Merkle, Johann Georg		3 Dec 1826	Isingen	Sulz	bef 1863	N.-Amer	849636
Merz, Andreas		1 Jul 1856	Hallwangen	Frd.	Feb 1861	N.-Amer	577778

Merz, Andreas & F	5 Aug 1826	Hallwangen	Frd.	Feb 1861	N.-Amer	577778
Merz, Andreas & F		Lossburg	Frd.	Aug 1845	N.-Amer	569769
Merz, Christian	31 Mar 1835	Aach	Frd.	bef 1864	Baden	577779
Merz, Creszentia		Ottersweier/Baden	Frd.	Aug 1845	N.-Amer	569269
Merz, Elisabetha (wife)	6 Jan 1829	Aach	Frd.	Feb 1861	N.-Amer	577778
Merz, Jakob	28 Jul 1834	Glatten	Frd.	Jan 1863	N.-Amer	577778
Merz, Johann Georg	1819	Lossburg	Frd.	bef 1844	N.-Amer	569272
Merz, Johannes	12 Dec 1856	Hallwangen	Frd.	Feb 1861	N.-Amer	577778
Merz, Johannes	2 Dec 1848	Bickelsberg	Sulz	Mar 1867	N.-Amer	849630
Merz, Johannes	26 May 1848	Trichtingen	Sulz	Apr 1867	N.-Amer	849642
Merz, Mathaeus	7 Jul 1862	Bickelsberg	Sulz	May 1879	N.-Amer	849630
Merz, Rosina	18 Oct 1828	Aach	Frd.	Jul 1861	Baden	577778
Merz, Xaver		Leinstetten	Sulz	Sep 1854	N.-Amer	849638
Merz, female		Hossingen	Bal.	Mar 1852	N.-Amer	555964
Messerschmid, Anna Maria	4 Nov 1846	Tailfingen	Herr.	Feb 1849	N.-Amer	834627
Messerschmid, Catharina	4 Jan 1839	Tailfingen	Herr.	Feb 1849	N.-Amer	834627
Messerschmid, Catharina (wife)	15 Jul 1810	Tailfingen	Herr.	Feb 1849	N.-Amer	834627
Messerschmid, Christina Marg.		Moenchberg	Herr.	Mar 1836	N.-Amer	834624
Messerschmid, Johannes		Tailfingen	Herr.	Mar 1836	N.-Amer	834624
Messerschmid, Johannes & F		Tailfingen	Herr.	Feb 1849	N.-Amer	834627
Messerschmid, Martin	54 yrs.	Tailfingen	Herr.	May 1849	N.-Amer	834627
Messmer, Margaretha		Rosenfeld	Sulz	Mar 1858	Switz.	849640
Messner, Anna		Leidringen	Sulz	bef 1853	N.-Amer	849637
Messner, Anna Susanna (wife)	16 Apr 1833	Rosenfeld	Sulz	Jul 1885	N.-Amer	849626
Messner, Barbara (wife) & F	24 Oct 1825	Laufen	Sulz	1858	N.-Amer	849641
Messner, Dorothea	26 yrs.	Untermusbach	Frd.	Mar 1833	N.-Amer	569268
Messner, Eva Maria	30 yrs.	Untermusbach	Frd.	Mar 1833	N.-Amer	569268
Messner, Johann		Neubulach	Calw	Mar 1873	N.-Amer	563212
Messner, Johann Friedrich	7 Sep 1851	Rosenfeld	Sulz	1858	N.-Amer	849641
Messner, Johann Georg	3 Dec 1852	Rosenfeld	Sulz	1858	N.-Amer	849641
Messner, Johann Georg & F	7 Jun 1827	Rosenfeld	Sulz	Jul 1885	N.-Amer	849626
Messner, Johannes	31 yrs.	Neubulach	Calw	1866	N.-Amer	563212
Messner, Johannes	7 Apr 1822	Leidringen	Sulz	Aug 1845	N.-Amer	849637
Messner, Johannes	21 Jan 1823	Rosenfeld	Sulz	1852	N.-Amer	849641
Messner, Johannes	27 Apr 1849	Laufen	Sulz	1858	N.-Amer	849641
Messner, Johannes	17 Jun 1850	Rosenfeld	Sulz	1858	N.-Amer	849641
Messner, Luise	4 May 1869	Rosenfeld	Sulz	Jul 1885	N.-Amer	849626
Messner, Wilhelm	28 May 1866	Rosenfeld	Sulz	Jul 1885	N.-Amer	849626
Metschler, Sabina Elisabeth	May 1837	Schoenmuenzbach	Frd.	bef 1863	Baden	577778
Metz, Adam Karl	15 Jul 1842	Rosenfeld	Sulz	Aug 1849	N.-Amer	849640
Metz, Catharine Luise	10 Aug 1847	Rosenfeld	Sulz	Aug 1849	N.-Amer	849640
Metz, Christian	15 Dec 1809	Rosenfeld	Sulz	Jun 1838	Kiel	849640
Metz, Jacob Konrad		Rosenfeld	Sulz	Apr 1889	N.-Amer	849626
Metz, Johann Friedrich	17 May 1841	Rosenfeld	Sulz	Aug 1849	N.-Amer	849640
Metz, Johann Georg	4 Dec 1838	Rosenfeld	Sulz	Aug 1849	N.-Amer	849640
Metz, Johann Georg	2 Feb 1815	Rosenfeld	Sulz	Mar 1840	Hamburg	849640
Metz, Johann Georg & F		Rosenfeld	Sulz	Aug 1849	N.-Amer	849640
Metz, Maria (wife)		Rosenfeld	Sulz	Aug 1849	N.-Amer	849640
Metz, Marie Friederike	18 May 1849	Rosenfeld	Sulz	Aug 1849	N.-Amer	849640
Metzger, Christiane Heinrike	16 Sep 1816	Herrenberg	Herr.	Mar 1846	Prussia	834626

Name		Birth		Emigration			Film
Last	First	Date	Place	O'amt	Appl. Date	Dest.	Number
Metzger, Christine Margarete			Dornstetten	Frd.	Apr 1850	N.-Amer	569271
Metzler, Christoph Friedrich		1850	Dennjaecht	Calw	1867	N.-Amer	563212
Metzler, Louise			Unterreichenbach	Calw	1854	N.-Amer	563212
Meyer, Johann Ulrich			Buedingen	– –	Dec 1751	N.-Amer	550803
Mezger, Balthas		6 Mar 1838	Bergfelden	Sulz	Apr 1858	N.-Amer	849629
Mezger, Catharina Paul. Wilh.		27 Feb 1820	Herrenberg	Herr.	Aug 1849	Bavaria	834627
Mezger, Friedrich			Bergfelden	Sulz	Aug 1854	N.-Amer	849629
Mezger, Johannes			Bickelsberg	Sulz	Oct 1852	N.-Amer	849630
Mezger, Karl Heinrich		20 Jun 1826	Reusten	Herr.	Sep 1862	N.-Amer	834624
Mezger, Maria Margaretha		29 Aug 1818	Herrenberg	Herr.	Jul 1863	Austral	834624
Michael, Anna Maria (wife)			Sulz	Sulz	Apr 1834	N.-Amer	849627
Michael, Johann Christoph		1 Jan 1825	Sulz	Sulz	Apr 1834	N.-Amer	849627
Michael, Johann Gottlieb		7 Sep 1817	Sulz	Sulz	Apr 1834	N.-Amer	849627
Michael, Johann Gottlieb & F		25 Jan 1798	Sulz	Sulz	Apr 1834	N.-Amer	849627
Michael, Johann Jonathan		16 Nov 1830	Sulz	Sulz	Apr 1834	N.-Amer	849627
Michel, Andreas		16 Jan 1835	Bergfelden	Sulz	Feb 1857	N.-Amer	849629
Michel, Andreas & F		16 Oct 1841	Bergfelden	Sulz	Nov 1866	N.-Amer	849629
Michel, Elisabetha Barbara		25 Apr 1866	Bergfelden	Sulz	Sep 1866	N.-Amer	849629
Michel, Elisabetha Barbara		1 Dec 1845	Bergfelden	Sulz	Sep 1866	N.-Amer	849629
Michel, Eva			Voehringen	Sulz	Apr 1833	N.-Amer	849643
Michel, Eva & C			Voehringen	Sulz	Jun 1817	Russia	849643
Michel, Johann Georg		21 Jan 1838	Bergfelden	Sulz	Jan 1857	N.-Amer	849629
Michel, Johanna (wife)		15 Apr 1843	Bergfelden	Sulz	Nov 1866	N.-Amer	849629
Michel, Johannes		14 Dec 1864	Bergfelden	Sulz	Nov 1866	N.-Amer	849629
Michel, Johannes		25 Sep 1839	Bergfelden	Sulz	Sep 1866	N.-Amer	849629
Michel, Juliane		14 Feb 1866	Bergfelden	Sulz	Nov 1866	N.-Amer	849629
Michel, Margaretha & C		3 Dec 1841	Bergfelden	Sulz	Sep 1866	N.-Amer	849629
Michelin, Catharina			Sigmarswangen	Sulz	Apr 1817	Polen	849642
Miedert, Hermine Christine		31 Oct 1847	Dornhan	Sulz	1869	N.-Amer	849634
Millhauer, Jacob & F		28 Oct 1774	Leinstetten	Sulz	Jun 1817	N.-Amer	849638
Millhauer, Joseph		9 Mar 1811	Leinstetten	Sulz	Jun 1817	N.-Amer	849638
Millhauer, Maria Anna (wife)		7 Apr 1769	Leinstetten	Sulz	Jun 1817	N.-Amer	849638
Millhauer, Xaverius		5 Jan 1802	Leinstetten	Sulz	Jun 1817	N.-Amer	849638
Minster, Gottfried			Freudenstadt	Frd.	1817	Russia	569269
Mitsch, Johann Friedrich			Calw	Calw	1849	France	563212
Mitschdoerfer, Michael			Unterhaugstett	Calw	1852	N.-Amer	563212
Mockler, Christina		5 Mar 1819	Goettelfingen	Frd.	May 1851	N.-Amer	569271
Moehle, Christine Barbara			Sulz	Sulz	Oct 1861	Switz.	849628
Moehrle, Agatha			Baiersbronn	Frd.	bef 1817	Poland	569267
Moehrle, Carl			Baiersbronn	Frd.	bef 1817	Poland	569267
Moehrle, Catharina		24 Apr 1802	Baiersbronn	Frd.	Apr 1846	N.-Amer	569271
Moehrle, Christian David		1 Jan 1852	Freudenstadt	Frd.	Sep 1854	N.-Amer	569274
Moehrle, Christiane & C		Apr 1826	Freudenstadt	Frd.	Sep 1854	N.-Amer	569274
Moehrle, Johann David		9 Apr 1834	Tonbach	Frd.	Feb 1854	N.-Amer	569273
Moehrle, Johann Heinr.			Freudenstadt	Frd.	bef 1854	N.-Amer	569273
Moehrle, Mathaeus & F			Neuneck	Frd.	Mar 1851	N.-Amer	569271
Moehrlen, Christoph & F			Baiersbronn	Frd.	bef 1856	Switz.	569275
Moench, Catharina			Geradstetten	Schd.	Mar 1837	N.-Amer	801461
Moench, Christina Barbara		25 yrs.	Rodt	Frd.	May 1750	Pen.N-A	550803
Moench, Johannes & F		60 yrs.	Rodt	Frd.	May 1750	Pen.N-A	550803

Moench, Margaretha	40 yrs.	Rodt	Frd.	May 1750	Pen.N-A 550803
Moench, Maria Magdalena	24 yrs.	Rodt	Frd.	May 1750	Pen.N-A 550803
Moench, Tobias		Dietersweiler	Frd.	Apr 1865	N.-Amer 577779
Moerk, Gottlob & F		Gechingen	Calw	1852	N.-Amer 563212
Moerle, Agatha	28 Jun 1829	Baiersbronn	Frd.	Mar 1849	N.-Amer 569270
Moersch, Johann Georg		Elsstadt	— —	Dec 1751	N.-Amer 550803
Moessner, Johann Martin	13 Jan 1823	Affstaett	Herr.	bef 1862	N.-Amer 834624
Mohr, Agnes Barbara		Freudenstadt	Frd.	Mar 1847	France 569271
Mohr, Caroline Sophie	13 Jul 1829	Freudenstadt	Frd.	Sep 1858	Baden 577776
Mohr, Christian Friedrich & F		Freudenstadt	Frd.	Sep 1854	N.-Amer 569274
Mohr, Christiane Rosine	5 Jun 1835	Freudenstadt	Frd.	Sep 1854	N.-Amer 569274
Mohr, Johann Georg	4 May 1830	Simmozheim	Calw	1868	Baden 563212
Mohr, Johann Ludwig & F		Simmozheim	Calw	Jun 1877	Switz. 563212
Mohr, Johanna Eva		Simmozheim	Calw	1868	Bohemia 563212
Mohr, Rosine		Freudenstadt	Frd.	Oct 1854	N.-Amer 569274
Mohr, Sophie Marie	4 Apr 1833	Freudenstadt	Frd.	Sep 1854	N.-Amer 569274
Mohr, Sophie Wilhelmine	8 yrs.	Simmozheim	Calw	1864	Baden 563212
Mohr, Wilhelmine Catharine & C		Simmozheim	Calw	1864	Baden 563212
Mohrdott, Eva Maria		Schoenegruend	Frd.	Jun 1832	N.-Amer 569268
Mohrenweeg, Friedrich	19 yrs.	Oberwaldach	Frd.	Mar 1837	N.-Amer 569269
Mohrhardt, Anna Maria (wife)		Herrenberg	Herr.	Mar 1831	N.-Amer 834624
Mohrhardt, Catharina Dor. (wife)		Herrenberg	Herr.	Mar 1831	N.-Amer 834624
Mohrhardt, Gottlieb Fried. & W		Herrenberg	Herr.	Mar 1831	N.-Amer 834624
Mohrhardt, Johann Christ. & W		Herrenberg	Herr.	Mar 1831	N.-Amer 834624
Mohrhardt, Johannes		Gaertringen	Herr.	Feb 1828	Berlin 834624
Mohrhardt, Michael		Vesperweiler	Frd.	Mar 1856	N.-Amer 569275
Mohrlok, Christina	22 yrs.	Roet	Frd.	Apr 1860	N.-Amer 577777
Mohrlok, Karolina	19 yrs.	Roet	Frd.	Apr 1860	N.-Amer 577777
Mokler, Anna Maria		Goettelfingen	Frd.	Jul 1854	N.-Amer 569274
Mokler, Friederike		Goettelfingen	Frd.	Jul 1854	N.-Amer 569274
Moraller, Marie Anna & C	23 May 1815	Freudenstadt	Frd.	Sep 1854	N.-Amer 569274
Moraller, Marie Friederike	25 May 1851	Freudenstadt	Frd.	Sep 1854	N.-Amer 569274
Morgenthaler, Andreas	20 yrs.	Rosenfeld	Sulz	Mar 1853	N.-Amer 849640
Morgenthaler, Christian	1 yrs.	Rosenfeld	Sulz	Mar 1853	N.-Amer 849640
Morgenthaler, Jacob Fried. & F		Rosenfeld	Sulz	Mar 1853	N.-Amer 849640
Morgenthaler, Jacob Friedrich	21 yrs.	Rosenfeld	Sulz	Mar 1853	N.-Amer 849640
Morgenthaler, Jakob Friedrich	13 Jul 1875	Rosenfeld	Sulz	Apr 1890	N.-Amer 849626
Morgenthaler, Johannes	15 yrs.	Rosenfeld	Sulz	Mar 1853	N.-Amer 849640
Morgenthaler, Marie Rosine	4 yrs.	Rosenfeld	Sulz	Mar 1853	N.-Amer 849640
Morgenthaler, Regine Christ.	16 yrs.	Rosenfeld	Sulz	Mar 1853	N.-Amer 849640
Morgenthaler, Rosina (wife)		Rosenfeld	Sulz	Mar 1853	N.-Amer 849640
Morlock, Catharina	7 Mar 1852	Tonbach	Frd.	Aug 1854	N.-Amer 569274
Morlock, Catharina (wife)	2 Feb 1822	Tonbach	Frd.	Aug 1854	N.-Amer 569274
Morlock, Johannes	22 Feb 1842	Tonbach	Frd.	Aug 1854	N.-Amer 569274
Morlock, Ludwig	9 Mar 1846	Tonbach	Frd.	Aug 1854	N.-Amer 569274
Morlock, Ludwig & F	28 Feb 1815	Tonbach	Frd.	Aug 1854	N.-Amer 569274
Morlock, Regina	12 Jun 1836	Baiersbronn	Frd.	Aug 1854	N.-Amer 569274
Morlock, Rosine Catharine		Roet	Frd.	Jul 1852	N.-Amer 569271
Morlock, Salome	14 Jul 1847	Tonbach	Frd.	Aug 1854	N.-Amer 569274
Morlok, Agnes Catharine	30 Mar 1810	Baiersbronn	Frd.	Dec 1853	N.-Amer 569272

Name		Birth		Emigration			Film
Last	First	Date	Place	O'amt	Appl. Date	Dest.	Number
Morlok, Christian			Schoenegruend	Frd.	Apr 1857	N.-Amer	577776
Morlok, Christian			Moetzingen	Herr.	Feb 1834	N.-Amer	834624
Morlok, Friedrich		24 Nov 1825	Baiersbronn	Frd.	Mar 1849	N.-Amer	569270
Morlok, Jacob		17 Aug 1832	Moetzingen	Herr.	Apr 1847	N.-Amer	834626
Morlok, Jacob Friedrich & F			Freudenstadt	Frd.	Mar 1817	Russia	569267
Morlok, Margaretha		11 Jul 1818	Tailfingen	Herr.	Jan 1868	N.-Amer	834624
Morlok, Michael			Schoenegruend	Frd.	Apr 1857	N.-Amer	577776
Mornhinweg, Johann			Gaertringen	Herr.	bef 1838	Berlin	834625
Moser, Andreas		24 Mar 1848	Frutenhof	Frd.	Nov 1855	N.-Amer	569275
Moser, Anna Maria		25 May 1847	Baiersbronn	Frd.	Nov 1853	N.-Amer	569272
Moser, Anna Maria		18 Sep 1844	Frutenhof	Frd.	Nov 1855	N.-Amer	569275
Moser, Carl		17 Apr 1838	Frutenhof	Frd.	Nov 1855	N.-Amer	569275
Moser, Catharine Friederike			Sulz	Sulz	Jan 1843	Baden	849627
Moser, Christina Catharina		18 Feb 1842	Schramberg	Frd.	Aug 1854	N.-Amer	569274
Moser, Johann		23 Apr 1794	Dornstetten	Frd.	bef 1856	France	569275
Moser, Johann Karl		8 Jan 1845	Schramberg	Frd.	Aug 1854	N.-Amer	569274
Moser, Johannes & F			Aach	Frd.	Sep 1817	Poland	569267
Moser, Johannes & F		2 Aug 1819	Schramberg	Frd.	Aug 1854	N.-Amer	569274
Moser, Karl Jakob		26 Apr 1828	Pfalzgrafenweiler	Frd.	Oct 1858	N.-Amer	577776
Moser, Katharina		9 Feb 1834	Frutenhof	Frd.	Nov 1855	N.-Amer	569275
Moser, Katharina (wid.) & F			Frutenhof	Frd.	Nov 1855	N.-Amer	569275
Moser, Margaretha		21 Mar 1811	Baiersbronn	Frd.	Dec 1853	N.-Amer	569272
Moser, Maria		4 Jun 1840	Frutenhof	Frd.	Nov 1855	N.-Amer	569275
Moser, Matthaeus		1 Dec 1847	Schramberg	Frd.	Aug 1854	N.-Amer	569274
Moser, Regina		26 Jul 1843	Schramberg	Frd.	Aug 1854	N.-Amer	569274
Moser, Sophia (wife)		5 Apr 1820	Schramberg	Frd.	Aug 1854	N.-Amer	569274
Moser, Sophie Charlotte Louise		30 Mar 1833	Sulz	Sulz	Sep 1853	Baden	849627
Mosser, Johannes			Glatten	Frd.	1817	Russia	569269
Most, Agnes Barbara			Freudenstadt	Sulz	bef 1854	N.-Amer	849627
Most, Johann Georg		23 Apr 1828	Gaertringen	Herr.	bef 1862	N.-Amer	834624
Most, Paul Emil		10 Jul 1832	Herrenberg	Herr.	Sep 1850	Austria	834627
Motteler, Georg Friedrich		1 Mar 1831	Gaertringen	Herr.	Sep 1851	N.-Amer	834627
Mozer, Anna Barbara		29 May 1830	Unterjesingen	Herr.	Sep 1848	N.-Amer	834626
Mozer, Anna Barbara (wife)			Unterjesingen	Herr.	Sep 1848	N.-Amer	834626
Mozer, Christian Gottlob		12 Jan 1835	Unterjesingen	Herr.	Sep 1848	N.-Amer	834626
Mozer, Gottlieb & F			Unterjesingen	Herr.	Sep 1848	N.-Amer	834626
Mozer, Hermann Oskar		8 Feb 1872	Sulz	Sulz	Dec 1889	N.-Amer	849626
Mozer, Jakob Friedrich Gotth.		1 Nov 1841	Unterjesingen	Herr.	Sep 1848	N.-Amer	834626
Mozer, Johann Adam & F			Oberhaugstett	Calw	1864	N.-Amer	563212
Mozer, Johann Gottlieb		25 May 1837	Unterjesingen	Herr.	Sep 1848	N.-Amer	834626
Mozer, Julius Reinhold		23 Feb 1848	Unterjesingen	Herr.	Sep 1848	N.-Amer	834626
Mozer, Karl August		15 Apr 1844	Unterjesingen	Herr.	Sep 1848	N.-Amer	834626
Muck, Christine Wilhelmine			Hirsau	Calw	1868	Prussia	563212
Mueller, Agatha		15 May 1838	Besenfeld	Frd.	May 1848	N.-Amer	569270
Mueller, Albert Friedrich		16 yrs.	Wildbad	Calw	1869	N.-Amer	563212
Mueller, Andreas		9 Jan 1831	Besenfeld	Frd.	May 1846	N.-Amer	569271
Mueller, Andreas		13 Apr 1856	Dornhan	Sulz	May 1872	N.-Amer	849634
Mueller, Ann Maria			Rosenfeld	Sulz	bef 1829	Switz.	849625
Mueller, Anna Maria			Boeffingen	Frd.	May 1854	N.-Amer	569273
Mueller, Anna Maria		30 Mar 1837	Hallwangen	Frd.	Feb 1861	N.-Amer	577778

Mueller, Anna Maria		Wittendorf	Frd.	Apr 1817	Russia	569268
Mueller, Anna Maria	18 May 1849	Hoerschweiler	Frd.	Oct 1854	N.-Amer	569274
Mueller, Anna Maria	15 May 1844	Trichtingen	Sulz	Apr 1867	N.-Amer	849642
Mueller, Anna Maria	15 Feb 1835	Dornhan	Sulz	Apr 1849	N.-Amer	849633
Mueller, Anna Maria	9 Oct 1832	Bondorf	Herr.	Jul 1847	N.-Amer	834626
Mueller, Anna Maria (wife)		Rosenfeld	Sulz	Oct 1879	N.-Amer	849641
Mueller, Anna Maria Cath. (wife)	27 Feb 1808	Bondorf	Herr.	Jul 1847	N.-Amer	834626
Mueller, August Friedrich	28 Sep 1844	Freudenstadt	Frd.	Sep 1854	N.-Amer	569274
Mueller, Auguste		Bergfelden	Sulz	Oct 1853	N.-Amer	849629
Mueller, Barbara	23 Jan 1840	Dietersweiler	Frd.	bef 1861	Switz.	577778
Mueller, Barbara	16 yrs.	Rosenfeld	Sulz	Aug 1855	N.-Amer	849640
Mueller, Barbara (wid.) & F	22 May 1793	Dornhan	Sulz	Apr 1849	N.-Amer	849633
Mueller, Benjamin Heinrich	13 Feb 1852	Weiden	Sulz	Sep 1871	N.-Amer	849644
Mueller, Bernhardt	1 mon.	Frutenhof	Frd.	Jun 1853	N.-Amer	569272
Mueller, Carl		Calw	Calw	1853	N.-Amer	563212
Mueller, Carl	2 Nov 1833	Moetzingen	Herr.	1847	N.-Amer	834626
Mueller, Carl Christian	6 Jun 1841	Nagold	Nag.	Jan 1854	N.-Amer	838491
Mueller, Carl Friedrich	17 Mar 1851	Freudenstadt	Frd.	Sep 1854	N.-Amer	569274
Mueller, Carl Friedrich & F	12 Jun 1802	Moetzingen	Herr.	Apr 1848	N.-Amer	834626
Mueller, Caroline F. M. L.	24 yrs.	Calw	Calw	Dec 1868	France	563212
Mueller, Caroline Wilhelmine	29 Nov 1846	Freudenstadt	Frd.	Sep 1854	N.-Amer	569274
Mueller, Catharina	29 Dec 1830	Lauterbad	Frd.	bef 1853	Switz.	569272
Mueller, Catharina	19 Nov 1844	Besenfeld	Frd.	May 1846	N.-Amer	569271
Mueller, Catharina	4 Nov 1823	Unterjettingen	Herr.	Jun 1867	N.-Amer	834624
Mueller, Catharina Christina		Oberjettingen	Herr.	Feb 1839	Switz.	834625
Mueller, Catharine & F		Nagold	Nag.	Jan 1854	N.-Amer	838491
Mueller, Charlotte		Calw	Calw	1869	Baden	563212
Mueller, Christian		Wittendorf	Frd.	Apr 1854	N.-Amer	569273
Mueller, Christian	10 Feb 1830	Dornhan	Sulz	Apr 1849	N.-Amer	849633
Mueller, Christian	17 yrs.	Rosenfeld	Sulz	Aug 1855	N.-Amer	849640
Mueller, Christian		Rosenfeld	Sulz	1864	N.-Amer	849641
Mueller, Christian	20 Jul 1849	Rosenfeld	Sulz	Apr 1865	N.-Amer	849641
Mueller, Christian & F		Freudenstadt	Frd.	Sep 1854	N.-Amer	569274
Mueller, Christian Jakob	5 Nov 1838	Freudenstadt	Frd.	Sep 1854	N.-Amer	569274
Mueller, Christiana	13 May 1840	Nagold	Nag.	Jan 1854	N.-Amer	838491
Mueller, Christiane Caroline	11 Jul 1825	Moetzingen	Herr.	Apr 1848	N.-Amer	834626
Mueller, Christiane M. J. (wife)	10 Dec 1800	Moetzingen	Herr.	Apr 1848	N.-Amer	834626
Mueller, Christina	17 yrs.	Lossburg	Frd.	1817	Russia	569269
Mueller, Christina	10 Nov 1832	Besenfeld	Frd.	May 1846	N.-Amer	569271
Mueller, Christina & C	28 yrs.	Frutenhof	Frd.	Jun 1853	N.-Amer	569272
Mueller, Christine (wife)	61 yrs.	Oberjettingen	Herr.	Jun 1852	N.-Amer	834627
Mueller, Dorothea		Dornhan	Sulz	Apr 1854	N.-Amer	849633
Mueller, Elisabeth	18 Mar 1836	Dietersweiler	Frd.	bef 1864	Switz.	577779
Mueller, Elisabeth	28 Apr 1839	Hoerschweiler	Frd.	Oct 1854	N.-Amer	569274
Mueller, Elisabetha	9 Aug 1841	Renfrizhausen	Sulz	Sep 1868	N.-Amer	849639
Mueller, Elisabetha Margar.	36 yrs.	Rosenfeld	Sulz	Aug 1854	N.-Amer	849640
Mueller, Ernst Gottlieb	18 Oct 1847	Gueltstein	Herr.	Apr 1869	N.-Amer	834624
Mueller, Eva Maria & C	5 Dec 1815	Besenfeld	Frd.	May 1848	N.-Amer	569270
Mueller, Friederike		Huzenbach	Frd.	bef 1865	Bavaria	577779
Mueller, Friedrich		Protenhof	Frd.	1817	Russia	569269

| Name | | Birth | | Emigration | | | Film |
Last	First	Date	Place	O'amt	Appl. Date	Dest.	Number
Mueller, Friedrich		27 May 1872	Rosenfeld	Sulz	Apr 1887	N.-Amer	849626
Mueller, Friedrich & F			Boeffingen	Frd.	May 1854	N.-Amer	569273
Mueller, Friedrich Ludwig			Lauterbad	Frd.	Aug 1804	Baden	550803
Mueller, Georg		15 Sep 1806	Gueltstein	Herr.	Mar 1848	N.-Amer	834626
Mueller, Georg Friedrich			Wittlensweiler	Frd.	1817	Russia	569269
Mueller, Georg Jakob & F			Trichtingen	Sulz	Jun 1817	Russia	849642
Mueller, Gottlieb			Bergfelden	Sulz	Oct 1853	N.-Amer	849629
Mueller, Gottlieb		40 yrs.	Zavelstein	Calw	1855	N.-Amer	563212
Mueller, Heinrich		6 Sep 1831	Rosenfeld	Sulz	Feb 1860	N.-Amer	849640
Mueller, Heinrich Benjamin		10 Mar 1843	Moetzingen	Herr.	1847	N.-Amer	834626
Mueller, Heinrich Eduard		11 Oct 1836	Dornstetten	Frd.	Mar 1854	N.-Amer	569273
Mueller, Jacob		7 Nov 1815	Glatten	Frd.	Jul 1852	Austria	569271
Mueller, Jacob & F		1 Apr 1813	Hoerschweiler	Frd.	Oct 1854	N.-Amer	569274
Mueller, Jacob & F			Alzenberg	Calw	1847	N.-Amer	563212
Mueller, Jacob & F		16 Dec 1803	Bondorf	Herr.	Jul 1847	N.-Amer	834626
Mueller, Jacob Friedrich		28 Dec 1833	Dornhan	Sulz	Apr 1849	N.-Amer	849633
Mueller, Jakob			Frutenhof	Frd.	Dec 1853	N.-Amer	569272
Mueller, Jakob Bernhard		27 Jul 1839	Besenfeld	Frd.	May 1846	N.-Amer	569271
Mueller, Jakob Friedrich		1826	Wuerzbach	Calw	1857	N.-Amer	563212
Mueller, Johann Christian		8 Sep 1866	Rosenfeld	Sulz	Sep 1881	N.-Amer	849626
Mueller, Johann Christian		20 Dec 1839	Bondorf	Herr.	Jul 1847	N.-Amer	834626
Mueller, Johann Friedrich		8 Aug 1849	Freudenstadt	Frd.	Sep 1854	N.-Amer	569274
Mueller, Johann Friedrich			Freudenstadt	Frd.	bef 1866	Venedig	577780
Mueller, Johann Friedrich		Aug 1828	Rosenfeld	Sulz	Oct 1857	N.-Amer	849640
Mueller, Johann Friedrich		3 Aug 1873	Rosenfeld	Sulz	Apr 1887	N.-Amer	849626
Mueller, Johann Georg		5 Nov 1828	Wittendorf	Frd.	Mar 1854	N.-Amer	569273
Mueller, Johann Georg		7 Jul 1830	Balingen	Bal.	Apr 1857	Switz.	555962
Mueller, Johann Georg		35 yrs.	Oberjettingen	Herr.	Jun 1852	N.-Amer	834627
Mueller, Johann Georg		3 yrs.	Oberjettingen	Herr.	Jun 1852	N.-Amer	834627
Mueller, Johann Georg			Gueltstein	Herr.	May 1852	N.-Amer	834627
Mueller, Johann Gottlieb			Ebingen	Bal.	1844	Switz.	555963
Mueller, Johann Heinrich		3 Apr 1840	Rosenfeld	Sulz	Jun 1859	N.-Amer	849640
Mueller, Johann Jacob			Lauterbad	Frd.	Aug 1804	Baden	550803
Mueller, Johann Jacob		27 Oct 1834	Rosenfeld	Sulz	Apr 1854	N.-Amer	849640
Mueller, Johann Jacob		8 Feb 1879	Rosenfeld	Sulz	Oct 1879	N.-Amer	849641
Mueller, Johann Jacob		2 Nov 1835	Bondorf	Herr.	Jul 1847	N.-Amer	834626
Mueller, Johann Jacob		24 Nov 1838	Moetzingen	Herr.	1847	N.-Amer	834626
Mueller, Johann Jakob		28 May 1847	Untermusbach	Frd.	Aug 1866	N.-Amer	577780
Mueller, Johann Jakob & F			Rosenfeld	Sulz	Oct 1879	N.-Amer	849641
Mueller, Johann Michael			Unterjettingen	Herr.	Jun 1852	Austral	834627
Mueller, Johann Michael & F			Unterbraendi	Sulz	Feb 1817	Russia	849635
Mueller, Johann Peter & F			Oberjesingen	Herr.	May 1852	N.-Amer	834627
Mueller, Johanna			Schoenbronn	Nag.	Mar 1854	Bavaria	838491
Mueller, Johanna		24 yrs.	Rosenfeld	Sulz	Aug 1854	N.-Amer	849640
Mueller, Johanna Margaretha			Herrenberg	Herr.	bef 1839	Switz.	834625
Mueller, Johannes			Dietersweiler	Frd.	1847	N.-Amer	577777
Mueller, Johannes		18 yrs.	Voehringen	Sulz	Oct 1853	N.-Amer	849643
Mueller, Johannes		16 Apr 1841	Trichtingen	Sulz	bef 1867	N.-Amer	849642
Mueller, Johannes		23 Nov 1841	Rosenfeld	Sulz	Nov 1863	N.-Amer	849641
Mueller, Johannes		14 May 1867	Rosenfeld	Sulz	May 1883	N.-Amer	849626

Mueller, Johannes	17 Jan 1842	Bondorf	Herr.	Jul 1847	N.-Amer	834626
Mueller, Josef	7 yrs.	Dietersweiler	Frd.	1817	Russia	569269
Mueller, Joseph & F		Dietersweiler	Frd.	1817	Russia	569269
Mueller, Julius Adolf & F		Simmozheim	Calw	1855	Saxony	563212
Mueller, Karl	4 Nov 1829	Besenfeld	Frd.	May 1846	N.-Amer	569271
Mueller, Karl	1 Jan 1874	Rosenfeld	Sulz	Oct 1889	N.-Amer	849626
Mueller, Karl Robert	28 Mar 1868	Rosenfeld	Sulz	May 1882	N.-Amer	849626
Mueller, Klara	10 Mar 1841	Altheim	Horb	bef 1869	Baden	835929
Mueller, Ludwig Gottlieb	16 Apr 1835	Dornstetten	Frd.	Mar 1854	N.-Amer	569273
Mueller, Magdalena	24 May 1841	Hoerschweiler	Frd.	Oct 1854	N.-Amer	569274
Mueller, Margaretha	30 May 1846	Hoerschweiler	Frd.	Oct 1854	N.-Amer	569274
Mueller, Maria	4 Apr 1812	Lombach	Frd.	Apr 1846	N.-Amer	569271
Mueller, Maria Barbara	7 Jul 1847	Renfrizhausen	Sulz	Sep 1868	N.-Amer	849639
Mueller, Maria Catharina (wife)		Aistaig	Sulz	Jun 1835	N.-Amer	849628
Mueller, Maria Catharina (wife)	28 Sep 1795	Aistaig	Sulz	1817	Russia	849628
Mueller, Maria Franziska & F	20 Oct 1804	Besenfeld	Frd.	May 1846	N.-Amer	569271
Mueller, Marie Margaretha		Althengstett	Calw	1869	Baden	563212
Mueller, Martin		Rosenfeld	Sulz	bef 1834	Poland	849625
Mueller, Mathaeus & F		Aistaig	Sulz	Jun 1835	N.-Amer	849628
Mueller, Mathaeus & W	21 Aug 1786	Aistaig	Sulz	1817	Russia	849628
Mueller, Mathias	11 Sep 1867	Dornhan	Sulz	Jul 1884	N.-Amer	849626
Mueller, Matthaeus	21 Aug 1845	Freudenstadt	Frd.	Apr 1864	N.-Amer	577779
Mueller, Matthias	12 Apr 1821	Wittendorf	Frd.	May 1856	N.-Amer	569275
Mueller, Matthias	16 Feb 1829	Frutenhof	Frd.	bef 1861	N.-Amer	577778
Mueller, Michael	18 Feb 1836	Besenfeld	Frd.	May 1846	N.-Amer	569271
Mueller, Michael	26 Mar 1812	Unterjettingen	Herr.	Feb 1852	N.-Amer	834627
Mueller, Pauline	28 yrs.	Oberjettingen	Herr.	Jun 1852	N.-Amer	834627
Mueller, Pauline Henriette	1 Sep 1839	Moetzingen	Herr.	1847	N.-Amer	834626
Mueller, Philipp	26 Sep 1839	Bondorf	Herr.	Jan 1865	N.-Amer	834624
Mueller, Philipp & F	73 yrs.	Oberjettingen	Herr.	Jun 1852	N.-Amer	834627
Mueller, Philipp Jacob		Oberjettingen	Herr.	Dec 1844	Bavaria	834626
Mueller, Philippine Auguste		Baiersbronn	Frd.	Apr 1808	Baden	569267
Mueller, Regina		Groembach	Frd.	Aug 1851	N.-Amer	569271
Mueller, Regina Catharina	9 Nov 1846	Bondorf	Herr.	Jul 1847	N.-Amer	834626
Mueller, Rosina	25 Jun 1817	Cresbach	Frd.	Oct 1854	N.-Amer	569274
Mueller, Sibilla Cathar. (wife)		Freudenstadt	Frd.	Sep 1854	N.-Amer	569274
Mueller, Susanna (wid.) & F		Rosenfeld	Sulz	Aug 1854	N.-Amer	849640
Mueller, Sybilla	7 Jun 1820	Dietersweiler	Frd.	Mar 1861	N.-Amer	577778
Mueller, Theodor Otto	19 yrs.	Calw	Calw	1866	N.-Amer	563212
Mueller, Theodosius		Geislingen	Bal.	1862	Baden	555962
Mueller, Theresia		Wildberg	Nag.	bef 1856	N.-Amer	838492
Mueller, Wilhelm	10 Nov 1842	Besenfeld	Frd.	May 1846	N.-Amer	569271
Mueller, Wilhelm	18 Jul 1876	Rosenfeld	Sulz	Apr 1890	N.-Amer	849626
Mueller, Wilhelmine	12 Dec 1845	Nagold	Nag.	Jan 1854	N.-Amer	838491
Muenchbach, Margretha Magd.	21 yrs.	Freudenstadt	Frd.	Jan 1843	Baden	569269
Muenster, Christian Jakob		Freudenstadt	Frd.	May 1850	France	569271
Muenster, Georg Friedrich		Freudenstadt	Frd.	Mar 1850	France	569271
Muenster, Gottfried & F		Freudenstadt	Frd.	Apr 1817	Russia	569267
Muenster, Karl Friedrich	27 Jan 1840	Freudenstadt	Frd.	Feb 1854	N.-Amer	569273
Muenster, Maria Barbara		Freudenstadt	Frd.	Apr 1843	France	569269

Name		Birth		Emigration			Film
Last	First	Date	Place	O'amt	Appl. Date	Dest.	Number
Muenster, Maria Christiane		21 Sep 1825	Freudenstadt	Frd.	Nov 1860	France	577777
Muessigman, Johann Georg			Untermusbach	Frd.	May 1840	France	569268
Mussbach, Johann georg		12 Dec 1803	Reusten	Herr.	1838	Baden	834625
Mutschler, Agnes Catharina			Sulz	Sulz	1833	N.-Amer	849625
Mutschler, Andreas		20 Apr 1869	Sterneck	Sulz	Mar 1883	N.-Amer	849642
Mutschler, Anna		3 Dec 1874	Wittershausen	Sulz	Jan 1881	Switz.	849626
Mutschler, Anna Barbara			Sulz	Sulz	1833	N.-Amer	849625
Mutschler, Anna Dorothea			Sulz	Sulz	1833	N.-Amer	849625
Mutschler, Bertha		26 Sep 1878	Wittershausen	Sulz	Jan 1881	Switz.	849626
Mutschler, Christian		16 Jan 1867	Sterneck	Sulz	Mar 1883	N.-Amer	849642
Mutschler, Christina		4 Jan 1848	Dornhan	Sulz	Sep 1869	N.-Amer	849634
Mutschler, Christine Elis. & F		6 Sep 1819	Baiersbronn	Frd.	Nov 1853	N.-Amer	569272
Mutschler, Dorothea		7 Apr 1864	Sterneck	Sulz	Mar 1883	N.-Amer	849642
Mutschler, Friederike		4 Mar 1823	Sulz	Sulz	1833	N.-Amer	849627
Mutschler, Heinrich		12 Mar 1835	Sulz	Sulz	Feb 1854	N.-Amer	849627
Mutschler, Jacob			Alpirsbach	Sulz	Aug 1825	Hungary	849625
Mutschler, Jacob & F		9 Jun 1833	Sterneck	Sulz	Mar 1883	N.-Amer	849642
Mutschler, Johann		11 May 1845	Dornhan	Sulz	Sep 1864	N.-Amer	849634
Mutschler, Johann Georg		6 Apr 1862	Sterneck	Sulz	May 1880	N.-Amer	849626
Mutschler, Johann Georg & F		18 Jun 1843	Wittershausen	Sulz	Jan 1881	Switz.	849626
Mutschler, Johann Gottlieb		20 yrs.	Sulz	Sulz	Aug 1852	N.-Amer	849627
Mutschler, Johann Jacob			Sulz	Sulz	1833	N.-Amer	849625
Mutschler, Johannes			Sulz	Sulz	1833	N.-Amer	849625
Mutschler, Johannes		1 Jun 1846	Wittershausen	Sulz	Aug 1866	N.-Amer	849644
Mutschler, Johannes		13 Nov 1875	Sterneck	Sulz	Mar 1883	N.-Amer	849642
Mutschler, Karoline		1 Aug 1871	Wittershausen	Sulz	Jan 1881	Switz.	849626
Mutschler, Karoline & C			Baiersbronn	Frd.	bef 1865	Hesse	577779
Mutschler, Luise Wil.Kar. (wife)		2 Feb 1846	Wittershausen	Sulz	Jan 1881	Switz.	849626
Mutschler, Maria (wife)		17 Aug 1833	Sterneck	Sulz	Mar 1883	N.-Amer	849642
Mutschler, Matthaeus		3 Aug 1843	Baiersbronn	Frd.	Nov 1853	N.-Amer	569272
Mutschler, Rosine Magdalene		24 Jun 1849	Baiersbronn	Frd.	Nov 1853	N.-Amer	569272
Mutschler, Sophie Louise			Sulz	Sulz	1833	N.-Amer	849625
Mutz, Adam & F		14 Jun 1814	Besenfeld	Frd.	Mar 1855	N.-Amer	569275
Mutz, Agatha		11 Nov 1854	Besenfeld	Frd.	Mar 1855	N.-Amer	569275
Mutz, Andreas		15 Dec 1840	Duerrenmettstetten	Sulz	Feb 1860	N.-Amer	849635
Mutz, Anna Maria			Cresbach	Frd.	Aug 1852	N.-Amer	569271
Mutz, Anna Maria		3 Jul 1823	Glatten	Frd.	Oct 1854	S.-Amer	569274
Mutz, Barbara		31 Dec 1841	Voehringen	Sulz	1869	N.-Amer	849643
Mutz, Eva Maria		1 May 1853	Besenfeld	Frd.	Mar 1855	N.-Amer	569275
Mutz, Eva Maria		22 Jul 1827	Besenfeld	Frd.	Mar 1855	N.-Amer	569275
Mutz, Jakob		19 yrs.	Voehringen	Sulz	Feb 1854	N.-Amer	849643
Mutz, Johann Georg		10 Aug 1810	Glatten	Frd.	Jun 1854	N.-Amer	569274
Mutz, Johann Georg		23 Sep 1867	Duerrenmettstetten	Sulz	Mar 1882	N.-Amer	849635
Mutz, Johannes		21 Sep 1848	Schopfloch	Frd.	Oct 1854	S.-Amer	569274
Mutz, Maria Magdalena			Freudenstadt	Frd.	Sep 1854	N.-Amer	569274
Mutz, Michael			Duerrenmettstetten	Sulz	Feb 1854	N.-Amer	849635
Muz, Barbara			Besenfeld	Frd.	Apr 1855	N.-Amer	569275
Muz, Jakob		31 yrs.	Glatten	Frd.	Mar 1857	N.-Amer	577776
Naeher, Franz		14 Aug 1840	Binsdorf	Sulz	Apr 1868	N.-Amer	849631
Nafz, Adele		18 Aug 1848	Altheim	Horb	bef 1869	Switz.	835929

Nafz, Christian	16 May 1828	Altheim	Horb	Apr 1854	N.-Amer	835929
Nafz, Franziska	5 Mar 1808	Altheim	Horb	Oct 1853	N.-Amer	835929
Nafz, Genovefa		Altheim	Horb	bef 1867	Prussia	835929
Nafz, Leonhardt	3 yrs.	Altheim	Horb	Jul 1849	N.-Amer	835929
Nafz, Magdalena & C	31 yrs.	Altheim	Horb	Jul 1849	N.-Amer	835929
Nafz, Scholastika	2 mon.	Altheim	Horb	Jul 1849	N.-Amer	835929
Nafz, Walburga & C	14 Apr 1824	Altheim	Horb	Apr 1850	N.-Amer	835929
Nagel, Anna	5 Jan 1838	Rosenfeld	Sulz	Aug 1865	N.-Amer	849641
Nagel, Anna Maria (wife)		Fuernsal	Sulz	Oct 1853	N.-Amer	849635
Nagel, Christian Israel	2 Feb 1840	Rosenfeld	Sulz	Apr 1870	N.-Amer	849641
Nagel, Conrad Friedrich	14 Sep 1853	Rosenfeld	Sulz	Jun 1871	N.-Amer	849641
Nagel, Elisabeth	2 Mar 1827	Marschalkenzimmern	Sulz	bef 1862	France	849638
Nagel, Friedrich	4 Jan 1846	Gaertringen	Herr.	Nov 1866	N.-Amer	834624
Nagel, Gottlieb		Neubulach	Calw	1860	N.-Amer	563212
Nagel, Jakob	3 May 1865	Floezlingen/Rottw.	Sulz	May 1885	N.-Amer	849644
Nagel, Jakob	21 Mar 1869	Rosenfeld	Sulz	Aug 1885	N.-Amer	849626
Nagel, Jakob	3 May 1865	Weiden	Sulz	May 1885	N.-Amer	849626
Nagel, Jakob & F		Fuernsal	Sulz	Oct 1853	N.-Amer	849635
Nagel, Johann Georg	7 Dec 1862	Fuernsal	Sulz	Sep 1882	N.-Amer	849626
Nagel, Johann Jacob		Rosenfeld	Sulz	Aug 1852	N.-Amer	849640
Nagel, Johann Jacob	4 Oct 1821	Kuppingen	Herr.	Dec 1865	N.-Amer	834624
Nagel, Johann Michael	9 Mar 1832	Kuppingen	Herr.	Jul 1865	N.-Amer	834624
Nagel, Karl Friedrich	5 Nov 1866	Rosenfeld	Sulz	Jun 1883	N.-Amer	849626
Nagel, Margaretha	2 Sep 1829	Kuppingen	Herr.	Dec 1865	N.-Amer	834624
Nagel, Mathias	20 Mar 1861	Fuernsal	Sulz	Nov 1880	N.-Amer	849626
Nagel, Sophie	15 Jul 1815	Bickelsberg	Sulz	Apr 1870	N.-Amer	849641
Narr, Barbara & C	13 Jun 1810	Glatten	Frd.	Oct 1854	S.-Amer	569274
Narr, Charlotte	29 Mar 1831	Loechgau	Sulz	Feb 1854	N.-Amer	849633
Narr, Katharina & C	4 Apr 1829	Aistaig	Sulz	Sep 1864	N.-Amer	849628
Narr, Luise	15 Nov 1854	Aistaig	Sulz	Sep 1864	N.-Amer	849628
Narr, Pauline	2 Mar 1838	Loechgau	Sulz	Feb 1854	N.-Amer	849633
Naschold, Christine	2 yrs.	Nagold	Nag.	Mar 1854	N.-Amer	838491
Naschold, Friedrich	5 yrs.	Nagold	Nag.	Mar 1854	N.-Amer	838491
Naschold, Johann Jacob & F		Nagold	Nag.	Mar 1854	N.-Amer	838491
Naschold, Luise		Nagold	Nag.	Mar 1854	N.-Amer	838491
Naschold, Wilhelm	8 yrs.	Nagold	Nag.	Mar 1854	N.-Amer	838491
Necker, Elise Sophia		Althenstett	Calw	1861	Baden	563212
Neher, Catharina		Boll	Sulz	bef 1863	Switz.	849632
Neher, Jacob		Balingen	Bal.	Oct 1863	Switz.	555962
Neissle, Catharina Magdalena		Simmozheim	Calw	1853	N.-Amer	563212
Nekermann, Johann & F		Sigmarswangen	Sulz	Jan 1817	Russia	849642
Nerdlinger, Johann Georg		Unterjesingen	Herr.	Sep 1846	France	834626
Nestle, August Friedrich	16 Oct 1849	Baiersbronn	Frd.	Aug 1854	N.-Amer	569274
Nestle, Barbara & C	30 yrs.	Dornstetten	Frd.	Mar 1865	N.-Amer	577779
Nestle, Bernhard David	7 Apr 1835	Freudenstadt	Frd.	Sep 1853	N.-Amer	569274
Nestle, Carl	2 yrs.	Dornstetten	Frd.	Mar 1865	N.-Amer	577779
Nestle, Carl Eberhard	25 Dec 1846	Baiersbronn	Frd.	Aug 1854	N.-Amer	569274
Nestle, Carl Friedrich		Klosterreichenbach	Frd.	May 1816	France	569268
Nestle, Catharina	13 yrs.	Altenstaig	Nag.	Jul 1852	N.-Amer	838490
Nestle, Christian	15 yrs.	Altenstaig	Nag.	Jul 1852	N.-Amer	838490

| Name | | Birth | | Emigration | | | Film |
Last	First	Date	Place	O'amt	Appl. Date	Dest.	Number
Nestle,	Christian	5 Nov 1844	Kniebis	Frd.	bef 1864	Baden	577779
Nestle,	Christian Friedrich	20 Dec 1826	Freudenstadt	Frd.	Aug 1859	France	577776
Nestle,	Christian Friedrich	22 Apr 1857	Besenfeld	Frd.	Jan 1860	Baden	577777
Nestle,	Christiane	24 yrs.	Altenstaig	Nag.	Jul 1852	N.-Amer	838490
Nestle,	Christiane Friederike		Freudenstadt	Frd.	bef 1854	Switz.	569273
Nestle,	Christina	22 yrs.	Altenstaig	Nag.	Jul 1852	N.-Amer	838490
Nestle,	Christoph & F	27 Sep 1813	Baiersbronn	Frd.	Aug 1854	N.-Amer	569274
Nestle,	Elisabetha (wife)	16 Sep 1812	Baiersbronn	Frd.	Aug 1854	N.-Amer	569274
Nestle,	Franziska	2 Oct 1832	Freudenstadt	Frd.	Sep 1859	Switz.	577776
Nestle,	Friederich	7 yrs.	Dornstetten	Frd.	Mar 1865	N.-Amer	577779
Nestle,	Friedrich		Dornstetten	Frd.	bef 1838	Switz.	569269
Nestle,	Georg Christoph	25 Feb 1837	Baiersbronn	Frd.	Aug 1854	N.-Amer	569274
Nestle,	Georg Friedrich		Dornstetten	Frd.	Mar 1807	France	569269
Nestle,	Georg Friedrich	19 Sep 1779	Dornstetten	Frd.	bef 1844	Switz.	569269
Nestle,	Jacob & F		Dornstetten	Frd.	Jun 1817	Russia	569269
Nestle,	Johann Ulrich		Klosterreichenbach	Frd.	May 1816	France	569268
Nestle,	Johannes		Freudenstadt	Frd.	Mar 1854	N.-Amer	569273
Nestle,	Julius Ferdinand	24 Jun 1831	Baiersbronn	Frd.	Aug 1854	N.-Amer	569274
Nestle,	Louise Charlotte	25 Dec 1846	Baiersbronn	Frd.	Aug 1854	N.-Amer	569274
Nestle,	Maria Cath. (wid.) & F		Altenstaig	Nag.	Jul 1852	N.-Amer	838490
Nestle,	Mathilde Cathar. Mar.	19 Oct 1844	Baiersbronn	Frd.	Aug 1854	N.-Amer	569274
Nestle,	Michael	30 Nov 1815	Pfalzgrafenweiler	Frd.	bef 1846	N.-Amer	569271
Nestle,	Rosina Dorothea & C	25 Feb 1835	Besenfeld	Frd.	Jan 1860	Baden	577777
Nestle,	Rosina Magdalena		Reichenbach	Frd.	bef 1865	France	577779
Nestle,	Rosine		Freudenstadt	Frd.	bef 1857	N.-Amer	577776
Neth,	Anna Maria (wife)		Leidringen	Sulz	Jul 1837	N.-Amer	849637
Neth,	Catharina		Leidringen	Sulz	Jul 1837	N.-Amer	849637
Neth,	Jakob		Leidringen	Sulz	bef 1837	N.-Amer	849625
Neth,	Johann Georg		Leidringen	Sulz	bef 1837	N.-Amer	849625
Neth,	Johann Jacob & F	11 Mar 1805	Leidringen	Sulz	Jul 1837	N.-Amer	849637
Neth,	Johannes		Leidringen	Sulz	bef 1827	Augsb.	849637
Neth,	Rosina		Leidringen	Sulz	May 1837	Augsb.	849637
Nettrumpf,	Johann Heinrich	1828	Neubulach	Calw	1856	N.-Amer	563212
Neuchel,	Agnes		Baiersbronn	Frd.	Mar 1857	N.-Amer	577776
Neuchel,	Karl Ludwig	21 Sep 1855	Baiersbronn	Frd.	Mar 1857	N.-Amer	577776
Neuchel,	Maria	13 Jan 1852	Baiersbronn	Frd.	Mar 1857	N.-Amer	577776
Neuchel,	Matthaeus	13 Aug 1853	Baiersbronn	Frd.	Mar 1857	N.-Amer	577776
Neuchel,	Matthaeus & F	17 Sep 1826	Baiersbronn	Frd.	Mar 1857	N.-Amer	577776
Neufer,	Margaretha & C	44 yrs.	Oberjesingen	Herr.	Jun 1832	N.-Amer	834624
Neumaier,	Georg Jakob		Stammheim	Calw	May 1874	N.-Amer	563212
Niebel,	Andreas & F	4 Oct 1798	Aistaig	Sulz	Mar 1836	N.-Amer	849628
Niebel,	Andreas & F		Dornhan	Sulz	May 1817	Russia	849633
Niebel,	Anna		Dornhan	Sulz	May 1817	Russia	849633
Niebel,	Anna Maria	24 Aug 1821	Sigmarswangen	Sulz	May 1834	N.-Amer	849627
Niebel,	Barbara		Dornhan	Sulz	Apr 1881	N.-Amer	849626
Niebel,	Christian & F	25 Nov 1792	Sigmarswangen	Sulz	May 1834	N.-Amer	849627
Niebel,	Christina		Dornhan	Sulz	May 1817	Russia	849633
Niebel,	Christina Barbara	5 May 1830	Sigmarswangen	Sulz	May 1834	N.-Amer	849627
Niebel,	Christine Barb. (wife)		Sigmarswangen	Sulz	May 1834	N.-Amer	849627
Niebel,	Gottlieb Friedrich	14 Oct 1812	Sigmarswangen	Sulz	May 1834	N.-Amer	849627

Niebel, Jacob		Dornhan	Sulz	May 1817	Russia	849633
Niebel, Johann Christian	12 Aug 1832	Sigmarswangen	Sulz	May 1834	N. Amer	849627
Niebel, Johann Georg		Fuernsal	Sulz	1829	France	849635
Niebel, Johanne Christine	7 Feb 1827	Sigmarswangen	Sulz	May!1834	N.-Amer	849627
Niebel, Johannes	5 Jun 1824	Sigmarswangen	Sulz	May 1834	N.-Amer	849627
Niebel, Mathias		Dornhan	Sulz	May 1817	Russia	849633
Niebel, Ursula (wife)		Aistaig	Sulz	Mar 1836	N.-Amer	849628
Niethammer, Andreas	19 Apr 1847	Rohrau	Herr.	Feb 1870	N.-Amer	834624
Niethammer, Anna Cathar. (wife)		Unterjettingen	Herr.	Jun 1831	N.-Amer	834624
Niethammer, Anna Maria	17 Aug 1851	Rohrau	Herr.	Feb 1870	N.-Amer	834624
Niethammer, Anna Maria (wife)		Trichtingen	Sulz	bef 1867	Switz.	849636
Niethammer, Barbara		Holzbronn	Calw	1856	Switz.	563212
Niethammer, Eugen Friedrich	1839	Hirsau	Calw	1859	N.-Amer	563212
Niethammer, Johann Christian		Nagold	Nag.	bef 1864	N.-Amer	838494
Niethammer, Johann Georg	1836	Holzbronn	Calw	1854	N.-Amer	563212
Niethammer, Johann Georg	29 Jun 1815	Unterjettingen	Herr.	Jul 1852	N.-Amer	834627
Niethammer, Johann Georg & F		Unterjettingen	Herr.	Apr 1836	N.-Amer	834624
Niethammer, Johann Gottlieb	1830	Holzbronn	Calw	1854	N.-Amer	563212
Niethammer, Johann Jacob		Holzbronn	Calw	1859	Prussia	563212
Niethammer, Johann Jacob & W		Unterjettingen	Herr.	Jun 1831	N.-Amer	834624
Niethammer, Magdalena		Sulz	Nag.	Feb 1854	N.-Amer	838491
Niethammer, Maria		Holzbronn	Calw	1861	Frankf.	563212
Niethammer, Mathias & F		Trichtingen	Sulz	bef 1867	Switz.	849636
' Niethhammer, Albert	12 Nov 1848	Moetzingen	Herr.	May 1852	N.-Amer	834627
Niethhammer, Dorothea Elisab.	31 Dec 1840	Moetzingen	Herr.	May 1852	N.-Amer	834627
Niethhammer, Georg Fried. & F	4 Oct 1807	Moetzingen	Herr.	May 1852	N.-Amer	834627
Niethhammer, Georg Friedrich	11 Feb 1842	Moetzingen	Herr.	May 1852	N.-Amer	834627
Niethhammer, Gottliebin	12 Feb 1837	Moetzingen	Herr.	May 1852	N.-Amer	834627
Niethhammer, Johann Georg	5 Feb 1846	Moetzingen	Herr.	May 1852	N.-Amer	834627
Niethhammer, Maria Regina	28 Nov 1833	Moetzingen	Herr.	May 1852	N.-Amer	834627
Niethhammer, Regina Gottl.wife	6 Jan 1809	Moetzingen	Herr.	May 1852	N.-Amer	834627
Niggel, Anton & F		Binsdorf	Sulz	Feb 1839	N.-Amer	849630
Niggel, Dominika	30 Nov 1839	Binsdorf	Sulz	Jun 1854	N.-Amer	849630
Niggel, Elisabetha (wife)		Binsdorf	Sulz	Mar 1851	N.-Amer	849630
Niggel, Fidel	19 yrs.	Binsdorf	Sulz	Apr 1835	Wien	849630
Niggel, Franziska	28 yrs.	Binsdorf	Sulz	Jul 1863	Baden	849631
Niggel, Franziska (wife)		Binsdorf	Sulz	Apr 1835	Wien	849630
Niggel, Genovefa	9 Dec 1836	Binsdorf	Sulz	Jun 1854	N.-Amer	849630
Niggel, Johann	14 Aug 1806	Binsdorf	Sulz	Feb 1834	Wien	849630
Niggel, Johann Georg		Binsdorf	Sulz	Feb 1834	Wien	849630
Niggel, Johannes	27 Dec 1848	Binsdorf	Sulz	Mar 1866	N.-Amer	849631
Niggel, Jordan	27 yrs.	Binsdorf	Sulz	Apr 1835	Wien	849630
Niggel, Joseph	12 yrs.	Binsdorf	Sulz	Apr 1835	Wien	849630
Niggel, Juditha	18 yrs.	Binsdorf	Sulz	Apr 1835	Wien	849630
Niggel, Konrad	26 Nov 1845	Binsdorf	Sulz	bef 1871	N.-Amer	849631
Niggel, Maria & C		Binsdorf	Sulz	Feb 1852	N.-Amer	849630
Niggel, Marianne	4 Dec 1838	Binsdorf	Sulz	Jun 1854	N.-Amer	849630
Niggel, Markus	25 Apr 1849	Binsdorf	Sulz	Apr 1869	N.-Amer	849631
Niggel, Mathaeus	8 Sep 1849	Binsdorf	Sulz	Apr 1869	N.-Amer	849631
Niggel, Matheus	17 Sep 1828	Binsdorf	Sulz	Jun 1854	N.-Amer	849630

Name		Birth		Emigration			Film
Last	First	Date	Place	O'amt	Appl. Date	Dest.	Number
Niggel, Matheus		5 yrs.	Binsdorf	Sulz	Mar 1851	N.-Amer	849630
Niggel, Maximillian		17 Nov 1847	Binsdorf	Sulz	Jun 1866	N.-Amer	849631
Niggel, Peter		9 Apr 1849	Binsdorf	Sulz	Apr 1867	N.-Amer	849631
Niggel, Philipina		18 mon.	Binsdorf	Sulz	Feb 1839	N.-Amer	849630
Niggel, Regulat & F		5 Oct 1806	Binsdorf	Sulz	Mar 1851	N.-Amer	849630
Niggel, Richard		18 yrs.	Binsdorf	Sulz	Mar 1851	N.-Amer	849630
Niggel, Roman			Binsdorf	Sulz	May 1817	Poland	849630
Niggel, Roman		23 Sep 1856	Binsdorf	Sulz	Apr 1872	N.-Amer	849631
Niggel, Rudolf		18 Apr 1865	Binsdorf	Sulz	Feb 1882	N.-Amer	849631
Niggel, Rudolph		6 Dec 1804	Binsdorf	Sulz	Apr 1835	Wien	849630
Niggel, Rudolph & F		9 Mar 1774	Binsdorf	Sulz	Apr 1835	Wien	849630
Niggel, Sales			Binsdorf	Sulz	Apr 1835	Wien	849630
Niggel, Therese		22 Sep 1833	Binsdorf	Sulz	Jun 1854	N.-Amer	849630
Niggel, Viktoria		8 yrs.	Binsdorf	Sulz	Mar 1851	N.-Amer	849630
Nikel, Dominik			Binsdorf	Sulz	Feb 1817	Russia	849630
Nikel, Joseph		22 Sep 1789	Leinstetten	Sulz	Jun 1817	N.-Amer	849638
Nikolaus, Catharina Regina		59 yrs.	Teinach	Calw	Mar 1847	N.-Amer	563212
Nixdorf, Louis & F			Rosenfeld	Sulz	Jul 1853	N.-Amer	849640
Nolle, Christiane			Calw	Calw	1869	Baden	563212
Nolle, Johann Georg		26 yrs.	Zwerenberg	Calw	1869	N.-Amer	563212
Nonnenmacher, Anna Maria (wife)		18 Sep 1802	Moetzingen	Herr.	Feb 1847	N.-Amer	834626
Nonnenmacher, Catharina Barb.		26 Nov 1832	Moetzingen	Herr.	Feb 1847	N.-Amer	834626
Nonnenmacher, Christian		2 Jun 1838	Moetzingen	Herr.	Mar 1847	N.-Amer	834626
Nonnenmacher, Christoph & F		14 Dec 1801	Moetzingen	Herr.	Feb 1847	N.-Amer	834626
Nonnenmacher, Johann Georg		31 Dec 1828	Moetzingen	Herr.	Feb 1847	N.-Amer	834626
Nonnenmacher, Magdalena		27 May 1842	Moetzingen	Herr.	Mar 1847	N.-Amer	834626
Nonnenmann, Jakob			Unterreichenbach	Calw	Nov 1873	Palest.	563212
Nopfeld, Maria Friedrike			Calw	Calw	bef 1855	N.-Amer	563212
Noppel, Sibilla			Hildrizhausen	Herr.	Jun 1841	Switz.	834625
Nothacker, Anna Barbara			Sommenhardt	Calw	May 1871	N.-Amer	563212
Nothacker, Dorothea			Sommenhardt	Calw	May 1871	N.-Amer	563212
Nothacker, Johannes & F			Roetenbach	Calw	1852	N.-Amer	563212
Nothacker, Ludwig (wid.) & F			Roetenbach	Calw	1854	N.-Amer	563212
Nothacker, Peter		1836	Emberg	Calw	1856	N.-Amer	563212
Nothardt, Mathaeus		1834	Emberg	Calw	1857	N.-Amer	563212
Nothfelder, Regina		Jan 1834	Ostelsheim	Calw	1854	N.-Amer	563212
Nuebel, (wid.) & F			Freudenstadt	Frd.	Sep 1854	N.-Amer	569274
Nuebel, Anna maria		2 Oct 1834	Wittlensweiler	Frd.	Aug 1854	N.-Amer	569274
Nuebel, Carl Friedrich		17 Jan 1844	Freudenstadt	Frd.	Sep 1854	N.-Amer	569274
Nuebel, Friederike			Freudenstadt	Frd.	Mar 1854	N.-Amer	569273
Nuebel, Gustav Adolph		16 Jul 1847	Freudenstadt	Frd.	Sep 1854	N.-Amer	569274
Nuebel, Johann Jakob		3 Apr 1845	Freudenstadt	Frd.	Sep 1854	N.-Amer	569274
Nuebel, Johann Jakob Georg		28 Apr 1841	Freudenstadt	Frd.	Sep 1854	N.-Amer	569274
Nuebel, Johanna Sophie		25 Mar 1839	Freudenstadt	Frd.	Sep 1854	N.-Amer	569274
Nuessle, Anna Catharina		27 Jun 1845	Kuppingen	Herr.	Mar 1848	N.-Amer	834626
Nuessle, Anna Maria		22 May 1843	Kuppingen	Herr.	Mar 1848	N.-Amer	834626
Nuessle, Anna Maria & C			Deckenpfronn	Calw	1855	N.-Amer	563212
Nuessle, Anna Maria & C			Kuppingen	Herr.	Feb 1847	N.-Amer	834626
Nuessle, Anna Maria & C		16 Jan 1823	Kuppingen	Herr.	Mar 1848	N.-Amer	834626
Nuessle, Anna Maria (wife)		26 Aug 1815	Kuppingen	Herr.	Feb 1847	N.-Amer	834626

Nuessle, Caroline	17 Oct 1845	Kuppingen	Herr.	Feb 1847	N.-Amer	834626
Nuessle, Caroline	17 Oct 1845	Kuppingen	Herr.	Mar 1848	N.-Amer	834626
Nuessle, Daniel	2 Sep 1834	Affstaett	Herr.	Apr 1847	N.-Amer	834626
Nuessle, Eva Catharina & C	26 Sep 1825	Kuppingen	Herr.	Mar 1848	N.-Amer	834626
Nuessle, Friedrich & F		Affstaett	Herr.	Apr 1847	N.-Amer	834626
Nuessle, Gottliebin	12 Jan 1842	Affstaett	Herr.	Apr 1847	N.-Amer	834626
Nuessle, Gottliebin (wife)	49 yrs.	Affstaett	Herr.	Apr 1847	N.-Amer	834626
Nuessle, Jakob Friedrich	18 Sep 1845	Kuppingen	Herr.	Feb 1847	N.-Amer	834626
Nuessle, Jakob Friedrich	28 yrs.	Kuppingen	Herr.	Feb 1847	N.-Amer	834626
Nuessle, Jakob Friedrich & F	57 yrs.	Kuppingen	Herr.	Mar 1848	N.-Amer	834626
Nuessle, Johann Friedrich	11 Aug 1830	Oberjesingen	Herr.	May 1862	N.-Amer	834624
Nuessle, Johann Georg	20 Feb 1846	Oberjesingen	Herr.	May 1862	N.-Amer	834624
Nuessle, Johann Georg	26 Mar 1826	Affstaett	Herr.	Apr 1847	N.-Amer	834626
Nuessle, Jost & F	26 Jan 1817	Kuppingen	Herr.	Feb 1847	N.-Amer	834626
Nuessle, Maria Magdalena	28 Aug 1824	Kuppingen	Herr.	Feb 1847	N.-Amer	834626
Nuessle, Simon Friedrich	47 Yrs.	Affstaett	Herr.	Apr 1847	N.-Amer	834626
Nuessle, Simon Friedrich	12 Mar 1830	Affstaett	Herr.	Apr 1847	N.-Amer	834626
Nufer, Anna Maria	16 Dec 1824	Oberjesingen	Herr.	1848	N.-Amer	834626
Nufer, Christian	28 Nov 1846	Oberjesingen	Herr.	1848	N.-Amer	834626
Nufer, Christiane (wife)	29 May 1813	Oberjesingen	Herr.	1848	N.-Amer	834626
Nufer, Daniel	9 May 1848	Oberjesingen	Herr.	1848	N.-Amer	834626
Nufer, Jakob Friedrich	20 Mar 1835	Oberjesingen	Herr.	1848	N.-Amer	834626
Nufer, Johann Friedrich & F	1 Jan 1799	Oberjesingen	Herr.	1848	N.-Amer	834626
Nufer, Johann Georg	8 Oct 1840	Oberjesingen	Herr.	1848	N.-Amer	834626
Nuffer, Anna Barbara	15 Jul 1829	Oberjesingen	Herr.	bef 1852	N.-Amer	834627
Nuffer, Jakob Friedrich	3 Sep 1838	Oberjesingen	Herr.	Sep 1852	N.-Amer	834627
Nuffer, Johann	24 Jan 1824	Oberjesingen	Herr.	Sep 1852	N.-Amer	834627
Nuffer, Johann Michael	11 Mar 1821	Oberjesingen	Herr.	Sep 1852	N.-Amer	834627
Nuffer, Johann Michael & F		Oberjesingen	Herr.	Sep 1852	N.-Amer	834627
Nuffer, Johann Peter	14 Sep 1833	Oberjesingen	Herr.	bef 1852	N.-Amer	834627
Nuffer, Johannes	19 Nov 1826	Oberjesingen	Herr.	Sep 1852	N.-Amer	834627
Nuoffer, Catharina Friedrike	17 Aug 1850	Gueltstein	Herr.	Apr 1852	N.-Amer	834627
Nuoffer, Ferdinand & F		Gueltstein	Herr.	Apr 1852	N.-Amer	834627
Nuoffer, Jakob	10 Dec 1812	Herrenberg	Herr.	bef 1846	Hungary	834626
Nuoffer, Johann Martin & F		Gechingen	Calw	1855	N.-Amer	563212
Nuoffer, Johanna Philippine	14 Sep 1851	Gueltstein	Herr.	Apr 1852	N.-Amer	834627
Nuoffer, Philippine (wife)		Gueltstein	Herr.	Apr 1852	N.-Amer	834627
Nusskern, Magdalena		Wittlensweiler	Frd.	Apr 1817	Russia	569268
Nusskern, Sophie Christiane	1 Jun 1845	Freudenstadt	Frd.	Nov 1865	Saxony	577780
Obergfell, Andreas	Jul 1780	Dornstetten	Frd.	bef 1839	Austria	569269
Obergfell, Andreas	22 Aug 1809	Dornstetten	Frd.	Jun 1838	N.-Amer	569269
Obergfell, Barbara		Dornstetten	Frd.	Jul 1866	N.-Amer	577780
Obergfell, Christian	9 Jun 1824	Dornstetten	Frd.	Apr 1847	N.-Amer	569270
Obergfell, Friedrich	19 Sep 1806	Dornstetten	Frd.	Jun 1838	N.-Amer	569269
Obergfell, Gottlieb	1 Feb 1815	Dornstetten	Frd.	Feb 1846	N.-Amer	569271
Obergfell, Johann Friedrich	25 Jan 1834	Dornstetten	Frd.	bef 1854	N.-Amer	569273
Obergfell, Johann Jakob	16 Dec 1825	Dornstetten	Frd.	May 1848	N.-Amer	569270
Obergfell, Johann Jakob	30 Apr 1836	Dornstetten	Frd.	Feb 1853	N.-Amer	569272
Oehler, Anna Maria		Dornhan	Sulz	bef 1815	Russia	849625
Oehlschlaeger, Margarethe		Moettlingen	Calw	1853	N.-Amer	563212

Name		Birth		Emigration			Film
Last	First	Date	Place	O'amt	Appl. Date	Dest.	Number
Oehrlich, Anna Maria (wife)		28 Feb 1794	Bondorf	Herr.	Jul 1847	N.-Amer	834626
Oehrlich, Barbara (wife)		26 Aug 1837	Bondorf	Herr.	Oct 1865	N.-Amer	834624
Oehrlich, Christian			Bondorf	Herr.	Apr 1836	N.-Amer	834624
Oehrlich, Christian & F		24 Sep 1797	Bondorf	Herr.	Jul 1847	N.-Amer	834626
Oehrlich, Christian Friedrich			Bondorf	Herr.	bef 1848	N.-Amer	834626
Oehrlich, Friedrich Christian		30 May 1828	Bondorf	Herr.	Jun 1848	N.-Amer	834626
Oehrlich, Johann Michael		8 May 1835	Bondorf	Herr.	Jul 1862	N.-Amer	834624
Oehrlich, Katharina Wilhelm.		7 Mar 1862	Bondorf	Herr.	Oct 1865	N.-Amer	834624
Oehrlich, Maria		12 Oct 1807	Bondorf	Herr.	Apr 1847	N.-Amer	834626
Oehrlich, Maria Friederike		18 Oct 1832	Bondorf	Herr.	Jul 1847	N.-Amer	834626
Oehrlich, Wilhelm Friedr. & F		6 Dec 1835	Bondorf	Herr.	Oct 1865	N.-Amer	834624
Oerthle, Jakob		10 Dec 1812	Herrenberg	Herr.	bef 1846	Hungary	834626
Oerthle, Johann Gottlieb		24 Jan 1812	Herrenberg	Herr.	Jul 1846	N.-Amer	834626
Oesterle, Anna Catharina		3 Dec 1836	Affstaett	Herr.	Apr 1847	N.-Amer	834626
Oesterle, Anna Catharina (wife)		45 yrs.	Affstaett	Herr.	Apr 1847	N.-Amer	834626
Oesterle, Anna Maria		1 yrs.	Edelweiler	Frd.	Jul 1857	N.-Amer	577776
Oesterle, Anna Maria & F		6 Jan 1815	Groembach	Frd.	Sep 1848	N.-Amer	569270
Oesterle, Christian		16 Feb 1837	Groembach	Frd.	Sep 1848	N.-Amer	569270
Oesterle, Christiana		26 May 1841	Groembach	Frd.	Sep 1848	N.-Amer	569270
Oesterle, Christine		31 Jan 1838	Pfalzgrafenweiler	Frd.	Mar 1855	N.-Amer	569275
Oesterle, David		24 Sep 1845	Groembach	Frd.	Sep 1848	N.-Amer	569270
Oesterle, Elisabetha		18 Jan 1843	Affstaett	Herr.	Apr 1847	N.-Amer	834626
Oesterle, Elisabetha & C			Edelweiler	Frd.	Jul 1857	N.-Amer	577776
Oesterle, Eva			Tumlingen	Frd.	Feb 1855	N.-Amer	569275
Oesterle, Friederich			Tumlingen	Frd.	Mar 1856	N.-Amer	569275
Oesterle, Friedrich		24 Nov 1833	Pfalzgrafenweiler	Frd.	bef 1853	N.-Amer	569272
Oesterle, Friedrich			Roet	Frd.	Aug 1865	N.-Amer	577779
Oesterle, Jacob			Aichelberg	Calw	1860	N.-Amer	563212
Oesterle, Jacob Friedrich		14 Nov 1850	Gaertringen	Herr.	Sep 1869	N.-Amer	834624
Oesterle, Jakob Friedrich		5 Apr 1839	Groembach	Frd.	Sep 1848	N.-Amer	569270
Oesterle, Johann			Woernersberg	Frd.	Jan 1809	Baden	569268
Oesterle, Johann Adam		18 Jun 1841	Pfalzgrafenweiler	Frd.	Mar 1855	N.-Amer	569275
Oesterle, Johann Georg		4 Mar 1833	Groembach	Frd.	Sep 1848	N.-Amer	569270
Oesterle, Johann Georg			Groembach	Frd.	bef 1848	N.-Amer	569270
Oesterle, Johann Georg		4 Dec 1830	Affstaett	Herr.	Apr 1847	N.-Amer	834626
Oesterle, Johann Georg & F		48 yrs.	Affstaett	Herr.	Apr 1847	N.-Amer	834626
Oesterle, Johann Jacob		7 May 1844	Unterjettingen	Herr.	Apr 1862	N.-Amer	834624
Oesterle, Johann Michael		22 Nov 1833	Affstaett	Herr.	Apr 1847	N.-Amer	834626
Oesterle, Johannes			Tumlingen	Frd.	bef 1854	N.-Amer	569273
Oesterle, Margaretha		8 May 1840	Affstaett	Herr.	Apr 1847	N.-Amer	834626
Oesterle, Maria		25 Jan 1835	Groembach	Frd.	Sep 1848	N.-Amer	569270
Oesterle, Michael & F			Rodt	Frd.	Apr 1817	Russia	569268
Oesterle, Michael Friedrich			Roet	Frd.	Apr 1865	N.-Amer	577779
Oesterle, Rosina		24 Sep 1831	Pfalzgrafenweiler	Frd.	Mar 1854	N.-Amer	569273
Oetinger, Carl Friedrich		12 Aug 1834	Grunbach	Schd.	Mar 1844	Austria	801461
Oetinger, Caroline Jacobine		1 Dec 1805	Grunbach	Schd.	Mar 1844	Austria	801461
Oettle, Johannes		6 Nov 1819	Oberurbach	Schd.	Mar 1844	N.-Amer	801461
Oettle, Sabina		8 Jun 1807	Streich	Schd.	Apr 1842	N.-Amer	801461
Ohngemach, Christina Barbara			Liebelsberg	Calw	1856	N.-Amer	563212
Ohngemach, Jacob Friedrich			Neubulach	Calw	1852	France	563212

Ohngemach, Johann Georg		Altbulach	Calw	1860	Graz	563212
Ohngemach, Johann Georg		Stammheim	Calw	1853	N. Amer	563212
Ohngemach, Maria Agnes		Liebelsberg	Calw	1856	N.-Amer	563212
Ohngemach, Wilhelmine		Stammheim	Calw	Jun 1873	N.-Amer	563212
Ohnmacht, Johann Martin	22 Jun 1808	Nennethausen	Sulz	Aug 1833	Baden	849636
Oster, Andreas	28 Jan 1803	Moetzingen	Herr.	May 1852	N.-Amer	834627
Oster, Anna Barbara	10 Jun 1835	Reusten	Herr.	May 1854	N.-Amer	834624
Oster, Catharina	18 Jun 1826	Reusten	Herr.	May 1854	N.-Amer	834624
Oster, Elisabeth (wid.) & F		Gueltstein	Herr.	Apr 1831	N.-Amer	834624
Oster, Jonathan	24 Jun 1831	Reusten	Herr.	May 1867	N.-Amer	834624
Ostertag, Anna Maria	22 Feb 1825	Dornstetten	Frd.	Mar 1848	N.-Amer	569270
Ostertag, Anna Maria (wid.)& F		Dornstetten	Frd.	Aug 1850	N.-Amer	569271
Ostertag, Gottlieb & W		Dornstetten	Frd.	Nov 1848	N.-Amer	569270
Ostertag, Johann Friedrich	19 Feb 1832	Dornstetten	Frd.	Aug 1850	N.-Amer	569271
Ostertag, Johann Gottlieb	31 Aug 1816	Dornstetten	Frd.	Apr 1847	N.-Amer	569270
Ostertag, Johann Jakob	5 Aug 1828	Dornstetten	Frd.	Aug 1850	N.-Amer	569271
Ostertag, Johanna Friederika	30 Apr 1822	Dornstetten	Frd.	Apr 1847	N.-Amer	569270
Ostertag, Ludwig		Dornstetten	Frd.	1817	Russia	569269
Ostertag, Ludwig	16 Aug 1814	Dornstetten	Frd.	Oct 1850	N.-Amer	569271
Ostertag, Ludwig & F		Dornstetten	Frd.	1817	Russia	569269
Oswald, Carl Christoph	19 yrs.	Klosterreichenbach	Frd.	Apr 1832	N.-Amer	569268
Oswald, Chrischona		Dornstetten	Frd.	Sep 1853	N.-Amer	569272
Oswald, Christian Ludwig	17 yrs.	Klosterreichenbach	Frd.	Apr 1832	N.-Amer	569268
Ott, Anna	5 yrs.	Bickelsberg	Sulz	Jun 1817	Hungary	849625
Ott, Anna Maria	26 Jun 1818	Bickelsberg	Sulz	May 1837	N.-Amer	849625
Ott, Anna Maria	26 yrs.	Freudenstadt	Frd.	May 1752	Pen.N-A	550803
Ott, Anna Maria	7 yrs.	Bickelsberg	Sulz	Jun 1817	Hungary	849625
Ott, Anna Maria		Bickelsberg	Sulz	Feb 1837	N.-Amer	849644
Ott, Anna Maria	27 Jun 1818	Bickelsberg	Sulz	Mar 1837	N.-Amer	849630
Ott, Barbara (wife)		Bickelsberg	Sulz	Apr 1838	N.-Amer	849630
Ott, Christina	12 yrs.	Bickelsberg	Sulz	Jun 1817	Hungary	849625
Ott, Clemens		Bickelsberg	Sulz	May 1837	N.-Amer	849625
Ott, Clemens	9 yrs.	Bickelsberg	Sulz	Jun 1817	Hungary	849625
Ott, Clemens & F	36 yrs.	Bickelsberg	Sulz	Jun 1817	Hungary	849625
Ott, Clemens & F		Bickelsberg	Sulz	Jul 1817	Russia	849630
Ott, Clemenz		Bickelsberg	Sulz	Apr 1838	N.-Amer	849630
Ott, Clemenz & F	11 Oct 1808	Bickelsberg	Sulz	Apr 1838	N.-Amer	849630
Ott, Cosmos David	19 Jan 1877	Bettenhausen	Sulz	Dec 1884	N.-Amer	849626
Ott, Friedrich	4 Mar 1838	Hallwangen	Frd.	May 1860	N.-Amer	577777
Ott, Johann Georg		Bickelsberg	Sulz	Apr 1838	N.-Amer	849630
Ott, Johann Georg & F	32 yrs.	Freudenstadt	Frd.	May 1752	Pen.N-A	550803
Ott, Johann Jacob	11 yrs.	Bickelsberg	Sulz	Jun 1817	Hungary	849625
Ott, Johann Jacob		Bickelsberg	Sulz	Apr 1838	N.-Amer	849630
Ott, Johannes	6 mon.	Freudenstadt	Frd.	May 1752	Pen.N-A	550803
Ott, Johannes	4 Dec 1807	Bickelsberg	Sulz	Jul 1851	N.-Amer	849630
Ott, Johannes	25 Apr 1878	Dornhan	Sulz	Jul 1893	N.-Amer	849626
Ott, Johannes & F	22 Apr 1844	Bettenhausen	Sulz	Dec 1884	N.-Amer	849626
Ott, Maximillian	28 Dec 1877	Bettenhausen	Sulz	Dec 1884	N.-Amer	849626
Ott, Rosina	2 yrs.	Freudenstadt	Frd.	May 1752	Pen.N-A	550803
Ott, Theresia (wife)	30 Aug 1850	Bettenhausen	Sulz	Dec 1884	N.-Amer	849626

Name		Birth		Emigration			Film
Last	First	Date	Place	O'amt	Appl. Date	Dest.	Number
Ott, Ursula (wife)		38 yrs.	Bickelsberg	Sulz	Jun 1817	Hungary	849625
Ottmar, Anna Maria			Zwerenberg	Calw	1853	N.-Amer	563212
Ottmar, Jacob		21 yrs.	Zwerenberg	Calw	1867	N.-Amer	563212
Ottmar, Jakob Friedrich		1838	Zwerenberg	Calw	1856	N.-Amer	563212
Ottmar, Johann		1836	Zwerenberg	Calw	1854	N.-Amer	563212
Ottmar, Michael		1840	Zwerenberg	Calw	1857	N.-Amer	563212
Pabst, Creszentia			Ottersweier/Baden	Frd.	Aug 1845	N.-Amer	569269
Palm, Gottfried			Ebingen	Bal.	Sep 1844	N.-Amer	555964
Palmer, Johann David & F			Hebsack	Schd.	Feb 1834	N.-Amer	801460
Palmer, Johann Dorothea			Hebsack	Schd.	Feb 1834	N.-Amer	801460
Palmer, Louise Heinrika		6 yrs.	Hebsack	Schd.	Feb 1834	N.-Amer	801460
Palmer, Philipp Jacob		3 yrs.	Hebsack	Schd.	Feb 1834	N.-Amer	801460
Palmer, Rosina Magdalena			Hebsack	Schd.	Jun 1833	Russia	801460
Paulus, Johann Gottlieb		32 yrs.	Deckenpfronn	Calw	Mar 1847	N.-Amer	563212
Pfaeffle, Christina & C		9 Aug 1833	Rosenfeld	Sulz	bef 1861	Switz.	849641
Pfaeffle, Johannes			Ostelsheim	Calw	1853	N.-Amer	563212
Pfaeffle, Maria Adelheid		27 Apr 1858	Rosenfeld	Sulz	Feb 1861	Switz.	849641
Pfaeffle, Martha		22 Oct 1818	Tailfingen	Herr.	Sep 1852	N.-Amer	834627
Pfaefflin, Albert Wilhelm Fr.			Rosenfeld	Sulz	Jul 1853	N.-Amer	849640
Pfaefflin, Carl Christian Fr.		6 Jul 1837	Rosenfeld	Sulz	Apr 1854	N.-Amer	849640
Pfaefflin, Carl Friedrich			Rosenfeld	Sulz	May 1815	Austria	849625
Pfaefflin, Christoph Friedr.		25 May 1829	Rosenfeld	Sulz	May 1854	N.-Amer	849640
Pfaefflin, Paul Friedr. Eugen			Rosenfeld	Sulz	Aug 1852	N.-Amer	849640
Pfau, Anna & C			Boeffingen	Frd.	Jan 1854	N.-Amer	569273
Pfau, Anna Maria			Boeffingen	Frd.	Feb 1854	N.-Amer	569273
Pfau, Barbara			Boeffingen	Frd.	Feb 1854	N.-Amer	569273
Pfau, Barbara		16 Oct 1838	Dornhan	Sulz	Apr 1854	N.-Amer	849633
Pfau, Christina (wife)			Aistaig	Sulz	Mar 1833	N.-Amer	849628
Pfau, Christine			Boeffingen	Frd.	Feb 1854	N.-Amer	569273
Pfau, Christine		18 Feb 1804	Reinerzau	Frd.	Jun 1837	Basel	569268
Pfau, Dorothea			Boeffingen	Frd.	Jan 1854	N.-Amer	569273
Pfau, Dorothea		7 May 1819	Lossburg	Frd.	May 1847	N.-Amer	569271
Pfau, Dorothea		2 mo.	Aistaig	Sulz	Mar 1833	N.-Amer	849628
Pfau, Eva		26 Apr 1811	Reinerzau	Frd.	Jan 1845	France	569271
Pfau, Friedrich & F		5 Mar 1802	Aistaig	Sulz	Mar 1833	N.-Amer	849628
Pfau, Georg			Boeffingen	Frd.	Feb 1854	N.-Amer	569273
Pfau, Georg		25 Jun 1834	Dornhan	Sulz	May 1853	N.-Amer	849633
Pfau, Jacob			Dornhan	Sulz	Apr 1847	N.-Amer	849633
Pfau, Jakob		7 Jan 1868	Dottenweiler	Sulz	May 1883	N.-Amer	849626
Pfau, Johann Georg		24 Apr 1834	Unteriflingen	Frd.	Jun 1854	N.-Amer	569274
Pfau, Johann Georg			Geroldsweiler	Sulz	Apr 1873	N.-Amer	849642
Pfau, Johann Georg		28 Jul 1835	Hopfau	Sulz	Nov 1866	Baden	849636
Pfau, Johannes		2 yrs.	Aistaig	Sulz	Mar 1833	N.-Amer	849628
Pfau, Johannes			Dornhan	Sulz	1847	N.-Amer	849633
Pfau, Mathes		24 Aug 1820	Unterwies	Frd.	Aug 1854	N.-Amer	569274
Pfau, Mathias		28 Sep 1870	Dornhan	Sulz	Jan 1888	N.-Amer	849626
Pfaus, Anna Maria			Zavelstein	Calw	Oct 1870	Tyrol	563212
Pfaus, Anna Maria			Zavelstein	Calw	1849	Baden	563212
Pfaus, Augustin		33 yrs.	Oberjesingen	Herr.	Oct 1846	N.-Amer	834626
Pfaus, Catharina (wid.)		49 yrs.	Oberjesingen	Herr.	Oct 1846	N.-Amer	834626

Pfaus, Michael	9 yrs	Oberjesingen	Herr.	Oct 1846	N.-Amer	834626
Pfaus, Salome	18 yrs.	Oberjesingen	Herr.	Oct 1846	N.-Amer	834626
Pfaus, Thomas	21 yrs.	Oberjesingen	Herr.	Oct 1846	N.-Amer	834626
Pfautz, Adolph	1840	Calw	Calw	1860	N.-Amer	563212
Pfeffer, Christian	21 Nov 1827	Calw	Calw	bef 1857	N.-Amer	563212
Pfeffer, Josefine (wife)		Poltringen	Herr.	Jan 1852	N.-Amer	834627
Pfeffer, Magdalena	20 Feb 1851	Poltringen	Herr.	Jan 1852	N.-Amer	834627
Pfeffer, Rochus	3 Feb 1850	Poltringen	Herr.	Jan 1852	N.-Amer	834627
Pfeffer, Rochus & F		Poltringen	Herr.	Jan 1852	N.-Amer	834627
Pfefferle, Barbara		Oberiflingen	Frd.	Apr 1847	N.-Amer	569270
Pfefferle, Christine	26 Nov 1822	Neuneck	Frd.	Feb 1850	N.-Amer	569271
Pfefferle, Elisabetha		Oberiflingen	Frd.	Apr 1847	N.-Amer	569270
Pfefferle, Eva & F		Oberiflingen	Frd.	Apr 1847	N.-Amer	569270
Pfefferle, Friedrich		Oberiflingen	Frd.	Apr 1847	N.-Amer	569270
Pfefferle, Johann Burkhard		Endingen	Bal.	Jul 1853	Berlin	555962
Pfefferle, Johann Fridrich	20 yrs.	Neuneck	Frd.	May 1752	Pen.N-A	550803
Pfefferle, Johann Georg		Oberiflingen	Frd.	Apr 1847	N.-Amer	569270
Pfefferle, Johannes		Oberiflingen	Frd.	Mar 1847	N.-Amer	569270
Pfefferle, Martin		Endingen	Bal.	Dec 1844	N.-Amer	555964
Pfeifer, Johann Jakob	6 Apr 1816	Groembach	Frd.	Oct 1846	N.-Amer	569271
Pfeifer, Johannes Martin & F		Gechingen	Calw	1853	N.-Amer	563212
Pfeifer, Rosina	18 yrs.	Calw	Calw	Mar 1847	N.-Amer	563212
Pfeiffer, Adam	23 yrs.	Wittlensweiler	Frd.	Nov 1810	Baden	569268
Pfeiffer, Adolph	17 yrs.	Freudenstadt	Frd.	Jun 1854	N.-Amer	569274
Pfeiffer, Anna Maria	11 yrs.	Freudenstadt	Frd.	May 1752	Pen.N-A	550803
Pfeiffer, Barbara & F	25 Jul 1823	Gruental	Frd.	Apr 1865	N.-Amer	577779
Pfeiffer, Christian	20 yrs.	Freudenstadt	Frd.	Jun 1854	N.-Amer	569274
Pfeiffer, Emilie		Freudenstadt	Frd.	bef 1866	Baden	577780
Pfeiffer, Friedrich	5 yrs.	Hallwangen	Frd.	May 1860	N.-Amer	577777
Pfeiffer, Friedrich		Bergfelden	Sulz	Jan 1807	France	849625
Pfeiffer, Jacob		Bergfelden	Sulz	Jul 1852	N.-Amer	849629
Pfeiffer, Johann & F	3 Jun 1804	Bergfelden	Sulz	Mar 1836	N.-Amer	849629
Pfeiffer, Johann Adam	23 Nov 1845	Gruental	Frd.	Apr 1865	N.-Amer	577779
Pfeiffer, Johann Friedrich	16 yrs.	Gruental	Frd.	Jul 1854	N.-Amer	569274
Pfeiffer, Johann Paul	22 May 1854	Bergfelden	Sulz	Aug 1869	N.-Amer	849629
Pfeiffer, Johannes	28 yrs.	Bergfelden	Sulz	1817	Russia	849629
Pfeiffer, Karl		Freudenstadt	Frd.	Jun 1855	N.-Amer	569275
Pfeiffer, Katharina	26 yrs.	Gruental	Frd.	Jul 1854	N.-Amer	569274
Pfeiffer, Ludwig Heinrich	5 yrs.	Freudenstadt	Frd.	May 1752	Pen.N-A	550803
Pfeiffer, Magdalena	24 Nov 1832	Gruental	Frd.	1853	N.-Amer	577776
Pfeiffer, Magdalena & C	14 Jun 1826	Hallwangen	Frd.	May 1860	N.-Amer	577777
Pfeiffer, Maria Agnes	14 yrs.	Freudenstadt	Frd.	May 1752	Pen.N-A	550803
Pfeiffer, Maria Kleophe	1839	Bergfelden	Su,z	Mar 1857	N.-Amer	849629
Pfeiffer, Philipp Andreas	7 yrs.	Freudenstadt	Frd.	May 1752	Pen.N-A	550803
Pfeiffer, Rosina (wife)		Bergfelden	Sulz	Mar 1836	N.-Amer	849629
Pfeiffer, Wilelm		Freudenstadt	Frd.	Aug 1859	N.-Amer	577776
Pfeiffer, Wilhelm	17 Oct 1850	Bergfelden	Sulz	Apr 1865	N.-Amer	849629
Pfeiffle, Christina	13 Apr 1843	Hornberg	Calw	1855	N.-Amer	563212
Pfeiffle, Dorothea		Hornberg	Calw	1867	N.-Amer	563212
Pfeiffle, Elisabetha Kathar.	1841	Hornberg	Calw	1854	Canada	563212

Name		Birth		Emigration			Film
Last	First	Date	Place	O'amt	Appl. Date	Dest.	Number
Pfeiffle, Jakob		19 Oct 1829	Gueltlingen	Nag.	Feb 1860	N.-Amer	838493
Pfeiffle, Jakob		1834	Liebenzell	Calw	1854	N.-Amer	563212
Pfeiffle, Johann Adam		1835	Hornberg	Calw	1854	Canada	563212
Pfeiffle, Johann Friedrich		8 Apr 1837	Hornberg	Calw	1855	N.-Amer	563212
Pfeiffle, Johann Georg		17 Feb 1838	Gueltlingen	Nag.	Apr 1860	N.-Amer	838493
Pfeiffle, Margarethe		10 Nov 1838	Hornberg	Calw	1855	N.-Amer	563212
Pfeiffle, Sophie			Teinach	Calw	bef 1855	Baden	563212
Pfeifle, Agatha		50 yrs.	Cresbach	Frd.	Apr 1837	N.-Amer	569269
Pfeifle, Andreas		14 Apr 1851	Goettelfingen	Frd.	May 1853	N.-Amer	569272
Pfeifle, Anna Barbara		27 Jul 1822	Beuren	Frd.	May 1853	N.-Amer	569272
Pfeifle, Anna Maria		3 Oct 1829	Goettelfingen	Frd.	Jan 1847	N.-Amer	569270
Pfeifle, Anna Maria			Huzenbach	Frd.	Jan 1847	N.-Amer	569270
Pfeifle, Carl		6 yrs.	Freudenstadt	Frd.	Sep 1854	N.-Amer	569274
Pfeifle, Christian Friedrich		26 Feb 1837	Goettelfingen	Frd.	Jan 1847	N.-Amer	569270
Pfeifle, Christina		24 Aug 1845	Goettelfingen	Frd.	May 1853	N.-Amer	569272
Pfeifle, Christina		10 yrs.	Roet	Frd.	Apr 1854	N.-Amer	569273
Pfeifle, Georg			Freudenstadt	Frd.	Nov 1853	N.-Amer	569272
Pfeifle, Jacob		4 yrs.	Freudenstadt	Frd.	Sep 1854	N.-Amer	569274
Pfeifle, Johann			Liebenzell	Calw	1863	N.-Amer	563212
Pfeifle, Johann Adam & F		17 Jan 1819	Goettelfingen	Frd.	May 1853	N.-Amer	569272
Pfeifle, Johann Georg		13 Dec 1833	Goettelfingen	Frd.	Jan 1847	N.-Amer	569270
Pfeifle, Johann Georg		45 yrs.	Roet	Frd.	Apr 1854	N.-Amer	569273
Pfeifle, Johann Georg		4 Aug 1841	Goettelfingen	Frd.	Mar 1861	N.-Amer	577778
Pfeifle, Johann Georg		12 Jun 1849	Martinsmoos	Frd.	Jun 1866	N.-Amer	577780
Pfeifle, Johann Georg & F			Goettelfingen	Frd.	Jan 1847	N.-Amer	569270
Pfeifle, Johann Peter		1 yrs.	Roet	Frd.	Apr 1854	N.-Amer	569273
Pfeifle, Johanne Christina		8 Jan 1828	Goettelfingen	Frd.	Jan 1847	N.-Amer	569270
Pfeifle, Johannes		5 yrs.	Roet	Frd.	Apr 1854	N.-Amer	569273
Pfeifle, Margaretha		8 yrs.	Roet	Frd.	Apr 1854	N.-Amer	569273
Pfeifle, Michael		31 yrs.	Schoenmuenzach	Frd.	Mar 1847	N.-Amer	569270
Pfeifle, Michael Friedrich		7 yrs.	Roet	Frd.	Apr 1854	N.-Amer	569273
Pfeifle, Michael Friedrich & F			Roet	Frd.	Apr 1854	N.-Amer	569273
Pfeifle, Paul		9 yrs.	Freudenstadt	Frd.	Sep 1854	N.-Amer	569274
Pfeifle, Philipp Friedrich		15 Oct 1835	Goettelfingen	Frd.	Feb 1855	N.-Amer	569275
Pfeifle, Regina (wife)			Roet	Frd.	Apr 1854	N.-Amer	569273
Pfeifle, Sophie		2 yrs.	Freudenstadt	Frd.	Sep 1854	N.-Amer	569274
Pfeiflin, Christiane Frieder.		18 Mar 1805	Sulz	Sulz	Jan 1834	Augsb.	849627
Pfender, Jacob			Balingen	Bal.	Jul 1858	Switz.	555962
Pfister, Anna Maria (wife)			Binsdorf	Sulz	Apr 1853	N.-Amer	849630
Pfister, Blasius & F		3 Sep 1795	Binsdorf	Sulz	Apr 1853	N.-Amer	849630
Pfister, Josef		28 Oct 1865	Rosenfeld	Sulz	May 1882	N.-Amer	849626
Pfister, Magdalena			Binsdorf	Sulz	Jan 1847	Hohenz.	849630
Pfister, Roman & F		8 Aug 1822	Binsdorf	Sulz	Apr 1853	N.-Amer	849630
Pfister, Wilhelmine (wife)			Binsdorf	Sulz	Apr 1853	N.-Amer	849630
Pflaum, Dorothea & C			Reinerzau	Frd.	Mar 1817	Russia	569268
Pflum, Elisabetha Katharina		26 yrs.	Simmozheim	Calw	1856	Baden	563212
Pfroerer, Emilie Louise			Calw	Calw	1855	N.-Amer	563212
Pfroerer, Heinrich			Calw	Calw	1855	N.-Amer	563212
Pfroerer, Karl August			Calw	Calw	1855	N.-Amer	563212
Pfroerer, Ludwig Eugen			Calw	Calw	1855	N.-Amer	563212

Pfrommer, Johann Ulrich	7 Sep 1848	Oberkollbach	Calw	1868	N.-Amer	563212
Pfronner, Katharina (wid.)	1815	Oberhaugstett	Calw	1856	N.-Amer	563212
Pfund, Amasch	26 yrs.	Liebenzell	Calw	1866	N.-Amer	563212
Pfund, Georg August	25 yrs.	Liebenzell	Calw	1866	N.-Amer	563212
Plaetscher, Anna Maria		Gruental	Frd.	Mar 1833	N.-Amer	569268
Plag, Karl Ludwig Ferdinand		Baiersbronn	Frd.	bef 1860	N.-Amer	577777
Plaz, Michael	1810	Schopfloch	Frd.	bef 1848	Wien	569270
Plessen, Wilhelm von & F		Herrenberg	Herr.	bef 1846	Saxony	834626
Plocher, Agatha Martha Maria	6 Mar 1881	Holzhausen	Sulz	Jun 1882	N.-Amer	849635
Plocher, Andreas	19 Jun 1850	Muehlheim a.B.	Sulz	Mar 1868	N.-Amer	849639
Plocher, Andreas & F		Holzhausen	Sulz	May 1817	Russia	849635
Plocher, Anna		Holzhausen	Sulz	1853	N.-Amer	849635
Plocher, Anna & C	20 Aug 1795	Holzhausen	Sulz	Apr 1832	N.-Amer	849635
Plocher, Anna (wife)		Holzhausen	Sulz	Apr 1832	N.-Amer	849635
Plocher, Anna Maria	8 Feb 1838	Bergfelden	Sulz	1854	N.-Amer	849629
Plocher, Anna Maria	25 yrs.	Holzhausen	Sulz	Feb 1857	N.-Amer	849635
Plocher, Anna Maria	3 May 1809	Holzhausen	Sulz	Jun 1832	N.-Amer	849635
Plocher, Anna Maria (wid.) & F	11 Feb 1820	Muehlheim a.B.	Sulz	Oct 1872	N.-Amer	849639
Plocher, Barbara (wife)	7 Nov 1843	Holzhausen	Sulz	Jun 1882	N.-Amer	849635
Plocher, Benjamin Gottlieb		Holzhausen	Sulz	Apr 1853	N.-Amer	849635
Plocher, Christian		Bergfelden	Sulz	1855	N.-Amer	849629
Plocher, Christian	2 Oct 1839	Bergfelden	Sulz	Nov 1854	N.-Amer	849629
Plocher, Christian	7 Dec 1851	Muehlheim a.B.	Sulz	Mar 1867	N.-Amer	849639
Plocher, Christina Margaretha		Holzhausen	Sulz	Sep 1853	N.-Amer	849635
Plocher, Christine Barbara	10 Apr 1879	Holzhausen	Sulz	Jun 1882	N.-Amer	849635
Plocher, Christoph & F		Bergfelden	Sulz	bef 1830	Russia	849625
Plocher, Elisabeth	26 yrs.	Voehringen	Sulz	May 1867	N.-Amer	849643
Plocher, Ferdinand	16 Dec 1835	Holzhausen	Sulz	Nov 1853	N.-Amer	849635
Plocher, Friedrich & F	26 Oct 1801	Holzhausen	Sulz	Apr 1832	N.-Amer	849635
Plocher, Georg Jakob		Holzhausen	Sulz	Sep 1853	N.-Amer	849635
Plocher, Georg Michael & F	17 Aug 1835	Holzhausen	Sulz	Jun 1882	N.-Amer	849635
Plocher, Gottfried Ludwig		Holzhausen	Sulz	Sep 1853	N.-Amer	849635
Plocher, Gottlob		Holzhausen	Sulz	Sep 1853	N.-Amer	849635
Plocher, Gottlob Christian	24 Jan 1874	Holzhausen	Sulz	Jun 1882	N.-Amer	849635
Plocher, Jacob & F		Holzhausen	Sulz	May 1817	Russia	849635
Plocher, Jakob	1 Mar 1854	Muehlheim a.B.	Sulz	Oct 1872	N.-Amer	849639
Plocher, Johann Bernhard	13 Mar 1843	Heselbach	Frd.	Aug 1853	N.-Amer	569274
Plocher, Johann Georg	14 Mar 1808	Marschalkenzimmern	Frd.	Apr 1846	N.-Amer	569271
Plocher, Johann Georg	15 Jan 1875	Holzhausen	Sulz	Jun 1882	N.-Amer	849635
Plocher, Johann Gottfried		Holzhausen	Sulz	Sep 1853	N.-Amer	849635
Plocher, Johann Jakob & W		Holzhausen	Sulz	Jun 1817	Russia	849635
Plocher, Johann Ludwig		Holzhausen	Sulz	Sep 1853	N.-Amer	849635
Plocher, Johann Michael	25 Apr 1810	Holzhausen	Sulz	Apr 1832	N.Amer	849635
Plocher, Johannes	26 Dec 1794	Sigmarswangen	Sulz	Jun 1817	Russia	849642
Plocher, Johannes	29 Aug 1853	Dornhan	Sulz	Apr 1871	N.-Amer	849634
Plocher, Johannes	2 Apr 1868	Holzhausen	Sulz	Jul 1883	N.-Amer	849635
Plocher, Johannes		Holzhausen	Sulz	Apr 1853	N.-Amer	849635
Plocher, Johannes	25 Oct 1847	Muehlheim a.B.	Sulz	Mar 1867	N.-Amer	849639
Plocher, Karolina	28 Sep 1840	Heselbach	Frd.	Aug 1853	N.-Amer	569274
Plocher, Katharina	7 Nov 1838	Heselbach	Frd.	Aug 1853	N.-Amer	569274

Name		Birth		Emigration			Film
Last	First	Date	Place	O'amt	Appl. Date	Dest.	Number
Plocher, Katharina		29 May 1764	Wittershausen	Sulz	May 1817	N.-Amer	849644
Plocher, Katharina Barbara		8 Jul 1877	Holzhausen	Sulz	Jun 1882	N.-Amer	849635
Plocher, Louisa & C		11 Oct 1810	Holzhausen	Sulz	Mar 1857	N.-Amer	849635
Plocher, Ludwig & F		11 Jun 1775	Holzhausen	Sulz	Apr 1832	N.-Amer	849635
Plocher, Ludwig Peter & F			Holzhausen	Sulz	Sep 1853	N.-Amer	849635
Plocher, Magdalena			Voehringen	Sulz	Mar 1837	N.-Amer	849643
Plocher, Magdalena		19 Nov 1856	Muehlheim a.B.	Sulz	Oct 1872	N.-Amer	849639
Plocher, Maria Agatha			Holzhausen	Sulz	Sep 1853	N.-Amer	849635
Plocher, Maria Barbara (wife)			Bergfelden	Sulz	bef 1830	Russia	849625
Plocher, Maria Johanna		3 Apr 1828	Holzhausen	Sulz	1867	N.-Amer	849635
Plocher, Martin		19 Aug 1799	Holzhausen	Sulz	bef 1834	Baden	849635
Plocher, Matthias			Sigmarswangen	Sulz	bef 1840	N.-Amer	849642
Plocher, Michael			Holzhausen	Sulz	Jun 1817	Russia	849635
Plocher, Rebeka (wife)			Holzhausen	Sulz	Apr 1832	N.-Amer	849635
Plocher, Regina		17 Nov 1835	Heselbach	Frd.	Aug 1853	N.-Amer	569274
Plocher, Regina & F		22 Jul 1835	Wenden	Frd.	Aug 1853	N.-Amer	569274
Plocher, Wilhelm		12 Nov 1846	Holzhausen	Sulz	Mar 1857	N.-Amer	849635
Ploetscher, Catharina		27 Apr 1826	Wittlensweiler	Frd.	Mar 1847	N.-Amer	569271
Ploetscher, Georg Friedrich			Wittlensweiler	Frd.	Mar 1816	France	569268
Ploetscher, Johann Georg		10 Aug 1803	Wittlensweiler	Frd.	bef 1839	N.-Amer	569268
Pochard, Jean			Montbeilard	– –	Dec 1751	Mas.N-A	550803
Podervils Freiin, Elisabeth			Leinstetten	Sulz	Mar 1871	Austria	849638
Pommer, Christian		1835	Calw	Calw	1854	N.-Amer	563212
Pommer, Wilhelm Friedrich			Calw	Calw	1859	N.-Amer	563212
Poppele, Carl		28 yrs.	Alzenberg	Calw	1866	England	563212
Pregizer, Gustav			Moetzingen	Herr.	Mar 1843	Baden	834625
Preising, Johannes			Ulm	– –	Dec 1751	Mas.N-A	550803
Press, Jakob		17 Jan 1831	Neuweiler	Calw	1857	N.-Amer	563212
Pressler, Johann Martin & W			Muehlheim a.B.	Sulz	Jun 1847	N.-Amer	849639
Pressler, Susanna (wife)			Muehlheim a.B.	Sulz	Jun 1847	N.-Amer	849639
Prez, Philipp Jacob Friedrich		32 yrs.	Geradstetten	Schd.	Jan 1833	Erfurt	801460
Probst, Anna Maria		6 yrs.	Gaertringen	Herr.	Oct 1846	N.-Amer	834626
Probst, Anna Maria (wid.)		18 Nov 1807	Gaertringen	Herr.	Jul 1869	N.-Amer	834624
Probst, Eva & C		54 yrs.	Gaertringen	Herr.	Oct 1846	N.-Amer	834626
Probst, Friederke Dorothea		12 May 1845	Unterjesingen	Herr.	Jan 1867	N.-Amer	834624
Probst, Johann Georg		30 yrs.	Gaertringen	Herr.	Oct 1846	N.-Amer	834626
Probst, Lucia & C		35 yrs.	Gaertringen	Herr.	Oct 1846	N.-Amer	834626
Probst, Margaretha		20 yrs.	Gaertringen	Herr.	Oct 1846	N.-Amer	834626
Probst, Margaretha (wid.) & F		61 yrs.	Gaertringen	Herr.	Oct 1846	N.-Amer	834626
Probst, Margaretha Elisabeth		12 yrs.	Gaertringen	Herr.	Oct 1846	N.-Amer	834626
Pross, Anna			Breitenberg	Calw	1855	N.-Amer	563212
Pross, Anna Maria & F			Dachteln	Calw	1852	N.-Amer	563212
Pross, Christine Katharina		1832	Neuweiler	Calw	1854	N.-Amer	563212
Pross, Daniel		12 Nov 1817	Oberjesingen	Herr.	Jun 1846	Bavaria	834626
Pross, Dorothea			Huzenbach	Frd.	bef 1865	France	577779
Pross, Georg Adam			Sulz	Nag.	Feb 1854	N.-Amer	838491
Prothmueller, Georg & F			Stammheim	Calw	1854	N.-Amer	563212
Pulvermueller, Christian & F			Freudenstadt	Frd.	Jul 1854	N.-Amer	569274
Pulvermueller, Rosine			Freudenstadt	Frd.	Mar 1843	Hesse	569269
Rahl, Paulina		7 May 1840	Gaertringen	Herr.	Dec 1868	Wien	834624

Raible, Anna Maria		Bickelsberg	Sulz	Feb 1837	N.-Amer	849644
Raible, Catharina		Untermusbach	Frd.	Apr 1752	Pen.N-A	550803
Raible, Hans Martin		Untermusbach	Frd.	Apr 1752	Pen.N-A	550803
Raible, Jakob & W	12 Aug 1809	Wittershausen	Sulz	Feb 1837	N.-Amer	849644
Raible, Johannes		Untermusbach	Frd.	Apr 1752	Pen.N-A	550803
Rais, Mathias	2 Jan 1830	Dornhan	Sulz	Mar 1854	N.-Amer	849633
Raisch, Anna (wife)		Oberjettingen	Herr.	May 1830	N.-Amer	834624
Raisch, Catharina		Walddorf	Nag.	Mar 1854	N.-Amer	838491
Raisch, Gottlieb	11 Dec 1833	Pfalzgrafenweiler	Frd.	bef 1862	France	577778
Raisch, Michael & F		Oberjettingen	Herr.	May 1830	N.-Amer	834624
Raisele, Anna Maria	6 Nov 1830	Hopfau	Sulz	Jan 1867	Switz.	849636
Raiser, Gustav Adolf	18 Mar 1843	Entringen	Herr.	Feb 1869	N.-Amer	834624
Raissle, Johannes (wid.) & F	50 yrs.	Oberjesingen	Herr.	Jun 1832	N.-Amer	834624
Raith, Anna Maria	30 Oct 1838	Breitenholz	Herr.	Sep 1865	N.-Amer	834624
Raith, Johann Jacob & F	53 yrs.	Nufringen	Herr.	Apr 1838	N.-Amer	834625
Raith, Maria Catharina	9 Aug 1806	Nufringen	Herr.	Apr 1838	N.-Amer	834625
Raith, Maria Catharina (wife)	58 yrs.	Nufringen	Herr.	Apr 1838	N.-Amer	834625
Raith, Wilhelm Gottlob	23 Jan 1801	Herrenberg	Herr.	bef 1845	N.-Amer	834626
Rall, Hermann Friedrich	1 Apr 1850	Unterjesingen	Herr.	Oct 1869	N.-Amer	834624
Rall, Johann Christoph & F		Reusten	Herr.	Apr 1835	N.-Amer	834624
Rall, Johann Gottlieb	13 yrs.	Althengstett	Calw	1860	N.-Amer	563212
Rall, Wilhelmine Dorothea	6 Mar 1832	Unterjesingen	Herr.	May 1869	N.-Amer	834624
Rampp, Georg Friedrich	4 Feb 1819	Klosterreichenbach	Frd.	Mar 1847	N.-Amer	569271
Ranler, Anna Maria & C		Oberkollwangen	Calw	1857	N.-Amer	563212
Ranler, Johann Georg	1855	Oberkollwangen	Calw	1857	N.-Amer	563212
Ranler, Michael	1852	Oberkollwangen	Calw	1857	N.-Amer	563212
Rapp, Anna Barbara		Neuneck	Frd.	Apr 1752	Pen.N-A	550803
Rapp, Anna Maria	1 Apr 1827	Bergfelden	Sulz	Feb 1856	Switz.	849629
Rapp, Babara		Fuernsal	Sulz	bef 1848	Switz.	849635
Rapp, Catharina		Fuernsal	Sulz	Apr 1837	N.-Amer	849635
Rapp, Elisabetha	22 Nov 1832	Bergfelden	Sulz	1858	Switz.	849629
Rapp, Georg Heinrich	32 yrs.	Calw	Calw	1866	N.-Amer	563212
Rapp, Jakob		Renfrizhausen	Sulz	Sep 1847	N.-Amer	849639
Rapp, Karoline & C		Schramberg	Frd.	Apr 1864	N.-Amer	577779
Rapp, Martin & F		Aichhalden	Calw	1853	N.-Amer	563212
Raster, Johann Philipp		Bondorf	Herr.	Nov 1829	Hungary	834624
Rath, Anna Maria	15 Nov 1843	Hopfau	Sulz	Nov 1866	N.-Amer	849636
Rath, Christian		Althengstett	Calw	1860	N.-Amer	563212
Rath, Gottlieb & F		Pfalzgrafenweiler	Frd.	Feb 1817	Russia	569268
Rath, Gottlob	13 Feb 1866	Dornhan	Sulz	Oct 1881	N.-Amer	849626
Rath, Jacob & F		Dornhan	Sulz	May 1817	Russia	849633
Rath, Johann Georg	22 May 1788	Pfalzgrafenweiler	Frd.	Jan 1817	N.-Amer	569268
Rath, Johann Georg	30 yrs.	Cresbach	Frd.	Feb 1837	Baden	569269
Rath, Johann Georg	30 Nov 1856	Dornhan	Sulz	Sep 1872	N.-Amer	849634
Rath, Johann Georg & F		Neuneck	Frd.	1817	Russia	569269
Rath, Michael & F		Cresbach	Frd.	1817	Russia	569269
Rathgeb, Johann Adam & W	34 yrs.	Rohrau	Herr.	Apr 1849	N.-Amer	834627
Rathgeb, Johanna		Rohrau	Herr.	Sep 1835	Greece	834624
Rathgeb, Sarina Regina (wife)	33 yrs.	Rohrau	Herr.	Apr 1849	N.-Amer	834627
Rau, Carl Ferdinand		Liebenzell	Calw	1867	Turkey	563212

| Name | | Birth | | Emigration | | | Film |
Last	First	Date	Place	O'amt	Appl. Date	Dest.	Number
Rau, Christian Gottlob		19 Aug 1820	Unterjesingen	Herr.	May 1869	N.-Amer	834624
Rau, Eva Barbara			Liebelsberg	Calw	1868	N.-Amer	563212
Rau, Georg Jakob		15 yrs.	Liebelsberg	Calw	1869	N.-Amer	563212
Rau, Gilpus		17 yrs.	Liebesberg	Calw	1866	N.-Amer	563212
Rau, Gottlob Friedrich		19 Jun 1825	Unterjesingen	Herr.	May 1869	N.-Amer	834624
Rau, Johann Georg		25 Jul 1870	Fuernsal	Sulz	Jun 1887	N.-Amer	849626
Rau, Johann Michael		14 yrs.	Liebesberg	Calw	1866	N.-Amer	563212
Rau, Ludwig Friedrich & F			Neubulach	Calw	1852	N.-Amer	563212
Rau, Maria Agnes			Liebelsberg	Calw	1869	N.-Amer	563212
Rauch, Agatha		23 Dec 1844	Voehringen	Sulz	Sep 1852	N.-Amer	849643
Rauch, Andreas		3 mon.	Voehringen	Sulz	Apr 1833	N.-Amer	849643
Rauch, Anna		16 Jan 1847	Voehringen	Sulz	Sep 1852	N.-Amer	849643
Rauch, Anna			Voehringen	Sulz	Mar 1836	N.-Amer	849643
Rauch, Anna			Voehringen	Sulz	Apr 1833	N.-Amer	849643
Rauch, Anna (wife)			Voehringen	Sulz	Sep 1852	N.-Amer	849643
Rauch, Anna Barbara			Voehringen	Sulz	Apr 1833	N.-Amer	849643
Rauch, Anna Barbara (wife)			Voehringen	Sulz	Apr 1833	N.-Amer	849643
Rauch, Anna Catharina			Voehringen	Sulz	Apr 1833	N.-Amer	849643
Rauch, Anna Maria			Voehringen	Sulz	1833	Russia	849625
Rauch, Anna Maria			Voehringen	Sulz	Apr 1833	N.-Amer	849643
Rauch, Anna Maria (wife)			Voehringen	Sulz	Apr 1833	N.-Amer	849643
Rauch, Caspar			Voehringen	Sulz	Jul 1847	N.-Amer	849643
Rauch, Catharina			Voehringen	Sulz	Mar 1836	N.-Amer	849643
Rauch, Catharina (wife)			Voehringen	Sulz	Apr 1833	N.-Amer	849643
Rauch, Elisabeth		22 yrs.	Voehringen	Sulz	Aug 1854	N.-Amer	849643
Rauch, Eva			Voehringen	Sulz	Apr 1845	N.-Amer	849643
Rauch, Eva			Voehringen	Sulz	Apr 1833	N.-Amer	849643
Rauch, Friedrich		27 May 1810	Voehringen	Sulz	bef 1843	N.-Amer	849643
Rauch, Heinrich		5 Feb 1864	Bickelsberg	Sulz	May 1879	N.-Amer	849630
Rauch, Jacob			Voehringen	Sulz	bef 1825	St-burg	849643
Rauch, Johann Jacob & F			Voehringen	Sulz	Apr 1833	N.-Amer	849643
Rauch, Johann Martin		24 Feb 1852	Voehringen	Sulz	Aug 1872	N.-Amer	849643
Rauch, Johann Martin		4 Apr 1842	Voehringen	Sulz	Sep 1852	N.-Amer	849643
Rauch, Johann Martin & F			Voehringen	Sulz	Apr 1833	N.-Amer	849643
Rauch, Johannes			Voehringen	Sulz	1843	Russia	849625
Rauch, Johannes			Voehringen	Sulz	bef 1842	N.-Amer	849643
Rauch, Konrad & F			Voehringen	Sulz	bef 1844	N.-Amer	849625
Rauch, Marie Magdalena			Voehringen	Sulz	bef 1844	N.-Amer	849625
Rauch, Mathias & F			Voehringen	Sulz	Sep 1852	N.-Amer	849643
Rauch, Tobias & F			Voehringen	Sulz	Apr 1833	N.-Amer	849643
Rauch, Ursula			Voehringen	Sulz	Apr 1833	N.-Amer	849643
Rausch, Christian Wilhelm		20 yrs.	Rosenfeld	Sulz	Apr 1854	N.-Amer	849640
Rausch, Jakob		2 Sep 1849	Rosenfeld	Sulz	Mar 1867	N.-Amer	849641
Rauschenberger, Anna Maria			Unterwaldach	Frd.	Mar 1854	N.-Amer	569273
Rauschenberger, Eva			Unterwaldach	Frd.	Mar 1854	N.-Amer	569273
Rauschenberger, Friederika		31 Dec 1833	Neunuifra	Frd.	Apr 1861	N.-Amer	577778
Rauschenberger, Jakob Friedr.		9 Sep 1841	Herzogsweiler	Frd.	May 1860	N.-Amer	577777
Rauschenberger, Johannes		2 Aug 1833	Unterwaldach	Frd.	Apr 1853	N.-Amer	569272
Rauschenberger, Margaretha		11 May 1836	Unterwaldach	Frd.	Apr 1853	N.-Amer	569272
Rauschenberger, Maria El. (wife)			Moetzingen	Herr.	May 1831	N.-Amer	834624

Rauschenberger, Martin & W		Moetzingen	Herr.	May 1831	N.-Amer	834624
Rauscher, Carl Christian	23 Aug 1852	Freudenstadt	Frd.	Aug 1866	N.-Amer	577780
Rauscher, Christian	23 Mar 1849	Freudenstadt	Frd.	Aug 1866	N.-Amer	577780
Rauscher, David Wilhelm	19 Jan 1838	Freudenstadt	Frd.	Jun 1864	N.-Amer	577779
Rauser, Christian	21 Mar 1831	Nagold	Nag.	bef 1857	N.-Amer	838492
Rauser, Friedrich		Cresbach	Frd.	Apr 1856	N.-Amer	569275
Rauser, Heinrich Christof		Calw	Calw	1852	N.-Amer	563212
Rauser, Johann Gottlob	20 yrs.	Nagold	Nag.	Jul 1854	N.-Amer	838491
Rauser, Maria Catharina & F		Nagold	Nag.	Jul 1854	N.-Amer	838491
Rauser, Rudolf August		Calw	Calw	1852	N.-Amer	563212
Rauser, Salome	1 Aug 1847	Aach	Frd.	Feb 1866	N.-Amer	577780
Rauss, Adam	25 yrs.	Cresbach	Frd.	Apr 1837	N.-Amer	569269
Rauss, Adelheide	2 yrs.	Unterschwandorf	Nag.	Jul 1852	N.-Amer	838490
Rauss, Agatha	50 yrs.	Cresbach	Frd.	Apr 1837	N.-Amer	569269
Rauss, Andreas	6 mon.	Unterschwandorf	Nag.	Jul 1852	N.-Amer	838490
Rauss, Carl Christian & F		Unterschwandorf	Nag.	Jul 1852	N.-Amer	838490
Rauss, Christian Jakob	24 Feb 1831	Haiterbach	Nag.	Feb 1854	N.-Amer	838491
Rauss, Christina		Unterschwandorf	Nag.	Jul 1852	N.-Amer	838490
Rauss, Christine	16 yrs.	Cresbach	Frd.	Apr 1837	N.-Amer	569269
Rauss, Elisabethe Karoline	24 Jul 1833	Haiterbach	Nag.	Feb 1854	N.-Amer	838491
Rauss, Eva	23 yrs.	Cresbach	Frd.	Apr 1837	N.-Amer	569269
Rauss, Franz Jakob		Klosterreichenbach	Frd.	Jan 1848	France	569270
Rauss, Friederike Elisabetha	12 Jan 1830	Haiterbach	Nag.	Feb 1854	N.-Amer	838491
Rauss, Johann Peter	19 yrs.	Cresbach	Frd.	Apr 1837	N.-Amer	569269
Rauss, Johannes		Klosterreichenbach	Frd.	Nov 1841	France	569268
Rauss, Johannes	14 yrs.	Cresbach	Frd.	Apr 1837	N.-Amer	569269
Rauss, Louise Wilhelmine	13 Feb 1835	Haiterbach	Nag.	Feb 1854	N.-Amer	838491
Rauss, Martin & F	55 yrs.	Cresbach	Frd.	Apr 1837	N.-Amer	569269
Rauss, Maximilian	4 Sep 1828	Haiterbach	Nag.	Feb 1854	N.-Amer	838491
Rausser, Johann Georg	30 May 1832	Baiersbronn	Frd.	Nov 1854	N.-Amer	569274
Rauter, Martin	21 yrs.	Wittlensweiler	Frd.	Mar 1837	N.-Amer	569268
Rautter, Barbara	14 Jan 1836	Wittlensweiler	Frd.	Mar 1854	N.-Amer	569273
Rebholz, Andreas	23 Feb 1872	Bettenhausen	Sulz	Feb 1887	N.-Amer	849626
Rebholz, Anna		Leinstetten	Sulz	Jun 1854	N.-Amer	849638
Rebholz, Barbara & C		Bettenhausen	Sulz	Mar 1836	Hohenz.	849630
Rebholz, Barbara & C		Leinstetten	Sulz	Jun 1854	N.-Amer	849638
Rebholz, Franziska	13 Feb 1836	Bettenhausen	Sulz	Mar 1836	Hohenz.	849630
Rebstock, Adolph	8 yrs.	Binsdorf	Sulz	Feb 1839	N.-Amer	849630
Rebstock, Aloysia	3 yrs.	Binsdorf	Sulz	Feb 1839	N.-Amer	849630
Rebstock, Georg Benjamin	22 Jul 1850	Unterjesingen	Herr.	Oct 1868	N.-Amer	834624
Rebstock, Johannes & W	14 Oct 1814	Gueltstein	Herr.	Mar 1866	N.-Amer	834624
Rebstock, Maria Magdalena (wife)	9 Apr 1818	Gueltstein	Herr.	Mar 1866	N.-Amer	834624
Rebstok, Adolf		Binsdorf	Sulz	bef 1869	N.-Amer	849631
Rebstok, Christian	20 yrs.	Unterjesingen	Herr.	Aug 1849	N.-Amer	834627
Rebstok, Christof & F	49 yrs.	Unterjesingen	Herr.	Aug 1849	N.-Amer	834627
Rebstok, Christof Friedrich	12 yrs.	Unterjesingen	Herr.	Aug 1849	N.-Amer	834627
Rebstok, Ernst Wilhelm	17 yrs.	Unterjesingen	Herr.	Aug 1849	N.-Amer	834627
Rebstok, Fiedel	15 Oct 1872	Binsdorf	Sulz	Jul 1886	N.-Amer	849631
Rebstok, Jacob	30 Apr 1851	Rottenburg	Sulz	May 1869	N.-Amer	849631
Rebstok, Johann Georg	7 yrs.	Unterjesingen	Herr.	Aug 1849	N.-Amer	834627

Name		Birth		Emigration			Film
Last	First	Date	Place	O'amt	Appl. Date	Dest.	Number
Rebstok, Joseph		15 Mar 1857	Binsdorf	Sulz	Feb 1872	N.-Amer	849631
Rebstok, Maria Agnes (wife)		47 yrs.	Unterjesingen	Herr.	Aug 1849	N.-Amer	834627
Rebstok, Tabitha Dorothea		11 yrs.	Unterjesingen	Herr.	Aug 1849	N.-Amer	834627
Rebstok, Wilhelm Friedrich		15 yrs.	Unterjesingen	Herr.	Aug 1849	N.-Amer	834627
Rech, Christina		19 Mar 1843	Glatten	Frd.	Oct 1854	S.-Amer	569274
Recherer, Karl August Julius		9 Mar 1866	Sulz	Sulz	Oct 1882	N.-Amer	849626
Reck, Andreas		8 Aug 1837	Hopfau	Sulz	Mar 1857	N.-Amer	849636
Reck, Anna		24 Nov 1845	Hopfau	Sulz	Jun 1860	N.-Amer	849636
Reck, Anna Maria		27 Nov 1826	Hopfau	Sulz	Nov 1858	N.-Amer	849636
Reck, Barbara		14 Jun 1840	Hopfau	Sulz	Jun 1860	N.-Amer	849636
Reck, Catharina (wid.) & F		15 Oct 1805	Hopfau	Sulz	Jun 1860	N.-Amer	849636
Reck, Christina		2 Apr 1832	Hopfau	Sulz	1851	N.-Amer	849636
Reck, Jacob		17 Mar 1843	Hopfau	Sulz	Jun 1860	N.-Amer	849636
Reck, Johann Georg		1 Nov 1820	Hopfau	Sulz	bef 1860	N.-Amer	849636
Reck, Johannes		19 Dec 1818	Hopfau	Sulz	bef 1860	N.-Amer	849636
Reck, Johannes		3 Jul 1850	Hopfau	Sulz	Jun 1860	N.-Amer	849636
Reck, Katharina & C		29 Nov 1823	Hopfau	Sulz	Jun 1860	N.-Amer	849636
Reck, Matthaeus		30 Jul 1830	Hopfau	Sulz	1854	N.-Amer	849636
Reck, Rosina		20 Apr 1834	Hopfau	Sulz	1854	N.-Amer	849636
Reebig, Christina Catharina		13 Sep 1868	Breitenholz	Herr.	Oct 1868	N.-Amer	834624
Reebig, Jacob Friedrich		16 Sep 1863	Breitenholz	Herr.	Oct 1868	N.-Amer	834624
Reebig, Magdalena		14 Dec 1866	Breitenholz	Herr.	Oct 1868	N.-Amer	834624
Reebig, Maria Catharina & C		11 Nov 1835	Breitenholz	Herr.	Oct 1868	N.-Amer	834624
Reger, Barbara			Roetenbach	Calw	1853	N.-Amer	563212
Rehfuss, Bertha		4 yrs.	Sulz	Sulz	May 1857	N.-Amer	849628
Rehfuss, Carl		1 yrs.	Sulz	Sulz	May 1857	N.-Amer	849628
Rehfuss, Christian Hermann		2 Jul 1847	Aach	Frd.	Aug 1866	N.-Amer	577780
Rehfuss, Christina & F		4 Mar 1819	Dornhan	Sulz	Feb 1857	N.-Amer	849633
Rehfuss, Georg		2 Oct 1853	Waelde	Sulz	Mar 1872	N.-Amer	849644
Rehfuss, Jakob		30 Apr 1858	Dornhan	Sulz	May 1873	N.-Amer	849634
Rehfuss, Jakob		11 Feb 1850	Dornhan	Sulz	May 1869	N.-Amer	849634
Rehfuss, Jakob		5 Oct 1848	Dornhan	Sulz	Feb 1857	N.-Amer	849633
Rehfuss, Johann		15 Nov 1825	Dornhan	Sulz	Jul 1848	N.-Amer	849633
Rehfuss, Johann Adam		18 Jun 1855	Dornhan	Sulz	Apr 1864	N.-Amer	849634
Rehfuss, Johann Georg		15 Jan 1847	Dornhan	Sulz	Feb 1857	N.-Amer	849633
Rehfuss, Johann Martin		8 Nov 1818	Dornhan	Sulz	1854	N.-Amer	849633
Rehfuss, Ludwig Joh.Gottl. & F			Sulz	Sulz	May 1857	N.-Amer	849628
Rehfuss, Mathaeus			Ebingen	Bal.	bef 1849	Switz.	555963
Rehfuss, Mathilde		3 yrs.	Sulz	Sulz	May 1857	N.-Amer	849628
Rehfuss, Melchior			Ebingen	Bal.	Jun 1850	Switz.	555962
Rehfuss, Rosina			Aach	Frd.	bef 1804	France	550803
Rehfuss, Rosine (wife)			Sulz	Sulz	May 1857	N.-Amer	849628
Rehm, Jacob & F			Gueltstein	Herr.	Apr 1835	N.-Amer	834624
Reich, Anna		30 Aug 1838	Voehringen	Sulz	Mar 1866	N.-Amer	849643
Reich, Anna & C		9 Mar 1807	Voehringen	Sulz	Mar 1866	N.-Amer	849643
Reich, Anna (wife)			Rosenfeld	Sulz	Aug 1854	N.-Amer	849640
Reich, Anna Maria			Wittlensweiler	Frd.	Jun 1856	N.-Amer	569275
Reich, Christian		22 Feb 1846	Rosenfeld	Sulz	Aug 1865	N.-Amer	849641
Reich, Christina		22 Jul 1835	Trichtingen	Sulz	bef 1859	N.-Amer	849642
Reich, Christina (wife)			Wittlensweiler	Frd.	Jun 1856	N.-Amer	569275

Reich, Conrad		Rosenfeld	Sulz	bef 1852	N.-Amer	849640
Reich, Friederich		Wittlensweiler	Frd.	Jun 1856	N.-Amer	569275
Reich, Friederich & F		Wittlensweiler	Frd.	Jun 1856	N.-Amer	569275
Reich, Jacob		Marschalkenzimmern	Sulz	Feb 1846	Austria	849638
Reich, Jakob	18 May 1861	Trichtingen	Sulz	Nov 1882	Switz.	849626
Reich, Jakob & F		Rosenfeld	Sulz	bef 1861	N.-Amer	849641
Reich, Johann Georg	14 yrs.	Rosenfeld	Sulz	Aug 1854	N.-Amer	849640
Reich, Johann Georg & F		Rosenfeld	Sulz	Aug 1854	N.-Amer	849640
Reich, Johann Jacob	18 Nov 1835	Rosenfeld	Sulz	Aug 1852	N.-Amer	849640
Reich, Johann Michael	16 Dec 1841	Rosenfeld	Sulz	May 1859	N.-Amer	849640
Reich, Johannes		Klosterreichenbach	Frd.	Apr 1848	N.-Amer	569270
Reich, Johannes		Rheinduerckheim	– –	Dec 1751	N.-Amer	550803
Reich, Joseph	1 Dec 1856	Binsdorf	Sulz	Feb 1872	N.-Amer	849631
Reich, Margarethe	16 yrs.	Rosenfeld	Sulz	Aug 1854	N.-Amer	849640
Reich, Maria Johanna (wife)		Rosenfeld	Sulz	bef 1861	N.-Amer	849641
Reich, Martin		Rosenfeld	Sulz	Aug 1852	N.-Amer	849640
Reich, Mathaeus	9 Oct 1849	Binsdorf	Sulz	Feb 1866	N.-Amer	849631
Reichardt, Anna Maria	30 Apr 1849	Kuppingen	Herr.	May 1867	N.-Amer	834624
Reichardt, Anna Maria	24 Dec 1844	Hildrizhausen	Herr.	Mar 1870	N.-Amer	834624
Reichardt, Johann Michael & F		Reusten	Herr.	Apr 1831	N.-Amer	834624
Reichardt, Johannes		Hildrizhausen	Herr.	Apr 1833	Bavaria	834624
Reichert, Anna Maria	3 Dec 1831	Nufringen	Herr.	Jun 1839	N.-Amer	834625
Reichert, Anna Maria	30 Sep 1835	Hildrizhausen	Herr.	Apr 1852	N.-Amer	834627
Reichert, Barbara (wife)		Herrenberg	Herr.	Apr 1852	N.-Amer	834627
Reichert, Catharina Dorothea	2 Mar 1838	Nufringen	Herr.	Jun 1839	N.-Amer	834625
Reichert, Christiana	22 Apr 1833	Nufringen	Herr.	Jun 1839	N.-Amer	834625
Reichert, Christiana Dor. (wife)	28 Sep 1807	Nufringen	Herr.	Jun 1839	N.-Amer	834625
Reichert, Christiane (wife)		Hildrizhausen	Herr.	Apr 1852	N.-Amer	834627
Reichert, Christiane Barbara	24 Dec 1842	Moetzingen	Herr.	Apr 1847	N.-Amer	834626
Reichert, Georg Friedrich	25 Nov 1849	Pfaeffingen	Herr.	Feb 1869	N.-Amer	834624
Reichert, Gottlieb & W	1 May 1807	Herrenberg	Herr.	Apr 1852	N.-Amer	834627
Reichert, Jacob	24 yrs.	Reusten	Herr.	May 1831	N.-Amer	834624
Reichert, Jakob & F	1 Apr 1827	Hildrizhausen	Herr.	Apr 1852	N.-Amer	834627
Reichert, Johann Georg	12 Jul 1828	Hildrizhausen	Herr.	Nov 1868	N.-Amer	834624
Reichert, Johanna Sabina	25 Mar 1820	Nufringen	Herr.	Feb 1848	N.-Amer	834626
Reichert, Johannes	30 Oct 1809	Moetzingen	Herr.	May 1852	N.-Amer	834627
Reichert, Johannes	4 Mar 1822	Nufringen	Herr.	Feb 1869	N.-Amer	834624
Reichert, Johannes	5 Sep 1856	Nufringen	Herr.	Feb 1869	N.-Amer	834624
Reichert, Johannes	12 Mar 1831	Hildrizhausen	Herr.	Apr 1852	N.-Amer	834627
Reichert, Lorenz	2 Oct 1833	Hildrizhausen	Herr.	Apr 1852	N.-Amer	834627
Reichert, Margaretha	58 yrs.	Affstaett	Herr.	Apr 1847	N.-Amer	834626
Reichert, Margaretha	17 Feb 1839	Hildrizhausen	Herr.	Apr 1852	N.-Amer	834627
Reichert, Maria Catharina	1 Feb 1840	Hildrizhausen	Herr.	Apr 1852	N.-Amer	834627
Reichert, Michael	20 Feb 1833	Hildrizhausen	Herr.	Apr 1852	N.-Amer	834627
Reichert, Michael		Reusten	Herr.	Mar 1829	N.-Amer	834624
Reichert, Peter & F	49 yrs.	Nufringen	Herr.	Jun 1839	N.-Amer	834625
Reichert, Rosina & C	20 Jan 1815	Moetzingen	Herr.	Apr 1847	N.-Amer	834626
Reichert, Wilhelm Heinrich	29 Dec 1851	Pfaeffingen	Herr.	Feb 1869	N.-Amer	834624
Reichle, (wid.) & F		Dornhan	Sulz	Mar 1847	N.-Amer	849633
Reichle, Johann Robert	1 Jan 1849	Sulz	Sulz	Sep 1868	N.-Amer	849628

| Name | | Birth | | Emigration | | | Film |
Last	First	Date	Place	O'amt	Appl. Date	Dest.	Number
Reichle, Karl Gottfried		13 Feb 1856	Sulz	Sulz	Jun 1872	N.-Amer	849628
Reichle, Rosine Catharina		5 mon.	Dornstetten	Frd.	Apr 1857	N.-Amer	577776
Reichle, Rosine Catharine & C			Dornstetten	Frd.	Apr 1857	N.-Amer	577776
Reichle, Rosine Friederike		3 yrs.	Dornstetten	Frd.	Apr 1857	N.-Amer	577776
Reichmann, Emanuel Gustav		20 yrs.	Calw	Calw	1866	N.-Amer	563212
Reichstadt, Anna Maria		17 Jan 1829	Reinerzau	Frd.	Dec 1858	Switz.	577776
Reif, Jacob & F			Oberjettingen	Herr.	May 1836	N.-Amer	834624
Reiff, Elisabetha & C		27 Dec 1843	Muehlheim a.b.	Sulz	Jan 1884	N.-Amer	849639
Reigel, Anna & C		15 Apr 1785	Dornhan	Sulz	Jun 1817	N.-Amer	849633
Reigel, Barbara		15 Apr 1785	Dornhan	Sulz	Jun 1817	N.-Amer	849633
Reilin, Anna & C		28 yrs.	Hornberg	Calw	1854	N.-Amer	563212
Reinhard, Caroline Maxim.			Unterreichenbach	Calw	1861	N.-Amer	563212
Reinhard, Johannes			Duerrenmettstetten	Sulz	Feb 1852	N.-Amer	849635
Reinhardt, Elisabetha		28 Aug 1810	Wittlensweiler	Frd.	Oct 1836	France	569268
Reinhardt, Georg Friedrich		20 yrs.	Oberkollwangen	Calw	1866	N.-Amer	563212
Reinhardt, Ulrich		16 yrs.	Oberkollwangen	Calw	1869	Palest.	563212
Reinhart, Christiane Renate		22 Oct 1808	Wittlensweiler	Frd.	Jan 1841	France	569268
Reiser, Christina		3 Feb 1826	Dornhan	Sulz	Oct 1853	N.-Amer	849633
Reiser, Johannes		18 Feb 1833	Dornhan	Sulz	Sep 1853	N.-Amer	849633
Reiser, Matthias		14 Apr 1840	Dornhan	Sulz	Jun 1857	N.-Amer	849633
Reisser, Heinrich & F			Unterjesingen	Herr.	1826	N.-Amer	834624
Reisslin, Rosina Catharina			Bondorf	Herr.	Apr 1848	Bavaria	834626
Rempfer, Andreas		26 Mar 1830	Dornhan	Sulz	Mar 1857	N.-Amer	849633
Rempfer, Anreas		28 Sep 1856	Marschalkenzimmern	Sulz	Jul 1860	N.-Amer	849638
Rempp, Barbara (wid.)			Dornstetten	Frd.	1817	Russia	569269
Rempp, Christiana		31 Aug 1845	Bickelsberg	Sulz	Dec 1866	N.-Amer	849630
Rempp, Friedrich		15 May 1846	Wildberg	Nag.	May 1865	N.-Amer	838494
Rempp, Jacob		23 Jul 1833	Bickelsberg	Sulz	Apr 1852	N.-Amer	849630
Rempp, Johann Georg & W			Gueltstein	Herr.	Apr 1831	N.-Amer	834624
Rempp, Johann Jacob		31 Oct 1828	Oeschelbronn	Herr.	Sep 1869	France	834624
Rempp, Regina Marta (wife)			Gueltstein	Herr.	Apr 1831	N.-Amer	834624
Renschler, Anna Maria			Wuerzbach	Calw	1855	N.-Amer	563212
Renschler, Anna Maria			Sommenhardt	Calw	1855	N.-Amer	563212
Renschler, Johannes		25 yrs.	Sommenhardt	Calw	1855	N.-Amer	563212
Renschler, Johannes & W			Unterjettingen	Herr.	Apr 1837	N.-Amer	834624
Renschler, Marie			Holzbronn	Calw	1854	N.-Amer	563212
Rentscher, Agatha		25 Sep 1832	Groembach	Frd.	Feb 1860	N.-Amer	577777
Rentschler, Agatha		6 Jun 1859	Groembach	Frd.	Sep 1865	N.-Amer	577779
Rentschler, Anna Maria		11 May 1842	Groembach	Frd.	Sep 1865	N.-Amer	577779
Rentschler, Anna Maria			Zwerenberg	Calw	1868	N.-Amer	563212
Rentschler, Anna Marie			Liebelsberg	Calw	1862	England	563212
Rentschler, Anna Marie & C			Wuerzbach	Calw	1853	N.-Amer	563212
Rentschler, Barbara		19 Dec 1828	Altburg	Calw	1847	N.-Amer	563212
Rentschler, Barbara & C			Altbulach	Calw	1852	N.-Amer	563212
Rentschler, Carl Leopold			Oberreichenbach	Calw	1853	N.-Amer	563212
Rentschler, Catharina		10 yrs.	Rotfelden	Nag.	Jan 1854	N.-Amer	838491
Rentschler, Catharina Barbara		40 yrs.	Rotfelden	Nag.	Jan 1854	N.-Amer	838491
Rentschler, Christian		17 Jun 1850	Groembach	Frd.	Sep 1865	N.-Amer	577779
Rentschler, Christiane		19 Mar 1848	Groembach	Frd.	Sep 1865	N.-Amer	577779
Rentschler, Christina Barbara		13 yrs.	Rotfelden	Nag.	Jan 1854	N.-Amer	838491

Rentschler, Dorothea	25 yrs.	Zwerenberg	Calw	1854	N.-Amer	563212
Rentschler, Dorothea	10 Apr 1832	Altburg	Calw	1847	N.-Amer	563212
Rentschler, Elisabeth Cath.	22 Jul 1856	Groembach	Frd.	Sep 1865	N.-Amer	577779
Rentschler, Elisabetha Cath.		Walddorf	Nag.	Oct 1854	N.-Amer	838491
Rentschler, Friedrich	6 yrs.	Rotfelden	Nag.	Jan 1854	N.-Amer	838491
Rentschler, Friedrich	17 yrs.	Sommenhardt	Calw	1859	N.-Amer	563212
Rentschler, Gottfried	17 Jun 1846	Groembach	Frd.	Sep 1865	N.-Amer	577779
Rentschler, Gottlieb	8 yrs.	Rotfelden	Nag.	Jan 1854	N.-Amer	838491
Rentschler, Gottlieb		Wuerzbach	Calw	1853	N.-Amer	563212
Rentschler, Jacob	1 yrs.	Walddorf	Nag.	Oct 1854	N.-Amer	838491
Rentschler, Jacob & F		Oberhaugstett	Calw	1852	N.-Amer	563212
Rentschler, Jacob Friedrich	22 Oct 1844	Groembach	Frd.	Sep 1865	N.-Amer	577779
Rentschler, Jacob Jr. & F		Walddorf	Nag.	Oct 1854	N.-Amer	838491
Rentschler, Jakob		Edelweiler	Frd.	Oct 1854	N.-Amer	569274
Rentschler, Jakob & F		Schmieh	Calw	1854	N.-Amer	563212
Rentschler, Jakob Friedr. & F	12 Sep 1817	Groembach	Frd.	Sep 1865	N.-Amer	577779
Rentschler, Johann Adam		Aichelberg	Calw	Jul 1870	N.-Amer	563212
Rentschler, Johann Georg	infant	Walddorf	Nag.	Oct 1854	N.-Amer	838491
Rentschler, Johann Georg	19 yrs.	Rotfelden	Nag.	Jan 1854	N.-Amer	838491
Rentschler, Johann Gottlob	1839	Holzbronn	Calw	1857	N.-Amer	563212
Rentschler, Johann Jacob		Simmonzheim	Calw	1866	Holst.	563212
Rentschler, Johann Jacob		Oberhengstett	Calw	1858	N.-Amer	563212
Rentschler, Johann Michael		Schmieh	Calw	1868	N.-Amer	563212
Rentschler, Johann Michael		Oberhaugstett	Calw	1861	Bavaria	563212
Rentschler, Johannes	25 yrs.	Weltenschwann	Calw	1847	N.-Amer	563212
Rentschler, Lorenz	28 yrs.	Breitenberg	Calw	1867	N.-Amer	563212
Rentschler, Margaretha		Altburg	Calw	1856	Switz.	563212
Rentschler, Margarethe		Altburg	Calw	1853	N.-Amer	563212
Rentschler, Martin	16 yrs.	Rotfelden	Nag.	Jan 1854	N.-Amer	838491
Rentschler, Martin & F	41 yrs.	Rotfelden	Nag.	Jan 1854	N.-Amer	838491
Rentschler, Mathaeus	21 yrs.	Liebelsberg	Calw	1866	N.-Amer	563212
Rentschler, Michael	16 Oct 1853	Groembach	Frd.	Sep 1865	N.-Amer	577779
Rentschler, Michael		Monakam	Calw	1864	Baden	563212
Rentschler, Michael	1840	Zwerenberg	Calw	1854	N.-Amer	563212
Rentschler, Regine		Dennjaecht	Calw	May 1870	Baden	563212
Rentschler, Ulrich		Vesperweiler	Frd.	Mar 1856	N.-Amer	569275
Renz, Anna Maria (wife)	45 yrs.	Oberjettingen	Herr.	1838	Poland	834625
Renz, Barbara	28 Oct 1822	Oberjettingen	Herr.	bef 1862	N.-Amer	834624
Renz, Christian		Rohrau	Herr.	Jul 1833	Rus-Pol	834624
Renz, Elisabeth		Leinstetten	Sulz	Jun 1854	N.-Amer	849638
Renz, Johann Georg	31 Dec 1806	Herrenberg	Herr.	May 1844	N.-Amer	834626
Renz, Johann Jacob & W	6 Jun 1791	Oberjettingen	Herr.	1838	Poland	834625
Renz, Johann Magnus	23 Feb 1821	Ebhausen	Nag.	bef 1856	France	838492
Renz, Johann Micheal	23 Oct 1827	Oberjesingen	Herr.	May 1867	N.-Amer	834624
Renz, Johanne Margaretha		Nagold	Nag.	Jan 1854	N.-Amer	838491
Renz, Katharina	26 Oct 1820	Ebhausen	Nag.	Jul 1854	Switz.	838491
Renz, Rosina		Leinstetten	Sulz	Jun 1854	N.-Amer	849638
Renz, Theresia & C		Leinstetten	Sulz	Jun 1854	N.-Amer	849638
Repphun, Johann Ulrich		Simmozheim	Calw	Jun 1874	N.-Amer	563212
Retter, Augusta		Geradstetten	Schd.	Mar 1834	N.-Amer	801460

| Name | | Birth | | Emigration | | | Film |
Last	First	Date	Place	O'amt	Appl. Date	Dest.	Number
Retter, Daniel & F			Geradstetten	Schd.	Mar 1834	N.-Amer	801460
Reule, Anna Maria			Oberweiler	Calw	1867	N.-Amer	563212
Reule, Conrad			Oberweiler	Calw	1867	N.-Amer	563212
Reulin, Christine Magdalena			Aichhalden	Calw	1854	N.-Amer	563212
Reuter, Christina		23 Nov 1823	Pfalzgrafenweiler	Frd.	Jul 1854	N.-Amer	569274
Reuter, Rosine			Wittlensweiler	Frd.	Nov 1860	N.-Amer	577777
Reutter, Christian		5 Feb 1820	Pfalzgrafenweiler	Frd.	Apr 1844	France	569269
Reutter, Friedrich		10 Jul 1836	Glatten	Frd.	bef 1856	N.-Amer	569275
Reutter, Johann Martin		12 Mar 1826	Dornstetten	Frd.	Sep 1850	N.-Amer	569271
Reutter, Magdalena			Neubulach	Calw	1859	Switz.	563212
Reutter, Matthaeus		22 Dec 1841	Glatten	Frd.	May 1860	N.-Amer	577777
Reutter, Michael		18 Apr 1824	Dornstetten	Frd.	Mar 1847	N.-Amer	569271
Reutter, Rosina		18 Feb 1796	Pfalzgrafenweiler	Frd.	Apr 1846	N.-Amer	569271
Rexer, Georg Friedrich & F			Sommenhardt	Calw	Mar 1847	N.-Amer	563212
Richter, Nothburga			Effringen	Nag.	Sep 1854	N.-Amer	838491
Ricker, Sophie		13 Nov 1834	Freudenstadt	Frd.	Jun 1854	N.-Amer	569274
Rieber, Johannes			Ebingen	Bal.	bef 1846	Switz.	555963
Riecker, Paul Friedrich			Calw	Calw	Jul 1870	N.-Amer	563212
Rieder, Barbara & C		16 Jan 1832	Marschalkenzimmern	Sulz	Jul 1860	N.-Amer	849638
Rieder, Carl Jacob		10 Feb 1828	Aistaig	Sulz	May 1862	Switz.	849628
Rieder, Christine		8 May 1830	Aistaig	Sulz	Jun 1862	Bremen	849628
Riedt, Johann Adam		6 Jan 1825	Rosenfeld	Sulz	Jun 1850	Bavaria	849640
Rieger, Carl		20 yrs.	Altensteig	Nag.	Aug 1854	N.-Amer	838491
Rieger, Jeremias			Baiersbronn	Frd.	Dec 1807	France	569267
Rieger, Johanna Karoline			Freudenstadt	Frd.	May 1825	Rhld.	569267
Rieger, Xaver			Bettenhausen	Sulz	Feb 1854	N.-Amer	849630
Riehen, Anna		18 yrs.	Calw	Calw	1868	N.-Amer	563212
Riehen, Jakobine Magdalene		23 yrs.	Calw	Calw	1868	N.-Amer	563212
Riehen, Maria		18 yrs.	Calw	Calw	1868	N.-Amer	563212
Riehm, Anna Maria		25 Apr 1832	Oberjesingen	Herr.	Jan 1866	N.-Amer	834624
Rieker, Franziska		13 Jan 1816	Freudenstadt	Frd.	Sep 1846	N.-Amer	569271
Rieker, Johann Sigmund		4 Sep 1835	Freudenstadt	Frd.	1851	N.-Amer	569275
Rieker, Sophie		13 Nov 1834	Freudenstadt	Frd.	bef 1862	N.-Amer	577778
Riekert, Johann Christian			Hagelloch/Tuebingen	Herr.	Apr 1837	N.-Amer	834624
Riep, Jacob		28 yrs.	Ernstmuehl	Calw	Mar 1847	N.-Amer	563212
Riepp, Philipp Friedrich			Calw	Calw	1852	N.-Amer	563212
Riesel, Jacob			Liebenzell	Calw	1853	N.-Amer	563212
Riesemann, Elisabetha			Marschalkenzimmern	Sulz	Mar 1826	France	849638
Riesemann, Marie Katharina		11 Aug 1821	Trichtingen	Sulz	bef 1833	N.-Amer	849642
Riesenmann, Anna Maria & C		24 Feb 1842	Trichtingen	Sulz	bef 1870	Baden	849642
Riesenmann, Christine & C		29 yrs.	Trichtingen	Sulz	bef 1864	Baden	849642
Riesenmann, Johann Martin			Trichtingen	Sulz	Sep 1854	N.-Amer	849642
Rieser, Philipp Jakob & F			Huernerberg/Bergorte	Calw	1854	N.-Amer	563212
Riether, Anna Maria		27 Dec 1806	Sigmarswangen	Sulz	bef 1836	France	849642
Riethmueller, Christian Tob.		27 Mar 1851	Gueltstein	Herr.	Jul 1852	N.-Amer	834627
Riethmueller, Christina & C		11 Mar 1840	Nufringen	Herr.	Jan 1865	Baden	834624
Riethmueller, Gottlob Friedr.		14 Oct 1811	Gueltstein	Herr.	Mar 1847	N.-Amer	834626
Riethmueller, Jacob Oswald		18 Feb 1864	Nufringen	Herr.	Jan 1865	Baden	834624
Riethmueller, Johann Georg		29 Nov 1829	Kayh	Herr.	Jan 1865	N.-Amer	834624
Riethmueller, Johann Jacob		8 Nov 1839	Gueltstein	Herr.	Aug 1867	N.-Amer	834624

Name	Date	Place	Region	Emig. Date	Destination	Number
Riethmueller, Johann Martin		Tailfingen	Herr.	Jun 1837	N.-Amer	834624
Riethmueller, Johannes		Gueltstein	Herr.	Sep 1852	N.-Amer	834627
Riethmueller, Maria Kath. (wife)		Gueltstein	Herr.	Jul 1852	N.-Amer	834627
Riethmueller, Michael & F		Gueltstein	Herr.	Mar 1836	N.-Amer	834624
Riethmueller, Tobias & F		Gueltstein	Herr.	Jul 1852	N.-Amer	834627
Rietmueller, Christina Cath.	21 Aug 1838	Gueltstein	Herr.	Feb 1867	N.-Amer	834624
Riexinger, Magdalena	17 yrs.	Hildrizhausen	Herr.	Jul 1831	N.-Amer	834624
Rinderknecht, Christina Joh.	12 Apr 1810	Bondorf	Herr.	1848	N.-Amer	834626
Rinderknecht, Friedrich B. & F		Unterjettingen	Herr.	May 1832	N.-Amer	834624
Rinderknecht, Johann Jakob & F	20 Apr 1820	Bondorf	Herr.	1848	N.-Amer	834626
Rinderknecht, Johanne Christ.	27 Jun 1846	Bondorf	Herr.	1848	N.-Amer	834626
Rinderknecht, Marie Regine	31 Jan 1848	Bondorf	Herr.	1848	N.-Amer	834626
Ringel, Johann Michael		Hassloch	– –	Dec 1751	Mas.N-A	550803
Rink, Johann Georg		Wildberg	Nag.	Oct 1852	N.-Amer	838490
Rinler, Oskar	10 Aug 1822	Beutelsbach	Schd.	Apr 1841	Baden	801461
Ritt, Katharina		Ottenbronn	Calw	1857	N.-Amer	563212
Ritter, Rosa		Binsdorf	Sulz	Mar 1815	Bavaria	849625
Rittmann, Johann Georg		Baiersbronn	Frd.	Aug 1845	France	569269
Rittmann, Mathaeus & F	29 yrs.	Schoenmuenzach	Frd.	Jul 1832	N.-Amer	569267
Rittmann, Matthaeus	2 Jan 1836	Baiersbronn	Frd.	Apr 1856	N.-Amer	569275
Rixinger, Johannes	1834	Altburg	Calw	1854	N.-Amer	563212
Rixinius, Christoph		Hirsau	Calw	Jul 1848	N.-Amer	563212
Rockburger, Christian & F		Marschalkenzimmern	Sulz	bef 1853	N.-Amer	849638
Rodel, Anna Maria & C		Rosenfeld	Sulz	Jun 1817	Russia	849640
Roefler, Daniel Friedrich		Freudenstadt	Frd.	bef 1829	Paris	569267
Roehm, Andreas	25 yrs.	Wittershausen	Sulz	bef 1839	N.-Amer	849644
Roehm, Anna Maria		Sulz	Nag.	Feb 1854	N.-Amer	838491
Roehm, Barbara (wife)	6 Sep 1805	Bergfelden	Sulz	Apr 1860	N.-Amer	849629
Roehm, Catharina (wife)		Bickelsberg	Sulz	Feb 1834	N.-Amer	849644
Roehm, Christian	23 Aug 1840	Bergfelden	Sulz	Apr 1860	N.-Amer	849629
Roehm, Christian		Deckenpfronn	Calw	1852	N.-Amer	563212
Roehm, Christian & F	28 Dec 1811	Bergfelden	Sulz	Apr 1860	N.-Amer	849629
Roehm, Christina Marg.(wid.)		Sulz	Nag.	Apr 1849	N.-Amer	838490
Roehm, Christoph Friedrich	8 Apr 1829	Nufringen	Herr.	May 1851	N.-Amer	834627
Roehm, Dorothea & C		Deckenpfronn	Calw	1853	N.-Amer	563212
Roehm, Dorothea (wid.) & F	26 Sep 1793	Nufringen	Herr.	May 1851	N.-Amer	834627
Roehm, Eva Catharina		Sulz	Nag.	Feb 1854	N.-Amer	838491
Roehm, Friedrich & F	24 Dec 1801	Bickelsberg	Sulz	Feb 1834	N.-Amer	849644
Roehm, Georg Balthas		Deckenpfronn	Calw	1852	N.-Amer	563212
Roehm, Jacob (wid.) & F		Deckenpfronn	Calw	1853	N.-Amer	563212
Roehm, Johann Georg		Wittershausen	Sulz	bef 1842	N.-Amer	849644
Roehm, Johann Michael		Sulz	Nag.	Feb 1854	N.-Amer	838491
Roehm, Johanna Louise		Tailfingen	Herr.	Mar 1836	N.-Amer	834624
Roehm, Johannes		Deckenpfronn	Calw	1853	N.-Amer	563212
Roehm, Johannes	1 Aug 1840	Nufringen	Herr.	May 1851	N.-Amer	834627
Roehm, Philipp Gottlieb		Sulz	Nag.	Feb 1854	N.-Amer	838491
Roehne, Christian	23 Dec 1805	Oberjettingen	Herr.	Jun 1868	N.-Amer	834624
Roehr, Fridrich		Dornstetten	Frd.	Apr 1752	Pen.N-A	550803
Roehrer, Adam		Dornstetten	Frd.	bef 1853	N.-Amer	569272
Roehrer, Charlotte	14 yrs.	Dornstetten	Frd.	Sep 1853	N.-Amer	569272

Name		Birth		Emigration			Film
Last	First	Date	Place	O'amt	Appl. Date	Dest.	Number
Roehrer, Chrischona			Dornstetten	Frd.	Sep 1853	N.-Amer	569272
Roehrer, Christian		29 Apr 1838	Dornstetten	Frd.	bef 1864	Baden	577779
Roehrer, Emma		5 yrs.	Dornstetten	Frd.	Sep 1853	N.-Amer	569272
Roehrer, Jakob		16 yrs.	Dornstetten	Frd.	Sep 1853	N.-Amer	569272
Roehrer, Margaretha		9 yrs.	Dornstetten	Frd.	Sep 1853	N.-Amer	569272
Roehrer, Susanna		10 yrs.	Dornstetten	Frd.	Sep 1853	N.-Amer	569272
Roempp, Christian		19 Nov 1849	Weiden	Sulz	bef 1877	Switz.	849644
Roesch, Mathilde		12 Aug 1851	Haiterbach	Nag.	Sep 1853	N.-Amer	838490
Roesch, Regina		65 yrs.	Haiterbach	Nag.	Sep 1853	N.-Amer	838490
Roesle, Johannes & W			Herrenberg	Herr.	Jun 1831	N.-Amer	834624
Roesle, Maria Magdalena (wife)			Herrenberg	Herr.	Jun 1831	N.-Amer	834624
Roggenstein, Christoph		22 Jan 1795	Rosenfeld	Sulz	Oct 1836	N.-Amer	849640
Roh, Amalie		29 Jan 1844	Pfalzgrafenweiler	Frd.	Jul 1861	N.-Amer	577778
Roh, Anna Maria			Altenstaig	Nag.	Jun 1856	N.-Amer	838492
Roh, Christiane Friederike		28 Jul 1842	Pfalzgrafenweiler	Frd.	Jul 1861	N.-Amer	577778
Roh, Wilhelmine Sophie			Freudenstadt	Frd.	Apr 1857	D.-dorf	577776
Rohl, Paul Eduard			Calw	Calw	bef 1857	N.-Amer	563212
Rohmann, Ludwig Friedrich		23 Jan 1797	Sulz	Sulz	Sep 1832	Bohemia	849627
Rohrer, Anna		9 May 1829	Dornhan	Sulz	Dec 1856	N.-Amer	849633
Rohrer, Anna Maria		23 May 1806	Baiersbronn	Frd.	Dec 1853	N.-Amer	569272
Rohrer, Anna Maria		16 Apr 1837	Durrweiler	Frd.	May 1854	N.-Amer	569273
Rohrer, Eva Christine		10 Dec 1792	Baiersbronn	Frd.	Apr 1847	N.-Amer	569270
Rohrer, Jakob			Geisburg/Stuttgart	Sulz	bef 1848	N.-Amer	849643
Rohrer, Johann Georg & F			Kniebis	Frd.	Apr 1817	Russia	569267
Rohrer, Johann Martin		11 Jul 1839	Durrweiler	Frd.	May 1854	N.-Amer	569273
Rohrer, Martin			Bergfelden	Sulz	May 1855	N.-Amer	849629
Rolerer, Auguste Christiane		3 Nov 1839	Freudenstadt	Frd.	Sep 1854	N.-Amer	569274
Rolerer, Carl		15 Jun 1846	Freudenstadt	Frd.	Sep 1854	N.-Amer	569274
Rolerer, Caroline Sophie		3 Jul 1849	Freudenstadt	Frd.	Sep 1854	N.-Amer	569274
Rolerer, Catharina Sophie			Freudenstadt	Frd.	Sep 1854	N.-Amer	569274
Rolerer, David & F			Freudenstadt	Frd.	Sep 1854	N.-Amer	569274
Rolerer, Wilhelm David		28 Jul 1842	Freudenstadt	Frd.	Sep 1854	N.-Amer	569274
Roll, Christian		28 Mar 1867	Renfrizhausen	Sulz	May 1883	N.-Amer	849639
Roll, Georg Friedrich		25 Nov 1843	Oberjettingen	Herr.	Jul 1866	N.-Amer	834624
Roll, Johann Michael			Oeschelbronn	Herr.	Apr 1831	N.-Amer	834624
Roller, Anna Maria			Zwerenberg	Calw	1861	N.-Amer	563212
Roller, Anna Maria		18 yrs.	Altburg	Calw	Mar 1847	N.-Amer	563212
Roller, Barbara			Neubulach	Calw	1860	N.-Amer	563212
Roller, Carl			Calw	Calw	1852	N.-Amer	563212
Roller, Christiane Friederike		29 yrs.	Calw	Calw	Jan 1848	Baden	563212
Roller, Eva Maria (wife)			Neubulach	Calw	1860	N.-Amer	563212
Roller, Georg			Balingen	Bal.	bef 1848	Switz.	555963
Roller, Georg David			Neubulach	Calw	1864	France	563212
Roller, Georg David		1839	Oberhaugstett	Calw	1856	N.-Amer	563212
Roller, Gottfried		1835	Calw	Calw	1854	N.-Amer	563212
Roller, Gotthilf			Neubulach	Calw	1860	N.-Amer	563212
Roller, Hiob			Goettelfingen	Frd.	1817	Russia	569269
Roller, Jacob & F			Neubulach	Calw	1860	N.-Amer	563212
Roller, Jacob Friedrich			Neubulach	Calw	1860	N.-Amer	563212
Roller, Jakob			Glatten	Frd.	1817	Russia	569269

Roller, Jakob & F		Kuppingen	Herr.	Mar 1848	N.-Amer	834626
Roller, Johann Georg	25 yrs.	Sommenhardt	Calw	1867	N.-Amer	563212
Roller, Johann Georg	1836	Aichhalden	Calw	1854	N.-Amer	563212
Roller, Johann Georg		Meistern/Bergorte	Calw	1852	N.-Amer	563212
Roller, Johann Jacob	27 yrs.	Stammheim	Calw	1868	N.-Amer	563212
Roller, Johann Jacob	23 Jan 1844	Moetzingen	Herr.	Jan 1848	N.-Amer	834626
Roller, Johann Jakob	12 Jun 1824	Kuppingen	Herr.	Mar 1848	N.-Amer	834626
Roller, Johann Martin		Kuppingen	Herr.	Feb 1845	France	834626
Roller, Johann Martin	19 Apr 1845	Kuppingen	Herr.	Mar 1848	N.-Amer	834626
Roller, Johann Peter	6 Apr 1849	Kuppingen	Herr.	Aug 1869	N.-Amer	834624
Roller, Johanne Gottliebin		Wildberg	Nag.	1852	N.-Amer	838491
Roller, Johannes		Neubulach	Calw	1860	N.-Amer	563212
Roller, Johannes		Altburg	Calw	1852	N.-Amer	563212
Roller, Karolina		Wildberg	Nag.	Jun 1852	N.-Amer	838490
Roller, Katharina		Neubulach	Calw	1860	N.-Amer	563212
Roller, Katharina Barb. (wife)		Kuppingen	Herr.	Mar 1848	N.-Amer	834626
Roller, Katharina Barbara	9 Dec 1829	Kuppingen	Herr.	Mar 1848	N.-Amer	834626
Roller, Margaretha	1 Jan 1823	Kuppingen	Herr.	Mar 1848	N.-Amer	834626
Roller, Maria Dorothea	29 Jun 1817	Kuppingen	Herr.	Mar 1848	N.-Amer	834626
Roller, Maria Magdalena	24 Jun 1827	Kuppingen	Herr.	Mar 1848	N.-Amer	834626
Rominger, Gottlieb	1819	Ebingen	Bal.	1845	Switz.	555963
Rominger, Johann Georg & F		Ebingen	Bal.	Jan 1852	N.-Amer	555964
Rommann, Barbara		Reutin	Sulz	Oct 1854	N.-Amer	849642
Rommann, Friedrich & F		Trichtingen	Sulz	Oct 1854	N.-Amer	849642
Rommann, Matthias		Reutin	Sulz	1852	N.-Amer	849642
Rommann, Wilhelm		Reutin	Sulz	Oct 1854	N.-Amer	849642
Rommelin, Friedrike		Herrenberg	Herr.	Dec 1839	Switz.	834625
Rommer, Johannes & F		Glatten	Frd.	1817	Russia	569269
Rommer, Martin		Aach	Frd.	1817	Russia	569269
Roth, Andreas	28 Jun 1845	Duerrenmettstetten	Sulz	Apr 1864	N.-Amer	849635
Roth, Anna Maria	30 Jan 1835	Dornhan	Sulz	Apr 1861	N.-Amer	849634
Roth, Anna Maria	21 yrs.	Muehlheim a.B.	Sulz	1859	N.-Amer	849639
Roth, Barbara	19 yrs.	Voehringen	Sulz	Apr 1867	N.-Amer	849643
Roth, Barbara		Duerrenmettstetten	Sulz	Mar 1854	N.-Amer	849635
Roth, Carl		Laufen	Bal.	Oct 1849	Chili	555964
Roth, Christian		Guckersberg	--	1752	Pen.N-A	550803
Roth, Christian		Renfrizhausen	Sulz	Feb 1817	Russia	849639
Roth, Johann Georg	18 Jun 1848	Duerrenmettstetten	Sulz	Jul 1866	N.-Amer	849635
Roth, Johann Georg	26 Dec 1854	Duerrenmettstetten	Sulz	Mar 1860	N.-Amer	849635
Roth, Johann Ludwig		Simmozheim	Calw	May 1870	N.-Amer	563212
Roth, Johannes	3 Dec 1846	Bergfelden	Sulz	Sep 1866	N.-Amer	849629
Roth, Johannes	26 Dec 1854	Duerrenmettstetten	Sulz	Mar 1860	N.-Amer	849635
Roth, Lisette		Winterbach	Schd.	Mar 1844	Baden	801461
Roth, Magdalena	26 yrs.	Tailfingen	Herr.	Jul 1848	N.-Amer	834626
Roth, Walpurga		Dornhan	Sulz	Mar 1817	Russia	849633
Roth, Wilhelm		Laufen	Bal.	Oct 1849	Chili	555964
Rothdach, Michael		Cresbach	Frd.	1817	Russia	569269
Rothfuss, Adolf	20 May 1838	Roehrsbaechle	Frd.	Jul 1855	N.-Amer	569275
Rothfuss, Anna Maria	23 Dec 1818	Oberiflingen	Frd.	Jan 1855	N.-Amer	569275
Rothfuss, Anna Maria	18 Apr 1828	Aach	Frd.	Jul 1857	N.-Amer	577776

| Name | | Birth | | Emigration | | | Film |
Last	First	Date	Place	O'amt	Appl. Date	Dest.	Number
Rothfuss, Anna Maria & C		7 Mar 1822	Baiersbronn	Frd.	Mar 1849	N.-Amer	569270
Rothfuss, Barbara		23 May 1817	Tumlingen	Frd.	Mar 1837	N.-Amer	569268
Rothfuss, Carl Bernhardt		6 Aug 1844	Baiersbronn	Frd.	Mar 1849	N.-Amer	569270
Rothfuss, Carl Friedrich		9 May 1834	Baiersbronn	Frd.	Oct 1854	N.-Amer	569274
Rothfuss, Christian		5 Nov 1814	Dietersweiler	Frd.	Mar 1848	Baden	569270
Rothfuss, Christian		21 Jul 1814	Klosterreichenbach	Frd.	bef 1847	Wien	569270
Rothfuss, Friedrich		10 Feb 1809	Tumlingen	Frd.	Feb 1837	N.-Amer	569268
Rothfuss, Friedrich Aug.		16 Aug 1835	Baiersbronn	Frd.	Dec 1853	N.-Amer	569272
Rothfuss, Georg David & F		37 yrs.	Aach	Frd.	Mar 1837	N.-Amer	569267
Rothfuss, Georg Friedrich		19 yrs.	Dennjaecht	Calw	1866	N.-Amer	563212
Rothfuss, Georg Ulrich		20 Aug 1829	Baiersbronn	Frd.	Aug 1854	N.-Amer	569274
Rothfuss, Gottlieb		17 yrs.	Dennjaecht	Calw	1866	N.-Amer	563212
Rothfuss, Gottliebin			Altbulach	Calw	1860	Switz.	563212
Rothfuss, Jakob Friedrch		14 Apr 1846	Baiersbronn	Frd.	Jun 1864	N.-Amer	577779
Rothfuss, Jakob Friedrich			Vesperweiler	Frd.	Mar 1856	N.-Amer	569275
Rothfuss, Johann David		24 Jan 1824	Baiersbronn	Frd.	Dec 1853	N.-Amer	569272
Rothfuss, Johanne Elisabeth		31 Jan 1835	Aach	Frd.	Mar 1837	N.-Amer	569267
Rothfuss, Johannes		13 May 1836	Roehrsbaechle	Frd.	Jul 1855	N.-Amer	569275
Rothfuss, Johannes			Besenfeld	Frd.	Mar 1865	N.-Amer	577779
Rothfuss, Johannes		21 May 1836	Baiersbronn	Frd.	Aug 1854	N.-Amer	569274
Rothfuss, Magdalena		29 yrs.	Simmersfeld	Nag.	May 1856	N.-Amer	838492
Rothfuss, Maria Helena		26 May 1865	Liebenzell	Calw	1867	Baden	563212
Rothfuss, Marie Dorothee		3 Dec 1828	Aach	Frd.	Mar 1837	N.-Amer	569267
Rothfuss, Marie Luise		18 Sep 1832	Aach	Frd.	Mar 1837	N.-Amer	569267
Rothfuss, Michael Friedrich			Besenfeld	Frd.	bef 1863	Baden	577778
Rothfuss, Rosine Christine		23 Jul 1817	Aach	Frd.	Mar 1837	N.-Amer	569267
Rothfuss, Rosine Christine		9 Jun 1837	Aach	Frd.	Mar 1837	N.-Amer	569267
Rothfuss, Ulrich		16 yrs.	Heselbach	Frd.	Apr 1860	N.-Amer	577777
Rothfuss, Wilhelmine Frieder.		26 Sep 1830	Aach	Frd.	Mar 1837	N.-Amer	569267
Rotter, Anna Maria (wife)			Bondorf	Herr.	Jun 1832	N.-Amer	834624
Rotter, Anna Maria (wife)			Bondorf	Herr.	Jun 1832	N.-Amer	834624
Rotter, Catharina (wife)		32 yrs.	Bondorf	Herr.	Jun 1832	N.-Amer	834624
Rotter, Christian & F		28 yrs.	Bondorf	Herr.	Jun 1832	N.-Amer	834624
Rotter, Johann Georg & F		30 yrs.	Bondorf	Herr.	Jun 1832	N.-Amer	834624
Rotter, Sebastian & W		56 yrs.	Bondorf	Herr.	Jun 1832	N.-Amer	834624
Royhfuss, Margaretha & C			Liebenzell	Calw	1867	Baden	563212
Royhfuss, Maria Catharina		24 Nov 1863	Liebenzell	Calw	1867	Baden	563212
Ruckhaber, Christiane Friedr.		18 May 1820	Herrenberg	Herr.	Feb 1852	N.-Amer	834627
Rudolph, Wilhelm Friedrich		18 May 1831	Unterjesingen	Herr.	Jul 1866	N.-Amer	834624
Rueffle, Johannes		43 yrs.	Gechingen	Calw	1869	N.-Amer	563212
Ruegner, Elisabetha			Freudenstadt	Frd.	1851	N.-Amer	577778
Ruegner, Regina		24 yrs.	Dornstetten	Frd.	Oct 1851	N.-Amer	569271
Ruehle, Anna Maria			Gaertringen	Herr.	Mar 1834	N.-Amer	834626
Ruehle, Dorothea (wife)			Gaertringen	Herr.	Aug 1852	N.-Amer	834627
Ruehle, Heinrich		14 Jan 1839	Gaertringen	Herr.	Aug 1852	N.-Amer	834627
Ruehle, Jakob Friedrich		13 Feb 1849	Gaertringen	Herr.	Aug 1852	N.-Amer	834627
Ruehle, Jeremias		3 Apr 1835	Gaertringen	Herr.	Aug 1852	N.-Amer	834627
Ruehle, Johann (wid.) & F			Gaertringen	Herr.	Mar 1834	N.-Amer	834626
Ruehle, Johann Georg		21 Sep 1847	Gaertringen	Herr.	Aug 1852	N.-Amer	834627
Ruehle, Johann Georg & F			Gaertringen	Herr.	Aug 1852	N.-Amer	834627

Ruehle, Justine Dorothea	29 Aug 1837	Gaertringen	Herr.	Aug 1852	N.-Amer	834627
Ruehle, Wilhelm	19 Jun 1842	Gaertringen	Herr.	Aug 1852	N.-Amer	834627
Ruemelin, Elisabeth	20 yrs.	Pfalzgrafenweiler	Frd.	Aug 1842	Switz.	569269
Ruemmele, Anna Maria	22 yrs.	Pfalzgrafenweiler	Frd.	Mar 1846	Switz.	569271
Rues, Johann Georg		Wittershausen	Sulz	1782	Poland	849625
Ruess, Johann Georg	28 Sep 1845	Kuppingen	Herr.	Feb 1847	N.-Amer	834626
Ruess, Johann Georg & F		Kuppingen	Herr.	Feb 1847	N.-Amer	834626
Ruess, Johannes	12 Sep 1834	Kuppingen	Herr.	Feb 1847	N.-Amer	834626
Ruess, Jonas	8 Dec 1832	Kuppingen	Herr.	Feb 1847	N.-Amer	834626
Ruess, Joseph Friedrich	12 Sep 1839	Kuppingen	Herr.	Feb 1847	N.-Amer	834626
Ruess, Rosina Barbara (wife)		Kuppingen	Herr.	Feb 1847	N.-Amer	834626
Ruess, Rosine Barbara	1 Oct 1843	Kuppingen	Herr.	Feb 1847	N.-Amer	834626
Ruf, Johannes	11 Dec 1811	Renfrizhausen	Sulz	Oct 1844	Baden	849639
Ruf, Karl	4 Feb 1849	Altheim	Horb	Apr 1850	N.-Amer	835929
Ruff, Anna Maria	2 Aug 1841	Dornstetten	Frd.	Mar 1846	N.-Amer	569271
Ruff, Christian & F	1 Aug 1814	Dornstetten	Frd.	Mar 1846	N.-Amer	569271
Ruff, Margaritha		Friedrichstal	Frd.	Mar 1805	Austria	569267
Ruff, Maria Magdalena	15 Mar 1808	Dornstetten	Frd.	Mar 1846	N.-Amer	569271
Ruffle, Johannes	1825	Gechingen	Calw	1856	N.-Amer	563212
Rukler, Johann Martin	1839	Hornberg	Calw	1857	N.-Amer	563212
Rummelin, Elisabeth Salome	7 Oct 1830	Pfalzgrafenweiler	Frd.	bef 1863	Italia	577778
Rumpel, Johann Georg	3 Jan 1834	Bergfelden	Sulz	May 1853	N.-Amer	849629
Rumpel, Johann Georg	30 Mar 1822	Voehringen	Sulz	1850	N.-Amer	849643
Rumpel, Johannes & F		Bergfelden	Sulz	Jul 1854	N.-Amer	849629
Rumpel, Maria		Bergfelden	Sulz	bef 1851	N.-Amer	849629
Rumpel, Mathias	27 Sep 1835	Bergfelden	Sulz	bef 1851	N.-Amer	849629
Rumppel, Erasmus & F		Bergfelden	Sulz	May 1817	Russia	849629
Ruof, Anna Maria		Brittheim	Sulz	bef 1863	N.-Amer	849632
Ruof, Barbara	14 Mar 1842	Renfrizhausen	Sulz	Mar 1860	N.-Amer	849639
Ruof, Christoph		Dornstetten	Frd.	Oct 1830	Bavaria	569269
Ruof, Demuth		Sulz	Sulz	Jan 1815	Bavaria	849625
Ruof, Johannesa	11 Jun 1853	Renfrizhausen	Sulz	Apr 1871	N.-Amer	849639
Ruof, Katharina	11 Jun 1848	Renfrizhausen	Sulz	Apr 1871	N.-Amer	849639
Ruof, Maria Rebekka		Sulz	Sulz	Jul 1815	Switz.	849627
Ruof, Mathaeus		Duerrenmettstetten	Sulz	bef 1828	France	849635
Ruof, Rosina	9 Apr 1844	Renfrizhausen	Sulz	Apr 1871	N.-Amer	849639
Ruoff, Anna	3 yrs.	Isingen	Sulz	Sep 1854	N.-Amer	849636
Ruoff, Anna Barbara	24 yrs.	Isingen	Sulz	Sep 1854	N.-Amer	849636
Ruoff, Barbara		Dornstetten	Frd.	Apr 1838	N.-Amer	569269
Ruoff, Christian	26 Feb 1826	Isingen	Sulz	1852	N.-Amer	849636
Ruoff, Eva Marie		Dornstetten	Frd.	Apr 1838	N.-Amer	569269
Ruoff, Jacob & F		Dornstetten	Frd.	Apr 1838	N.-Amer	569269
Ruoff, Jakob	5 Jun 1851	Holzhausen	Sulz	Oct 1867	N.-Amer	849635
Ruoff, Jakob	1 yrs.	Isingen	Sulz	Sep 1854	N.-Amer	849636
Ruoff, Jakob & F		Isingen	Sulz	Sep 1854	N.-Amer	849636
Ruoff, Johann Georg	22 Oct 1816	Isingen	Sulz	Mar 1852	N.-Amer	849636
Ruoff, Johann Georg	20 Apr 1833	Leidringen	Sulz	Oct 1852	N.-Amer	849637
Ruoff, Johann Georg		Leidringen	Sulz	Aug 1853	N.-Amer	849637
Ruoff, Johann Ludwig & F	27 Sep 1804	Dornstetten	Frd.	Apr 1838	N.-Amer	569269
Ruoff, Johann Martin		Bondorf	Herr.	Mar 1831	N.-Amer	834624

Name		Birth		Emigration			Film
Last	First	Date	Place	O'amt	Appl. Date	Dest.	Number
Ruoff, Johann Michael		5 Feb 1826	Bondorf	Herr.	Jul 1847	N.-Amer	834626
Ruoff, Johannes			Leidringen	Sulz	Aug 1854	N.-Amer	849637
Ruoff, Karl		23 Feb 1870	Dornhan	Sulz	Apr 1884	N.-Amer	849634
Ruoff, Katharina			Isingen	Sulz	Apr 1840	N.-Amer	849636
Ruoff, Katharina (wife)			Isingen	Sulz	Sep 1854	N.-Amer	849636
Ruoff, Ludwig		7 Nov 1802	Dornstetten	Frd.	Mar 1851	France	569271
Ruoff, Ludwig		4 Oct 1836	Freudenstadt	Frd.	Jun 1854	N.-Amer	569274
Ruoff, Martin		9 Mar 1854	Leidringen	Sulz	Jul 1871	N.-Amer	849637
Ruoff, Pauline			Herrenberg	Herr.	Nov 1843	Baden	834625
Ruoff, Philippina Fried. Lis.		25 yrs.	Sulz	Sulz	Mar 1815	Bavaria	849625
Ruoff, Wilhelm Georg		10 Nov 1838	Sulz	Sulz	Apr 1858	N.-Amer	849628
Ruoss, Johann Georg		8 Feb 1837	Schopfloch	Frd.	Jul 1856	N.-Amer	569275
Ruoss, Johann Georg		2 Jul 1809	Dornhan	Frd.	bef 1854	N.-Amer	569274
Rupp, Andreas		1820	Neubulach	Calw	1856	N.-Amer	563212
Rupp, Anna Maria		16 Jul 1838	Reusten	Herr.	Jul 1870	N.-Amer	834624
Rupp, Anna Maria (wife)			Neubulach	Calw	1860	N.-Amer	563212
Rupp, Anton & F			Neubulach	Calw	1860	N.-Amer	563212
Rupp, Barbara & C		35 yrs.	Reusten	Herr.	Apr 1843	N.-Amer	834625
Rupp, Christian		17 yrs.	Neubulach	Calw	1860	N.-Amer	563212
Rupp, David Jacob		31 Mar 1830	Reusten	Herr.	Apr 1843	N.-Amer	834625
Rupp, Eva		1829	Neubulach	Calw	1856	N.-Amer	563212
Rupp, Eva Maria		19 yrs.	Neubulach	Calw	1860	N.-Amer	563212
Rupp, Johann Georg		1834	Neubulach	Calw	1856	N.-Amer	563212
Rupp, Johannes		41 yrs.	Teinach	Calw	1856	N.-Amer	563212
Rupp, Johannes		20 Mar 1837	Bondorf	Herr.	Aug 1845	N.-Amer	834626
Rupp, Johannes		24 Jul 1831	Reusten	Herr.	Apr 1843	N.-Amer	834625
Rupp, Joseph		1840	Neubulach	Calw	1856	N.-Amer	563212
Rupp, Karl Albert Viktor		9 Oct 1840	Reusten	Herr.	Apr 1843	N.-Amer	834625
Rupp, Maria		4 Feb 1835	Reusten	Herr.	Apr 1843	N.-Amer	834625
Rupp, Marianna		1832	Neubulach	Calw	1856	N.-Amer	563212
Rupp, Mathaeus		2 Feb 1842	Reusten	Herr.	Apr 1843	N.-Amer	834625
Rupp, Vincenz		1 Jul 1847	Oberjettingen	Herr.	Jul 1866	N.-Amer	834624
Ruthart, Gotthilf Adolf		9 Feb 1849	Herrenberg	Herr.	Jul 1869	Switz.	834624
Sachs, Daniel			Oggersheim	– –	Dec 1751	N.-Amer	550803
Sackler, Magdalena			Deckenpfronn	Calw	1857	Austria	563212
Sackmann, Anna			Vesperweiler	Frd.	Sep 1846	N.-Amer	569271
Sackmann, Anna Maria		15 Oct 1823	Vesperweiler	Frd.	Sep 1846	N.-Amer	569271
Sackmann, Barbara		10 Sep 1826	Vesperweiler	Frd.	Sep 1846	N.-Amer	569271
Sackmann, Jakob Bernhardt		11 Jan 1835	Heselbach	Frd.	Mar 1854	N.-Amer	569273
Sackmann, Johann Georg		11 Jul 1843	Voehringen	Sulz	bef 1873	Switz.	849643
Sackmann, Johann Georg & F			Voehringen	Sulz	Jan 1894	Switz.	849626
Saemann, Anna (wife)			Isingen	Sulz	Apr 1840	N.-Amer	849636
Saemann, Catharina			Isingen	Sulz	Apr 1840	N.-Amer	849636
Saemann, Christian		2 Mar 1840	Isingen	Sulz	Apr 1840	N.-Amer	849636
Saemann, Christine		3 Nov 1825	Isingen	Sulz	Apr 1840	N.-Amer	849636
Saemann, Jacob Friedrich		27 Feb 1827	Rosenfeld	Sulz	bef 1857	N.-Amer	849640
Saemann, Martin		1 Jan 1823	Isingen	Sulz	Apr 1840	N.-Amer	849636
Saemann, Martin & F			Isingen	Sulz	Apr 1840	N.-Amer	849636
Saengle, Friedrich		14 yrs.	Freudenstadt	Frd.	Jun 1854	N.-Amer	569274
Saengle, Sophia			Freudenstadt	Frd.	Apr 1854	N.-Amer	569273

Said, Anna Maria	2 Apr 1836	Groembach	Frd.	Aug 1856	N.-Amer	569275
Sailer, Bonifaz	5 Jun 1832	Oberndorf	Herr.	Aug 1867	N.-Amer	834624
Sailer, Carl	12 Apr 1851	Poltringen	Herr.	Oct 1869	N.-Amer	834624
Sailer, Catharina & C		Simmozheim	Calw	1853	N.-Amer	563212
Sailer, Christian & F		Freudenstadt	Frd.	1851	N.-Amer	577778
Sailer, Christian & F		Dornstetten	Frd.	May 1851	N.-Amer	569271
Sailer, David & F		Dornstetten	Frd.	1817	Odessa	569269
Sailer, Eva Marie		Dornstetten	Frd.	Apr 1838	N.-Amer	569269
Sailer, Felex	14 Feb 1853	Oberndorf	Herr.	Aug 1866	N.-Amer	834624
Sailer, Franziska (wife)		Poltringen	Herr.	Apr 1848	N.-Amer	834626
Sailer, Jacob Friedrich		Freudenstadt	Frd.	1851	N.-Amer	577778
Sailer, Jakob Friedrich		Dornstetten	Frd.	May 1851	N.-Amer	569271
Sailer, Johann & F		Dornstetten	Frd.	1817	Poland	569269
Sailer, Johann Christian	9 yrs.	Dornstetten	Frd.	May 1851	N.-Amer	569271
Sailer, Johannes	18 Apr 1829	Dornstetten	Frd.	Feb 1854	N.-Amer	569273
Sailer, Johannes		Dornstetten	Frd.	1817	Russia	569269
Sailer, Johannes	5 Jun 1815	Oberndorf	Herr.	Aug 1866	N.-Amer	834624
Sailer, Josef	4 Mar 1847	Oberndorf	Herr.	Aug 1866	N.-Amer	834624
Sailer, Josef	12 Oct 1847	Poltringen	Herr.	Oct 1869	N.-Amer	834624
Sailer, Joseph & F		Poltringen	Herr.	Apr 1848	N.-Amer	834626
Sailer, Katharina	1 yrs.	Dornstetten	Frd.	May 1851	N.-Amer	569271
Sailer, Maria Elisabeth		Dornstetten	Frd.	Jul 1866	N.-Amer	577780
Sailer, Maria Rosine	8 yrs.	Dornstetten	Frd.	May 1851	N.-Amer	569271
Sailer, Michael & F		Gueltstein	Herr.	Mar 1836	N.-Amer	834624
Sailer, Rosina Maria	6 yrs.	Dornstetten	Frd.	May 1851	N.-Amer	569271
Sailer, Sebast		Oberndorf	Herr.	Jul 1841	Prussia	834625
Sailer, Wilhelm	23 Nov 1838	Dornstetten	Frd.	Feb 1854	N.-Amer	569273
Sailer, Ziprian		Oberndorf	Herr.	Apr 1830	N.-Amer	834624
Sakmann, Christina		Bickelsberg	Sulz	Jun 1849	N.-Amer	849630
Sarrler, Anna Maria		Oberjesingen	Herr.	May 1852	N.-Amer	834627
Sassauer, Joseph & F		Kohlwald	Frd.	Apr 1817	N.-Amer	569268
Sassauer, Mathias		Pfaffenwald	Frd.	Mar 1817	N.-Amer	569268
Sassler, Jacob & F		Frommern	Bal.	Aug 1847	N.-Amer	555964
Satorius, Carl Christ. Fr. G.	30 May 1820	Herrenberg	Herr.	Nov 1851	N.-Amer	834627
Satter, Anna Barbara	25 Oct 1842	Moetzingen	Herr.	May 1852	N.-Amer	834627
Satter, Johannes	13 Dec 1850	Moetzingen	Herr.	May 1852	N.-Amer	834627
Satter, Regina & C	4 Jun 1814	Moetzingen	Herr.	May 1852	N.-Amer	834627
Sattler, Christiana Dorothea	25 Oct 1860	Oberjesingen	Herr.	Aug 1869	N.-Amer	834624
Sattler, Elisabetha Wilhelm.	27 Apr 1837	Gaertringen	Herr.	Feb 1862	Switz	834624
Sattler, Friederike	1 Mar 1817	Unterjesingen	Herr.	Jun 1839	Switz.	834625
Sattler, Friederike & C		Deckenpfronn	Calw	1853	N.-Amer	563212
Sattler, Georg Michael	10 Mar 1830	Oberjesingen	Herr.	Aug 1869	N.-Amer	834624
Sattler, Hermann	17 yrs.	Deckenpfronn	Calw	1868	N.-Amer	563212
Sattler, Johann Georg	39 yrs.	Affstaett	Herr.	Jun 1850	N.-Amer	834627
Sattler, Johann Martin & F		Tailfingen	Herr.	Mar 1836	N.-Amer	834624
Sattler, Ludwig Friedrich	31 Jan 1842	Moetzingen	Herr.	May 1869	N.-Amer	834624
Sattler, Maria Catharina	30 Aug 1858	Oberjesingen	Herr.	Aug 1869	N.-Amer	834624
Sattler, Markus		Deckenpfronn	Calw	1853	N.-Amer	563212
Sattler, Stefan	46 yrs.	Tailfingen	Herr.	May 1849	N.-Amer	834627
Sattler, Stephan (wid.)		Tailfingen	Herr.	May 1832	N.-Amer	834624

| Name | | Birth | | Emigration | | | Film |
Last	First	Date	Place	O'amt	Appl. Date	Dest.	Number
Sattler, Wilhelm		20 Nov 1868	Oberjesingen	Herr.	Aug 1869	N.-Amer	834624
Sauer, Anna Maria		1812	Aistaig	Sulz	Jun 1837	N.-Amer	849628
Sauer, Christina			Sigmarswangen	Sulz	Jun 1885	N.-Amer	849626
Sauer, Dorothea & C		27 Sep 1828	Reinerzau	Frd.	bef 1865	Switz.	577780
Sauer, Emerenzia		23 Jan 1844	Leinstetten	Sulz	Apr 1866	N.-Amer	849638
Sauer, Georg Jacob			Aistaig	Sulz	bef 1851	France	849628
Sauer, Jakob		4 May 1854	Reinerzau	Frd.	bef 1865	Switz.	577780
Sauer, Johannes			Lossburg	Frd.	bef 1855	Baden	569275
Sauer, Johannes		7 Mar 1860	Hopfau	Sulz	Apr 1882	N.-Amer	849636
Sauer, Johannes		28 Apr 1865	Wei-herhof/Muehlheim	Sulz	Jul 1885	N.-Amer	849639
Sauer, Karl Friedrich		22 Jan 1850	Sulz	Sulz	Nov 1873	N.-Amer	849628
Sauer, Mathilde Wilh.		19 May 1835	Aistaig	Sulz	Jan 1859	France	849628
Sauer, Rosine			Aistaig	Sulz	1863	Paris	849628
Saur, Joseph		26 Oct 1837	Leinstetten	Sulz	Apr 1855	N.-Amer	849638
Saur, Paulina		15 May 1868	Leinstetten	Sulz	Sep 1869	Prussia	849638
Saur, Pauline & C		9 Dec 1839	Leinstetten	Sulz	Sep 1869	Prussia	849638
Saur, Theresia			Leinstetten	Sulz	Jun 1854	N.-Amer	849638
Saur, Xaver			Leinstetten	Sulz	Apr 1855	N.-Amer	849638
Sauter, Agnes (wid.)			Reusten	Herr.	May 1830	N.-Amer	834624
Sauter, Catharina & F			Reusten	Herr.	Jun 1832	N.-Amer	834624
Sauter, Christina		15 yrs.	Duerrenmettstetten	Sulz	Aug 1854	N.-Amer	849635
Sauter, Dorothea			Reusten	Herr.	Jun 1848	N.-Amer	834626
Sauter, Dorothea		23 Nov 1839	Reusten	Herr.	Mar 1868	N.-Amer	834624
Sauter, Georg Michael			Weilheim	Bal.	1821	Switz.	555963
Sauter, Gottlieb & W			Reusten	Herr.	1848	N.-Amer	834626
Sauter, Imanuel			Oberdigisheim	Bal.	1869	Switz.	555962
Sauter, J. Joseph			Onstmettingen	Bal.	bef 1851	Switz.	555962
Sauter, Johann			Duerrenmettstetten	Sulz	bef 1837	Russia	849625
Sauter, Johann Georg		29 Sep 1804	Voehringen	Sulz	Apr 1837	N.-Amer	849643
Sauter, Johann Georg			Balingen	Bal.	Jul 1858	France	555962
Sauter, Johann Georg			Weilheim	Bal.	Feb 1849	N.-Amer	555964
Sauter, Johann Jakob			Freudenstadt	Frd.	Sep 1820	Baden	569267
Sauter, Michael			Weilheim	Bal.	bef 1852	Switz.	555962
Sauter, Peter		11 Sep 1847	Reusten	Herr.	May 1870	N.-Amer	834624
Sautter, Anna Maria (wife)		24 Mar 1818	Reusten	Herr.	Mar 1847	N.-Amer	834626
Sautter, Catharina		21 Sep 1850	Reusten	Herr.	Jul 1852	N.-Amer	834627
Sautter, Catharina Barbara		14 Feb 1843	Aach	Frd.	Apr 1846	N.-Amer	569271
Sautter, Christina		6 Dec 1827	Leidringen	Sulz	Sep 1855	N.-Amer	849643
Sautter, Dorothea Magdalena		5 Jul 1818	Sulz	Sulz	May 1845	Switz.	849627
Sautter, Jacob			Freudenstadt	Frd.	Mar 1817	Russia	569267
Sautter, Jacob		6 Nov 1846	Dornhan	Sulz	Sep 1866	N.-Amer	849634
Sautter, Jakob		19 yrs.	Reusten	Herr.	Feb 1848	N.-Amer	834627
Sautter, Johann Christian		11 Dec 1839	Bondorf	Herr.	Apr 1847	N.-Amer	834626
Sautter, Johann Friedrich		11 Dec 1839	Bondorf	Herr.	Apr 1847	N.-Amer	834626
Sautter, Johann Georg		8 Aug 1843	Haslach	Herr.	Mar 1869	N.-Amer	834624
Sautter, Johann Georg		26 yrs.	Reusten	Herr.	Mar 1852	N.-Amer	834627
Sautter, Johann Georg			Reusten	Herr.	Jun 1834	N.-Amer	834624
Sautter, Johann Gottlieb & F		51 yrs.	Herrenberg	Herr.	Apr 1846	N.-Amer	834626
Sautter, Johann Jacob		6 Sep 1840	Aach	Frd.	Apr 1846	N.-Amer	569271
Sautter, Johann Jakob		6 Aug 1830	Bondorf	Herr.	Apr 1847	N.-Amer	834626

Sautter, Johann Martin	8 Nov 1825	Bondorf	Herr.	Jun 1850	N.-Amer	834627
Sautter, Johann Martin & F	22 Feb 1799	Bondorf	Herr.	Apr 1847	N.-Amer	834626
Sautter, Johann Michael	23 Nov 1851	Reusten	Herr.	Jul 1852	N.-Amer	834627
Sautter, Johanna Catharina	2 May 1824	Bondorf	Herr.	Apr 1847	N.-Amer	834626
Sautter, Johanna Fried. (wife)	36 yrs.	Herrenberg	Herr.	Apr 1846	N.-Amer	834626
Sautter, Johannes	13 Aug 1838	Aach	Frd.	Apr 1846	N.-Amer	569271
Sautter, Johannes	8 Jan 1844	Bondorf	Herr.	Apr 1847	N.-Amer	834626
Sautter, Johannes	6 Mar 1801	Gueltstein	Herr.	Mar 1849	N.-Amer	834627
Sautter, Maria Catharina	3 Nov 1841	Bondorf	Herr.	Apr 1847	N.-Amer	834626
Sautter, Maria Catharina (wife)	46 yrs.	Bondorf	Herr.	Apr 1847	N.-Amer	834626
Sautter, Maria Friedrike	12 Dec 1841	Herrenberg	Herr.	Apr 1846	N.-Amer	834626
Sautter, Michael & F		Reusten	Herr.	Jul 1852	N.-Amer	834627
Sautter, Michael & W	2 Nov 1818	Reusten	Herr.	Mar 1847	N.-Amer	834626
Sautter, Pauline Louise	3 Jun 1839	Herrenberg	Herr.	Apr 1846	N.-Amer	834626
Sautter, Salome	29 Mar 1809	Reusten	Herr.	Apr 1840	Switz.	834625
Sautter, Stephan	36 yrs.	Reusten	Herr.	May 1852	N.-Amer	834627
Sautter, Ursula	30 Sep 1834	Voehringen	Sulz	Sep 1855	N.-Amer	849643
Sautter, Wilhelmine Tabitha	8 Nov 1840	Herrenberg	Herr.	Apr 1846	N.-Amer	834626
Sayer, Johann Andreas	9 Sep 1831	Unterjettingen	Herr.	Mar 1848	N.-Amer	834626
Sayer, Johann Georg	14 Sep 1842	Unterjettingen	Herr.	Mar 1848	N.-Amer	834626
Sayer, Johann Jacob & F	12 Jul 1803	Unterjettingen	Herr.	Mar 1848	N.-Amer	834626
Sayer, Johann Jakob	3 Jun 1845	Unterjettingen	Herr.	Mar 1848	N.-Amer	834626
Sayer, Johannes	4 May 1834	Unterjettingen	Herr.	Mar 1848	N.-Amer	834626
Sayer, Justina Marg. Ba. (wife)	14 Feb 1802	Unterjettingen	Herr.	Mar 1848	N.-Amer	834626
Sayer, Rosina Barbara	27 Oct 1839	Unterjettingen	Herr.	Mar 1848	N.-Amer	834626
Schaad, Andreas	1 Oct 1844	Sigmarswangen	Sulz	Oct 1863	N.-Amer	849642
Schaad, Andreas & F	27 Mar 1796	Sigmarswangen	Sulz	May 1834	N.-Amer	849642
Schaad, Catharina (wife)		Sigmarswangen	Sulz	May 1834	N.-Amer	849642
Schaad, Catharina Johanna	3 Apr 1826	Sigmarswangen	Sulz	May 1834	N.-Amer	849642
Schaad, Christina Louisa	6 Oct 1823	Sigmarswangen	Sulz	May 1834	N.-Amer	849642
Schaad, Johann Martin	30 Jan 1833	Sigmarswangen	Sulz	May 1834	N.-Amer	849642
Schaad, Margaretha	16 May 1821	Sigmarswangen	Sulz	May 1834	N.-Amer	849642
Schaal, Friederike & C	1830	Teinach	Calw	1854	N.-Amer	563212
Schaal, Rosina	25 yrs.	Calw	Calw	Oct 1848	Switz.	563212
Schaber, Andreas		Tuebingen	Herr.	Apr 1850	N.-Amer	834627
Schaber, Hans Georg		Dornstetten	Frd.	Apr 1752	Pen.N-A	550803
Schad, Anna Maria	2 Sep 1827	Sigmarswangen	Sulz	Mar 1833	N.-Amer	849642
Schad, Johann Friederich	14 May 1823	Sigmarswangen	Sulz	Mar 1833	N.-Amer	849642
Schad, Johannes & F	11 Nov 1802	Sigmarswangen	Sulz	Mar 1833	N.-Amer	849642
Schad, Joseph & F		Sigmarswangen	Sulz	Apr 1817	Russia	849642
Schad, Margaretha	25 Dec 1826	Sigmarswangen	Sulz	Mar 1833	N.-Amer	849642
Schad, Sibilla (wife)		Sigmarswangen	Sulz	Mar 1833	N.-Amer	849642
Schaeberle, Heinrich		Oeschelbronn	Herr.	May 1827	Austria	834624
Schaeberle, Katharina Barbara	30 Sep 1836	Reusten	Herr.	Apr 1869	N.-Amer	834624
Schaedle, August	28 Aug 1826	Binsdorf	Sulz	Mar 1862	Austria	849631
Schaedle, Donat	4 Mar 1852	Binsdorf	Sulz	Apr 1869	N.-Amer	849631
Schaedle, Markus	14 Jan 1850	Binsdorf	Sulz	Apr 1867	N.-Amer	849631
Schaedle, Mathias	4 Aug 1850	Binsdorf	Sulz	Dec 1870	N.-Amer	849631
Schaefer, Christina	30 May 1825	Nufringen	Herr.	May 1839	N.-Amer	834625
Schaefer, Christina Barbara	31 May 1820	Nufringen	Herr.	May 1839	N.-Amer	834625

| Name | | Birth | | Emigration | | | Film |
Last	First	Date	Place	O'amt	Appl. Date	Dest.	Number
Schaefer, Christof		24 Jul 1872	Leidringen	Sulz	Mar 1889	N.-Amer	849626
Schaefer, Eva Maria (wid.)& F		23 Dec 1791	Nufringen	Herr.	May 1839	N.-Amer	834625
Schaefer, Georg		9 Jun 1818	Gueltstein	Herr.	Mar 1849	N.-Amer	834627
Schaefer, Georg Michael		29 May 1841	Gaertringen	Herr.	Jul 1866	N.-Amer	834624
Schaefer, Jacob Friedrich		18 mon.	Boll	Sulz	Jul 1871	N.-Amer	849632
Schaefer, Jakob & F		4 Jul 1849	Voehringen	Sulz	Jul 1890	Switz.	849626
Schaefer, Johann Georg		21 Jan 1816	Nufringen	Herr.	May 1839	N.-Amer	834625
Schaefer, Johann Georgerike			Gechingen	Calw	1853	N.-Amer	563212
Schaefer, Johann Jacob		9 Jan 1823	Nufringen	Herr.	May 1839	N.-Amer	834625
Schaefer, Johann Jacob & F			Bondorf	Herr.	Apr 1836	N.-Amer	834624
Schaefer, Johann Martin		23 Nov 1810	Unterjettingen	Herr.	May 1868	N.-Amer	834624
Schaefer, Johann Michael		20 Dec 1831	Nufringen	Herr.	May 1839	N.-Amer	834625
Schaefer, Johann Michael		6 Feb 1828	Tailfingen	Herr.	Apr 1852	N.-Amer	834627
Schaefer, Karl		17 May 1885	Voehringen	Sulz	Jul 1890	Switz.	849626
Schaefer, Karl		1 Oct 1846	Leinstetten	Sulz	Sep 1866	N.-Amer	849638
Schaefer, Kaspar			Leinstetten	Sulz	Jun 1854	N.-Amer	849638
Schaefer, Leonhardt		1835	Gechingen	Calw	1854	N.-Amer	563212
Schaefer, Xaver		8 Dec 1833	Bettenhausen	Sulz	Jan 1859	Prussia	849630
Schaeffer, Anna Maria		15 Feb 1832	Oeschelbronn	Herr.	May 1852	N.-Amer	834627
Schaeffer, Dorothea		30 Mar 1839	Oeschelbronn	Herr.	May 1852	N.-Amer	834627
Schaeffer, Georg		Feb 1837	Sulz	Sulz	Jun 1856	N.-Amer	849627
Schaeffer, Jacob Friedrich		22 May 1822	Oberjettingen	Herr.	Feb 1852	N.-Amer	834627
Schaeffer, Jacobina		24 Jan 1837	Oeschelbronn	Herr.	May 1852	N.-Amer	834627
Schaeffer, Johann Georg			Voehringen	Sulz	May 1817	Russia	849627
Schaeffer, Karolina		22 Jun 1842	Oeschelbronn	Herr.	May 1852	N.-Amer	834627
Schaeffer, Sophie		1824	Sulz	Sulz	Nov 1855	Switz.	849627
Schaeuble, Agatha & C			Voehringen	Sulz	Feb 1855	N.-Amer	849643
Schaeuble, Andreas		4 Dec 1814	Wittershausen	Sulz	Jan 1817	Russia	849644
Schaeuble, Andreas		14 Nov 1795	Wittershausen	Sulz	Jan 1817	Russia	849644
Schaeuble, Anna			Voehringen	Sulz	Feb 1855	N.-Amer	849643
Schaeuble, Anna (wife)		30 Dec 1810	Bickelsberg	Sulz	May 1860	N.-Amer	849644
Schaeuble, Barbara		8 Oct 1812	Wittershausen	Sulz	Jan 1817	Russia	849644
Schaeuble, Catharina			Wittershausen	Sulz	Sep 1854	N.-Amer	849644
Schaeuble, Christina		1 Feb 1789	Wittershausen	Sulz	Mar 1837	N.-Amer	849644
Schaeuble, Christina			Wittershausen	Sulz	Jan 1817	Russia	849644
Schaeuble, Christine			Voehringen	Sulz	Oct 1851	N.-Amer	849643
Schaeuble, Friedrich		10 Nov 1829	Erkenbrechtsweiler	Sulz	bef 1864	France	849643
Schaeuble, Friedrich		10 Jul 1853	Voehringen	Sulz	Feb 1855	N.-Amer	849643
Schaeuble, Johann Georg		17 Mar 1853	Wittershausen	Sulz	May 1860	N.-Amer	849644
Schaeuble, Johann Georg & F		20 Apr 1806	Wittershausen	Sulz	1853- 60	N.-Amer	849644
Schaeuble, Ursula		18 Jun 1809	Wittershausen	Sulz	Oct 1860	N.-Amer	849644
Schaeuble, Wilhelm			Nagold	Nag.	Feb 1854	N.-Amer	838491
Schaeufele, Friedrich & F			Leidringen	Sulz	Jun 1817	Russia	849637
Schaffauer, Christina Marg.& F		24 Jun 1786	Herrenberg	Herr.	Jul 1846	N.-Amer	834626
Schaffauer, Friederike Phil.		20 Mar 1827	Herrenberg	Herr.	Jul 1846	N.-Amer	834626
Schaffauer, Maria Theresia		20 Mar 1827	Herrenberg	Herr.	Jul 1846	N.-Amer	834626
Schaible, Agatha		12 Nov 1847	Grombach	Frd.	Mar 1853	N.-Amer	569272
Schaible, Agatha & C		3 Sep 1832	Sigmarswangen	Sulz	Sep 1868	N.-Amer	849642
Schaible, Andreas		24 Aug 1851	Wittershausen	Sulz	May 1866	N.-Amer	849644
Schaible, Anna		1 Nov 1844	Wittershausen	Sulz	May 1866	N.-Amer	849644

Schaible, Anna Barbara (wife)		Voehringen	Sulz	Apr 1832	N.-Amer	849643
Schaible, Anna Maria	2 Nov 1847	Groembach	Frd.	bef 1856	N.-Amer	569275
Schaible, Anna Maria	19 Dec 1840	Wittershausen	Sulz	May 1866	N.-Amer	849644
Schaible, Anton	19 yrs.	Poltringen	Herr.	Mar 1851	N.-Amer	834627
Schaible, Barbara	20 Jan 1837	Wittershausen	Sulz	May 1866	N.-Amer	849644
Schaible, Barbara	4 yrs.	Sigmarswangen	Sulz	Sep 1868	N.-Amer	849642
Schaible, Barbara (wife)	28 Feb 1812	Fuernsal	Sulz	May 1866	N.-Amer	849644
Schaible, Christian		Dornstetten	Frd.	bef 1850	N.-Amer	569271
Schaible, Christina	6 Mar 1843	Wittershausen	Sulz	May 1866	N.-Amer	849644
Schaible, Christoph & F		Leidringen	Sulz	Jun 1817	Russia	849637
Schaible, David	7 Feb 1833	Durrweiler	Frd.	Mar 1851	N.-Amer	569271
Schaible, Eva	7 Oct 1821	Voehringen	Sulz	Mar 1834	N.-Amer	849643
Schaible, Eva Maria	22 Nov 1844	Groembach	Frd.	Jun 1856	N.-Amer	569275
Schaible, Eva Maria & C	14 Jul 1828	Groembach	Frd.	Mar 1858	N.-Amer	577776
Schaible, Friederich	31 Dec 1836	Groembach	Frd.	Mar 1854	N.-Amer	569273
Schaible, Georg Adam	25 Apr 1847	Hochdorf	Frd.	Jun 1866	N.-Amer	577780
Schaible, Jacob	16 Oct 1831	Voehringen	Sulz	Mar 1834	N.-Amer	849643
Schaible, Jacob	41 yrs.	Aichhalden	Calw	1867	N.-Amer	563212
Schaible, Jacob & F		Rohrau	Herr.	Jun 1833	Rus-Pol	834624
Schaible, Jakob	11 yrs.	Voehringen	Sulz	Apr 1832	N.-Amer	849643
Schaible, Jakob	31 Aug 1834	Sigmarswangen	Sulz	bef 1867	France	849642
Schaible, Jakob & F		Aichhalden	Calw	1854	N.-Amer	563212
Schaible, Jakob & F		Agenbach	Calw	1854	N.-Amer	563212
Schaible, Johann Friedrich	6 Dec 1856	Groembach	Frd.	Mar 1858	N.-Amer	577776
Schaible, Johann Georg	21 Apr 1847	Wittershausen	Sulz	May 1866	N.-Amer	849644
Schaible, Johann Georg	11 Feb 1829	Voehringen	Sulz	Mar 1834	N.-Amer	849643
Schaible, Johann Georg	27 yrs.	Aichhalden	Calw	1867	N.-Amer	563212
Schaible, Johann Georg & F		Oberjettingen	Herr.	Apr 1836	N.-Amer	834624
Schaible, Johann Jacob		Hornberg	Calw	1861	N.-Amer	563212
Schaible, Johann Jacob & F	5 Jan 1792	Voehringen	Sulz	Mar 1834	N.-Amer	849643
Schaible, Johann Jakob	26 Jan 1844	Rosenfeld	Sulz	Apr 1859	N.-Amer	849640
Schaible, Johann Jakob & F	1 Jul 1787	Voehringen	Sulz	Apr 1832	N.-Amer	849643
Schaible, Johannes	26 Jan 1828	Voehringen	Sulz	May 1866	France	849643
Schaible, Johannes	6 Jun 1826	Voehringen	Sulz	Mar 1834	N.-Amer	849643
Schaible, Johannes		Marschalkenzimmern	Sulz	Mar 1830	Switz.	849638
Schaible, Johannes		Rosenfeld	Sulz	May 1855	N.-Amer	849640
Schaible, Johannes	1823	Hornberg	Calw	1854	N.-Amer	563212
Schaible, Johannes	29 yrs.	Zwerenberg	Calw	1847	N.-Amer	563212
Schaible, Josua Hermann	7 Oct 1857	Leidringen	Sulz	Feb 1874	N.-Amer	849637
Schaible, Karl Jakob		Rosenfeld	Sulz	Apr 1893	N.-Amer	849626
Schaible, Katharina	18 Mar 1839	Wittershausen	Sulz	May 1866	N.-Amer	849644
Schaible, Katharina	10 yrs.	Voehringen	Sulz	Apr 1832	N.-Amer	849643
Schaible, Katharina	22 yrs.	Aichhalden	Calw	1854	N.-Amer	563212
Schaible, Konrad		Groembach	Frd.	Jun 1856	N.-Amer	569275
Schaible, Maria Elisabetha	25 yrs.	Dornstetten	Frd.	Oct 1860	France	577777
Schaible, Maria Magdalena	7 Jul 1823	Voehringen	Sulz	Mar 1834	N.-Amer	849643
Schaible, Maria Magdalena (wife)		Voehringen	Sulz	Mar 1834	N.-Amer	849643
Schaible, Martin	23 yrs.	Aichhalden	Calw	1866	N.-Amer	563212
Schaible, Mathaeus	16 Jan 1846	Schernbach	Frd.	Mar 1863	N.-Amer	577778
Schaible, Matthaeus	1836	Aichhalden	Calw	1856	N.-Amer	563212

Name		Birth			Emigration		Film
Last	First	Date	Place	O'amt	Appl. Date	Dest.	Number
Schaible, Matthias & F		26 Feb 1812	Wittershausen	Sulz	May 1866	N.-Amer	849644
Schaible, Michael		14 Mar 1843	Hornberg	Calw	1863	N.-Amer	563212
Schaible, Michael			Martinsmoos	Calw	1854	N.-Amer	563212
Schaible, Michael & F			Voehringen	Sulz	Mar 1846	N.-Amer	849643
Schaible, Michael & F			Zwerenberg	Calw	1853	N.-Amer	563212
Schaible, Rosina		31 Jan 1850	Wittershausen	Sulz	May 1866	N.-Amer	849644
Schaible, Wilhelm		1849	Oberhengstett	Calw	1869	France	563212
Schaible, Wilhelm		29 Jun 1846	Rosenfeld	Sulz	Jun 1866	N.-Amer	849641
Schairer, Jakob			Erzingen	Bal.	bef 1852	Switz.	555962
Schairer, Mathaeus			Margarethenhausen	Bal.	bef 1848	Switz.	555963
Schall, Agnes		15 Sep 1838	Marschalkenzimmern	Sulz	bef 1862	Hamburg	849638
Schanbacher, Andreas		11 yrs.	Wintersbach	Schd.	Mar 1833	N.-Amer	801460
Schanbacher, Andreas & F		48 yrs.	Winterbach	Schd.	Mar 1833	N.-Amer	801460
Schanbacher, Anna Maria		9 mon.	Wintersbach	Schd.	Mar 1833	N.-Amer	801460
Schanbacher, Georg Michael		14 yrs.	Wintersbach	Schd.	Mar 1833	N.-Amer	801460
Schanbacher, Johann Georg		7 yrs.	Wintersbach	Schd.	Mar 1833	N.-Amer	801460
Schanbacher, Johann Jacob		4 yrs.	Wintersbach	Schd.	Mar 1833	N.-Amer	801460
Schanbacher, Katharina Margar.		21 yrs.	Wintersbach	Schd.	Mar 1833	N.-Amer	801460
Schanbacher, Maria Catharina		44 yrs.	Wintersbach	Schd.	Mar 1833	N.-Amer	801460
Schanbacher, Maria Magdalena		9 yrs.	Wintersbach	Schd.	Mar 1833	N.-Amer	801460
Schanz, Adam		12 Jul 1861	Gaertringen	Herr.	Aug 1863	N.-Amer	834624
Schanz, Agatha		25 Nov 1844	Voehringen	Sulz	Sep 1852	N.-Amer	849643
Schanz, Andreas		19 yrs.	Voehringen	Sulz	Oct 1853	N.-Amer	849643
Schanz, Anna Barbara			Voehringen	Sulz	Sep 1852	N.-Amer	849643
Schanz, Anna Maria		29 Aug 1834	Dornhan	Sulz	Oct 1854	N.-Amer	849633
Schanz, Barbara		18 Mar 1832	Dornhan	Sulz	Oct 1862	Baden	849634
Schanz, Eva Catharina			Oberkollbach	Calw	1860	N.-Amer	563212
Schanz, Eva Maria		1834	Oberkollbach	Calw	1857	N.-Amer	563212
Schanz, Johann Georg		16 Jun 1845	Dornhan	Sulz	Sep 1864	N.-Amer	849634
Schanz, Johann Georg			Neuweiler	Calw	1855	N.-Amer	563212
Schanz, Johann Georg		25 yrs.	Neuweiler	Calw	1854	N.-Amer	563212
Schanz, Katharina Dorothea			Neuweiler	Calw	1855	N.-Amer	563212
Schanz, Margaretha Magdalena		6 Nov 1827	Gaertringen	Herr.	Aug 1863	N.-Amer	834624
Schanz, Martin			Breitenberg	Calw	1852	N.-Amer	563212
Schanz, Martin & F			Voehringen	Sulz	Sep 1852	N.-Amer	849643
Schanz, Peter		12 Mar 1836	Moenchberg	Herr.	Jul 1865	N.-Amer	834624
Schanz, Samuel			Neuweiler	Calw	1864	Bavaria	563212
Schanz, Wilhelm		34 yrs.	Neuweiler	Calw	1864	N.-Amer	563212
Schatz, Agnes Katharina & F			Isingen	Sulz	Mar 1854	N.-Amer	849636
Schatz, Andreas		4 Dec 1867	Waelde	Sulz	Nov 1884	N.-Amer	849644
Schatz, Andreas		7 Feb 1836	Rotenzimmern	Sulz	Jul 1852	N.-Amer	849642
Schatz, Andreas		4 Dec 1867	Waelde	Sulz	Nov 1884	N.-Amer	849626
Schatz, Anna		2 yrs.	Isingen	Sulz	Mar 1854	N.-Amer	849636
Schatz, Anna Barbara		8 Jan 1806	Leidringen	Sulz	Jun 1817	Rus-Pol	849637
Schatz, Anna Catharina		24 May 1864	Isingen	Sulz	Mar 1866	N.-Amer	849636
Schatz, Anna Maria		12 May 1845	Rotenzimmern	Sulz	May 1866	N.-Amer	849642
Schatz, Anna Maria		19 Dec 1803	Leidringen	Sulz	Jun 1817	Rus-Pol	849637
Schatz, Barbara			Hopfau	Sulz	bef 1868	N.-Amer	849636
Schatz, Catharina		11 Aug 1796	Weiler	Schd.	Jun 1833	Russia	801460
Schatz, Christian		2 May 1853	Rotenzimmern	Sulz	Apr 1872	N.-Amer	849642

Schatz, Christian	30 Dec 1848	Rotenzimmern	Sulz	Apr 1868	N.-Amer	849642
Schatz, Christina	24 Dec 1840	Rotenzimmern	Sulz	Jan 1871	Switz.	849642
Schatz, Christina	4 Apr 1865	Rotenzimmern	Sulz	May 1866	N.-Amer	849642
Schatz, Christina		Hopfau	Sulz	bef 1868	N.-Amer	849636
Schatz, Christina	2 Oct 1809	Leidringen	Sulz	Jun 1817	Rus-Pol	849637
Schatz, Christina & C	9 Jan 1846	Rotenzimmern	Sulz	May 1866	N.-Amer	849642
Schatz, Christina Catharina	27 Dec 1825	Weiler	Schd.	Jun 1833	Russia	801460
Schatz, Christine		Rodt	Frd.	Dec 1822	Baden	569268
Schatz, Elisabeth	15 May 1837	Baiersbronn	Frd.	Dec 1853	N.-Amer	569272
Schatz, Friederike	1 Sep 1834	Freudenstadt	Frd.	Mar 1865	N.-Amer	577779
Schatz, Friedrich	23 Aug 1867	Dornhan	Sulz	Jan 1885	N.-Amer	849634
Schatz, Gottfried	16 Dec 1801	Leidringen	Sulz	Jun 1817	Rus-Pol	849637
Schatz, Jakob	3 Jun 1849	Baiersbronn	Frd.	Dec 1853	N.-Amer	569272
Schatz, Jakob	16 May 1873	Breitenau	Sulz	Apr 1889	N.-Amer	849626
Schatz, Johann Georg	28 Apr 1823	Weiler	Schd.	Jun 1833	Russia	801460
Schatz, Johann Georg	16 Apr 1870	Rotenzimmern	Sulz	Oct 1884	N.-Amer	849642
Schatz, Johann Georg	31 Dec 1873	Dornhan	Sulz	Sep 1888	N.-Amer	849634
Schatz, Johann Georg	11 Sep 1862	Isingen	Sulz	Mar 1866	N.-Amer	849636
Schatz, Johann Georg & F	8 Oct 1793	Weiler	Schd.	Jun 1833	Russia	801460
Schatz, Johann Gottlieb	4 Dec 1820	Weiler	Schd.	Jun 1833	Russia	801460
Schatz, Johann Jakob	21 Sep 1865	Rotenzimmern	Sulz	May 1866	N.-Amer	849642
Schatz, Johann Jakob	22 Aug 1833	Rotenzimmern	Sulz	Oct 1860	N.-Amer	849642
Schatz, Johann Jakob & F	17 Oct 1839	Isingen	Sulz	Mar 1866	N.-Amer	849636
Schatz, Johannes	4 Oct 1847	Rotenzimmern	Sulz	Mar 1866	N.-Amer	849642
Schatz, Johannes	15 yrs.	Isingen	Sulz	Mar 1854	N.-Amer	849636
Schatz, Johannes & F	7 Feb 1838	Rotenzimmern	Sulz	May 1866	N.-Amer	849642
Schatz, Katharine Rosine	24 Oct 1851	Baiersbronn	Frd.	Dec 1853	N.-Amer	569272
Schatz, Louise	1838	Freudenstadt	Frd.	bef 1866	France	577780
Schatz, Magdalena	12 Nov 1799	Leidringen	Sulz	Jun 1817	Rus-Pol	849637
Schatz, Magdalena (wid.) & F	23 Feb 1772	Leidringen	Sulz	Jun 1817	Rus-Pol	849637
Schatz, Margaretha	24 Jun 1840	Baiersbronn	Frd.	Dec 1853	N.-Amer	569272
Schatz, Margaretha	21 Mar 1811	Baiersbronn	Frd.	Dec 1853	N.-Amer	569272
Schatz, Martin	1863	Rotenzimmern	Sulz	1872	N.-Amer	849642
Schatz, Martin	18 May 1848	Rotenzimmern	Sulz	Mar 1868	N.-Amer	849642
Schatz, Mattheus & F	14 Jun 1808	Baiersbronn	Frd.	Dec 1853	N.-Amer	569272
Schatz, Matthias	29 Mar 1846	Rotenzimmern	Sulz	Sep 1866	N.-Amer	849642
Schatz, Regina (wife)	22 Oct 1841	Isingen	Sulz	Mar 1866	N.-Amer	849636
Schatz, Wilhelm	19 Jun 1881	Dornhan	Sulz	Oct 1895	N.-Amer	849626
Schatz, Wilhelm Abraham	9 May 1832	Weiler	Schd.	Jun 1833	Russia	801460
Schatz, Wilhelmine Friederike	17 Mar 1828	Weiler	Schd.	Jun 1833	Russia	801460
Schaub, Johannes	17 Aug 1864	Dornhan	Sulz	Aug 1883	N.-Amer	849634
Schaufelberger, Carl Ludwig		Oberreichenbach	Calw	1853	N.-Amer	563212
Schaufelberger, Friedrich		Oberreichenbach	Calw	1853	N.-Amer	563212
Schaufelberger, Johannes		Oberreichenbach	Calw	1853	N.-Amer	563212
Schaufelberger, Magdalene		Oberreichenbach	Calw	1853	N.-Amer	563212
Schaufelberger, Michael		Oberreichenbach	Calw	1853	N.-Amer	563212
Schaumann, Sophie Friederike	26 Apr 1846	Sulz	Sulz	Sep 1866	Nassau	849628
Schaupp, Andreas	7 Feb 1874	Dornhan/Sterneck	Sulz	Aug 1883	N.-Amer	849634
Schaupp, Anna Maria	25 Sep 1833	Gundelshausen	Sulz	Oct 1853	N.-Amer	849633
Schaupp, Johann Michael & F	21 Mar 1819	Altensteig	Frd.	Feb 1848	N.-Amer	569270

| Name | | Birth | | Emigration | | | Film |
Last	First	Date	Place	O'amt	Appl. Date	Dest.	Number
Schaupp, Louise		8 Dec 1823	Dornstetten	Frd.	Feb 1848	N.-Amer	569270
Schaupp, Louise Wilhelmine		31 Oct 1846	Dornstetten	Frd.	Feb 1848	N.-Amer	569270
Schauppe, Christian Friedrich		26 Oct 1831	Erzgrube	Frd.	bef 1866	Prussia	577780
Schaz, Anna Maria			Leidringen	Sulz	bef 1815	Russia	849625
Schaz, Christina			Schoemberg	Frd.	Jul 1853	N.-Amer	569272
Schaz, Magdalena			Leidringen	Sulz	bef 1815	Russia	849625
Schaz, Martin			Rotenzimmern	Sulz	May 1817	Russia	849642
Schechinger, Anna Maria			Sulz	Nag.	Feb 1854	N.-Amer	838491
Schechinger, Caroline Frieder.			Sulz	Nag.	Feb 1854	N.-Amer	838491
Schechinger, Georg Friedrich			Sulz	Nag.	Feb 1854	N.-Amer	838491
Scheerer, Anna Maria		10 May 1813	Oberiflingen	Frd.	Sep 1854	N.-Amer	569274
Scheerer, Anna Maria		12 May 1840	Oberiflingen	Frd.	Sep 1854	N.-Amer	569274
Scheerer, August Gottlob		3 Jan 1854	Sulz	Sulz	Jul 1871	N.-Amer	849628
Scheerer, Barbara		18 Apr 1843	Oberiflingen	Frd.	Sep 1854	N.-Amer	569274
Scheerer, Christine		3 May 1838	Oberiflingen	Frd.	Sep 1854	N.-Amer	569274
Scheerer, Elisabetha & C		18 Aug 1819	Oberiflingen	Frd.	Sep 1854	N.-Amer	569274
Scheerer, Johann Christian		24 Oct 1850	Sulz	Sulz	Mar 1869	N.-Amer	849628
Scheffenacker, Heinrich		16 Oct 1847	Rosenfeld	Sulz	Jun 1866	N.-Amer	849641
Scheffenacker, Johann Friedr.		6 Feb 1841	Rosenfeld	Sulz	May 1867	N.-Amer	849641
Scheffenaker, Katharina		30 Jun 1820	Rosenfeld	Sulz	Nov 1852	N.-Amer	849640
Scheible, Christina		10 Jul 1831	Groembach	Frd.	Jun 1854	N.-Amer	569274
Scheible, Conrad		11 Mar 1838	Schernbach	Frd.	Jul 1854	N.-Amer	569274
Scheible, Elisabetha Marg. & F		18 Feb 1801	Groembach	Frd.	Jun 1854	N.-Amer	569274
Scheible, Johannes		25 Feb 1834	Schernbach	Frd.	Jul 1854	N.-Amer	569274
Scheifele, Juliane			Christophstal	Frd.	Mar 1854	N.-Amer	569273
Schek, Agatha		14 Aug 1858	Sigmarswangen	Sulz	Aug 1860	N.-Amer	849642
Schek, Catharina (wife)		15 Dec 1836	Sigmarswangen	Sulz	Aug 1860	N.-Amer	849642
Schek, Johann Georg		20 Oct 1859	Sigmarswangen	Sulz	Aug 1860	N.-Amer	849642
Schek, Johann Georg & F		26 Jul 1833	Sigmarswangen	Sulz	Aug 1860	N.-Amer	849642
Schele, Georg Jakob			Calw	Calw	bef 1855	Austria	563212
Schelling, Christian			Calw	Calw	1852	N.-Amer	563212
Schenk, Anna		19 Sep 1816	Bergfelden	Sulz	1839	Hohenz.	849629
Schenk, Anna Maria		31 Dec 1853	Dietersweiler	Frd.	Jan 1855	N.-Amer	569275
Schenk, Anna Maria (wife)		23 Dec 1818	Oberiflingen	Frd.	Jan 1855	N.-Amer	569275
Schenk, Bernhard		12 Dec 1849	Dietersweiler	Frd.	Jan 1855	N.-Amer	569275
Schenk, Christian		23 Jul 1846	Dietersweiler	Frd.	Jan 1855	N.-Amer	569275
Schenk, Friedrich			Hagelloch/Tuebingen	Herr.	May 1831	N.-Amer	834624
Schenk, Johannes		30 Sep 1843	Dietersweiler	Frd.	Jan 1855	N.-Amer	569275
Schenk, Johannes & F		3 Jul 1808	Dietersweiler	Frd.	Jan 1855	N.-Amer	569275
Schenk, Johannes & F			Fuernsal	Sulz	May 1852	N.-Amer	849635
Schenk, Matthaeus		3 Aug 1851	Dietersweiler	Frd.	Jan 1855	N.-Amer	569275
Schenk, Michael		1 Oct 1847	Dietersweiler	Frd.	Jan 1855	N.-Amer	569275
Schenkel, Christian & F		27 Jul 1763	Muehlheim a.B.	Sulz	May 1817	Russia	849639
Schenkel, Elisabeth (wife)		3 Oct 1759	Muehlheim a.B.	Sulz	May 1817	Russia	849639
Schenkel, Katharina Barbara		7 Apr 1793	Muehlheim a.B.	Sulz	May 1817	Russia	849639
Scherer, Barbara		30 Nov 1844	Duerrenmettstetten	Sulz	Jan 1856	N.-Amer	849635
Scherer, Carl			Duerrenmettstetten	Sulz	Sep 1853	N.-Amer	849635
Scherer, Carl Gustav		16 Sep 1852	Duerrenmettstetten	Sulz	Jan 1856	N.-Amer	849635
Scherer, Christian		11 Aug 1829	Duerrenmettstetten	Sulz	Mar 1854	N.-Amer	849635
Scherer, Christian			Duerrenmettstetten	Sulz	Sep 1853	N.-Amer	849635

Scherer, Christina & F	5 Mar 1810	Duerrenmettstetten	Sulz	Jan 1856	N.-Amer	849635
Scherer, Christine	8 yrs.	Duerrenmettstetten	Sulz	Mar 1854	N.-Amer	849635
Scherer, Emma		Duerrenmettstetten	Sulz	Sep 1853	N.-Amer	849635
Scherer, Johann Jacob	29 Jan 1809	Duerrenmettstetten	Sulz	1854	N.-Amer	849635
Scherer, Johannes		Duerrenmettstetten	Sulz	Aug 1848	N.-Amer	849635
Scherer, Johannes & F		Duerrenmettstetten	Sulz	Sep 1853	N.-Amer	849635
Scherer, Lina		Duerrenmettstetten	Sulz	Sep 1853	N.-Amer	849635
Scherer, Magdalena & C		Duerrenmettstetten	Sulz	Mar 1854	N.-Amer	849635
Scherer, Susanna (wife)		Duerrenmettstetten	Sulz	Sep 1853	N.-Amer	849635
Schermann, Andreas	13 Sep 1825	Altheim	Horb	bef 1857	N.-Amer	835929
Schermann, Simon	2 Dec 1833	Altheim	Horb	bef 1857	N.-Amer	835929
Scherrmann, Josef	14 Feb 1834	Altheim	Horb	Mar 1854	N.-Amer	835929
Schertle, -- & F		Freudenstadt	Frd.	Mar 1817	Russia	569267
Schertlin, Rosine	21 Sep 1816	Baiersbronn	Frd.	Dec 1853	N.-Amer	569272
Scheuerle, Carl	1834	Calw	Calw	1854	N.-Amer	563212
Scheurer, Carl Heinrich		Calw	Calw	1849	France	563212
Scheurer, Johann Christian		Sulz	Sulz	Aug 1861	Austria	849628
Scheurer, Johann Georg, Sr.	28 Jun 1798	Bondorf	Herr.	Jan 1868	N.-Amer	834624
Scheurer, Maria Catharina	24 Mar 1811	Bondorf	Herr.	Apr 1869	N.-Amer	834624
Scheuter, Rosina Magdalena		Hebsack	Schd.	Jun 1833	Russia	801460
Scheutter, Johannes		Hebsack	Schd.	Jun 1833	Russia	801460
Schick, Anna Elisabetha	4 Jan 1808	Isingen	Sulz	Apr 1817	Russia	849636
Schick, Anna Maria	6 May 1809	Isingen	Sulz	Apr 1817	Russia	849636
Schick, Anna Maria (wife)	31 Dec 1774	Isingen	Sulz	Apr 1817	Russia	849636
Schick, Christian Gottlieb		Balingen	Bal.	Dec 1862	Switz.	555962
Schick, Conrad	26 Jul 1813	Isingen	Sulz	Apr 1817	Russia	849636
Schick, Conrad		Bitz	Bal.	bef 1852	Israel	555962
Schick, Gottlieb	29 Mar 1806	Isingen	Sulz	Apr 1817	Russia	849636
Schick, Johann Georg	27 Nov 1804	Isingen	Sulz	Apr 1817	Russia	849636
Schick, Johann Georg & F	5 Mar 1773	Isingen	Sulz	Apr 1817	Russia	849636
Schick, Johann Martin	3 Jul 1867	Isingen	Sulz	Apr 1884	N.-Amer	849636
Schick, Johann Martin	20 Sep 1810	Isingen	Sulz	Apr 1817	Russia	849636
Schick, Ludwig Friederich	15 Feb 1817	Isingen	Sulz	Apr 1817	Russia	849636
Schiebel, Margaretha		Cresbach	Frd.	Mar 1837	N.-Amer	569269
Schiehle, Anna Maria (wife)		Leidringen	Sulz	1799	W.-Prs.	849625
Schiehle, Johann Martin & F		Leidringen	Sulz	1799	W.-Prs.	849625
Schiek, Jakob	6 Jan 1799	Oberurbach	Schd.	Mar 1844	N.-Amer	801461
Schiek, Johann Jakob		Oberurbach	Schd.	Nov 1835	Hungary	801460
Schiele, Carl		Leidringen	Sulz	bef 1847	Poland	849637
Schill, Eva Dorothea	9 Sep 1827	Kuppingen	Herr.	bef 1862	N.-Amer	834624
Schill, Hermann Carl		Calw	Calw	1861	England	563212
Schill, Maria Magdalena	9 Apr 1818	Gueltstein	Herr.	Mar 1866	N.-Amer	834624
Schill, Rosina Dorothea		Hirsau	Calw	1869	Italia	563212
Schilling, Caroline Henriette	12 Jul 1834	Erzgrube	Frd.	Jan 1858	Bavaria	577776
Schilling, Friedrich Wilh. Eu.	7 Jan 1840	Erzgrube	Frd.	Jul 1858	N.-Amer	577776
Schillinger, Andreas	18 May 1840	Gruental	Frd.	Apr 1860	N.-Amer	577777
Schillinger, Anna Maria	9 Apr 1848	Gruental	Frd.	Apr 1860	N.-Amer	577777
Schillinger, Barbara	26 May 1837	Gruental	Frd.	Apr 1860	N.-Amer	577777
Schillinger, Christian	5 Aug 1851	Gruental	Frd.	Apr 1860	N.-Amer	577777
Schillinger, Christina	30 Mar 1803	Gruental	Frd.	Apr 1860	N.-Amer	577777

| Name | | Birth | | | Emigration | | Film |
Last	First	Date	Place	O'amt	Appl. Date	Dest.	Number
Schillinger,	Friedrich	18 Jul 1841	Gruental	Frd.	Apr 1860	N.-Amer	577777
Schillinger,	Friedrich & F	8 Jan 1812	Gruental	Frd.	Apr 1860	N.-Amer	577777
Schillinger,	Jakob	11 Dec 1842	Gruental	Frd.	Apr 1860	N.-Amer	577777
Schillinger,	Johann Georg	26 Apr 1850	Gruental	Frd.	Apr 1860	N.-Amer	577777
Schillinger,	Johann Georg	10 Aug 1848	Schoemberg	Frd.	Jun 1866	N.-Amer	577780
Schillinger,	Johannes	7 Apr 1845	Gruental	Frd.	Apr 1860	N.-Amer	577777
Schillinger,	Magdalena & C		Reinerzau	Frd.	bef 1866	Baden	577780
Schillinger,	Mathaeus	8 Jul 1838	Gruental	Frd.	Apr 1860	N.-Amer	577777
Schillinger,	Mathias	1 Jun 1810	Reinerzau	Frd.	Apr 1833	N.-Amer	569268
Schimpf,	Anna Catharina (wife)		Unterjettingen	Herr.	Jun 1831	N.-Amer	834624
Schimpf,	Carl Friedrich	31 Jan 1864	Althengstett	Calw	Apr 1870	N.-Amer	563212
Schimpf,	Gottlob Samuel	26 Mar 1861	Althengstett	Calw	Apr 1870	N.-Amer	563212
Schimpf,	Johann	26 Sep 1858	Althengstett	Calw	Apr 1870	N.-Amer	563212
Schimpf,	Johann Georg & F		Althengstett	Calw	Apr 1870	N.-Amer	563212
Schimpf,	Johann Georg & W		Unterjettingen	Herr.	Jun 1831	N.-Amer	834624
Schimpf,	Simon	14 Mar 1844	Gueltstein	Herr.	Sep 1867	N.-Amer	834624
Schinck,	Hans Georg		Neuneck	Frd.	Apr 1752	Pen.N-A	550803
Schindel,	Theresia		Leinstetten	Sulz	Jan 1816	--	849638
Schipfer,	Gottlieb	32 yrs.	Brittheim	Sulz	Dec 1861	N.-Amer	849632
Schipfer,	Jacob Friedrich		Brittheim	Sulz	Jun 1858	N.-Amer	849632
Schipfer,	Johann Michael	8 May 1837	Brittheim	Sulz	May 1855	N.-Amer	849632
Schipfer,	Wilhelm		Brittheim	Sulz	Jun 1858	N.-Amer	849632
Schittenhelm,	-- (wife)		Pfalzgrafenweiler	Frd.	Feb 1817	Russia	569268
Schittenhelm,	Andreas	9 yrs.	Cresbach	Frd.	Aug 1852	N.-Amer	569271
Schittenhelm,	Andreas	13 Feb 1840	Boll	Sulz	Apr 1860	N.-Amer	849632
Schittenhelm,	Anna	15 Dec 1835	Aistaig	Sulz	Aug 1860	N.-Amer	849628
Schittenhelm,	Anna	6 Jan 1865	Boll	Sulz	Sep 1867	N.-Amer	849632
Schittenhelm,	Anna & C	25 Dec 1807	Tumlingen	Frd.	Aug 1845	N.-Amer	569269
Schittenhelm,	Anna Catharina	16 yrs.	Voehringen	Sulz	Mar 1866	N.-Amer	849643
Schittenhelm,	Anna Katharina	18 Oct 1842	Aistaig	Sulz	Mar 1858	N.-Amer	849628
Schittenhelm,	Anna Magdalena		Cresbach	Frd.	Mar 1837	N.-Amer	569269
Schittenhelm,	Anna Maria	2 Jul 1836	Tumlingen	Frd.	Aug 1845	N.-Amer	569269
Schittenhelm,	Anna Maria		Cresbach	Frd.	Aug 1852	N.-Amer	569271
Schittenhelm,	Anna Maria	5 Jan 1838	Bergfelden	Sulz	Jul 1861	N.-Amer	849629
Schittenhelm,	Barbara		Wittlensweiler	Frd.	Jun 1856	N.-Amer	569275
Schittenhelm,	Barbara	15 Jan 1839	Tumlingen	Frd.	Aug 1845	N.-Amer	569269
Schittenhelm,	Barbara & C	4 Oct 1844	Boll	Sulz	Jul 1871	N.-Amer	849632
Schittenhelm,	Carl Friedrich	20 Feb 1846	Wittlensweiler	Frd.	Sep 1866	N.-Amer	577780
Schittenhelm,	Catharina		Wittlensweiler	Frd.	Jun 1856	N.-Amer	569275
Schittenhelm,	Catharina		Rodt	Frd.	Oct 1850	N.-Amer	569271
Schittenhelm,	Christian	15 yrs.	Cresbach	Frd.	Aug 1852	N.-Amer	569271
Schittenhelm,	Christian	29 Oct 1845	Bergfelden	Sulz	Jul 1861	N.-Amer	849629
Schittenhelm,	Christian	29 Jun 1845	Boll	Sulz	Apr 1860	N.-Amer	849632
Schittenhelm,	Christian		Fuernsaal	Sulz	1817	Rus-Pol	849637
Schittenhelm,	Christian & F		Cresbach	Frd.	Aug 1852	N.-Amer	569271
Schittenhelm,	Christina		Wittlensweiler	Frd.	Jun 1856	N.-Amer	569275
Schittenhelm,	Christina		Oberwaldach	Frd.	Mar 1837	N.-Amer	569269
Schittenhelm,	Christina	8 Nov 1842	Sigmarswangen	Sulz	Sep 1860	N.-Amer	849642
Schittenhelm,	Christoph Fr.		Freudenstadt	Frd.	May 1840	France	569267
Schittenhelm,	Eva Maria	8 Jan 1845	Sigmarswangen	Sulz	Sep 1860	N.-Amer	849642

Schittenhelm, Friedrich	11 Dec 1832	Tumlingen	Frd.	Aug 1845	N.-Amer	569269
Schittenhelm, Friedrich	Aug 1852	Boll	Sulz	Apr 1871	N.-Amer	049632
Schittenhelm, Jacob	10 yrs.	Cresbach	Frd.	Aug 1852	N.-Amer	569271
Schittenhelm, Jacob		Bergfelden	Sulz	Jun 1855	N.-Amer	849629
Schittenhelm, Jakob	7 Jan 1834	Boll	Sulz	Apr 1853	N.-Amer	849632
Schittenhelm, Jakob		Boll	Sulz	Aug 1852	N.-Amer	849632
Schittenhelm, Jakob	19 Dec 1844	Duerrenmettstetten	Sulz	Mar 1860	N.-Amer	849635
Schittenhelm, Johann Adam	30 Dec 1835	Herzogsweiler	Frd.	Mar 1864	N.-Amer	577779
Schittenhelm, Johann Adam		Pfalzgrafenweiler	Frd.	May 1806	Baden	569268
Schittenhelm, Johann Friedrich	23 Aug 1835	Untermusbach	Frd.	Jan 1854	N.-Amer	569273
Schittenhelm, Johann Friedrich	8 Jul 1834	Wittlensweiler	Frd.	Mar 1854	N.-Amer	569274
Schittenhelm, Johann Georg		Oberwaldach	Frd.	Mar 1837	N.-Amer	569269
Schittenhelm, Johann Georg	4 yrs.	Cresbach	Frd.	Aug 1852	N.-Amer	569271
Schittenhelm, Johann Georg & F		Cresbach	Frd.	Mar 1837	N.-Amer	569269
Schittenhelm, Johann Mart. & F		Muehlheim a.B.	Sulz	Jul 1847	N.-Amer	849639
Schittenhelm, Johannes	1 yrs.	Cresbach	Frd.	Aug 1852	N.-Amer	569271
Schittenhelm, Johannes	28 Oct 1847	Bergfelden	Sulz	Jul 1861	N.-Amer	849629
Schittenhelm, Johannes	21 Aug 1847	Voehringen	Sulz	Sep 1865	N.-Amer	849643
Schittenhelm, Johannes	30 Sep 1847	Boll	Sulz	Jul 1867	N.-Amer	849632
Schittenhelm, Johannes	20 Oct 1835	Boll	Sulz	Apr 1853	N.-Amer	849632
Schittenhelm, Johannes	22 Jun 1846	Muehlheim a.B.	Sulz	Dec 1865	N.-Amer	849639
Schittenhelm, Johannes & F		Oberwaldach	Frd.	Mar 1837	N.-Amer	569269
Schittenhelm, Ludwig & F	20 Mar 1810	Bergfelden	Sulz	Jul 1861	N.-Amer	849629
Schittenhelm, Margaretha (wife)	9 Dec 1812	Bergfelden	Sulz	Jul 1861	N.-Amer	849629
Schittenhelm, Maria Barbara	13 May 1835	Bergfelden	Sulz	Jul 1861	N.-Amer	849629
Schittenhelm, Mathaeus	13 Jun 1838	Duerrenmettstetten	Sulz	Feb 1854	N.-Amer	849635
Schittenhelm, Mathias	15 Nov 1848	Boll	Sulz	Aug 1865	N.-Amer	849632
Schittenhelm, Rosine	8 yrs.	Cresbach	Frd.	Aug 1852	N.-Amer	569271
Schittenhelm, Sibila & C	20 Sep 1836	Boll	Sulz	Sep 1867	N.-Amer	849632
Schiz, Catharina Barbara		Holzbronn	Calw	1852	N.-Amer	563212
Schlack, Carl Gottlieb	20 Nov 1808	Pfalzgrafenweiler	Frd.	bef 1847	N.-Amer	569270
Schlack, Hermann Christian	21 Oct 1818	Pfalzgrafenweiler	Frd.	1837	N.-Amer	569269
Schlack, Johann Carl	4 Jul 1850	Freudenstadt	Frd.	Jul 1866	N.-Amer	577780
Schlagenhauf, Johannes		Bergfelden	Sulz	Feb 1851	N.-Amer	849629
Schlagenhauf, Johannes	25 May 1822	Oberdigisheim	Bal.	bef 1846	Prussia	555963
Schlagenhauf, Johannes & F	4 May 1807	Leidringen	Sulz	Oct 1852	N.-Amer	849637
Schlagenhauff, Friedrich		Rosenfeld	Sulz	1854	N.-Amer	849641
Schlagenhauff, Johann Georg	3 Jul 1853	Rosenfeld	Sulz	Jan 1881	N.-Amer	849626
Schlaich, Caroline Sabine		Calw	Calw	Jan 1848	N.-Amer	563212
Schlaich, Christian & F		Glatten	Frd.	1817	Russia	569269
Schlaich, Louise Friederike		Calw	Calw	1853	N.-Amer	563212
Schlanderer, Christian	9 Nov 1838	Altingen	Herr.	May 1866	Bavaria	834624
Schlatterer, Pauline		Calw	Calw	1869	Bavaria	563212
Schlatterer, Pauline Eug. Mag.		Calw	Calw	1861	Prussia	563212
Schlauch, Christian		Glatten	Frd.	1817	Russia	569269
Schlecht, Johannes	16 Apr 1833	Entringen	Herr.	Mar 1852	N.-Amer	834627
Schlee, Anton & W	17 Jun 1794	Fuernsal	Sulz	Apr 1837	N.-Amer	849635
Schlee, Christian	22 Jan 1835	Herzogsweiler	Frd.	Apr 1853	N.-Amer	569272
Schlee, Christian	17 Dec 1836	Cresbach	Frd.	Aug 1853	N.-Amer	569274
Schlee, Elisabetha		Pfalzgrafenweiler	Frd.	Jul 1854	N.-Amer	569274

Name		Birth		Emigration			Film
Last	First	Date	Place	O'amt	Appl. Date	Dest.	Number
Schlee, Johannes		3 Sep 1876	Sigmarswangen	Sulz	Aug 1893	N.-Amer	849642
Schlee, Maria (wife)			Fuernsal	Sulz	Apr 1837	N.-Amer	849635
Schlee, Peter & W			Fuernsal	Sulz	Apr 1837	N.-Amer	849635
Schlee, Rosina & C		25 Jun 1817	Cresbach	Frd.	Oct 1854	N.-Amer	569274
Schleeh, Christian		6 Nov 1833	Glatten	Frd.	Jun 1855	N.-Amer	569275
Schleeh, Johannes		3 Aug 1810	Unterweiler	Frd.	Mar 1841	Austria	569269
Schlegel, Johann Georg			Laufen	Bal.	bef 1853	Switz.	555962
Schleh, Anna		22 yrs.	Wittlensweiler	Frd.	Apr 1833	N.-Amer	569268
Schleh, Anna Maria			Pfalzgrafenweiler	Frd.	bef 1847	N.-Amer	569270
Schleh, Carl		29 Jan 1846	Baiersbronn	Frd.	May 1866	N.-Amer	577780
Schleh, Carl Friedrich		14 Dec 1833	Durrweiler	Frd.	Mar 1853	N.-Amer	569272
Schleh, Christian		16 Oct 1826	Pfalzgrafenweiler	Frd.	Apr 1846	N.-Amer	569271
Schleh, Friedrich & F		16 Sep 1819	Pfalzgrafenweiler	Frd.	Apr 1846	N.-Amer	569271
Schleh, Gottfried		3 Jan 1843	Herzogsweiler	Frd.	Jan 1866	N.-Amer	577780
Schleh, Gottlieb		4 yrs.	Igelsberg	Frd.	Apr 1857	N.-Amer	577776
Schleh, Jakob		27 Jun 1830	Durrweiler	Frd.	May 1853	N.-Amer	569272
Schleh, Jakob		8 Oct 1824	Glatten	Frd.	Apr 1846	N.-Amer	569271
Schleh, Jakob Friedrich		24 Jun 1835	Pfalzgrafenweiler	Frd.	Apr 1846	N.-Amer	569271
Schleh, Johann Adam		20 Jan 1833	Durrweiler	Frd.	Sep 1852	N.-Amer	569271
Schleh, Johann Georg		17 Aug 1821	Herzogsweiler	Frd.	1846	N.-Amer	569270
Schleh, Johann Georg		6 Jun 1836	Herzogsweiler	Frd.	May 1854	N.-Amer	569273
Schleh, Johann Georg		6 Feb 1836	Durrweiler	Frd.	Sep 1852	N.-Amer	569271
Schleich, Anna Maria			Dornstetten	Frd.	Aug 1850	N.-Amer	569271
Schleich, Elisabeth			Dornstetten	Frd.	bef 1831	Odessa	569269
Schleich, Jakob & F			Dornstetten	Frd.	Feb 1817	Odessa	569269
Schlichter, Maria B.(wid.)& F			Gueltstein	Herr.	Mar 1836	N.-Amer	834624
Schloderer, Georg Christian		7 May 1840	Freudenstadt	Frd.	Jun 1854	N.-Amer	569274
Schlopp, Eva Catharina			Oberkollwangen	Calw	1859	N.-Amer	563212
Schlopp, Johann Georg			Calw	Calw	1859	N.-Amer	563212
Schlopp, Johann Ludwig			Calw	Calw	1858	N.-Amer	563212
Schlotter, Anna			Leidringen	Sulz	May 1854	N.-Amer	849637
Schlotter, Christina		10 Dec 1838	Leidringen	Sulz	May 1856	N.-Amer	849637
Schlotter, Christina (wife)		22 Jan 1804	Leidringen	Sulz	May 1856	N.-Amer	849637
Schlotter, Friedrich			Leidringen	Sulz	Mar 1854	N.-Amer	849637
Schlotter, Georg		24 Sep 1835	Leidringen	Sulz	Feb 1854	N.-Amer	849637
Schlotter, Georg & F		6 Sep 1802	Leidringen	Sulz	May 1856	N.-Amer	849637
Schlotter, Jakob		10 Aug 1875	Leidringen	Sulz	Sep 1893	N.-Amer	849626
Schlotter, Jakob		1 Jun 1856	Leidringen	Sulz	Apr 1873	N.-Amer	849637
Schlotter, Johann Georg		16 Apr 1847	Leidringen	Sulz	Mar 1866	N.-Amer	849637
Schlotter, Johann Georg & F			Leidringen	Sulz	Mar 1854	N.-Amer	849637
Schlotter, Martin		6 Jul 1844	Leidringen	Sulz	Mar 1866	N.-Amer	849637
Schlotter, Martin Friedrich		10 Jun 1841	Leidringen	Sulz	May 1856	N.-Amer	849637
Schlotter, Ursula			Leidringen	Sulz	Mar 1854	N.-Amer	849637
Schlotter, Ursula		13 Dec 1836	Leidringen	Sulz	Jul 1864	Bavaria	849637
Schlotterbeck, Christina Barb.		22 Aug 1818	Nufringen	Herr.	Feb 1847	N.-Amer	834626
Schlotterbeck, Georg Mich. & F			Nufringen	Herr.	Feb 1847	N.-Amer	834626
Schlotterbeck, Jacob Friedr.		22 May 1842	Nufringen	Herr.	Feb 1847	N.-Amer	834626
Schlotterbeck, Johannes			Nufringen	Herr.	Jul 1832	N.-Amer	834624
Schlotterbek, (family)			Renfrizhausen	Sulz	Aug 1846	N.-Amer	849639
Schlotterbek, Andreas		21 Dec 1804	Muehlheim a.B.	Sulz	bef 1844	N.-Amer	849625

Schlotterbek, Andreas		Muehlheim a.B.	Sulz	bef 1841	N.-Amer 849639
Schlotterbek, Anna Katharina		Muehlheim a.B.	Sulz	Mar 1847	N.-Amer 849639
Schlotterbek, Anna Maria		Muehlheim a.B.	Sulz	Mar 1847	N.-Amer 849639
Schlotterbek, Anna Maria (wife)		Muehlheim a.B.	Sulz	Mar 1847	N.-Amer 849639
Schlotterbek, Anna Maria (wife)	26 yrs.	Nufringen	Herr.	May 1832	N.-Amer 834624
Schlotterbek, Christian		Renfrizhausen	Sulz	Jun 1847	N.-Amer 849639
Schlotterbek, Elisabetha (wife)		Holzhausen	Sulz	Mar 1852	Hamburg 849635
Schlotterbek, Eva	8 Jun 1804	Voehringen	Sulz	Feb 1833	N.-Amer 849643
Schlotterbek, Eva Elisabetha		Muehlheim a.B.	Sulz	Apr 1833	N.-Amer 849639
Schlotterbek, Georg		Renfrizhausen	Sulz	Jun 1847	N.-Amer 849639
Schlotterbek, Jacob & W	51 yrs.	Nufringen	Herr.	May 1832	N.-Amer 834624
Schlotterbek, Johann Friedrich		Muehlheim a.B.	Sulz	Mar 1847	N.-Amer 849639
Schlotterbek, Johann Jac. & F		Nufringen	Herr.	Mar 1835	Rus-Pol 834624
Schlotterbek, Johann Jakob		Muehlheim a.B.	Sulz	Apr 1833	N.-Amer 849639
Schlotterbek, Johann Jakob & F	18 Feb 1781	Muehlheim a.B.	Sulz	Apr 1833	N.-Amer 849639
Schlotterbek, Johannes	21 Jul 1807	Holzhausen	Sulz	bef 1844	Hamburg 849635
Schlotterbek, Johannes	35 Yrs.	Renfrizhausen	Sulz	Jun 1854	N.-Amer 849639
Schlotterbek, Johannes	27 yrs.	Renfrizhausen	Sulz	Jun 1849	N.-Amer 849639
Schlotterbek, Johannes		Muehlheim a.B.	Sulz	Mar 1847	N.-Amer 849639
Schlotterbek, Johannes & F		Muehlheim a.B.	Sulz	Mar 1847	N.-Amer 849639
Schlotterbek, Johannes & W		Holzhausen	Sulz	Mar 1852	Hamburg 849635
Schlotterbek, Katharina (wife)	28 Oct 1786	Muehlheim a.B.	Sulz	Apr 1833	N.-Amer 849639
Schlotterbek, Maria Barbara	21 yrs.	Muehlheim a.B.	Sulz	Apr 1833	N.-Amer 849639
Schlotterbek, Martha		Muehlheim a.B.	Sulz	Mar 1847	N.-Amer 849639
Schlotterbek, Sabina	15 yrs.	Muehlheim a.B.	Sulz	Apr 1833	N.-Amer 849639
Schlottterbek, Wilhelm Friedr.		Reusten	Herr.	Feb 1836	France 834624
Schmaelzle, Esther (wife)		Wittendorf	Frd.	Mar 1833	N.-Amer 569268
Schmaelzle, Jacob & F		Aach	Frd.	Apr 1817	Russia 569267
Schmaelzle, Johanna Elisabetha	12 May 1833	Freudenstadt	Frd.	bef 1861	France 577778
Schmaelzle, Johannes & F		Wittendorf	Frd.	Mar 1833	N.-Amer 569268
Schmaelzle, Wilhelmine Carol.	20 Jul 1840	Freudenstadt	Frd.	bef 1861	N.-Amer 577778
Schmalz, Anna Maria	26 Dec 1820	Herzogsweiler	Frd.	Apr 1846	N.-Amer 569271
Schmalz, Anna Maria	3 May 1840	Herzogsweiler	Frd.	Apr 1846	N.-Amer 569271
Schmalz, Christina	23 Oct 1828	Herzogsweiler	Frd.	Apr 1846	N.-Amer 569271
Schmalz, Elisabetha Barbara	15 Nov 1816	Herzogsweiler	Frd.	Apr 1846	N.-Amer 569271
Schmalz, Elisabetha Katharina	18 Nov 1825	Herzogsweiler	Frd.	Apr 1846	N.-Amer 569271
Schmalz, Elisabetha Katharina	7 Nov 1845	Herzogsweiler	Frd.	Apr 1846	N.-Amer 569271
Schmalz, Eva	5 Sep 1843	Herzogsweiler	Frd.	Apr 1846	N.-Amer 569271
Schmalz, Gottlieb & F	17 Dec 1813	Herzogsweiler	Frd.	Apr 1846	N.-Amer 569271
Schmalzle, David	25 Jun 1834	Baiersbronn	Frd.	Sep 1854	N.-Amer 569274
Schmauk, Johann Philipp	23 Sep 1802	Voehringen	Sulz	bef 1837	Baden 849643
Schmauk, Johanna Philippina	51 yrs.	Voehringen	Sulz	Mar 1815	Bavaria 849625
Schmeikle, Anna Maria	25 Sep 1829	Wittlensweiler	Frd.	bef 1854	France 569273
Schmeltzle, Agatha	11 yrs.	Freudenstadt	Frd.	May 1752	Pen.N-A 550803
Schmeltzle, Barbara	19 yrs.	Freudenstadt	Frd.	May 1752	Pen.N-A 550803
Schmeltzle, Eva (wid.) & F	49 yrs.	Freudenstadt	Frd.	May 1752	Pen.N-A 550803
Schmeltzle, Simon	14 yrs.	Freudenstadt	Frd.	May 1752	Pen.N-A 550803
Schmelzle, Agnes		Schoenegruend	Frd.	bef 1861	Baden 577778
Schmelzle, Anna Maria	13 yrs.	Hoerschweiler	Frd.	Aug 1854	N.-Amer 569274
Schmelzle, Barbara		Hoerschweiler	Frd.	Aug 1854	N.-Amer 569274

Name		Birth		Emigration			Film
Last	First	Date	Place	O'amt	Appl. Date	Dest.	Number
Schmelzle, Christina		21 Dec 1830	Hallwangen	Frd.	May 1860	N.-Amer	577777
Schmelzle, Friedrich		7 Apr 1827	Hallwangen	Frd.	Feb 1849	N.-Amer	569270
Schmelzle, Friedrich		26 Jan 1845	Rosenfeld	Sulz	Jun 1865	N.-Amer	849641
Schmelzle, Georg Friedrich		19 yrs.	Hallwangen	Frd.	Sep 1866	N.-Amer	577780
Schmelzle, Johann Georg			Haiterbach	Nag.	Feb 1854	N.-Amer	838491
Schmelzle, Louise		18 May 1825	Dornstetten	Frd.	May 1858	Switz.	577776
Schmelzle, Ludwig		23 Sep 1795	Baiersbronn	Frd.	bef 1844	France	569269
Schmelzle, Matthaeus		9 Feb 1837	Kniebis	Frd.	Jan 1857	N.-Amer	577776
Schmetzle, Christian		Jul 1812	Vesperweiler	Frd.	Mar 1837	N.-Amer	569269
Schmetzle, Johann Georg		3 Jul 1810	Vesperweiler	Frd.	Mar 1837	N.-Amer	569269
Schmid, Adam		3 yrs.	Aichelberg	Calw	1860	N.-Amer	563212
Schmid, Agatha		18 Nov 1819	Cresbach	Frd.	Apr 1844	N.-Amer	569269
Schmid, Agatha		13 Oct 1834	Voehringen	Sulz	1848	N.-Amer	849643
Schmid, Agatha			Aichelberg	Calw	1860	N.-Amer	563212
Schmid, Andreas			Zwieselberg	Frd.	bef 1863	Baden	577778
Schmid, Andreas		17 Jan 1860	Bergfelden	Sulz	Mar 1881	N.-Amer	849629
Schmid, Andreas		24 Apr 1847	Erkenbrechtsweiler	Sulz	Jul 1864	France	849643
Schmid, Andreas & F		53 yrs.	Freudenstadt	Frd.	May 1752	Pen.N-A	550803
Schmid, Anna		5 Oct 1838	Tumlingen	Frd.	Jan 1855	N.-Amer	569275
Schmid, Anna		51 yrs.	Freudenstadt	Frd.	May 1752	Pen.N-A	550803
Schmid, Anna		15 Jun 1839	Voehringen	Sulz	Apr 1883	N.-Amer	849643
Schmid, Anna			Voehringen	Sulz	Apr 1833	N.-Amer	849643
Schmid, Anna		30 yrs.	Aichelberg	Calw	1854	N.-Amer	563212
Schmid, Anna Barbara		15 Mar 1764	Voehringen	Sulz	bef 1817	--	849643
Schmid, Anna Christine		13 Jan 1866	Bergfelden	Sulz	Apr 1881	N.-Amer	849626
Schmid, Anna Elisabetha		18 yrs.	Freudenstadt	Frd.	May 1752	Pen.N-A	550803
Schmid, Anna Maria		11 Jan 1848	Tumlingen	Frd.	Jan 1855	N.-Amer	569275
Schmid, Anna Maria			Voehringen	Sulz	bef 1815	Russia	849625
Schmid, Anna Maria		9 Dec 1815	Schopfloch	Frd.	Apr 1851	N.-Amer	569271
Schmid, Anna Maria		14 Aug 1824	Bergfelden	Sulz	Oct 1867	France	849629
Schmid, Anna Maria		22 yrs.	Cresbach	Frd.	Dec 1864	N.-Amer	577779
Schmid, Anna Maria		14 Jan 1849	Voehringen	Sulz	Sep 1855	N.-Amer	849643
Schmid, Anna Maria		30 Dec 1838	Voehringen	Sulz	Jun 1860	N.-Amer	849643
Schmid, Anna Maria		20 Jun 1833	Rosenfeld	Sulz	Apr 1854	N.-Amer	849640
Schmid, Anna Maria		12 yrs.	Rosenfeld	Sulz	Jun 1817	Russia	849640
Schmid, Anna Maria (wife)		22 Jan 1814	Cresbach	Frd.	Apr 1844	N.-Amer	569269
Schmid, Anna Maria (wid) & F		22 Nov 1812	Tumlingen	Frd.	Jan 1855	N.-Amer	569275
Schmid, Barbara		3 Jan 1847	Tumlingen	Frd.	Jan 1855	N.-Amer	569275
Schmid, Barbara		28 Dec 1805	Tumlingen	Frd.	Jan 1855	N.-Amer	569275
Schmid, Barbara		4 Nov 1849	Marschalkenzimmern	Sulz	Aug 1869	Switz.	849638
Schmid, Barbara		18 yrs.	Rosenfeld	Sulz	Jun 1817	Russia	849640
Schmid, Carl Friedrich		28 Dec 1846	Unterjesingen	Herr.	Mar 1868	N.-Amer	834624
Schmid, Caspar			Geislingen	Bal.	bef 1861	Switz.	555962
Schmid, Catharina		6 Feb 1836	Voehringen	Sulz	1854	N.-Amer	849643
Schmid, Catharina Magdalena		9 yrs.	Beutelsbach	Schd.	May 1833	N.-Amer	801460
Schmid, Christian		16 Apr 1850	Tumlingen	Frd.	Jan 1855	N.-Amer	569275
Schmid, Christian		18 Jul 1867	Bergfelden	Sulz	Apr 1881	N.-Amer	849626
Schmid, Christian		17 yrs.	Beutelsbach	Schd.	May 1833	N.-Amer	801460
Schmid, Christian			Aichelberg	Calw	1860	N.-Amer	563212
Schmid, Christian & F			Freudenstadt	Frd.	Sep 1854	N.-Amer	569274

Schmid, Christian & F	21 Nov 1836	Bergfelden	Sulz	Apr 1881	N.-Amer	849626
Schmid, Christiane Barbara		Freudenstadt	Frd.	Jul 1852	N. Amer	569271
Schmid, Christina		Rosenfeld	Sulz	1834	N.-Amer	849625
Schmid, Christina		Voehringen	Sulz	Jun 1817	Russia	849643
Schmid, Christina	30 May 1877	Fuernsal	Sulz	Sep 1882	N.-Amer	849626
Schmid, Christina & C	9 Mar 1826	Erkenbrechtsweiler	Sulz	Sep 1855	Switz.	849643
Schmid, Christina (wid.) & F	37 yrs.	Rosenfeld	Sulz	Jun 1817	Russia	849640
Schmid, Christina Barbara		Voehringen	Sulz	Apr 1833	N.-Amer	849643
Schmid, Christine Doroth. (wife)		Freudenstadt	Frd.	Sep 1854	N.-Amer	569274
Schmid, Christoph Friedrich	5 yrs.	Freudenstadt	Frd.	Jul 1852	N.-Amer	569271
Schmid, Conrad	3 Jan 1863	Rosenfeld	Sulz	Mar 1864	N.-Amer	849641
Schmid, Dorothea	7 Feb 1828	Boeffingen	Frd.	Sep 1854	N.-Amer	569274
Schmid, Dorothea	16 Apr 1834	Oberiflingen	Frd.	Apr 1860	N.-Amer	577777
Schmid, Dorothea & F	4 Dec 1835	Fuernsal	Sulz	Sep 1882	N.-Amer	849626
Schmid, Elisabeth Luise & F		Sulz	Sulz	Oct 1857	Canada	849628
Schmid, Elisabetha	2 Feb 1833	Cresbach	Frd.	Apr 1844	N.-Amer	569269
Schmid, Elisabetha		Beutelsbach	Schd.	May 1833	N.-Amer	801460
Schmid, Elisabetha	11 yrs.	Beutelsbach	Schd.	May 1833	N.-Amer	801460
Schmid, Elisabetha Cathar.	22 May 1836	Tumlingen	Frd.	Jan 1855	N.-Amer	569275
Schmid, Elisabethe Barb. (wife)		Bergfelden	Sulz	Aug 1853	N.-Amer	849629
Schmid, Emilie Franziska	18 yrs.	Freudenstadt	Frd.	Jul 1852	N.-Amer	569271
Schmid, Ernestine Sophie	14 yrs.	Freudenstadt	Frd.	Jul 1852	N.-Amer	569271
Schmid, Ernst Carl		Sulz	Sulz	Oct 1850	N.-Amer	849628
Schmid, Ernst Christoph Fried.	9 yrs.	Freudenstadt	Frd.	Jul 1852	N.-Amer	569271
Schmid, Friederike	5 yrs.	Beutelsbach	Schd.	May 1833	N.-Amer	801460
Schmid, Friedrich		Bergfelden	Sulz	Dec 1854	N.-Amer	849629
Schmid, Friedrich	3 Oct 1800	Holzhausen	Sulz	Apr 1833	N.-Amer	849635
Schmid, Friedrich & F		Bergfelden	Sulz	Feb 1846	N.-Amer	849629
Schmid, Friedrich & F		Calw	Calw	Jun 1847	N.-Amer	563212
Schmid, Georg David	16 yrs.	Freudenstadt	Frd.	Jul 1852	N.-Amer	569271
Schmid, Georg Jakob	18 Feb 1806	Holzhausen	Sulz	Apr 1832	N.-Amer	849635
Schmid, Gottfried	27 Jan 1831	Boeffingen	Frd.	Sep 1859	N.-Amer	577776
Schmid, Gottfried	23 Nov 1799	Voehringen	Sulz	bef 1817	--	849643
Schmid, Gottfried & F		Wittershausen	Sulz	Jun 1817	N.-Amer	849644
Schmid, Gottfried & W		Voehringen	Sulz	Apr 1833	N.-Amer	849643
Schmid, Gottlieb	25 Feb 1877	Bergfelden	Sulz	Apr 1881	N.-Amer	849626
Schmid, Gottlieb	3 Feb 1860	Rosenfeld	Sulz	Mar 1864	N.-Amer	849641
Schmid, Gustav		Calw	Calw	1853	N.-Amer	563212
Schmid, Heinrich		Freudenstadt	Frd.	Aug 1851	N.-Amer	569271
Schmid, Heinrich	2 yrs.	Sulz	Sulz	Oct 1857	Canada	849628
Schmid, Hermine Sophie	10 Feb 1839	Sulz	Sulz	Nov 1860	Baden	849628
Schmid, Imanuel		Affstaett	Herr.	bef 1848	N.-Amer	834627
Schmid, Jacob		Bergfelden	Sulz	bef 1855	N.-Amer	849629
Schmid, Jakob	30 Aug 1840	Tumlingen	Frd.	Jan 1855	N.-Amer	569275
Schmid, Jakob		Wittershausen	Sulz	Jul 1815	Bavaria	849644
Schmid, Jakob	4 Feb 1862	Bergfelden	Sulz	Apr 1881	N.-amer	849626
Schmid, Jakob	16 Jan 1854	Sigmarswangen	Sulz	Jun 1871	N.-Amer	849642
Schmid, Johann & F		Voehringen	Sulz	Jan 1848	N.-Amer	849643
Schmid, Johann Caspar	20 Jun 1812	Rosenfeld	Sulz	Apr 1834	N.-Amer	849640
Schmid, Johann Caspar	5 yrs.	Rosenfeld	Sulz	Jun 1817	Russia	849640

Name		Birth		Emigration			Film
Last	First	Date	Place	O'amt	Appl. Date	Dest.	Number
Schmid, Johann Christian		22 Aug 1841	Dornstetten	Frd.	Mar 1861	N.-Amer	577778
Schmid, Johann David & F			Freudenstadt	Frd.	Jul 1852	N.-Amer	569271
Schmid, Johann Friedrich		40 yrs.	Agenbach	Calw	1856	Bavaria	563212
Schmid, Johann Georg			Cresbach	Frd.	May 1840	N.-Amer	569269
Schmid, Johann Georg			Herzogsweiler	Frd.	1817	Russia	569269
Schmid, Johann Georg		28 Oct 1832	Bergfelden	Sulz	Apr 1860	N.-Amer	849629
Schmid, Johann Georg		9 mon.	Cresbach	Frd.	Dec 1864	N.-Amer	577779
Schmid, Johann Georg		7 Aug 1879	Bergfelden	Sulz	Apr 1881	N.-Amer	849626
Schmid, Johann Georg		29 Nov 1830	Gueltstein	Herr.	bef 1862	N.-Amer	834624
Schmid, Johann Georg & F			Bergfelden	Sulz	Jul 1854	N.-Amer	849629
Schmid, Johann Jacob		24 Apr 1839	Rosenfeld	Sulz	1853	N.-Amer	849640
Schmid, Johann Jacob		20 Jan 1840	Rosenfeld	Sulz	Apr 1854	N.-Amer	849640
Schmid, Johann Jakob		29 May 1834	Dornstetten	Frd.	Apr 1853	N.-Amer	569272
Schmid, Johann Jakob & F			Voehringen	Sulz	Jun 1817	Rus-Pol	849643
Schmid, Johann Jakob & F		26 Apr 1823	Rosenfeld	Sulz	Mar 1864	N.-Amer	849641
Schmid, Johann Martin		20 Nov 1845	Voehringen	Sulz	Jun 1860	N.-Amer	849643
Schmid, Johann Martin		18 yrs.	Voehringen	Sulz	Oct 1853	N.-Amer	849643
Schmid, Johann Martin		10 Mar 1873	Bergfelden	Sulz	Apr 1881	N.-Amer	849626
Schmid, Johann Martin		3 Jun 1851	Isingen	Sulz	Mar 1866	N.-Amer	849636
Schmid, Johanna Elisab. (wife)			Sulz	Sulz	Apr 1834	N.-Amer	849627
Schmid, Johanna Sophie		7 Jan 1854	Freudenstadt	Frd.	Sep 1854	N.-Amer	569274
Schmid, Johannes		2 Aug 1844	Tumlingen	Frd.	Jan 1855	N.-Amer	569275
Schmid, Johannes		20 Mar 1848	Bergfelden	Sulz	May 1868	N.-Amer	849629
Schmid, Johannes		25 Mar 1819	Voehringen	Sulz	Nov 1844	N.-Amer	849643
Schmid, Johannes			Voehringen	Sulz	Apr 1833	N.-Amer	849643
Schmid, Johannes		16 Apr 1788	Voehringen	Sulz	bef 1817	--	849643
Schmid, Johannes			Fuernsal	Sulz	Nov 1881	N.-Amer	849635
Schmid, Johannes			Ostelsheim	Calw	1860	N.-Amer	563212
Schmid, Johannes		26 Sep 1808	Rosenfeld	Sulz	Jun 1817	Russia	849640
Schmid, Johannes			Beutelsbach	Schd.	May 1833	N.-Amer	801460
Schmid, Johannes		7 yrs.	Ostelsheim	Calw	1854	N.-Amer	563212
Schmid, Johannes & F		26 Sep 1808	Sulz	Sulz	Apr 1834	N.-Amer	849627
Schmid, Johannes & F			Bergfelden	Sulz	Aug 1853	N.-Amer	849629
Schmid, Johannes & F			Dachtel	Calw	1852	N.-Amer	563212
Schmid, Justine Barbara		12 yrs.	Freudenstadt	Frd.	Jul 1852	N.-Amer	569271
Schmid, Karl		3 Mar 1871	Bergfelden	Sulz	Apr 1881	N.-Amer	849626
Schmid, Karl		11 Jun 1857	Rosenfeld	Sulz	Mar 1864	N.-Amer	849641
Schmid, Karl Ferdinand		11 Apr 1840	Rosenfeld	Sulz	Jul 1863	N.-Amer	849641
Schmid, Katharina			Oberiflingen	Frd.	May 1854	N.-Amer	569273
Schmid, Louise Friederike W.		7 Dec 1835	Sulz	Sulz	Apr 1860	Baden	849628
Schmid, Magdalena		10 Jun 1842	Tumlingen	Frd.	Jan 1855	N.-Amer	569275
Schmid, Magdalena			Aichelberg	Calw	1860	N.-Amer	563212
Schmid, Magdalena (wife)			Voehringen	Sulz	Apr 1833	N.-Amer	849643
Schmid, Margaretha (wife)		30 Jul 1839	Bergfelden	Sulz	Apr 1881	N.-Amer	849626
Schmid, Maria Dorothea		8 Jun 1851	Freudenstadt	Frd.	Sep 1854	N.-Amer	569274
Schmid, Maria Dorothea		2 yrs.	Sulz	Sulz	Apr 1834	N.-Amer	849627
Schmid, Maria Friederike		20 yrs.	Freudenstadt	Frd.	Jul 1852	N.-Amer	569271
Schmid, Martin		21 Jan 1840	Renfrizhausen	Sulz	Oct 1859	N.-Amer	849639
Schmid, Martin & F			Voehringen	Sulz	Jul 1817	Russia	849627
Schmid, Martin & F		23 May 1757	Voehringen	Sulz	bef 1817	--	849643

Name	Date	Place		Dest.	Ref.
Schmid, Martin Leopold & F		Bergfelden	Sulz	May 1853	N.-Amer 849629
Schmid, Mathias	22 Nov 1863	Bergfelden	Sulz	Jul 1880	N.-Amer 849626
Schmid, Mathias (wid.)		Voehringen	Sulz	Apr 1833	N.-Amer 849643
Schmid, Matthias & F	29 Jun 1835	Cresbach	Frd.	Dec 1864	N.-Amer 577779
Schmid, Pauline	24 Aug 1833	Baiersbronn	Frd.	Apr 1857	Baden 577776
Schmid, Rosina & C		Aichelberg	Calw	1860	N.-Amer 563212
Schmid, Rosina Katharina (wife)	25 Jan 1827	Herrenberg	Sulz	Mar 1864	N.-Amer 849641
Schmid, Rudolph Caspar	3 yrs.	Freudenstadt	Frd.	Jul 1852	N.-Amer 569271
Schmid, Sabina & C	14 Apr 1819	Nebringen	Herr.	May 1847	N.-Amer 834626
Schmid, Stephania Louise	8 yrs.	Freudenstadt	Frd.	Jul 1852	N.-Amer 569271
Schmid, Wilhelm		Freudenstadt	Frd.	Jun 1854	N.-Amer 569273
Schmidberger, Agatha & C	36 yrs.	Bondorf	Herr.	Aug 1845	N.-Amer 834626
Schmidberger, Antonia	17 Apr 1845	Bondorf	Herr.	Aug 1845	N.-Amer 834626
Schmidberger, Catharina	6 Apr 1844	Bondorf	Herr.	Aug 1845	N.-Amer 834626
Schmidberger, Eleonoea	24 Dec 1838	Bondorf	Herr.	Aug 1845	N.-Amer 834626
Schmidberger, Eleonora & C	30 yrs.	Bondorf	Herr.	Aug 1845	N.-Amer 834626
Schmidberger, Herrmann	8 May 1846	Bondorf	Herr.	Aug 1845	N.-Amer 834626
Schmidberger, Rosalie	21 Sep 1840	Bondorf	Herr.	Aug 1845	N.-Amer 834626
Schmider, Conrad & F	7 May 1843	Altheim	Horb	Aug 1868	N.-Amer 835929
Schmider, Johannes	13 Apr 1867	Altheim	Horb	Aug 1868	N.-Amer 835929
Schmider, Maria	8 Apr 1868	Altheim	Horb	Aug 1868	N.-Amer 835929
Schmider, Rosalia & F	52 yrs.	Altheim	Horb	Apr 1855	N.-Amer 835929
Schmider, Victoria	17 Sep 1843	Altheim	Horb	Aug 1868	N.-Amer 835929
Schmider, Wilhelm	15 Oct 1846	Altheim	Horb	Jul 1866	N.-Amer 835929
Schmider, Wilhelm	12 Aug 1831	Altheim	Horb	bef 1854	N.-Amer 835929
Schmidt, Agatha	13 Apr 1835	Holzhausen	Sulz	Aug 1858	N.-Amer 849635
Schmidt, Andreas	29 Nov 1845	Binsdorf	Sulz	Feb 1846	Austria 849630
Schmidt, Anna Maria	29 Oct 1825	Unterjesingen	Herr.	May 1852	N.-Amer 834627
Schmidt, Balbina		Binsdorf	Sulz	Feb 1846	Austria 849630
Schmidt, Christian		Voehringen	Sulz	Aug 1840	N.-Amer 849643
Schmidt, Christian & F	28 Nov 1798	Aistaig	Sulz	Jul 1837	N.-Amer 849628
Schmidt, Christina (wife)		Aistaig	Sulz	Jul 1837	N.-Amer 849628
Schmidt, Eva Margaretha	23 Sep 1812	Unterjesingen	Herr.	May 1867	N.-Amer 834624
Schmidt, Georg Simon	41 yrs.	Gechingen	Calw	1868	N.-Amer 563212
Schmidt, Gottlieb		Rosenfeld	Sulz	1839	N.-Amer 849625
Schmidt, Jakob	27 Jul 1832	Unterjesingen	Herr.	May 1852	N.-Amer 834627
Schmidt, Johann Catharina	12 May 1852	Unterjesingen	Herr.	Feb 1869	N.-Amer 834624
Schmidt, Johann Georg & F		Rohrau	Herr.	May 1835	Rus-Pol 834624
Schmidt, Johann Jacob	23 Oct 1840	Hildrizhausen	Herr.	Nov 1865	Baden 834624
Schmidt, Joseph	15 Jan 1841	Binsdorf	Sulz	Feb 1846	Silesia 849630
Schmidt, Karoline		Gaertringen	Herr.	bef 1844	Switz. 834626
Schmidt, Maria Dorothea	6 Sep 1824	Unterjesingen	Herr.	May 1852	N.-Amer 834627
Schmidt, Maria Kathar. (wid.)	10 Dec 1793	Holzhausen	Sulz	Apr 1832	N.-Amer 849635
Schmidt, Maria Katharina	20 Feb 1836	Unterjesingen	Herr.	May 1852	N.-Amer 834627
Schmidt, Marianne (wife)	20 Nov 1814	Binsdorf	Sulz	Feb 1846	Silesia 849630
Schmidt, Mathias		Hildrizhausen	Herr.	Mar 1828	Baden 834624
Schmidt, Peter & F	29 Jan 1801	Binsdorf	Sulz	Feb 1846	Silesia 849630
Schmidt, Robert	15 Nov 1816	Baiersbronn	Frd.	Jun 1849	N.-Amer 569270
Schmidt, Simon Friedrich	22 yrs.	Gechingen	Calw	1867	N.-Amer 563212
Schmidt, Wilhelm Gottlob	10 Jan 1833	Unterjesingen	Herr.	Sep 1850	N.-Amer 834627

Name		Birth		Emigration			Film
Last	First	Date	Place	O'amt	Appl. Date	Dest.	Number
Schmied, Barbara (wife)			Bergfelden	Sulz	1846	Austria	849625
Schmied, Friedrich & F			Bergfelden	Sulz	1846	Austria	849625
Schmied, Theresia			Reinerzau	Frd.	Apr 1833	Baden	569268
Schmiele, Gottlob Friedrich			Dachtel	Calw	Oct 1870	N.-Amer	563212
Schmitt, Johanne Dorothea			Hirsau	Calw	1858	N.-Amer	563212
Schmollinger, Jacob		5 Jun 1835	Altingen	Herr.	Jan 1865	N.-Amer	834624
Schmollinger, Jonas			Altingen	Herr.	Nov 1843	France	834625
Schmollinger, Magdalena		20 Dec 1828	Altingen	Herr.	Dec 1828	N.-Amer	834624
Schmollinger, Maria Anna			Altingen	Herr.	Apr 1845	France	834626
Schnabel, Gottlieb			Wintersbach	Schd.	Nov 1834	Pommern	801460
Schnabel, Magdalena		20 Nov 1819	Winterbach	Schd.	Mar 1844	Baden	801461
Schnaible, Johann			Breitenberg	Calw	May 1873	N.-Amer	563212
Schnaible, Michael & F			Breitenberg	Calw	1853	N.-Amer	563212
Schnaidt, Eva Margaretha			Unterjesingen	Herr.	Apr 1830	N.-Amer	834624
Schnaidt, Jacob Friedrich			Unterjesingen	Herr.	Apr 1830	N.-Amer	834624
Schnaidt, Johann Friedrich & F			Unterjesingen	Herr.	1826	N.-Amer	834624
Schnaidt, Johann Martin			Unterjesingen	Herr.	Feb 1828	--	834624
Schnaufer, Christian Friedr.		1840	Calw	Calw	1860	N.-Amer	563212
Schneck, Gottlieb		15 Jun 1822	Entringen	Herr.	bef 1862	N.-Amer	834624
Schneck, Immanuel Wilhelm		13 Nov 1825	Entringen	Herr.	bef 1862	N.-Amer	834624
Schneck, Jacob		10 Nov 1819	Entringen	Herr.	bef 1862	N.-Amer	834624
Schneckenburger, Anna B. (wife)			Bergfelden	Sulz	Mar 1833	N.-Amer	849629
Schneckenburger, Anna Barbara		8 yrs.	Bergfelden	Sulz	Mar 1833	N.-Amer	849629
Schneckenburger, Christian		22 Dec 1867	Bergfelden	Sulz	Sep 1882	N.-Amer	849626
Schneckenburger, Friedrich			Binsdorf	Sulz	bef 1859	Bremen	849630
Schneckenburger, Jakob		18 mon.	Bergfelden	Sulz	Mar 1833	N.-Amer	849629
Schneckenburger, Johann Jacob		1 Jul 1848	Trichtingen	Sulz	Oct 1868	N.-Amer	849642
Schneckenburger, Johannes		4 yrs.	Bergfelden	Sulz	Mar 1833	N.-Amer	849629
Schneckenburger, Johannes & F		27 Sep 1800	Bergfelden	Sulz	Mar 1833	N.-Amer	849629
Schneckenburger, Margaretha			Bergfelden	Sulz	Apr 1881	N.-Amer	849626
Schneider, Agnes			Aach	Frd.	Aug 1817	Rus-Pol	569267
Schneider, Andreas		15 yrs.	Wittendorf	Frd.	Oct 1854	N.-Amer	569274
Schneider, Andreas & F		53 yrs.	Freudenstadt	Frd.	May 1752	Pen.N-A	550803
Schneider, Anna			Voehringen	Sulz	Mar 1837	N.-Amer	849643
Schneider, Anna & C		7 Apr 1819	Aach	Frd.	Mar 1847	N.-Amer	569270
Schneider, Anna (wife)		51 yrs.	Freudenstadt	Frd.	May 1752	Pen.N-A	550803
Schneider, Anna Elisabetha		18 yrs.	Freudenstadt	Frd.	May 1752	Pen.N-A	550803
Schneider, Anna Maria			Enztal	Nag.	Jul 1852	N.-Amer	838490
Schneider, Anna Maria		21 Apr 1838	Wittlensweiler	Frd.	bef 1863	France	577778
Schneider, Anna Maria			Deckenpfronn	Calw	1854	N.-Amer	563212
Schneider, Anna Maria (wife)		52 yrs.	Gaertringen	Herr.	Sep 1851	N.-Amer	834627
Schneider, Anna Maria (wife)			Hildrizhausen	Herr.	Mar 1831	N.-Amer	834624
Schneider, August		14 Feb 1844	Freudenstadt	Frd.	Aug 1864	N.-Amer	577779
Schneider, Barbara		4 Dec 1847	Hallwangen	Frd.	Sep 1853	N.-Amer	569274
Schneider, Barbara Magda. (wife)		30 Mar 1815	Hallwangen	Frd.	Sep 1853	N.-Amer	569274
Schneider, Bernhardt			Enztal	Nag.	Jul 1852	N.-Amer	838490
Schneider, Carl			Calw	Calw	1853	N.-Amer	563212
Schneider, Catharina (wife)			Wittendorf	Frd.	Jun 1855	N.-Amer	569275
Schneider, Catharina Dorothea			Deckenpfronn	Calw	1853	N.-Amer	563212
Schneider, Christian			Enztal	Nag.	Jul 1852	N.-Amer	838490

Schneider, Christian	8 yrs	Wittendorf	Frd.	Oct 1854	N.-Amer	569274
Schneider, Christian & F		Wittendorf	Frd.	Oct 1854	N.-Amer	569274
Schneider, Christian Friedr.		Calw	Calw	1860	N.-Amer	563212
Schneider, Christina	16 Nov 1778	Heselbach	Frd.	Apr 1847	N.-Amer	569270
Schneider, Christina	3 Apr 1825	Wittlensweiler	Frd.	Jun 1854	N.-Amer	569274
Schneider, Christina	12 Jun 1795	Voehringen	Sulz	Mar 1834	N.-Amer	849643
Schneider, Dorothea	30 Dec 1824	Weiler	Schd.	Mar 1835	N.-Amer	801460
Schneider, Elisabeth		Freudenstadt	Frd.	Mar 1851	N.-Amer	569271
Schneider, Esther	27 May 1842	Aach	Frd.	Mar 1847	N.-Amer	569270
Schneider, Eva Marie	25 Jul 1844	Hallwangen	Frd.	Sep 1853	N.-Amer	569274
Schneider, Franziska	8 Mar 1832	Zwieslberg	Frd.	Jan 1860	France	577777
Schneider, Friederike	22 May 1838	Hallwangen	Frd.	Sep 1853	N.-Amer	569274
Schneider, Friederike	5 Oct 1830	Weiler	Schd.	Mar 1835	N.-Amer	801460
Schneider, Friedrich		Enztal	Nag.	Jul 1852	N.-Amer	838490
Schneider, Friedrich	17 Feb 1820	Lombach	Frd.	1841	N.-Amer	569269
Schneider, Friedrich		Freudenstadt	Frd.	Sep 1860	N.-Amer	577777
Schneider, Friedrich		Unterjesingen	Herr.	Feb 1829	N.-Amer	834624
Schneider, Georg Friedrich	22 Dec 1839	Hallwangen	Frd.	Sep 1853	N.-Amer	569274
Schneider, Gottfried		Balingen	Bal.	Aug 1853	Switz.	555962
Schneider, Gottfried		Onstmettingen	Bal.	bef 1860	Switz.	555962
Schneider, Gottlieb & W		Hildrizhausen	Herr.	Mar 1831	N.-Amer	834624
Schneider, Gottlob	2 Mar 1836	Altingen	Herr.	1853	N.-Amer	834624
Schneider, Heinrich		Gechingen	Calw	May 1870	N.-Amer	563212
Schneider, Jacob Friedrich	10 Nov 1826	Weiler	Schd.	Mar 1835	N.-Amer	801460
Schneider, Jacob Friedrich & F		Deckenpfronn	Calw	1852	N.-Amer	563212
Schneider, Jakob	18 Jan 1845	Leidringen	Sulz	Apr 1865	N.-Amer	849637
Schneider, Johann Adam & F	2 Apr 1811	Hallwangen	Frd.	Sep 1853	N.-Amer	569274
Schneider, Johann Christian	26 Dec 1846	Aach	Frd.	Mar 1847	N.-Amer	569270
Schneider, Johann Friedr. & F		Enztal	Nag.	Jul 1852	N.-Amer	838490
Schneider, Johann Georg	13 Sep 1851	Leidringen	Sulz	Mar 1869	N.-Amer	849637
Schneider, Johann Georg & W		Wittendorf	Frd.	Jun 1855	N.-Amer	569275
Schneider, Johann Jacob	17 Jan 1844	Geschingen	Calw	1864	N.-Amer	563212
Schneider, Johann Jacob		Unterjesingen	Herr.	bef 1839	Saxony	834625
Schneider, Johann Martin	31 Aug 1841	Schernberg	Frd.	Apr 1861	N.-Amer	577778
Schneider, Johann Martin	11 Apr 1830	Hallwangen	Frd.	Sep 1853	N.-Amer	569274
Schneider, Johann Michael	10 Oct 1845	Schernbach	Frd.	Mar 1864	N.-Amer	577779
Schneider, Johann Michael	13 Feb 1842	Hallwangen	Frd.	Sep 1853	N.-Amer	569274
Schneider, Johannes	3 Jul 1853	Hallwangen	Frd.	Sep 1853	N.-Amer	569274
Schneider, Johannes	25 Sep 1838	Aistaig	Sulz	Dec 1865	N.-Amer	849628
Schneider, Johannes	27 Dec 1831	Weiler	Schd.	Mar 1835	N.-Amer	801460
Schneider, Johannes Fried. & W	45 yrs.	Gaertringen	Herr.	Sep 1851	N.-Amer	834627
Schneider, Katharina Barbara	1824	Gechingen	Calw	1854	N.-Amer	563212
Schneider, Magdalena	12 yrs.	Wittendorf	Frd.	Oct 1854	N.-Amer	569274
Schneider, Magdalena	23 yrs.	Unterjesingen	Herr.	May 1829	N.-Amer	834624
Schneider, Magdalena & C		Unterjesingen	Herr.	Apr 1830	N.-Amer	834624
Schneider, Margaretha		Unterjesingen	Herr.	Apr 1830	N.-Amer	834624
Schneider, Maria	1 yrs.	Wittendorf	Frd.	Oct 1854	N.-Amer	569274
Schneider, Maria Agnes		Gechingen	Calw	1861	France	563212
Schneider, Maria Agnes	1835	Gechingen	Calw	1854	N.-Amer	563212
Schneider, Maria Barbara		Deckenpfronn	Calw	1857	N.-Amer	563212

| Name | | Birth | | Emigration | | | Film |
Last	First	Date	Place	O'amt	Appl. Date	Dest.	Number
Schneider, Marie Friederike			Simmozheim	Calw	1868	France	563212
Schneider, Martin		19 Jul 1846	Hallwangen	Frd.	Sep 1853	N.-Amer	569274
Schneider, Michael			Glatten	Frd.	1817	Russia	569269
Schneider, Michael & F			Aach	Frd.	Aug 1817	Rus-Pol	569267
Schneider, Rosina		16 May 1822	Weiler	Schd.	Mar 1835	N.-Amer	801460
Schneider, Rosine			Enztal	Nag.	Jul 1852	N.-Amer	838490
Schneider, Rosine Elisab. & C			Gechingen	Calw	1856	France	563212
Schneider, Sigismund David			Freudenstadt	Frd.	Oct 1816	Switz.	569267
Schneider, Sophia Maria			Sulz	Sulz	bef 1859	N.-Amer	849628
Schneider, Sophie Friederike		22 Apr 1841	Freudenstadt	Frd.	bef 1864	France	577779
Schneider, Wilhelm		19 yrs.	Calw	Calw	1866	N.-Amer	563212
Schnekenburger, Eva Dorothea		25 Jul 1775	Voehringen	Sulz	Apr 1817	Polen	849642
Schnekenburger, Jacob & F			Sigmarswangen	Sulz	Apr 1817	Russia	849642
Schnekenburger, Johann Georg		6 Jul 1809	Bergfelden	Sulz	Apr 1817	Polen	849642
Schnekenburger, Johann Martin		19 May 1811	Bickelsberg	Sulz	Apr 1817	Polen	849642
Schnekenburger, Margaretha & F			Voehringen	Sulz	Mar 1846	N.-Amer	849643
Schnekenburger, Martin & F		14 Apr 1771	Trichtingen	Sulz	Apr 1817	Polen	849642
Schnierle, Jacob Philipp		17 Sep 1865	Kuppingen	Herr.	Mar 1869	Hesse	834624
Schnierle, Katharina Paul. & C		18 Feb 1845	Kuppingen	Herr.	Mar 1869	Hesse	834624
Schnierle, Matthaeus		1 Feb 1839	Groembach	Frd.	Feb 1855	N.-Amer	569275
Schnuerle, Adam & F			Beuren	Nag.	Jun 1852	N.-Amer	838490
Schnuerle, Anna Maria			Beuren	Nag.	Jun 1852	N.-Amer	838490
Schnuerle, Benjamin & F			Altburg	Calw	1852	N.-Amer	563212
Schnuerle, Christina			Beuren	Nag.	Jun 1852	N.-Amer	838490
Schnuerle, Elisabeth Cathar.			Oberkollbach	Calw	1869	N.-Amer	563212
Schnuerle, Eva			Beuren	Nag.	Jun 1852	N.-Amer	838490
Schnuerle, Jacob			Oberkollwangen	Calw	1853	N.-Amer	563212
Schnuerle, Johann Georg		21 Mar 1836	Schernbach	Frd.	Mar 1854	N.-Amer	569273
Schnuerle, Michael & F			Monakam	Calw	1852	N.-Amer	563212
Schnuerle, Wilhelm Friedrich			Calw	Calw	1852	N.-Amer	563212
Schober, Anna Maria		30 Aug 1829	Dornhan	Sulz	bef 1882	Switz.	849634
Schober, Johann Gottlob			Calw	Calw	1862	Saxony	563212
Schoch, Andreas		10 May 1850	Schoemberg	Frd.	May 1866	N.-Amer	577780
Schoch, Barbara		14 Jul 1854	Schoemberg	Frd.	May 1866	N.-Amer	577780
Schoch, Friedrich		13 Mar 1848	Schoemberg	Frd.	May 1866	N.-Amer	577780
Schoch, Johann Georg		20 Oct 1851	Schoemberg	Frd.	May 1866	N.-Amer	577780
Schoch, Philipp Jacob & F			Schoemberg	Frd.	May 1866	N.-Amer	577780
Schoeberle, Jakob Martin		20 Dec 1839	Oeschelbronn	Herr.	May 1862	N.-Amer	834624
Schoeffler, Christoph Heinrich			Ostelsheim	Calw	Dec 1870	N.-Amer	563212
Schoeffler, Johannes & F			Simmozheim	Calw	1853	N.-Amer	563212
Schoeffler, Wilhelm		19 yrs.	Ostelsheim	Calw	1869	N.-Amer	563212
Schoelle, Johann Georg & F			Stammheim	Calw	1853	N.-Amer	563212
Schoellhammer, Johannes		6 Jul 1841	Wittershausen	Sulz	1867	Switz.	849644
Schoellkopf, Charlotte Gottl.			Herrenberg	Herr.	May 1865	N.-Amer	834624
Schoenhardt, Anna Maria			Oberkollwangen	Calw	1869	N.-Amer	563212
Schoenhardt, Johann Ulrich		19 yrs.	Oberkollwangen	Calw	1869	N.-Amer	563212
Schoester, Johann Georg & F			Voehringen	Sulz	1817	Hungary	849643
Schoettle, Anna Barbara		19 Mar 1839	Woernersberg	Frd.	Mar 1860	N.-Amer	577777
Schoettle, Anna Maria		27 Apr 1833	Ebhausen	Nag.	Apr 1854	N.-Amer	838491
Schoettle, Anna Maria		2 Jul 1835	Woernersberg	Frd.	May 1856	N.-Amer	569275

Name	Date	Place	Dist.	Emig.	Dest.	Film
Schoettle, Elisabetha Cath.	27 Oct 1830	Groembach	Frd.	Jun 1854	N.-Amer	569273
Schoettle, Friedrich	11 Dec 1832	Tumlingen	Frd.	Aug 1845	N.-Amer	569269
Schoettle, Friedrich & F		Altburg	Calw	1853	N.-Amer	563212
Schoettle, Johannes	1 Nov 1830	Muehlheim a.B.	Sulz	1857	N.-Amer	849639
Schoettle, Katharina		Neubulach	Calw	1860	Hesse	563212
Scholderer, Catharina		Rosenfeld	Sulz	bef 1833	Poland	849625
Scholderer, Eleonore	5 yrs.	Rosenfeld	Sulz	May 1854	N.-Amer	849640
Scholderer, Elisabetha Cathar.	31 Jan 1836	Freudenstadt	Frd.	bef 1863	Baden	577778
Scholderer, Gottlieb Christian		Rosenfeld	Sulz	bef 1833	Russia	849625
Scholderer, Jacob & F		Rosenfeld	Sulz	May 1854	N.-Amer	849640
Scholderer, Jacob Friedrich		Rosenfeld	Sulz	bef 1833	Russia	849625
Scholderer, Johanna Chr. (wife)		Rosenfeld	Sulz	May 1854	N.-Amer	849640
Scholderer, Johannes	3 yrs.	Rosenfeld	Sulz	May 1854	N.-Amer	849640
Scholderer, Luise Christine	infant	Rosenfeld	Sulz	May 1854	N.-Amer	849640
Scholderer, Maria Barbara	7 yrs.	Rosenfeld	Sulz	May 1854	N.-Amer	849640
Scholl, Ernst Benjamin	30 Jan 1833	Breitenholz	Herr.	Dec 1863	Bavaria	834624
Schon, Andreas & F	22 Aug 1799	Hopfau	Sulz	Mar 1833	N.-Amer	849636
Schon, Anna Barbara (wife)		Hopfau	Sulz	Mar 1833	N.-Amer	849636
Schon, Anna Maria	21 Oct 1808	Hopfau	Sulz	Mar 1836	N.-Amer	849636
Schon, Barbara (wife)	13 Mar 1809	Glatten	Frd.	Oct 1854	S.-Amer	569274
Schon, Christian	8 Jan 1843	Glatten	Frd.	Oct 1854	S.-Amer	569274
Schon, Elisabetha	23 Jul 1846	Glatten	Frd.	Oct 1854	S.-Amer	569274
Schon, Johannes	22 Nov 1801	Hopfau	Sulz	Mar 1833	N.-Amer	849636
Schon, Johannes & F	22 Nov 1801	Glatten	Frd.	Oct 1854	S.-Amer	569274
Schon, Magdalena	10 Jun 1837	Glatten	Frd.	Oct 1854	S.-Amer	569274
Schon, Margaretha	1 May 1850	Glatten	Frd.	Oct 1854	S.-Amer	569274
Schrade, Johann Michael	29 Sep 1839	Nufringen	Herr.	Mar 1868	N.-Amer	834624
Schraegle, Anna	14 May 1840	Hopfau	Sulz	Feb 1860	N.-Amer	849636
Schraegle, Anna	abt 1802	Poland	Sulz	Sep 1816	Russia	849636
Schraegle, Anna (wife)		Wittendorf	Sulz	Sep 1816	Russia	849636
Schraegle, Anna (wid.) & F	19 Mar 1824	Hopfau	Sulz	Feb 1860	N.-Amer	849636
Schraegle, Anna Maria	7 Oct 1854	Hopfau	Sulz	Aug 1869	N.-Amer	849636
Schraegle, Eva	abt 1807	Poland	Sulz	Sep 1816	Russia	849636
Schraegle, Johann Michael	13 Aug 1845	Hopfau	Sulz	Feb 1860	N.-Amer	849636
Schraegle, Johannes	12 Feb 1849	Hopfau	Sulz	Feb 1860	N.-Amer	849636
Schraegle, Johannes	9 Dec 1766	Hopfau	Sulz	bef 1816	Poland	849636
Schraegle, Johannes	abt 1810	Poland	Sulz	Sep 1816	Russia	849636
Schraegle, Johannes & F	9 Dec 1766	Hopfau	Sulz	Sep 1816	Russia	849636
Schraegle, Maria	25 Sep 1842	Hopfau	Sulz	Feb 1860	N.-Amer	849636
Schraegle, Mathaeus	11 Mar 1815	Hopfau	Sulz	Sep 1816	Russia	849636
Schraegle, Mathias	15 Sep 1857	Hopfau	Sulz	Aug 1871	N.-Amer	849636
Schrai, Anna Maria		Dornstetten	Frd.	Jun 1817	Russia	569269
Schramm, Ludwig Rudolf	15 yrs.	Calw	Calw	1866	N.-Amer	563212
Schray, Heinrich	20 Aug 1835	Lossburg	Frd.	Jan 1853	N.-Amer	569272
Schray, Johann Martin	1 Oct 1837	Hallwangen	Frd.	Apr 1854	N.-Amer	569273
Schreivogel, Louise Agatha		Pfalzgrafenweiler	Frd.	Mat 1854	N.-Amer	569273
Schrempf, Wilhelmine		Simmozheim	Calw	Jan 1870	France	563212
Schrenk, Jakob	27 May 1848	Glatten	Frd.	Aug 1866	N.-Amer	577780
Schrenk, Johann Georg	1 Feb 1840	Glatten	Frd.	May 1858	N.-Amer	577776
Schrenk, Johannes	24 Jun 1845	Glatten	Frd.	Sep 1865	N.-Amer	577779

Name		Birth		Emigration			Film
Last	First	Date	Place	O'amt	Appl. Date	Dest.	Number
Schrenk, Johannes & F		5 Apr 1810	Glatten	Frd.	Aug 1866	N.-Amer	577780
Schrenk, Margaretha (wife)		10 Apr 1819	Glatten	Frd.	Aug 1866	N.-Amer	577780
Schrenk, Matthaeus		21 Sep 1843	Glatten	Frd.	Aug 1866	N.-Amer	577780
Schrizgaeble, Luise			Nagold	Nag.	Mar 1854	N.-Amer	838491
Schroeter, Anna Maria		9 Oct 1811	Kaelbersbronn	Frd.	Apr 1844	N.-Amer	569269
Schroth, Barbara Pauline & F			Calw	Calw	1867	Prussia	563212
Schroth, Carl		1838	Teinach	Calw	1856	N.-Amer	563212
Schroth, Catharine & C			Oberreichenbach	Calw	1853	N.-Amer	563212
Schroth, Christian Friedrich			Calw	Calw	1853	N.-Amer	563212
Schroth, Christine			Monakam	Calw	1863	Baden	563212
Schroth, Jacob		27 yrs.	Sommenhardt	Calw	1866	N.-Amer	563212
Schroth, Jakob		6 Apr 1835	Sommenhardt	Calw	1854	N.-Amer	563212
Schroth, Jakob Friedrich			Liebelsberg	Calw	1855	N.-Amer	563212
Schroth, Johann Georg		32 yrs.	Sommenhardt	Calw	1866	N.-Amer	563212
Schroth, Johann Georg			Teinach	Calw	1860	N.-Amer	563212
Schroth, Johann Ulrich			Sommenhardt	Calw	1868	Prussia	563212
Schroth, Ulrich		30 yrs.	Sommenhardt	Calw	1866	N.-Amer	563212
Schroth, Wilhelm		1836	Teinach	Calw	1854	N.-Amer	563212
Schroth, Wilhelmine			Calw	Calw	1852	N.-Amer	563212
Schubert, Johann Peter			Aach	Frd.	Oct 1846	France	569271
Schuebel, Anna Maria			Schopfloch	Frd.	Mar 1865	N.-Amer	577779
Schuebel, Barbara			Schopfloch	Frd.	Mar 1865	N.-Amer	577779
Schuebel, Eva			Schopfloch	Frd.	Mar 1865	N.-Amer	577779
Schuebel, Katharina			Schopfloch	Frd.	Mar 1865	N.-Amer	577779
Schuehle, Andreas		29 Apr 1876	Leidringen	Sulz	Mar 1891	N.-Amer	849626
Schuehle, Andreas		21 Jun 1857	Leidringen	Sulz	Jun 1872	N.-Amer	849637
Schuele, Anna		1 yrs.	Leidringen	Sulz	Mar 1837	N.-Amer	849637
Schuele, Anna (wife)			Leidringen	Sulz	Mar 1837	N.-Amer	849637
Schuele, Anna Regina		5 May 1878	Rosenfeld	Sulz	Jun 1881	N.-Amer	849626
Schuele, Johann Georg		1 May 1878	Rosenfeld	Sulz	Jun 1895	N.-Amer	849626
Schuele, Johann Jacob			Leidringen	Sulz	Feb 1846	Austria	849637
Schuele, Johannes & F		27 Jun 1847	Rosenfeld	Sulz	Jun 1881	N.-Amer	849626
Schuele, Josias		27 yrs.	Bickelsberg	Sulz	May 1856	N.-Amer	849630
Schuele, Maria Agnes		19 Dec 1874	Rosenfeld	Sulz	Jun 1881	N.-Amer	849626
Schuele, Martin & F		1 May 1805	Leidringen	Sulz	Mar 1837	N.-Amer	849637
Schuele, Regina (wife)		18 Dec 1849	Rosenfeld	Sulz	Jun 1881	N.-Amer	849626
Schuerle, Johann Georg		1 May 1878	Rosenfeld	Sulz	Jun 1895	N.-Amer	849641
Schuetz, Georg Michael			Holzbronn	Calw	1862	N.-Amer	563212
Schuetz, Johann Georg		21 Aug 1845	Hildrizhausen	Herr.	Aug 1865	N.-Amer	834624
Schuez, Johann Georg			Rohrau	Herr.	bef 1845	Switz.	834626
Schule, Marie			Oberhaugstett	Calw	1858	N.-Amer	563212
Schuler, Adam			Dietersweiler	Frd.	bef 1813	Baden	569269
Schuler, Adam		12 Feb 1835	Renfrizhausen	Sulz	Jan 1854	N.-Amer	849639
Schuler, Agnes Catharina		7 Jun 1812	Leidringen	Sulz	May 1832	Rus-Pol	849637
Schuler, Anna		25 Jul 1828	Herrenberg	Herr.	Feb 1852	N.-Amer	834627
Schuler, Anna Barbara		30 Jul 1818	Leidringen	Sulz	May 1832	Rus-Pol	849637
Schuler, Anna Catharina		11 May 1829	Leidringen	Sulz	May 1832	Rus-Pol	849637
Schuler, Anna Maria		28 Aug 1813	Leidringen	Sulz	May 1832	Rus-Pol	849637
Schuler, Anna Maria		4 Sep 1826	Herrenberg	Herr.	Feb 1852	N.-Amer	834627
Schuler, Anna Maria (wife)			Herrenberg	Herr.	Feb 1852	N.-Amer	834627

Schuler, Carl August	21 Mar 1841	Freudenstadt	Frd.	Apr 1865	N.-Amer	577779
Schuler, Christian	27 Jul 1827	Freudenstadt	Frd.	Aug 1859	Switz.	577776
Schuler, Christian	25 Jul 1846	Herrenberg	Herr.	Feb 1852	N.-Amer	834627
Schuler, Christiane Louise	28 Aug 1811	Schorndorf	Schd.	Aug 1842	Baden	801461
Schuler, Friedrich	17 Apr 1857	Sterneck	Sulz	Apr 1873	N.-Amer	849642
Schuler, Jacob & F		Leidringen	Sulz	Sep 1816	Russia	849637
Schuler, Jakob	30 Jul 1815	Leidringen	Sulz	May 1832	Rus-Pol	849637
Schuler, Johann Georg	16 Mar 1832	Leidringen	Sulz	May 1832	Rus-Pol	849637
Schuler, Johann Jacob	13 Apr 1832	Herrenberg	Herr.	Feb 1852	N.-Amer	834627
Schuler, Johann Jacob & F		Herrenberg	Herr.	Feb 1852	N.-Amer	834627
Schuler, Johann Jakob & F	24 Jan 1783	Leidringen	Sulz	May 1832	Rus-Pol	849637
Schuler, Johann Martin	12 Aug 1819	Renfrizhausen	Sulz	1857	N.-Amer	849639
Schuler, Johannes	23 May 1826	Leidringen	Sulz	May 1832	Rus-Pol	849637
Schuler, Johannes	24 Apr 1841	Herrenberg	Herr.	Feb 1852	N.-Amer	834627
Schuler, Magdalena (wife)		Leidringen	Sulz	May 1832	Rus-Pol	849637
Schuler, Maria Katharina	21 Sep 1834	Herrenberg	Herr.	Feb 1852	N.-Amer	834627
Schuler, Martin	10 May 1820	Leidringen	Sulz	May 1832	Rus-Pol	849637
Schuler, Mathias	24 Jan 1822	Leidringen	Sulz	May 1832	Rus-Pol	849637
Schuler, Mathilda		Freudenstadt	Frd.	bef 1856	N.-Amer	569275
Schultheiss, Catharina Christ.		Steinenberg	Schd.	Apr 1842	N.-Amer	801461
Schultheiss, Elisabetha Marg.		Neubulach	Calw	1859	N.-Amer	563212
Schultheiss, Gottfried		Steinenberg	Schd.	Apr 1842	N.-Amer	801461
Schultheiss, Gottlieb		Steinenberg	Schd.	Apr 1842	N.-Amer	801461
Schultheiss, Heinrich		Neubulach	Calw	1860	N.-Amer	563212
Schultheiss, Johann Georg		Neubulach	Calw	1860	N.-Amer	563212
Schultheiss, Rosine Catharina		Steinenberg	Schd.	Apr 1842	N.-Amer	801461
Schulz, Carl Johann		Hirsau	Calw	1858	N.-Amer	563212
Schulz, Christian	1835	Hirsau	Calw	1855	N.-Amer	563212
Schulz, Gustav		Simmozheim	Calw	1861	N.-Amer	563212
Schulz, Johanna Heinrike		Hirsau	Calw	1858	N.-Amer	563212
Schulz, Johanne Dorothea		Hirsau	Calw	1858	N.-Amer	563212
Schulz, Otto	1837	Simmozheim	Calw	1854	N.-Amer	563212
Schumacher, Anna Barbara & C	5 Apr 1821	Durrweiler	Frd.	Aug 1848	N.-Amer	569270
Schumacher, Anna Maria	5 Jun 1838	Durrweiler	Frd.	Apr 1853	France	569272
Schumacher, Anna Maria	2 Jul 1840	Goettelfingen	Frd.	Mar 1854	N.-Amer	569273
Schumacher, Caroline Christ.		Sulz	Sulz	Sep 1857	Hohenz.	849628
Schumacher, Catharina Barbara		Stammheim	Calw	1858	N.-Amer	563212
Schumacher, Christian	23 Dec 1828	Durrweiler	Frd.	Apr 1849	N.-Amer	569270
Schumacher, Christian	12 Apr 1838	Goettelfingen	Frd.	Mar 1854	N.-Amer	569273
Schumacher, Christine	25 Jul 1834	Goettelfingen	Frd.	Mar 1854	N.-Amer	569273
Schumacher, Conrad Friedrich	13 Aug 1875	Rosenfeld	Sulz	Mar 1892	N.-Amer	849626
Schumacher, Eva Regina	17 Dec 1783	Rosenfeld	Sulz	Jul 1830	Austria	849640
Schumacher, Friederike	27 May 1831	Goettelfingen	Frd.	Mar 1854	N.-Amer	569273
Schumacher, Friedrich	7 Jan 1836	Goettelfingen	Frd.	Mar 1854	N.-Amer	569273
Schumacher, Georg Adam	13 Oct 1831	Goettelfingen	Frd.	Mar 1854	N.-Amer	569273
Schumacher, Gottlieb		Stammheim	Calw	1849	N.-Amer	563212
Schumacher, Gustav Adolph	16 Sep 1844	Sigmarswangen	Sulz	Aug 1860	N.-Amer	849642
Schumacher, Jakob	21 Aug 1841	Durrweiler	Frd.	Oct 1853	N.-Amer	569272
Schumacher, Jakob Gottlieb	9 Aug 1790	Goettelfingen	Frd.	Mar 1854	N.-Amer	569273
Schumacher, Jakob Gottlieb	14 Aug 1843	Goettelfingen	Frd.	Mar 1854	N.-Amer	569273

| Name | | Birth | | Emigration | | | Film |
Last	First	Date	Place	O'amt	Appl. Date	Dest.	Number
Schumacher, Johann Friedr.			Stammheim	Calw	1868	N.-Amer	563212
Schumacher, Johann Georg		14 Jun 1826	Durrweiler	Frd.	Oct 1853	N.-Amer	569272
Schumacher, Johann Georg		9 May 1828	Goettelfingen	Frd.	Mar 1854	N.-Amer	569273
Schumacher, Johannes		24 yrs.	Durrweiler	Frd.	Aug 1848	N.-Amer	569270
Schumacher, Karl		11 Jul 1842	Sigmarswangen	Sulz	Aug 1860	N.-Amer	849642
Schumacher, Katharina		27 Nov 1837	Durrweiler	Frd.	Oct 1853	N.-Amer	569272
Schumacher, Maria Dorothea		Sep 1832	Entringen	Herr.	May 1869	N.-Amer	834624
Schumacher, Maria Friederika		20 Nov 1847	Sulz	Sulz	Nov 1867	Pfalz	849628
Schumacher, Maria Magdal. (wife)		10 Apr 1806	Huzenbach	Frd.	Mar 1854	N.-Amer	569273
Schunk, Johannes & F			Bergfelden	Sulz	May 1817	Russia	849629
Schuon, Johann Georg			Haiterbach	Frd.	Jun 1856	N.-Amer	569275
Schurer, Andreas			Tailfingen	Herr.	Apr 1830	N.-Amer	834624
Schurer, Conrad		26 Feb 1859	Nufringen	Herr.	Apr 1867	N.-Amer	834624
Schurer, Johann Georg		24 Sep 1825	Tailfingen	Herr.	Apr 1847	N.-Amer	834626
Schurer, Johann Georg & F			Nufringen	Herr.	Jun 1833	Rus-Pol	834624
Schurer, Maria Agnes & C		10 Mar 1832	Nufringen	Herr.	Apr 1867	N.-Amer	834624
Schurer, Stephan & F			Nufringen	Herr.	Mar 1835	Rus-Pol	834624
Schuster, Carl Gottlob		9 Nov 1843	Nufringen	Herr.	May 1866	N.-Amer	834624
Schuster, Justina Louisa			Nufringen	Herr.	May 1866	N.-Amer	834624
Schwaab, Christina Barbara		22 yrs.	Freudenstadt	Frd.	May 1752	Pen.N-A	550803
Schwaab, Dorothea		14 yrs.	Freudenstadt	Frd.	May 1752	Pen.N-A	550803
Schwaab, Elisabetha (wife)		45 yrs.	Freudenstadt	Frd.	May 1752	Pen.N-A	550803
Schwaab, Elisabetha Catharina		8 yrs.	Freudenstadt	Frd.	May 1752	Pen.N-A	550803
Schwaab, Jacob Bernhard & F		52 yrs.	Freudenstadt	Frd.	May 1752	Pen.N-A	550803
Schwaab, Jocob Bernhard		16 yrs.	Freudenstadt	Frd.	May 1752	Pen.N-A	550803
Schwaab, Johann Adam		20 yrs.	Freudenstadt	Frd.	May 1752	Pen.N-A	550803
Schwaab, Johann Fridrich		18 yrs.	Freudenstadt	Frd.	May 1752	Pen.N-A	550803
Schwab, Barbara		16 Aug 1839	Dornhan	Sulz	Apr 1859	N.-Amer	849633
Schwab, Christian			Breitenau	Sulz	Apr 1893	N.-Amer	849626
Schwab, Christian		16 Nov 1876	Waelde	Sulz	Apr 1893	N.-Amer	849644
Schwab, Christiane Fr.			Calw	Calw	1869	Hesse	563212
Schwab, Christine		2 yrs.	Altenstaig	Nag.	Jul 1852	N.-Amer	838490
Schwab, Elisabeth Caroline			Calw	Calw	1869	France	563212
Schwab, Gottfried		11 yrs.	Altenstaig	Nag.	Jul 1852	N.-Amer	838490
Schwab, Johann Georg		9 yrs.	Altenstaig	Nag.	Jul 1852	N.-Amer	838490
Schwab, Johann Georg & F			Altenstaig	Nag.	Jul 1852	N.-Amer	838490
Schwab, Johann Ludwig		42 yrs.	Calw	Calw	1869	Prussia	563212
Schwab, Magdalena			Freudenstadt	Frd.	Sep 1854	N.-Amer	569274
Schwab, Margaretha		6 mon.	Altenstaig	Nag.	Jul 1852	N.-Amer	838490
Schwab, Maria		6 yrs.	Altenstaig	Nag.	Jul 1852	N.-Amer	838490
Schwab, Michael		12 Aug 1829	Schernbach	Frd.	May 1862	N.-Amer	577778
Schwaegler, Anna Maria		7 Mar 1821	Bondorf	Herr.	Jul 1869	Switz.	834624
Schwaegler, Johannes & W		6 Dec 1831	Bondorf	Herr.	Jul 1869	Switz.	834624
Schwaemmele, Carl Heinrich			Calw	Calw	1863	Augsb.	563212
Schwaemmle, Christian Friedr.			Hirsau	Calw	1852	N.-Amer	563212
Schwaemmle, Johann Adam			Unterhaugstett	Calw	1854	N.-Amer	563212
Schwaemmle, Johann Georg & F			Oberkollbach	Calw	1853	N.-Amer	563212
Schwaemmle, Johann Ludwig			Hirsau	Calw	1852	N.-Amer	563212
Schwaemmle, Martin & F			Calw	Calw	1852	N.-Amer	563212
Schwaemmle, Wilhelmine			Hirsau	Calw	1853	N.-Amer	563212

Name	Date/Age	Place	Region	Date	Destination	Number
Schwander, Elisabetha		Rodt	Frd.	May 1860	N.-Amer	577777
Schwank, Christina		Hoerschweiler	Frd.	1851	N.-Amer	577770
Schwank, Christina & C	40 yrs.	Hoerschweiler	Frd.	May 1851	N.-Amer	569271
Schwann, Johann		Dornhan	Sulz	1807	Austria	849633
Schwanz, Andreas	22 Apr 1840	Dornhan	Sulz	Sep 1854	N.-Amer	849633
Schwanz, Anna Maria	11 May 1823	Dornhan	Sulz	Oct 1865	N.-Amer	849634
Schwanz, Christine & C		Dornhan	Sulz	Sep 1853	N.-Amer	849633
Schwanz, Matheus		Dornhan	Sulz	bef 1816	Russia	849633
Schwanz, Sibilla & C	3 May 1807	Dornhan	Sulz	Jul 1867	N.-Amer	849634
Schwartz, Agnes	9 yrs.	Unteriflingen	Frd.	May 1752	Pen.N-A	550803
Schwartz, Anna Maria & C		Deckenpfronn	Calw	1855	N.-Amer	563212
Schwartz, Catharina	40 yrs.	Unteriflingen	Frd.	May 1752	Pen.N-A	550803
Schwartz, Christian		Kaelbersbronn	Frd.	Apr 1752	Pen.N-A	550803
Schwartz, Elisabetha	4 yrs.	Unteriflingen	Frd.	May 1752	Pen.N-A	550803
Schwartz, Jacob	20 yrs.	Unteriflingen	Frd.	May 1752	Pen.N-A	550803
Schwartz, Johann	24 May 1846	Deckenpfronn	Calw	1855	N.-Amer	563212
Schwartz, Johannes		Sulz	Sulz	bef 1811	Poland	849625
Schwartz, Maria	4 yrs.	Unteriflingen	Frd.	May 1752	Pen.N-A	550803
Schwarz, Adelheit		Leinstetten	Sulz	Sep 1841	Prussia	849638
Schwarz, Agnesia		Leidringen	Sulz	bef 1842	Poland	849637
Schwarz, Agnesia	6 yrs.	Leidringen	Sulz	Feb 1817	Russia	849637
Schwarz, Andreas	16 Oct 1838	Leidringen	Sulz	Jan 1857	N.-Amer	849637
Schwarz, Andreas & F		Renfrizhausen	Sulz	Apr 1891	Switz.	849626
Schwarz, Andreas & W	2 Jun 1853	Renfrizhausen	Sulz	1875	Switz.	849639
Schwarz, Anna	2 yrs.	Voehringen	Sulz	Apr 1832	N.-Amer	849643
Schwarz, Anna	9 yrs.	Leidringen	Sulz	Feb 1817	Russia	849637
Schwarz, Anna (wife)		Voehringen	Sulz	Mar 1837	N.-Amer	849643
Schwarz, Anna (wife)		Voehringen	Sulz	Apr 1832	N.-Amer	849643
Schwarz, Anna (wife)		Leidringen	Sulz	Feb 1817	Russia	849637
Schwarz, Anna Barbara & C	19 Nov 1787	Leinstetten	Sulz	Jun 1817	N.-Amer	849638
Schwarz, Anna Catharina		Leidringen	Sulz	bef 1863	N.-Amer	849637
Schwarz, Anna Maria		Grunbach	Schd.	May 1834	N.-Amer	801460
Schwarz, Anna Maria	12 yrs.	Leidringen	Sulz	Feb 1817	Russia	849637
Schwarz, Anna Maria		Muehlheim a.B.	Sulz	Apr 1855	N.-Amer	849639
Schwarz, Anna Maria (wife)		Voehringen	Sulz	Mar 1834	N.-Amer	849643
Schwarz, Barbara		Voehringen	Sulz	Apr 1832	N.-Amer	849643
Schwarz, Barbara	23 Sep 1844	Muehlheim a.B.	Sulz	Jun 1869	Switz.	849639
Schwarz, Carl Friedrich		Grunbach	Schd.	May 1834	N.-Amer	801460
Schwarz, Caroline		Deckenpfronn	Calw	1852	N.-Amer	563212
Schwarz, Caroline		Deckenpfronn	Calw	1852	N.-Amer	563212
Schwarz, Christian	23 Sep 1807	Oberiflingen	Frd.	Mar 1833	N.-Amer	569268
Schwarz, Christian	16 yrs.	Isingen	Sulz	Aug 1855	N.-Amer	849636
Schwarz, Christian	2 Jan 1836	Leidringen	Sulz	Apr 1856	N.-Amer	849637
Schwarz, Christian & F		Voehringen	Sulz	Mar 1837	N.-Amer	849643
Schwarz, Christian & W	11 Oct 1800	Voehringen	Sulz	Mar 1837	N.-Amer	849643
Schwarz, Christian Daniel		Grunbach	Schd.	May 1834	N.-Amer	801460
Schwarz, Christina	10 Oct 1829	Voehringen	Sulz	Mar 1834	N.-Amer	849643
Schwarz, Christina & C	34 yrs.	Cresbach	Frd.	Apr 1833	N.-Amer	569269
Schwarz, Christine		Freudenstadt	Frd.	Jul 1812	Baden	569267
Schwarz, Christine	10 May 1834	Leidringen	Sulz	bef 1857	N.-Amer	849637

Name		Birth		Emigration			Film
Last	First	Date	Place	O'amt	Appl. Date	Dest.	Number
Schwarz, Chrysostomus		2 Jan 1814	Leinstetten	Sulz	Jun 1817	N.-Amer	849638
Schwarz, Daniel		3 Jul 1847	Isingen	Sulz	May 1867	N.-Amer	849636
Schwarz, Dorothea			Deckenpfronn	Calw	1853	N.-Amer	563212
Schwarz, Eva			Muehlheim a.B.	Sulz	Apr 1855	N.-Amer	849639
Schwarz, Franziska		7 Oct 1810	Leinstetten	Sulz	Jun 1817	N.-Amer	849638
Schwarz, Friedrich			Lombach	Frd.	Aug 1854	N.-Amer	569274
Schwarz, Hans Martin & F		40 yrs.	Unteriflingen	Frd.	May 1752	Pen.N-A	550803
Schwarz, Heinrich		20 Aug 1855	Leidringen	Sulz	Sep 1871	N.-Amer	849637
Schwarz, Jacob		10 Jul 1813	Cresbach	Frd.	Aug 1845	N.-Amer	569269
Schwarz, Jacob		19 Nov 1853	Leidringen	Sulz	Jun 1869	N.-Amer	849637
Schwarz, Jakob			Bergfelden	Sulz	Jan 1854	N.-Amer	849629
Schwarz, Johann Friedrich		10 Jun 1847	Freudenstadt	Frd.	May 1866	N.-Amer	577780
Schwarz, Johann Friedrich			Muehlheim a.B.	Sulz	Apr 1855	N.-Amer	849639
Schwarz, Johann Georg		9 yrs.	Cresbach	Frd.	Apr 1833	N.-Amer	569269
Schwarz, Johann Georg			Grunbach	Schd.	May 1834	N.-Amer	801460
Schwarz, Johann Georg		3 Feb 1815	Rotenzimmern	Sulz	Jan 1846	N.-Amer	849642
Schwarz, Johann Georg			Leidringen	Sulz	Jul 1853	N.-Amer	849637
Schwarz, Johann Georg		28 Feb 1846	Gaertringen	Herr.	Jul 1866	N.-Amer	834624
Schwarz, Johann Gottfried		19 Jan 1834	Sulz	Sulz	Aug 1853	N.-Amer	849627
Schwarz, Johann Gottlieb			Grunbach	Schd.	May 1834	N.-Amer	801460
Schwarz, Johann Jakob		8 Jun 1845	Leidringen	Sulz	Dec 1865	N.-Amer	849637
Schwarz, Johann Jakob & F		10 Feb 1804	Voehringen	Sulz	Mar 1834	N.-Amer	849643
Schwarz, Johann Jakob & F			Leidringen	Sulz	Feb 1817	Russia	849637
Schwarz, Johann Joseph			Grunbach	Schd.	May 1834	N.-Amer	801460
Schwarz, Johann Justus Heinr.			Grunbach	Schd.	May 1834	N.-Amer	801460
Schwarz, Johann Martin		17 yrs.	Voehringen	Sulz	Apr 1832	N.-Amer	849643
Schwarz, Johann Michael		6 yrs.	Cresbach	Frd.	Apr 1833	N.-Amer	569269
Schwarz, Johanna Friederike			Grunbach	Schd.	May 1834	N.-Amer	801460
Schwarz, Johanna Margar. & F			Grunbach	Schd.	May 1834	N.-Amer	801460
Schwarz, Johannes		4 Mar 1829	Bergfelden	Sulz	Jul 1860	N.-Amer	849629
Schwarz, Johannes		11 Aug 1832	Voehringen	Sulz	Mar 1834	N.-Amer	849643
Schwarz, Johannes		14 Mar 1865	Muehlheim a.B.	Sulz	bef 1897	Switz.	849639
Schwarz, Johannes		4 Jul 1866	Leidringen	Sulz	Mar 1881	N.-Amer	849626
Schwarz, Johannes & F		14 Mar 1789	Voehringen	Sulz	Apr 1832	N.-Amer	849643
Schwarz, Katharina		11 Feb 1840	Freudenstadt	Frd.	Mar 1865	N.-Amer	577779
Schwarz, Katharina			Voehringen	Sulz	Apr 1832	N.-Amer	849643
Schwarz, Louise Friederike			Freudenstadt	Frd.	Aug 1860	N.-Amer	577777
Schwarz, Magdalena (wife)			Voehringen	Sulz	Mar 1837	N.-Amer	849643
Schwarz, Maria			Voehringen	Sulz	Apr 1832	N.-Amer	849643
Schwarz, Maria (wife)		1 Dec 1857	Renfrizhausen	Sulz	1875	Switz.	849639
Schwarz, Maria Catharina			Neubulach	Calw	1863	N.-Amer	563212
Schwarz, Maria Salome		23 Oct 1807	Leidringen	Sulz	Mar 1833	N.-Amer	849637
Schwarz, Marianne			Leinstetten	Sulz	Jun 1817	N.-Amer	849638
Schwarz, Martin		21 Oct 1856	Leidringen	Sulz	Apr 1873	N.-Amer	849637
Schwarz, Mathaeus Ludwig			Grunbach	Schd.	May 1834	N.-Amer	801460
Schwarz, Michael			Voehringen	Sulz	Mar 1837	N.-Amer	849643
Schwarz, Michael		2 Oct 1852	Leidringen	Sulz	Sep 1869	N.-Amer	849637
Schwarz, Sabina			Bergfelden	Sulz	Apr 1851	N.-Amer	849629
Schwarz, Ursula		18 Jan 1846	Muehlheim a.B.	Sulz	Jun 1868	N.-Amer	849639
Schwarz, Xaver			Bettenhausen	Sulz	Feb 1816	Switz.	849625

Schwarzach, Leopold	19 Nov 1793	Altingen	Herr.	Feb 1867	Russia	834624
Schwarzmaier, Carl Michael	28 Jan 1835	Affstaett	Herr.	May 1862	N.-Amer	834624
Schwarzwaelder, Catharina	1831	Wittershausen	Sulz	bef 1858	Switz.	849644
Schwarzwaelder, Christian		Sigmarswangen	Sulz	Oct 1854	N.-Amer	849642
Schwarzwaelder, Friedrich Ad.	13 Apr 1847	Sulz	Sulz	Oct 1866	N.-Amer	849628
Schwarzwaelder, Georg Ludwig		Sigmarswangen	Sulz	Oct 1854	N.-Amer	849642
Schwarzwaelder, Johann Gottf.		Sulz	Sulz	Nov 1852	N.-Amer	849627
Schwarzwaelder, Mathias	19 yrs.	Wittershausen	Sulz	Aug 1871	N.-Amer	849644
Schwarzwaelder, Rosina Cath.	12 Aug 1785	Sulz	Sulz	May 1832	N.-Amer	849627
Schwegler, Anna Maria	24 yrs.	Beutelsbach	Schd.	Jun 1833	N.-Amer	801460
Schweible, Christian	5 Jan 1835	Dornstetten	Frd.	Feb 1853	N.-Amer	569272
Schweickle, Gottlieb		Sulz	Sulz	bef 1824	Danzig	849625
Schweiglin, Margaretha	21 yrs.	Wittlensweiler	Frd.	bef 1846	N.-Amer	569271
Schweikardt, Christiane Marg.		Freudenstadt	Frd.	Sep 1854	N.-Amer	569274
Schweiker, Johannes	6 Jan 1821	Dornstetten	Frd.	Oct 1844	Hesse	569269
Schweikert, Andreas	30 Dec 1840	Moetzingen	Herr.	May 1852	N.-Amer	834627
Schweikert, Anna Maria	19 Nov 1832	Moetzingen	Herr.	Apr 1847	N.-Amer	834626
Schweikert, Anna Maria (wife)	10 Oct 1802	Moetzingen	Herr.	Apr 1847	N.-Amer	834626
Schweikert, Benjamin & F	18 Feb 1797	Moetzingen	Herr.	Apr 1847	N.-Amer	834626
Schweikert, Carl August	23 Aug 1827	Moetzingen	Herr.	Apr 1847	N.-Amer	834626
Schweikert, Heinrich Phil. & F	30 Sep 1802	Moetzingen	Herr.	May 1852	N.-Amer	834627
Schweikert, Katharina		Freudenstadt	Frd.	Mar 1854	N.-Amer	569273
Schweikert, Leokadine (wife)	27 Nov 1802	Moetzingen	Herr.	May 1852	N.-Amer	834627
Schweikert, Martin & F		Freudenstadt	Frd.	Apr 1817	Russia	569267
Schweikert, Philipp Heinrich	30 Apr 1831	Moetzingen	Herr.	Apr 1847	N.-Amer	834626
Schweikert, Wilhelmine Pauline		Freudenstadt	Frd.	Mar 1860	France	577777
Schweikhardt, Carolina	10 Dec 1842	Gueltstein	Herr.	Jan 1870	Baden	834624
Schweikle, Anna Barbara		Wittlensweiler	Frd.	Jul 1865	N.-Amer	577779
Schweikle, Catharina		Dornstetten	Frd.	Mar 1837	N.-Amer	569269
Schweikle, Gottfried		Freudenstadt	Frd.	Jul 1865	N.-Amer	577779
Schweikle, Jakob Friedrich	6 Dec 1837	Wittlensweiler	Frd.	Aug 1857	N.-Amer	577776
Schweikle, Johann Adam		Wittlensweiler	Frd.	Jul 1865	N.-Amer	577779
Schweikle, Maria Katharina	8 Nov 1855	Muehlheim a.B.	Sulz	Aug 1860	Prussia	849639
Schweitzer, Christian & F		Oberhaugstett	Calw	1854	N.-Amer	563212
Schweitzer, Christian Fr. & F		Liebelsberg	Calw	1855	N.-Amer	563212
Schweitzer, Jacob Friedrich	25 yrs.	Reinerzau	Frd.	Mar 1817	Russia	569268
Schweizer, Anna Maria	6 May 1839	Gruental	Frd.	Sep 1854	N.-Amer	569274
Schweizer, Anna Maria		Altburg	Calw	1868	M-burg	563212
Schweizer, Christiane	9 yrs.	Berneck	Nag.	Jul 1852	N.-Amer	838490
Schweizer, Christina	2 Mar 1831	Hallwangen	Frd.	Mar 1847	N.-Amer	569271
Schweizer, Eva	23 May 1841	Hallwangen	Frd.	Jun 1857	N.-Amer	577776
Schweizer, Eva Catharina & C	31 Dec 1805	Hallwangen	Frd.	Jun 1857	N.-Amer	577776
Schweizer, Gottlob Jakob & F		Berneck	Nag.	Jul 1852	N.-Amer	838490
Schweizer, Jakob Friedrich	4 yrs.	Berneck	Nag.	Jul 1852	N.-Amer	838490
Schweizer, Johann Conrad		Altingen	Herr.	1842		834627
Schweizer, Johann Georg	7 yrs.	Berneck	Nag.	Jul 1852	N.-Amer	838490
Schweizer, Johannes	11 yrs.	Berneck	Nag.	Jul 1852	N.-Amer	838490
Schweizer, Magdalena Rosina	9 May 1831	Altingen	Herr.	Feb 1867	N.-Amer	834624
Schweizer, Margaretha	1 yrs.	Berneck	Nag.	Jul 1852	N.-Amer	838490
Schweizer, Maria Friederike		Ostelsheim	Calw	Sep 1869	N.-Amer	563212

Name		Birth		Emigration			Film
Last	First	Date	Place	O'amt	Appl. Date	Dest.	Number
Schwenk, Albert		28 Jan 1878	Dornhan	Sulz	Jun 1892	N.-Amer	849634
Schwenk, Anna			Rodt	Frd.	bef 1855	Switz.	569275
Schwenk, Anna Maria			Schoemberg	Frd.	Jun 1854	N.-Amer	569273
Schwenk, Anna Maria		11 Aug 1858	Hallwangen	Frd.	May 1860	N.-Amer	577777
Schwenk, Barbara		6 yrs.	Rodt	Frd.	Oct 1850	N.-Amer	569271
Schwenk, Caroline & C		11 Sep 1821	Freudenstadt	Frd.	Sep 1854	N.-Amer	569274
Schwenk, Catharina			Rodt	Frd.	Oct 1850	N.-Amer	569271
Schwenk, Catharina Barbara		19 Jun 1813	Gruental	Frd.	Feb 1847	N.-Amer	569271
Schwenk, Christian Jakob		19 May 1839	Freudenstadt	Frd.	Sep 1853	N.-Amer	569274
Schwenk, Christina			Schoemberg	Frd.	Jun 1854	N.-Amer	569273
Schwenk, Christina		21 Dec 1830	Hallwangen	Frd.	May 1860	N.-Amer	577777
Schwenk, Christine		46 yrs.	Rodt	Frd.	Oct 1850	N.-Amer	569271
Schwenk, Christine		12 Jan 1852	Hallwangen	Frd.	May 1860	N.-Amer	577777
Schwenk, Dorothea			Schoemberg	Frd.	Jul 1849	N.-Amer	569270
Schwenk, Dorothea			Schoemberg	Frd.	Jun 1854	N.-Amer	569273
Schwenk, Dorothea		2 Jun 1853	Hallwangen	Frd.	May 1860	N.-Amer	577777
Schwenk, Friedrich		28 Apr 1856	Waelde	Sulz	Jun 1872	N.-Amer	849644
Schwenk, Georg Heinrich			Teinach	Calw	1858	N.-Amer	563212
Schwenk, Jacob		7 Jun 1841	Schoemberg	Frd.	Sep 1866	N.-Amer	577780
Schwenk, Jacob		11 Sep 1839	Dornhan	Sulz	Aug 1866	N.-Amer	849634
Schwenk, Jacob & F			Rodt	Frd.	Oct 1850	N.-Amer	569271
Schwenk, Jakob			Rodt	Frd.	bef 1855	N.-Amer	569275
Schwenk, Johann Friedrich			Freudenstadt	Frd.	Apr 1852	Austria	569272
Schwenk, Johann Friedrich		22 Sep 1843	Freudenstadt	Frd.	Sep 1854	N.-Amer	569274
Schwenk, Johann Martin			Gruental	Frd.	Feb 1847	N.-Amer	569271
Schwenk, Johanna		15 Apr 1843	Bergfelden	Sulz	Nov 1866	N.-Amer	849629
Schwenk, Johanne Christiane		25 Feb 1846	Freudenstadt	Frd.	Sep 1854	N.-Amer	569274
Schwenk, Johannes		9 yrs.	Rodt	Frd.	Oct 1850	N.-Amer	569271
Schwenk, Justine & C		6 Nov 1829	Freudenstadt	Frd.	Sep 1854	N.-Amer	569274
Schwenk, Katharina		13 Dec 1856	Hallwangen	Frd.	May 1860	N.-Amer	577777
Schwenk, Katharina Maria			Freudenstadt	Frd.	bef 1850	Switz.	569271
Schwenk, Magdalena			Schoemberg	Frd.	Jun 1854	N.-Amer	569273
Schwenk, Margaretha			Freudenstadt	Frd.	Apr 1813	France	569267
Schwenk, Margaretha			Klosterreichenbach	Frd.	Apr 1817	Russia	569268
Schwenk, Margaretha		17 yrs.	Rodt	Frd.	Oct 1850	N.-Amer	569271
Schwenk, Maria		12 yrs.	Rodt	Frd.	Oct 1850	N.-Amer	569271
Schwenk, Marie Friederike		29 Jan 1854	Freudenstadt	Frd.	Sep 1854	N.-Amer	569274
Schwenk, Martin & F		4 Sep 1828	Hallwangen	Frd.	May 1860	N.-Amer	577777
Schwenk, Mathias & F			Schoemberg	Frd.	Jul 1817	N.-Amer	569268
Schwenk, Matthias		13 Aug 1838	Schoemberg	Frd.	Sep 1866	N.-Amer	577780
Schwenk, Rosine		15 yrs.	Rodt	Frd.	Oct 1850	N.-Amer	569271
Schwenk, Sophie Friederika		10 Jan 1825	Freudenstadt	Frd.	bef 1863	France	577778
Schwenk, Ursula (wid.)		25 Aug 1824	Leidringen	Sulz	bef 1866	N.-Amer	849637
Schwitzgaebele, Katharina		1834	Liebenzell	Calw	1854	N.-Amer	563212
Schwitzgaebele, Maria Wilhel.		1830	Unterreichenbach	Calw	1856	N.-Amer	563212
Schwitzgaebele, Wilhelm Chr.			Unterreichenbach	Calw	1853	N.-Amer	563212
Schwitzgaebele, Wilhelmine			Unterreichenbach	Calw	1852	N.-Amer	563212
Schwitzgaeble, Johann Friedr.			Hirsau	Calw	1853	N.-Amer	563212
Schwizgaebele, Rosine Margar.			Unterreichenbach	Calw	1853	N.-Amer	563212
Schwizgaebele, Wilhelm		30 yrs.	Liebenzell	Calw	1866	N.-Amer	563212

Seeburger, Anna Maria & F	7 Sep 1799	Bickelsberg	Sulz	Jun 1849	N.-Amer	849630
Seeburger, David	12 Sep 1793	Trichtingen	Sulz	May 1817	Russia	849642
Seeburger, Georg		Bickelsberg	Sulz	Jun 1849	N.-Amer	849630
Seeburger, Lorenz	9 yrs.	Bickelsberg	Sulz	Jun 1849	N.-Amer	849630
Seeburger, Maria		Bettenhausen	Sulz	Jun 1854	N.-Amer	849630
Seeburger, Mathias		Trichtingen	Sulz	May 1817	Russia	849625
Seeburger, Matthaeus	10 Apr 1788	Trichtingen	Sulz	May 1817	Russia	849642
Seeger, Agatha	8 Dec 1836	Woernersberg	Frd.	Feb 1860	N.-Amer	577777
Seeger, Agatha	1838	Neuweiler	Calw	1857	N.-Amer	563212
Seeger, Anna	25 yrs.	Neuweiler	Calw	1855	N.-Amer	563212
Seeger, Anna Catharina		Stammheim	Calw	1853	N.-Amer	563212
Seeger, Anna Kath. (wid.) & F	23 Jan 1798	Bondorf	Herr.	Jul 1847	N.-Amer	834626
Seeger, Anna Maria	9 Dec 1815	Schopfloch	Frd.	Apr 1851	N.-Amer	569271
Seeger, Anna Maria	23 Dec 1816	Pfalzgrafenweiler	Frd.	Jul 1854	N.-Amer	569274
Seeger, Anna Maria		Hochdorf	Frd.	Jun 1832	N.-Amer	577776
Seeger, Anna Maria	1844	Neuweiler	Calw	1857	N.-Amer	563212
Seeger, Anna Maria	7 Apr 1826	Unterjettingen	Herr.	1847	N.-Amer	834626
Seeger, Catharina		Dornstetten	Frd.	Mar 1840	France	569269
Seeger, Catharina		Teinach	Calw	1864	N.-Amer	563212
Seeger, Catharina & C		Oberweiler	Calw	May 1847	N.-Amer	563212
Seeger, Christian		Hochdorf	Frd.	Jun 1832	N.-Amer	577776
Seeger, Christina	6 Dec 1845	Woernersberg	Frd.	Sep 1866	N.-Amer	577780
Seeger, Hans Georg		Schopfloch	Frd.	Apr 1752	Pen.N-A	550803
Seeger, Jacob	21 yrs.	Neuweiler	Calw	1867	N.-Amer	563212
Seeger, Jacob & F		Hornberg	Calw	1852	N.-Amer	563212
Seeger, Jacob Friedrich	19 yrs.	Zwerenberg	Calw	1867	N.-Amer	563212
Seeger, Johann Georg		Ettmannsweiler	Nag.	Sep 1854	N.-Amer	838491
Seeger, Johann Georg & F		Schopfloch	Frd.	Apr 1851	N.-Amer	569271
Seeger, Johann Jakob	13 Feb 1829	Unterjettingen	Herr.	1847	N.-Amer	834626
Seeger, Johann Michael	1 Nov 1832	Unterjettingen	Herr.	1847	N.-Amer	834626
Seeger, Johann Wilelm	10 Sep 1827	Unterjettingen	Herr.	1847	N.-Amer	834626
Seeger, Johanne		Freudenstadt	Frd.	Sep 1842	France	569269
Seeger, Johannes		Oberiflingen	Frd.	1851	N.-Amer	577778
Seeger, Johannes	24 Mar 1845	Glatten	Frd.	Apr 1864	N.-Amer	577779
Seeger, Johannes		Freudenstadt	Frd.	May 1851	N.-Amer	569271
Seeger, Johannes	1834	Neuweiler	Calw	1854	N.-Amer	563212
Seeger, Johannes	53 yrs.	Aichhalden	Calw	1854	N.-Amer	563212
Seeger, Karl	26 Jul 1833	Woernersberg	Frd.	Sep 1865	N.-Amer	577779
Seeger, Katharina	3 Jan 1831	Unterjettingen	Herr.	1847	N.-Amer	834626
Seeger, Katharina Elisabetha	9 Nov 1837	Woernersberg	Frd.	Feb 1860	N.-Amer	577777
Seeger, Mathaeus		Dornstetten	Frd.	Jun 1830	France	569269
Seeger, Mathaeus	1 Nov 1834	Schopfloch	Frd.	May 1851	N.-Amer	569271
Seeger, Matthaeus		Freudenstadt	Frd.	1851	N.-Amer	577778
Seeger, Matthaeus		Dornstetten	Frd.	Apr 1752	Pen.N-A	550803
Seeger, Michael	1841	Neuweiler	Calw	1857	N.-Amer	563212
Seeger, Philipp	1835	Neuweiler	Calw	1855	N.-Amer	563212
Seeger, Regine	1834	Hornberg	Calw	1854	N.-Amer	563212
Seegis, Anna Maria	26 Feb 1857	Dornhan	Sulz	Feb 1869	N.-Amer	849634
Seeker, Lorenz	1820	Ostelsheim	Calw	1857	N.-Amer	563212
Seemann, Agnes	6 Sep 1857	Leidringen	Sulz	Jun 1865	N.-Amer	849637

Name		Birth		Emigration			Film
Last	First	Date	Place	O'amt	Appl. Date	Dest.	Number
Seemann, Agnes (wife)		13 May 1826	Leidringen	Sulz	Jun 1865	N.-Amer	849637
Seemann, Andreas		20 Jun 1863	Leidringen	Sulz	Jun 1865	N.-Amer	849637
Seemann, Andreas & F		16 Mar 1823	Rotenzimmern	Sulz	Jun 1865	N.-Amer	849637
Seemann, Anna Maria		11 Nov 1843	Brittheim	Sulz	Mar 1863	Bavaria	849632
Seemann, Christian		29 Mar 1855	Leidringen	Sulz	Jun 1865	N.-Amer	849637
Seemann, Friedrich		13 Apr 1849	Leidringen	Sulz	Jun 1865	N.-Amer	849637
Seemann, Georg		3 Jul 1861	Leidringen	Sulz	Jun 1865	N.-Amer	849637
Seemann, Jakob		1 May 1867	Rotenzimmern	Sulz	Oct 1884	N.-Amer	849642
Seemann, Johann Georg		11 Jun 1856	Brittheim	Sulz	Apr 1872	N.-Amer	849632
Seemann, Johann Martin		3 Nov 1851	Brittheim	Sulz	Dec 1870	N.-Amer	849632
Seemann, Johannes		14 sep 1845	Erkenbrechtsweiler	Sulz	Oct 1864	Baden	849643
Seemann, Johannes		2 Mar 1829	Bickelsberg	Sulz	Mar 1865	Baden	849630
Seemann, Martin			Brittheim	Sulz	bef 1863	N.-Amer	849632
Seemann, Martin		15 Aug 1830	Leidringen	Sulz	Jun 1865	N.-Amer	849637
Sehburger, Johann Georg & F			Trichtingen	Sulz	Apr 1817	Russia	849642
Sehburger, Lucas			Trichtingen	Sulz	1822	France	849642
Seibold, Jacob			Nebringen	Herr.	Mar 1831	N.-Amer	834624
Seibold, Johann Christian		3 Apr 1826	Unterjesingen	Herr.	Mar 1870	Bavaria	834624
Seibold, Johann Gottfried		24 Dec 1830	Unterjesingen	Herr.	Aug 1846	Austria	834626
Seibold, Wilhelm Friedrich		8 Mar 1835	Unterjesingen	Herr.	Aug 1846	Austria	834626
Seid, Andreas		7 Jun 1849	Besenfeld	Frd.	Jun 1854	N.-Amer	569274
Seid, Anna Barbara (wife)		30 Apr 1825	Besenfeld	Frd.	Jun 1854	N.-Amer	569274
Seid, Anna Catharina		25 yrs.	Igelsberg	Frd.	Nov 1857	Switz.	577776
Seid, Barbara		25 Jun 1853	Besenfeld	Frd.	Jun 1854	N.-Amer	569274
Seid, Bernhard		3 Jul 1833	Igelsberg	Frd.	Feb 1853	N.-Amer	569272
Seid, Christian		4 Apr 1834	Igelsberg	Frd.	Jul 1854	N.-Amer	569274
Seid, Christina		23 Mar 1831	Groembach	Frd.	Feb 1854	N.-Amer	569273
Seid, Elisabetha Cath.			Walddorf	Nag.	Oct 1854	N.-Amer	838491
Seid, Eva Maria		29 Aug 1847	Besenfeld	Frd.	Jun 1854	N.-Amer	569274
Seid, Eva Maria			Igelsberg	Frd.	bef 1859	N.-Amer	577776
Seid, Eva Maria		15 Jan 1835	Tonbach	Frd.	bef 1860	N.-Amer	577777
Seid, Johann Friedrich		24 Sep 1840	Igelsberg	Frd.	Dec 1860	N.-Amer	577777
Seid, Johannes		9 Nov 1827	Igelsberg	Frd.	Feb 1853	N.-Amer	569272
Seid, Johannes		17 yrs.	Igelsberg	Frd.	Apr 1854	N.-Amer	569274
Seid, Johannes & F		19 Feb 1824	Igelsberg	Frd.	Jun 1854	N.-Amer	569274
Seid, Rosalie Lissette		27 Jul 1834	Igelsberg	Frd.	bef 1857	Switz.	577776
Seidt, Andreas		30 yrs.	Roet	Frd.	bef 1858	N.-Amer	577776
Seidt, Anna Maria		23 May 1806	Baiersbronn	Frd.	Dec 1853	N.-Amer	569272
Seidt, Beata		28 Feb 1835	Baiersbronn	Frd.	Dec 1853	N.-Amer	569272
Seidt, Christina Dorothea & F		8 Oct 1793	Besenfeld	Frd.	Jun 1854	N.-Amer	569274
Seidt, Christine		13 Dec 1814	Schoenegruend	Frd.	Apr 1836	N.-Amer	569268
Seidt, Christine Barbara		30 Apr 1852	Baiersbronn	Frd.	Dec 1853	N.-Amer	569272
Seidt, Eva Maria		2 Jul 1840	Baiersbronn	Frd.	Dec 1853	N.-Amer	569272
Seidt, Johann Matthias		25 Mar 1845	Baiersbronn	Frd.	Dec 1853	N.-Amer	569272
Seidt, Johannes		12 Aug 1823	Roet	Frd.	bef 1848	N.-Amer	569270
Seidt, Johannes		19 Feb 1824	Besenfeld	Frd.	Jun 1854	N.-Amer	569274
Seidt, Johannes & F		27 Oct 1810	Baiersbronn	Frd.	Dec 1853	N.-Amer	569272
Seidt, Katharina Elisabetha		27 Oct 1830	Besenfeld	Frd.	Jun 1854	N.-Amer	569274
Seiferheld, Gottlob C. W. F.		17 Sep 1795	Tailfingen	Sulz	bef 1835	France	849642
Seifried, Anna Maria (wife)			Hildrizhausen	Herr.	Mar 1831	N.-Amer	834624

Name	Date	Place	Region	Emig. Date	Destination	Film
Seifried, Barbara		Liebenzell	Calw	1866	Baden	563212
Seifried, Georg		Unterhenstett	Calw	Mar 1871	N.-Amer	563212
Seifried, Jacob Friedrich & W		Hildrizhausen	Herr.	Mar 1831	N.-Amer	834624
Seifried, Johannes	3 Oct 1846	Goettelfingen	Frd.	Dec 1866	Switz.	577780
Seifried, Katharine		Liebenzell	Calw	1863	Bavaria	563212
Seifried, Marie Jacobine		Liebenzell	Calw	1863	Baden	563212
Seiler, Friedrich		Dornstetten	Frd.	1817	Russia	569269
Seiler, Rosa	5 Oct 1846	Poltringen	Herr.	Jul 1868	N.-Amer	834624
Seissle, Michael & F		Moettlingen	Calw	1853	N.-Amer	563212
Seitz, Adolph	6 Apr 1849	Herrenberg	Herr.	Apr 1866	N.-Amer	834624
Seitz, Johann Georg	9 Sep 1840	Groembach	Frd.	Feb 1863	N.-Amer	577778
Seitz, Michael Friedrich & F	6 Oct 1825	Groembach	Frd.	May 1853	N.-Amer	569272
Sekinger, Gottlieb	4 Jun 1835	Holzhausen	Sulz	Dec 1853	N.-Amer	849635
Sekinger, Johannes	18 yrs.	Holzhausen	Sulz	Feb 1855	N.-Amer	849635
Sekmeyer, Georg		Schoenegrund	Frd.	Apr 1817	Russia	569268
Serger, Friedrich & F		Unterjettingen	Herr.	Apr 1836	N.-Amer	834624
Sessing, Daniel	Jun 1845	Calw	Calw	1863	England	563212
Sessing, James		Calw	Calw	1860	England	563212
Sessing, Samuel	1838	Calw	Calw	1858	England	563212
Sessler, Auguste	18 yrs.	Voehringen	Sulz	Feb 1867	N.-Amer	849643
Sessler, Karl	14 yrs.	Voehringen	Sulz	Oct 1851	N.-Amer	849643
Seutter, Carl von	1842	Edelweiler	Frd.	bef 1862	N.-Amer	577778
Seyd, Johannes & F		Baiersbronn	Frd.	Feb 1846	Austria	569271
Seydt, Johann Georg		Breitenberg	Calw	May 1873	N.-Amer	563212
Seydt, Michael		Breitenberg	Calw	May 1873	N.-Amer	563212
Seyfang, Georg Johann	12 Jan 1802	Schorndorf	Schd.	Nov 1837	Austria	801461
Seyfried, Christoph		Sommenhardt	Calw	1859	Baden	563212
Seyfried, Johann Adam	27 Jan 1845	Goettelfingen	Frd.	1865	N.-Amer	577779
Seyter, Rosina	28 yrs.	Liebenzell	Calw	Feb 1848	N.-Amer	563212
Sicher, Abraham	43 yrs.	Geradstetten	Schd.	May 1844	Bavaria	801461
Sickeler, Anna Amalie	22 Jan 1888	Bergfelden	Sulz	Mar 1891	Prussia	849626
Sickeler, Caroline Barbara		Sulz	Sulz	Sep 1836	Switz.	849627
Sickeler, Emerentia (wife)	12 Nov 1848	Bergfelden	Sulz	Mar 1891	Prussia	849626
Sickeler, Frieda	13 Dec 1884	Bergfelden	Sulz	Mar 1891	Prussia	849626
Sickeler, Johannes	7 Dec 1881	Bergfelden	Sulz	Mar 1891	Prussia	849626
Sickeler, Johannes & F	27 May 1849	Bergfelden	Sulz	Mar 1891	Prussia	849626
Sickeler, Marie	22 Jun 1880	Bergfelden	Sulz	Mar 1891	Prussia	849626
Sickeler, Rosine	22 Oct 1886	Bergfelden	Sulz	Mar 1891	Prussia	849626
Sieber, Johannes	26 Dec 1867	Holzhausen	Sulz	Mar 1883	N.-Amer	849635
Sieber, Mathias (wid.)	7 Sep 1801	Duerrenmettstetten	Sulz	Mar 1854	N.-Amer	849635
Siegel, Alexander	20 Jul 1845	Baihingen	Frd.	May 1851	N.-Amer	569271
Siegel, Anna Maria	18 yrs.	Bickelsberg	Sulz	Feb 1853	N.-Amer	849630
Siegel, Anna Maria Rosina		Holzhausen	Sulz	Sep 1853	N.-Amer	849635
Siegel, Barbara	20 Jan 1842	Baisingen	Frd.	May 1851	N.-Amer	569271
Siegel, Barbara	5 May 1814	Betzenweiler	Frd.	May 1851	N.-Amer	569271
Siegel, Barbara (wife)		Bickelsberg	Sulz	Feb 1853	N.-Amer	849630
Siegel, Christian	2 Apr 1813	Schopfloch	Frd.	bef 1848	N.-Amer	569270
Siegel, Christian	14 Dec 1834	Schopfloch	Frd.	May 1851	N.-Amer	569271
Siegel, Christine	2 Dec 1831	Schopfloch	Frd.	May 1851	N.-Amer	569271
Siegel, Elisabetha	13 Apr 1841	Schopfloch	Frd.	Aug 1848	N.-Amer	569270

Name		Birth		Emigration			Film
Last	First	Date	Place	O'amt	Appl. Date	Dest.	Number
Siegel, Elisabetha		20 Jan 1847	Baihingen	Frd.	May 1851	N.-Amer	569271
Siegel, Elisabetha & F		30 Jul 1814	Schopfloch	Frd.	Aug 1848	N.-Amer	569270
Siegel, Georg		16 Oct 1835	Schopfloch	Frd.	Aug 1848	N.-Amer	569270
Siegel, Jacob Friedrich & F			Freudenstadt	Frd.	1851	N.-Amer	577778
Siegel, Jakob Friedrich & F		19 Nov 1803	Schopfloch	Frd.	May 1851	N.-Amer	569271
Siegel, Johann Friederich		25 Feb 1836	Schopfloch	Frd.	May 1851	N.-Amer	569271
Siegel, Johann Georg		6 Feb 1840	Schopfloch	Frd.	May 1851	N.-Amer	569271
Siegel, Johann Jakob			Holzhausen	Sulz	Sep 1853	N.-Amer	849635
Siegel, Johann Martin & F			Holzhausen	Sulz	Sep 1853	N.-Amer	849635
Siegel, Johann Michael		28 yrs.	Bickelsberg	Sulz	Feb 1853	N.-Amer	849630
Siegel, Johannes			Schopfloch	Frd.	Mar 1837	N.-Amer	569268
Siegel, Johannes		13 Dec 1843	Baihingen	Frd.	May 1851	N.-Amer	569271
Siegel, Johannes			Duerrenmettstetten	Sulz	Mar 1857	N.-Amer	849635
Siegel, Johannes			Muehlheim a.B.	Sulz	bef 1852	France	849639
Siegel, Mathaeus		20 Mar 1833	Schopfloch	Frd.	May 1851	N.-Amer	569271
Siegel, Mathias		8 Sep 1834	Duerrenmettstetten	Sulz	Mar 1854	N.-Amer	849635
Siegel, Mathias & F			Glatten	Frd.	1817	Russia	569269
Siegel, Matthaeus		12 Jun 1846	Schopfloch	Frd.	Aug 1848	N.-Amer	569270
Siegel, Michael & F		1 Oct 1792	Bickelsberg	Sulz	Feb 1853	N.-Amer	849630
Siegel, Rebekka			Holzhausen	Sulz	Sep 1853	N.-Amer	849635
Siegel, Tobias		14 May 1862	Voehringen	Sulz	Jan 1879	N.-Amer	849643
Siegel, Veronika		9 Oct 1849	Baisingen	Frd.	May 1851	N.-Amer	569271
Siegle, Johann Jacob			Rosenfeld	Sulz	Mar 1816	France	849640
Siegle, Leonhard		2 Aug 1862	Leidringen	Sulz	Sep 1869	N.-Amer	849637
Sigel, Agatha (wife)			Voehringen	Sulz	Jul 1837	N.-Amer	849643
Sigel, Andreas & F		20 Sep 1796	Voehringen	Sulz	Jul 1837	N.-Amer	849643
Sigel, Jakob		1 Oct 1866	Voehringen	Sulz	Mar 1883	N.-Amer	849626
Sigel, Johann Jakob		1 yrs.	Voehringen	Sulz	Jul 1837	N.-Amer	849643
Sigel, Johannes		24 yrs.	Voehringen	Sulz	Feb 1854	N.-Amer	849643
Sigel, Tobias		18 yrs.	Voehringen	Sulz	Oct 1853	N.-Amer	849643
Sikeler, Dorothea			Trichtingen	Sulz	Mar 1833	N.-Amer	849642
Silberradt, Luise			Rosenfeld	Sulz	bef 1838	N.-Amer	849625
Simen, Anna Maria (wid.) & F			Sulz	Sulz	May 1856	N.-Amer	849627
Simen, Gottfried Daniel		5 Jan 1844	Sulz	Sulz	May 1856	N.-Amer	849627
Simen, Jacob Friedrich		21 Apr 1847	Sulz	Sulz	May 1856	N.-Amer	849627
Simen, Johanne Friederike		28 Aug 1841	Sulz	Sulz	May 1856	N.-Amer	849627
Simon, Auguste Friederike		8 Jun 1841	Sulz	Sulz	Sep 1860	Switz.	849628
Simon, Dorothea Friederika		15 Jan 1838	Sulz	Sulz	Aug 1857	N.-Amer	849628
Sindlinger, Andreas		20 Jan 1848	Moetzingen	Herr.	May 1852	N.-Amer	834627
Sindlinger, Anna Maria		6 May 1842	Moetzingen	Herr.	May 1852	N.-Amer	834627
Sindlinger, Anna Maria (wife)		26 May 1809	Moetzingen	Herr.	May 1852	N.-Amer	834627
Sindlinger, Christina (wife)		9 Jun 1801	Moetzingen	Herr.	Mar 1847	N.-Amer	834626
Sindlinger, Christina Barbara		30 Sep 1833	Moetzingen	Herr.	Mar 1847	N.-Amer	834626
Sindlinger, Jacob & F		13 Aug 1807	Moetzingen	Herr.	May 1852	N.-Amer	834627
Sindlinger, Jacob Friedrich		22 Oct 1845	Moetzingen	Herr.	Mar 1847	N.-Amer	834626
Sindlinger, Jakob		9 Nov 1844	Moetzingen	Herr.	May 1852	N.-Amer	834627
Sindlinger, Johann Martin		26 Jan 1843	Moetzingen	Herr.	May 1852	N.-Amer	834627
Sindlinger, Johann Ulrich		17 Feb 1831	Altingen	Herr.	Jun 1866	N.-Amer	834624
Sindlinger, Katharina & C		23 Apr 1811	Moetzingen	Herr.	May 1852	N.-Amer	834627
Sindlinger, Katharina Barb.		2 Sep 1847	Moetzingen	Herr.	May 1852	N.-Amer	834627

Sindlinger, Margaretha	16 Nov 1844	Moetzingen	Herr.	May 1852	N.-Amer	834627
Sindlinger, Margaretha & F	25 Feb 1809	Moetzingen	Herr.	May 1852	N.-Amer	834627
Sindlinger, Simon	28 Oct 1841	Moetzingen	Herr.	Mar 1847	N.-Amer	834626
Sindlinger, Simon & F	20 Jul 1810	Moetzingen	Herr.	Mar 1847	N.-Amer	834626
Sindlinger, Sophia	13 May 1813	Moetzingen	Herr.	Mar 1847	N.-Amer	834626
Sindlinger, Wilhelmina	10 Oct 1839	Moetzingen	Herr.	Mar 1847	N.-Amer	834626
Sing, Johann Martin	36 yrs.	Dornstetten	Frd.	Mar 1865	N.-Amer	577779
Singer, Johann Jacob	21 Aug 1842	Sulz	Sulz	bef 1873	Switz.	849628
Singer, Maria Anna		Altheim	Horb	Jun 1865	Baden	835929
Single, Adolf Julius	16 Jun 1848	Winterlingen	Bal.	Aug 1858	Switz.	555962
Single, Anna Maria	19 yrs.	Isingen	Sulz	May 1840	N.-Amer	849636
Single, Catharina		Trichtingen	Sulz	Feb 1817	Russia	849642
Single, Catharina (wid.) & F		Trichtingen	Sulz	May 1817	Rus-Pol	849642
Single, Charlotte Friederike	10 Nov 1846	Winterlingen	Bal.	Aug 1858	Switz.	555962
Single, Christina & C		Isingen	Sulz	Jan 1856	N.-Amer	849636
Single, Johann Martin		Balingen	Bal.	bef 1882	N.-Amer	555964
Single, Johannes		Erzingen	Bal.	Jun 1865	Switz.	555962
Single, Johannes & F		Trichtingen	Sulz	Feb 1817	Russia	849642
Single, Louise Magdalena (wife)	5 Mar 1827	Winterlingen	Bal.	Aug 1858	Switz.	555962
Single, Mathilde Friederike	5 Nov 1850	Winterlingen	Bal.	Aug 1858	Switz.	555962
Single, Otto Friedrich	2 Aug 1854	Winterlingen	Bal.	Aug 1858	Switz.	555962
Single, Rosina	20 May 1833	Aach	Frd.	Sep 1854	N.-Amer	569274
Single, Wilhelm & F	26 Sep 1817	Winterlingen	Bal.	Aug 1858	Switz.	555962
Sinn, Anna Maria	22 yrs.	Rodt	Frd.	May 1752	Pen.N-A	550803
Sinn, Barbara	2 yrs.	Rodt	Frd.	May 1752	Pen.N-A	550803
Sinn, Catharina	23 yrs.	Rodt	Frd.	May 1752	Pen.N-A	550803
Sinn, Christian	46 yrs.	Rodt	Frd.	May 1752	Pen.N-A	550803
Sinn, Elisabetha	15 yrs.	Rodt	Frd.	May 1752	Pen.N-A	550803
Sinn, Eva	19 yrs.	Rodt	Frd.	May 1752	Pen.N-A	550803
Sinn, Frantz Anton & F	50 yrs.	Rodt	Frd.	May 1752	Pen.N-A	550803
Sinn, Hans Jerg	6 yrs.	Rodt	Frd.	May 1752	Pen.N-A	550803
Sinn, Jacob	14 yrs.	Rodt	Frd.	May 1752	Pen.N-A	550803
Sinn, Michel	10 yrs.	Rodt	Frd.	May 1752	Pen.N-A	550803
Sinz, Karl	11 May 1847	Altheim	Horb	Feb 1867	N.-Amer	835929
Sixt, Michael & F		Ostelheim	Calw	1853	N.-Amer	563212
Snitz, Adolf	6 Apr 1849	Herrenberg	Herr.	Dec 1867	N.-Amer	834624
Snitz, Friedrike Wilhelmine	29 Dec 1846	Herrenberg	Herr.	Dec 1867	N.-Amer	834624
Solleder, Jacob		Sulz	Sulz	Sep 1816	Switz.	849627
Solleder, Johann Carl		Sulz	Sulz	Oct 1816	France	849627
Solleder, Wilhelmine Rosine		Sulz	Sulz	Sep 1842	Switz.	849627
Sommer, Luise		Calw	Calw	1856	Austria	563212
Sommer, Martin & F		Aach	Frd.	1817	Russia	569269
Sonn, Agatha (wife)		Isingen	Sulz	Jan 1817	Russia	849635
Sonn, Jakob & W		Isingen	Sulz	Jan 1817	Russia	849635
Sonntag, Friedrich		Freudenstadt	Frd.	Dec 1854	N.-Amer	569274
Spaeht, Anna Maria	4 Dec 1830	Glatten	Frd.	Oct 1854	S.-Amer	569274
Spaeth, Andreas	22 Feb 1876	Dornhan	Sulz	Sep 1895	N.-Amer	849626
Spaeth, Andreas & F	6 Apr 1808	Nennethausen	Sulz	Jun 1837	Korsika	849636
Spaeth, Anna	22 yrs.	Boeffingen	Frd.	May 1752	Pen.N-A	550803
Spaeth, Anna (wife)		Nennethausen	Sulz	Jun 1837	Korsika	849636

Name		Birth		Emigration			Film
Last	First	Date	Place	O'amt	Appl. Date	Dest.	Number
Spaeth, Barbara		50 yrs.	Boeffingen	Frd.	May 1752	Pen.N-A	550803
Spaeth, Catharina		20 yrs.	Boeffingen	Frd.	May 1752	Pen.N-A	550803
Spaeth, Christian		14 yrs.	Boeffingen	Frd.	May 1752	Pen.N-A	550803
Spaeth, Christian		8 Feb 1860	Dornhan	Sulz	Nov 1875	N.-Amer	849634
Spaeth, Christina & C		25 Oct 1820	Glatten	Frd.	Oct 1854	S.-Amer	569274
Spaeth, Christof Gottlieb		16 Mar 1844	Dornhan	Sulz	Sep 1864	N.-Amer	849634
Spaeth, Eva Margaretha		26 yrs.	Boeffingen	Frd.	May 1752	Pen.N-A	550803
Spaeth, Hans Georg		12 yrs.	Boeffingen	Frd.	May 1752	Pen.N-A	550803
Spaeth, Hans Georg & F		56 yrs.	Boeffingen	Frd.	May 1752	Pen.N-A	550803
Spaeth, Hans Jacob		17 yrs.	Boeffingen	Frd.	May 1752	Pen.N-A	550803
Spaeth, Hans Martin		7 yrs.	Boeffingen	Frd.	May 1752	Pen.N-A	550803
Spaeth, Jacob		20 Apr 1814	Glatten O/A Frd.	Sulz	Apr 1846	Austria	849638
Spaeth, Jakob		29 Apr 1840	Hopfau	Sulz	Mar 1860	N.-Amer	849636
Spaeth, Jakob		11 Mar 1868	Dornhan	Sulz	Jan 1887	N.-Amer	849626
Spaeth, Johann Michael		22 Oct 1842	Glatten	Frd.	Oct 1854	S.-Amer	569274
Spaeth, Johannes		18 Dec 1845	Dornhan	Sulz	Aug 1864	N.-Amer	849634
Spaeth, Johannes		8 Dec 1857	Hopfau	Sulz	Feb 1873	N.-Amer	849636
Spaeth, Magdalena		18 yrs.	Boeffingen	Frd.	May 1752	Pen.N-A	550803
Spath, Elisabetha		8 Nov 1817	Glatten	Frd.	Mar 1847	N.-Amer	569271
Speer, Jakob & F			Wittendorf	Frd.	May 1817	Rus-Pol	569268
Speidel, Adolf Julius		8 Jul 1850	Bondorf	Herr.	May 1869	N.-Amer	834624
Speidel, Carl		27 Oct 1829	Klingenberg	Frd.	Jul 1849	N.-Amer	569270
Speidel, Eduard (Pastor) & F			Pfalzgrafenweiler	Frd.	Jun 1854	N.-Amer	569273
Speiser, Anna Barbara		16 Feb 1830	Moetzingen	Herr.	Apr 1847	N.-Amer	834626
Speiser, Anna Maria		25 Dec 1837	Moetzingen	Herr.	Apr 1847	N.-Amer	834626
Speiser, Maria Catharina		24 Nov 1832	Moetzingen	Herr.	Apr 1847	N.-Amer	834626
Spengler, Anna Marie (wid.)& F			Wuerzbach	Calw	1853	N.-Amer	563212
Spiegel, Anna		5 Aug 1810	Isingen	Sulz	May 1838	N.-Amer	849636
Spiegel, Anna Barbara		1 Aug 1822	Isingen	Sulz	May 1838	N.-Amer	849636
Spiegel, Anna Maria		22 Jul 1820	Isingen	Sulz	May 1838	N.-Amer	849636
Spiegel, Christian		2 Dec 1843	Isingen	Sulz	Feb 1859	N.-Amer	849636
Spiegel, Gottlieb		2 Jul 1850	Isingen	Sulz	May 1868	N.-Amer	849636
Spiegel, Gottlieb		28 Jul 1815	Isingen	Sulz	May 1838	N.-Amer	849636
Spiegel, Johann Georg		1 Oct 1847	Isingen	Sulz	Apr 1867	N.-Amer	849636
Spiegel, Johann Georg			Isingen	Sulz	Apr 1840	N.-Amer	849636
Spiegel, Johannes & W			Isingen	Sulz	Apr 1840	N.-Amer	849636
Spiegel, Katharina		22 Oct 1824	Isingen	Sulz	May 1838	N.-Amer	849636
Spiegel, Ludwig		26 Jun 1846	Isingen	Sulz	Feb 1866	N.-Amer	849636
Spiegel, Ludwig		25 Aug 1804	Isingen	Sulz	May 1845	Austria	849636
Spiegel, Philipp J. (wid.) & F		7 Feb 1782	Isingen	Sulz	May 1838	N.-Amer	849636
Spiegel, Rosine (wife)			Isingen	Sulz	Apr 1840	N.-Amer	849636
Spiegel, Wilhelm		25 Apr 1849	Isingen	Sulz	Apr 1868	N.-Amer	849636
Spiegel, Wilhelm		1 Oct 1818	Isingen	Sulz	Mar 1852	N.-Amer	849636
Spiess, Johann Jacob		5 Sep 1848	Unterjesingen	Herr.	May 1866	N.-Amer	834624
Spitz, Michael & F			Altburg	Calw	1854	N.-Amer	563212
Spoehr, Jacob & F			Stammheim	Calw	1853	N.-Amer	563212
Sponfail, Catharina			Ernstmuehl	Calw	1853	N.-Amer	563212
Sponnagel, Louise (wid.)			Dennjaecht	Calw	1854	Baden	563212
Sprenger, Anna Maria		5 Nov 1821	Oberjettingen	Herr.	1838	Rus-Pol	834625
Sprenger, Anna Maria (wife)		43 yrs.	Oberjettingen	Herr.	1838	Rus-Pol	834625

Sprenger, David Wilhelm	17 Jul 1825	Oberjettingen	Herr.	1838	Rus-Pol	834625
Sprenger, Friedrich & F	44 yrs.	Oberjettingen	Herr.	1838	Rus-Pol	834625
Sprenger, Maria Wilhelmine		Oeschelbronn	Herr.	Sep 1842	Hesse	834625
Sprenger, Rosina Barbara	2 Nov 1819	Oberjettingen	Herr.	1838	Rus-Pol	834625
Springer, Anna Maria		Freudenstadt	Frd.	Aug 1811	Baden	569267
Springer, Caroline	11 yrs.	Freudenstadt	Frd.	Oct 1850	N.-Amer	569271
Springer, Christian	17 yrs.	Freudenstadt	Frd.	Oct 1850	N.-Amer	569271
Springer, Christian	22 Sep 1843	Rosenfeld	Sulz	Aug 1858	N.-Amer	849640
Springer, Christian & F		Freudenstadt	Frd.	Oct 1850	N.-Amer	569271
Springer, Christina Cath. (wife)		Rosenfeld	Sulz	Mar 1836	N.-Amer	849640
Springer, Conrad	19 yrs.	Calw	Calw	1866	N.-Amer	563212
Springer, Conrad (wid.)	28 Jul 1763	Voehringen	Sulz	Mar 1834	N.-Amer	849643
Springer, Dorothea	30 Dec 1830	Rosenfeld	Sulz	Aug 1858	N.-Amer	849640
Springer, Dorothea (wife)	44 yrs.	Rosenfeld	Sulz	Jun 1817	Russia	849640
Springer, Friederike	13 yrs.	Freudenstadt	Frd.	Oct 1850	N.-Amer	569271
Springer, Friedrich	9 yrs.	Freudenstadt	Frd.	Oct 1850	N.-Amer	569271
Springer, Friedrich & F	48 yrs.	Rosenfeld	Sulz	Jun 1817	Russia	849640
Springer, Johann Adam		Rosenfeld	Sulz	bef 1831	Russia	849640
Springer, Johann Adam	6 yrs.	Rosenfeld	Sulz	Jun 1817	Russia	849640
Springer, Johann Georg	11 Oct 1831	Freudenstadt	Frd.	Aug 1857	N.-Amer	577776
Springer, Johann Martin		Rosenfeld	Sulz	bef 1831	Russia	849640
Springer, Johann Martin	8 yrs.	Rosenfeld	Sulz	Jun 1817	Russia	849640
Springer, Johann Michael	15 Jan 1821	Rosenfeld	Sulz	Feb 1849	Baden	849640
Springer, Johann Philipp & F	19 Feb 1792	Rosenfeld	Sulz	Mar 1836	N.-Amer	849640
Springer, Karl		Rosenfeld	Sulz	Apr 1893	N.-Amer	849626
Springer, Katharine Frieder.	7 Apr 1835	Freudenstadt	Frd.	bef 1864	Baden	577779
Springer, Louise	6 yrs.	Freudenstadt	Frd.	Oct 1850	N.-Amer	569271
Springer, Margarethe	4 Apr 1835	Rosenfeld	Sulz	Sep 1859	Switz.	849640
Springer, Marie	1 yrs.	Freudenstadt	Frd.	Oct 1850	N.-Amer	569271
Springer, Martin		Rosenfeld	Sulz	Aug 1852	N.-Amer	849640
Springer, Martin & F	4 Feb 1834	Voehringen	Sulz	Sep 1882	Switz.	849643
Springer, Ottmar	11 Nov 1832	Herrenberg	Herr.	Nov 1863	N.-Amer	834624
Springer, Regina	24 Aug 1831	Rosenfeld	Sulz	Nov 1857	Switz.	849640
Springer, Wilhelm Friedrich	7 Feb 1833	Freudenstadt	Frd.	bef 1862	Baden	577778
Springmann, Jacob		Lossburg	Frd.	1817	Russia	569269
Springmann, Johann Martin	24 Aug 1811	Freudenstadt	Frd.	bef 1840	N.-Amer	577777
Springmann, Johannes	22 Aug 1837	Gruental	Frd.	Apr 1856	N.-Amer	569275
Springmann, Matthaeus		Dietersweiler	Frd.	Apr 1865	N.-Amer	577779
Staebler, Johann Jakob	15 Dec 1807	Schoenmuenzach	Frd.	Aug 1836	Prussia	569268
Staebler, Wilhelmine Catharine		Schoenmuenzach	Frd.	Oct 1844	Baden	569269
Staeffler, Baltas	22 yrs.	Deckenpfronn	Calw	1854	N.-Amer	563212
Staehle, Barbara (wife)		Isingen	Sulz	Jul 1837	Switz.	849636
Staehle, Bertha Katharina	15 Jun 1874	Isingen	Sulz	Sep 1883	Switz.	849626
Staehle, Carl	23 Sep 1867	Bergfelden	Sulz	May 1883	N.-Amer	849629
Staehle, Christian & F		Isingen	Sulz	Jul 1837	Switz.	849636
Staehle, Friedrich	6 Mar 1806	Bondorf	Herr.	Nov 1849	N.-Amer	834627
Staehle, Jacob	16 Apr 1863	Bergfelden	Sulz	Sep 1880	N.-Amer	849626
Staehle, Jakob	1833	Isingen	Sulz	Oct 1852	N.-Amer	849636
Staehle, Johann Georg & F	11 Apr 1842	Isingen	Sulz	Sep 1883	Switz.	849636
Staehle, Johann Martin	8 Sep 1842	Bondorf	Herr.	May 1869	N.-Amer	834624

Name		Birth		Emigration			Film
Last	First	Date	Place	O'amt	Appl. Date	Dest.	Number
Staehle, Johann Michael		2 Mar 1848	Isingen	Sulz	Apr 1866	N.-Amer	849636
Staehle, Karl		23 Mar 1871	Isingen	Sulz	Sep 1883	Switz.	849626
Staehle, Karolina (wife)			Isingen	Sulz	Sep 1883	Switz.	849626
Staehle, Maria		4 yrs.	Isingen	Sulz	Jul 1837	Switz.	849636
Staehle, Maria Louise		6 mon.	Isingen	Sulz	Jul 1837	Switz.	849636
Staengle, Johann Jacob		1840	Gechingen	Calw	1854	N.-Amer	563212
Staeudinger, Jakob Friedrich		7 Feb 1846	Wittershausen	Sulz	Dec 1866	N.-Amer	849644
Stahl, Anna Maria			Dornstetten	Frd.	1817	Russia	569269
Stahl, Christian		10 yrs.	Dornstetten	Frd.	Jun 1853	N.-Amer	569272
Stahl, Friederike (wid.) & F			Dornstetten	Frd.	Apr 1817	Russia	569269
Stahl, Friedrich & F			Gechingen	Calw	1852	N.-Amer	563212
Stahl, Jakob Friedrich		19 May 1809	Dornstetten	Frd.	Mar 1833	N.-Amer	569269
Stahl, Johann Georg		21 Jun 1831	Dornstetten	Frd.	Mar 1846	N.-Amer	569271
Stahl, Katharina		29 yrs.	Dornstetten	Frd.	Apr 1817	Russia	569269
Stahl, Katharina		3 Jul 1829	Dornstetten	Frd.	Mar 1846	N.-Amer	569271
Stahl, Katharina & C			Dornstetten	Frd.	Jun 1853	N.-Amer	569272
Stahl, Maria Christiane		28 Feb 1829	Dornstetten	Frd.	Mar 1846	N.-Amer	569271
Stahl, Matthaeus		6 Apr 1823	Dornstetten	Frd.	Aug 1846	N.-Amer	569271
Stahl, Rosine Margaretha		10 Jan 1836	Dornstetten	Frd.	Mar 1846	N.-Amer	569271
Staib, Tobias Friedrich		11 Sep 1811	Schnait	Schd.	Feb 1834	S.-Russ	801460
Staib, Tobias Friedrich			Schnait	Schd.	1833	Russia	801460
Staidinger, Ludwig			Voehringen	Sulz	bef 1848	N.-Amer	849643
Staiger, Carl Friedrich		16 Mar 1845	Tailfingen	Herr.	Oct 1862	N.-Amer	834624
Staiger, Paul		26 Dec 1855	Tailfingen	Herr.	Nov 1869	N.-Amer	834624
Stanger, Anna Barbara			Unterhaugstett	Calw	1866	Baden	563212
Stark, August		14 yrs.	Sulz	Sulz	Jul 1843	N.-Amer	849627
Stark, Auguste Luise		15 yrs.	Sulz	Sulz	Jul 1840	N.-Amer	849627
Stark, Christian Wilhelm		25 Oct 1828	Sulz	Sulz	Aug 1866	N.-Amer	849628
Stark, Christiane Rosine (wife)			Sulz	Sulz	Jul 1843	N.-Amer	849627
Stark, Christine		26 yrs.	Sulz	Sulz	Jul 1843	N.-Amer	849627
Stark, Marie Pauline		16 yrs.	Sulz	Sulz	Jul 1843	N.-Amer	849627
Stark, Philipp Jakob Chr. & F			Sulz	Sulz	Jul 1843	N.-Amer	849627
Stark, Sophie Caroline		17 yrs.	Sulz	Sulz	Jul 1840	N.-Amer	849627
Stauss, Agnes		1783	Bettenhausen	Sulz	Jun 1817	N.-Amer	849630
Stauss, Gottlob		11 Apr 1875	Rosenfeld	Sulz	Mar 1891	N.-Amer	849626
Stauss, Johann Georg		9 Nov 1870	Rosenfeld	Sulz	Sep 1887	N.-Amer	849626
Stauss, Johann Martina		3 Apr 1872	Rosenfeld	Sulz	Oct 1888	N.-Amer	849626
Stauss, Philipp		1834	Bettenhausen	Sulz	Jun 1817	N.-Amer	849630
Steck, Barbara (wid.)		63 yrs.	Nufringen	Herr.	Apr 1838	N.-Amer	834625
Steeb, Johann Gottlieb			Sulz	Sulz	bef 1855	N.-Amer	849628
Steeb, Michael		18 Dec 1848	Huzenbach	Frd.	Jan 1866	N.-Amer	577780
Steegmaier, Anna Maria		22 Oct 1813	Waldhausen	Schd.	May 1844	Bavaria	801461
Stehle, Afra		6 Jan 1857	Binsdorf	Sulz	May 1869	N.-Amer	849631
Stehle, Agnes		29 Jan 1826	Binsdorf	Sulz	May 1865	Hohenz.	849631
Stehle, Andreas		22 May 1849	Binsdorf	Sulz	Apr 1869	N.-Amer	849631
Stehle, Anna Karoline			Binsdorf	Sulz	Nov 1861	Italy	849631
Stehle, Anton & F		2 Oct 1774	Binsdorf	Sulz	May 1817	Poland	849630
Stehle, Carolina		26 Jan 1816	Binsdorf	Sulz	Apr 1833	N.-Amer	849630
Stehle, Catharina (wife)			Binsdorf	Sulz	Apr 1853	N.-Amer	849630
Stehle, Chrisostomus		1794	Rosenfeld	Sulz	1817	Russia	849625

Stehle, Christof		Binsdorf	Sulz	Apr 1858	Switz.	849630
Stehle, David	5 Apr 1849	Binsdorf	Sulz	Aug 1868	N. Amer	849631
Stehle, David & F	21 Mar 1816	Binsdorf	Sulz	Feb 1852	N.-Amer	849630
Stehle, Donat	24 Feb 1850	Binsdorf	Sulz	Sep 1868	N.-Amer	849631
Stehle, Dorothea (wife)	13 Mar 1787	Binsdorf	Sulz	Apr 1833	N.-Amer	849630
Stehle, Elisabetha	25 Jun 1846	Reichenbach	Frd.	Jan 1865	N.-Amer	577779
Stehle, Elisabetha	4 Nov 1833	Binsdorf	Sulz	Oct 1860	Prussia	849630
Stehle, Elisabetha	26 Dec 1844	Binsdorf	Sulz	Oct 1868	N.-Amer	849631
Stehle, Fabian & F	6 Dec 1822	Binsdorf	Sulz	Dec 1852	N.-Amer	849630
Stehle, Fridolin & F	24 Feb 1785	Binsdorf	Sulz	Apr 1833	N.-Amer	849630
Stehle, Friederike	1 Jun 1843	Binsdorf	Sulz	Feb 1852	N.-Amer	849630
Stehle, Friedrich	11 Feb 1842	Binsdorf	Sulz	Feb 1852	N.-Amer	849630
Stehle, Genovefa		Binsdorf	Sulz	Aug 1855	Hohenz.	849630
Stehle, Gertrud	17 Mar 1820	Binsdorf	Sulz	Apr 1833	N.-Amer	849630
Stehle, Gotthardt Gustav Emil	13 Nov 1839	Binsdorf	Sulz	May 1858	N.-Amer	849630
Stehle, Gottlieb	7 Nov 1815	Binsdorf	Sulz	May 1817	Poland	849630
Stehle, Helene	21 May 1822	Binsdorf	Sulz	Apr 1833	N.-Amer	849630
Stehle, Isidor	29 Mar 1827	Binsdorf	Sulz	Jun 1866	Bavaria	849631
Stehle, Johann Evangelist	6 Dec 1846	Binsdorf	Sulz	Sep 1866	N.-Amer	849631
Stehle, Johanna	17 Feb 1832	Binsdorf	Sulz	Nov 1842	Austria	849630
Stehle, Johanna	13 Sep 1809	Binsdorf	Sulz	May 1817	Poland	849630
Stehle, Johannes	22 May 1876	Binsdorf	Sulz	Aug 1892	N.-Amer	849626
Stehle, Johannes	22 May 1876	Binsdorf	Sulz	Aug 1892	N.-Amer	849631
Stehle, Jordan	14 Feb 1849	Binsdorf	Sulz	Apr 1869	N.-Amer	849631
Stehle, Josefine	28 Jan 1864	Binsdorf	Sulz	May 1886	Switz.	849631
Stehle, Josefine	24 Jan 1867	Binsdorf	Sulz	Apr 1889	Switz.	849626
Stehle, Joseph & F	17 May 1821	Binsdorf	Sulz	Apr 1853	N.-Amer	849630
Stehle, Joseph Anton	7 May 1805	Binsdorf	Sulz	May 1817	Poland	849630
Stehle, Josepha Amanda	2 Feb 1832	Binsdorf	Sulz	Mar 1863	Baden	849631
Stehle, Juliane	9 Jan 1825	Binsdorf	Sulz	Apr 1833	N.-Amer	849630
Stehle, Justine (wife)	12 Jul 1819	Binsdorf	Sulz	Feb 1852	N.-Amer	849630
Stehle, Leonhard	28 Oct 1851	Binsdorf	Sulz	Sep 1868	N.-Amer	849631
Stehle, Ludwig	31 Dec 1878	Binsdorf	Sulz	May 1893	N.-Amer	849631
Stehle, Luzia	10 Dec 1811	Binsdorf	Sulz	May 1817	Poland	849630
Stehle, Magdalena	7 Mar 1827	Binsdorf	Sulz	Jul 1860	Prussia	849630
Stehle, Magdalena	11 Jul 1777	Binsdorf	Sulz	May 1817	Poland	849630
Stehle, Marianne	12 Mar 1819	Binsdorf	Sulz	Feb 1846	Switz.	849630
Stehle, Markus	14 Apr 1856	Binsdorf	Sulz	Sep 1872	N.-Amer	849631
Stehle, Markus	4 Jan 1850	Binsdorf	Sulz	May 1869	N.-Amer	849631
Stehle, Marzelle		Binsdorf	Sulz	May 1842	Hohenz.	849630
Stehle, Reinhard	29 Jan 1848	Binsdorf	Sulz	Mar 1868	N.-Amer	849631
Stehle, Reinhold	11 Sep 1847	Binsdorf	Sulz	Jun 1866	N.-Amer	849631
Stehle, Richard	17 May 1848	Binsdorf	Sulz	Oct 1868	N.-Amer	849631
Stehle, Rosalie		Binsdorf	Sulz	bef 1857	N.-Amer	849630
Stehle, Rosina & F		Altheim	Horb	Feb 1849	N.-Amer	835929
Stehle, Sabina		Binsdorf	Sulz	Jun 1863	Baden	849631
Stehle, Sofie (wife)		Binsdorf	Sulz	Dec 1852	N.-Amer	849630
Stehle, Theresia	11 Oct 1847	Binsdorf	Sulz	Feb 1852	N.-Amer	849630
Stehle, Theresia		Binsdorf	Sulz	Jan 1846	Baden	849630
Stehle, Thomas	19 Dec 1813	Binsdorf	Sulz	Apr 1833	N.-Amer	849630

| Name | | Birth | | Emigration | | | Film |
Last	First	Date	Place	O'amt	Appl. Date	Dest.	Number
Stehle, Verena		25 Dec 1860	Binsdorf	Sulz	Apr 1881	N.-Amer	849631
Stehle, Wendelin		17 Jul 1852	Binsdorf	Sulz	May 1869	N.-Amer	849631
Stehle, Wilhelm		24 Mar 1852	Binsdorf	Sulz	Apr 1869	N.-Amer	849631
Steidinger, Andreas			Dornhan	Sulz	bef 1818	Switz.	849625
Steidinger, Andreas			Aistaig	Sulz	bef 1864	N.-Amer	849628
Steidinger, Andreas		1 Nov 1854	Aistaig	Sulz	bef 1892	N.-Amer	849626
Steidinger, Anna (wife)			Dornhan	Sulz	Mar 1817	Russia	849633
Steidinger, Anna Barbara		11 May 1840	Aistaig	Sulz	Oct 1851	N.-Amer	849628
Steidinger, Anna Maria		21 Sep 1836	Aistaig	Sulz	Oct 1851	N.-Amer	849628
Steidinger, Anna Maria		10 Sep 1833	Erkenbrechtsweiler	Sulz	Mar 1865	Baden	849643
Steidinger, Barbara			Aistaig	Sulz	Apr 1867	N.-Amer	849628
Steidinger, Barbara		21 Nov 1825	Sigmarswangen	Sulz	Apr 1880	N.-Amer	849642
Steidinger, Christina			Aistaig	Sulz	bef 1864	N.-Amer	849628
Steidinger, Christina & F		22 Sep 1810	Aistaig	Sulz	Oct 1851	N.-Amer	849628
Steidinger, Elisabetha		15 yrs.	Dornhan	Sulz	Mar 1817	Russia	849633
Steidinger, Johann & F			Dornhan	Sulz	Mar 1817	Russia	849633
Steidinger, Johann August			Aistaig	Sulz	bef 1864	N.-Amer	849628
Steidinger, Johann Georg			Aistaig	Sulz	bef 1828	Berlin	849628
Steidinger, Johannes			Sulz	Sulz	Apr 1815	Switz.	849625
Steidinger, Joseph		1 Oct 1802	Aistaig	Sulz	bef 1828	France	849628
Steidinger, Margaretha		19 Feb 1836	Dornhan	Sulz	Oct 1854	N.-Amer	849633
Steidinger, Mathias			Dornhan	Sulz	Feb 1848	N.-Amer	849633
Steiger, Paul Samuel			Aistaig	Sulz	Mar 1848	N.-Amer	849628
Steimle, Anna Maria			Altbulach	Calw	1866	Baden	563212
Steimle, Christine (wid.) & F			Liebelsberg	Calw	1859	N.-Amer	563212
Stein, Anna Maria		23 Mar 1833	Cresbach	Frd.	May 1835	N.-Amer	569269
Stein, Christian		7 Aug 1842	Lombach	Frd.	Jul 1861	N.-Amer	577778
Stein, Christian Friedrich		2 May 1867	Renfrizhausen	Sulz	May 1883	N.-Amer	849639
Stein, Christina (wife)			Duerrenmettstetten	Sulz	Mar 1833	N.-Amer	849635
Stein, Elisabetha Barbara		18 Jun 1844	Bergfelden	Sulz	Sep 1865	N.-Amer	849629
Stein, Friedrich		12 Jul 1844	Muehlheim a.B.	Sulz	Feb 1859	N.-Amer	849639
Stein, Gottlieb & F		29 Oct 1788	Duerrenmettstetten	Sulz	Mar 1833	N.-Amer	849635
Stein, Jacob			Renfrizhausen	Sulz	1815	Bavaria	849639
Stein, Johann Jakob		30 Jan 1850	Bergfelden	Sulz	Jul 1867	N.-Amer	849629
Stein, Johann Martin		2 Nov 1850	Bergfelden	Sulz	Sep 1865	N.-Amer	849629
Stein, Johannes			Renfrizhausen	Sulz	Sep 1853	N.-Amer	849639
Stein, Katharina (wid.) & F		10 Dec 1829	Bergfelden	Sulz	Sep 1865	N.-Amer	849629
Stein, Ludwig		13 Oct 1851	Muehlheim a.B.	Sulz	Mar 1869	N.-Amer	849639
Stein, Magdalena		25 yrs.	Cresbach	Frd.	May 1835	N.-Amer	569269
Stein, Mathaeus Bernhardt		21 Nov 1856	Bergfelden	Sulz	Sep 1865	N.-Amer	849629
Stein, Michael & F		30 yrs.	Cresbach	Frd.	May 1835	N.-Amer	569269
Steiner, Agatha (wife)			Klosterreichenbach	Frd.	Jul 1832	N.-Amer	569268
Steiner, Anna		3 Apr 1803	Graubuenden/Switz.	Frd.	Mar 1846	N.-Amer	569271
Steiner, Anna Katharina		1 May 1834	Freudenstadt	Frd.	Mar 1846	N.-Amer	569271
Steiner, Auguste		21 Oct 1839	Freudenstadt	Frd.	Mar 1846	N.-Amer	569271
Steiner, Carolina Magdalena		Feb 1837	Winnenden	Frd.	Mar 1854	N.-Amer	569273
Steiner, Christian & F		2 Feb 1804	Freudenstadt	Frd.	Mar 1846	N.-Amer	569271
Steiner, Christiane		9 Mar 1834	Freudenstadt	Frd.	Mar 1846	N.-Amer	569271
Steiner, Elisabeth		13 Jul 1828	Freudenstadt	Frd.	Mar 1846	N.-Amer	569271
Steiner, Eva Anna Maria		28 Oct 1821	Baiersbronn	Frd.	Apr 1856	N.-Amer	569275

Name	Date	Place	Region	Date2	Dest	Code
Steiner, Gottlieb		Liebenzell	Calw	1860	Hamburg	563212
Steiner, Jacob Fried.	6 Nov 1833	Winnenden	Frd.	Mar 1854	N.-Amer	569273
Steiner, Jacob Fried. & F	24 Feb 1800	Winnenden	Frd.	Mar 1854	N.-Amer	569273
Steiner, Jacobina Fried.	28 Apr 1825	Winnenden	Frd.	Mar 1854	N.-Amer	569273
Steiner, Jakob Bernhardt & F		Klosterreichenbach	Frd.	Jul 1832	N.-Amer	569268
Steiner, Johann Friedrich	21 Oct 1839	Freudenstadt	Frd.	Mar 1846	N.-Amer	569271
Steiner, Maria Louise	8 Oct 1839	Winnenden	Frd.	Mar 1854	N.-Amer	569273
Steiner, Martin & F		Klosterreichenbach	Frd.	Jul 1832	N.-Amer	569268
Steiner, Rosine Barbara		Baiersbronn	Frd.	Mar 1814	Baden	569267
Steiner, Sabina (wife)		Klosterreichenbach	Frd.	Jul 1832	N.-Amer	569268
Steiner, Wilhelmine	25 May 1844	Winnenden	Frd.	Mar 1854	N.-Amer	569273
Steinhauer, Christian Jakob	24 May 1848	Renfrizhausen	Sulz	Sep 1865	N.-Amer	849639
Steinhilber, Jacob & F		Bondorf	Herr.	Mar 1831	N.-Amer	834624
Steiniger, Mathaeus	1829	Altbulach	Calw	1854	N.-Amer	563212
Steinle, Gottlieb & F		Liebelsberg	Calw	1847	N.-Amer	563212
Steinwand, Andreas	30 Nov 1827	Dornhan	Sulz	Mar 1854	N.-Amer	849633
Steinwand, Catharina & C		Dornhan	Sulz	Jun 1817	Russia	849633
Steinwand, Johann & F		Dornhan	Sulz	May 1817	Russia	849633
Steinwand, Johann Georg		Marschalkenzimmern	Sulz	bef 1887	Switz.	849638
Steinwand, Johannes	13 Dec 1824	Dornhan	Sulz	Mar 1854	N.-Amer	849633
Steinwand, Mathias	21 Feb 1832	Dornhan	Sulz	bef 1892	Switz.	849634
Steinwandt, Jacob	4 Apr 1832	Dornhan	Sulz	Jun 1859	Switz.	849633
Steinwandt, Margaretha		Sulz	Sulz	Apr 1869	Bavaria	849628
Stelzer, Anna Maria	9 Jul 1834	Neunuifra	Frd.	bef 1863	Hesse	577778
Stelzer, Christina Margaretha		Dornstetten	Frd.	Apr 1850	N.-Amer	569271
Stelzer, Johann Jakob	21 Jan 1833	Dornstetten	Frd.	Feb 1853	N.-Amer	569272
Stelzig, Rosina		Renfrizhausen	Sulz	bef 1831	Russia	849625
Stepper, Anna Catharina (wife)	22 Dec 1800	Oeschelbronn	Herr.	Apr 1847	N.-Amer	834626
Stepper, Eva Maria	4 Dec 1840	Oeschelbronn	Herr.	Apr 1847	N.-Amer	834626
Stepper, Jacob		Oeschelbronn	Herr.	1834	N.-Amer	834625
Stepper, Johann Georg	28 Sep 1834	Oeschelbronn	Herr.	Apr 1847	N.-Amer	834626
Stepper, Johann Georg & F	9 Apr 1802	Oeschelbronn	Herr.	Apr 1847	N.-Amer	834626
Stepper, Justine Barbara	30 Dec 1831	Oeschelbronn	Herr.	Apr 1847	N.-Amer	834626
Sterzer, Johann Martin		Gueltstein	Herr.	Apr 1830	N.-Amer	834624
Steudinger, Katharina & C	1 Nov 1788	Schoenegrund	Frd.	Apr 1836	N.-Amer	569268
Stickel, Agatha	27 yrs.	Spielberg	Nag.	Jun 1854	N.-Amer	838491
Stickel, Elisabeth	infant	Spielberg	Nag.	Jun 1854	N.-Amer	838491
Stickel, Gotthilf & F	31 yrs.	Spielberg	Nag.	Jun 1854	N.-Amer	838491
Stickel, Johann Georg	1840	Neubulach	Calw	bef 1857	N.-Amer	563212
Stickel, Johannes		Egenhausen	Nag.	bef 1852	Austria	838490
Stickel, Ludwig		Calw	Calw	1869	Bavaria	563212
Stickel, Margaretha		Neubulach	Calw	1869	Bavaria	563212
Stickel, Sophia		Calw	Calw	1869	N.-Amer	563212
Stickels, Johannes		Neuweiler	Calw	1869	N.-Amer	563212
Stickle, Caroline Louise	29 Jan 1818	Freudenstadt	Frd.	bef 1861	France	577778
Stiegelmaier, Catharina M. & C	23 Feb 1832	Kuppingen	Herr.	Mar 1865	N.-Amer	834624
Stiegelmaier, Martha Maria	3 Jul 1863	Kuppingen	Herr.	Mar 1865	N.-Amer	834624
Stierle, Anna Maria		Sigmarswangen	Sulz	Nov 1853	N.-Amer	849642
Stierle, Anna Maria		Muehlheim a.B.	Sulz	Sep 1856	Baden	849639
Stierle, Katharina & C	67 yrs.	Sigmarswangen	Sulz	Nov 1853	N.-Amer	849642

| Name | | Birth | | | Emigration | | Film |
Last	First	Date	Place	O'amt	Appl. Date	Dest.	Number
Stikel, Mathaeus & F			Schopfloch	Frd.	Mar 1833	N.-Amer	569268
Stimle, Leonhardt			Altbulach	Calw	1863	Prussia	563212
Sting, Ludwig			Dornstetten	Frd.	Apr 1857	N.-Amer	577776
Sting, Michael			Balingen	Bal.	Apr 1857	Switz.	555962
Stingel, Johannes			Balingen	Bal.	Oct 1862	Switz.	555962
Stizelmeier, Heinrich Wilhelm		1839	Gechingen	Calw	1854	N.-Amer	563212
Stockburger, Christian		1827	Marschalkenzimmern	Sulz	Jan 1848	N.-Amer	849638
Stockburger, Gottlieb		18 Jun 1886	Dornhan	Sulz	Jul 1900	N.-Amer	849634
Stockburger, Johann Georg		10 Jul 1878	Dornhan	Sulz	Jul 1893	N.-Amer	849626
Stockburger, Johannes		11 Oct 1795	Marschalkenzimmern	Sulz	Mar 1836	N.-Amer	849638
Stocker, Andreas		22 Aug 1852	Bergfelden	Sulz	Oct 1872	N.-Amer	849629
Stocker, Christian		10 Aug 1857	Bergfelden	Sulz	Jul 1872	N.-Amer	849629
Stocker, Christian		7 Apr 1872	Bergfelden	Sulz	Apr 1889	N.-Amer	849626
Stocker, Elisabetha Margaretha		14 Aug 1843	Bergfelden	Sulz	bef 1866	N.-Amer	849629
Stocker, Jakob		23 Jun 1874	Bergfelden	Sulz	Jun 1888	N.-Amer	849626
Stocker, Johann Jacob		2 Jun 1849	Bergfelden	Sulz	Aug 1869	N.-Amer	849629
Stockinger, Johann Ulrich & F			Pfalzgrafenweiler	Frd.	Apr 1817	Russia	569268
Stockinger, Ulrich			Freudenstadt	Frd.	1817	Russia	569269
Stoeckel, Wilhelm		30 Nov 1837	Unterjesingen	Herr.	Nov 1863	Baden	834624
Stoeffler, Gustav Christian		7 Aug 1850	Herrenberg	Herr.	Jul 1869	N.-Amer	834624
Stoeffler, Johann Martin		22 Aug 1821	Pfalzgrafenweiler	Frd.	Jun 1857	N.-Amer	577776
Stoehr, Barbara		5 yrs.	Pfalzgrafenweiler	Frd.	Apr 1835	N.-Amer	569268
Stoehr, Christina			Pfalzgrafenweiler	Frd.	Apr 1835	N.-Amer	569268
Stoehr, Elisabetha (wife)			Gruental	Frd.	Apr 1819	N.-Amer	569268
Stoehr, Johannes		10 yrs.	Pfalzgrafenweiler	Frd.	Apr 1835	N.-Amer	569268
Stoehr, Johannes & F			Pfalzgrafenweiler	Frd.	Apr 1835	N.-Amer	569268
Stoehr, Johannes & F		5 Mar 1795	Schopfloch	Frd.	Apr 1819	N.-Amer	569268
Stoehr, Mathaeus		13 Dec 1805	Schopfloch	Frd.	Apr 1819	N.-Amer	569268
Stoelle, Johann Gottlieb & F			Kuppingen	Herr.	Jun 1833	Rus-Pol	834624
Stoerr, Friederike			Calw	Calw	1867	Bavaria	563212
Stoetzer, Catharina Val. (wife)			Sulz	Sulz	Apr 1834	N.-Amer	849627
Stoetzer, Jacob Otto		18 Apr 1868	Sulz	Sulz	Apr 1885	N.-Amer	849628
Stoetzer, Johann Christoph & F		21 Jan 1792	Sulz	Sulz	Apr 1834	N.-Amer	849627
Stoetzer, Johann Georg		19 Nov 1805	Sulz	Sulz	Feb 1837	France	849627
Stoetzer, Johann Ludwig		26 Mar 1787	Sulz	Sulz	bef 1832	Switz.	849627
Stoffler, Balthas & F			Deckenpfronn	Calw	1852	N.-Amer	563212
Stoffler, Jacob Friedrich & F			Deckenpfronn	Calw	1852	N.-Amer	563212
Stoker, Andreas			Bergfelden	Sulz	Aug 1854	N.-Amer	849629
Stoker, Barbara			Bergfelden	Sulz	1846	Austria	849625
Stoker, Christina (wid.) & F			Bergfelden	Sulz	Aug 1854	N.-Amer	849629
Stoker, Christine			Bergfelden	Sulz	Jun 1855	N.-Amer	849629
Stoker, Jacob			Bergfelden	Sulz	Jun 1855	N.-Amer	849629
Stoker, Johann Martin			Bergfelden	Sulz	Aug 1853	N.-Amer	849629
Stoker, Johannes			Bergfelden	Sulz	Feb 1851	N.-Amer	849629
Stoker, Maria Barbara			Bergfelden	Sulz	Feb 1851	N.-Amer	849629
Stoker, Rosina			Bergfelden	Sulz	Jan 1854	N.-Amer	849629
Stokinger, Carl Albert		6 Jul 1815	Pfalzgrafenweiler	Frd.	bef 1847	Baden	569270
Stokinger, Dorothea		9 yrs.	Oberjesingen	Herr.	May 1845	N.-Amer	834626
Stokinger, Friedrich Ludwig		16 Aug 1840	Oberjettingen	Herr.	Apr 1867	N.-Amer	834624
Stokinger, Jacob Friedrich		12 yrs.	Oberjesingen	Herr.	May 1845	N.-Amer	834626

Stokinger, Jacob Friedrich & F		Oberjesingen	Herr.	May 1845	N.-Amer	834626
Stokinger, Luise		Pforzheim	Herr.	May 1845	N.-Amer	834626
Stokinger, Philipp	2 yrs.	Oberjesingen	Herr.	May 1845	N.-Amer	834626
Stoll, Andreas	30 Nov 1829	Brittheim	Sulz	1853	N.-Amer	849632
Stoll, Anna	20 Jun 1833	Brittheim	Sulz	Feb 1859	N.-Amer	849632
Stoll, Anna Maria	20 Mar 1827	Dornstetten	Frd.	Oct 1856	France	569275
Stoll, Anna Maria		Voehringen	Sulz	bef 1869	N.-Amer	849643
Stoll, Anna Maria (wife)		Sigmarswangen	Sulz	Apr 1833	N.-Amer	849642
Stoll, Anna Maria (wife)		Leidringen	Sulz	Jul 1837	N.-Amer	849637
Stoll, Barbara		Trichtingen	Sulz	bef 1830	Switz.	849642
Stoll, Barbara	1 Jun 1849	Brittheim	Sulz	Nov 1868	N.-Amer	849632
Stoll, Barbara	12 Dec 1849	Dornhan	Sulz	Jul 1870	N.-Amer	849634
Stoll, Catharina		Beuren	Nag.	Jun 1852	N.-Amer	838490
Stoll, Catharina	25 Nov 1835	Brittheim	Sulz	Jan 1857	N.-Amer	849632
Stoll, Catharine Wilhelmine	25 Sep 1822	Sigmarswangen	Sulz	Apr 1833	N.-Amer	849642
Stoll, Christian		Pfalzgrafenweiler	Frd.	Jul 1832	N.-Amer	569268
Stoll, Christian		Dornstetten	Frd.	Oct 1860	N.-Amer	577777
Stoll, Christian	28 Mar 1867	Renfrizhausen	Sulz	May 1883	N.-Amer	849626
Stoll, Christina		Glatten	Frd.	Mar 1847	N.-Amer	569271
Stoll, Christine	66 yrs.	Aach	Frd.	Oct 1835	Baden	569267
Stoll, Christoph		Ludwigsburg	Sulz	bef 1815	Wien	849625
Stoll, Christoph		Calw	Calw	1853	N.-Amer	563212
Stoll, David	35 yrs.	Dornstetten	Frd.	Oct 1860	N.-Amer	577777
Stoll, Friedrich		Aach	Frd.	1817	Russia	569269
Stoll, Friedrich & F		Aach	Frd.	Sep 1817	Rus-Pol	569267
Stoll, Georg		Beuren	Nag.	Jun 1852	N.-Amer	838490
Stoll, Georg	2 Feb 1839	Brittheim	Sulz	Jan 1857	N.-Amer	849632
Stoll, Georg	9 Apr 1807	Dornhan	Sulz	bef 1848	N.-Amer	849633
Stoll, Georg Friedrich		Dornstetten	Frd.	bef 1826	Koblenz	569269
Stoll, Georg Friedrich		Dornhan	Sulz	Mar 1817	Russia	849633
Stoll, Johann		Dornhan	Sulz	Mar 1835	Baden	849633
Stoll, Johann Eberhart	10 Mar 1824	Sigmarswangen	Sulz	Apr 1833	N.-Amer	849642
Stoll, Johann Georg		Brittheim	Sulz	Oct 1863	N.-Amer	849632
Stoll, Johann Georg	21 Aug 1819	Brittheim	Sulz	1857	N.-Amer	849632
Stoll, Johann Martin	May 1832	Brittheim	Sulz	Oct 1860	N.-Amer	849632
Stoll, Johannes		Beuren	Nag.	Jun 1852	N.-Amer	838490
Stoll, Johannes	13 Aug 1780	Sigmarswangen	Sulz	Jul 1817	Russia	849642
Stoll, Johannes	5 yrs.	Brittheim	Sulz	1862	N.-Amer	849632
Stoll, Johannes & F		Voehringen	Sulz	Jun 1817	N.-Amer	849643
Stoll, Johannes (wid)		Aach	Frd.	Apr 1817	Russia	569267
Stoll, Karl & F		Leidringen	Sulz	Jul 1837	N.-Amer	849637
Stoll, Katharina	25 Nov 1835	Brittheim	Sulz	1857	N.-Amer	849632
Stoll, Magdalena	19 yrs.	Dornstetten	Frd.	Sep 1857	N.-Amer	577776
Stoll, Martin	18 Oct 1830	Sigmarswangen	Sulz	Apr 1833	N.-Amer	849642
Stoll, Martin	13 Jan 1825	Brittheim	Sulz	1857	N.-Amer	849632
Stoll, Martin & F	4 Aug 1788	Brittheim	Sulz	Apr 1833	N.-Amer	849642
Stoll, Mathias		Brittheim	Sulz	bef 1823	Hungary	849625
Stoll, Mathias	3 yrs.	Brittheim	Sulz	1862	N.-Amer	849632
Stoll, Matthias & F		Sigmarswangen	Sulz	May 1817	Russia	849642
Stoll, Michael & F		Brittheim	Sulz	1862	N.-Amer	849632

| Name | | Birth | | Emigration | | | Film |
Last	First	Date	Place	O'amt	Appl. Date	Dest.	Number
Stolle, Johannes		1837	Altburg	Calw	1857	N.-Amer	563212
Stolzer, Jakob Otto		18 Apr 1868	Sulz	Sulz	Apr 1885	N.-Amer	849626
Stortz, Andreas		11 Jan 1868	Rosenfeld	Sulz	May 1884	N.-Amer	849626
Stortz, Katharina		12 Jan 1842	Rosenfeld	Sulz	Jun 1865	N.-Amer	849641
Storz, Andreas		11 Apr 1816	Rosenfeld	Sulz	Sep 1869	Switz.	849641
Storz, Andreas		1 Aug 1850	Rosenfeld	Sulz	Jun 1869	N.-Amer	849641
Storz, Christina		26 yrs.	Holzhausen	Sulz	Mar 1864	N.-Amer	849635
Storz, Franziska (wife)			Renfrizhausen	Sulz	Aug 1890	Prussia	849626
Storz, Gottlob		1 Jul 1864	Renfrizhausen	Sulz	bef 1890	Prussia	849639
Storz, Gottlob & F			Renfrizhausen	Sulz	Aug 1890	Prussia	849626
Storz, Johann Friedrich		6 Sep 1847	Fuernsal	Sulz	Aug 1866	N.-Amer	849635
Storz, Johann Jakob		13 Feb 1857	Trichtingen	Sulz	bef 1880	Switz.	849642
Storz, Mathias		15 Jan 1870	Fuernsal	Sulz	Apr 1886	N.-Amer	849626
Stotz, Agnese (wid.) & F			Rosenfeld	Sulz	Aug 1853	N.-Amer	849640
Stotz, Anna Christine		2 yrs.	Rosenfeld	Sulz	bef 1840	Switz.	849640
Stotz, Anna Dorothea			Sulz	Sulz	Apr 1833	N.-Amer	849627
Stotz, Anna Maria		20 Apr 1842	Holzhausen	Sulz	Jul 1860	N.-Amer	849635
Stotz, Barbara			Rosenfeld	Sulz	bef 1856	N.-Amer	849640
Stotz, Barbara (wid.)			Holzhausen	Sulz	Jun 1866	Prussia	849635
Stotz, Caspar		7 Apr 1825	Rosenfeld	Sulz	Aug 1852	N.-Amer	849640
Stotz, Elisabetha		20 yrs.	Rosenfeld	Sulz	Jun 1817	Russia	849640
Stotz, Elisabetha		2 Feb 1848	Rosenfeld	Sulz	Apr 1864	Austria	849641
Stotz, Elisabetha (wife)			Sulz	Sulz	Apr 1834	N.-Amer	849627
Stotz, Friedrich		30 Sep 1850	Dornhan	Sulz	Jul 1872	N.-Amer	849634
Stotz, Friedrich Christoph & F		29 Jan 1787	Sulz	Sulz	Apr 1834	N.-Amer	849627
Stotz, Gottlib Christoph & F		8 Aug 1783	Sulz	Sulz	Apr 1833	N.-Amer	849627
Stotz, Heinrich			Rosenfeld	Sulz	bef 1856	N.-Amer	849640
Stotz, Hermann		23 Apr 1831	Rosenfeld	Sulz	Jul 1856	Switz.	849640
Stotz, Hermann Friedrich		6 Apr 1832	Rosenfeld	Sulz	Aug 1880	Austria	849626
Stotz, Jacob Friedrich		5 May 1815	Sulz	Sulz	Apr 1834	N.-Amer	849627
Stotz, Jakob		18 Jun 1845	Dornhan	Sulz	Jun 1892	Switz.	849626
Stotz, Johann Friedrich		5 Jan 1826	Sulz	Sulz	Apr 1834	N.-Amer	849627
Stotz, Johann Peter		6 Jul 1831	Rosenfeld	Sulz	1861	Switz.	849641
Stotz, Johannes Georg		15 yrs.	Rosenfeld	Sulz	Aug 1853	N.-Amer	849640
Stotz, Karl Friedrich		6 Nov 1833	Rosenfeld	Sulz	bef 1865	Baden	849641
Stotz, Karl Michael		16 Mar 1866	Sulz	Sulz	Jan 1883	N.-Amer	849626
Stotz, Maria Catharina		29 Apr 1830	Sulz	Sulz	Apr 1834	N.-Amer	849627
Stotz, Maria Karoline		30 Jan 1838	Rosenfeld	Sulz	bef 1865	Paris	849641
Stotz, Martin			Rosenfeld	Sulz	Feb 1857	Baden	849640
Stotz, Pauline Caroline			Calw	Calw	Mar 1870	Merzig	563212
Stotz, Philipp Heinrich		24 Jul 1835	Sulz	Sulz	Oct 1854	N.-Amer	849627
Stotz, Sibylla Elisabetha		4 Jan 1828	Sulz	Sulz	Apr 1834	N.-Amer	849627
Stoz, Conrad			Rosenfeld	Sulz	Aug 1852	N.-Amer	849640
Stoz, Jacob		2 May 1836	Rosenfeld	Sulz	Apr 1854	N.-Amer	849640
Straehler, Michael		28 Jul 1807	Cresbach	Frd.	Jul 1832	N.-Amer	569268
Straub, Anna (wife)			Aistaig	Sulz	1817	N.-Amer	849628
Straub, Anna Barbara			Aistaig	Sulz	1817	N.-Amer	849628
Straub, Johanna		32 yrs.	Altheim	Horb	1853	N.-Amer	835929
Straub, Johannes		30 yrs.	Altheim	Horb	1853	N.-Amer	835929
Straub, Johannes & F			Aistaig	Sulz	1817	N.-Amer	849628

Name	Date	Place	Region	Date2	Dest	Number
Straub, Martin		Wittlensweiler	Frd.	Apr 1752	Pen.N-A	550803
Straub, Michael & F	28 Sep 1813	Altheim	Horb	1853	N. Amer	835929
Straub, Rosina	11 yrs.	Altheim	Horb	1853	N.-Amer	835929
Strehler, Johann Georg	21 yrs.	Neuweiler	Calw	1869	N.-Amer	563212
Strehler, Philipp	1835	Neuweiler	Calw	1855	N.-Amer	563212
Strienz, Johann Wilhelm	29 Apr 1824	Wildberg	Nag.	Nov 1860	Hesse	838493
Strobel, Andreas	7 Mar 1835	Bickelsberg	Sulz	May 1855	N.-Amer	849630
Strobel, Anna Katharina		Leidringen	Sulz	Jul 1871	N.-Amer	849637
Strobel, Anna Maria	16 Jun 1835	Brittheim	Sulz	Feb 1854	N.-Amer	849632
Strobel, Anna Maria		Leidringen	Sulz	Jul 1871	N.-Amer	849637
Strobel, Anna Maria & C	37 yrs.	Dornstetten	Frd.	Oct 1854	N.-Amer	569274
Strobel, Barbara		Liebenzell	Calw	1867	Austria	563212
Strobel, Catharina	8 Mar 1837	Brittheim	Sulz	Feb 1859	N.-Amer	849632
Strobel, Catharina Barbara	10 Feb 1805	Gueltstein	Herr.	Mar 1849	N.-Amer	834627
Strobel, Christian & F		Roetenbach	Calw	1854	N.-Amer	563212
Strobel, Christina	30 Dec 1843	Brittheim	Sulz	Feb 1866	N.-Amer	849632
Strobel, Elisabetha & C	15 Mar 1832	Muehlheim a.B.	Sulz	Aug 1860	Prussia	849639
Strobel, Elisabetha Barbara	30 Yrs.	Renfrizhausen	Sulz	Mar 1854	N.-Amer	849639
Strobel, Gotthilf Friedrich	4 May 1848	Muehlheim a.B.	Sulz	Sep 1867	N.-Amer	849639
Strobel, Gottlieb	22 Mar 1847	Voehringen	Sulz	Jun 1867	N.-Amer	849643
Strobel, Gottlob	28 Oct 1834	Muehlheim a.B.	Sulz	Jan 1854	N.-Amer	849639
Strobel, Jakob	14 Aug 1817	Leidringen	Sulz	Mar 1833	N.-Amer	849637
Strobel, Jakob		Leidringen	Sulz	Jul 1871	N.-Amer	849637
Strobel, Jakob Friedrich	43 yrs.	Dornstetten	Frd.	Oct 1854	N.-Amer	569274
Strobel, Johann Georg		Brittheim	Sulz	Apr 1859	N.-Amer	849632
Strobel, Johann Georg	14 Oct 1850	Leidringen	Sulz	Mar 1869	N.-Amer	849637
Strobel, Johann Jacob		Leidringen	Sulz	bef 1847	S.-Russ	849637
Strobel, Johann Jacob		Leidringen	Sulz	1817	Rus-Pol	849637
Strobel, Johann Martin & F		Sigmarswangen	Sulz	May 1817	N.-Amer	849642
Strobel, Johannes	7 Jul 1813	Leidringen	Sulz	bef 1844	N.-Amer	849637
Strobel, Joseph	47 yrs.	Dornstetten	Frd.	Oct 1854	N.-Amer	569274
Strobel, Ludwig Friedrich	11 Jan 1836	Muehlheim a.B.	Sulz	Jun 1854	N.-Amer	849639
Strobel, Martin	24 Sep 1784	Leidringen	Sulz	1801	Poland	849625
Strobel, Martin		Frommern	Bal.	1844	Switz.	555963
Strobel, Michael	1832	Neuweiler	Calw	1854	N.-Amer	563212
Strobel, Rosina	2 yrs.	Dornstetten	Frd.	Oct 1854	N.-Amer	569274
Strobel, Wilhelm		Muehlheim a.B.	Sulz	Jul 1854	N.-Amer	849639
Strohfricker, Christiane Hein.	2 Mar 1834	Herrenberg	Herr.	Aug 1849	N.-Amer	834627
Strohl, Christina	14 Sep 1825	Messstetten	Bal.	Apr 1844	Baden	555962
Stroz, Christian	22 Aug 1851	Holzhausen	Sulz	May 1872	N.-Amer	849635
Stucke, Christian Friedrich	16 Oct 1849	Herrenberg	Herr.	Sep 1868	N.-Amer	834624
Stufft, Johann David	20 Dec 1847	Freudenstadt	Frd.	Jun 1866	N.-Amer	577780
Stuft, Caroline	18 May 1853	Freudenstadt	Frd.	Sep 1854	N.-Amer	569274
Stuft, Caroline Catharina	9 Sep 1840	Freudenstadt	Frd.	Sep 1854	N.-Amer	569274
Stuft, Catharina	20 Oct 1809	Freudenstadt	Frd.	Mar 1843	Hesse	569269
Stuft, Catharina Elisabetha	30 Sep 1837	Freudenstadt	Frd.	Sep 1854	N.-Amer	569274
Stuft, Catharine Marie	1 Aug 1842	Freudenstadt	Frd.	Sep 1854	N.-Amer	569274
Stuft, Christian Jakob	20 Dec 1852	Freudenstadt	Frd.	Sep 1854	N.-Amer	569274
Stuft, Christiane Rosine	26 Aug 1846	Freudenstadt	Frd.	Sep 1854	N.-Amer	569274
Stuft, Christiane Sofie	13 Jul 1853	Freudenstadt	Frd.	Sep 1854	N.-Amer	569274

Name		Birth		Emigration			Film
Last	First	Date	Place	O'amt	Appl. Date	Dest.	Number
Stuft, Christine & C		21 Jan 1824	Freudenstadt	Frd.	Sep 1854	N.-Amer	569274
Stuft, Johannes & F			Freudenstadt	Frd.	Sep 1854	N.-Amer	569274
Stuft, Marie & C		31 Dec 1828	Freudenstadt	Frd.	Sep 1854	N.-Amer	569274
Stuft, Marie Christiane (wife)			Freudenstadt	Frd.	Sep 1854	N.-Amer	569274
Stuft, Marie Friederika		30 Mar 1849	Freudenstadt	Frd.	Sep 1854	N.-Amer	569274
Stum, --			Bron/Swit	– –	1752	Pen.N-A	550803
Sturm, Andreas		4 yrs.	Hopfau	Sulz	Mar 1847	N.-Amer	849636
Sturm, Anna			Aistaig	Sulz	Jul 1843	Hesse	849628
Sturm, Anna (wife)			Hopfau	Sulz	Mar 1847	N.-Amer	849636
Sturm, Anna Maria		52 yrs.	Cresbach	Frd.	Aug 1832	N.-Amer	569269
Sturm, Anna Maria		14 yrs.	Hopfau	Sulz	Mar 1847	N.-Amer	849636
Sturm, Barbara		13 yrs.	Boeffingen	Frd.	Jan 1853	N.-Amer	569272
Sturm, Christian		15 Feb 1865	Sterneck	Sulz	May 1882	N.-Amer	849626
Sturm, Dorothea		18 yrs.	Boeffingen	Frd.	Jan 1853	N.-Amer	569272
Sturm, Eva		9 yrs.	Boeffingen	Frd.	Jan 1853	N.-Amer	569272
Sturm, Eva		6 yrs.	Hopfau	Sulz	Mar 1847	N.-Amer	849636
Sturm, Friederich & F			Hopfau	Sulz	Mar 1847	N.-Amer	849636
Sturm, Georg		8 yrs.	Boeffingen	Frd.	Jan 1853	N.-Amer	569272
Sturm, Johannes		16 yrs.	Boeffingen	Frd.	Jan 1853	N.-Amer	569272
Sturm, Johannes		17 Dec 1829	Hopfau	Sulz	Feb 1854	N.-Amer	849636
Sturm, Johannes		9 yrs.	Hopfau	Sulz	Mar 1847	N.-Amer	849636
Sturm, Johannes & F			Boeffingen	Frd.	Jan 1853	N.-Amer	569272
Sturm, Louise Margarethe		26 Mar 1813	Sulz	Sulz	Oct 1834	France	849627
Sturm, Maria		6 yrs.	Boeffingen	Frd.	Jan 1853	N.-Amer	569272
Sturm, Maria Pauline			Aistaig	Sulz	Sep 1846	N.-Amer	849628
Sturm, Mathaeus		11 yrs.	Hopfau	Sulz	Mar 1847	N.-Amer	849636
Sturm, Sophie Dorothea		16 May 1848	Sulz	Sulz	Jun 1869	Augsb.	849628
Stutz, August Robert			Altbulach	Calw	1853	N.-Amer	563212
Suelzle, Agatha			Voehringen	Sulz	Apr 1833	N.-Amer	849643
Suelzle, Anna Maria			Voehringen	Sulz	Apr 1833	N.-Amer	849643
Suelzle, Anna Maria (wife)			Voehringen	Sulz	Apr 1833	N.-Amer	849643
Suelzle, Christina			Voehringen	Sulz	Apr 1833	N.-Amer	849643
Suelzle, Christina		27 Mar 1826	Trichtingen	Sulz	1853	N.-Amer	849642
Suelzle, Elisabetha (wife)			Rosenfeld	Sulz	Mar 1836	N.-Amer	849640
Suelzle, Eva			Voehringen	Sulz	Apr 1833	N.-Amer	849643
Suelzle, Jacob			Busenweiler	Sulz	bef 1818	Hungary	849625
Suelzle, Jakob Friedrich		26 Jul 1842	Rosenfeld	Sulz	Sep 1859	N.-Amer	849640
Suelzle, Johann Georg			Voehringen	Sulz	Apr 1833	N.-Amer	849643
Suelzle, Johann Georg & F			Voehringen	Sulz	Apr 1833	N.-Amer	849643
Suelzle, Johann Georg & F		25 Aug 1793	Rosenfeld	Sulz	Mar 1836	N.-Amer	849640
Suelzle, Johannes			Nebringen	Herr.	Apr 1836	N.-Amer	834624
Suelzle, Johannes			Voehringen	Sulz	Apr 1833	N.-Amer	849643
Suelzle, Johannes		13 Jan 1876	Bickelsberg	Sulz	Sep 1893	N.-Amer	849626
Suepple, Anna Maria		22 Oct 1813	Waldhausen	Schd.	May 1844	N.-Amer	801461
Suepple, Catharina		10 Feb 1840	Waldhausen	Schd.	May 1844	N.-Amer	801461
Suepple, Gottlieb		26 Oct 1836	Waldhausen	Schd.	May 1844	N.-Amer	801461
Suepple, Johannes		8 Jun 1842	Waldhausen	Schd.	May 1844	N.-Amer	801461
Suepple, Johannes & F		29 Apr 1806	Alfdorf	Schd.	May 1844	N.-Amer	801461
Suesser, Balthas & F			Deckenpfronn	Calw	1852	N.-Amer	563212
Suesser, Christina Cath. (wife)			Oberjettingen	Herr.	Jun 1832	N.-Amer	834624

Suesser, Jacob Adam		Deckenpfronn	Calw	1849	N.-Amer 563212
Suesser, Jacob Leonhart		Deckenpfronn	Calw	Sep 1847	N.-Amer 563212
Suesser, Johann Baltas		Calw	Calw	1853	N.-Amer 563212
Suesser, Johann Georg		Deckenpfronn	Calw	1852	N.-Amer 563212
Suesser, Johann Georg		Deckenpfronn	Calw	Jul 1848	Switz. 563212
Suesser, Johannes & W		Oberjettingen	Herr.	Jun 1832	N.-Amer 834624
Suessle, Christian	18 Jul 1836	Sulz	Sulz	Mar 1854	N.-Amer 849627
Suessle, Johannes	7 Dec 1830	Brittheim	Sulz	1853	N.-Amer 849632
Suessle, Johannes		Deckenpfronn	Calw	1852	N.-Amer 563212
Suessler, Sebastian		Voehringen	Sulz	Mar 1812	Nimweg. 849625
Sulzle, Johann Georg	5 Jun 1845	Trichtingen	Sulz	Oct 1866	N.-Amer 849642
Supper, Anna Maria (wife)	28 yrs.	Nufringen	Herr.	May 1832	N.-Amer 834624
Supper, Christiana	10 Dec 1816	Nufringen	Herr.	Apr 1839	N.-Amer 834625
Supper, Christina	8 May 1788	Nufringen	Herr.	Apr 1838	N.-Amer 834625
Supper, Georg Heinrich		Herrenberg	Herr.	Apr 1838	N.-Amer 834625
Supper, Jacob		Herrenberg	Herr.	May 1830	N.-Amer 834624
Supper, Jacob & W	72 yrs.	Nufringen	Herr.	May 1832	N.-Amer 834624
Supper, Johann Miachael		Nufringen	Herr.	Jan 1831	Switz. 834624
Supper, Johannes		Kuppingen	Herr.	Nov 1826	France 834624
Tade, Mathias & F		Rosenfeld	Sulz	bef 1830	Russia 849625
Tafel, Christian Ferdinand	10 Oct 1834	Nagold	Nag.	Jan 1854	N.-Amer 838491
Tafel, Elisabeth		Sulz	Sulz	May 1817	N.-Amer 849627
Tafel, Gustav Rudolph		Sulz	Sulz	bef 1850	N.-Amer 849627
Tafel, Hugo		Sulz	Sulz	bef 1850	N.-Amer 849627
Tafel, Johann Christoph	13 Jun 1838	Rosenfeld	Sulz	Jul 1867	N.-Amer 849641
Tafel, Rudolf		Sulz	Sulz	bef 1853	N.-Amer 849627
Tag, Christiana		Sulz	Sulz	Apr 1833	N.-Amer 849627
Tag, Heinrich Christian	30 Nov 1847	Sulz	Sulz	Dec 1867	N.-Amer 849628
Talmon, Katharina Barbara		Neuhengstett	Calw	1866	Baden 563212
Talmon, Magdalena		Neuhengstett	Calw	1862	N.-Amer 563212
Talmon, Magdalena		Neuhengstett	Calw	1854	N.-Amer 563212
Talmon/Martinch, Eva Rosina		Neuhengstett	Calw	1858	Hesse 563212
Talmongros, Louise		Neuhengstett	Calw	1860	N.-Amer 563212
Teufel, Anna Maria	28 Nov 1840	Moetzingen	Herr.	Mar 1847	N.-Amer 834626
Teufel, Anton	28 Jun 1831	Tailfingen	Herr.	Aug 1852	N.-Amer 834627
Teufel, Barbara (wife)		Tailfingen	Herr.	Aug 1852	N.-Amer 834627
Teufel, Catharina	11 May 1844	Moetzingen	Herr.	Mar 1847	N.-Amer 834626
Teufel, Catharina & C		Schietingen	Nag.	Apr 1854	N.-Amer 838491
Teufel, Catharina Christine		Steinenberg	Schd.	Apr 1842	N.-Amer 801461
Teufel, Christian	10 May 1840	Tailfingen	Herr.	Aug 1852	N.-Amer 834627
Teufel, Christian & F		Moetzingen	Herr.	Oct 1830	N.-Amer 834624
Teufel, Christiana	25 Jul 1848	Moetzingen	Herr.	May 1852	N.-Amer 834627
Teufel, Christiane Magdalena	22 Feb 1847	Moetzingen	Herr.	May 1852	N.-Amer 834627
Teufel, Christoph (wid.) & F	21 Jan 1809	Moetzingen	Herr.	May 1852	N.-Amer 834627
Teufel, Dorothea	28 May 1838	Tailfingen	Herr.	Aug 1852	N.-Amer 834627
Teufel, Elisabetha	28 Mar 1851	Moetzingen	Herr.	May 1852	N.-Amer 834627
Teufel, Eva Barbara	8 Apr 1830	Tailfingen	Herr.	Aug 1852	N.-Amer 834627
Teufel, Jacob		Moetzingen	Herr.	Jul 1827	France 834624
Teufel, Jacob		Moetzingen	Herr.	Sep 1827	France 834624
Teufel, Jacob Friedrich		Moetzingen	Herr.	Oct 1830	N.-Amer 834624

Name		Birth		Emigration			Film
Last	First	Date	Place	O'amt	Appl. Date	Dest.	Number
Teufel, Jakob Friedrich		24 Aug 1845	Moetzingen	Herr.	May 1852	N.-Amer	834627
Teufel, Johann & F			Unterwaldach	Frd.	1817	Russia	569269
Teufel, Johann Adam		8 Apr 1834	Durrweiler	Frd.	Apr 1853	N.-Amer	569272
Teufel, Johann Friedrich & F			Bondorf	Herr.	Sep 1847	N.-Amer	834626
Teufel, Johann Georg		31 Mar 1847	Bondorf	Herr.	Dec 1866	N.-Amer	834624
Teufel, Johann Georg		21 Dec 1825	Unterjettingen	Herr.	Mar 1849	N.-Amer	834627
Teufel, Johann Georg		50 yrs.	Moetzingen	Herr.	Jan 1831	Baden	834624
Teufel, Johann Jacob & F			Tailfingen	Herr.	Aug 1852	N.-Amer	834627
Teufel, Johann Martin		23 Mar 1843	Tailfingen	Herr.	Aug 1852	N.-Amer	834627
Teufel, Johann Michael		13 Aug 1848	Tailfingen	Herr.	Aug 1852	N.-Amer	834627
Teufel, Katharina & C		22 Apr 1819	Moetzingen	Herr.	May 1852	N.-Amer	834627
Teufel, Maria		11 May 1836	Moetzingen	Herr.	May 1852	N.-Amer	834627
Teufel, Maria Catharina (wife)			Moetzingen	Herr.	Oct 1830	N.-Amer	834624
Teufel, Maria Elisabeth		3 Apr 1834	Tailfingen	Herr.	Aug 1852	N.-Amer	834627
Teufel, Maria Katharina		22 Apr 1840	Moetzingen	Herr.	May 1852	N.-Amer	834627
Teufel, Michael & F		16 Jun 1794	Moetzingen	Herr.	Oct 1847	N.-Amer	834626
Teufel, Philippine Luise & C		23 May 1811	Moetzingen	Herr.	Mar 1847	N.-Amer	834626
Teufel, Rosina		7 yrs.	Schietingen	Nag.	Apr 1854	N.-Amer	838491
Teufel, Rosina Margaretha		30 Oct 1846	Moetzingen	Herr.	Mar 1847	N.-Amer	834626
Teufel, Simon		3 Dec 1831	Unterjettingen	Herr.	Oct 1847	N.-Amer	834626
Teufel, Wilhelm			Moetzingen	Herr.	Feb 1847	N.-Amer	834626
Teufel, Wilhelmine		15 Mar 1838	Moetzingen	Herr.	May 1852	N.-Amer	834627
Thender, Theodor		26 Sep 1829	Unterjesingen	Herr.	May 1866	N.-Amer	834624
Theurer, Anna		15 yrs.	Altenstaig	Nag.	Jul 1852	N.-Amer	838490
Theurer, Anna Maria		3 yrs.	Altenstaig	Nag.	Jul 1852	N.-Amer	838490
Theurer, Anna Maria		1 Sep 1840	Entringen	Herr.	Jun 1867	Switz.	834624
Theurer, Ernst Wilhelm		28 Nov 1849	Unterjesingen	Herr.	May 1852	N.-Amer	834627
Theurer, Friedrike		13 yrs.	Altenstaig	Nag.	Jul 1852	N.-Amer	838490
Theurer, Friedrike		12 Dec 1834	Entringen	Herr.	Feb 1867	Hesse	834624
Theurer, Imanuel David & F			Unterjesingen	Herr.	May 1852	N.-Amer	834627
Theurer, Johann Georg		14 Oct 1850	Eisenbach	Frd.	bef 1864	N.-Amer	577779
Theurer, Johann Gottf. Peter			Unterwaldach	Frd.	1816	Baden	569269
Theurer, Johann Jacob		11 Jan 1845	Moenchberg	Herr.	Aug 1865	N.-Amer	834624
Theurer, Johann Michael & F			Altenstaig	Nag.	Jul 1852	N.-Amer	838490
Theurer, Margaretha		17 yrs.	Altenstaig	Nag.	Jul 1852	N.-Amer	838490
Theurer, Maria Dorothea		31 Dec 1831	Unterjesingen	Herr.	May 1852	N.-Amer	834627
Theurer, Maria Katharina (wife)			Unterjesingen	Herr.	May 1852	N.-Amer	834627
Theurer, Martin		29 yrs.	Altenstaig	Nag.	Jul 1852	N.-Amer	838490
Theurer, Michael		18 yrs.	Altenstaig	Nag.	Jul 1852	N.-Amer	838490
Theurer, Philipp		31 Jul 1831	Unterjesingen	Herr.	Aug 1850	N.-Amer	834627
Theurer, Rosina			Neunuifra	Frd.	bef 1862	N.-Amer	577778
Theurer, Sabina Barbara		30 Jun 1835	Unterjesingen	Herr.	May 1862	N.-Amer	834624
Theurer, Wilhelmine		6 yrs.	Altenstaig	Nag.	Jul 1852	N.-Amer	838490
Thies, Johann Ludwig			Rheinhardt-Muenster	– –	Dec 1751	N.-Amer	550803
Toepfer, Georg			Wittlensweiler	Frd.	1817	Russia	569269
Traeger, Anna Maria		30 Jun 1836	Wittendorf	Frd.	Sep 1854	N.-Amer	569274
Traeger, Anna Maria		16 Nov 1803	Fuernsal	Sulz	Apr 1847	N.-Amer	849635
Traeger, Anna Maria		5 Jan 1830	Fuernsal	Sulz	Apr 1847	N.-Amer	849635
Traeger, Barbara		3 Mar 1837	Fuernsal	Sulz	Apr 1847	N.-Amer	849635
Traeger, Catharine		18 yrs.	Pfalzgrafenweiler	Frd.	Jul 1832	N.-Amer	569268

Traeger, Christina	1 Dec 1832	Fuernsal	Sulz	Apr 1847	N.-Amer	849635
Traeger, Elisabetha Dor. & F		Pfalzgrafenweiler	Frd.	Apr 1835	N.-Amer	569268
Traeger, Georg & F	9 Oct 1802	Fuernsal	Sulz	Apr 1847	N.-Amer	849635
Traeger, Jakob & F		Pfalzgrafenweiler	Frd.	Jul 1832	N.-Amer	569268
Traeger, Johann	19 Oct 1841	Fuernsal	Sulz	Apr 1847	N.-Amer	849635
Traeger, Johann Georg	10 Sep 1839	Fuernsal	Sulz	Apr 1847	N.-Amer	849635
Traeger, Katharina	29 Nov 1829	Wittendorf	Frd.	Nov 1853	N.-Amer	569272
Traeger, Katharina	24 Dec 1826	Fuernsal	Sulz	Apr 1847	N.-Amer	849635
Traeger, Maria	17 Aug 1833	Sterneck	Sulz	Mar 1883	N.-Amer	849642
Traub, Adam	37 yrs.	Rosenfeld	Sulz	Jun 1851	N.-Amer	849640
Traub, Andreas		Rosenfeld	Sulz	Dec 1845	France	849640
Traub, Christiana Elisacetha	5 May 1863	Rosenfeld	Sulz	Jul 1863	N.-Amer	849641
Traub, Conrad Friedrich	13 Jan 1842	Rosenfeld	Sulz	Feb 1864	N.-Amer	849641
Traub, Jacob		Rosenfeld	Sulz	Dec 1852	N.-Amer	849640
Traub, Johann Friedrich	3 Oct 1850	Rosenfeld	Sulz	bef 1894	Switz.	849641
Traub, Johann Jacob		Rosenfeld	Sulz	Mar 1816	Switz.	849625
Traub, Johann Martin	6 Mar 1859	Rosenfeld	Sulz	Jul 1863	N.-Amer	849641
Traub, Johann Wilhelm	25 Dec 1844	Rosenfeld	Sulz	Feb 1864	N.-Amer	849641
Traub, Maria Katharina & F	20 Aug 1825	Rosenfeld	Sulz	Jul 1863	N.-Amer	849641
Traub, Rosina	25 yrs.	Rosenfeld	Sulz	Jun 1851	N.-Amer	849640
Treffs, Amalie Rosine Charl.	8 Feb 1857	Pfalzgrafenweiler	Frd.	Aug 1860	N.-Amer	577777
Treffs, Ernestine Adelheid	30 May 1826	Pfalzgrafenweiler	Frd.	Aug 1860	N.-Amer	577777
Treffs, Friedrich Theodor	6 Aug 1850	Pfalzgrafenweiler	Frd.	Aug 1860	N.-Amer	577777
Treffs, Luise Dorothea	8 Dec 1854	Pfalzgrafenweiler	Frd.	Aug 1860	N.-Amer	577777
Treffs, Mathilde Wilhel. Chr.	20 Sep 1852	Pfalzgrafenweiler	Frd.	Aug 1860	N.-Amer	577777
Treffs, Philipp Friedr.Theod.	13 Jan 1824	Ludwigsburg	Frd.	Aug 1860	N.-Amer	577777
Tressel, Johannes		Leinstetten	Sulz	Mar 1816	Austria	849638
Treudel, Anna Maria & C		Liebenzell	Calw	1867	N.-Amer	563212
Treudel, Christian Gottfried	7 yrs.	Liebenzell	Calw	1867	N.-Amer	563212
Trick, Theresia	29 May 1823	Bettenhausen	Sulz	Apr 1857	N.-Amer	849630
Trik, Anna Maria	7 Jun 1838	Muehlheim a.B.	Sulz	Jun 1865	N.-Amer	849639
Trik, Christine & F	25 Apr 1828	Sulz	Sulz	Sep 1876	N.-Amer	849628
Trik, Maria Charlotte	28 Feb 1864	Sulz	Sulz	Sep 1876	N.-Amer	849628
Trik, Pauline	12 Nov 1839	Mindersbach	Nag.	Jun 1862	England	838493
Tritschler, Barbara		Bergfelden	Sulz	Apr 1833	N.-Amer	849629
Trogler, Carolina Friederika	7 Apr 1809	Schorndorf	Schd.	Oct 1837	Hesse	801461
Trost, Konrad	37 yrs.	Simmozheim	Calw	1857	N.-Amer	563212
Trost, Zacharias	24 May 1839	Freudenstadt	Frd.	Sep 1866	N.-Amer	577780
Trueck, Agnes	16 Mar 1792	Leinstetten	Sulz	Jun 1817	N.-Amer	849638
Trueck, Anna (wife)		Freudenstadt	Frd.	Sep 1854	N.-Amer	569274
Trueck, Anna Maria & C	28 Jun 1819	Glatten	Frd.	Oct 1854	S.-Amer	569274
Trueck, Auguste Justine		Kniebis	Frd.	Nov 1809	Baden	569267
Trueck, Barbara	18 Nov 1853	Glatten	Frd.	Oct 1854	S.-Amer	569274
Trueck, Barbara	13 Jun 1788	Leinstetten	Sulz	Jun 1817	N.-Amer	849638
Trueck, Christian		Lombach	Frd.	Sep 1853	N.-Amer	569272
Trueck, Christian	21 Apr 1876	Hopfau	Sulz	May 1891	N.-Amer	849626
Trueck, Christian Friedrich	8 Jul 1838	Freudenstadt	Frd.	Sep 1854	N.-Amer	569274
Trueck, Christiane Johanne	17 Jul 1832	Freudenstadt	Frd.	Sep 1854	N.-Amer	569274
Trueck, Christine Johanne		Freudenstadt	Frd.	Jan 1855	N.-Amer	569275
Trueck, Christoph Friedr. & F		Freudenstadt	Frd.	Sep 1854	N.-Amer	569274

Name		Birth		Emigration			Film
Last	First	Date	Place	O'amt	Appl. Date	Dest.	Number
Trueck, Franziska		13 Nov 1809	Leinstetten	Sulz	Jun 1817	N.-Amer	849638
Trueck, Gottlieb		6 Mar 1846	Glatten	Frd.	Oct 1854	S.-Amer	569274
Trueck, Jakob			Lombach	Frd.	Apr 1856	N.-Amer	569275
Trueck, Johann		9 Apr 1842	Freudenstadt	Frd.	Sep 1854	N.-Amer	569274
Trueck, Johann Georg		20 Apr 1875	Hopfau	Sulz	May 1891	N.-Amer	849626
Trueck, Johannes			Lombach	Frd.	Apr 1856	N.-Amer	569275
Trueck, Johannes		21 Sep 1846	Freudenstadt	Frd.	Oct 1866	N.-Amer	577780
Trueck, Joseph Daniel		14 Apr 1780	Kniebis	Frd.	bef 1810	Paris	569267
Trueck, Kaspar (wid.) & F		6 Jan 1756	Bettenhausen	Sulz	Jun 1817	N.-Amer	849638
Trueck, Katharina		18 Oct 1798	Leinstetten	Sulz	Jun 1817	N.-Amer	849638
Trueck, Margaretha		3 May 1843	Glatten	Frd.	Oct 1854	S.-Amer	569274
Trueck, Maria Barbara		24 Apr 1828	Freudenstadt	Frd.	bef 1864	Switz.	577779
Trueck, Zaecilia (wife)		3 Aug 1765	Leinstetten	Sulz	Jun 1817	N.-Amer	849638
Truek, Anna Maria (wid) & F		11 Sep 1810	Dornstetten	Frd.	Apr 1854	N.-Amer	569273
Truek, Christian		29 Jan 1832	Dornstetten	Frd.	bef 1854	N.-Amer	569273
Truek, Christiane Katharine		23 Nov 1834	Dornstetten	Frd.	bef 1854	N.-Amer	569273
Truek, Jakob		18 Oct 1839	Dornstetten	Frd.	Apr 1854	N.-Amer	569273
Truek, Katharina Barbara		14 Jul 1838	Dornstetten	Frd.	Apr 1854	N.-Amer	569273
Trum, Elisabetha			Oberwaldach	Frd.	Feb 1847	N.-Amer	569271
Trum, Eva (wid.) & F			Oberwaldach	Frd.	Feb 1847	N.-Amer	569271
Tuerck, Christian		29 Jan 1832	Dornstetten	Frd.	Apr 1853	N.-Amer	569272
Tuerck, Christiane Katharina		23 Nov 1834	Dornstetten	Frd.	Apr 1853	N.-Amer	569272
Uber, Dorothea Magdalena			Freudenstadt	Frd.	Sep 1854	N.-Amer	569274
Ueber, Johann David		7 yrs.	Freudenstadt	Frd.	May 1752	Pen.N-A	550803
Ueber, Johann Ludwig		3 yrs.	Freudenstadt	Frd.	May 1752	Pen.N-A	550803
Ueber, Johann Ludwig & F		30 yrs.	Freudenstadt	Frd.	May 1752	Pen.N-A	550803
Ueber, Margaretha Barbara		30 yrs.	Freudenstadt	Frd.	May 1752	Pen.N-A	550803
Uetz, Johann Christian		23 Dec 1815	Winterbach	Schd.	Feb 1836	N.-Amer	801460
Uhlmann, Catharina			Neubulach	Calw	1861	Bohemia	563212
Ullrich, Johannes		19 yrs.	Calw	Calw	1854	N.-Amer	563212
Ulrich, Amalie		3 Jan 1841	Freudenstadt	Frd.	Apr 1864	Bavaria	577779
Ulrich, Franz Fr. Ferd. & F			Christophstal	Frd.	Mar 1854	N.-Amer	569273
Ulrich, Friedrich Karl		25 Oct 1844	Christophstal	Frd.	Mar 1854	N.-Amer	569273
Ulrich, Juliane (wife)			Christophstal	Frd.	Mar 1854	N.-Amer	569273
Ulrich, Mathilde		1 Apr 1849	Christophstal	Frd.	Mar 1854	N.-Amer	569273
Ulrich, Pauline Dorothea		22 Sep 1847	Christophstal	Frd.	Mar 1854	N.-Amer	569273
Ulrich, Wilhelm		18 Nov 1851	Christophstal	Frd.	Mar 1854	N.-Amer	569273
Ulrich, Wilhelm Fried. Alb.		22 Feb 1838	Stuttgart	Frd.	Mar 1854	N.-Amer	569273
Umbrecht, Maximillian			Ahldorf	Horb	Nov 1833	Baden	835928
Umhofer, Christian		4 yrs.	Freudenstadt	Frd.	Jul 1854	N.-Amer	569274
Umhofer, Karolie Barbara		25 Mar 1850	Freudenstadt	Frd.	Aug 1866	N.-Amer	577780
Umhofer, Wilhelmine & C			Freudenstadt	Frd.	Jul 1854	N.-Amer	569274
Unfried, Johann Georg		2 Nov 1819	Herrenberg	Herr.	Jul 1846	N.-Amer	834626
Ungemach, Eva Catharina		23 yrs.	Neuweiler	Calw	Apr 1847	N.-Amer	563212
Ungemach, Johann Martina		15 Sep 1832	Neuweiler	Calw	1854	N.-Amer	563212
Ungerer, Albert Heinrich		29 Nov 1830	Sulz	Sulz	May 1856	Baden	849627
Unkel, Christian Eduard		2 Aug 1849	Herrenberg	Herr.	Apr 1866	N.-Amer	834624
Unmuth, Margaretha Barbara			Zavelstein	Calw	1868	N.-Amer	563212
Uxkull, Anna von (Graefin)			Holzhausen	Sulz	Jun 1864	Saxony	849635
Uxkull, Ida von (Graefin)		30 Jul 1837	Holzhausen	Sulz	May 1870	N.-Amer	849635

Vayhinger, Carl Ludwig		Sulz	Sulz	bef 1854	N.-Amer	849627
Vayhinger, Charlotte Auguste	19 yrs.	Sulz	Sulz	Jun 1833	N.-Amer	849627
Vayhinger, Gottfried Ima. & F	18 Feb 1766	Sulz	Sulz	Jun 1833	N.-Amer	849627
Vayhinger, Ludwig Heinrich	19 Jul 1836	Sulz	Sulz	Aug 1852	N.-Amer	849627
Vayhinger, Luise Friedrike		Sulz	Sulz	Jun 1833	N.-Amer	849627
Veil, Carl Wilhelm		Calw	Calw	1853	N.-Amer	563212
Veil, Magdalena & C		Althengstett	Calw	1852	N.-Amer	563212
Veil, Philipp		Althengstett	Calw	1852	N.-Amer	563212
Vetter, Barbara	27 Feb 1835	Pfalzgrafenweiler	Frd.	Jun 1854	N.-Amer	569273
Vetter, Friederike	12 Nov 1842	Vesperweiler	Frd.	Mar 1856	N.-Amer	569275
Vetter, Georg	10 Apr 1841	Vesperweiler	Frd.	Mar 1856	N.-Amer	569275
Vetter, Georg Martin & F	1 Dec 1789	Gaertringen	Herr.	Oct 1851	N.-Amer	834627
Vetter, Johann Georg		Vesperweiler	Frd.	Mar 1838	France	569269
Vetter, Johannes		Sigmarswangen	Sulz	Jan 1817	Russia	849642
Vetter, Joseph		Oberjettingen	Herr.	Nov 1852	N.-Amer	834627
Vetter, Maria Barbara	20 Nov 1798	Gaertringen	Herr.	Oct 1851	N.-Amer	834627
Vetter, Matthias		Sigmarswangen	Sulz	Jan 1817	Russia	849642
Vetter, Salome	18 Jan 1839	Gaertringen	Herr.	Oct 1851	N.-Amer	834627
Vetter, Sara	20 Jul 1835	Gaertringen	Herr.	Oct 1851	N.-Amer	834627
Vetter, Ursula (wid.) & F		Sigmarswangen	Sulz	Jan 1817	Russia	849642
Viesel, Anna Maria	4 Mar 1832	Gaertringen	Herr.	Sep 1852	N.-Amer	834627
Vischer, Christina Catharina		Holzbronn	Calw	Oct 1848	N.-Amer	563212
Voegele, Anna Barbara & F		Bergfelden	Sulz	May 1855	N.-Amer	849629
Voegele, Anna Maria	13 Mar 1852	Bergfelden	Sulz	May 1855	N.-Amer	849629
Voegele, August & F		Freudenstadt	Frd.	Sep 1854	N.-Amer	569274
Voegele, Carl	6 Apr 1838	Freudenstadt	Frd.	Sep 1854	N.-Amer	569274
Voegele, Caroline Rosine	5 Apr 1853	Freudenstadt	Frd.	Sep 1854	N.-Amer	569274
Voegele, Eva Maria	4 Feb 1845	Bergfelden	Sulz	May 1855	N.-Amer	849629
Voegele, Ferdinand	19 yrs.	Freudenstadt	Frd.	Aug 1865	N.-Amer	577779
Voegele, Friederike	8 Aug 1839	Freudenstadt	Frd.	Sep 1854	N.-Amer	569274
Voegele, Gottlieb	1 Sep 1843	Isingen	Sulz	Mar 1860	N.-Amer	849636
Voegele, Gustav	13 Jan 1841	Freudenstadt	Frd.	Sep 1854	N.-Amer	569274
Voegele, Jacob		Isingen	Sulz	bef 1862	N.-Amer	849636
Voegele, Jakob & F		Freudenstadt	Frd.	Sep 1854	N.-Amer	569274
Voegele, Johann Jacob	8 Jan 1839	Bergfelden	Sulz	May 1855	N.-Amer	849629
Voegele, Johann Martin	29 Sep 1842	Bergfelden	Sulz	May 1855	N.-Amer	849629
Voegele, Johann Martin		Isingen	Sulz	Aug 1852	N.-Amer	849636
Voegele, Johannes	23 Jan 1837	Bergfelden	Sulz	May 1855	N.-Amer	849629
Voegele, Johannes	19 yrs.	Isingen	Sulz	Apr 1854	N.-Amer	849636
Voegele, Louise Philipp. (wife)		Freudenstadt	Frd.	Sep 1854	N.-Amer	569274
Voegele, Louise Wilhelmine	26 Jul 1848	Freudenstadt	Frd.	Sep 1854	N.-Amer	569274
Voegele, Ludwig Heinrich	27 Jan 1846	Freudenstadt	Frd.	Sep 1854	N.-Amer	569274
Voegele, Magdalena (wife)		Freudenstadt	Frd.	Sep 1854	N.-Amer	569274
Voegele, Maria Barbara	24 Jul 1841	Bergfelden	Sulz	May 1855	N.-Amer	849629
Voegele, Martin		Bergfelden	Sulz	bef 1856	Switz.	849629
Voegele, Mathilde	19 Dec 1847	Freudenstadt	Frd.	Sep 1854	N.-Amer	569274
Voegele, Pauline	25 Dec 1842	Freudenstadt	Frd.	Sep 1854	N.-Amer	569274
Voegele, Sophie Wilhelmine	15 Aug 1850	Freudenstadt	Frd.	Sep 1854	N.-Amer	569274
Voelkle, Anna Maria	22 May 1839	Dornhan	Sulz	Jul 1870	N.-Amer	849634
Voelkle, Babara (wife)		Dornhan	Sulz	Jul 1870	N.-Amer	849634

| Name | | Birth | | Emigration | | | Film |
Last	First	Date	Place	O'amt	Appl. Date	Dest.	Number
Voelkle, Dorothea		6 Mar 1847	Dornhan	Sulz	Jul 1870	N.-Amer	849634
Voelkle, Johann georg		4 Feb 1871	Leidringen	Sulz	Jan 1888	N.-Amer	849626
Voelkle, Johannes		15 Sep 1835	Sigmarswangen	Sulz	Jun 1860	N.-Amer	849642
Voelkle, Johannes		11 Mar 1850	Duerrenmettstetten	Sulz	Apr 1867	N.-Amer	849635
Voelkle, Johannes & W		25 May 1807	Dornhan	Sulz	Jul 1870	N.-Amer	849634
Voeller, Anna Maria		9 Nov 1828	Hildrizhausen	Herr.	Nov 1862	N.-Amer	834624
Voeller, Johanna Dorothea		15 Oct 1826	Hildrizhausen	Herr.	Nov 1862	N.-Amer	834624
Voelmle, Johann Friedrich		6 Oct 1825	Wildberg	Nag.	Aug 1862	Hannov.	838493
Voeltner, Philipp Heinrich		11 Apr 1814	Schorndorf	Schd.	Mar 1837	N.-Amer	801461
Voetsch, Johannes		1 Nov 1810	Frommern	Bal.	1844	Switz.	555963
Voett, Johann Georg		5 Feb 1827	Reusten	Herr.	Sep 1862	N.-Amer	834624
Voetterle, Anna Maria		1 Dec 1819	Gueltstein	Herr.	Dec 1863	Leipzig	834624
Voetterle, Jacob			Gueltstein	Herr.	Apr 1831	N.-Amer	834624
Voetterle, Margarethe		23 Aug 1817	Hildrizhausen	Herr.	Apr 1865	N.-Amer	834624
Vogel, Heinrich & F			Oberhaugstett	Calw	1855	N.-Amer	563212
Vogt, Catharina Margaretha		27 yrs.	Winterbach	Schd.	Aug 1837	Baden	801461
Vogt, Georg Friedrich			Unterjesingen	Herr.	Jul 1866	N.-Amer	834624
Vogt, Margaretha			Isingen	Sulz	Sep 1854	N.-Amer	849636
Vohl, Andreas Ludwig		13 Oct 1840	Sulz	Sulz	May 1857	N.-Amer	849628
Vohl, Christian		10 Dec 1838	Sulz	Sulz	May 1857	N.-Amer	849628
Vohl, Johann Math. August		30 Sep 1837	Sulz	Sulz	May 1857	N.-Amer	849628
Volle, Ulrich			Weltenschwann	Calw	1862	N.-Amer	563212
Vollmar, Christian		17 Oct 1868	Dornhan	Sulz	Jun 1884	N.-Amer	849626
Vollmar, Johann Jacob		4 May 1838	Brittheim	Sulz	Jan 1857	N.-Amer	849632
Vollmar, Martina			Reusten	Herr.	Apr 1830	--	834624
Vollmer, Andreas		11 Jan 1856	Dornhan	Sulz	Sep 1872	N.-Amer	849634
Vollmer, Christina		21 Jan 1837	Dornhan	Sulz	Jun 1860	N.-Amer	849633
Vollmer, Dorothea			Marschalkenzimmern	Sulz	Feb 1880	N.-Amer	849626
Vollmer, Friedrich			Aichelberg	Calw	1852	N.-Amer	563212
Vollmer, Jacob			Calw	Calw	1861	N.-Amer	563212
Vollmer, Johann		20 May 1855	Dornhan	Sulz	May 1872	N.-Amer	849634
Vollmer, Johann Georg		19 Jul 1859	Dornhan	Sulz	Apr 1874	N.-Amer	849634
Vollmer, Johann Georg			Deckenpfronn	Calw	1852	N.-Amer	563212
Vollmer, Johann Jacob		18 yrs.	Deckenpfronn	Calw	1869	N.-Amer	563212
Vollmer, Johannes		24 Sep 1818	Marschalkenzimmern	Sulz	May 1861	Baden	849638
Vollmer, Johannes (wid.) & F			Deckenpfronn	Calw	1852	N.-Amer	563212
Vollmer, Joseph Friedrich			Beutelsbach	Schd.	1834	Russia	801460
Vollmer, Mathias		31 Jul 1848	Boll	Sulz	Sep 1867	N.-Amer	849632
Vollmer, Pauline & C			Gechingen	Calw	1852	N.-Amer	563212
Volz, Agatha Maria		5 Nov 1808	Baiersbronn	Frd.	Dec 1853	N.-Amer	569272
Volz, Anna Maria			Neubulach	Calw	1856	Baden	563212
Volz, Anna Maria			Liebenzell	Calw	1853	N.-Amer	563212
Volz, Caroline Sophie			Hirsau	Calw	1869	Bavaria	563212
Volz, Christian		3 Aug 1843	Baiersbronn	Frd.	Dec 1853	N.-Amer	569272
Volz, Elisabeth Katharina		26 Mar 1849	Baiersbronn	Frd.	Dec 1853	N.-Amer	569272
Volz, Georg Friedrich		17 Aug 1840	Baiersbronn	Frd.	Dec 1853	N.-Amer	569272
Volz, Georg Friedrich & F		29 Nov 1807	Baiersbronn	Frd.	Dec 1853	N.-Amer	569272
Volz, Johann Georg		24 Oct 1844	Baiersbronn	Frd.	Dec 1853	N.-Amer	569272
Vosseler, Anna Christina (wife)			Bergfelden	Sulz	Aug 1857	N.-Amer	849629
Vosseler, Anna Elisabetha		28 Jun 1847	Bergfelden	Sulz	Jul 1861	N.-Amer	849629

Vosseler, Christine Margaretha	11 Jan 1847	Bergfelden	Sulz	Aug 1857	N.-Amer	849629
Vosseler, Elisabetha M. (wife)	17 Sep 1822	Bergfelden	Sulz	Jul 1861	N.-Amer	849629
Vosseler, Jacob	13 Apr 1836	Bergfelden	Sulz	Oct 1856	N.-Amer	849629
Vosseler, Johann Georg	27 Oct 1857	Bergfelden	Sulz	Jul 1861	N.-Amer	849629
Vosseler, Johann Georg & F	16 Sep 1818	Bergfelden	Sulz	Jul 1861	N.-Amer	849629
Vosseler, Johann Martin	10 Jul 1859	Bergfelden	Sulz	Jul 1861	N.-Amer	849629
Vosseler, Johann Martin	8 Sep 1803	Voehringen	Sulz	May 1832	N.-Amer	849643
Vosseler, Johannes	19 yrs.	Bergfelden	Sulz	Oct 1853	N.-Amer	849629
Vosseler, Johannes & F		Bergfelden	Sulz	Aug 1857	N.-Amer	849629
Vossler, Friederike		Calw	Calw	1855	N.-Amer	563212
Wackenhut, Anna	21 yrs.	Zwerenberg	Calw	1854	N.-Amer	563212
Wackenhut, Carl	23 yrs.	Calw	Calw	1867	N.-Amer	563212
Wackenhut, Elisabetha	12 Jun 1829	Durrweiler	Frd.	Apr 1849	N.-Amer	569270
Wackenhut, Elisabetha & C	1807	Martinsmoos	Calw	1854	N.-Amer	563212
Wackenhut, Friederika	26 yrs.	Martinsmoos	Calw	1854	N.-Amer	563212
Wackenhut, Friedrich	16 yrs.	Zwerenberg	Calw	1866	N.-Amer	563212
Wackenhut, Jacob & F		Zwerenberg	Calw	1853	N.-Amer	563212
Wackenhut, Johann Georg		Cresbach	Frd.	Aug 1859	France	577776
Wackenhut, Johann Georg	25 yrs.	Oberreichenbach	Calw	1868	N.-Amer	563212
Wackenhut, Johann Georg	1839	Zwerenberg	Calw	1854	N.-Amer	563212
Wackenhut, Johann Georg & F		Aichelberg	Calw	1854	N.-Amer	563212
Wackenhut, Johann Michael		Oberreichenbach	Calw	1860	N.-Amer	563212
Wackenhut, Matthias	16 yrs.	Zwerenberg	Calw	1868	N.-Amer	563212
Wacker, Elisabeth		Oberhengstett	Calw	Jun 1870	Bavaria	563212
Wacker, Friederika Katharina		Zavelstein	Calw	Jun 1873	Switz.	563212
Wacker, Jacob	31 yrs.	Oberhaugstett	Calw	1866	Augsb.	563212
Wacker, Jacob Friedrich	19 yrs.	Deckenpfronn	Calw	1869	N.-Amer	563212
Wacker, Johann Georg		Dennjaecht	Calw	May 1871	Baden	563212
Wacker, Johannes		Kuppingen	Herr.	bef 1844	Frankf.	834626
Wackerhut, Johannes	25 yrs.	Zwerenberg	Calw	1869	N.-Amer	563212
Waegner, Christine	20 yrs.	Winterbach	Schd.	Apr 1844	Austria	801461
Waegner, Eberhardt	10 yrs.	Winterbach	Schd.	Apr 1844	Austria	801461
Waegner, Friedrich Wilhelm	6 yrs.	Winterbach	Schd.	Apr 1844	Austria	801461
Waegner, Jacob Friedrich	35 yrs.	Winterbach	Schd.	Apr 1844	Austria	801461
Waegner, Johann Georg	15 yrs.	Winterbach	Schd.	Apr 1844	Austria	801461
Waegner, Johann Gottlieb	8 yrs.	Winterbach	Schd.	Apr 1844	Austria	801461
Waegner, Johannes & F	27 Sep 1892	Winterbach	Schd.	Apr 1844	Austria	801461
Waegner, Maria Magdalena		Winterbach	Schd.	Apr 1844	Austria	801461
Waegner, Maria Magdalena	4 yrs.	Winterbach	Schd.	Apr 1844	Austria	801461
Waelde, August Adolf	25 Sep 1853	Untertuerkheim	Frd.	Nov 1853	N.-Amer	569272
Waelde, August Friedrich & F		Christophstal	Frd.	Nov 1844	N.-Amer	569272
Waelde, Carl		Freudenstadt	Frd.	Sep 1853	N.-Amer	569274
Waelde, Catharine Frieder.		Freudenstadt	Frd.	Oct 1853	Baden	569273
Waelde, Christine	13 Mar 1833	Dornhan	Sulz	Mar 1858	N.-Amer	849633
Waelde, Eberhardt		Altensteig	Nag.	Feb 1849	Baden	838490
Waelde, Friederika Carl. R. E.	26 Dec 1847	Untertuerkheim	Frd.	Nov 1853	N.-Amer	569272
Waelde, Friedrich & F		Fuernsal	Sulz	May 1847	N.-Amer	849635
Waelde, Gustav Adolph	18 Jan 1835	Freudenstadt	Frd.	Feb 1853	N.-Amer	569273
Waelde, Johannes		Fuernsal	Sulz	May 1847	N.-Amer	849635
Waelde, Louise Caroline		Schorndorf	Frd.	Nov 1853	N.-Amer	569272

| Name | | Birth | | Emigration | | | Film |
Last	First	Date	Place	O'amt	Appl. Date	Dest.	Number
Waelder, Friederike Margar.		4 Nov 1835	Freudenstadt	Frd.	Jul 1859	Switz.	577776
Waeldin, Friederika (wid)			Freudenstadt	Frd.	Apr 1817	Russia	569267
Wagner, Anna (wife)		8 Feb 1819	Oeschelbronn	Herr.	Sep 1852	N.-Amer	834627
Wagner, Anna Maria		8 Sep 1829	Pfalzgrafenweiler	Frd.	Apr 1849	N.-Amer	569270
Wagner, Anna Maria			Pfalzgrafenweiler	Frd.	May 1833	N.-Amer	569268
Wagner, Anna Maria		1 Aug 1842	Oeschelbronn	Herr.	Sep 1852	N.-Amer	834627
Wagner, Carl Friedrich & F		11 Sep 1807	Ludwigsburg	Herr.	Sep 1852	N.-Amer	834627
Wagner, Carl Friedrich Aug.		25 Aug 1843	Oeschelbronn	Herr.	Sep 1852	N.-Amer	834627
Wagner, Catharina Friedrich		10 Feb 1845	Oeschelbronn	Herr.	Sep 1852	N.-Amer	834627
Wagner, Christian		7 Aug 1811	Pfalzgrafenweiler	Frd.	Apr 1836	N.-Amer	569268
Wagner, Christiane			Pfalzgrafenweiler	Frd.	May 1833	N.-Amer	569268
Wagner, Christina Catharina		28 Mar 1847	Oeschelbronn	Herr.	Sep 1852	N.-Amer	834627
Wagner, Ernst		13 Jul 1845	Pfalzgrafenweiler	Frd.	Oct 1865	N.-Amer	577779
Wagner, Fridrika		15 Jan 1834	Pfalzgrafenweiler	Frd.	Apr 1849	N.-Amer	569270
Wagner, Gottfried		1 Aug 1818	Pfalzgrafenweiler	Frd.	Jun 1847	N.-Amer	569270
Wagner, Gottfried & F			Pfalzgrafenweiler	Frd.	Mar 1817	Russia	569268
Wagner, Gottlieb Friedricha		15 Jan 1849	Oeschelbronn	Herr.	Sep 1852	N.-Amer	834627
Wagner, Hermann Friedrich		16 May 1877	Dornhan	Sulz	Jun 1885	N.-Amer	849626
Wagner, Karl Gustav		20 Dec 1836	Pfalzgrafenweiler	Frd.	Apr 1855	N.-Amer	569275
Wagner, Karoline Frieder. & F		12 Oct 1849	Dornhan	Sulz	Jun 1885	N.-Amer	849626
Wagner, Karoline Friederike		1 Jul 1883	Dornhan	Sulz	Jun 1885	N.-Amer	849626
Wagner, Ludwig Friedrich			Calw	Calw	1849	N.-Amer	563212
Wagner, Maria Barbara		2 Feb 1850	Oeschelbronn	Herr.	Sep 1852	N.-Amer	834627
Wagner, Maximillian		18 Oct 1881	Dornhan	Sulz	Jun 1885	N.-Amer	849626
Wagner, Michael (wid.) & F			Holzbronn	Calw	1854	N.-Amer	563212
Wagner, Rebecka			Pfalzgrafenweiler	Frd.	May 1833	N.-Amer	569268
Wagner, Rosina		15 Jan 1837	Pfalzgrafenweiler	Frd.	Aug 1853	N.-Amer	569272
Wagner, Rudolf Wilh. Alex.		1 Dec 1873	Dornhan	Sulz	Jun 1885	N.-Amer	849626
Waidelich, Christine			Aichhalden	Calw	1853	N.-Amer	563212
Waidelich, Eva Katharina			Aichhalden	Calw	1853	N.-Amer	563212
Waidelich, Johann Georg			Besenfeld	Frd.	May 1854	N.-Amer	569273
Waierle, Anna Maria			Steinenberg	Schd.	Apr 1842	N.-Amer	801461
Waierle, Christian Friedrich			Steinenberg	Schd.	Apr 1842	N.-Amer	801461
Waierle, Dorothea			Steinenberg	Schd.	Apr 1842	N.-Amer	801461
Waierle, Eva Barbara		14 Dec 1792	Steinenberg	Schd.	Apr 1842	N.-Amer	801461
Waierle, Eva Catharina			Steinenberg	Schd.	Apr 1842	N.-Amer	801461
Waierle, Friederika			Steinenberg	Schd.	Apr 1842	N.-Amer	801461
Waierle, Friedrich & F			Steinenberg	Schd.	Apr 1842	N.-Amer	801461
Waisch, Johann Georg		23 Feb 1830	Kayh	Herr.	Oct 1863	N.-Amer	834624
Wakenhut, Barbara		15 Mar 1847	Durrweiler	Frd.	Aug 1848	N.-Amer	569270
Wakenhut, Johann Friederich		21 Jan 1824	Durrweiler	Frd.	Aug 1848	N.-Amer	569270
Wakenhut, Johann Jacob			Pfalzgrafenweiler	Frd.	Apr 1807	Baden	569268
Waker, Anna Maria		23 yrs.	Kuppingen	Herr.	Mar 1831	N.-Amer	834624
Waker, Christina Elisabeth			Kuppingen	Herr.	Mar 1831	N.-Amer	834624
Waker, Imanuel Friedrich		2 Oct 1831	Unterjesingen	Herr.	Aug 1851	N.-Amer	834627
Waker, Johannes			Kuppingen	Herr.	Mar 1831	N.-Amer	834624
Waker, Magdalena		18 Dec 1830	Durrweiler	Frd.	Mar 1847	N.-Amer	569271
Waldschuh, Margaretha		23 Feb 1841	Oberndorf	Herr.	Jun 1867	N.-Amer	834624
Walker, Dorothea			Neuweiler	Calw	Jun 1870	N.-Amer	563212
Walker, Friedrich August		11 Nov 1813	Freudenstadt	Frd.	Oct 1860	Bavaria	577777

Name	Date/Age	Place		Date	Destination	ID
Walker, Hermann	36 yrs.	Dornstetten	Frd.	Jun 1851	N.-Amer	569271
Walker, Hermann Friedrich		Freudenstadt	Frd.	1851	N.-Amer	577778
Walker, Johann Martin	24 Oct 1850	Rosenfeld	Sulz	Aug 1867	N.-Amer	849641
Walker, Johannes	4 Nov 1810	Huzenbach	Frd.	1841	Baden	569269
Wallraff, Johannes & F		Altensteig	Frd.	May 1853	France	569272
Walten, Gustav	29 Nov 1831	Kuppingen	Herr.	Jan 1865	Saxony	834624
Walter, Anna	10 yrs.	Wittendorf	Frd.	Apr 1817	Poland	569268
Walter, Anna Maria	12 yrs.	Wittendorf	Frd.	Apr 1817	Poland	569268
Walter, Anna Maria	5 Jul 1833	Dornhan	Sulz	Apr 1861	N.-Amer	849634
Walter, Barbara	14 yrs.	Wittendorf	Frd.	Apr 1817	Poland	569268
Walter, Barbara	30 Sep 1841	Dornhan	Sulz	Apr 1861	N.-Amer	849634
Walter, Catharina	7 yrs.	Wittendorf	Frd.	Apr 1817	Poland	569268
Walter, Christina		Sigmarswangen	Sulz	May 1868	N.-Amer	849642
Walter, Christine	18 yrs.	Wittendorf	Frd.	Apr 1817	Poland	569268
Walter, Conrad Ludwig		Bondorf	Herr.	Apr 1847	N.-Amer	834626
Walter, Dorothea	7 Apr 1842	Marschalkenzimmern	Sulz	Sep 1867	N.-Amer	849638
Walter, Elisabetha	1 yrs.	Wittendorf	Frd.	Apr 1817	Poland	569268
Walter, Georg Friedrich & F		Agenbach	Calw	Feb 1848	N.-Amer	563212
Walter, Georg Jacob		Calw	Calw	Jun 1847	Austria	563212
Walter, Gottfried & F		Wittendorf	Frd.	Jul 1817	Russia	569268
Walter, Gottlieb	11 Jun 1879	Weiden	Sulz	Oct 1889	N.-Amer	849644
Walter, Gottlieb & F	42 yrs.	Wittendorf	Frd.	Apr 1817	Poland	569268
Walter, Heinrika & C		Sigmarswangen	Sulz	Mar 1817	N.-Amer	849642
Walter, Jakob	5 yrs.	Wittendorf	Frd.	Apr 1817	Poland	569268
Walter, Johann	17 Nov 1817	Dornhan	Sulz	Mar 1852	N.-Amer	849633
Walter, Johann		Kentheim	Calw	1862	N.-Amer	563212
Walter, Johann Friedrich	20 May 1877	Weiden	Sulz	Oct 1889	N.-Amer	849626
Walter, Johann Georg	23 Feb 1846	Dornhan	Sulz	May 1864	N.-Amer	849634
Walter, Johann Georg	27 Jan 1872	Bergfelden	Sulz	Jan 1888	N.-Amer	849626
Walter, Johann Georg & F	24 Jan 1839	Weiden	Sulz	Oct 1889	N.-Amer	849626
Walter, Johann Georg (wid.)& F	24 Jan 1839	Weiden	Sulz	Oct 1889	N.-Amer	849644
Walter, Johann georg		Dornhan	Sulz	May 1835	Bavaria	849633
Walter, Johannes	2 Nov 1833	Wittlensweiler	Frd.	May 1852	N.-Amer	569272
Walter, Johannes	16 Apr 1854	Dornhan	Sulz	Jun 1869	N.-Amer	849634
Walter, Johannes	7 Dec 1850	Hopfau	Sulz	Feb 1869	N.-Amer	849636
Walter, Johannes	29 May 1823	Hopfau	Sulz	Mar 1851	N.-Amer	849636
Walter, Joseph	27 Apr 1857	Binsdorf	Sulz	Mar 1872	N.-Amer	849631
Walter, Joseph & F		Muehlheim a.B.	Sulz	Aug 1847	N.-Amer	849639
Walter, Konrad	23 Jun 1850	Binsdorf	Sulz	Dec 1870	N.-Amer	849631
Walter, Leo		Balingen	Bal.	Feb 1859	Switz.	555962
Walter, Maria	40 yrs.	Wittendorf	Frd.	Feb 1846	Austria	569271
Walter, Maria Barbara	26 Apr 1799	Sulz	Sulz	Feb 1837	France	849627
Walter, Marie Margaretha	10 Sep 1875	Weiden	Sulz	Oct 1889	N.-Amer	849626
Walter, Mathaeus	31 Oct 1870	Bergfelden	Sulz	May 1886	N.-Amer	849626
Walter, Mathias		Marschalkenzimmern	Sulz	Mar 1836	N.-Amer	849625
Walter, Mathias		Marschalkenzimmern	Sulz	Apr 1833	N.-Amer	849638
Walter, Matthias	25 yrs.	Sigmarswangen	Sulz	Mar 1817	N.-Amer	849642
Walter, Philipp	14 Sep 1857	Binsdorf	Sulz	Mar 1872	N.-Amer	849631
Walter, Raphael	13 Mar 1856	Binsdorf	Sulz	Mar 1872	N.-Amer	849631
Walter, Sophie Dorothea		Sulz	Sulz	Aug 1838	Augsb.	849627

Name		Birth		Emigration			Film
Last	First	Date	Place	O'amt	Appl. Date	Dest.	Number
Walter, Theresia			Binsdorf	Sulz	Sep 1835	Baden	849630
Walther, Albrecht			Gruental	Frd.	Apr 1752	Pen.N-A	550803
Walther, Anna Barbara (wife)		12 Jul 1791	Rotenberg	Sulz	1817	Russia	849627
Walther, Carolina Louise & C			Sulz	Sulz	Aug 1864	Saxony	849628
Walther, Christian		14 Mar 1856	Bergfelden	Sulz	Apr 1872	N.-Amer	849629
Walther, Elisabetha			Rodt	Frd.	May 1860	N.-Amer	577777
Walther, Jacob		5 Apr 1842	Bergfelden	Sulz	Mar 1870	Paris	849629
Walther, Johann Georg			Sulz	Sulz	Mar 1811	France	849625
Walther, Johann Georg & F			Schernbach	Frd.	Aug 1857	N.-Amer	577776
Walther, Johann Georg & F		4 Mar 1790	Sulz	Sulz	1817	Russia	849627
Walther, Johann Gottlieb		11 Sep 1860	Sulz	Sulz	Jan 1883	Holland	849626
Walther, Karl Friedrich		4 Jul 1864	Sulz	Sulz	Aug 1864	Saxony	849628
Walther, Mathias & F		8 Nov 1806	Rodt	Frd.	May 1860	N.-Amer	577777
Walther, Philippine Dorothea			Schernbach	Frd.	Aug 1857	N.-Amer	577776
Walz, Anna Maria		1 Jun 1827	Tonbach	Frd.	bef 1864	N.-Amer	577779
Walz, Barbara (wife)			Wittlensweiler	Frd.	Feb 1849	N.-Amer	569270
Walz, Catharina Barbara			Sulz	Sulz	May 1817	N.-Amer	849627
Walz, Christian		inf.	Ebhausen	Nag.	Apr 1854	N.-Amer	838491
Walz, Christian		10 yrs.	Altenstaig	Nag.	Oct 1849	N.-Amer	838490
Walz, Christian & W			Wittlensweiler	Frd.	Feb 1849	N.-Amer	569270
Walz, Christina Barbara			Rosenfeld	Sulz	1834	N.-Amer	849625
Walz, Elise			Altenstaig	Nag.	Oct 1849	N.-Amer	838490
Walz, Elise Katharine		9 mon.	Altenstaig	Nag.	Oct 1849	N.-Amer	838490
Walz, Eva Maria		27 yrs.	Ebhausen	Nag.	Apr 1854	N.-Amer	838491
Walz, Friedrich		27 Mar 1820	Freudenstadt	Frd.	Sep 1854	N.-Amer	569274
Walz, Friedrich & F		31 yrs.	Ebhausen	Nag.	Apr 1854	N.-Amer	838491
Walz, Georg		4 Jun 1828	Altheim	Horb	bef 1853	N.-Amer	835929
Walz, Jacob Friedrich			Nagold	Nag.	Jul 1854	N.-Amer	838491
Walz, Jacob Friedrich		11 Jul 1857	Kuppingen	Herr.	Mar 1865	N.-Amer	834624
Walz, Johann		11 Feb 1830	Lossburg	Frd.	bef 1861	Bavaria	577778
Walz, Johann Friedrich		3 yrs.	Ebhausen	Nag.	Apr 1854	N.-Amer	838491
Walz, Johann Jacob		5 Feb 1836	Walddorf	Nag.	Apr 1854	N.-Amer	838491
Walz, Johann Jacob			Liebenzell	Calw	1864	N.-Amer	563212
Walz, Johann Martin			Oberschwandorf	Nag.	Sep 1854	N.-Amer	838491
Walz, Johannes		12 Oct 1833	Groembach	Frd.	Jun 1854	N.-Amer	569274
Walz, Justina Katharina		31 Jan 1844	Kuppingen	Herr.	May 1867	N.-Amer	834624
Walz, Karl		9 yrs.	Altenstaig	Nag.	Oct 1849	N.-Amer	838490
Walz, Karoline		7 yrs.	Altenstaig	Nag.	Oct 1849	N.-Amer	838490
Walz, Katharina		12 Jul 1797	Wittlensweiler	Frd.	Jul 1847	N.-Amer	569270
Walz, Kunigunda		16 Jul 1830	Hochdorf	Frd.	bef 1863	Switz.	577778
Walz, Louis		2 yrs.	Altenstaig	Nag.	Oct 1849	N.-Amer	838490
Walz, Magdalena			Ueberberg	Nag.	Feb 1852	N.-Amer	838490
Walz, Maria Catharina (wife)		23 Feb 1829	Kuppingen	Herr.	Mar 1865	N.-Amer	834624
Walz, Martha			Oberhaugstett	Calw	1858	N.-Amer	563212
Walz, Mathias		14 Oct 1822	Altheim	Horb	Sep 1857	N.-Amer	835929
Walz, Michael & F			Altenstaig	Nag.	Oct 1849	N.-Amer	838490
Walz, Michael Friedrich		12 yrs.	Altenstaig	Nag.	Oct 1849	N.-Amer	838490
Walz, Paul		5 yrs.	Altenstaig	Nag.	Oct 1849	N.-Amer	838490
Walz, Regine		7 Nov 1836	Tonbach	Frd.	bef 1864	N.-Amer	577779
Walz, Rosina			Zavelstein	Calw	1868	Prussia	563212

Walz, Rosina		Altingen	Herr.	bef 1838	Austria	834625
Walz, Rosine Barbara & F		Walddorf	Nag.	Aug 1854	N.-Amer	838491
Walz, Rudolf Johann & F	26 Dec 1828	Kuppingen	Herr.	Mar 1865	N.-Amer	834624
Wandel, Tobias		Freudenstadt	– –	Mar 1753	Pen.N-A	550803
Wanner, Michael & F	12 Jun 1807	Kayh	Herr.	Dec 1848	N.-Amer	834626
Weber, Anna Maria		Neuweiler	Calw	1868	N.-Amer	563212
Weber, Anton	10 Jul 1839	Leinstetten	Sulz	May 1868	N.-Amer	849638
Weber, Carl Adolph	7 Jan 1847	Freudenstadt	Frd.	Aug 1866	N.-Amer	577780
Weber, Caroline Fr. Chr.		Calw	Calw	1868	Baden	563212
Weber, Caroline Franziska	23 Sep 1830	Freudenstadt	Frd.	bef 1862	France	577778
Weber, Caroline Maria	22 Mar 1842	Christophstal	Frd.	Aug 1861	N.-Amer	577778
Weber, Christian		Friedrichstal	Frd.	bef 1864	N.-Amer	577779
Weber, Christian Heinrich	27 Mar 1841	Unterjesingen	Herr.	Jun 1865	N.-Amer	834624
Weber, Christiane	22 Jul 1819	Sulz	Sulz	Mar 1836	N.-Amer	849627
Weber, Christiane Barbara		Freudenstadt	Frd.	Jul 1852	N.-Amer	569271
Weber, Christine Magdalena	18 yrs.	Oberkollbach	Calw	Apr 1848	N.-Amer	563212
Weber, Christoph Friedrich	10 Apr 1813	Sulz	Sulz	Mar 1836	N.-Amer	849627
Weber, Friederike		Schoemberg	Frd.	Sep 1853	N.-Amer	569272
Weber, Friederike Barbara & C	18 Jan 1832	Christophstal	Frd.	Dec 1858	Baden	577776
Weber, Friedrich	18 Mar 1810	Freudenstadt	Frd.	Oct 1836	Prussia	569267
Weber, Friedrich	16 Jul 1843	Baiersbronn	Frd.	Aug 1854	N.-Amer	569274
Weber, Friedrich	21 Apr 1854	Baiersbronn	Frd.	Aug 1854	N.-Amer	569274
Weber, Friedrich	23 yrs.	Neuweiler	Calw	1867	N.-Amer	563212
Weber, Friedrich Eberhardt	20 Mar 1841	Freudenstadt	Frd.	Jun 1864	N.-Amer	577779
Weber, Georg David		Baiersbronn	Frd.	May 1847	N.-Amer	569270
Weber, Georg Heinrich		Wiesenbachen	– –	Dec 1751	Mas.N-A	550803
Weber, Gottlieb	19 Feb 1830	Baiersbronn	Frd.	Aug 1853	N.-Amer	569272
Weber, Gottlieb	27 Oct 1871	Sigmarswangen	Sulz	May 1889	N.-Amer	849642
Weber, Gottlieb Ferdinand	28 Feb 1821	Sulz	Sulz	Mar 1836	N.-Amer	849627
Weber, Jacob Fridrich		Christophstal	Frd.	Apr 1817	Prussia	569267
Weber, Jakob Friedrich	23 Jun 1851	Freudenstadt	Frd.	Sep 1866	N.-Amer	577780
Weber, Johann	1 Jun 1833	Haslach	Herr.	Sep 1867	N.-Amer	834624
Weber, Johann Christian	28 Nov 1840	Christophstal	Frd.	Jul 1856	N.-Amer	569275
Weber, Johann David		Freudenstadt	Frd.	Mar 1851	N.-Amer	569271
Weber, Johann David		Sulz	Sulz	1834	N.-Amer	849627
Weber, Johann Friedrich		Holzbronn	Calw	1852	N.-Amer	563212
Weber, Johann Mathias		Freudenstadt	Frd.	Dec 1843	Baden	569269
Weber, Johanne Friederike	16 Jan 1817	Sulz	Sulz	Mar 1836	N.-Amer	849627
Weber, Johannes	9 Jan 1833	Baiersbronn	Frd.	Aug 1853	N.-Amer	569272
Weber, Johannes	7 Feb 1849	Baiersbronn	Frd.	Aug 1854	N.-Amer	569274
Weber, Johannes	13 Jul 1848	Bickelsberg	Sulz	Apr 1868	N.-Amer	849630
Weber, Karl	16 May 1842	Baiersbronn	Frd.	Aug 1854	N.-Amer	569274
Weber, Katharina	4 Sep 1851	Baiersbronn	Frd.	Aug 1854	N.-Amer	569274
Weber, Katharina		Neuweiler	Calw	1864	N.-Amer	563212
Weber, Magdalena (wid.) & F		Sommenhardt	Calw	1853	N.-Amer	563212
Weber, Maria	1 Jun 1810	Leinstetten	Sulz	Nov 1861	Prussia	849638
Weber, Martin	28 Jun 1807	Bickelsberg	Sulz	1849	N.-Amer	849630
Weber, Regine Helene & F		Sulz	Sulz	Mar 1836	N.-Amer	849627
Weber, Rosine Johanne Marie	10 Mar 1815	Sulz	Sulz	Mar 1836	N.-Amer	849627
Weber, Sophie	16 Dec 1822	Baiersbronn	Frd.	Aug 1854	N.-Amer	569274

222

| Name | | Birth | | Emigration | | | Film |
Last	First	Date	Place	O'amt	Appl. Date	Dest.	Number
Weber, Sophie		15 Jul 1845	Baiersbronn	Frd.	Aug 1854	N.-Amer	569274
Weber, Wilhelm			Freudenstadt	Frd.	Jul 1850	N.-Amer	569271
Weber, Wilhelm		23 Mar 1878	Leinstetten	Sulz	bef 1891	Switz.	849626
Weber, Wilhelm & F		10 May 1807	Baiersbronn	Frd.	Aug 1854	N.-Amer	569274
Weber, Wilhelm Friedrich		21 Sep 1845	Freudenstadt	Frd.	Apr 1860	N.-Amer	577777
Weber, Wilhelm Philipp		22 Aug 1834	Friedrichstal	Frd.	Apr 1854	N.-Amer	569273
Wechselberger, Anna Marie		1 yrs.	Oberkollbach	Calw	1860	N.-Amer	563212
Wechselberger, Marie & C			Oberkollbach	Calw	1860	N.-Amer	563212
Weck, Louise Heinrike			Hirsau	Calw	1867	Hesse	563212
Weckerle, Emanuel		24 yrs.	Freudenstadt	Frd.	May 1752	Pen.N-A	550803
Weckerle, Jacob		1834	Hirsau	Calw	1854	N.-Amer	563212
Weckerle, Jeramias Fridrich		3 yrs.	Freudenstadt	Frd.	May 1752	Pen.N-A	550803
Weckerle, Juliane Dorothea		6 mon.	Freudenstadt	Frd.	May 1752	Pen.N-A	550803
Weckerle, Maria Elisabetha		32 yrs.	Freudenstadt	Frd.	May 1752	Pen.N-A	550803
Weckerle, Rosine Christine			Calw	Calw	1864	Baden	563212
Weckerle, Sabina Margaretha		4 yrs.	Freudenstadt	Frd.	May 1752	Pen.N-A	550803
Weckerlin, Marie Magdalena		14 Jul 1819	Freudenstadt	Frd.	bef 1858	Baden	577779
Weckherlin, Christian Johann		7 May 1819	Stuttgart	Frd.	1847	Lemberg	569275
Wegenast, Anna		17 Nov 1847	Muehlheim a.B.	Sulz	Mar 1857	N.-Amer	849639
Wegenast, Anna Maria		14 Jul 1838	Holzhausen	Sulz	Mar 1859	N.-Amer	849635
Wegenast, Anna Maria		9 Sep 1844	Muehlheim a.B.	Sulz	Mar 1857	N.-Amer	849639
Wegenast, Christina		24 yrs.	Holzhausen	Sulz	Sep 1854	N.-Amer	849635
Wegenast, Christina (wife)			Holzhausen	Sulz	Apr 1832	N.-Amer	849635
Wegenast, Eva Margaretha (wife)		1813	Muehlheim a.B.	Sulz	Mar 1857	N.-Amer	849639
Wegenast, Jakob Friedrich & F		1806	Muehlheim a.B.	Sulz	Mar 1857	N.-Amer	849639
Wegenast, Johann & F			Renfrizhausen	Sulz	Mar 1817	Russia	849639
Wegenast, Johann Friedrich		5 Mar 1824	Muehlheim a.B.	Sulz	Nov 1859	N.-Amer	849639
Wegenast, Johann Georg			Holzhausen	Sulz	Apr 1832	N.-Amer	849635
Wegenast, Johann Georg		28 Oct 1870	Duerrenmettstetten	Sulz	Mar 1889	N.-Amer	849626
Wegenast, Johann Georg & F		29 Sep 1788	Holzhausen	Sulz	Apr 1832	N.-Amer	849635
Wegenast, Johannes		4 Mar 1855	Duerrenmettstetten	Sulz	Jan 1872	N.-Amer	849635
Wegenast, Katharina		30 Mar 1838	Muehlheim a.B.	Sulz	bef 1857	N.-Amer	849639
Wegenast, Maria Paulina			Holzhausen	Sulz	Apr 1832	N.-Amer	849635
Wegenast, Matheis			Holzhausen	Sulz	Apr 1832	N.-Amer	849635
Wegenast, Mathias		21 Sep 1835	Holzhausen	Sulz	Mar 1859	N.-Amer	849635
Wegenast, Michael & W			Holzhausen	Sulz	Apr 1817	Russia	849635
Wehle, Elisabetha & F		27 Aug 1841	Bettenhausen	Sulz	May 1885	N.-Amer	849630
Wehle, Elise Therese		10 Jun 1878	Bettenhausen	Sulz	May 1885	N.-Amer	849630
Weick, Marie Katharine			Liebenzell	Calw	1863	Baden	563212
Weidelich, Agatha			Aichhalden	Calw	1857	N.-Amer	563212
Weidelich, Johannes			Aichhalden	Calw	1852	N.-Amer	563212
Weidelich, Ludwig Heinrich		1843	Aichhalden	Calw	1857	N.-Amer	563212
Weidler, Catharina			Calw	Calw	1853	N.-Amer	563212
Weigandt, Catharina Dorothea		6 Sep 1809	Schorndorf	Schd.	Dec 1832	Baden	801460
Weigold, Andreas		24 May 1847	Hopfau	Sulz	May 1866	N.-Amer	849636
Weigold, Anna Maria		19 Jan 1846	Glatten	Frd.	Jan 1847	N.-Amer	569271
Weigold, Anna Maria			Glatten	Frd.	Jan 1847	N.-Amer	569271
Weigold, Anna Maria & C		3 Feb 1827	Glatten	Frd.	Oct 1854	S.-Amer	569274
Weigold, Anna Maria (wife)			Gueltstein	Herr.	Sep 1852	N.-Amer	834627
Weigold, Barbara		11 Jun 1844	Glatten	Frd.	Jan 1847	N.-Amer	569271

Weigold, Carl & F		Gueltstein	Herr.	Sep 1852	N.-Amer	834627
Weigold, Carl Andreas	23 Jan 1850	Gueltstein	Herr.	Sep 1852	N.-Amer	834627
Weigold, Christina	28 Sep 1839	Glatten	Frd.	Jan 1847	N.-Amer	569271
Weigold, Friedrich	26 Mar 1841	Gueltstein	Herr.	Sep 1852	N.-Amer	834627
Weigold, Jacob		Schoemberg	Frd.	Nov 1853	N.-Amer	569272
Weigold, Johann Georg		Schoemberg	Frd.	Jun 1854	N.-Amer	569273
Weigold, Johannes		Lauterbad	Frd.	bef 1816	Baden	569269
Weigold, Johannes	30 Sep 1842	Glatten	Frd.	Jan 1847	N.-Amer	569271
Weigold, Johannes & F		Glatten	Frd.	Jan 1847	N.-Amer	569271
Weigold, Katharina Dorothea	11 Dec 1844	Gueltstein	Herr.	Sep 1852	N.-Amer	834627
Weigold, Margaretha	2 Aug 1851	Glatten	Frd.	Oct 1854	S.-Amer	569274
Weigold, Martin		Schoemberg	Frd.	Jun 1854	N.-Amer	569273
Weik, Anna Barbara	28 Jun 1867	Renfrizhausen	Sulz	Mar 1884	N.-Amer	849639
Weik, Anna Maria (wife)		Bergfelden	Sulz	Feb 1883	N.-Amer	849626
Weik, Christian	10 Mar 1865	Renfrizhausen	Sulz	Feb 1881	N.-Amer	849639
Weik, Elisabetha & C	40 yrs.	Renfrizhausen	Sulz	Mar 1817	Russia	849639
Weik, Gottlieb Friedrich & F		Hirsau	Calw	1856	N.-Amer	563212
Weik, Jakobine		Renfrizhausen	Sulz	1853	N.-Amer	849639
Weik, Johann Martin	21 Aug 1868	Bergfelden	Sulz	Feb 1883	N.-Amer	849626
Weik, Johannes	3 Dec 1867	Renfrizhausen	Sulz	Feb 1881	N.-Amer	849639
Weik, Maria & C		Calw	Calw	1856	Switz.	563212
Weikardt, Christina (wife)		Sulz	Sulz	Jul 1854	N.-Amer	849627
Weikardt, Gottlieb & F	10 Oct 1825	Sulz	Sulz	Jul 1854	N.-Amer	849627
Weike, Gottlob	29 Nov 1870	Renfrizhausen	Sulz	Jan 1887	N.-Amer	849639
Weike, Jacob & F	31 Dec 1839	Renfrizhausen	Sulz	Jan 1887	N.-Amer	849639
Weike, Johann Jacob	5 Aug 1866	Renfrizhausen	Sulz	Jan 1887	N.-Amer	849639
Weike, Theresia (wife)	22 Sep 1846	Renfrizhausen	Sulz	Jan 1887	N.-Amer	849639
Weikert, Elisabetha Barbara		Freudenstadt	Frd.	May 1855	France	569275
Weikert, Jacob Friedrich		Freudenstadt	Frd.	Apr 1858	France	577776
Weikert, Johann Christian	14 Dec 1826	Freudenstadt	Frd.	Dec 1860	Austria	577777
Weikert, Johann Georg	14 Jun 1831	Freudenstadt	Frd.	bef 1860	France	577778
Weikh, Heinrich	7 Feb 1835	Herrenberg	Herr.	Dec 1868	N.-Amer	834624
Weimer, Christina		Bondorf	Herr.	Jun 1833	N.-Amer	834624
Weimer, Elisabeth	22 May 1837	Bondorf	Herr.	Mar 1846	Austria	834626
Weimer, Elisabeth	11 Sep 1835	Bondorf	Herr.	1848	N.-Amer	834626
Weimer, Elisabetha (wife)		Bondorf	Herr.	Apr 1831	N.-Amer	834624
Weimer, Friedrich	29 Aug 1812	Oeschelbronn	Herr.	Feb 1866	Bavaria	834624
Weimer, Friedrich	36 yrs.	Bondorf	Herr.	Mar 1831	N.-Amer	834624
Weimer, Jacob & F		Bondorf	Herr.	Mar 1846	Austria	834626
Weimer, Johann Christian	25 Nov 1832	Bondorf	Herr.	Mar 1846	Austria	834626
Weimer, Johann Friedrich	8 Dec 1842	Bondorf	Herr.	Mar 1846	Austria	834626
Weimer, Johann Jacob		Bondorf/Herrenberg	Calw	1869	N.-Amer	563212
Weimer, Johann Jacob	25 Mar 1837	Bondorf	Herr.	Jun 1867	France	834624
Weimer, Johann Jacob	16 Nov 1845	Bondorf	Herr.	Aug 1869	N.-Amer	834624
Weimer, Johann Martin	14 Mar 1827	Bondorf	Herr.	1846	N.-Amer	834624
Weimer, Johann Michael	2 Aug 1820	Bondorf	Herr.	Mar 1847	N.-Amer	834626
Weimer, Johannes & W		Bondorf	Herr.	Apr 1831	N.-Amer	834624
Weimer, Maria Barbara	31 Jan 1844	Bondorf	Herr.	Mar 1846	Austria	834626
Weimer, Regina Barbara (wife)	31 yrs.	Bondorf	Herr.	Mar 1846	Austria	834626
Weimer, Regina Catharina	9 Sep 1845	Bondorf	Herr.	Mar 1846	Austria	834626

Name		Birth		Emigration			Film
Last	First	Date	Place	O'amt	Appl. Date	Dest.	Number
Wein, Bernhardt		7 Apr 1836	Tonbach	Frd.	Apr 1856	N.-Amer	569275
Wein, Catharina		29 Jun 1841	Baiersbronn	Frd.	Aug 1854	N.-Amer	569274
Wein, Catharina (wife)		5 Apr 1821	Tonbach	Frd.	Aug 1854	N.-Amer	569274
Wein, Christian & F			Kniebis	Frd.	Mar 1817	Russia	569267
Wein, Christian Friedrich		25 Dec 1843	Baiersbronn	Frd.	Aug 1854	N.-Amer	569274
Wein, Friederike		20 Apr 1842	Baiersbronn	Frd.	Aug 1854	N.-Amer	569274
Wein, Gottfried		11 Aug 1834	Baiersbronn	Frd.	Aug 1854	N.-Amer	569274
Wein, Johannes & F		31 May 1818	Tonbach	Frd.	Aug 1854	N.-Amer	569274
Wein, Mathaeus			Baiersbronn	Frd.	bef 1817	Wien	569267
Wein, Regina		21 Mar 1813	Baiersbronn	Frd.	Sep 1848	N.-Amer	569270
Wein, Rosina		19 May 1831	Baiersbronn	Frd.	Mar 1854	N.-Amer	569273
Weinberger, Christiane Fried.			Calw	Calw	1858	Prussia	563212
Weinlaeder, Anna Maria		13 Sep 1824	Dornstetten	Frd.	Feb 1847	N.-Amer	569271
Weinlaeder, Catharina		19 Mar 1865	Dornstetten	Frd.	Jul 1866	N.-Amer	577780
Weinlaeder, Christian		26 Oct 1861	Dornstetten	Frd.	Jul 1866	N.-Amer	577780
Weinlaeder, Jakob Friedr.		27 Aug 1851	Dornstetten	Frd.	Jul 1866	N.-Amer	577780
Weinlaeder, Jakob Friedr. & F			Dornstetten	Frd.	Jul 1866	N.-Amer	577780
Weinlaeder, Johann			Dornstetten	Frd.	bef 1821	Odessa	569269
Weinlaeder, Katharina & C			Dornstetten	Frd.	Apr 1857	N.-Amer	577776
Weinlaeder, Katharina Margar.		25 Feb 1838	Dornstetten	Frd.	Feb 1847	N.-Amer	569271
Weinlaeder, Margaretha & F		10 May 1800	Dornstetten	Frd.	Feb 1847	N.-Amer	569271
Weinlaeder, Maria Catharina		25 Nov 1858	Dornstetten	Frd.	Jul 1866	N.-Amer	577780
Weinlaeder, Maria Elisab. (wife)			Dornstetten	Frd.	Jul 1866	N.-Amer	577780
Weinmann, Andreas			Fuernsal	Sulz	May 1866	N.-Amer	849635
Weinmann, Jakob		6 Jul 1862	Fuernsal	Sulz	Sep 1882	N.-Amer	849626
Weinmann, Johann Georg & F			Wittendorf	Frd.	Apr 1817	Russia	569268
Weippert, Anna Marie			Deckenpfronn	Calw	1853	N.-Amer	563212
Weippert, Anton (wid.) & F			Nebringen	Herr.	Jun 1834	N.-Amer	834624
Weippert, Christof & F			Nebringen	Herr.	Jun 1834	N.-Amer	834624
Weippert, Georg Friedrich		17 yrs.	Sulz	Nag.	Jan 1852	N.-Amer	838490
Weippert, Johann Georg		20 Mar 1836	Nebringen	Herr.	Apr 1869	N.-Amer	834624
Weippert, Johann Jacob		26 Jun 1825	Tailfingen	Herr.	Jun 1865	Hesse	834624
Weippert, Ludwig Christian		2 Oct 1848	Pfaeffingen	Herr.	Dec 1868	N.-Amer	834624
Weippert, Michael & F			Nebringen	Herr.	Apr 1835	N.-Amer	834624
Weischert, Jacob			Deckenpfronn	Calw	1852	N.-Amer	563212
Weisenfahrt, Anna Maria (wife)		42 yrs.	Unterjesingen	Herr.	Sep 1843	N.-Amer	834625
Weisenfahrt, Caspar		32 yrs.	Unterjesingen	Herr.	Sep 1843	N.-Amer	834625
Weisenfahrt, Catharina		12 yrs.	Unterjesingen	Herr.	Sep 1843	N.-Amer	834625
Weisenfahrt, Catharina		8 yrs.	Unterjesingen	Herr.	Sep 1843	N.-Amer	834625
Weisenfahrt, Eleonora Magd.		14 yrs.	Unterjesingen	Herr.	Sep 1843	N.-Amer	834625
Weisenfahrt, Franziska		7 yrs.	Unterjesingen	Herr.	Sep 1843	N.-Amer	834625
Weisenfahrt, Franziska & C		38 yrs.	Unterjesingen	Herr.	Sep 1843	N.-Amer	834625
Weisenfahrt, Gordonus		13 yrs.	Unterjesingen	Herr.	Sep 1843	N.-Amer	834625
Weisenfahrt, Johann Georg		17 yrs.	Unterjesingen	Herr.	Sep 1843	N.-Amer	834625
Weisenfahrt, Johannes		1 yrs.	Unterjesingen	Herr.	Sep 1843	N.-Amer	834625
Weisenfahrt, Johannes		10 yrs.	Unterjesingen	Herr.	Sep 1843	N.-Amer	834625
Weisenfahrt, Johannes & F		42 yrs.	Unterjesingen	Herr.	Sep 1843	N.-Amer	834625
Weisenfahrt, Maria		6 yrs.	Unterjesingen	Herr.	Sep 1843	N.-Amer	834625
Weisenfahrt, Mathaeus		40 yrs.	Unterjesingen	Herr.	Sep 1843	N.-Amer	834625
Weisenfahrt, Rosine		5 yrs.	Unterjesingen	Herr.	Sep 1843	N.-Amer	834625

Weisenfahrt, Rosine & C	36 yrs.	Unterjesingen	Herr.	Sep 1843	N.-Amer	834625
Weisenfahrt, Sebast	1 yrs.	Unterjesingen	Herr.	Sep 1843	N.-Amer	834625
Weisenfahrt, Wilhelmine	1 yrs.	Unterjesingen	Herr.	Sep 1843	N.-Amer	834625
Weisenfahrt, Wilhelmine	20 yrs.	Unterjesingen	Herr.	Sep 1843	N.-Amer	834625
Weiser, Adam		Durrweiler	Frd.	1817	Russia	569269
Weiss, Anna Maria	18 yrs.	Wittershausen	Sulz	Sep 1846	--	849644
Weiss, Carl Adolph	1840	Calw	Calw	1860	N.-Amer	563212
Weiss, Christian		Moetzingen	Herr.	Jul 1830	N.-Amer	834624
Weiss, Christiane & C	11 Dec 1839	Gaertringen	Herr.	Sep 1868	Baden	834624
Weiss, Elisabeth & C	7 Feb 1828	Gaertringen	Herr.	Nov 1865	France	834624
Weiss, Eva Maria	28 yrs.	Oberweiler	Calw	1857	N.-Amer	563212
Weiss, Georg Friedrich	19 Jul 1840	Sulz	Sulz	May 1867	Baden	849628
Weiss, Georg Friedrich		Moetzingen	Herr.	Oct 1830	N.-Amer	834624
Weiss, Heinrike		Unterjettingen	Herr.	Feb 1852	N.-Amer	834627
Weiss, Johann Friedrich	1817	Calw	Calw	1854	N.-Amer	563212
Weiss, Johanna	17 yrs.	Dornstetten	Frd.	Oct 1850	N.-Amer	569271
Weiss, Sophia Friedrika Dor.	16 Oct 1849	Gaertringen	Herr.	Sep 1868	Baden	834624
Weissburger, Georg Friedrich		Sulz	Sulz	May 1867	Baden	849628
Weisser, Anna Maria		Aistaig	Sulz	Sep 1855	Baden	849628
Weisser, Barbara		Oberiflingen	Frd.	Apr 1854	N.-Amer	569273
Weisser, Emilie	24 Oct 1818	Herrenberg	Herr.	Dec 1849	Baden	834627
Weisser, Jacob & F		Wittlensweiler	Frd.	Apr 1817	Russia	569268
Weisser, Johann Georg	10 Aug 1811	Oberwaldach	Frd.	Feb 1833	N.-Amer	569269
Weisser, Johannes	29 Sep 1845	Goettelfingen	Frd.	Feb 1864	N.-Amer	577779
Weisser, Johannes		Aistaig	Sulz	bef 1858	N.-Amer	849628
Weisser, Juliane	24 Feb 1812	Pfalzgrafenweiler	Frd.	Sep 1853	N.-Amer	569272
Weisser, Michael	11 Oct 1823	Groembach	Frd.	bef 1849	France	569270
Weisser, Michael	12 Jan 1809	Oberwaldach	Frd.	Feb 1833	N.-Amer	569269
Weisser, Regine		Friedrichstal	Frd.	May 1813	Baden	569267
Weisser, Sophie Caroline	23 Mar 1826	Unterjettingen	Herr.	Apr 1850	Switz.	834627
Weissert, Adam Friedrich & F		Durrweiler	Frd.	Jun 1817	Russia	569269
Wekherle, Wilhelmine		Calw	Calw	1861	Switz.	563212
Wekner, Gottlieb	1840	Gechingen	Calw	1854	N.-Amer	563212
Welcker, Jacob		Freudenstadt	--	Dec 1751	N.-Amer	550803
Welker, Christine	22 Dec 1825	Pfalzgrafenweiler	Frd.	Jun 1857	N.-Amer	577776
Welker, Johann Jacob (wid.)	21 Jul 1761	Holzhausen	Sulz	May 1817	N.-Amer	849635
Wellhaeuser, Barbara & C		Poltringen	Herr.	Mar 1852	N.-Amer	834627
Wellhaeuser, Konrad	42 yrs.	Oberndorf	Herr.	Jun 1852	N.-Amer	834627
Wellhaeuser, Maria & C	30 Oct 1810	Oberndorf	Herr.	Mar 1847	N.-Amer	834626
Wellhaeuser, Theresia	26 Mar 1836	Poltringen	Herr.	Apr 1870	N.-Amer	834624
Wellhaeuser, Theresia	15 Jun 1835	Oberndorf	Herr.	Mar 1847	N.-Amer	834626
Wellner, Jacob & F		Gechingen	Calw	1853	N.-Amer	563212
Welmaier, Johann Ludwig	38 yrs.	Althengstett	Calw	1868	N.-Amer	563212
Wendel, Friedrich	4 Feb 1847	Rodt	Frd.	Sep 1866	N.-Amer	577780
Weng, Anna	24 yrs.	Duerrenmettstetten	Sulz	Feb 1854	N.-Amer	849635
Weng, Anna (wid.) & F		Duerrenmettstetten	Sulz	Feb 1854	N.-Amer	849635
Weng, Anna Maria	21 yrs.	Duerrenmettstetten	Sulz	Feb 1854	N.-Amer	849635
Weng, Christina	11 yrs.	Duerrenmettstetten	Sulz	Feb 1854	N.-Amer	849635
Weng, Rosina	19 yrs.	Duerrenmettstetten	Sulz	Feb 1854	N.-Amer	849635
Weng, Zacharias	16 yrs.	Duerrenmettstetten	Sulz	Feb 1854	N.-Amer	849635

Name		Birth		Emigration			Film
Last	First	Date	Place	O'amt	Appl. Date	Dest.	Number
Wenkler, Maria Dorothea		19 yrs.	Gaertringen	Herr.	Oct 1846	N.-Amer	834626
Wennagel, Christiana		32 yrs.	Dornstetten	Frd.	Sep 1853	N.-Amer	569272
Wennagel, Jakob		16 Feb 1844	Dornstetten	Frd.	Nov 1862	N.-Amer	577778
Wennagel, Martin & F			Dornstetten	Frd.	Apr 1817	Russia	569269
Wenne, Johannes		22 yrs.	Zwerenberg	Calw	1857	N.-Amer	563212
Wentsch, Christine			Altburg	Calw	Apr 1870	Hesse	563212
Wentsch, Georg Friedrich		1839	Liebelsberg	Calw	1859	N.-Amer	563212
Wentsch, Johann Georg		1837	Liebelsberg	Calw	1856	N.-Amer	563212
Wentsch, Johann Jakob & F		36 yrs.	Liebelsberg	Calw	1854	N.-Amer	563212
Wentsch, Johann Martin		1841	Liebelsberg	Calw	1859	N.-Amer	563212
Wentsch, Katharina Barbara		19 yrs.	Liebelsberg	Calw	1854	N.-Amer	563212
Wentsch, Ulrich & F			Moettlingen	Calw	1853	N.-Amer	563212
Wenz, Agnes		11 Jun 1835	Schoenegruend	Frd.	bef 1863	Baden	577778
Wenz, Christian Adam		20 Jul 1828	Entringen	Herr.	Sep 1869	N.-Amer	834624
Wenzel, Christiane Rosine		25 Oct 1817	Herrenberg	Herr.	Nov 1843	Switz.	834625
Wenzler, Catharina (wife)			Aistaig	Sulz	Mar 1836	N.-Amer	849628
Wenzler, Johann Georg & W		11 Mar 1808	Aistaig	Sulz	Mar 1836	N.-Amer	849628
Wenzler, Johann Martin		22 May 1799	Bickelsberg	Sulz	Feb 1833	N.-Amer	849630
Wenzler, Mathilde & C			Binsdorf	Sulz	Apr 1817	Russia	849630
Werner, Barbara (wife)		34 yrs.	Bondorf	Herr.	Jun 1832	N.-Amer	834624
Werner, Carl Friedrich		1 Mar 1842	Bondorf	Herr.	Oct 1866	N.-Amer	834624
Werner, Christian		1 Feb 1848	Bondorf	Herr.	Dec 1868	N.-Amer	834624
Werner, Gotthilf			Bergfelden	Sulz	Oct 1880	N.-Amer	849626
Werner, Gotthilf Richard		1 Feb 1864	Bergfelden	Sulz	Oct 1880	N.-Amer	849629
Werner, Jacob & W		44 yrs.	Bondorf	Herr.	Jun 1832	N.-Amer	834624
Werner, Johann & F			Rodt	Frd.	Jun 1817	N.-Amer	569268
Werner, Johann Christian		9 Dec 1832	Bondorf	Herr.	Dec 1863	N.-Amer	834624
Werner, Johann Georg		27 Aug 1840	Bondorf	Herr.	Jan 1865	N.-Amer	834624
Werner, Johann Jacob & W		50 yrs.	Bondorf	Herr.	Jun 1832	N.-Amer	834624
Werner, Johann Martin		24 Sep 1849	Bondorf	Herr.	Oct 1866	N.-Amer	834624
Werner, Louisa (wife)			Bondorf	Herr.	Jun 1832	N.-Amer	834624
Weser, Agnes		29 Jan 1825	Binsdorf	Sulz	Apr 1833	N.-Amer	849630
Weser, Anna Maria			Fuernsal	Sulz	Oct 1853	N.-Amer	849635
Weser, Apolonia		7 Feb 1832	Binsdorf	Sulz	Apr 1833	N.-Amer	849630
Weser, Ferdinand & F		4 Feb 1785	Binsdorf	Sulz	Apr 1833	N.-Amer	849630
Weser, Franz Xaver		16 Dec 1823	Binsdorf	Sulz	Apr 1833	N.-Amer	849630
Weser, Johann Nepomuk		12 Feb 1868	Binsdorf	Sulz	Jul 1881	N.-Amer	849631
Weser, Katharina & F			Binsdorf	Sulz	Aug 1854	N.-Amer	849630
Weser, Loise			Binsdorf	Sulz	Aug 1854	N.-Amer	849630
Weser, Lotte			Binsdorf	Sulz	Aug 1854	N.-Amer	849630
Weser, Matthias			Binsdorf	Sulz	bef 1855	N.-Amer	849630
Weser, Roman		27 Feb 1822	Binsdorf	Sulz	Feb 1866	N.-Amer	849631
Weser, Rosa		30 Aug 1830	Binsdorf	Sulz	Apr 1833	N.-Amer	849630
Weser, Rudolf		12 Sep 1846	Binsdorf	Sulz	Sep 1866	N.-Amer	849631
Weser, Sofie			Binsdorf	Sulz	Aug 1854	N.-Amer	849630
Weser, Ursula (wife)		6 Jan 1799	Binsdorf	Sulz	Apr 1833	N.-Amer	849630
Wesser, Johann Georg		10 Jul 1843	Tailfingen	Herr.	Mar 1869	N.-Amer	834624
Westle, Georg Christoph & F		42 yrs.	Freudenstadt	Frd.	May 1752	Pen.N-A	550803
Westle, Rosina Margaretha		34 yrs.	Freudenstadt	Frd.	May 1752	Pen.N-A	550803
Wetzel, Christian		23 Nov 1847	Brittheim	Sulz	Apr 1867	N.-Amer	849632

Wetzel, Christian	22 Nov 1827	Unterjesingen	Herr.	bef 1863	N.-Amer	834624
Wetzel, Maria Dorothea	30 Jan 1837	Unterjesingen	Herr.	bef 1863	N.-Amer	834624
Wetzler, Johann	Nov 1825	Altheim	Horb	bef 1847	N.-Amer	835929
Weydman, Christian Wilhelm		Meerfelden	– –	Dec 1751	N.-Amer	550803
Weydman, Nicolaus		Meerfelden	– –	Dec 1751	N.-Amer	550803
Wezel, Anna & C	11 Jun 1835	Groembach	Frd.	Aug 1865	N.-Amer	577779
Wezel, Gotthold	23 Apr 1831	Unterjesingen	Herr.	Apr 1851	N.-Amer	834627
Wezel, Johann Adam	27 Jun 1846	Schwarzenberg	Frd.	Jan 1866	N.-Amer	577780
Wezel, Karl	13 Feb 1865	Groembach	Frd.	Aug 1865	N.-Amer	577779
Wezel, Ludwig	18 Mar 1829	Unterjesingen	Herr.	Apr 1851	N.-Amer	834627
Wezger, Gustav Adolf Ferdin.	5 Oct 1847	Herrenberg	Herr.	Dec 1867	N.-Amer	834624
Widemaier, Johann Georg	30 Aug 1835	Wittlensweiler	Frd.	May 1853	France	569272
Wider, Christian		Dornhan	Sulz	Jun 1852	N.-Amer	849633
Wider, Ferdinand Friedrich	1 May 1833	Rosenfeld	Sulz	Aug 1852	N.-Amer	849640
Wider, Friedrich	7 Nov 1838	Rosenfeld	Sulz	Aug 1854	N.-Amer	849640
Wider, Jacob		Rosenfeld	Sulz	bef 1858	N.-Amer	849640
Wider, Maria Charlotta	22 Apr 1835	Rosenfeld	Sulz	Jun 1865	N.-Amer	849641
Wider, Wilhelm	9 Nov 1839	Dornhan	Sulz	May 1859	England	849633
Wider, Wilhelm	20 Oct 1851	Rosenfeld	Sulz	Aug 1869	N.-Amer	849641
Widmaier, Anna Barbara	26 Oct 1828	Kuppingen	Herr.	bef 1862	N.-Amer	834624
Widmaier, Anna Maria	7 Jan 1787	Sigmarswangen	Sulz	Feb 1817	Russia	849642
Widmaier, Barbara	15 May 1834	Wittlensweiler	Frd.	bef 1864	Baden	577779
Widmaier, Christian		Kuppingen	Herr.	May 1836	N.-Amer	834624
Widmaier, Christian Friedrich	23 Nov 1823	Kuppingen	Herr.	Mar 1865	N.-Amer	834624
Widmaier, Daniel	25 Sep 1837	Oberjesingen	Herr.	May 1852	N.-Amer	834627
Widmaier, Elisabeth (wife)	25 Apr 1809	Oberjesingen	Herr.	May 1852	N.-Amer	834627
Widmaier, Elisabetha	15 Jul 1839	Oberjesingen	Herr.	May 1852	N.-Amer	834627
Widmaier, Eva Dorothea	9 Sep 1827	Kuppingen	Herr.	bef 1862	N.-Amer	834624
Widmaier, Friedrich	3 Aug 1849	Oberjesingen	Herr.	May 1852	N.-Amer	834627
Widmaier, Georg Balthasar	6 Nov 1845	Oberjesingen	Herr.	May 1852	N.-Amer	834627
Widmaier, Hermann	19 yrs.	Calw	Calw	1854	N.-Amer	563212
Widmaier, Jakob		Oberjesingen	Herr.	May 1852	N.-Amer	834627
Widmaier, Johann Friedrich	21 Apr 1841	Oberjesingen	Herr.	May 1852	N.-Amer	834627
Widmaier, Johann Friedrich & F		Oberjesingen	Herr.	May 1852	N.-Amer	834627
Widmaier, Johann Georg		Stammheim	Calw	1853	N.-Amer	563212
Widmaier, Johann Georg	29 Oct 1832	Oberjesingen	Herr.	May 1852	N.-Amer	834627
Widmaier, Johann Georg	Aug 1842	Oberjesingen	Herr.	May 1852	N.-Amer	834627
Widmaier, Johann Georg & F	8 Nov 1803	Oberjesingen	Herr.	May 1852	N.-Amer	834627
Widmaier, Johann Jakob	17 Oct 1843	Oberjesingen	Herr.	May 1852	N.-Amer	834627
Widmaier, Johann Peter	17 Jan 1834	Oberjesingen	Herr.	May 1852	N.-Amer	834627
Widmaier, Josua	29 Oct 1817	Kuppingen	Herr.	bef 1862	N.-Amer	834624
Widmaier, Justine	21 Jan 1830	Kuppingen	Herr.	bef 1862	N.-Amer	834624
Widmaier, Margaretha	23 Oct 1841	Oberjesingen	Herr.	May 1852	N.-Amer	834627
Widmaier, Maria Katharina	28 Apr 1841	Oberjesingen	Herr.	May 1852	N.-Amer	834627
Widmaier, Regina Heinrika		Kayh	Herr.	Mar 1847	N.-Amer	834626
Widmaier, Regina Magdalena	7 Jan 1848	Oberjesingen	Herr.	May 1852	N.-Amer	834627
Widman, Mathias	17 Mar 1845	Dornhan	Sulz	Apr 1864	N.-Amer	849634
Widmann, Christian		Enztal	Nag.	Jul 1852	N.-Amer	838490
Widmann, Christian & F		Enztal	Nag.	Jul 1852	N.-Amer	838490
Widmann, Christiane	29 yrs.	Simmozheim	Calw	1866	Baden	563212

228

Name		Birth		Emigration			Film
Last	First	Date	Place	O'amt	Appl. Date	Dest.	Number
Widmann, Christina			Enztal	Nag.	Jul 1852	N.-Amer	838490
Widmann, Johann Martin			Enztal	Nag.	Jul 1852	N.-Amer	838490
Widmann, Johannes		5 Nov 1859	Dornhan	Sulz	Jul 1874	N.-Amer	849634
Widmann, Michael Friedrich		14 Jul 1836	Goettelfingen	Frd.	Feb 1855	N.-Amer	569275
Widmann, Veronika			Enztal	Nag.	Jul 1852	N.-Amer	838490
Widmann, Veronika			Allmandle	Frd.	Aug 1856	N.-Amer	569275
Widmayer, Margaretha		29 yrs.	Kuppingen	Herr.	Apr 1831	N.-Amer	834624
Widmer, Jakob			Boll	Sulz	Aug 1852	N.-Amer	849632
Widmer, Johann Adam		12 Jun 1812	Aistaig	Sulz	bef 1841	N.-Amer	849628
Widmer, Johann Georg			Marschalkenzimmern	Sulz	bef 1807	Bessar.	849638
Widmer, Margaretha			Boll	Sulz	Feb 1847	N.-Amer	849632
Widmer, Maria			Marschalkenzimmern	Sulz	bef 1829	Bessar.	849638
Wiedmaier, Michael		16 Aug 1842	Rodt	Frd.	May 1860	N.-Amer	577777
Wiedmann, Jakob		10 Jan 1834	Allmandle	Frd.	Feb 1854	N.-Amer	569273
Wiedmann, Johann Georg		15 Apr 1829	Goettelfingen	Frd.	Jul 1857	N.-Amer	577776
Wiedmann, Johann Georg		14 Sep 1834	Marschalkenzimmern	Sulz	Sep 1854	N.-Amer	849638
Wiedmeyer, Catharina			Schoemberg	Frd.	Jun 1854	N.-Amer	569273
Wieland, Eva Catharina		15 Oct 1822	Unterweissach	Bckn.	bef 1868	N.-Amer	555959
Wieland, Jacob Friedrich		5 May 1852	Unterweissach	Bckn.	bef 1868	N.-Amer	555959
Wieland, Ludwig Wilhelm		1 Sep 1853	Unterweissach	Bckn.	bef 1868	N.-Amer	555959
Wierz, Carl Friedrich			Calw	Calw	1853	N.-Amer	563212
Wiesenhofer, Ambrosius		18 Dec 1820	Unterjesingen	Herr.	Sep 1843	N.-Amer	834625
Wiesotha, Maria (wife)		37 yrs.	Oberjettingen	Herr.	Jul 1847	N.-Amer	834626
Wiesotha, Mathaeus Fried. & F		38 yrs.	Oberjettingen	Herr.	Jul 1847	N.-Amer	834626
Wiezenmann, Johannes & F			Brittheim	Sulz	Apr 1817	Russia	849632
Wiezenmann, Mathaeus & F			Brittheim	Sulz	Apr 1817	Russia	849632
Wild, Martin & F			Wildberg	Frd.	1817	Russia	569269
Wildschuetz, Margaretha		24 Aug 1804	Baiersbronn	Frd.	Aug 1854	N.-Amer	569274
Wilhelm, Carl Hottlieb		21 Dec 1803	Rosenfeld	Sulz	Jul 1834	France	849640
Wille, Gottlob Friedrich		15 May 1852	Leidringen	Sulz	Mar 1871	N.-Amer	849637
Wille, Maria Wilhelmine			Leidringen	Sulz	Mar 1866	N.-Amer	849637
Winkler, Anna		16 Sep 1852	Dornhan	Sulz	May 1858	N.-Amer	849633
Winkler, Caroline			Stammheim	Calw	1853	N.-Amer	563212
Winkler, Christina & C		30 Dec 1828	Dornhan	Sulz	May 1858	N.-Amer	849633
Winkler, Jacob Friedrich			Stammheim	Calw	1860	N.-Amer	563212
Winkler, Mathias Gottlieb			Sulz	Sulz	Apr 1841	Bavaria	849627
Winnagel, Johann Martin			Dornstetten	Frd.	1817	Russia	569269
Winter, Eva		32 yrs.	Reinerzau	Frd.	Mar 1817	Russia	569268
Winterschmid, Elisabetha		27 yrs.	Sulz	Sulz	Feb 1818	N.-Amer	849627
Wirth, Anna Maria		18 Jul 1841	Klosterreichenbach	Frd.	Apr 1847	N.-Amer	569270
Wirth, Anna Maria		18 yrs.	Baiersbronn	Frd.	Jun 1855	N.-Amer	569275
Wirth, Carl		29 Mar 1851	Baiersbronn	Frd.	Jul 1866	N.-Amer	577780
Wirth, Catharina		5 Oct 1845	Baiersbronn	Frd.	Dec 1853	N.-Amer	569272
Wirth, Christine Magdalene		4 Jan 1843	Klosterreichenbach	Frd.	Apr 1847	N.-Amer	569270
Wirth, Friederike		31 Mar 1852	Baiersbronn	Frd.	Dec 1853	N.-Amer	569272
Wirth, Friedrich		29 Nov 1846	Baiersbronn	Frd.	Oct 1866	N.-Amer	577780
Wirth, Georg Friedrich			Freudenstadt	Frd.	Nov 1843	Augsb.	569269
Wirth, Jacob Friedrich & F		4 Jul 1819	Baiersbronn	Frd.	Dec 1853	N.-Amer	569272
Wirth, Jakob Friedrich		20 Nov 1849	Baiersbronn	Frd.	Dec 1853	N.-Amer	569272
Wirth, Johann Friedrich		5 Mar 1844	Baiersbronn	Frd.	Dec 1853	N.-Amer	569272

Wirth, Johannes & F	8 Aug 1816	Klosterreichenbach	Frd.	Apr 1847	N.-Amer	569270
Wirth, Johannes & F		Baiersbronn	Frd.	Jun 1855	N.-Amer	569275
Wirth, Karl David	18 May 1847	Baiersbronn	Frd.	May 1866	N.-Amer	577780
Wirth, Karl Friedrich	17 Jan 1846	Klosterreichenbach	Frd.	Apr 1847	N.-Amer	569270
Wirth, Ludwig	7 Jan 1846	Baiersbronn	Frd.	Aug 1866	N.-Amer	577780
Wirth, Regina (wife)		Baiersbronn	Frd.	Jun 1855	N.-Amer	569275
Wirth, Regine Rosine	26 Aug 1847	Baiersbronn	Frd.	Dec 1853	N.-Amer	569272
Wirth, Rosine	21 Sep 1816	Baiersbronn	Frd.	Dec 1853	N.-Amer	569272
Wirth, Rosine Barbara	2 Nov 1821	Baiersbronn	Frd.	Apr 1847	N.-Amer	569270
Wissmann, Balthas		Pfeffingen	Bal.	bef 1845	Switz.	555962
Wittmann, Margaretha		Freudenstadt	Frd.	Mar 1815	France	569267
Wizemann, Catharina & C	32 yrs.	Herrenberg	Herr.	Jun 1832	N.-Amer	834624
Wizemann, Johannes		Wittershausen	Sulz	Aug 1852	N.-Amer	849644
Wobler, Johann Friedrich & F		Voehringen	Sulz	Jul 1817	Russia	849627
Wochele, Friedrich		Calw	Calw	1853	N.-Amer	563212
Woehr, Hyancinthia		Binsdorf	Sulz	Mar 1815	Bavaria	849625
Woehr, Karl Fr. Albert	8 Sep 1829	Stuttgart	Sulz	Jun 1870	Switz.	849635
Woehrl, Tobias & F	5 Mar 1811	Baiersbronn	Frd.	Aug 1854	N.-Amer	569274
Woehrle, Catharina	19 Sep 1851	Baiersbronn	Frd.	Aug 1854	N.-Amer	569274
Woehrle, Catharina (wife)	1 Apr 1819	Baiersbronn	Frd.	Aug 1854	N.-Amer	569274
Woehrle, Christian	24 Jan 1842	Baiersbronn	Frd.	Aug 1854	N.-Amer	569274
Woehrle, Christina	4 Jun 1796	Freudenstadt	Frd.	Mar 1833	Baden	569267
Woehrle, Johann Georg		Baiersbronn	Frd.	Aug 1854	N.-Amer	569274
Woehrle, Johann Georg	12 Feb 1840	Baiersbronn	Frd.	Aug 1854	N.-Amer	569274
Woehrle, Marie	19 Apr 1845	Baiersbronn	Frd.	Aug 1854	N.-Amer	569274
Woehrle, Simon Friedrich & F		Calw	Calw	1854	N.-Amer	563212
Woehrle, Tobias	28 Oct 1847	Baiersbronn	Frd.	Aug 1854	N.-Amer	569274
Woelpper, Friederike Barbara	5 Sep 1837	Freudenstadt	Frd.	Jul 1858	France	577776
Woelpper, Jakob Friedrich & F		Freudenstadt	Frd.	Apr 1853	N.-Amer	569272
Woelpper, Johann Martin	19 yrs.	Freudenstadt	Frd.	May 1750	Pen.N-A	550803
Woelpper, Karoline		Freudenstadt	Frd.	Apr 1853	N.-Amer	569272
Woelpper, Marie Louise		Erzgrube	Frd.	Jun 1858	N.-Amer	577776
Woelpper, Rosine Margaretha		Freudenstadt	Frd.	Nov 1857	Sardin.	577776
Woerger, Sara & C		Nufringen	Herr.	Jun 1833	Rus-Pol	834624
Woerner, Andreas	14 yrs.	Schoemberg	Frd.	Nov 1851	N.-Amer	569271
Woerner, Andreas	8 Jan 1834	Kuppingen	Herr.	Mar 1848	N.-Amer	834626
Woerner, Anna Barbara	16 Jan 1816	Sulz	Sulz	Jul 1817	Russia	849627
Woerner, Anna Margaretha	3 Oct 1810	Hoesslinswart	Schd.	Jul 1834	N.-Amer	801460
Woerner, Anna Maria	15 yrs.	Schoemberg	Frd.	Nov 1851	N.-Amer	569271
Woerner, Anna Maria	27 Feb 1853	Glatten	Frd.	Oct 1854	S.-Amer	569274
Woerner, Anna Maria	10 Jan 1824	Rohrau	Herr.	Mar 1843	Rus-Pol	834625
Woerner, Anna Maria (wife)	12 Sep 1775	Sulz	Sulz	Jul 1817	Russia	849627
Woerner, Anna Maria (wife)	24 Dec 1844	Hildrizhausen	Herr.	Mar 1870	N.-Amer	834624
Woerner, Barbara	5 May 1808	Rodt	Frd.	Jan 1842	France	569269
Woerner, Barbara	1 yrs.	Schoemberg	Frd.	Nov 1851	N.-Amer	569271
Woerner, Barbara	13 Oct 1838	Sulz	Sulz	Mar 1870	N.-Amer	849628
Woerner, Bartholomaeus & F		Rohrau	Herr.	Mar 1835	Rus-Pol	834624
Woerner, Caroline & C	3 Feb 1825	Glatten	Frd.	Oct 1854	S.-Amer	569274
Woerner, Catharina Margaretha		Grunbach	Schd.	Mar 1837	N.-Amer	801461
Woerner, Christian	25 Dec 1822	Entringen	Herr.	Jan 1866	N.-Amer	834624

| Name | | Birth | | Emigration | | | Film |
Last	First	Date	Place	O'amt	Appl. Date	Dest.	Number
Woerner,	Christiana Regina		Voehringen	Sulz	1834	N.-Amer	849625
Woerner,	Christina	16 yrs.	Schoemberg	Frd.	Nov 1851	N.-Amer	569271
Woerner,	Christina	28 Jun 1797	Sulz	Sulz	Jul 1817	Russia	849627
Woerner,	Christina Rosine		Herrenberg	Herr.	May 1845	Baden	834626
Woerner,	Conrad Friedrich		Grunbach	Schd.	Mar 1837	N.-Amer	801461
Woerner,	Dorothea	8 Apr 1811	Sulz	Sulz	Jul 1817	Russia	849627
Woerner,	Elisabeth	26 Oct 1800	Sulz	Sulz	Jul 1817	Russia	849627
Woerner,	Friederike Cath. & C	14 Jul 1833	Sulz	Sulz	Sep 1866	N.-Amer	849628
Woerner,	Friedrich	27 Apr 1828	Nufringen	Herr.	bef 1870	N.-Amer	834624
Woerner,	Friedrich & F	22 Jul 1771	Sulz	Sulz	Jul 1817	Russia	849627
Woerner,	Gabriel	29 Nov 1835	Rohrau	Herr.	Mar 1843	Rus-Pol	834625
Woerner,	Georg Joseph & F		Gueltstein	Herr.	Apr 1835	N.-Amer	834624
Woerner,	Gottfried	8 Mar 1843	Boeffingen	Frd.	Aug 1866	N.-Amer	577780
Woerner,	Gottlieb		Grunbach	Schd.	Mar 1837	N.-Amer	801461
Woerner,	Jacob	3 Sep 1818	Rohrau	Herr.	Mar 1843	Rus-Pol	834625
Woerner,	Jacob & F	3 Mar 1793	Rohrau	Herr.	Mar 1843	Rus-Pol	834625
Woerner,	Jacob Friedrich	16 Jan 1816	Sulz	Sulz	Jul 1817	Russia	849627
Woerner,	Jacob Friedrich		Grunbach	Schd.	1834	Russia	801460
Woerner,	Jacobine Friederike	24 Jan 1805	Herrenberg	Herr.	Jul 1846	N.-Amer	834626
Woerner,	Jakob	9 Jun 1860	Dornhan	Sulz	Apr 1878	N.-Amer	849634
Woerner,	Jakob Friedrich		Sulz	Sulz	Jul 1863	Switz.	849628
Woerner,	Jakobine Friederike		Grunbach	Schd.	Mar 1837	N.-Amer	801461
Woerner,	Johann Adam & F		Schoemberg	Frd.	Nov 1851	N.-Amer	569271
Woerner,	Johann Andreas		Sulz	Sulz	May 1846	N.-Amer	849627
Woerner,	Johann Andreas & F		Freudenstadt	Frd.	1851	N.-Amer	577778
Woerner,	Johann Friedrich		Voehringen	Sulz	1834	N.-Amer	849625
Woerner,	Johann Georg	12 yrs.	Schoemberg	Frd.	Nov 1851	N.-Amer	569271
Woerner,	Johann Georg	19 Sep 1842	Rohrau	Herr.	Mar 1843	Rus-Pol	834625
Woerner,	Johann Georg & F		Kuppingen	Herr.	Mar 1848	N.-Amer	834626
Woerner,	Johann Georg & F	26 Dec 1842	Hildrizhausen	Herr.	Mar 1870	N.-Amer	834624
Woerner,	Johann Georg & F		Bondorf	Herr.	Apr 1835	N.-Amer	834624
Woerner,	Johann Gottlieb		Voehringen	Sulz	1834	N.-Amer	849625
Woerner,	Johanna	15 Jan 1820	Rohrau	Herr.	Mar 1843	Rus-Pol	834625
Woerner,	Johannes	17 Oct 1849	Glatten	Frd.	Oct 1854	S.-Amer	569274
Woerner,	Johannes	26 Apr 1811	Grunbach	Schd.	1834	Russia	801460
Woerner,	Johannes		Grunbach	Schd.	Mar 1837	N.-Amer	801461
Woerner,	Johannes	16 May 1831	Rohrau	Herr.	Mar 1870	N.-Amer	834624
Woerner,	Johannes August	3 May 1866	Hildrizhausen	Herr.	Mar 1870	N.-Amer	834624
Woerner,	Karl August	13 Jun 1843	Nufringen	Herr.	bef 1870	N.-Amer	834624
Woerner,	Katharina	8 Apr 1811	Sulz	Sulz	Jul 1817	Russia	849627
Woerner,	Maria Agnes	2 Oct 1829	Rohrau	Herr.	Mar 1843	Rus-Pol	834625
Woerner,	Maria Catharina	18 Jan 1821	Rohrau	Herr.	Mar 1843	Rus-Pol	834625
Woerner,	Maria Catharina (wife)	18 Nov 1797	Rohrau	Herr.	Mar 1843	Rus-Pol	834625
Woerner,	Maria Elisabetha		Voehringen	Sulz	1834	N.-Amer	849625
Woerner,	Maria Friederike	6 Dec 1860	Sulz	Sulz	Sep 1866	N.-Amer	849628
Woerner,	Mathias	21 May 1827	Rohrau	Herr.	Mar 1843	Rus-Pol	834625
Woerner,	Peter		Grunbach	Schd.	Mar 1837	N.-Amer	801461
Woerner,	Rosina Magdalena	23 Jul 1838	Entringen	Herr.	May 1866	Baden	834624
Woesner,	Anna Maria	13 Jul 1812	Marschalkenzimmern	Sulz	Jul 1817	Russia	849638
Woesner,	Anna Maria (wife)	44 yrs.	Rosenfeld	Sulz	Jun 1817	Russia	849640

Woesner, Carl Friedrich & W	40 yrs.	Rosenfeld	Sulz	Jun 1817	Russia	849640
Woesner, Christina Barbara		Sulz	Sulz	Aug 1812	France	849625
Woesner, Johannes	9 Dec 1816	Marschalkenzimmern	Sulz	Jul 1817	Russia	849638
Woesner, Veronika	12 Feb 1804	Marschalkenzimmern	Sulz	Jul 1817	Russia	849638
Woesner, Veronika & C	25 Nov 1781	Marschalkenzimmern	Sulz	Jul 1817	Russia	849638
Woessner, Andreas	10 Aug 1832	Wittendorf	Frd.	Jun 1860	France	577777
Woessner, Andreas	4 Apr 1808	Voehringen	Sulz	bef 1817	--	849643
Woessner, Andreas	9 Mar 1869	Sigmarswangen	Sulz	Aug 1872	N.-Amer	849642
Woessner, Andreas	30 Nov 1840	Marschalkenzimmern	Sulz	May 1864	N.-Amer	849638
Woessner, Andreas	26 Apr 1828	Muehlheim a.B.	Sulz	bef 1865	N.-Amer	849639
Woessner, Anna	19 Jul 1861	Voehringen	Sulz	bef 1883	N.-Amer	849643
Woessner, Anna	3 Oct 1856	Sigmarswangen	Sulz	Aug 1872	N.-Amer	849642
Woessner, Anna	5 Feb 1840	Dornhan	Sulz	Feb 1860	N.-Amer	849633
Woessner, Anna	19 Jul 1861	Voehringen	Sulz	Apr 1883	N.-Amer	849626
Woessner, Anna & C	7 Apr 1842	Boll	Sulz	Jun 1866	Baden	849632
Woessner, Anna & F	9 Jun 1849	Brittheim	Sulz	Nov 1884	N.-Amer	849632
Woessner, Anna (wife)	15 Jun 1839	Voehringen	Sulz	Apr 1883	N.-Amer	849643
Woessner, Anna (wife)		Voehringen	Sulz	Apr 1883	N.-Amer	849626
Woessner, Anna Maria	30 Nov 1780	Voehringen	Sulz	bef 1817	--	849643
Woessner, Anna Maria	11 Dec 1847	Sigmarswangen	Sulz	Sep 1869	N.-Amer	849642
Woessner, Anna Maria & C	27 Apr 1845	Dornhan	Sulz	Sep 1869	N.-Amer	849634
Woessner, Auguste		Sulz	Sulz	Jul 1851	Switz.	849627
Woessner, Balbina	20 Sep 1848	Leinstetten	Sulz	Dec 1856	Hungary	849638
Woessner, Balbina		Leinstetten	Sulz	bef 1842	Hungary	849638
Woessner, Balbina	24 Sep 1816	Leinstetten	Sulz	Jun 1817	N.-Amer	849638
Woessner, Barbara	18 Oct 1864	Voehringen	Sulz	bef 1883	N.-Amer	849643
Woessner, Barbara	12 Dec 1847	Voehringen	Sulz	Aug 1871	N.-Amer	849643
Woessner, Barbara	28 Jul 1845	Hopfau	Sulz	Oct 1853	N.-Amer	849636
Woessner, Barbara	6 May 1832	Leinstetten	Sulz	Dec 1856	Hungary	849638
Woessner, Barbara	18 Oct 1864	Voehringen	Sulz	Apr 1883	N.-Amer	849626
Woessner, Barbara (wife)	29 Jan 1844	Sigmarswangen	Sulz	Aug 1872	N.-Amer	849642
Woessner, Catharina		Marschalkenzimmern	Sulz	bef 1862	Switz.	849638
Woessner, Catharina Barb. (wife)		Muehlheim a.B.	Sulz	Aug 1832	N.-Amer	849639
Woessner, Catharine		Sulz	Sulz	Oct 1835	France	849627
Woessner, Christian	10 Nov 1836	Hopfau	Sulz	Feb 1854	N.-Amer	849636
Woessner, Christian	27 May 1848	Hopfau	Sulz	Oct 1853	N.-Amer	849636
Woessner, Christian	10 Sep 1795	Hopfau	Sulz	Feb 1834	Baden	849636
Woessner, Christian	19 Feb 1879	Dornhan	Sulz	Feb 1897	N.-Amer	849626
Woessner, Christian & F		Hopfau	Sulz	Oct 1853	N.-Amer	849636
Woessner, Christian Ludwig	7 Oct 1831	Sulz	Sulz	Mar 1833	N.-Amer	849627
Woessner, Christiana Elisab.	23 Jun 1830	Sulz	Sulz	Mar 1833	N.-Amer	849627
Woessner, Christiane Gottlieb.	14 Apr 1829	Sulz	Sulz	1855	N.-Amer	849628
Woessner, Christina	30 Jan 1869	Voehringen	Sulz	Apr 1883	N.-Amer	849643
Woessner, Christina	30 Jan 1869	Voehringen	Sulz	Apr 1883	N.-Amer	849626
Woessner, Christina (wife)		Sulz	Sulz	Apr 1833	N.-Amer	849627
Woessner, Christina Barbara	28 Feb 1844	Sigmarswangen	Sulz	1859	N.-Amer	849642
Woessner, Christine	9 Apr 1867	Dornhan	Sulz	Sep 1869	N.-Amer	849634
Woessner, Dorothea	5 Jul 1848	Aistaig	Sulz	Mar 1866	N.-Amer	849628
Woessner, Dorothea	27 Jun 1863	Sigmarswangen	Sulz	Aug 1872	N.-Amer	849642
Woessner, Elisabetha	4 Aug 1799	Voehringen	Sulz	bef 1817	--	849643

Name		Birth		Emigration			Film
Last	First	Date	Place	O'amt	Appl. Date	Dest.	Number
Woessner, Elisabetha		31 Oct 1772	Dornhan	Sulz	bef 1817	--	849643
Woessner, Elisabetha Catharina		10 Mar 1839	Untermusbach	Frd.	Dec 1857	N.-Amer	577776
Woessner, Georg Andreas		11 Jun 1829	Sulz	Sulz	Mar 1833	N.-Amer	849627
Woessner, Georg Jacob		30 Jan 1803	Voehringen	Sulz	bef 1817	--	849643
Woessner, Georg Jacob		25 Jan 1852	Sigmarswangen	Sulz	1869	N.-Amer	849642
Woessner, Jacob		22 May 1837	Brittheim	Sulz	Apr 1853	N.-Amer	849632
Woessner, Jakob		8 Jul 1876	Voehringen	Sulz	Apr 1883	N.-Amer	849643
Woessner, Jakob		25 Jan 1852	Sigmarswangen	Sulz	Sep 1869	N.-Amer	849642
Woessner, Jakob		27 Jun 1876	Brittheim	Sulz	Nov 1884	N.-Amer	849632
Woessner, Jakob		24 Aug 1823	Brittheim	Sulz	Oct 1853	N.-Amer	849632
Woessner, Jakob			Tischardt	Sulz	Apr 1841	Baden	849633
Woessner, Jakob		2 Jun 1849	Muehlheim a.B.	Sulz	May 1866	N.-Amer	849639
Woessner, Jakob		8 Jul 1876	Voehringen	Sulz	Apr 1883	N.-Amer	849626
Woessner, Johann & W		11 Mar 1804	Sulz	Sulz	Apr 1833	N.-Amer	849627
Woessner, Johann Adam		2 Feb 1828	Hopfau	Sulz	bef 1861	N.-Amer	849636
Woessner, Johann Georg		3 Nov 1820	Sulz	Sulz	May 1832	N.-Amer	849627
Woessner, Johann Georg		3 Feb 1867	Voehringen	Sulz	Apr 1883	N.-Amer	849643
Woessner, Johann Georg		28 Jul 1877	Brittheim	Sulz	Nov 1884	N.-Amer	849632
Woessner, Johann Georg		16 Feb 1842	Dornhan	Sulz	Feb 1860	N.-Amer	849633
Woessner, Johann Georg			Dornhan	Sulz	bef 1838	N.-Amer	849633
Woessner, Johann Georg		3 Feb 1867	Voehringen	Sulz	Apr 1883	N.-Amer	849626
Woessner, Johann Georg & F			Sulz	Sulz	Mar 1833	N.-Amer	849627
Woessner, Johann Georg & W		12 Dec 1800	Sulz	Sulz	Mar 1833	N.-Amer	849627
Woessner, Johann Jacob		14 Sep 1805	Voehringen	Sulz	bef 1817	--	849643
Woessner, Johann Jakob			Brittheim	Sulz	Jul 1884	N.-Amer	849632
Woessner, Johann Jakob		18 Mar 1839	Hopfau	Sulz	Oct 1853	N.-Amer	849636
Woessner, Johann Johann Georg		23 May 1870	Dornhan	Sulz	Sep 1889	N.-Amer	849626
Woessner, Johann Ludwig		23 Jul 1816	Sulz	Sulz	May 1832	N.-Amer	849627
Woessner, Johann Ludwig		22 Jan 1841	Muehlheim a.B.	Sulz	1857	N.-Amer	849639
Woessner, Johann Ludwig		22 Jan 1846	Muehlheim a.B.	Sulz	Mar 1857	N.-Amer	849639
Woessner, Johann Ludwig & F		10 Nov 1791	Sulz	Sulz	May 1832	N.-Amer	849627
Woessner, Johann Martin		13 Nov 1852	Bickelsberg	Sulz	May 1871	N.-Amer	849630
Woessner, Johann Martin & F			Brittheim	Sulz	Jul 1846	N.-Amer	849632
Woessner, Johann Ulrich & W			Muehlheim a.B.	Sulz	Aug 1832	N.-Amer	849639
Woessner, Johanna		6 Mar 1841	Dornhan	Sulz	Aug 1855	N.-Amer	849633
Woessner, Johanna Gottliebin		8 Nov 1818	Sulz	Sulz	May 1832	N.-Amer	849627
Woessner, Johannes		13 Feb 1828	Sulz	Sulz	May 1832	N.-Amer	849627
Woessner, Johannes		30 Aug 1863	Bickelsberg	Sulz	May 1879	N.-Amer	849630
Woessner, Johannes		12 Oct 1879	Brittheim	Sulz	Nov 1884	N.-Amer	849632
Woessner, Johannes		4 Apr 1851	Hopfau	Sulz	Oct 1853	N.-Amer	849636
Woessner, Johannes		4 Sep 1845	Leinstetten	Sulz	Dec 1856	Hungary	849638
Woessner, Johannes		2 Apr 1807	Leinstetten	Sulz	Jun 1817	N.-Amer	849638
Woessner, Johannes		20 Jun 1829	Muehlheim a.B.	Sulz	bef 1865	N.-Amer	849639
Woessner, Johannes		19 Dec 1874	Dornhan	Sulz	Sep 1889	N.-Amer	849626
Woessner, Johannes & F		1 Oct 1764	Voehringen	Sulz	bef 1817	--	849643
Woessner, Johannes (wid.)		14 Apr 1805	Bergfelden	Sulz	Mar 1857	N.-Amer	849629
Woessner, Josef (wid.) & F		23 Nov 1804	Leinstetten	Sulz	Dec 1856	Hungery	849638
Woessner, Joseph		23 Nov 1804	Leinstetten	Sulz	Jun 1817	N.-Amer	849638
Woessner, Katharina		30 Nov 1880	Voehringen	Sulz	Apr 1883	N.-Amer	849643
Woessner, Katharina		16 Jan 1866	Sigmarswangen	Sulz	Aug 1872	N.-Amer	849642

Woessner, Katharina	30 Nov 1880	Voehringen	Sulz	Apr 1883	N.-Amer	849626
Woessner, Lorenz	24 Nov 1808	Leinstetten	Sulz	Jun 1817	N.-Amer	849638
Woessner, Lorenza	19 Jul 1842	Leinstetten	Sulz	Dec 1856	Hungary	849638
Woessner, Luise (wife)	2 May 1784	Sulz	Sulz	May 1832	N.-Amer	849627
Woessner, Maria	26 Aug 1830	Leinstetten	Sulz	Dec 1856	Hungary	849638
Woessner, Maria Anna (wife)	19 Dec 1797	Leinstetten	Sulz	Jun 1817	N.-Amer	849638
Woessner, Maria Elisab. (wife)		Sulz	Sulz	Mar 1833	N.-Amer	849627
Woessner, Maria Luise	21 Jan 1823	Sulz	Sulz	May 1832	N.-Amer	849627
Woessner, Martin	24 Feb 1863	Voehringen	Sulz	Apr 1883	N.-Amer	849643
Woessner, Martin	26 Oct 1811	Voehringen	Sulz	bef 1817	--	849643
Woessner, Martin	24 Feb 1863	Voehringen	Sulz	Apr 1883	N.-Amer	849626
Woessner, Martin & F	29 Mar 1831	Voehringen	Sulz	Apr 1883	N.-Amer	849643
Woessner, Martin & F	24 Oct 1763	Leinstetten	Sulz	Jun 1817	N.-Amer	849638
Woessner, Martin & F		Voehringen	Sulz	Apr 1883	N.-Amer	849626
Woessner, Mathaeus	19 Apr 1842	Hopfau	Sulz	Oct 1853	N.-Amer	849636
Woessner, Mathias	15 Aug 1832	Brittheim	Sulz	bef 1863	N.-Amer	849632
Woessner, Mathias & F	8 Feb 1820	Sigmarswangen	Sulz	Aug 1872	N.-Amer	849642
Woessner, Matthaeus	30 Aug 1849	Marschalkenzimmern	Sulz	Oct 1869	N.-Amer	849638
Woessner, Regina	20 Oct 1846	Aistaig	Sulz	Mar 1866	N.-Amer	849628
Woessner, Regina Christ. (wife)		Sulz	Sulz	Mar 1833	N.-Amer	849627
Woessner, Rosina (wid.) & F	17 Mar 1809	Muehlheim a.B.	Sulz	May 1866	N.-Amer	849639
Woessner, Ulrich & F		Muehlheim a.B.	Sulz	May 1817	Russia	849639
Woessner, Wilhelm	1 Jun 1881	Brittheim	Sulz	Nov 1884	N.-Amer	849632
Woessner, Wilhelm	12 Jun 1842	Muehlheim a.B.	Sulz	1856	N.-Amer	849639
Wohlbold, Dorothea	4 Oct 1834	Gaertringen	Herr.	Dec 1866	N.-Amer	834624
Wohlbold, Johann Ludwig	21 Apr 1821	Herrenberg	Herr.	bef 1845	Bavaria	834626
Wohlgemuth, Agnes Maria		Freudenstadt	Frd.	Sep 1856	N.-Amer	577779
Wohlgemuth, Anna Maria		Agenbach	Calw	1868	N.-Amer	563212
Wohlgemuth, August	1 Aug 1845	Freudenstadt	Frd.	Nov 1865	N.-Amer	577779
Wohlgemuth, Michael & F		Monakam	Calw	1852	N.-Amer	563212
Wohlgemuth, Philippine Doro.		Schernbach	Frd.	Aug 1857	N.-Amer	577776
Wohllaber, Wilhelmine Dorothea		Liebenzell	Calw	1864	Baden	563212
Wohlleber, Christian Friedr.		Liebenzell	Calw	1859	N.-Amer	563212
Wolber, Anna & C	14 Sep 1830	Schopfloch	Frd.	Mar 1859	N.-Amer	577776
Wolber, Christian	18 Feb 1858	Schopfloch	Frd.	Mar 1859	N.-Amer	577776
Wolber, Gottlieb	3 Dec 1854	Schopfloch	Frd.	Mar 1859	N.-Amer	577776
Wolber, Jakob	27 Jun 1852	Schopfloch	Frd.	Mar 1859	N.-Amer	577776
Wolber, Johann Georg		Duerrenmettstetten	Sulz	bef 1834	Poland	849625
Wolber, Johannes	9 Apr 1840	Schopfloch	Frd.	Mar 1859	N.-Amer	577776
Wolber, Maria Anna	10 Apr 1842	Bettenhausen	Sulz	Sep 1866	N.-Amer	849630
Wolbold, Franz & F		Gueltstein	Herr.	Apr 1834	N.-Amer	834624
Wolbold, Johannes & F		Calw	Calw	Apr 1847	N.-Amer	563212
Wolf, Adam	29 Jun 1829	Dornhan	Sulz	1852	N.-Amer	849633
Wolf, Andreas		Sigmarswangen	Sulz	Oct 1853	N.-Amer	849642
Wolf, August Franz	6 Oct 1843	Freudenstadt	Frd.	Sep 1854	N.-Amer	569274
Wolf, Carl Christian	13 May 1851	Freudenstadt	Frd.	Sep 1854	N.-Amer	569274
Wolf, Catharina	20 Apr 1853	Freudenstadt	Frd.	Mar 1854	N.-Amer	569273
Wolf, Catharine Pauline	21 Feb 1838	Freudenstadt	Frd.	Sep 1854	N.-Amer	569274
Wolf, Christian	1855	Renfrizhausen	Sulz	Jul 1861	N.-Amer	849639
Wolf, Christiane & C		Freudenstadt	Frd.	Mar 1854	N.-Amer	569273

234

| Name | | Birth | | Emigration | | | Film |
Last	First	Date	Place	O'amt	Appl. Date	Dest.	Number
Wolf, Elisabetha & C			Dachteln	Calw	1852	N.-Amer	563212
Wolf, Friedrich		27 Jul 1848	Freudenstadt	Frd.	Mar 1854	N.-Amer	569273
Wolf, Friedrich		21 Sep 1828	Tumlingen	Frd.	bef 1856	N.-Amer	569275
Wolf, Gottlieb		28 Oct 1831	Dornhan	Sulz	Dec 1862	Switz.	849634
Wolf, Jacob		32 yrs.	Geschingen	Calw	1864	N.-Amer	563212
Wolf, Johann Christian			Freudenstadt	Frd.	Mar 1858	N.-Amer	577776
Wolf, Johann David		4 Apr 1846	Freudenstadt	Frd.	Sep 1854	N.-Amer	569274
Wolf, Johann Georg			Tumlingen	Frd.	Jun 1862	Bavaria	577778
Wolf, Magdalena			Freudenstadt	Frd.	Aug 1844	Baden	569269
Wolf, Magdalena		1831	Oberjesingen	Herr.	Mar 1867		834624
Wolf, Maria Ursula		20 Sep 1831	Sigmarswangen	Sulz	bef 1861	N.-Amer	849642
Wolf, Mathias		7 Jan 1834	Dietersweiler	Frd.	bef 1854	N.-Amer	569274
Wolf, Rosine			Gechingen	Calw	1863	Bavaria	563212
Wolf, Rosine Friederike		5 Apr 1832	Freudenstadt	Frd.	Oct 1858	France	577776
Wolf, Sophie		12 yrs.	Freudenstadt	Frd.	Mar 1854	N.-Amer	569273
Wolff, August Franz		6 Oct 1843	Freudenstadt	Frd.	Sep 1854	N.-Amer	569274
Wolff, Carl Christian		13 May 1851	Freudenstadt	Frd.	Sep 1854	N.-Amer	569274
Wolff, Catharine Pauline		21 Feb 1838	Freudenstadt	Frd.	Sep 1854	N.-Amer	569274
Wolff, Christian & F			Freudenstadt	Frd.	Sep 1854	N.-Amer	569274
Wolff, Christian Jacob		19 Aug 1826	Freudenstadt	Frd.	Sep 1854	N.-Amer	569274
Wolff, Christine Friederike			Freudenstadt	Frd.	Sep 1854	N.-Amer	569274
Wolff, David & F			Freudenstadt	Frd.	Sep 1854	N.-Amer	569274
Wolff, Dorothea Barbara		6 Mar 1830	Freudenstadt	Frd.	Oct 1859	Hesse	577776
Wolff, Gottlieb		31 May 1842	Freudenstadt	Frd.	Sep 1854	N.-Amer	569274
Wolff, Gottlieb & F			Freudenstadt	Frd.	Sep 1854	N.-Amer	569274
Wolff, Jacob Heinrich			Freudenstadt	Frd.	May 1860	Bavaria	577777
Wolff, Johann David		4 Apr 1846	Freudenstadt	Frd.	Sep 1854	N.-Amer	569274
Wolff, Joseph		6 Feb 1842	Sigmarswangen	Sulz	Jul 1860	N.-Amer	849642
Wolff, Maria Christiane			Freudenstadt	Frd.	Sep 1854	N.-Amer	569274
Wolff, Maria Christiane (wife)			Freudenstadt	Frd.	Sep 1854	N.-Amer	569274
Wolff, Sophie Friederike		4 Feb 1834	Freudenstadt	Frd.	Sep 1854	N.-Amer	569274
Wolpert, Barbara			Duerrenmettstetten	Sulz	bef 1823	Russia	849625
Wolpold, Johann Jacob		31 yrs.	Affstaett	Herr.	Sep 1843	Baden	834625
Wolpper, (male)		9 Apr 1813	Freudenstadt	Frd.	Sep 1854	N.-Amer	569274
Wolz, Johannes		30 yrs.	Calw	Calw	1856	N.-Amer	563212
Wosselberger, Catharina			Oberkollbach	Calw	1849	N.-Amer	563212
Wuensch, Johannes		16 Nov 1844	Nufringen	Herr.	Jan 1867	N.-Amer	834624
Wuerth, Gottlieb		6 Jul 1849	Schwarzenberg	Frd.	Oct 1866	N.-Amer	577780
Wuerth, Johann Friedrich		15 Jun 1842	Baiersbronn	Frd.	Apr 1856	N.-Amer	569275
Wuerth, Johannes		8 Oct 1838	Kniebis	Frd.	Jan 1857	N.-Amer	577776
Wuerth, Magdalena		10 Nov 1835	Baiersbronn	Frd.	Mar 1857	N.-Amer	577776
Wuestling, Regina		4 Nov 1847	Bondorf	Herr.	Feb 1869	Hesse	834624
Wunderlich, Albert		12 Mar 1837	Sulz	Sulz	Jan 1855	N.-Amer	849627
Wunderlich, Carl Chr. Reinh.			Sulz	Sulz	Sep 1853	N.-Amer	849627
Wunderlich, Carl Theodor		10 Oct 1834	Sulz	Sulz	Sep 1854	N.-Amer	849627
Wunderlich, Hermann		2 Jan 1839	Sulz	Sulz	Jan 1855	N.-Amer	849627
Wunderlich, Julius		19 Mar 1843	Sulz	Sulz	Jan 1855	N.-Amer	849627
Wunsch, Jakob		19 Sep 1832	Baiersbronn	Frd.	Dec 1853	N.-Amer	569272
Wunsch, Katharina		23 Jan 1837	Baiersbronn	Frd.	Apr 1866	Baden	577780
Wurst, Christina & C		21 Jun 1811	Schnait	Schd.	May 1837	N.-Amer	801461

Wurst, Georg & F		Moettlingen	Calw	1853	N.-Amer	563212
Wurst, Gottlieb	21 Aug 1834	Schnait	Schd.	May 1837	N.-Amer	801461
Wurst, Johann Christian	1836	Calw	Calw	1856	N.-Amer	563212
Wurst, Johannes	10 Oct 1809	Calw	Calw	1854	N.-Amer	563212
Wurster, Adam Friedrich & F		Agenbach	Calw	1854	N.-Amer	563212
Wurster, Andreas	2 Jan 1842	Glatten	Frd.	Mar 1847	N.-Amer	569270
Wurster, Andreas	23 Dec 1829	Pfalzgrafenweiler	Frd.	Apr 1846	N.-Amer	569271
Wurster, Anna Catharina	18 Oct 1815	Pfalzgrafenweiler	Frd.	Apr 1836	N.-Amer	569268
Wurster, Anna Maria	11 Aug 1818	Pfalzgrafenweiler	Frd.	Apr 1846	N.-Amer	569271
Wurster, Anna Maria		Wittlensweiler	Frd.	Aug 1857	N.-Amer	577776
Wurster, Anna Maria		Freudenstadt	Frd.	Jan 1839	Switz.	569267
Wurster, Barbara (wife)		Untermusbach	Frd.	Mar 1833	N.-Amer	569268
Wurster, Catharina		Baiersbronn	Frd.	Aug 1860	Mainz	577777
Wurster, Catharina Margaretha	14 Feb 1822	Glatten	Frd.	Mar 1847	N.-Amer	569270
Wurster, Christian	1836	Agenbach	Calw	1854	N.-Amer	563212
Wurster, Christian & F	14 Dec 1821	Untermusbach	Frd.	Apr 1848	N.-Amer	569270
Wurster, Christiane Frieder.	24 Aug 1834	Freudenstadt	Frd.	bef 1862	France	577778
Wurster, Christina	4 yrs.	Untermusbach	Frd.	Mar 1833	N.-Amer	569268
Wurster, Christina Fried. & C		Sulz	Sulz	Aug 1832	Baden	849627
Wurster, Christina Magdal. & C		Neubulach	Calw	1862	Baden	563212
Wurster, Christine Katharine		Oberkollbach	Calw	1863	Switz.	563212
Wurster, Elisabeth Catharina		Ottenbronn	Calw	1867	Baden	563212
Wurster, Eva		Wittlensweiler	Frd.	Aug 1857	N.-Amer	577776
Wurster, Eva Dorothea		Ottenbronn	Calw	1867	Baden	563212
Wurster, Eva Margaretha	4 Aug 1819	Pfalzgrafenweiler	Frd.	Apr 1854	N.-Amer	569273
Wurster, Eva Maria	10 Nov 1824	Pfalzgrafenweiler	Frd.	Apr 1846	N.-Amer	569271
Wurster, Friedrich	1833	Hornberg	Calw	1854	N.-Amer	563212
Wurster, Georg Friedrich		Freudenstadt	Frd.	Mar 1844	Bavaria	569269
Wurster, Jacob	26 yrs.	Breitenberg	Calw	1867	N.-Amer	563212
Wurster, Jacob & F		Sommenhardt	Calw	Mar 1847	N.-Amer	563212
Wurster, Jacob Friedrich & F		Hirsau	Calw	1847	N.-Amer	563212
Wurster, Jacobine	14 Aug 1827	Pfalzgrafenweiler	Frd.	Apr 1846	N.-Amer	569271
Wurster, Jakob	30 Oct 1829	Pfalzgrafenweiler	Frd.	Sep 1854	N.-Amer	569274
Wurster, Jakob	3 yrs.	Neubulach	Calw	1862	Baden	563212
Wurster, Jakob Friedrich & F		Freudenstadt	Frd.	Mar 1833	N.-Amer	569267
Wurster, Johann Friedrich	19 yrs.	Aichelberg	Calw	1869	N.-Amer	563212
Wurster, Johann Georg	27 Apr 1809	Woernersberg	Frd.	Jul 1864	N.-Amer	577779
Wurster, Johann Georg	14 Jun 1816	Goettelfingen	Frd.	May 1844	A-dam	569269
Wurster, Johann Georg & F	4 May 1809	Glatten	Frd.	Mar 1847	N.-Amer	569270
Wurster, Johann Georg & F	30 yrs.	Untermusbach	Frd.	Mar 1833	N.-Amer	569268
Wurster, Johann Georg & F	2 Aug 1792	Pfalzgrafenweiler	Frd.	Apr 1846	N.-Amer	569271
Wurster, Johanna	10 Oct 1827	Freudenstadt	Frd.	bef 1853	Switz.	569272
Wurster, Johanna Sophie	6 Jun 1839	Freudenstadt	Frd.	Sep 1859	N.-Amer	577776
Wurster, Johannes		Ebershardt	Nag.	Mar 1854	N.-Amer	838491
Wurster, Johannes		Untermusbach	Frd.	Jul 1854	N.-Amer	569274
Wurster, Johannes	1 Dec 1848	Groembach	Frd.	Jan 1866	N.-Amer	577780
Wurster, Johannes		Neubulach	Calw	Feb 1848	Poland	563212
Wurster, Johannes & F		Zwerenberg	Calw	1853	N.-Amer	563212
Wurster, Justina	6 Nov 1819	Altensteig	Frd.	Feb 1861	N.-Amer	577778
Wurster, Magdalena		Schoemberg	Frd.	Jun 1854	N.-Amer	569273

Name		Birth		Emigration			Film
Last	First	Date	Place	O'amt	Appl. Date	Dest.	Number
Wurster, Magdalena		2 yrs.	Untermusbach	Frd.	Mar 1833	N.-Amer	569268
Wurster, Regine			Baiersbronn	Frd.	Mar 1817	Russia	569268
Wurster, Rosina		18 Feb 1796	Pfalzgrafenweiler	Frd.	Apr 1846	N.-Amer	569271
Wurster, Rosine		23 Mar 1810	Pfalzgrafenweiler	Frd.	Mar 1837	N.-Amer	569268
Wurster, Rosine Barbara		19 yrs.	Freudenstadt	Frd.	Mar 1833	N.-Amer	569267
Wurster, Veronika		25 Jul 1823	Woernersbach	Frd.	bef 1856	Baden	577779
Wurster, Wilhelmina		28 Apr 1845	Altensteig	Frd.	Feb 1861	N.-Amer	577778
Wurtz, Anna Maria		54 yrs.	Rodt	Frd.	May 1750	Pen.N-A	550803
Wurtz, Anna Maria		5 yrs.	Rodt	Frd.	May 1750	Pen.N-A	550803
Wurtz, Jacob		14 yrs.	Rodt	Frd.	May 1750	Pen.N-A	550803
Wurtz, Jeremias		18 yrs.	Rodt	Frd.	May 1750	Pen.N-A	550803
Wurtz, Johann Heinrich & F		44 yrs.	Rodt	Frd.	May 1750	Pen.N-A'	550803
Wurtz, Johannes		11 yrs.	Rodt	Frd.	May 1750	Pen.N-A	550803
Wurz, Johann Georg		16 Jan 1846	Gruental	Frd.	Jun 1866	N.-Amer	577780
Wurz, Rosine Barbara		2 Nov 1821	Baiersbronn	Frd.	Apr 1847	N.-Amer	569270
Zahn, Carl Gustav			Calw	Calw	Dec 1870	N.-Amer	563212
Zahn, Friederike Wilhelmine		1823	Hirsau	Calw	1854	Silesia	563212
Zahn, Richard		19 yrs.	Liebenzell	Calw	1867	N.-Amer	563212
Zahn, Viktor			Calw	Calw	1861	Greece	563212
Zaiser, Johannes		11 Nov 1821	Dietersweiler	Frd.	Jun 1854	N.-Amer	569273
Zanker, Sabine			Liebenzell	Calw	1853	N.-Amer	563212
Zeeb, (male) & F			Freudenstadt	Frd.	Sep 1854	N.-Amer	569274
Zeeb, Andreas		40 yrs.	Hagelloch/Tuebingen	Herr.	May 1831	N.-Amer	834624
Zeeb, Anna Maria		26 Apr 1835	Freudenstadt	Frd.	Feb 1865	Switz.	577779
Zeeb, Catharina Maria		Aug 1827	Freudenstadt	Frd.	Nov 1860	N.-Amer	577777
Zeeb, Christiane Friederike		12 Sep 1851	Freudenstadt	Frd.	Nov 1860	N.-Amer	577777
Zeeb, Christiane Rosine		7 Jul 1829	Freudenstadt	Frd.	Sep 1854	N.-Amer	569274
Zeeb, Elisabeth			Freudenstadt	Frd.	Dec 1854	N.-Amer	569274
Zeeb, Elisabetha			Hagelloch	Herr.	Apr 1831	N.-Amer	834624
Zeeb, Friederike Magdalena		9 yrs.	Freudenstadt	Frd.	Jul 1850	N.-Amer	569271
Zeeb, Friederike Wilhelmine		30 May 1838	Freudenstadt	Frd.	Sep 1854	N.-Amer	569274
Zeeb, Friedrich		3 Oct 1797	Freudenstadt	Frd.	Sep 1854	N.-Amer	569274
Zeeb, Georg David		11 yrs.	Freudenstadt	Frd.	Jul 1850	N.-Amer	569271
Zeeb, Jakob Friedrich		10 Oct 1843	Freudenstadt	Frd.	Sep 1854	N.-Amer	569274
Zeeb, Johann August		12 yrs.	Freudenstadt	Frd.	Jul 1850	N.-Amer	569271
Zeeb, Johann Friedrich & F			Freudenstadt	Frd.	Jul 1850	N.-Amer	569271
Zeeb, Johann Heinrich			Herrenberg	Herr.	bef 1840	Breslau	834625
Zeeb, Johannes Jakob & F		1790	Freudenstadt	Frd.	Sep 1854	N.-Amer	569274
Zeeb, Margarethe Barbara		5 Jun 1842	Freudenstadt	Frd.	Sep 1854	N.-Amer	569274
Zeeb, Marie Friederike		21 Feb 1845	Freudenstadt	Frd.	Sep 1854	N.-Amer	569274
Zeeb, Rosina Johanna		17 Feb 1835	Freudenstadt	Frd.	Sep 1854	N.-Amer	569274
Zeeb, Sophie Catharina		31 Oct 1834	Freudenstadt	Frd.	Sep 1854	N.-Amer	569274
Zeeb, Sophie Friederike (wife)			Freudenstadt	Frd.	Sep 1854	N.-Amer	569274
Zefler, Adam			Hallwangen	Frd.	1817	Russia	569269
Zehender, Johann Gottlieb		4 Jul 1809	Haubersbronn	Schd.	Apr 1834	N.-Amer	801460
Zehnder, Mathias & F			Gueltstein	Herr.	Apr 1835	N.-Amer	834624
Zeiger, Christina (wife)			Trichtingen	Sulz	Mar 1837	N.-Amer	849642
Zeiger, Johann Georg & F			Trichtingen	Sulz	Mar 1837	N.-Amer	849642
Zeiher, Philipp Friedrich		28 Apr 1798	Grunbach	Schd.	Sep 1816	Russia	801461
Zeiler, Christina Magdalena		29 yrs.	Nufringen	Herr.	Mar 1832	N.-Amer	834624

Zeiler, Georg Adam		Stammheim	Calw	1854	N.-Amer	563212
Zeiler, Sophie		Unterhaugstett	Calw	1866	Baden	563212
Zeiner, Barbara	3 Jun 1825	Goettelfingen	Frd.	Nov 1853	N.-Amer	569272
Zeller, Andreas (wid.) & F	26 May 1818	Holzhausen	Sulz	Feb 1881	N.-Amer	849635
Zeller, Anna	15 Jan 1850	Holzhausen	Sulz	Feb 1881	N.-Amer	849635
Zeller, Anna Barbara	28 Sep 1834	Voehringen	Sulz	May 1871	N.-Amer	849643
Zeller, Anna Barbara		Renfrizhausen	Sulz	bef 1829	Hungary	849639
Zeller, Anna Maria	1 Feb 1863	Muehlheim a.B.	Sulz	Oct 1865	N.-Amer	849639
Zeller, Anna Maria (wife)	30 Nov 1780	Voehringen	Sulz	bef 1817	--	849643
Zeller, Anna Maria (wife)	13 May 1832	Muehlheim a.B.	Sulz	Oct 1865	N.-Amer	849639
Zeller, Auguste	9 Jul 1851	Renfrizhausen	Sulz	Mar 1860	N.-Amer	849639
Zeller, Barbara		Renfrizhausen	Sulz	bef 1831	Russia	849625
Zeller, Barbara	6 Jun 1832	Durrweiler	Frd.	Feb 1847	N.-Amer	569271
Zeller, Christian		Renfrizhausen	Sulz	bef 1831	Russia	849625
Zeller, Christian	20 Aug 1816	Voehringen	Sulz	bef 1817	--	849643
Zeller, Christian	23 Nov 1848	Renfrizhausen	Sulz	Mar 1860	N.-Amer	849639
Zeller, Christian & F		Renfrizhausen	Sulz	bef 1829	Hungary	849639
Zeller, Christiana	5 Feb 1836	Durrweiler	Frd.	Feb 1847	N.-Amer	569271
Zeller, Christina	14 May 1842	Durrweiler	Frd.	Feb 1847	N.-Amer	569271
Zeller, Christina (wife)		Dornhan	Sulz	Mar 1817	Russia	849633
Zeller, Friedrich	10 Sep 1846	Voehringen	Sulz	Aug 1867	N.-Amer	849643
Zeller, Gottlieb	5 Oct 1816	Voehringen	Sulz	Aug 1867	N.-Amer	849643
Zeller, Jacob	4 Sep 1866	Renfrizhausen	Sulz	Mar 1881	N.-Amer	849639
Zeller, Jacob & F		Bergfelden	Sulz	Apr 1817	Russia	849629
Zeller, Jakob	15 Aug 1834	Durrweiler	Frd.	Feb 1847	N.-Amer	569271
Zeller, Jakob & F	28 Nov 1827	Muehlheim a.B.	Sulz	Oct 1865	N.-Amer	849639
Zeller, Johann & F		Renfrizhausen	Sulz	bef 1831	Russia	849625
Zeller, Johann Georg & F	16 Nov 1815	Renfrizhausen	Sulz	Mar 1860	N.-Amer	849639
Zeller, Johann Gottlieb	3 Nov 1862	Holzhausen	Sulz	Feb 1881	N.-Amer	849635
Zeller, Johann Jacob	9 Sep 1850	Bergfelden	Sulz	bef 1860	Nuernb.	849629
Zeller, Johann Jacob	19 Sep 1812	Voehringen	Sulz	bef 1817	--	849643
Zeller, Johann Jacob		Muehlheim a.B.	Sulz	bef 1869	Switz.	849639
Zeller, Johann Jacob & F		Voehringen	Sulz	Jul 1817	Russia	849627
Zeller, Johann Jacob & F	19 Aug 1780	Renfrizhausen	Sulz	bef 1817	--	849643
Zeller, Johann Ludwig		Muehlheim a.B.	Sulz	Oct 1854	N.-Amer	849639
Zeller, Johann Martin	5 Jun 1838	Muehlheim a.B.	Sulz	Mar 1865	N.-Amer	849639
Zeller, Johann Martin	17 Apr 1867	Voehringen	Sulz	1882	N.-Amer	849626
Zeller, Johann Philipp		Renfrizhausen	Sulz	bef 1831	Russia	849625
Zeller, Johanna	13 Jun 1866	Holzhausen	Sulz	Feb 1881	N.-Amer	849626
Zeller, Johannes	20 Jun 1875	Dornhan	Sulz	Mar 1893	N.-Amer	849634
Zeller, Johannes & F		Dornhan	Sulz	Mar 1817	Russia	849633
Zeller, Katharina	4 Jan 1857	Holzhausen	Sulz	Feb 1881	N.-Amer	849635
Zeller, Katharina	4 Mar 1860	Muehlheim a.B.	Sulz	Oct 1865	N.-Amer	849639
Zeller, Katharina (wife)	12 Apr 1821	Renfrizhausen	Sulz	Mar 1860	N.-Amer	849639
Zeller, Luise	9 Mar 1841	Voehringen	Sulz	Aug 1867	N.-Amer	849643
Zeller, Magdalena	1 Sep 1852	Muehlheim a.B.	Sulz	Oct 1865	N.-Amer	849639
Zeller, Maria (wife)	1761	Renfrizhausen	Sulz	bef 1829	Hungary	849639
Zeller, Matheis & F		Voehringen	Sulz	bef 1817	--	849643
Zeller, Mathias	7 Aug 1867	Dornhan	Sulz	Apr 1882	N.-Amer	849634
Zeller, Regina	5 Feb 1812	Voehringen	Sulz	Aug 1867	N.-Amer	849643

Name		Birth		Emigration			Film
Last	First	Date	Place	O'amt	Appl. Date	Dest.	Number
Zerr, Christina (wife)			Holzhausen	Sulz	Aug 1832	N.-Amer	849635
Zerr, Jakob & W		2 Jul 1800	Holzhausen	Sulz	Aug 1832	N.-Amer	849635
Zerwek, Christian David Carl		26 Jul 1848	Herrenberg	Herr.	Dec 1868	N.-Amer	834624
Ziefle, Friedrich		17 Jun 1842	Hallwangen	Frd.	May 1860	N.-Amer	577777
Ziefle, Johann Georg		18 yrs.	Schoenengrund	Frd.	Apr 1860	N.-Amer	577777
Ziegele, Johann Friedrich			Schorndorf	Schd.	Sep 1834	Bavaria	801460
Ziegler, Agnes Catharina		5 yrs.	Freudenstadt	Frd.	May 1752	Pen.N-A	550803
Ziegler, Andreas		27 Jun 1866	Dornhan	Sulz	Mar 1884	N.-Amer	849634
Ziegler, Andreas		14 Jan 1835	Dornhan	Sulz	Sep 1854	N.-Amer	849633
Ziegler, Andreas & F			Muehlheim a.B.	Sulz	May 1854	N.-Amer	849639
Ziegler, Anna		30 Dec 1810	Bickelsberg	Sulz	May 1860	N.-Amer	849644
Ziegler, Anna		18 yrs.	Bickelsberg	Sulz	Apr 1852	N.-Amer	849630
Ziegler, Anna		16 yrs.	Bickelsberg	Sulz	Jul 1851	N.-Amer	849630
Ziegler, Anna		9 Feb 1846	Dornhan	Sulz	Sep 1867	N.-Amer	849634
Ziegler, Anna (wife)		17 Aug 1814	Bickelsberg	Sulz	bef 1865	N.-Amer	849630
Ziegler, Anna Catharina (wife)			Bickelsberg	Sulz	Jul 1851	N.-Amer	849630
Ziegler, Anna Maria		15 yrs.	Freudenstadt	Frd.	May 1752	Pen.N-A	550803
Ziegler, Anna Maria		11 Jan 1830	Dornhan	Sulz	Aug 1854	N.-Amer	849633
Ziegler, Anna Maria			Renfrizhausen	Sulz	Oct 1867	N.-Amer	849639
Ziegler, Anna Maria & C			Bickelsberg	Sulz	May 1871	N.-Amer	849630
Ziegler, Barbara			Bickelsberg	Sulz	May 1837	N.-Amer	849625
Ziegler, Barbara		4 Jun 1843	Hopfau	Sulz	Aug 1869	N.-Amer	849636
Ziegler, Christian		9 Jan 1842	Schopfloch	Frd.	Jul 1856	N.-Amer	569275
Ziegler, Christian			Hopfau	Sulz	Sep 1853	N.-Amer	849636
Ziegler, Christian		3 Mar 1872	Fuernsal	Sulz	Feb 1889	N.-Amer	849626
Ziegler, Christiane		18 Apr 1854	Muehlheim a.B.	Sulz	May 1854	N.-Amer	849639
Ziegler, Christina		6 Jun 1841	Dornhan	Sulz	Apr 1861	N.-Amer	849634
Ziegler, Christina			Dornhan	Sulz	Jan 1861	France	849634
Ziegler, Christina Barb. (wife)			Sulz	Sulz	May 1834	N.-Amer	849627
Ziegler, Christina Margaretha		7 yrs.	Freudenstadt	Frd.	May 1752	Pen.N-A	550803
Ziegler, Christine		2 May 1842	Bickelsberg	Sulz	bef 1865	N.-Amer	849630
Ziegler, Elisabetha		19 Jan 1831	Schoenbrunn	Nag.	bef 1860	N.-Amer	838493
Ziegler, Friedrich			Wittendorf	Frd.	Mar 1837	N.-Amer	569268
Ziegler, Friedrich Wilhelm		19 Jan 1872	Rosenfeld	Sulz	Feb 1888	N.-Amer	849626
Ziegler, Georg		14 May 1843	Bickelsberg	Sulz	bef 1865	N.-Amer	849630
Ziegler, Georg & F		43 yrs.	Freudenstadt	Frd.	May 1752	Pen.N-A	550803
Ziegler, Georg & F		10 Feb 1821	Bickelsberg	Sulz	Jul 1851	N.-Amer	849630
Ziegler, Georg Adam		13 Feb 1839	Rosenfeld	Sulz	Mar 1859	N.-Amer	849640
Ziegler, Georg Bernhard		6 mon.	Freudenstadt	Frd.	May 1752	Pen.N-A	550803
Ziegler, Georg Jacob		11 yrs.	Freudenstadt	Frd.	May 1752	Pen.N-A	550803
Ziegler, Gottfried		18 yrs.	Duerrenmettstetten	Sulz	Aug 1854	N.-Amer	849635
Ziegler, Gottlieb		18 yrs.	Brittheim	Sulz	Oct 1853	N.-Amer	849632
Ziegler, Jacobina		42 yrs.	Freudenstadt	Frd.	May 1752	Pen.N-A	550803
Ziegler, Jakob & F			Sigmarswangen	Sulz	Jan 1817	Russia	849642
Ziegler, Joh. Friedrich Bern.		12 Jun 1844	Dornhan	Sulz	Jan 1871	Hamburg	849634
Ziegler, Johann Georg		24 Feb 1844	Dornhan	Sulz	Apr 1861	N.-Amer	849634
Ziegler, Johann Georg		12 Feb 1837	Dornhan	Sulz	Aug 1854	N.-Amer	849633
Ziegler, Johann Georg		12 Jun 1852	Renfrizhausen	Sulz	Mar 1869	N.-Amer	849639
Ziegler, Johann Georg & F		10 Dec 1818	Bickelsberg	Sulz	1865	N.-Amer	849630
Ziegler, Johann Gottlieb & F		29 Jun 1794	Sulz	Sulz	May 1834	N.-Amer	849627

Ziegler, Johann Ludwig	5 Sep 1852	Muehlheim a.B.	Sulz	May 1854	N.-Amer	849639
Ziegler, Johann Martin	12 Oct 1863	Bickelsberg	Sulz	Jul 1880	N.-Amer	849626
Ziegler, Johann Martin & F	24 Oct 1802	Bickelsberg	Sulz	Apr 1852	N.-Amer	849630
Ziegler, Johannes	20 Sep 1832	Schopfloch	Frd.	Apr 1851	N.-Amer	569271
Ziegler, Johannes		Dornhan	Sulz	Mar 1811	Saxony	849625
Ziegler, Johannes	17 Sep 1871	Dornhan	Sulz	Sep 1888	N.-Amer	849634
Ziegler, Johannes	16 Jan 1840	Hopfau	Sulz	Nov 1866	N.-Amer	849636
Ziegler, Johannes	21 Jul 1850	Renfrizhausen	Sulz	Mar 1869	N.-Amer	849639
Ziegler, Johannes	27 Jul 1873	Dorhan	Sulz	Oct 1889	N.-Amer	849626
Ziegler, Josias	10 Mar 1877	Bickelsberg	Sulz	Jul 1893	N.-Amer	849630
Ziegler, Katharina (wife)		Muehlheim a.B.	Sulz	May 1854	N.-Amer	849639
Ziegler, Ludwig & F		Muehlheim a.B.	Sulz	Sep 1856	N.-Amer	849639
Ziegler, Magdalena		Wittendorf	Frd.	Apr 1817	Russia	569268
Ziegler, Magdalena	3 yrs.	Freudenstadt	Frd.	May 1752	Pen.N-A	550803
Ziegler, Margaretha	8 Aug 1838	Dornhan	Sulz	Sep 1867	N.-Amer	849634
Ziegler, Maria & C		Bickelsberg	Sulz	May 1871	N.-Amer	849628
Ziegler, Mathaeus	6 Aug 1819	Dornhan	Sulz	bef 1856	N.-Amer	849633
Ziegler, Mathias	22 Apr 1846	Dornhan	Sulz	Sep 1866	N.-Amer	849634
Ziegler, Mathias	13 Mar 1874	Dornhan	Sulz	Oct 1893	N.-Amer	849626
Ziegler, Michael		Aach	Frd.	Apr 1817	Russia	569267
Ziegler, Wilhelm August	17 Aug 1852	Muehlheim a.B.	Sulz	Sep 1856	N.-Amer	849639
Zifle, Agatha	29 Dec 1802	Gruental	Frd.	Mar 1847	N.-Amer	569271
Ziflin, Anna Katharina	4 Feb 1833	Hallwangen	Frd.	Apr 1854	N.-Amer	569273
Ziflin, Elisabeth Katharina	4 Apr 1852	Untermusbach	Frd.	Feb 1854	N.-Amer	569273
Ziflin, Katharina & C	16 Feb 1832	Untermusbach	Frd.	Feb 1854	N.-Amer	569273
Zimmermann, Johann Georg		Voehringen	Sulz	Apr 1866	France	849643
Zimmermann, Johann Georg		Balingen	Bal.	Mar 1864	Bavaria	555962
Zimmermann, Johannes	27 Mar 1844	Boll	Sulz	May 1864	N.-Amer	849632
Zinck, Agnes	18 yrs.	Rodt	Frd.	May 1752	Pen.N-A	550803
Zinck, Catharina	17 yrs.	Rodt	Frd.	May 1752	Pen.N-A	550803
Zinck, Cleopha	3 yrs.	Rodt	Frd.	May 1752	Pen.N-A	550803
Zinck, Dorothea	12 yrs.	Rodt	Frd.	May 1752	Pen.N-A	550803
Zinck, Elisabetha	46 yrs.	Rodt	Frd.	May 1752	Pen.N-A	550803
Zinck, Georg	10 yrs.	Rodt	Frd.	May 1752	Pen.N-A	550803
Zinck, Gottlieb	22 yrs.	Rodt	Frd.	May 1752	Pen.N-A	550803
Zinck, Hans Georg & F	52 yrs.	Rodt	Frd.	May 1752	Pen.N-A	550803
Zinck, Jacob	7 yrs.	Rodt	Frd.	May 1752	Pen.N-A	550803
Zinck, Margarethe	15 yrs.	Rodt	Frd.	May 1752	Pen.N-A	550803
Zinser, Anna Maria	31 Dec 1827	Gaertringen	Herr.	Oct 1851	N.-Amer	834627
Zinser, Anna Maria	23 May 1844	Gaertringen	Herr.	Sep 1851	N.-Amer	834627
Zinser, Jakob Friedrich	9 Nov 1846	Gaertringen	Herr.	Sep 1851	N.-Amer	834627
Zinser, Johann Christian & W		Herrenberg	Herr.	Jun 1831	N.-Amer	834624
Zinser, Johann Michael		Gaertringen	Herr.	Jan 1838	Baden	834625
Zinser, Johann Michael	20 Jun 1850	Gaertringen	Herr.	Sep 1851	N.-Amer	834627
Zinser, Johanna Dorothea (wife)		Herrenberg	Herr.	Jun 1831	N.-Amer	834624
Zinser, Magdalena (wife)	27 yrs.	Gaertringen	Herr.	Sep 1851	N.-Amer	834627
Zinser, Peter & F	33 yrs.	Gaertringen	Herr.	Sep 1851	N.-Amer	834627
Zipperer, Jacob & W		Unterjesingen	Herr.	Mar 1846	N.-Amer	834626
Zipperer, Johann	16 Mar 1864	Moenchberg	Herr.	Apr 1869	N.-Amer	834624
Zipperer, Johann Jacob	20 Mar 1867	Moenchberg	Herr.	Apr 1869	N.-Amer	834624

| Name | | Birth | | Emigration | | | Film |
Last	First	Date	Place	O'amt	Appl. Date	Dest.	Number
Zipperer, Maria Agnes (wife)			Unterjesingen	Herr.	Mar 1846	N.-Amer	834626
Zipperer, Maria Saloma (wife)		30 Aug 1836	Moenchberg	Herr.	Apr 1869	N.-Amer	834624
Zipperer, Rudolf & F		19 Feb 1836	Moenchberg	Herr.	Apr 1869	N.-Amer	834624
Zobel, Christine Catharine			Unterreichenbach	Calw	1866	Switz.	563212
Zobel, Johann Wilhelm			Delckheim	– –	Dec 1751	N.-Amer	550803
Zoeppritz, Andreas Carl		6 Apr 1842	Schoemberg	Frd.	1866	N.-Amer	577780
Zoerr, Johann Martin			Voehringen	Sulz	bef 1817	France	849643
Zoller, Johann Michael		1841	Martinsmoos	Calw	1856	N.-Amer	563212
Zucker, Gottlieb			Sulz	Sulz	May 1846	N.-Amer	849627
Zueffle, Johann Ludwig			Baiersbronn	Frd.	Sep 1846	N.-Amer	569271
Zuefle, Agnes Barbara		5 May 1833	Tonbach	Frd.	Aug 1854	N.-Amer	569274
Zuefle, Catharina		8 Mar 1844	Tonbach	Frd.	Aug 1854	N.-Amer	569274
Zuefle, Christian			Baiersbronn	Frd.	Aug 1854	N.-Amer	569274
Zuefle, Christian		8 Jan 1846	Tonbach	Frd.	Aug 1854	N.-Amer	569274
Zuefle, Christina			Pfalzgrafenweiler	Frd.	Apr 1817	Russia	569268
Zuefle, Christina			Eisenbach	Frd.	May 1854	N.-Amer	569274
Zuefle, Jacob Friedrich		13 Mar 1848	Unterwies	Frd.	Aug 1854	N.-Amer	569274
Zuefle, Johann Friedrich			Baiersbronn	Frd.	Jun 1842	N.-Amer	569269
Zuefle, Johann Georg			Lombach	Frd.	bef 1854	N.-Amer	569274
Zuefle, Johann Georg		8 Nov 1837	Tonbach	Frd.	Aug 1854	N.-Amer	569274
Zuefle, Johann Georg		23 Jul 1843	Unterwies	Frd.	Aug 1854	N.-Amer	569274
Zuefle, Johanna		16 yrs.	Baiersbronn	Frd.	Aug 1854	N.-Amer	569274
Zuefle, Johannes		12 Sep 1835	Tonbach	Frd.	Aug 1854	N.-Amer	569274
Zuefle, Johannes & F		12 Feb 1809	Tonbach	Frd.	Aug 1854	N.-Amer	569274
Zuefle, Johannes & F			Eisenbach	Frd.	May 1854	N.-Amer	569274
Zuefle, Ludwig		6 Dec 1837	Unterwies	Frd.	Aug 1854	N.-Amer	569274
Zuefle, Mathaeus		22 Sep 1840	Unterwies	Frd.	Aug 1854	N.-Amer	569274
Zuefle, Mathaeus & F			Tonbach	Frd.	Jul 1832	N.-Amer	569267
Zuefle, Mathaeus & F		29 Aug 1810	Unterwies	Frd.	Aug 1854	N.-Amer	569274
Zuefle, Michael Friedrich			Goettelfingen	Frd.	Apr 1859	N.-Amer	577776
Zuefle, Regina			Pfalzgrafenweiler	Frd.	Apr 1817	Russia	569268
Zuefle, Regina (wife)		2 Aug 1815	Unterwies	Frd.	Aug 1854	N.-Amer	569274
Zuefle, Rosina		28 Feb 1806	Tonbach	Frd.	Aug 1854	N.-Amer	569274
Zuefle, Rosina Margaretha		14 Aug 1842	Tonbach	Frd.	Aug 1854	N.-Amer	569274
Zuefle, Tobias		12 May 1830	Tonbach	Frd.	Aug 1854	N.-Amer	569274
Zuefle, Wilhelm		28 Oct 1846	Tonbach	Frd.	Aug 1854	N.-Amer	569274
Zuern, Anna Maria		1 Nov 1801	Isingen	Sulz	Jun 1817	Russia	849636
Zuern, Christian			Boeffingen	Frd.	1817	Russia	569269
Zuern, Friederike		9 May 1848	Dornhan	Sulz	May 1871	N.-Amer	849634
Zuern, Johannes		26 Jun 1848	Isingen	Sulz	Apr 1868	N.-Amer	849636
Zuern, Maria Barbara & F		10 Sep 1770	Isingen	Sulz	Jun 1817	Russia	849636
Zufle, Agnes Catharine		23 Aug 1835	Tombach	Frd.	Aug 1861	N.-Amer	577778
Zufle, Catharina Dorothea		29 Sep 1836	Freudenstadt	Frd.	bef 1862	Paris	577778
Zugschwerdt, Anna		2 yrs.	Rodt	Frd.	May 1750	Pen.N-A	550803
Zugschwerdt, Barthle & F		31 yrs.	Rodt	Frd.	May 1750	Pen.N-A	550803
Zugschwerdt, Magdalena		41 yrs.	Rodt	Frd.	May 1750	Pen.N-A	550803
Zurr, Mathaeus		20 yrs.	Weltenschwann	Calw	1866	N.-Amer	563212
Zweig, Lucas & F			Baiersbronn	Frd.	Feb 1847	N.-Amer	569271
Zweig, Lucas Eduard		18 Apr 1846	Baiersbronn	Frd.	Mar 1847	N.-Amer	569271
Zwilling, – –			Ludwigsburg	– –	1752	Pen.N-A	550803